Gender and Physical Education

Gender and Physical Education offers a critical and comprehensive commentary on issues relating to gender in the context of physical education in schools and in teacher training. The book challenges our understandings of gender, equity and identity in physical education, establishing a conceptual and historical foundation for the issue, as well as presenting a wealth of original research material.

The book delivers a critical analysis of the progress and shortcomings of contemporary policies and practice in physical education as they relate to gender, and reflects on the similarities and differences between developments in the UK, US and Australia. It also offers new frameworks for research, policy and practice with a view to advancing gender equity, and addresses the roles that teachers, educators and policy-makers can play in challenging existing inequalities.

Gender and Physical Education is an important text for students and lecturers in education, teacher educators and providers of continuing professional development in physical education, and anybody concerned with gender issues in education, physical education or sport.

Dawn Penney is Senior Research Fellow at the Department of Physical Education, Sports Science and Recreation Management at the University of Loughborough. She is co-author of *Politics, Policy and Practice in Physical Education* (also published by Routledge).

Gender and Physical Education

Contemporary issues and future directions

Edited by Dawn Penney

London and New York

First published 2002 by Routledge
11 New Fetter Lane, London EC4P 3EE

Simultaneously published in the USA and Canada
by Routledge
29 West 35th Street, New York, NY 10001

Routledge is an imprint of the Taylor & Francis Group

Typeset in Times by Steven Gardiner Ltd, Cambridge
Printed and bound in Great Britain by Biddles Ltd,
Guildford and King's Lynn

British Library Cataloguing in Publication Data
A catalogue record for this book is available from the British Library

Library of Congress Cataloging in Publication Data
Gender and physical education: contemporary issues and future
directions / edited by Dawn Penney.
    p. cm.
  Includes bibliographical references and index.
  1. Physical education and training – Social aspects. 2. Sexism in
education. 3. Gender identity in education. I. Penney, Dawn, 1966–
GV342.27 .G46 2002
613.7'071 – dc21   2001048673

ISBN 0-415-23576-6 (pbk)
ISBN 0-415-23575-8 (hbk)

Contents

Contributors

Julie Bedward is a qualitative researcher who has conducted several major studies as a Research Fellow at the University of Birmingham since 1987. She is currently working on a number of projects in the School of Education, including a study of gender differences in learning.

Tansin Benn is a Senior Lecturer at the University of Birmingham. She is head of the Physical Education, Sports Studies and Dance Department. Her teaching and research interests cross arts, sport and teaching boundaries.

David Brown was formerly a teacher of physical education and French. David then became a lecturer in physical education with the Department of Physical Education, Sports Science and Recreation Management of Loughborough University. He is currently a lecturer in the School of Postgraduate Medicine and Health Sciences in the Department of Exercise and Sports Sciences at Exeter University.

Kim Bush is a doctoral candidate in sport pedagogy at Ohio State University. She is a former collegiate field hockey player and coach. Her research interests relate to feminist approaches to understanding urban adolescent girls and empowering them in relation to issues surrounding physical activity, sport and their bodies.

Gill Clarke is a Senior Lecturer in physical education and autobiographical studies in the Research and Graduate School of Education at the University of Southampton. Gill is also deputy director of the Centre for Biography and Education at the University of Southampton. Gill has published widely on issues around sexuality, physical education and sport.

John Evans is Professor of Physical Education in the Department of Physical Education, Sports Science and Recreation Management at Loughborough University. He is author of *Teaching in Transition: the Challenge of Mixed Ability Grouping* and editor of *PE, Sport and Schooling: Studies in the Sociology of PE*; *Teachers, Teaching and Control*; and *Equality, Education and Physical Education* (all by Falmer Press). John is editor of the international journal, *Sport Education and Society*. His research interests centre on the study of policy, teaching and equity issues in the secondary school curriculum.

Margaret Gehring is a faculty member at Ohio Weslyean College and a doctoral candidate in sport pedagogy at Ohio State University. She is a former collegiate cross country runner and coach. Her research interests are in using feminist perspectives to study female coaches in American collegiate ranks.

Jo Harris is currently Director of the Physical Education teacher education programmes at Loughborough University, where she also contributes to masters degree programmes in physical education. Jo taught for twelve years in state secondary schools and has twelve years' experience of teacher education. Jo gained her PhD in 1997 and has published articles in academic and professional journals, produced numerous teaching resources and directed many in-service training courses for both primary and secondary school teachers. Jo has a particular interest in physical education's contribution to health and associated issues relating to personal and social education, citizenship, inclusion and lifelong learning.

David Kirk joined Loughborough University in November 1998. He is currently Professor of Physical Education and Sport. His research interests include young people in sport, curriculum change in physical education, the body, schooling and culture, and situated learning in physical education and sport. His most recent book is *Schooling Bodies*, published in 1998 by Leicester University Press.

Doune Macdonald is a Reader in the School of Human Movement Studies, the University of Queensland. She coordinates the health and physical education teacher education programme and her current research interests include HPE curriculum construction and change, teachers' work, and young people and physical activity.

Mary O'Sullivan is an Associate Dean in the College of Education at Ohio State University. Her research interests are in teaching and teacher education reform. She teaches graduate classes in supervision, educational reform, curriculum and instruction in secondary physical education and an undergraduate class in social issues in physical education and sport. She is a former collegiate field hockey player and likes to travel, read and play golf.

Dawn Penney is a Senior Research Fellow at the Department of Physical Education, Sports Science and Recreation Management at Loughborough University. Dawn has previously held research positions at the University of Southampton, the University of Queensland and De Montfort University, and is the reviews editor for *Sport, Education and Society*. Since 1990 Dawn has been researching contemporary policy and curriculum developments in physical education and has published widely in academic and professional journals. She is co-author with John Evans of *Politics, Policy and Practice in Physical Education* (1999, E&FN Spon, an imprint of Routledge).

Emma Rich graduated from the Department of Physical Education, Sports Science and Recreation Management at Loughborough University with a first class Honours in Recreation Management in 1998. She was awarded a research scholarship at Loughborough where she is investigating the social (re)construction of gender in teaching physical education. Emma is also a member of Women in Sport Regional Advisory committee for the Sports Council. Emma is now a lecturer in Gender, Identity, Health and Physical Education in the Department of Physical Education, Sports Science and Recreation Management, Loughborough University.

Anne Williams is Professor and Head of the School of Education at King Alfred's College Winchester and Honorary Senior Lecturer at the University of Birmingham. Her research interests include teacher education and physical education. She has published widely on primary school physical education, gender issues in physical education and on teacher education.

Jan Wright is an Associate Professor and Research Director of the Graduate School of Education, University of Wollongong. She has taught in the areas of curriculum and pedagogy and socio-cultural perspectives of physical education to undergraduates for the last twenty years. She played a key role in the development of the new NSW Senior Syllabus in Personal Development, Health and Physical Education (PDHPE) and has been employed by the NSW Dept of Education and Training to provide professional development on the socio-cultural perspective that underpins this syllabus. Jan has published widely on gender and physical education and is co-author of *Becoming a Physical Education Teacher* (Addison-Wesley, 2000) with Richard Tinning, Doune Macdonald and Chris Hickey.

Preface

Why a book focusing upon gender and physical education? Gender has not been the major focus of my research or writing on contemporary physical education. I certainly do not consider myself an expert on gender issues and nor do I have the background of years of engagement with literature focusing upon issues of gender, sexuality and identity in education, physical education and sport that others (including contributors to this collection) can claim. In embarking upon this project, I was therefore acutely aware that my qualification to lead it could be questioned. However, I undertook the project in the hope that with the support and encouragement of colleagues, we could help to extend the accessibility of, and engagement with, literature and research focusing on gender. This book confirms (if we need any confirmation) that all of us, not only an 'expert few', need to be extending our understandings of the issues and pursuing ways in which we can better respond to them in policies and in practice in physical education teaching and teacher education.

The process of editing this collection and contributing to several chapters has greatly advanced my own understanding of gender and equity in physical education and I am therefore very grateful to have had the opportunity to work with the talented and remarkably understanding colleagues who are the contributors. It has been an opportunity that has enabled me to bring to the fore issues that I have often been aware have been present in my research and data, but that have remained marginal in my writing. It has been a challenging and rewarding experience, demanding that I not only ask new questions of data, but also of myself, my own experiences and attitudes. I hope that those reading the book will be encouraged to be similarly reflective and be inspired to continue to pursue the issues in their daily lives.

In producing the book I have also become aware of the limitations of any single text, and of the scope of current research in physical education. We certainly do not claim to have filled all the gaps in research or writing on gender, equity and identity in physical education. Rather, the hope has to be that we have highlighted the need for sustained and extended research and commentary on those issues. There is much that each of us can do individually, but also much to be achieved collectively. I hope that readers will see the benefits of bringing together people from different backgrounds, with knowledge of different literature, to speak on issues of shared interest and concern. The interchanges which I have had with the authors and which I have tried to facilitate between them, have demonstrated that by working together we can challenge each other in very positive and productive ways. My thanks therefore go to all involved in the production of the book and in the various research projects upon which I and the other contributors have drawn.

Part I
Setting the agenda

1 Introduction

John Evans and Dawn Penney

This chapter outlines our rationale for a focus upon gender and equity in contemporary physical education and draws attention to the breadth and complexity of the issues that this text seeks to address. It considers why professionals in all walks of physical education should be concerned with gender issues at the beginning of the twenty-first century, a period of rapidly changing lifestyles, life chances and expectations. We draw attention to long-standing inequities in the policies and practices of physical education in schools, and address the roles that teachers, teacher educators and researchers can play in either reinforcing or challenging sexism and inequity in physical education and sport.

Why do we need a gender agenda?

Gender has long been 'an issue' for physical educationalists in schools and in initial teacher education in the UK and elsewhere. As David Kirk illustrates in chapter 3, both as a school subject and as a 'profession', historically physical education in the UK has developed in explicitly gendered ways. While we cannot change that history, nor simply judge it comparatively against the standards of propriety and expectation of our now so-called (post) 'modern' world, neither can we overlook its contemporary relevance for the practices and policies of education and physical education. Several of the contributions within this collection show that physical educationalists have seemed slow to respond to debate and research that has highlighted sexism and sex differentiation in physical education and to confront inequitable gender relations in schools and the subject, sometimes despite their stated best intentions to entertain curriculum change. Why is this so? Why has there been so little surface level, let alone deep structural, change? The paucity of 'gender related' innovation evident in physical education over the last twenty years may have had as much, if not more, to do with the absence of a positive encouragement and steer on gender matters from central governments in the UK as any shortfall in the attitudes and interests of physical educationalists in schools and training institutions. The result is that many schools in the UK today entertain practices comparable to those that would have featured in physical education many decades ago. A tad more 'health related exercise' perhaps, a few more women 'heads of PE', but many single sex departments, dominated by male heads of PE, offering a thoroughly unreconstructed sex differentiated curriculum and pedagogy of sport and physical education. Current advertisements for jobs for teachers of boys', or alternatively girls' physical education are testimony to the fact that in many schools, organisational concerns continue to co-mingle with deep-seated stereotypical, ideological and cultural values to produce sex-differentiated curricula and single sex grouping, particularly in games. The experiences that girls and boys receive in physical education are likely to reinforce stereotypical images, attitudes and behaviours relating, amongst other things, to how they should feel about their own and other's bodies, who can legitimately participate in what physical activities, when and why.

Yet members of the physical education profession still frequently claim a commitment to ensuring that there is a place in physical education curriculum for *all* children irrespective of background; a place that they value and enjoy, not one in which they feel uncomfortable, unwelcome and marginalised. As we will see in the chapters that follow, we still have a long way to go in order to achieve these ideals – in arenas of policy making nationally, in schools and in training institutions. However, this book aims to go beyond critique. It seeks to not only demonstrate an undeniable need for a 'gender agenda' in contemporary policy, curriculum development and everyday pedagogical practice in physical education, but also to inform the development of that agenda and in particular, extend it beyond what we regard as longstanding and now outdated 'discursive boundaries', ways of thinking and acting in physical education and sport. We emphasise that what is needed in physical education is not *a* gender agenda but gender *agendas* – that engage with social and cultural diversity, are capable of providing for the needs of individual girls and individual boys, and that celebrate individuality. The contributions in this collection demonstrate the difficulties and challenges that arise in seeking to establish these agendas in policy and practice in physical education, but importantly, also point to the potential to do just that. Readers will see that there are pressures in contemporary society, often reflected in Government policies on education, that press the profession to maintain, rather than eradicate, inequities in the status quo. While acknowledging the desire for stability and the ongoing resistance from many sources to discourses and practices that seriously challenge inequities, we also celebrate the progress that has been made towards more equitable, innovative and inclusive practices in sport and physical education. It is talk of 'the possible' and evidence of progress and ideas for further advances that will enthuse and inspire yet more widespread innovative action. In these respects we highlight the value in looking beyond national boundaries and gaining insights and ideas from developments in other countries, where there may be greater support for and opportunities to develop 'new agendas' in and for physical education.

We are all players in this gender game

There are dangers inherent in talking abstractly about the 'subject' and 'the profession'. It incorrectly suggests that Physical Education is a unified and homogenous phenomenon, when it patently is not; and when understanding its diversity of cultures, of knowledge, values attitudes and practices needs to be acknowledged as a precursor to knowing better how it may change. It may also lead us to feel that we are somehow positioned outside of, or apart from, its 'discursive regimes'; its stereotypes, values, assumptions, ways of thinking and acting about its subject matter and those who are touched by it. The problems of sexism and inequity in physical education, and equally, the potential to address them, are easy to identify as someone else's concern. Thus, part of our emphasis here is to stress the need for each of us to position ourselves firmly within, rather than as somehow removed from, the gendered discourses of physical education. This may help us assess more adequately how, individually, departmentally and institutionally, we may be implicated in processes of social reproduction or change. The chapters that follow document the ways in which pupils, student teachers, teachers, teacher trainers, policy makers, politicians and researchers all variously play an active part in the production, reproduction and potential transformation of these discourses. Many readers will identify with one or more of these identities. In accepting those identities we may be able to more readily accept some of the roles and responsibilities that are inherent in them. In several chapters we also reflect on the power-relations in education and physical education. Once again, the temptation is to point to the constraints that we variously feel inhibit our attempts to 'do things differently'. But it must be acknowledged that a better understanding of the nature of these constraints is a precursor to moving beyond them. There is a critical need to counterbalance talk of constraint and restriction with that of opportunity, and to therefore acknowledge that education and physical education remain arenas in which we *are powerfully positioned* to influence children's and young people's attitudes, experiences and behaviours, for the better or worse.

None of this is neutral: we have an agenda

To talk in terms of 'better or worse' directs us to a further important characteristic of the work of all individuals' variously engaged in physical education; namely that it is inevitably, inescapably value laden and never 'interest free'. For our own part, we make no apologies for vigorously taking sides against those forms of oppression, including racism, sexism, homophobia and elitism, that debilitate, damage and ruin people's lives, alienating them not only from their own and other's bodies but from involvement in physical activity and sport. Elsewhere we have detailed the contested nature of physical education in schools, the struggles within and beyond the profession to determine how the subject should be defined, what form it should take, and what and whose values it should promote (see for example Evans and Penney, 1995; Penney and Evans, 1999). Throughout this book we will see further evidence of such contestation, highlighting that we cannot and should not expect agreement upon these issues, and that for those who do choose to challenge inequities in education, it will not be a comfortable ride. We all have particular visions of what the subject, the pupils or students that we may be engaged with, are and ought to be. We can, therefore, safely anticipate diversity in opinions about the ways in which (particular) gender identities can and should be expressed in physical education. Exploring that diversity may prompt us to either position, or potentially, *re*position ourselves in the debates and practices surrounding the issues of gender and physical education. Acknowledging that no one can claim value neutrality on this issue may be a first but critical step towards understanding it better. Identifying our position(s) and being honest about our agendas may take time and be uncomfortable. It is therefore appropriate at this point that we shed light on the personal agendas and values that have shaped our thinking on these issues, and for us to position ourselves in relation to the debates that follow.

'Futures have to be made, they do not just happen' (Young, 1998: 79). We have already alluded to the need for creativity and innovation in teaching and teacher training, that goes beyond the PE classroom and schools and relates fundamentally to the communities they serve. As Young (1998) has stated 'curriculum debates, implicitly or explicitly, are always debates about alternative views of society and its future' (ibid.: 9). Perhaps all too rarely do curriculum debates extend to these levels. Instead they remain conveniently confined to the detail and nuances of the curriculum, either overlooking or deliberately ignoring the implications of those intricacies in relation to whether they will serve 'a future society that we can endorse or a past society that we want to change' (ibid.: 21).

'In changing times *is it* time for change?' (Penney, 1999, our emphasis). Fashions change in social and educational theory with all the regularity of a manikin's poise and when they do it is all too easy to forget how the ideas, understandings and agendas of the 'old' have helped, and can help fashion the thinking and practices of the 'new'. Rarely are discursive developments, discrete, unrelated or ideologically pure. Fifteen years ago we may have approached the introduction to this book with the interests of 'equal opportunities' uppermost in mind. The concepts and language of Marxism and of interpretative sociology may usefully have shaped our thinking on gender and physical education. The former would have directed our attention to structural issues, in particular, to the relationships between education and the economy and how social class values, interests and hierarchies are reflected in schooling and physical education (Evans, 1984; 1986). Our attention may have centred on the organisation of schooling, on processes of selection, differentiation and socialisation (usually finding in favour of middle class, white, male values) and the structuring of work and leisure opportunities in and outside schools. The latter, would have drawn our attention to the processes of schooling. In particular, to the ways in which meanings and values are attributed to physical and social objects of the social world and how structures of convention, action and identity are created and reproduced in schooling and physical education. Together, these perspectives, especially when later integrated with the more liberating perspectives of feminism forced us to ask; who gets access to what forms of schooling, curriculum, knowledge, experience and opportunity in education and physical education? Whose values and interests are benefited and privileged in this process, and why? Before the advent of rampant neo-liberalism in the UK (reflected most obviously in the Governments of the Thatcher years), a variety of policy legislation in the UK and elsewhere broadly reflected these democratic concerns (Wright, 1999).

Although there were limits to the agendas of theoretical perspectives of this kind, they did help make more complex our view of schooling and physical education. And, to a degree, they pressed us to avoid thinking in crude generalisations about 'children', 'pupils', 'men', women', 'masculinity' and 'femininity' in education and physical education. They forced us to consider that 'individuals' and social groups may be positioned differently in the social order by virtue of their relationship to the means of production and the benefits (or otherwise) derived from their social class position as well as their culture, gender, ethnicity and physical ability. They illustrated that these factors co-mingle in education to belie crude claims about the way in which boys and girls, men and women differently experience the opportunities putatively available to them in education, physical education and wider society. They prompted acknowledgement that categories of identity, for example, of masculinity and femininity, are social realities that not only change historically but also are experienced differently according to specific economic, ideological, political and social structures (Hargreaves, 1994; Colwell, 1999). Sadly, the merits of this way of thinking all too rarely found expression either in research on physical education, or in the practices of teachers in physical education and sport in schools.

This remains the case today. For example, it is not uncommon to hear the over-generalised and undifferentiated wisdom, peddled by proponents of health in physical education, that 'individuals' should exercise for thirty (or so) minutes a day if cardiovascular health is to be achieved. Girls and women, of different class, culture and ethnicity, are likely to receive this news rather differently. The single woman raising a child and the person engaged in physical labour for the majority of their out-of-school waking hours, is not likely to treat this information in the same way as the child of middle-class parents enjoying time and opportunity to exercise at will. Neither are the concomitant feelings of inadequacy, guilt and pathology likely to be evenly shared. To talk of girls' or boys' interests in physical education as if each is a homogenous cultural category is, therefore, as unhelpful to the cause of theoretical progress in physical education as it is to the task of curriculum development in schools. Ethnicity, culture, ability and social class codetermine how an individual is likely to receive and respond to the experiences of physical education. As we emphasise in the following chapter, that the focus of this text is on 'gender issues' should not then lead us to either reduce the complexity of identity to sexism or gender alone, or fail to explore the interaction of these elements with the range of other identities that prevail on the sociocultural terrain. The historical paucity of research on ethnicity and disability in physical education, for example, is now matched only by the more contemporary deafening silence on social class as an 'object' of study and analysis in education and physical education. We share Skeggs' (1997) view that a retreat from class analyses whether in the corridors of academia, in the corridors of power or in schools and classrooms is distinctly disturbing, and we add, unhelpful to social progress in education and physical education. As Skeggs points out, 'retreatists' either ignore class or argue that it is an increasingly redundant issue. There have been plenty of politicians adopting this blinkered stance in recent years. She reminds us that when

> a retreat is being mounted we need to ask whose experiences are being silenced, whose lives are being ignored and whose lives are considered worthy of study . . . to ignore or make a class invisible is to abdicate responsibility (through privilege) from the effects it produces. To think that class does not matter is only a prerogative of those unaffected by the deprivations and exclusions it produces. Making class invisible represents a historical stage in which the identity of the middle classes is assumed.
>
> (Skeggs, 1997: 7)

It helps us avoid difficult and unpalatable questions relating to the material consequences of capitalism and inequalities in wealth and opportunity in education and wider society. It also reminds us that issues of class, ethnicity, disability, sexuality and gender have to be considered both independently and together, if we are to begin to appreciate the decisions and actions of teachers and pupils in education and physical education. The performance and educational achievements of girls and boys, of all classes, cultures and abilities in the curriculum should, then, occupy the attention of teachers, parents and politicians alike.

A decade ago educational researchers were revealing the social inequalities in both access to and success in physical education in schools. The curriculum in schools and furthermore, training institutions, was clearly gender differentiated. Boys and girls experienced a differentiated curriculum – sometimes rationalised with the powerful rhetorical logic of 'different but equal' – boys and girls having access to different forms of educational experience. Boys were shown to also enjoy more opportunities to engage in physical recreation, particularly out of school hours. It took researchers to point out that the games encouraged for girls – netball, hockey and dance not only carried less prestige than soccer, rugby and cricket but were also less readily pursued into adult life. A host of practices which seemed trivial on the surface, from the habit of calling girls and only girls by their first names, to the teasing remarks which teachers sometimes directed at their female pupils, transmitted messages concerning the appropriateness of gender as a differentiating principle. These contributed to the conceptions that pupils hold of masculinity and femininity and their place and their position in different forms of physical education, sport and recreation.

The task of generating and sustaining interest in seriously addressing these practices and their inherent inequities has been and remains far from easy. Twenty years of a Conservative government in the UK did very little to help teachers of physical education address these concerns. At a time when the profession was just beginning to think creatively about the curriculum content and teaching of physical education, a series of retrogressive educational policies brought them to a halt. As Penney discusses further in chapter 7, the educational agenda shifted perversely from issues of social inclusion and equity to how to manage the implementation of a profoundly conservative and retrospective national curriculum, including one for physical education. All attempts to embed a firm commitment to equal opportunities in the teaching of physical education via the new 'official texts' were progressively and often very obviously resisted by government ministers.

A decade on and one could be forgiven for presuming that the issue of 'access' no longer has relevance in discussions of the curriculum of physical education, particularly as the issue of social inclusion has, with the return in 1997 of a New Labour government, returned to the foreground of educational policy developments. However, we need to keep in mind that while the obvious common feature of the experience of migrants to the UK has been the prejudice that they have encountered during successive policies of assimilation and multiculturalism, they constitute an extraordinarily diverse set of communities. Gender differences in responses to school, and physical education within it, have been a salient feature amongst these groups and the under-use and under-representation of 'their' physical cultures in school physical education and sport, and in higher education, remains evident (Davies and Evans, 2001).

Meanwhile the position of women and men in Britain's mainstream cultures has shifted on a number of fronts (Davies and Evans, 2001). Statistics are now showing that girls are outperforming boys in just about every aspect of the curriculum at all levels (from schools to university), and that boys are badly underachieving in schools and have real problems ahead of them in coming to terms with the demands of a post-modern age. As we emphasise in the following chapter, such statistics and generalisations continue to hide important differences within the gender groups. But at the same time, differences between men and women remain very much an issue, not least because for all their achievements at school and university, many women continue to face real barriers in translating those achievements into leisure and work opportunities that are comparable with those enjoyed by their male counterparts. In physical education specifically, boys and girls may now enjoy equal access, albeit to a differentiated curricular, but not to extra curricular sport and physical education. As later chapters vividly illustrate, it is folly to assume that the goal of providing equal opportunities, either to the same range of curricular experiences or to a range diverse enough to capture the range of interests that children bring to school, has been achieved. Physical education still has some way to go before it can claim to be providing the skills, aptitudes and motivations for all pupils to enjoy involvement in physical recreation as a form of leisure. Furthermore, it still ensures that, having engaged with the subject, the majority of boys and girls will leave schools with their (perhaps stereotypical and prejudicial) conceptions of femininity and masculinity and their application in contexts of physical activity and sport, essentially intact and unchallenged. In the processes of schooling they will have learnt that for their particular gender there are appropriate forms of employment and leisure, and appropriate attitudes towards their own and others' bodies and sexuality in relation to physical activity and health.

Any serious consideration of the relationship between gender and education is, therefore, likely to generate questions that go to the heart of our teaching and curriculum in physical education. These concern how the curriculum is organised and selected; how teachers teach, how pupils are grouped for teaching purposes, how they are evaluated and assessed; how teacher and pupils are defined as competent or otherwise by their peers and how aims are formulated and operationalised in practice. Given that each or all of these questions may touch on deep-seated interests and identities of physical education teachers it is highly unlikely that answers will be easily or quickly obtained. Answers in terms of curricular and pedagogical reform are certainly not simply to be seen as a matter of implementing either mixed sex or single sex grouping, or of giving girls football, or boys netball and lacrosse. The problems of formulating and effecting curriculum change in physical education as in other areas of the school curriculum are both varied and substantial. There is a clear need for further investigations into the processes and challenges of curriculum reform and in particular, investigations which focus upon the way in which pupils of different class, culture, ethnicity, ability and sexuality differently relate to and experience various forms of physical activity. Issues of identity, as well as those of access and opportunity, will need to be forced to the fore in all this. Investigations will need to be as appreciative of the perspectives and problems of both teachers and pupils as of the social, organisational and political contexts in which they are located. Innovation uninformed by this form of enquiry may be as insubstantial as it is short lived.

Progressing our agenda

The following chapter pursues at a conceptual level the implications of the changes in society, youth culture, sporting cultures, body cultures and gender relations in all of these, for our work as researchers, policymakers, teachers and teacher trainers in physical education. These concepts are necessary if we are to advance upon what we have identified as notably limited progress in recent years in the UK in extending understandings of gender equity and in developing policies and practices that express and promote understandings that will pose serious challenges to established practices in physical education and sport at all levels.

A chapter by David Kirk then completes the first part of the text. Kirk's historical perspective provides a crucial reference point for our readings of debates about contemporary and possible future developments in physical education, particularly where gender issues are concerned. The strength and depth of influence of the historical foundations of the subject and the profession in contemporary times is vividly apparent in the chapters that comprise the second and third parts of the book.

In part 2, our concern has been to draw upon contemporary research that is actively seeking to 'extend gender agendas' within physical education teaching and teacher education. The chapters by Clarke, Benn, and Brown and Rich each reflect important endeavours to adopt and further extend existing conceptualisations of gender in contexts of physical education, and in so doing, challenge and advance established policies and practices. These chapters highlight the need, undoubted difficulties, but also potential rewards of policies and practices in physical education being shaped by under-standings of gender that embrace the inter-relationships between various dimensions of equity and seek to provide for the multiple identities that children and their teachers bring to school.

Part 3 reports research that has specifically explored the representation and expression of gender issues in contemporary policy and practice in physical education in England. Penney, Harris, and Williams and Bedward variously present data that tells us much about the work yet to be done if physical education in schools is to be a forum in which the pursuit of gender equity is to go beyond conceptually limited, sporadic and sometimes tokenistic gestures. In many respects these chapters do not celebrate the progress that we may have hoped would have been forthcoming with the development of a national curriculum in England and Wales. However, that should not deflect our attention from some of the crucial messages that they provide for prospective future developments in policy and practice. Both explicitly and implicitly their analyses say much about what could be done better and differently where gender equity is concerned in physical education.

The book ends with a section that seeks to locate the UK-focused initiatives and developments within an international context, and draw researchers and teacher educators from overseas into the debates about the 'state of play', progress and remaining shortcomings in relation to gender equity in physical education. The chapters by O'Sullivan, Bush and Gehring, and Wright, point to there being both important similarities in experiences relating to the pursuit of gender equity in physical education across international boundaries, but also diversity and differences in those experiences. Both characteristics are important in terms of what we can all learn from each other in looking to progress thinking and practices in our respective countries.

The future and in particular, future research concerned with gender equity in physical education, is the focus of Macdonald's concluding chapter. Macdonald's critical reflection on the work that has preceded provides us with substantive and conceptual challenges to take forward in development of research, policy and practice in physical education settings.

These are exciting and also challenging times for physical educationalists. Never before has the subject been so prominent in the public eye, as issues of health, sport performance and physical literacy continue to occupy the attention of politicians and parents alike. If nothing else we hope that this book will convince readers that unless issues of identity, gender, equity and sexuality are placed centre stage in all forthcoming debates, then we can have little hope that the best interests of all young people in physical education and sport will be well served. A reading of this modest text may help press the profession towards the pursuit of more worthy progressive educational ideals.

References

Colwell, S. (1999) Feminism and figurational sociology: contributions to understandings of sport, physical education and sex/gender, *European Physical Education Review* 5(3): 219–41.

Davies, B. and Evans, J. (2001) Changing cultures and schools in England and Wales, in J. Cairns, D. Lawton and R. Gardner (eds) *World Handbook of Education 2001: Values, Culture and Education*, London: Kegan Paul, pp. 190–206.

Evans, J. (1984) Muscle, sweat and showers. Girls' conceptions of physical education and sport: a challenge for research and curriculum reform, *European Physical Education Review* 7(1): 12–19.

Evans, J. (1986) Introduction: personal troubles and public issues. Studies in the sociology of physical education, in J. Evans (ed.) *Physical Education, Sport and Schooling. Studies in the Sociology of Physical Education*, London: Falmer Press.

Evans, J. and Penney, D. (1995) The politics of pedagogy: making a National Curriculum physical education. *Journal of Education Policy* 10(1): 27–44.

Evans, J., Davies, B. and Penney, D. (1994) Whatever happened to the subject and the State in policy research in education?, *Discourse: Studies in the Cultural Politics of Education* 14(2): 57–64.

Hargreaves, J. (1994) *Sporting Females: Critical Issues in the History and Sociology of Women's Sport*, London: Routledge.

Penney, D. (1999) Physical education: in changing times is it time for a change?, *British Journal of Physical Education* 30(4): 4–6.

Penney, D. and Evans, J. (1999) *Politics, Policy and Practice in Physical Education*, London: Routledge.

Skeggs, B. (1997) *Formations of Class and Gender*, London: Sage.

Wright, J. (1999) Changing gendered practices in physical education: working with teachers, *European Physical Education Review* 5(3): 181–99.

Young, M.F.D. (1998) *The Curriculum of The Future: From The 'New Sociology of Education' to a Critical Theory of Learning*, London: Falmer Press.

2   Talking gender

Dawn Penney and John Evans

Introduction

In the previous chapter we discussed a number of issues that point towards the conceptual underpinnings of the analyses that we and others present in this book. In this chapter we focus explicitly on conceptual matters. This provides an important foundation for reading the chapters that follow. In the first part of the chapter we direct attention to concepts that are central to debates about and understandings of 'gender issues' and 'gender equity' in physical education. We then shift the focus to concepts that in our view enable a more complete and better understanding of the representation, expression and exclusion of gender in policy and practice in physical education. We deconstruct familiar and established ways of thinking and conceptualising 'policy' and 'practice' and re-position these concepts within a view of policy as a complex, ongoing, relational and contested process in which many people at many sites (including schools, teacher training institutions and government departments) have a part to play in advancing gender equity in physical education. We present the concepts of *text* and *discourse* as key tools for the analyses of gender in physical education, enabling us to explore and reveal the ways in which particular values and interests find expression in the policies and practices of physical education, while others are not given scope to emerge. In the final section of the chapter we comment upon the role that research and researchers may play in furthering understandings and expressions of gender equity in the subject.

Setting the agenda: gender and equity

In seeking to clear some conceptual ground, the starting point probably needs to be 'gender' itself. Typically, the key distinction that is made is between 'sex' and 'gender'. It is not uncommon in the literature on 'gender' for sex to be identified with biological differences between men and women and gender with social/non-biological issues that are typically associated with talk of 'masculine' and 'feminine' identities, personal characteristics and social behaviours. However, this nature/culture division/dualism is itself deeply problematic. As the seminal work of Shilling (1993) illustrates, 'it is important to recognise that the body is not simply constrained by or invested with social relations, but also actually forms a basis for *and contributes towards* these relations' (p. 13). The biological body helps shape relations, it is not independent of them; we are embodied; 'Social relations may take up and transform our embodied capacities in all manner of ways, but they still have a basis in human bodies' (ibid.: 13). Like Shilling, we think the body is profitably conceptualised

> as an unfinished biological and social phenomenon which is transformed, within certain limits, as a result of its entry into, and participation in, society. It is this biological and social quality that makes the body at once such an obvious, and yet such an elusive phenomenon.
>
> (Shilling, 1993: 13)

Below and throughout the book we also point to other inherent short-comings of traditional but still commonplace conceptualisations of gender which reduce what are, in effect, complex socio/biological processes, to simplistic and specifically, to singular characteristics or traits. Such conceptual-isations may well be 'based on unitary conceptions of sexual character' (Hargeaves, J., 1994: 147) with the result that 'There is widespread assumption that all girls and women have a set of characteristics which is constant and common to them as females, and which is distinctly different from the set of characteristics common to boys and men' (ibid.: 147). As we and others in this text highlight, unitary conceptions of gender are highly problematic. In particular they serve to deny or conceal commonalities in the characteristics and experiences of some men and some women, but also ignore the diversity in the characteristics and experiences of women and men. The diversity reflects that we are not 'only' women or men, but also 'many other things'; we have multiple identities. Thus, when we talk of 'gender equity' we are referring not only to whether boys and girls/men and women have *access* to particular forms of experience, for example, in the physical education curriculum, but also to whether they can express and develop attitudes and behaviours relating, for example, to their sexuality, shape and physical cultures, that help frame their identity, define who they are and what they want to be. In this vein, any analysis of equity in physical education will necessarily embrace both structural and existential issues. It will embrace multiple identities and multiple differences and in particular, be concerned to consider 'when and how differences become disadvantages that threaten to undermine oppor-tunities for all individuals to enjoy meaningful and equitable participation in social and civic life' (Collins *et al.*, 2000: 38).

As these brief comments have already indicated, in 'talking gender' we are not only concerned with the experiences of women or girls. Although some of the authors contributing to the book have chosen to research and write about the experiences of women or girls, our emphasis is that boys and men are not absent from our text. In a sense males and females are always present discursively, even if not materially so. Indeed, in this vein we might argue that the identities of men and women are always and inevitably inextricably bound or related; and that analyses are incomplete if the relational elements of masculinity and femininity are not recognised and brought to the fore. In more than one sense then this must mean that our concern remains the interests and experiences of *all* children, girls and boys. Many of the issues that are discussed in relation to policy and practice in physical education have clear relevance for both girls and boys, even if some past and current work has focused attention on the interests of the former. Our emphasis is that gender needs to be recognised as an issue for men and women, boys and girls in arenas of physical education and sport. We have endeavoured to reflect this in our writing, but are also acutely aware that there will be readers who may feel that we have not achieved the right balance of representation of issues, or of people. Some will see absences, for example of a chapter that focuses explicitly on boys and/or masculinities and/or other particular groups of men or women. We recognise the arguments for such foci but also stress the need for more research into the experiences of various groups of people in physical education. Gaps remain in our understanding of whose experiences are represented in physical education research and literature. However, we also see dangers that research and/or writing (including our own) with a focus on groups of individuals bounded in relation to gender can appear to express and reinforce exactly the binary thinking that we are seeking to move beyond. Thus, our approach has been to press towards greater integration rather than polarity in discussions. It is an approach that both some men and some women may see as diluting the strength of arguments that relate specifically to either the interests of men and boys, or alternatively, those of women and girls within and beyond arenas of physical education and sport. In advocating integration are we saying that differences within these groups are more important than those between them? Our stance could certainly be read in that way. Our response is to say that it should be seen to reflect a concern that both differences between and within are important, and that our conceptual-isations of gender and our writing about gender issues in physical education needs to engage with that complexity. There is no one way of doing this, nor one way that should be seen as 'the right way'. As the various chapters within this text demonstrate, different authors will, in their own ways, make different contributions to the debates. We hope that collectively, the chapters will be regarded as a worthwhile contribution to debates about gender and identity in physical education and be seen as useful to both men and women within the profession who are concerned to advance gender equity in our subject and in our societies.

So what is advancement of gender equity really about? Literature in physical education and policies established for the subject have variously used the language of, and have stated commitments to 'equal opportunities', 'equality', 'equity' and most recently in the United Kingdom, 'inclusion'.

These terms continue to be interchanged without the meanings of particular terms in particular contexts being adequately pursued. Hence our concern to clarify our own focus on equity and the way in which this embraces a commitment primarily to social justice. We establish equity as a reference point from which talk of 'equal opportunities', 'equality' and 'inclusion' can all be critically explored to assess whether, in the ways in which they are used and in the proposals that they are associated with, they embrace a commitment to equity. We suggest that in some instances, the answer will be 'yes', but as Talbot (1993) has previously highlighted, more often than not, policies and practices couched in these various terms will fall short of this commitment.

'Shifting thinking' to embrace equity is as much about redefining what we regard as problems in physical education as it is about identifying solutions. It demands that we reflect upon the value judgements inherent in our defining certain things (behaviours, attitudes, practices) as problematic. Invariably, this will reveal that problems are defined as such in relation to a dominant set of values or behaviours that it is assumed should 'naturally' be embraced and celebrated by all. Many claims to be addressing equality and/or equity in physical education and sport have failed at this first hurdle in terms of demonstrating a commitment to equity. They include many initiatives directed towards increasing participation amongst 'target groups'. All too often a lack of participation in specific forms of sport valued by dominant groups in society is defined as problematic. Rarely is the cultural specificity of the celebrated form of sport questioned. From an equity perspective, the lack of participation that has been identified may not be a problem at all. Rather, the relative absence of opportunities for people to participate in other more culturally relevant forms of physical activity and sport (that are central to 'other' (non-dominant) cultures and that embrace 'other' values) may be the 'real' problem to address.

Language is a useful and powerful tool in critical discussions concerned with issues of equality and equity. A commitment to equity prompts us to question our use of the term 'other' and the value judgements inherent in its use. Are we implying different but equal status, or deficit? A commitment to equity is not about denying difference, but neither is it merely about recognising or respecting difference. It is about valuing and celebrating difference as *a resource*, in our schools, in physical education and sport, and in our societies. Thus, as Evans and Davies (1993) explain 'the issue must not be whether differences can be dissolved . . . but how they can be celebrated in ways which negate prejudice and stereotyping and at the same time respect individual cultural identity' (p. 19). These are clearly difficult issues to deal with conceptually and empirically. Celebrating 'difference' does not mean that we should accept that anything goes, that all attitudes and behaviours are of equal value and equally 'good'. This would quickly lead us into a deep and relativistic quagmire in which everything must be considered important but nothing of value; racism, sexism, elitism, poverty and squalor enjoy the same authority and standing as all other more liberal attitudes or goals. The social fact is that moral and ethical codes inevitably have to be considered in our judgements of the 'difference' that we see. But all the while we need to bear in mind that that we cannot assume that our codes are superior to others, or worse still that others do not possess a moral code at all. Thus, from an equity perspective, no *one* set of values or behaviours should be regarded automatically or straightforwardly as superior to others, or as 'the norm' against which others are measured or judged. There is recognition that at different times, in different places and cultures, different behaviours and values will be regarded as normal, legitimate and desirable. Furthermore, this diversity may be regarded as a richness to celebrate and explore rather than deny. Celebrating difference and ensuring that all individuals feel that they have a legitimate place in physical education, in schools and in contemporary societies are matters that are pursued throughout the subsequent chapters. We see that although some advances have been made towards greater gender equity in physical education, in arenas of both policy and practice there is a clear case for gender to be 'on the agenda'.

Extending agendas: the complexities of 'gender issues' and 'gender equity'

In this section we draw attention to some key characteristics that in our view need to be central to our conceptualisations of gender. First, we consider the fundamental shortcomings of talking of 'masculinity' and 'femininity'. In our view, acknowledging multiple masculinities and femininities is a first but crucial step if we are to broaden thinking in relation to the behaviours that we regard as legitimate for men and women, the body shapes they may have, the physical activities which they may participate in. All too often, judgements are made in relation to a single and stereotypical image of masculinity or femininity that has come, over time and because of powerful vested interests, to be viewed as the norm. It may be the case that for many people, the singular and dominant is an unproblematic norm. The social, cultural and historical specificity of the norm is overlooked or denied, as is the way in which the specificity serves to marginalise or exclude some members of our schools and societies. Recognition of these issues is crucial if we are to enable alternative identities, masculinities and femininities to be legitimately expressed and pursued, and to encourage appreciation of their value. The history of the women's movement, of anti-racism, or of gay rights is evidence that stereotypes rarely go uncontested, and that values are rarely allowed to stand still.

Talk of multiple masculinities and femininities directs us to the fact that gender can never be viewed in isolation from the many other dimensions of sociocultural and economic life that shape our identities. Our analyses and understandings will always fall short if we do not engage with the dynamics between gender and issues of class, ethnicity, ability, sexuality, age, and religious and cultural values. Lists such as these always need to be presented with caution. There are always dangers of overlooking a crucial 'identity' for someone. However, it serves to make the point that we all have multiple identities, that masculinities and femininities reflect and express. It also draws attention to the inherent shortcomings of making generalised statements, or developing policies and practices in physical education, that are directed towards 'girls' and 'boys' as if these were discrete and homogeneous groups. As teachers are all too aware, children – both girls and boys – are individuals. In 'talking gender' we need to be able to accommodate their individuality and acknowledge the ways in which gendered identities are embedded with and mediated by, other identities. As we see in subsequent chapters, these 'other identities' can have an important bearing upon the masculinities and femininities that any individual will relate to, value, and regard as legitimate and accessible to them. Broadening thinking in relation to these issues is critical if we are to move towards greater gender equity in physical education.

It is appropriate to acknowledge that a focus upon multiple masculinities and femininities is not without potential pitfalls. Francis (2000) notably makes the point that hegemonic notions of masculinity and femininity may be positioned at the top of a hierarchy, with other forms located below them. Furthermore, she argues that to suggest that there are different categories of masculinity and femininity is to imply 'something more fixed than is the case' (p. 14). Francis' work thus prompts us to seek to avoid polarising debates and to stress the dynamic nature of gender and gender relations in physical education and sport.

In the chapters that follow we see both evidence of progress towards a greater level of sophistication in addressing gender in physical education, and clear failure on the part of policy-makers and practitioners to embrace such complexities. Issues of class, ethnicity, sexuality, ability, age, religion and culture have obvious bearings upon the ways in which both men and women will be positioned socially, culturally and in status and value in contexts of physical education and sport. The same issues also impact upon the ways in which we may position ourselves. We are all differently positioned, but also in different positions to (re-)position ourselves in contexts of physical education and sport, in arenas of policy and curriculum development in education, and in society. Following Rich (2001) we use the term 'positioning' as an active as well as a passive verb. As Rich's research on the life histories of women (in physical education and sport) consistently indicates, the activity of 'positioning genders' is an act of agency as well as of passivity and constraint. Differences between us in these respects arise not only by virtue of our being either male or female. Inherent in our multiple identities is the potential for us to be subject to 'multiple forms of oppression and discrimination' (Cole and Hill, 1999: 3). Marginalisation is a reality for many women but also for many men in physical education and sport as in many other forms of socio-economic life. It is something that will be experienced to varying degrees by different people in particular settings. As indicated above, people are judged in relation to prevailing norms that are not arbitrary and that are defined by dominant groups. Consequently, some people will be viewed as deficient and/or deviant, and subjected to prejudice in physical education, education, sport and society. Throughout this book we point to the need to pursue who – and more specifically, *which* women and *which* men – are being positioned 'at the margins' in and by the policies and practices of physical education. In parallel we consider the different scope that particular women and particular men have to be proactive in seeking to reposition themselves and their values and interests in educational arenas, in sport and in society. Analysis is therefore, directed to both the positions accorded to individuals and the positions that they may access and legitimately occupy.

As is apparent from the discussion above, power-relations are central to achieving more comprehensive conceptualisations of gender equity. The identities and positions that are occupied and can potentially be occupied by particular women and men always need to be understood and explored 'in context'; specifically in the political, social, cultural, historical and institutional contexts in which they are set. Characteristics of these contexts create both opportunities and barriers for the expression of particular identities, masculinities and femininities and serve to position them as either legitimate and to be celebrated – or equally, as undesirable. But perhaps the most important way in which these contexts are relevant to our concerns for greater gender equity is in the way in which they influence and in many instances constrain our potential to actively redefine the norms that underpin the exclusion and marginalisation that we seek to eradicate. We, along with the other contributors to this collection, have experienced the limits to our own scope to access and influence those who hold central positions in policy and curriculum development in physical education. As other educational policy researchers have similarly observed, agendas for social justice will not be shared by all and nor are they welcome in all arenas (see for example, Griffiths, 1998; Ozga, 2000). As we discuss in later chapters, this is also vividly reflected in the policies and practices of physical education, as much by what is missing from those policies and practices as what is present in them.

Policies, practice and the pursuit of gender equity

Having pointed to the limits of contemporary policies and practice in physical education and furthermore, our scope to influence them, it is appropriate to shift to a more positive orientation. We may be able to extend our ability to influence future developments in physical education by developing a better understanding of the ways in which policies and practices take particular forms (forms which can either reinforce or challenge inequities). We therefore direct attention to work within the field of 'education policy sociology' and the key concepts that this has provided for critical sociological inquiry. The starting point is to deconstruct the familiar conceptualisations of 'policy' and 'practice'; of policy 'making' and 'implementation'. Work such as that undertaken by Stephen Ball and his colleagues (see for example Ball,

1990; Bowe *et al.*, 1992) has led the field in advancing our thinking on 'policy matters'. In many respects we have seen that the language of description and analysis is inherently problematic. This is a point reflected in the use of textual markers ('. ...') to indicate the shortcomings of particular words, and their inability (because of the likelihood that they will be understood within dominant and established frames of reference) to accurately portray the intended meanings. For the same reasons we often extend talk of 'policy' to 'policy and curriculum development'. Our emphasis is that the two are inextricably linked. Policy is not an isolated, abstract 'thing' set apart from the individuals and practices that are found within schools. It is a complex, ongoing, contested and relational process, that encompasses both what we may have in the past viewed as 'policy' and that which we term 'practice', and in which the boundaries between 'making' and 'implementation' are blurred and complex, involving many sites and many individuals, both within and beyond education systems (see Penney and Evans, 1999). Policy viewed from this standpoint 'is more about "*process*" than "product" ' (Ozga, 2000: 2); it is 'struggled over, not delivered, in tablets of stone, to a grateful or quiescent population' (ibid.: 1). Acknowledging that policy is a social process is at the same time to note that it is also likely to be an emotional process, inherent in which are issues of identity, gender and sexuality. In this sense the 'body' is fundamentally, inextricably implicated in the policy process and therefore has to be accommodated in any analysis of sociocultural and educational change.

The ongoing struggles and contestation over, and adaptation of, texts are also key characteristics of the policy process. As Bowe *et al.* (1992) emphasised, policy is about the creation and re-creation of texts in many sites and by many individuals. There is thus plenty of scope in this process for various interests to come into play, to be privileged or equally, marginalised or excluded, at various points in time. Who privileges or marginalises what interests, where and why, are important issues to consider in relation to gender equity in physical education. We point to the concept of discourse as probably our most potent tool in addressing these issues (Penney and Evans, 1999). In talking of discourses we are concerned with the interests and values that are reflected, legitimated, promoted, or equally subordinated or excluded via particular modes of communication (linguistic and corporeal) and the meanings attached to the form and content of that communication. Discourse is the concept that captures the way in which texts produced historically and contemporaneously within and beyond contexts of physical education shape thinking, particularly in this instance, about issues to do with gender. As we have identified in our previous explorations of policy, we can identify particular discourses with particular interests and values and, thus, the presence of various discourses in the texts of policy-makers, teachers and pupils. We have repeatedly emphasised that not all discourses are accorded equal status, or even a visible presence in those texts. Following Ball (1990) we note that in critically exploring texts, what is *not* said is as important as what is. Several chapters in this collection serve to demonstrate the 'power of silence' in subordinating or excluding particular interests, identities and individuals. In chapter 7 particularly we see that silence on issues should not be read as a signal of neutrality on gender issues. In that chapter and others we also see another important dimension to discourse, that identifies it as a concept that clearly engages with the notion of policy as 'process rather than product'. In Ball's (1990) words, discourses are also about 'who can speak where, when and with what authority' (p. 17). Anyone seeking to advance equity in physical education will be aware of these issues that turn our attention back once again to matters of 'position' and where we can locate ourselves in a policy process that is always and inevitably highly political (see for example, Ball, 1990; Graham with Tytler, 1993; Penney and Evans, 1999; Taylor *et al.*, 1997).

Understanding the form and content of particular texts (which may be policy documents issued by central government, curriculum materials produced by teachers or their 'act' of teaching itself, i.e. the pedagogical text), and our varying abilities to influence that form and content, demands that we locate texts 'in context'. More specifically, it demands that we explore the historical, political, economic, social, cultural and institutional contexts that locate, shape and are shaped by particular texts. Several points need to be considered here. First, the various dimensions of context always create both opportunities and set limits to the type of texts that can legitimately arise in a particular context. Second, those same dimensions also create both possibilities and set limits in relation to the ability of particular people to shape texts. Third, all texts are in a dynamic relationship with contexts and as such work to either legitimate, reinforce and reproduce the values, interests and inequities inherent in them, or serve to challenge and potentially re-shape contexts in these terms. Hence our emphasis that we are all actors in the policy process, albeit differently positioned and variously able to influence thinking and actions. We should never deny the importance of structural issues in the exploration of policy matters. Indeed, we have argued that the complexity and extent of these has placed a stranglehold upon teachers' work in contemporary England and Wales, if not internationally (see Evans, Davies and Penney, 1994; Hargreaves, 1994). However, this book is testimony to our continued belief in the significance of the 'spaces for action', the 'scope for slippage' (Bowe *et al.*, 1992); that is to say, in the capacity of teachers and teacher educators to reshape physical education in more equitable ways and to promote policies and practices that better respond to gender issues.

Finally, we should address the position of researchers in the policy process. In important respects both individually and collectively, the authors of the chapters in this book are speaking from the margins of policy and curriculum development in physical education. Neither they nor the agendas that they pursue enjoy central positions in that development. Many of us have seen and experienced that 'Policy influence is a struggle to be heard in an arena where only certain voices have legitimacy at any point in time' (Ball, 1994: 112), and that the voices of critical educational researchers rarely have this legitimacy. The term 'critical' refers to our underpinning interest in social change towards greater gender equity, in education, physical education and in society. Not surprisingly those whose interests serve an inequitable status quo, whose values currently dominate and are represented and promoted in the policies and practice of education and physical education, are unlikely to welcome the prospect of innovation and change. However, even if marginalised, research and researchers may play a key role in socio-educational change. Like Ozga (2000) we contend that inherent in research are 'opportunities for change' which 'contribute to its power as an *educational process*, and help to explain why policy-makers are so anxious to ensure that research is encountered by teachers only in predictable and limited ways' (p. 70). The change that is referred to here is change on the part of both 'the researched' and researchers themselves. Ozga explains that 'research may bring about further transformation of the researcher, as he or she is altered through the generation of new insights and attitudes' (ibid.: 70). Variously, those of us writing for this collection have experienced such transformation, both in the context of our respective fieldwork, but also in the act of writing. Our hope is that this book will further facilitate and promote new insights, extend discussions, and open up a dialogue between all parties committed to equity in physical education.

References

Ball, S.J. (1990) *Politics and Policy Making in Education: Explorations in Policy Sociology*, London: Routledge.

Ball, S.J. (1994) Researching inside the State: issues in the interpretation of elite interviews, in D. Halpin and B. Troyna (eds) *Researching Education Policy. Ethical and Methodological Issues*, London: The Falmer Press.

Bowe, R. and Ball, S.J. with Gold, A. (1992) *Reforming Education and Changing Schools: Case Studies in Policy Sociology*, London: Routledge.

Cole, M. and Hill, D. (1999) Equality and secondary education: what are the conceptual issues?, in D. Hill and M. Cole (eds) *Promoting Equality in Secondary Schools*, London: Cassell.

Collins, C., Kenway, J. and McLeod, J. (2000) Gender debates we still have to have, *The Australian Educational Researcher* 27(3): 37–48.

Evans, J. and Davies, B. (1993) Equality, equity and physical education, in J. Evans, (ed.) *Equality, Education and Physical Education*, London: Falmer Press.

Evans, J., Davies, B. and Penney, D. (1994) Whatever happened to the subject and the State in policy research in education?, *Discourse: Studies in the Cultural Politics of Education* 14(2): 57–64.

Francis, B. (2000) *Boys, Girls and Achievement: Addressing Classroom Issues*, London: Falmer Press.

Graham, D. with Tytler, D. (1993) *A Lesson for Us All. The Making of the National Curriculum*, London: Routledge.

Griffiths, M. (1998) *Educational Research for Social Justice: Getting Off the Fence*, Buckingham: Open University Press.

Hargreaves, A. (1994) *Changing Teachers, Changing Times: Teachers' Work and Culture in the Postmodern Age*, London: Cassell.

Hargreaves, J. (1994) *Sporting Females: Critical Issues in the History and Sociology of Women's Sport*, London: Routledge.

Ozga, J. (2000) *Policy Research in Educational Settings: Contested Terrain*, Buckingham: Open University Press.

Penney, D. and Evans, J. (1999) *Politics, Policy and Practice in Physical Education*, London: Routledge.

Rich, E. (2001) *Strong Words, Tough Minds, Trained Bodies. A Life History Narrative Analysis of Female Student Teachers of Physical Education*, unpublished Ph.D thesis, Loughborough University.

Shilling, C. (1993) *The Body and Social Theory*, London: Sage.

Talbot, M. (1993) Gender and physical education, in J. Evans (ed.) *Equality, Education and Physical Education*, London: Falmer Press.

Taylor, S., Rizvi, F., Lingard, B. and Henry, M. (1997) *Educational Policy and the Politics of Change*, London: Routledge.

3 Physical education: a gendered history

David Kirk

Introduction

Many people who grew to adulthood between the 1960s and 1990s in Britain will believe that British society has moved a long way to resolve gender issues in sport and physical education. They may point to women's participation in marathon running or rugby, or look to girls and boys playing together in co-educational physical education classes as proof that we now have equality between the sexes in sport and physical education. However, some less sanguine members of the public may remind us that girls remain more likely to drop out of sport than boys and that in some elite sport contexts women do not receive the same rewards as men for what are arguably as good or better performances. Others might suggest that in order to gain public recognition and acceptance of their participation, women have increasingly had to 'play like men' (Hargreaves, 1994), or rather, like certain men. As other authors in this collection emphasise, particular forms of masculinity remain dominant in many sporting contexts and this dominance serves to exclude both women and men from participation, enjoyment and/or achievement in sport.

Those people taking an optimistic view in these debates may argue that the barriers to girls' and women's full participation in physical education and sport have now been removed, and that whether and how to participate is now a matter of individual choice. They might concede that more could be done to motivate disaffected and inactive girls, but would still contend that the problem, if one still exists, is down to individual choice and enthusiasm rather than structural barriers. A historical perspective on this issue reveals that the optimists do have a point; there has indeed been some progress. However, history also shows that they may have underestimated the enormity and complexity of gender in physical education and overestimated what has been achieved (Mangan and Parks, 1987). In this chapter, I adopt an historical perspective, arguing that physical education as an activity in the school curriculum has been gendered since its first appearance in the modern era, which dates for our purposes here from the 1880s and the beginning of mass compulsory schooling in Britain. What this means is that for over one hundred years, the practices that make up physical education have been strongly associated with stereotypical views about the behaviours and activity that is appropriate for girls and boys respectively and with notably singular images of femininity and masculinity. I present three episodes from the history of physical education in Scotland between the 1950s and the 1970s to show that this gendering of the subject has been profound and far-reaching. I suggest that what we now regard as legitimate knowledge in physical education has been strongly influenced by this gendered history and that this influence is invariably overlooked. Many members of the general public and of the teaching profession do not recognise the gender dimensions of physical education and assume that the subject is unproblematically androgenous, or gender-neutral. The inability to recognise the lasting influence of the gendered history of physical education has serious consequences for children's experiences of and opportunities in physical education and sport. As other chapters in this book confirm, for many girls and more boys than is often acknowledged, these experiences and opportunities are limited because of the ongoing influence of the past.

The chapter begins by examining a 1954 conference debate between female and male physical educators in Scotland over the future of physical education and in particular, over which version of gymnastics should be taught to Scottish schoolboys. It then moves on to take a closer look at the debate through the writings of David Munrow (for the 'male perspective') and Marjorie Randall (for the 'female perspective'). These respective spokespeople for men and women demonstrate that the gendering of physical education was actually constitutive of the form the subject could take in schools and higher education institutions. Finally, the chapter turns to an investigation of the Munn Report of 1977 on the curriculum in Scottish schools (SED/CCC, 1977) and the separate submissions to the Committee from female and male physical educators. This episode in the history of physical education in Scotland represents the 'bottom line' in terms of the selection of versions of physical education for the official curriculum of government-funded schools. The debates that I report occurred in Scotland but serve to illustrate issues that have relevance well beyond this national context.

A debate in Scotland

From the 1880s up to the 1950s, gymnastics was the main content of physical education programmes in government schools. By the end of the Second World War, three distinct versions of gymnastics were competing for teaching time in school physical education programmes (Kirk, 1992); the Swedish (or Ling) gymnastics; educational gymnastics; and German or Olympic gymnastics. In November 1954, delegates from the Scottish Physical Education Association (SPEA) and the Scottish League of Physical Education (SLPE) met in Edinburgh to discuss 'Physical Education Today and in the Future' (The Leaflet, 1955: 6) and specifically to consider which of three versions of gymnastics should be taught to boys in Scottish schools. The SPEA represented male physical education teachers and the SLPE represented female teachers, with the conference being organised by the Scottish Joint Consultative Committee on Physical Education (SJCCPE).

At this 1954 conference delegates failed to reach an agreed position regarding the future provision of gymnastics in the physical education curriculum for boys in Scotland. The SJCCPE organised four further one day meetings to debate the issue. The outcome of these meetings was that boys would continue to be taught Swedish (or Ling) gymnastics on the grounds that the other contender for the 'top spot', educational gymnastics, would undermine the traditionally high standards of skill developed in Swedish gymnastics. This outcome was ironic given the title and focus of the conference, which was intended to make decisions about the future. Within a decade, the 'winner', Swedish gymnastics, had disappeared completely from the school curriculum, and the contender, educational gymnastics, had been embattled and bruised. The distant third placer in 1954, Olympic gymnastics, emerged to take pride of place in physical education programmes throughout Britain. How could this conference of physical educators have got things so badly wrong? To understand the issues debated and the decisions made we need to further explore the development of each of the three forms of gymnastics and the values and traditions that each was associated with in 1954.

Swedish (or Ling) gymnastics

Swedish (or Ling) gymnastics had been the hallmark of the professional female physical educator between the late 1890s to the 1940s, and the version of physical education officially approved by the then Board of Education (working in partnership with the Scottish Education Department[1]) for use in elementary schools in Scotland. The Swedish system was invented by Per Henrick Ling in the early decades of the nineteenth century and consolidated into a system of physical training at the Central Gymnastic Institute in Stockholm, which he founded. It involved mostly free-standing exercises that sought to systematically exercise each part of the body through increasingly intricate flexions and extensions. It also involved some apparatus work such as vaulting (see Board of Education, 1909). Teaching within the Ling system was highly formalised and particularly in the 1800s featured movements performed to militaristic commands such as 'at the double!' and 'fall in!' It was easily practised with large groups in confined spaces (Munrow, 1955). The Swedish system was boosted in Britain in the 1880s through the work of Swedish Gymnasts appointed by the Board of Education to organise physical education in its elementary schools. Swedish gymnastics formed the foundation of women's professional training and was supplemented by training in massage, remedial exercises and games.

Educational gymnastics

Educational gymnastics made a rapid and dramatic impact on female physical education from the first appearance of Rudolf Laban's ideas on movement and dance in Britain in the 1930s. Modern Dance was built on a radical critique of 'unnatural' movement patterns in industrial society that in Laban's opinion, had much to do with the presence of mental illness and personality disorders. Laban's philosophy argued for the release of dangerously pent up and inhibited energies through free, spontaneous movement. Although Laban's main concerns were focused on the theatre and industry, female physical educators quickly applied his ideas to gymnastics during the late 1930s and through the war years. Educational gymnastics borrowed from modern dance a concern for the qualitative dimensions of movement experience and selectively adopted some of the rhetoric and ideas of the fast growing and fashionable child-centred progressivism in British educational circles of the time. In particular, ideas associated with humanistic liberal individualism found expression in educational gymnastics (Ministry of Education, 1952).

German or Olympic gymnastics

The third form of gymnastics was witnessed in its modern form for the first time by British physical educators at the 1948 London Olympic Games. German gymnastics had been around at least as long as Ling's system and involved work on apparatus such as the rings, parallel bars and pummel horse. At the beginning of the twentieth century it had vied with the Swedish system for selection (by the Interdepartmental Committee set up by the Royal Commission on Physical Training (1903) to produce a Syllabus of Physical Exercises for British schools) as the official system of physical training. It lost that contest and suffered the stigma of its German origins after the First World War, being neglected by all but a handful of enthusiasts in Britain until the 1940s. However, following the 1948 Olympics, which presented gymnastics as a competitive sport made up of the six activities of floor-work, vaulting, rings, bars, beam and pommel horse, there was an increasing level of interest in this version of gymnastics and a growing number of advocacies for its inclusion in school programmes.

Gender and gymnastics

It is important to note that each of these three version of gymnastics had strong gender associations. Swedish gymnastics was the staple of women's physical education during the first half of the twentieth century, but it was also widely practised by men. When women performed Swedish gymnastics, their movements were required to be dainty, nimble and flexible. When men performed Swedish gymnastics, they were required to be strong and powerful.

Curiously, as it was practised in government schools with co-educational classes, Swedish gymnastics took on an androgynous form where the sex of the individual was made to appear irrelevant to the activity. I have speculated elsewhere that this may only have been possible when Swedish gymnastics was taught to pre-pubescent children and became problematic as older and physically more mature children were staying on at school (Kirk, 2000).

Educational gymnastics was invariably associated with women's and girls' physical education, and the education of young children in the infant school. The influence of Laban's philosophy and the ideology of child-centredness that was the orthodoxy of the 1950s and 1960s in primary schools added such depth and strength to the practice of educational gymnastics that it provoked both intense support and considerable hostility. While the hostility came mainly from men, there were also many women physical educators who regarded educational gymnastics with some suspicion. The focus of opposition from the men were the claims that it was possible to develop generalised movement competencies through gymnastics and that there was little or no place for competition in the gym. The men were also extremely uncomfortable with the women's interest in movement as an aesthetic activity. Meanwhile opposition from women can be associated mainly with those women who were members of the 'old school' of Swedish gymnastics, who decried the informality and apparent lack of discipline of educational gymnastics.

Olympic gymnastics was practised by both men and women, and practised differently according to dominant notions of femininity and masculinity. This was most obviously expressed in the different activities that comprised Olympic gymnastics for men and women respectively; namely rings, pommel and parallel bars for men, and asymmetric bars and the beam for women. In 1954 this form of gymnastics was too new to be a genuine contender in the deliberations over which form of gymnastics would dominate physical education. However, its ultimate victory in debates and developments signalled new gender associations in physical education, a matter that I return to later in the chapter. But first, let us return to the question posed earlier: how did the conference delegates in 1954 get it so wrong in their decision to support Swedish gymnastics for boys as the future of their subject? Quite clearly, even though educational gymnastics was the rising star of physical education in the early 1950s, its strong association with the education of girls and women probably ruled it out of contention for the men. However, we need to note that the decision required a conference and four one-day meetings, indicating that the result was far from a foregone conclusion and nor was it an uncontested decision. In the next section I pursue the gender issues involved in the choice between these forms of gymnastics and consider what it was about the activities themselves and the forms of movement that they required that meant that they were firmly aligned with dominant forms of femininity and masculinity.

Inside the debate

By the end of the 1950s, male physical educators were in the majority within the profession, something that had never happened before in Britain. Before long they began to champion two developments that up to this time were quite alien to physical education (Kirk, 1992). The first of these was the idea that physical education was not primarily about gymnastics at all or rather, should not be in Britain. Instead, they argued that physical education should be centred on the sports and games that first appeared in the mid- to late 1800s in the schools for social elites such as Eton, Harrow and Westminster. Hugh Brown, then Director of the Scottish School of Physical Education,[2] captured this important and dramatic shift in his comments on training programmes for male physical education teachers in the 1950s.

> The curriculum in the Colleges of PE is ever-widening. This is something that I rejoice to be able to report, and my only comment is 'high time, too!' We are British people – for which I can find no cause for apology – and we are a games-playing nation. It has always puzzled me, for instance, that gymnastics should be regarded as being synonymous with Physical Education. Gymnastics is a part – a very valuable part – of a vast subject, and in some countries it may have been looked on as being the main fraction of the whole. No longer is that so here. However good a system may be, the folly of adopting it in its entirety and foisting it upon people, unadapted to peculiar needs, is at last recognised. What may delight the Germans or the Danes, and what suits their national characteristics, does not necessarily make a similar appeal here. Now we are recognising this!
>
> (Brown, 1958: 92)

The second development that the male physical educators championed was the use of science in the service of physical performance. This work began in earnest after the Second World War in university departments of physical education, at Leeds and Birmingham in particular. The first and most prominent achievement of this scientific approach was the development of work in the areas of strength and endurance, two dimensions of physical performance closely associated with the sports that were then clearly identified as 'male' (primarily rugby, athletics and weight-lifting). The application of a scientific perspective also generated new developments in the area of skill acquisition and motor learning.

During this period, female physical educators had also been involved in debate about the desirable content of their subject. For them the issue was not the place of gymnastics, but the relative place of which form, and specifically, the respective merits of Swedish versus educational gymnastics. By the end of the 1950s the 'new school' of the educational gymnasts were in the ascendancy. As male antagonism to educational gymnastics began to become increasingly more vocal through the 1950s, two major issues focused the debate between the 'female' and 'male' perspectives that became very evident in physical education. The first issue was the controversy surrounding the level of specificity required for skill development and the matter of transfer of training. The second concerned the application of objective standards to gymnastic performance and the place of competition in the gym.

The specificity of skill development

In his book *Pure and Applied Gymnastics* first published in 1955, Munrow suggested that in moving away from the Swedish system after the Second World War, male and female physical educators had reacted in different ways to the question of skill specificity.

> The men have made overt acknowledgement that other skills are as important and have 'diluted' the gymnastic skill content of gymnasium work so that now boys may be seen practising basket-ball shots and manoeuvres, carrying out heading practices or practising sprint starting. . . . The women, in the main, have . . . 'diluted' the traditional gymnastic skills by a quite different device. They have ceased both to name and to teach them. Instead, a description is given, in general terms, of a task involving apparatus and individual solutions are encouraged. A much wider range of solutions is thus possible; some may include traditional skills but many will not.
>
> (Munrow, 1955: 276)

The problem with the female alternative to the Swedish system, as Munrow saw it, was that pupils rarely had the chance to consolidate their skills because no specific skill teaching took place.

The educational gymnasts' reply to Munrow's challenge came from Marjorie Randall in 1961 in her book, *Basic Movement*. In the opening chapter of the book, Randall contested Munrow's functional definition of gymnastics, suggesting that 'the masculine approach . . . has become largely outmoded so far as women's work is concerned' (Randall, 1961: 12). She claimed that 'Women's gymnastics . . . have been emancipated from the restricted practices of stereotyped patterns of movements based upon anatomical classification. The physiological and anatomical ends . . . are incidentally served' (ibid.: 12).

The major aim identified by Randall was the achievement of what she termed body awareness, which included neural control combined with a higher level kinesthetic awareness, that could be developed through experience into an intuitive control of movement. Also in contrast to the male approach she added to this the need to engage the child cognitively. She accused the men of stressing only the physical effects of exercise, and consequently regarding cognition as out of range. 'The masculine approach to gymnastics' she claimed separates content from method. Munrow's gymnastics exercises can be directly and formally taken or informally taken. Movement gymnastics requires the intelligent co-operation of the child, rendering command-response methods obsolete . . . this represents a big break-away from the traditional approach of the 'see this' and 'do it this way' school of thought.

(Randall, 1961: 25–6)

Randall's response showed that behind the less formal methods of educational gymnastics lay an attempt to treat the pupil holistically, encouraging the simultaneous development of intellectual and creative abilities in a movement medium and relegating the physical effect of movement to a level of lesser importance.

However, the notion of body awareness, which lay at the centre of the women's scheme, suggested a theory of learning that ran directly counter to the new knowledge being produced by motor learning theorists. The educational gymnasts claimed, in much the same way as the Swedish gymnasts had before them, that the movement experience that they had to offer was a general foundation upon which more specific skills could be built. The notion of body awareness expressed this idea as generalised kinesthetic control. As early as 1949 members of the Birmingham University staff including David Munrow and Barbara Knapp questioned whether there was such a thing as generalised skill training. In her book *Skill in Sport* (Knapp, 1963), published in 1963, Barbara Knapp argued that transfer of training was most likely to occur when the tasks in question were similar, and that the best way to learn a specific action was to perform that action repeatedly over a period of time. The main point of the motor learning theorists' criticisms, which the male physical educators championed vigorously, was that skill learning is specific and that repeated practice in the same or similar conditions is the key to mastery. Taking these principles to heart, male physical educators developed an approach to teaching skills that consisted of reducing a skill to its component parts, and learning each part separately before re-assembling them gradually until the entire skill had been learned. This appeared to make nonsense of the claim amongst female physical educators that it was possible, indeed preferable, to develop a general body awareness as a foundation on which to build more specific learning.

Standards and competition in the gym

A second objection to the educational gymnasts' perspective related to the place of standards and competition in the gym. From the male point of view, it seemed unlikely that the educational gymnasts' child-centred approach could continue to stimulate pupils beyond the early stages of learning. Munrow argued that it could not challenge older boys or girls. He contended that competitive activity was essential as a stimulant or incentive for advancing learning. In *Pure and Applied Gymnastics* he complained

> Allied to a teaching philosophy which seeks actively to avoid confronting less able children with failure, is the belief that the child's own solution to the problem being always valid and right. This makes more sense with young children than with older boys and girls and with first efforts at a skill rather than with later ones . . . to leave children floundering to evolve their own technique when we could guide them is a neglect of our professional duties.
>
> (Munrow, 1955: 280–1)

In response to Munrow's view that standards were a necessary and important means of challenging pupils to strive for excellence, Randall suggested that girls, particularly in adolescence, had quite different needs to boys. She argued that the growing boy 'derives considerable prestige and social prominence through physical advantage in competitive games which his increase in height, weight and strength gives him' (Randall, 1961: 20). Girls, on the other hand, may have little to gain from competitive sport during the adolescent period.

> In the gymnastic lesson let her be free from all this competition and let her progress at her own rate and find joy and satisfaction in the slow but sure progress of controlling her body. Through her pride in the mastery of her body in the gymnasium will grow a certain independence, security and emotional stability. . . . Teaching must be geared to the individual; it must be flexible and tolerant of a wide range in aptitude . . . no longer is her worth in the gymnasium measured by whether she can get over the box in long fly or whether she can put her head on her knees keeping her legs straight; but rather can she work to surpass her own standards without being harassed or harried because she cannot conform to a common one.
>
> (Randall, 1961: 21–2)

The aims of independence, security and emotional stability contrast sharply with the desire to develop strength, endurance, flexibility and particular skills, and to use these attributes in competitive situations. The contrasts reveal starkly the contested issues that divided the male and female physical educators. It is also important to reflect upon the degree to which both sides were effectively arguing that boys and girls have different needs in relation to physical education. Notably absent in these debates is a recognition of different needs amongst either girls or boys. The image legitimated and reinforced is of two homogeneous groups aligned with stereotypical perceptions of activities and behaviours of which they are capable and in which they should be engaging.

The debate between female and male physical educators continued around these issues throughout the 1960s and into the 1970s. The development of the four-year Bachelor of Education (BEd) degree during the 1960s to replace the three-year diploma as the main qualification for teaching physical education in Britain drew heavily on exercise physiology, biomechanics and motor learning for its subject matter. This focus advantaged the men over the women whose child-centred movement focus leant itself to the Arts as a knowledge base (Fletcher, 1984). By the time the BEd was in place towards the end of the 1960s, gymnastics no longer formed the core of physical education programmes. Researcher Nick Whitehead's 1969 survey of a range of secondary schools mainly in the North of England found that the 'national sports' of soccer, rugby and cricket for boys, hockey and netball for girls, and athletics for both, now dominated school physical education (Whitehead and Hendry, 1976). Swedish gymnastics had disappeared almost completely to be replaced by Olympic gymnastics for boys which also began to compete with educational gymnastics as the main form of gymnastics for girls. So which of these gendered forms of physical education had won the day?

And the winner is . . . ?

In the mid 1970s, curriculum and assessment in Scottish secondary schools was under review. Policy-makers and curriculum writers had been influenced by the work of a number of philosophers of education (e.g. Peters, 1966; White, 1973; Hirst, 1974) who argued that some knowledge was of greater educational worth than others. These arguments led policy-makers to the view that some school subjects should be regarded as 'core' or essential and others as optional. In 1975, the Scottish Education Department (SED) and its Consultative Committee on Curriculum (CCC) set up a committee under the chairmanship of Mr James Munn to examine the curriculum of Scottish secondary schools in the years leading up to the national examinations (years 3 and 4).

The Munn Committee received submissions from interested parties during 1975 and 1976 prior to making its report the following year (SED/CCC, 1977). Given the prevailing interest in the notion of core and elective subjects based on the 'educational' criteria of the philosophers of education, members of the physical education profession were nervous about the possibility that their subject may be excluded from the core curriculum. What they chose to say 'on behalf of physical education' was clearly a matter of importance to the future of the subject.

In 1975, the Scottish Central Committee on Physical Education (SCCPE) made a submission to the Munn Committee on behalf of all of the physical education profession in Scotland (SCCPE, 1975). The SCCPE began their submission by taking issue with what they called the 'Peters/Hirst initiation model' of education arguing that this model was biased against a practical subject such as 'physical education/movement', as they called it. They proposed that the Munn committee adopt the scheme devised by another philosopher of education (Philip Phenix, 1964) whose 'realms of meaning' thesis, they claimed, offered greater scope to a movement-based subject. In laying out their view of physical education/movement, the SCCPE claimed that

> The early stages of the curriculum should attempt to help the child to become more aware of his/her own movement responses through kinesthetic feedback . . . [and should] help guide the child to an understanding of his individual movement characteristics. Cognitive understanding of underlying concepts of the activities and of individual movement responses should be established by this stage.
>
> (SCCPE, 1975: 6)

The SCCPE submission also claimed that 'the pupil should have a reasonably sophisticated body concept . . . a concept of aesthetic demands (and) a concept of the competitive nature of certain activities' (SCCPE, 1975: 7).

The emphasis that the submission placed upon understanding, cognition and conceptual development and the prominence of notions such as the aesthetic, were characteristic of the female tradition and the influence of educational gymnastics and modern dance. Significantly, the female-only Dunfermline College of Physical Education endorsed the SCCPE submission, but the male-only Scottish School of Physical Education (SSPE) did not. Indeed, the SSPE not only refused to endorse the submission, but went a step further and made a rival submission the following year. This later submission by the SSPE was altogether different to that of the SCCPE. The SSPE made no comment on the philosophy underpinning the approach likely to be taken by the Munn Committee. They made the case for physical education's inclusion in the core curriculum on the basis of its contribution to health, to the development of perceptual-motor skills through games and sports and as a preparation for life-time leisure activity. Where it was available, the men produced evidence from scientific studies to support their argument in each of these three areas.

The Munn Committee reported in 1977. Physical education was granted a place in the core curriculum of years 3 and 4 of Scottish secondary schools, though with two periods per week as compared to the five allocated to each of mathematics and English, and four to science and social studies. In Paragraph 4.17 of the Report, the Committee suggested that physical education could contribute to the development of skilful movement, to preparation for leisure, and to the health of all pupils. In justifying their decision to recommend only two periods a week for physical education, the Committee also suggested that as a 'non-cognitive activity' physical education should supplement its curriculum time through the extra-curriculum.

The similarities between the SSPE submission and the recommendations of the Munn Report were all too apparent. By the mid-1970s the male view of physical education, in Scotland in this case but arguably throughout Britain, had become the dominant perspective. The female view, it seemed, had been openly contested. The Committee countered the SCCPE's claims by bluntly stating that physical education was a 'non-cognitive activity'. The significance of this shift in the gendered definition of physical education should not be underestimated. Gender was clearly shown to be *central* to defining the subject, not merely an additional factor in this process. What the subject is today, the forms of engagement that it requires from learners and the criteria by which success should be measured, are stereotypically masculine. It follows that in order to be successful in the subject girls and women need to perform in a masculinised way, and furthermore, a particular masculinised way. This is a profound development and one that requires close and critical scrutiny since it impacts on the quality of physical education for all young people, female and male.

Conclusion

This chapter has sought to illustrate the gendered history of physical education through three episodes from the subject's recent past. I began with the notion that many adults currently accept that while there may have been gender issues in the past, physical education has now resolved these and girls are treated equally to boys. The subsequent investigation of a conference in the mid-1950s, a debate that continued in the literature into the 1960s and a crucial curriculum development process in the mid-1970s were intended to show that the optimistic view is not sustainable. On the contrary, historical investigation can lead us to no other conclusion than that physical education as it currently exists in many British schools is a masculinised form of the subject. But it is not merely masculinised. A particularly narrow vision of masculinity informs and is expressed in this masculinisation. Should this situation be a matter for concern? I believe it should. As is clearly evident in the other contributions to this book and in wider literature, this masculinised form of physical education does not meet the needs of many girls and at least some boys. A consequence is that many young people may be prevented from acquiring the knowledge, skills and motivation they need to lead active and healthy lifestyles. In schools funded by public money, such a situation is simply unacceptable.

However, we need to end with a note of caution. The male version of physical education is not a totalising discourse. This means that while it has achieved dominance, there are spaces for teachers and students to practise alternative forms of physical education that do not ascribe to the values and assumptions of stereotypically masculinised physical education. Other chapters in this book provide evidence to suggest that it is possible to expand those spaces and to provide forms of physical education that are properly educational for all young people. We must learn the lessons of history if the hopes contained in these alternative practices are to become a reality in students' later lives.

Notes

1 The partnership between the Board of Education and the Scottish Education Department was reflected in the 1903 Royal Commission on Physical Training (Scotland), a joint project and publication. This commission had an important influence on the direction of physical training throughout the UK, not only in Scotland.
2 The Scottish School of Physical Education (SSPE) was formed in 1932 to prepare male teachers of physical education, and for much of its history was part of Jordanhill College of Education, Glasgow. The SSPE was formally amalgamated with the women's college, Dunfermline College of Physical Education, in the late 1990s and survives as the Department of Physical Education, Sport and Leisure at the University of Edinburgh.

References

Board of Education (1909) *Syllabus of Physical Exercises for Schools*, London: HMSO.

Brown, H.C. (1958) The training of the man teacher of physical education, *Physical Education* 50 (91–4).

Fletcher, S. (1984) *Women First: The Female Tradition in English Physical Education, 1880–1980*, London: Athlone.

Hargreaves, J.A. (1994) *Sporting Females: Critical Issues in the History and Sociology of Women's Sport*, London: Routledge.

Hirst, P.H. (1974) *Knowledge and the Curriculum,* London: Routledge & Kegan Paul.

Kirk, D. (1992) *Defining Physical Education: The Social Construction of a School Subject in Postwar Britain*, London: Falmer.

Kirk, D. (2000) Gender associations: sport, state schools and Australian culture, *The International Journal of Sport History* 17(2/3): 49–64.

Knapp, B. (1963) *Skill in Sport*, London: Routledge & Kegan Paul.

Mangan, J.A. and Parks, R.J. (eds) (1987) *From 'Fair Sex' to Feminism: Sport and the Socialisation of Women in the Industrial and Post-Industrial Eras*, London: Frank Cass.

Ministry of Education (1952) *Moving and Growing: Physical Education in the Primary School, Part 1*, London: HMSO.

Munrow, A.D. (1955) *Pure and Applied Gymnastics*, London: Arnold.

Peters, R.S. (1966) *Ethics and Education*, London: Allen & Unwin.

Phenix, P. (1964) *Realms of Meaning*, London: McGraw-Hill.

Randall, M. (1961) *Basic Movement: A New Approach to Gymnastics*, London: Bell.

Scottish Central Committee on Physical Education (1975) Submission to the Munn Committee, unpublished paper.

Scottish Education Department/Consultative Committee on Curriculum (1977) *The Structure of the Curriculum in Years Three and Four of the Scottish Secondary School*, Edinburgh: HMSO.

Scottish School of Physical Education (1976) Submission to the Munn Committee, unpublished paper.

The Leaflet (1955) Physical Education Today and in the Future, *The Leaflet* 56(1): 6.

White, J. (1973) *Towards a Compulsory Curriculum*, London: Routledge & Kegan Paul.

Whitehead, N. and Hendry, L. (1976) *Teaching Physical Education in England: Description and Analysis*, London: Lepus.

Part II
Gender agendas

4 Difference matters: sexuality and physical education

Gill Clarke

Introduction

Earlier chapters within this collection have pointed to the specific traditions of physical education and in particular to the highly gender differentiated nature of these. These markedly conservative traditions have had a deleterious impact not only on the teaching and nature of the subject but also on conceptions of masculinity and femininity. This has contributed to a situation whereby damaging myths and stereotypes specifically about the participation of women and girls in physical education and sport have largely gone unchallenged. These prejudices centre on issues to do with the athletic body, heterosexuality and physicality. This chapter consequently seeks to raise issues around sexuality and physical education. It focuses attention on Section 28 of the Local Government Act (1988) which sought to prohibit the promotion of homosexuality within schools, and thereby illustrates attitudes towards sexuality and the impact that these have had on the educative system. Biographical research which endeavoured to make sense of the life stories of lesbian physical education teachers within the English schooling system is utilised to explore the effects of heterosexual discourses on their professional lives. Although the focus is largely on the experiences of lesbian physical education teachers it is crucial to acknowledge the impact that heterosexism and homophobia has had on boys and men and gay teachers in physical education and sport. Heterosexism

> refers to the system of beliefs, attitudes and institutional arrangements which reinforce that everyone is, or should be heterosexual; that heterosexuality is the only valid and worthwhile form of sexual expression; and that relationships between people of the opposite sex are vastly superior to any other lifestyle whether lesbian, gay, bisexual or single.
>
> (Labour Research Department, 1992: 4).

Homophobia is commonly defined as 'the irrational fear or intolerance of homosexuality, gay men or lesbians, and even behaviour that is perceived to be outside the boundaries of traditional gender role expectations' (Griffin and

Genasci, 1990: 211). The silences, fears and phobias that surround these issues make it difficult, if not impossible, to locate gay teachers in the macho masculine world of physical education (Clarke, 1998a). By this I mean that physical education has certain 'normalised' expectations of what it is to be male and it is these privileged ways of being that are hegemonic and often unquestioned. Those who do not explicitly portray traditional macho characteristics of toughness, aggression and physical prowess are likely to be ridiculed and their performances trivialised and marginalised by the dominant masculine group (see Parker, 1996). Thus, my attention is directed initially to specific situations within physical education that create anxiety and potential risks for lesbian teachers, in particular the supervising of changing rooms and showers. However, it is my contention that these anxieties could also be experienced by gay physical education teachers.[1] The relationships of these lesbian teachers with pupils both within the classroom and the extended curriculum, and with teaching colleagues, are examined insofar as these are locations where their heterosexual 'cover' might be blown and where specific tactics are required to protect their 'real' sexual identity. Finally, I consider how they feel the need to be seen to be 'normal' and how they deal with verbal harassment largely by pupils.

The schooling context

As the body is central to physical education, and the key vehicle for the expression of subject knowledge it is continually exposed and open to the gaze of others. Traditionally, it has been schooled along restricted and prescribed gender regimes[2] (see Scraton, 1992; Talbot, 1993). It is evident that both the content and pedagogical practices of physical education are built (and reproduced) through narrow ideologies and stereotyped visions of hetero-sexual femininity and masculinity. Accordingly, pupils and teachers learn and recognise the required 'feminine' and 'masculine' codes for acceptance within physical education and schooling more generally. These codes have to be made sense of within the confines of heterosexuality.

Lees' (1986: 145) research about sexuality and adolescent girls found that 'many girls expressed marked prejudice against them' [lesbians]. One of her subjects said 'Poofs I can tolerate but lesbians I can't. I suppose because it's my own sex' (p. 145). Lees' (1987: 177) research also revealed that 'lezzie' was the worst label that a girl could be called, far worse than a ' "slag" (a girl who sleeps around) or a "drag" (a "nice" girl who does not . . .)'. Sanders and Burke (1994: 69) also note that 'lezzie' is used as an insult and as a means to 'pressure the "other" to conform to stereotypical roles'. It is no wonder that given such pressures girls and women disengage from actively participating in physical education and sport. Boys are also pressurised into conforming. Indeed Lees (1993: 90) claims 'that it is far worse for a boy to show feminine qualities than for a girl to show masculine qualities'. Masculine identity is constructed in critical opposition to heterosexual femininity and anything deemed to be associated with femininity is subordinated and stigmatised. For a boy to be labelled a 'wimp', 'sissy', 'poofter' and or 'gay'[3] is one of the most virulent forms of insult (Askew and Ross, 1988; Duncan, 1999). As Paechter (1998: 104) points out

> the abusive form of these terms is of course derived from homophobia; the reason that it can be oppressive to be called 'gay' or 'lesbian', whether you are or not, is that lesbians and gay men are, in fact stigmatised both in and outside school.

This stigmatisation is exacerbated in England and Wales by the continued existence of Section 28 of the Local Government Act. This repressive legislation passed in 1988 by the Conservative government under the premiership of Margaret Thatcher stated that

(1) A local authority shall not:
    (a) intentionally promote homosexuality or publish material with the intention of promoting homosexuality;
    (b) promote the teaching in any maintained school of the acceptability of homosexuality as a pretended family relationship.

This legislation exemplified not only legal disapproval of lesbian and gay lifestyles but also the power of the Conservative New Right to dictate what constituted acceptable/normal sexual identity. In doing so it legitimised dominant discourses of compulsory heterosexuality. A situation which Epstein (2000: 387) notes 'both reflects and produces inequalities'.

Although Section 28 has been summarily dismissed as ambiguously worded it remains dangerously open to misinterpretation (Colvin and Hawksley, 1989). This confusion has created a situation whereby some teachers use it as an excuse for failing to act in cases of homophobic abuse (Douglas *et al.*, 1997; Epstein, 2000). Thus, whilst the provisions of Section 28 have yet to be interpreted by the courts its passing has undoubtedly had a marked effect on the teaching of lesbian and gay issues in schools.

Given this socio-political climate it is perhaps unsurprising that the largely conservative physical education profession has in the main failed to bring these issues into the public domain. Indeed, this chilly silence is also evidenced in the 'official texts' of the NCPE (2000, see chapter 7). These omissions are all the more disturbing given that earlier versions of the NCPE made specific reference to issues of 'the emergence of sexuality' (NCPE Interim Report, 1991: 17). These silences are complex and hugely powerful and signal tacit disapproval of other ways of being. Further, like Section 28 they legitimate and perpetuate hegemonic conceptions of masculinity and femininity such that it becomes difficult to challenge from either within or without. Nevertheless, the dramatic increase in homophobic bullying within schools makes it imperative that counter and more inclusive discourses are produced (Wallace,

2001). As Veri (1999: 358) points out 'counterdiscourses are needed in policies, laws, and curricula in order to strategically resist institutionalized homophobia and heterosexism.'

In order to illustrate the 'institutionalized homophobia and heterosexism' within schools I turn now to analyse the significance and impact of the context and subject matter of physical education on lesbian teachers' lives. This is identified as a major contributory factor in their feeling the need to conceal their lesbian identity from pupils, teachers, governors and parents.

Teaching physical education: a unique context

The prejudicial and discriminatory attitudes of the last Conservative Government towards lesbians and gay men has already been illustrated through reference to Section 28. This situation has left most lesbian, gay and bisexual teachers afraid to reveal their sexual identity for fear of loss of employment. In a homophobic and heterosexist world where moral traditionalist discourses about the family hold hegemonic power over other lifestyles, to be a lesbian teacher working with children is to be seen by some as 'a paedophile or pervert' (Lucy[4]). The gendered bodily culture of physical education and sport creates a unique context for denial of a homosexual identity that might not be experienced by teachers within other subject disciplines. Further, regardless of a physical education teachers' sexual identity the ways in which female physical education teachers are stereotyped as lesbian are well documented (Griffin, 1992; Squires and Sparkes, 1996). As Harris and Griffin (1997: 78) reveal this 'Labeling (or rather mis-labeling) the majority of women physical educators as lesbian is inaccurate. Such a term can be used to intimidate, discourage, devalue, and control women.'

The muscular athletic female body stands in sharp contrast to cultural conceptions of what it is to be stereotypically female, namely, passive and having a 'feminine' appearance. To transgress these bodily boundaries is to be deviant, not normal. Sport in general is associated with the defeminisation of women and the masculinisation of men, hence women and girls who participate in the male domain of physical education and sport and specifically in those activities not seen as stereotypically feminine run the risk of their sexual identity being called into question and the pejorative label lesbian applied. Many therefore seek to distance themselves from any possible suggestion of or association with lesbianism, as a result we often see evidence of what has been described as hyperfemininity (Felshin, 1974; Lenskyj, 1994). The wearing of jewellery and make-up announces a so-called 'normal' sexuality. For men and boys a 'normal' sexuality is demonstrated and proved by prowess in sport (see Connell, 1995). Failure to sustain a skilful performance and or to exhibit physical and mental toughness is to run the risk of homophobic abuse and ridicule, a situation that Parker (1996) found amongst 13–14 year old boys when their peers performed badly in competitive sport. Further, as Harris (1995, cited in Sparkes and Silvennoinen, 1999) reveals

Competitive sports can be painful for those men [and boys] who feel inferior because they cannot perform to the standards expected of them. For other men [and boys] who do not succeed, the sportsman message can cause them to doubt their worth as men [and boys].

Although prowess in competitive sport can be seen to be a marker for hegemonic heterosexual masculinity, prowess or indeed liking a physical activity that is not stereotypically masculine is a risky occurrence. Boys and men who wish to participate in dance or other related activities where they are required to display grace and exhibit emotional characteristics that are not regarded as being traditionally and stereotypically masculine also run the risk of their sexual identity being called into question and the pejorative label gay applied. Flintoff (1995: 56) has also shown how in Initial Teacher Education (ITE) male students 'do masculinity' and go

> out of their way to demonstrate their lack of commitment to 'feminine' activities like dance by fooling around, and being generally disruptive. Homophobic comments were also common, acting to reinforce the display of appropriately 'gendered' behaviour by male and female students, but also to make virtually untenable the position of any student (or lecturer) whose sexual orientation was not heterosexual.[5]

The physical nature of the subject creates particular worries for lesbian teachers since they are extremely wary as to how they may be perceived by others when they have to support and/or touch pupils. Ethel acknowledged that she felt vulnerable when she was 'Supporting female pupils in gymnastics or helping pupils hold a racket correctly (or a) piece of athletics equipment correctly . . . or generally any situation where I come into physical contact with the pupil'. Both Barbara and Caroline also confirmed that they felt anxious when they had to support pupils in gymnastics. Fay was the only teacher to indicate that she felt less wary when she had to support pupils because she believed that 'they seem to accept that you are going to have to support them anyway and so they don't seem to mind in that situation and they don't seem to feel inhibited or constricted by you touching them in those situations'.

In relation to the worries expressed by these lesbian teachers about the potential for false allegations, it is important to acknowledge that hetero-sexual teachers are also vulnerable to such accusations, but these lesbian women felt that it was not to the same degree. Annie believed that 'any false allegation would be less believed if the governors found they had a lovely boyfriend, but if the governors found you had a lovely girlfriend I'm sure it would open some homophobic doors'. Kay also recognised that it was a problem and she pointed out that no teacher liked to be faced with such situations. However, she was at pains to explain that it was a particularly sensitive and threatening issue for a lesbian teacher (Clarke, 1995).

Supervising changing rooms and pupil folklore

The daily routine of supervising pupils in changing rooms is another potentially threatening situation to be safely negotiated. As Caroline commented 'I don't go into the changing rooms and ever stay there, I walk in and out until they are dressed and then I speak to them.' There was also much fear over the supervision of pupils through showers, relating to concerns about being seen to be watching pupils. Consequently, all of the teachers went to great lengths to avoid being in the showering area. However, such strategies did not prevent some pupils spreading rumours about their teachers. I received a letter from Ivy (19 November 1997) in which she described a number of incidents that had occurred in the school where she teaches and which were related to her being thought of as a lesbian. One of these was associated with the issue of showering. Accordingly it seems pertinent to report it here.

> Two Year 8 girls . . . came out with the following statement to my straight colleague – who I am 'out' to. (Sorry about the pun). Basically, they said that the only reason girls don't shower was that there had been something in the paper that I had been found to be looking at girls in the showers. They had supposedly got this story from their aunty. Penny (a colleague) was terrific. They said that I must therefore be a lesbian. She replied that there had been nothing in the papers and dispelled their 'allegations'. She pointed out the supervisory nature of our role, and said because of their allegations, she would take the matter further. In consultation with me, I contacted the year Co-ordinator – who in turn told the Head – who in turn called the parents in. The parents were very apologetic, and had no knowledge of where the girls got the story from. The aunty was apparently someone whom Penny and I had both taught. The incident was handled very sensitively.

This scenario also illustrates that it is not only pupils that stereotype and label physical education teachers as lesbian. Their families may also hold such beliefs. Scraton (1992: 102) found evidence of similar parental beliefs. Her research revealed that at Townley School 'parental pressure stopped showering', as they were concerned that 'physical education staff would be able to watch their daughters in the showers'. As Scraton (1992: 102) comments, what this reaction actually implies is 'not only a concern to protect their daughter's sexuality (i.e. a protected, hidden heterosexuality), but also a homophobic assumption that female physical education teachers' heterosexuality is "questionable"'. It is also important to note that teachers may have to deal with colleagues who are not supportive.

In considering where the pupils at Ivy's school got their story from it is worth considering the place of pupils' folklore in the stories about transfer from primary to secondary school. Pugsley *et al.* (1996) found that many of these stories related to sexuality and to showers.[6] They suggest that for girls it is the most common fear about secondary school physical education. The other main 'fear' about physical education is the presence of the teacher. The following statements were written by their research subjects.

> I was told by a friend that everyone had to have a shower, watched by a teacher after sports.

> Before I went to Westhaven High school I was told by my sister that the PE teacher was gay and watched while you changed for PE and made you have a shower and watched while you had it.

> All the girls feared Miss Alexander for PE. Rumour had it she stood by the showers in the changing room, made you take your towel off and watched you showering.

It is possible that the statements made about Ivy were part of pupils' folklore, but regardless of the origin it says much about how young people view lesbians (and gay men). As Woods (1992: 91) and others have shown physical education teachers are particularly vulnerable to homophobic accusations, 'to be athletic is equated with masculinity and masculine women are labelled as lesbian. Therefore, athletic women are stereotyped as lesbian.' Hence many women in the male domain of sport and physical education learn that to be physically active, to develop muscle is to be at 'odds' with what 'real', 'normal' and 'feminine' women do. Thus, it takes 'strong' women to challenge these messages, and it could be argued that women in physical education by their very presence teaching a 'physical' subject do indeed challenge these messages (see Griffin, 1998).

Risky situations: social relations with colleagues

For the lesbian teachers in my research situations which might lead to the revealing of a lesbian identity were either avoided or closely monitored for the degree of risk. Such strategies contributed to the successful passing of the heterosexual presumption. Accordingly there was much apprehension about the kinds of questions that colleagues might ask about personal lives, most felt it safer not to say too much and to suppress their desire to talk about their home lives. Within the gendered locale of staffrooms (see Shilling, 1991) the stories that do get told are largely heterosexual ones, as Swigonski (1995: 417–18) records 'Heterocentrism structures perceptions of reality so that heterosexual ways of being define the nature of human relationships', and, I would add, the nature of many conversations. Heterosexual discourses impact on all women (and men) in teaching and on gender relations within the teaching profession (De Lyon and Widdowson Migniuolo, 1989; Siraj-Blatchford, 1993), but in this particular study it was evident how they impacted on lesbian teachers in especially damaging ways. Ivy's experiences of life in the staffroom lend support to this contention. For Ivy, who had been married for over fifteen years before 'falling in love with a woman and becoming a lesbian', the contrast was dramatic. She described how previously she was 'very free, very open', and

> had been a very chatty person about my life and saying to people 'what did you do at the weekend?' . . . I was very much a sharer in my life and other people's lives, but from that moment on I suddenly, or dramatically started to spiral inwards and closed my world entirely.

Ivy's world is no longer so closed, she has now 'come out' to a very small number of teaching colleagues and is able to talk with them about her 'private' life and her relationship with her partner. These teachers learned how to manage staffroom conversations so as to minimise the likelihood of exposure of their lesbian identity. This entailed the steering away of conversations which focused on children and partners to less threatening frames of reference. This strategy was not without its costs in terms of the nature of friendships that could be safely established within school. For Harriet this led her to 'hold back a significant part of myself all the time. I don't have any sort of intimate friendships [at work]. I suppose for fear of being exposed and for the pain that would cause'.

These narratives illustrate how the self is censored and policed and how pupils are denied the visible and positive presence of lesbian role models. The following section reveals further strategies that these lesbian teachers employ so as to appear to comply with dominant discourses of compulsory heterosexuality.

Keeping your distance: social relations with pupils and the extended curriculum

Interactions with pupils were seen as a site for the possible exposure of a lesbian identity. All the teachers commented in some detail about how they avoided getting 'too close' to pupils so as not to place themselves in risky situations. Hence, they tended to 'back off' and keep their distance in their dealings with pupils particularly in after school activities where traditionally teachers have felt able to develop less formal relationships with pupils. Several of the women did not feel quite so anxious. For instance Jay, who taught in an inner city school, which she described as having 'a lot of social problems', was rarely involved in extra curricular activities. She made the point that 'it is extremely difficult to get the girls to stay behind after school, partly because their parents are very worried about them getting home late, it's impossible to get them out on a Saturday'.

The 900 pupils in Jay's school were mainly boys of whom 70–85 per cent were Bengali, and many of the girls were Muslim. The points I am making here relate to the need to remain aware that schools are not homogeneous and hence the experiences of lesbian teachers may vary. This may be due to the location and cultural mix of the school and the attitudes of staff, parents and pupils to activities after school. Further, what is acceptable in terms of dress, physical contact/display of the body will differ amongst different cultural groups. Additionally, it should not be assumed that pupils from some ethnic minority groups are less interested than their 'white' counterparts in physical activity (Verma and Darby, 1994; see also Benn in chapter 5). As Zaman (1997: 65) states

> it is clear that a major problem surrounding participation is the ways in which sport, physical activity and physical education are organised and made available and not necessarily the activities themselves. If we genuinely want to increase the participation of Muslim young women, then Muslim values need to influence and inform the context in the way activities are structured and accessed.

It is also pertinent to this discussion to recognise that participation in the extended curriculum may be less important in some schools than others and moreover what is on offer may be at odds with the culture of young people's leisure and lifestyles (Hendry *et al.*, 1993). In the specific case of girls there is considerable evidence to support the view that the culture of physical education clashes sharply with the culture of heterosexual and emphasised femininity (Scraton, 1987; 1992).

Being seen to be 'normal'

Being seen as 'normal', that is heterosexual, meant that many of the women felt the need to introduce male figures into conversations, be they real or mythical. This adopting of dual identities, pseudo-heterosexual and lesbian, created tensions for many of the women. This identity dilemma was not experienced uniformly by all the women. Ethel who had been teaching for over twenty years felt that although she needed to be two people, as she got older it was something that was quite easy to keep going. This interface between age and sexual identity is worthy of further exploration, for it would seem to be an issue that also is not exclusively a problem for lesbian women. Indeed, single women in their 40s or 50s can experience the same pressure to engage in denial about their relationships (Clarke, 1996). Increasingly, to be deemed normal is to have a partner of the opposite sex and as such a clear heterosexual identity is evidenced. Inherent in the expectation of an established partnership are assumptions about sexual identity and what it is to be a 'real' woman. Thus, those teachers choosing to remain single may well face scrutiny.

What emerges from these stories is that the younger women generally felt that their lesbian identities were relatively safe. But being younger also meant that they were likely to be asked more personal questions by pupils. A lacuna in previous research into the lives of lesbian physical education teachers seems to be consideration of those women who are more senior members of the profession and for whom the issue of retirement becomes a key factor. This could in part be due to the 'physical' nature/culture of the subject that leads physical education teachers to think that they should be 'Growing old gracefully' (Sikes, 1988). Hence many women and men look to move away from the bodily demands of teaching physical education to other arenas within schools, such as pastoral roles and/or to teach subjects that do not require the same degree of physical competence/activity. Such moves are also likely to be related to increased promotional prospects. For Ivy it is more a matter of having fourteen years left, or as she said, 'fourteen years to survive is how I view it to be quite honest.' She wrote

> I have ten years left in teaching before I retire. I often joke that I'll be working for Stonewall, or some other L/G [lesbian/gay] organisation because I'll not be able to teach P.E. But the joke is not all light-hearted. I need the salary my job pays. At 49 there are '0' options. If I could get a job with the same salary – £24,000! I would do so at once, rather than feel under the constant pressure of losing my job, or not being able to continue in my post due to my sexuality.
>
> (Personal correspondence, 19 November 1997)

Running through most of these life stories was the feeling that within school they were living a lie, for some this had a damaging effect on their self-esteem and led to them feeling dishonest. These stories vividly illustrate the embeddedness of heterosexual discourses and the negative impact that they have on the lives of lesbian teachers.

(Hetero) sexual harassment

Many of the women had been subject to harassment because of their sexuality. Although I am unable to describe here the myriad of behaviours that constitute harassment, for the purposes of this research I utilise Halson's (1991: 99) working definition that 'Whatever its particular form, the behaviour in question is experienced as humiliating, embarrassing, threatening. . . . It offends, it objectifies, it denies autonomy, it controls.' I share Epstein's view (1996: 203) that in order to develop 'a fuller understanding of sexist harassment we need to see it within the context of . . . "compulsory hetero-sexuality"'. These points are helpful in that they draw attention to just how powerful the discourses of heterosexuality are and how institutionalised they are particularly within the educative system. Indeed, Epstein discusses how harassment can be understood 'as a kind of pedagogy of heterosexuality (ibid.: 203) . . . which schools women and men into normative heterosexuality (but not always successfully)' (ibid.: 207). In other words girls, women, boys and men are schooled into appropriate ways of behaving sexually, that is heterosexually.

The harassment the lesbian teachers had been subjected to was mainly from pupils, in school this often took the form of name calling, such as 'lezzie', 'dyke', 'homo', and/or 'queer' and in some instances graffiti also appeared around the school about a teacher's lesbianism. The women ignored the verbal comments as much as possible for fear of bringing too much attention to themselves. Ivy felt that there had been 'a shift in society', she was of the opinion that

> whereas any hint/gossip was kept amongst pupils, and whereas if you were married then there could be no question of where your sexuality was centred, now, pupils feel that it is quite acceptable to bring these issues into the public domain with little understanding of the consequences of what they are saying.
>
> (Personal correspondence, 19 November 1997)

In connection with this contention Andrews' (1990: 351) earlier research reveals how

> The more public profile of homosexuality . . . inevitably means more chat and gossip in corridors and classrooms. 'Revelations' in the popular press about a gay judge or film star, . . . reference to gay love in a GCSE text, all these may provoke hostility and controversy. If you are lesbian or gay the potential abuse is an ever present threat to your sense of safety and well-being in the world. If you decide to challenge prejudice you risk personal abuse, ridicule and adverse publicity.

Challenging prejudice for some is not worth the possible risk entailed. Further it is manifest that these physical education teachers are doubly vulnerable, as women and as lesbians.

Concluding remarks

Schools and physical education departments are powerful social and patriarchal institutions structured along heterosexual lines that operate to suppress alternative ways of being and performing. The schooling process defines and regulates what is socially acceptable through adherence to the required heterosexual gender regimes and through the activities on offer. The life stories discussed in this chapter have illustrated the oppressive power of these hegemonic heterosexual discourses to control and constrain the lives of lesbian teachers within the schooling context in general and more specifically within that of physical education. As I have demonstrated the concept of heterosexuality as compulsory is a key element in understanding and making sense of the ways in which these lesbian teachers feel the need to conceal and protect their sexual identities from exposure to the scrutiny of heterosexual 'others'. Thus, it is essential that their actions are understood both within this heterosexual matrix and the specific bodily context of physical education. Further, it is evident just how pervasive and naturalised heterosexuality is, be it in the staffroom, the changing room or in relationships between pupils and their teachers. Moreover, it is also legitimised through the discourse of Section 28. Physical education in schools and Initial Teacher Education has much to do if it is to disrupt and redress this unjust situation. A first step would be to openly acknowledge how heterosexism and homophobia act as deterrents to participation in physical education and sport. Schools in general could contribute to a more equitable and inclusive environment for both pupils and staff by subjecting the curriculum, grouping polices and teaching and learning strategies to critical scrutiny and by establishing non-discrimination and anti-harassment policies that include sexual orientation. By explicitly broadening their policies and perceptions about the multiple and contested forms of masculinity, femininity and sexual identity, physical education departments could enable all young people to begin to experience the life-long pleasures of what it is to be physically active without fear of sanction and reprisal. The recommendations that follow are intended to aid this process. They begin from the premise that homophobia is another form of discrimination that must be overcome if all pupils, student teachers, and teachers are to be provided with inclusive, effective and safe learning and working environments.

Challenging and addressing homophobia and heterosexism requires a *whole-school* commitment to:

- no form of discrimination being tolerated;
- equal opportunities policies being extended to include sexual orientation;
- non-discrimination and anti-harassment policies and practices being enacted, monitored and reviewed for their effectiveness;
- homophobic slurs/jokes/bullying/graffiti/name-calling being challenged;
- heterosexual assumptions ceasing;
- resources being available in school and the community which dispel and counter the myths and stereotypes about sexuality and physical education and sport;
- providing support for pupils, staff, coaches, governors and parents/carers;
- schools providing awareness training/education for all pupils, staff, coaches, governors, parents/carers;
- providing positive images/role models of lesbian and gay athletes/ coaches/teachers;
- recognising that this is a key issue for citizenship education.

Notes

1 This difficulty led Sparkes (1997) to write an ethnographic fiction about a gay physical education teacher.

2 I use 'gender regime' in much the same way as Kessler *et al.* (1985, cited in Acker, 1994: 92) who explain it as 'the pattern of practices that constructs various kinds of masculinity and femininity among staff and students, orders them in terms of prestige and power, and constructs a sexual division of labor within the institution'.

3 Duncan (1999: 19) comments ' "Gay" seemed to have duality of meaning against boys in much the same way as "slag", "cow" or "dog" were used against girls. The word was recognised as meaning homosexual, but for most purposes it denoted a wider negative male role.'

4 The fourteen white, able bodied lesbian teachers involved in the research from 1993 to 1995 were from the outset given pseudonyms. They taught in a variety of secondary schools (i.e. mixed comprehensives, girls' schools, church and independent schools) and were aged between 23 and 47, some had just started their teaching careers, whilst others had been teaching for over 25 years. Their schools are located in inner cities, urban and or rural areas. Some of the women were single, some had been married, some were currently in long-standing relationships, and none had children. They came from a variety of working- and middle-class backgrounds. Making contact and gaining access was difficult due to the prevailing climate of fear of exposure and loss of employment that surrounds lesbian (and gay) teachers and forces many of them to remain an invisible and silent presence within our schools. Contact was therefore initially made through lesbians known to me, who contacted other lesbians, to see if they were willing to talk in confidence about their lives. This created a 'snowballing' effect where one woman put me in contact with another and so forth. Contact was also made in this manner because such are the silences and the relative secrecy that it is not always possible to identify through any other method, with any degree of certainty, those women who are lesbian.

A biographical methodology was utilised as an approach particularly well suited to gaining a closely textured account of lesbian lives within the educational system and for interpreting data generated by the life story interviews. As well as offering a detailed examination of selves in specific settings the research was additionally concerned to make visible the structural and interactional injustices confronting lesbian teachers. For more details about the research process, see Clarke, 1997; 1998b and 1998c.

5 I have written elsewhere about the experiences of lesbian physical education students and the verbal and physical abuse that they are subjected to largely by their heterosexual male peers (see Clarke, 1996; 2000).

6 Pugsley *et al.* (1996) only asked for 'scarey stories'.

References

Acker, S. (1994) *Gendered Education: Sociological Reflections on Women, Teaching and Feminism*, Buckingham: Open University Press.

Andrews, J. (1990) Don't pass us by: keeping lesbian and gay issues on the agenda, *Gender and Education* 2(3): 351–5.

Askew, S. and Ross, C. (1988) *Boys Don't Cry: Boys and Sexism in Education*, Milton Keynes: Open University Press.

Clarke, G. (1995) Outlaws in sport and education? Exploring the sporting and education experiences of lesbian physical education teachers, in L. Lawrence, E. Murdoch and S. Parker (eds) *Professional and Development Issues in Leisure, Sport and Education*, Eastbourne: Leisure Studies Association.

Clarke, G. (1996) Conforming and contesting with (a) difference: how lesbian students and teachers manage their identities, *International Studies in Sociology of Education* 6(2): 191–209.

Clarke, G. (1997) Playing a part: the lives of lesbian physical education teachers, in G. Clarke and B. Humberstone (eds) *Researching Women and Sport*, London: Macmillan.

Clarke, G. (1998a) Queering the pitch and coming out to play: lesbians in physical education and sport, *Sport, Education and Society* 3(2): 145–60.

Clarke, G. (1998b) *Voices from the Margins: Lesbian Teachers in Physical Education*, unpublished PhD thesis, Leeds Metropolitan University.

Clarke, G. (1998c) Voices from the margins: resistance and regulation in the lives of lesbian teachers, in M. Erben (ed.) *Biography and Education: An Edited Collection*, London: Falmer Press.

Clarke, G. (2000) Crossing borders: lesbian physical education students and the struggles for sexual spaces, in S. Scraton and B. Watson (eds) *Sport, Leisure and Gendered Spaces*, Eastbourne: Leisure Studies Association.

Colvin, M. with Hawksley, J. (1989) *Section 28: A Practical Guide to the Law and its Implications*, London: National Council for Civil Liberties.

Connell, R.W. (1995) *Masculinities*, Oxford: Polity Press.

De Lyon, H. and Widdowson Migniuolo, F. (eds) (1989) *Women Teachers: Issues and Experiences*, Milton Keynes: Open University Press.

Douglas, N., Warwick, I., Kemp, S. and Whitty, G. (1997) *Playing it Safe: Responses of Secondary School Teachers to Lesbian, Gay and Bisexual Pupils, Bullying, HIV and AIDS Education and Section 28*, Health and Education Research Unit, Institute of Education: University of London.

Duncan, N. (1999) *Sexual Bullying: Gender Conflict and Pupil Culture in Secondary Schools*, London: Routledge.

Epstein, D. (1996) Keeping them in their place: hetero/sexist harassment, gender and the enforcement of heterosexuality, in J. Holland and L. Adkins (eds) *Sex, Sensibility and the Gendered Body*, London: Macmillan.

Epstein, D. (2000) Sexualities and education: catch 28, *Sexualities* 3(4): 387–94.

Felshin, J. (1974) The dialectic of women and sport, in E.W. Gerber, J. Felshin, P. Berlin and W. Wyrick (eds) *The American Women in Sport*, Reading: Addison-Wesley.

Flintoff, A. (1995) Learning and teaching in PE: a lesson in gender?, in A. Tomlinson (ed.) *Gender, Sport and Leisure: Continuities and Challenges*, Eastbourne: Leisure Studies Association.

Griffin, P. (1992) Changing the game: homophobia, sexism, and lesbians in sport, *Quest* 44(2): 251–65.

Griffin, P. (1998) *Strong Women, Deep Closets: Lesbians and Homophobia in Sport*, Champaign: Human Kinetics.

Griffin, P. and Genasci, J. (1990) Addressing homophobia in physical education: responsibilities for teachers and researchers, in M.A. Messner and D.F. Sabo (eds) S*port, Men and the Gender Order*, Leeds: Human Kinetics.

Halson, J. (1991) Young women, sexual harassment and heterosexuality: violence, power relations and mixed-sex schooling, in P. Abbott and C. Wallace (eds) *Gender, Power and Sexuality*, London: Macmillan.

Harris, M.B. and Griffin, J. (1997) Stereotypes and personal beliefs about women physical education teachers' *Women in Sport and Physical Activity Journal* 6(1): 49–83.

Hendry, L.B., Shucksmith, J., Love, J.G. and Glendinning, A. (1993) *Young People's Leisure and Lifestyles*, London: Routledge.

Labour Research Department (1992) *Out at Work: Lesbian and Gay Workers' Rights*, London: LRD Publications Ltd.

Lees, S. (1986) *Losing Out: Sexuality and Adolescent Girls*, London: Hutchinson.

Lees, S. (1987) The structure of sexual relations in school, in M. Arnot and G. Weiner (eds) *Gender and the Politics of Schooling*, London: Unwin Hyman.

Lees, S. (1993) *Sexuality and Spice: Sexuality and Adolescent Girls*, London: Penguin.

Lenskyj, H. (1991) Combating homophobia in sport and physical education, *Sociology of Sport Journal* 8: 61–9.

Lenskyj, H. (1994) Sexuality and femininity in sport contexts: issues and alternatives, *Journal of Sport and Social Issues* 18(4): 356–76.

National Curriculum Physical Education Working Group (1991) *Interim Report*, London: Department of Education and Science.

Paechter, C. (1998) *Educating the Other: Gender, Power and Schooling*, London: Falmer Press.

Parker, A. (1996) The construction of masculinity within boys' physical education, *Gender and Education* 8(2): 141–57.

Pugsley, L., Coffey, A. and Delamont S. (1996) Daps, dykes and five mile hikes: physical education in pupils' folklore, *Sport, Education and Society* 1(2): 133–46.

Sanders, S.A.L. and Burke, H. (1994) 'Are you a lesbian Miss?' in D. Epstein (ed.) *Challenging Lesbian and Gay Inequalities in Education*, Buckingham: Open University Press.

Scraton, S. (1987) 'Boys muscle in where angels fear to tread' – girls' sub-cultures and physical activities, in J. Horne, D. Jary and A. Tomlinson (eds) *Sport, Leisure and Social Relations*, London: Routledge & Kegan Paul.

Scraton, S. (1992) *Shaping Up to Womanhood: Gender and Girls' Physical Education*, Buckingham: Open University Press.

Shilling, C. (1991) Social space, gender inequalities and educational differentiation, *British Journal of Sociology of Education* 12(1): 23–44.

Sikes, P.J. (1988) Growing old gracefully? Age, identity and physical education, in J. Evans (ed.) *Teachers, Teaching and Control in Physical Education*, Lewes: Falmer Press.

Siraj-Blatchford, I. (ed.) (1993) *'Race', Gender and the Education of Teachers*, Buckingham: Open University Press.

Sparkes, A. (1997) Ethnographic fiction and representing the absent other, *Sport, Education and Society* 2(1): 25–40.

Sparkes, A. and Silvennoinen, M. (eds) (1999) *Talking Bodies: Men's Narratives of the Body and Sport*, University of Jyvaskyla, Finland: SoPhi.

Squires, S.L. and Sparkes A.C. (1996) Circles of silence: sexual identity in physical education and sport, *Sport, Education and Society* 1(1): 77–101.

Swigonski, M.E. (1995) Claiming a lesbian identity as act of empowerment, *AFFILIA: Journal of Women and Social Work* 10(4): 413–25.

Talbot, M. (1993) A gendered physical education: equality and sexism, in J. Evans (ed.) *Equality, Education and Physical Education*, London: Falmer Press.

Veri, M.J. (1999) Homophobic discourse surrounding the female athlete, *Quest* 51(4): 355–68.

Verma, G.K. and Darby, D.S. (eds) (1994) *Winners and Losers: Ethnic Minorities in Sport and Recreation*, London: Falmer Press.

Wallace, W. (2001) Is this table gay? Anatomy of a classroom insult, *Times Educational Supplement*, 19 January: 9–10.

Woods, S. (1992) Describing the experiences of lesbian physical educators: a phenomenological study, in A.C. Sparkes (ed.) *Research in Physical Education and Sport: Exploring Alternative Visions*, London: Falmer Press.

Zaman, H. (1997) Islam, well-being and physical activity: perceptions of Muslim young women, in G. Clarke and B. Humberstone (eds) *Researching Women and Sport*, London: Macmillan.

5 Muslim women in teacher training: issues of gender, 'race' and religion

Tansin Benn

Introduction

The case study research that is reported in this chapter explored equity issues in relation to life-experiences, opportunities and constraints for Muslim women in teacher training, with a focus on subject experiences within physical education. The research was motivated by the fact that, despite Government efforts, ethnic minority students are still under-represented in higher education and the teaching profession (DES (1989) Circular 24/89; EOC, 1989). In England's second largest city, where part of this case study was located, it is predicted that by 2001, ethnic minorities will constitute one in three 16-year-old pupils in the schools, yet only 5 per cent of the City's teaching force. The data presented in this chapter pinpoints the complexity of overlays of disadvantage experienced by Muslim women, including inter-actions of 'race' (used, as by Siraj-Blatchford, 1993, in inverted commas to acknowledge the problematic nature of the term yet the significance of racism), ethnicity, religion, culture and gender. In the research a qualitative study with a group of Muslim women in initial teacher training, in one higher education institution (HEI) provided a 'micro' perspective of a particular group and situation. An accompanying questionnaire survey of all other higher education institutes in England and Wales offering initial teacher training with an element of physical education, was used to give a 'macro' perspective on the issues being explored. Research based in higher education is rare. Most sociological researchers pursue critical investigations of other sites in preference to their own. Siraj-Blatchford (ibid.: 35) has highlighted that 'the experiences of black students (Asian and African-Caribbean) in higher education have been largely ignored'. The data generated in this research can be seen to extend our knowledge and understanding of ways in which institutional and subject cultures, traditions, policies and practices, variously impact on particular and invariably marginalised, groups. We see the challenges that arise if teacher training is to embrace in policy and practice, conceptualisations of gender that acknowledge multiple identities and differences.

Theory and method

The research was a theoretically informed empirical study, underpinned by a process theory of identity (Elias, 1991; Mennel, 1994). This theory explores how identity is shaped and re-shaped in processes of interaction with others. As student-teachers in one HEI the Muslim women would be bound in 'figurations' or networks of mutually interested, differentially related, inter-dependent human beings. Seventeen self-declared Muslim women initially volunteered to take part in an interpretive, qualitative study. Their involvement in the research eventually spanned four years (from 1994 to 1998), the first two in initial teacher training the latter two in their early teaching careers. Discussion in this chapter draws upon data from the first two years of the study, gathered via interviews, participant diaries and observations. Throughout the research the focus was on the women's experiences and perceptions of the influence of others (including peers, tutors, school-experience teachers, parents, head teachers) on their professional and personal development in training. Analysis of the data highlighted the process of negotiation and change that was occurring within one HEI as a result of increasing numbers of Muslim women entering the teacher-training programme. Lecturing and management staff were making changes in the direction of providing a more compatible environment for the Muslim students, and were learning much in this process of development. Arguably, the negotiations and changes that occurred in this HEI are required in all training institutions and not only in relation to the needs of Muslim students.

The qualitative research focused on one particular group, defined by sex and religious belief. Although clearly not a homogeneous group, Muslims are united globally by the basic tenets of their faith. Whilst many are born into Islam, many others across the world choose to embrace the faith. It is not only a religion but a way of life, providing frames within which followers endeavour to live their lives as 'good Muslims', following religious guidance for men and women on diet, dress, prayer and behaviour. Respect for others, humility, and the importance of family, are key aspects of their faith. Focusing on Muslim women's experiences meant that issues of gender, 'race', ethnicity and culture, emerged alongside and inter-twined with religion. Since such terms are often confused and used loosely, later I clarify the ways in which they were approached in this study.

In order to gain a wider picture of awareness and the needs of Muslim students in higher education, lessons learned from the qualitative study were used in a subsequent questionnaire survey (conducted in the 1999/2000 academic year) of seventy higher education institutions in England and Wales offering teacher training in physical education at either primary or secondary level. The survey was directed to the relevant heads of department within these institutions and received a 50 per cent return. The heads of department were recognised as key people challenging or perpetuating institutional/ departmental ethos, policies, practices and procedures. The questionnaire focused on the extent to which, if at all, other institutions were able to meet and/or respond to the needs of Muslim student teacher-trainees. More specifically it addressed:

- awareness of numbers of Muslim students entering higher education;
- whether Muslim students had ever raised issues of religious requirements;
- to what extent the institution addressed general Islamic requirements such as single sex accommodation, dietary requirements, the honouring of Muslim Festival days or provision of a prayer room;
- whether issues of religious requirements had ever been raised in relation to participation in physical education, for example the need for single-sex groups, same-sex environments, privacy of accommodation or kit requirements;
- where colleagues had no experience to date of accommodating Muslim students' needs, hypothetical views were sought.

Although the questionnaire was designed to elicit quantitative data, questions were also incorporated that would enable colleagues to expand answers, qualitatively, where they wished. Before discussing the data generated by the research, there is a need to address my own location and identity; as a researcher, but also a lecturer in the HEI being investigated.

The researcher's position

The power differentials between researcher and researched in the qualitative dimension of this study may be seen by some as problematic. As a researcher I am positioned as a white, non-Muslim woman and head of physical education in the HEI investigated. The respondents were Muslim, predominantly of Asian heritage and students. Fellow researchers are divided over the effects of such differentials. For example, Essed (1991) suggested that black respondents would not talk freely to white researchers whilst Rhodes (1994, cited in Mirza, 1995) suggested that black respondents would be less happy talking to black researchers. Haw (1996) believes in the possibility of dialogue despite these differentials and that the future of research should be open to possibilities rather than closed by the creation of boundaries. She suggested success in cross-structural research as related to 'travelling sensitively and judiciously' (ibid.: 329).

Requirements relating to Islam would have prohibited some of the respondents from participating in one-to-one interviews with a male researcher. Ultimately, being non-Muslim appeared to be an asset since the women were not threatened by fear of any judgements on their religiosity.[1] Being non-Asian was perhaps, however, the greatest barrier in this research. There were deeply ingrained differences between myself and the participants, rooted in social habitus that limited some aspects of understanding the life-experiences of others.

The tutor/student relationship is probably best understood through the notion of relational power. As Brown and Rich (in chapter 6) also discuss, this concept is helpful in analysing power balances between groups of people, or ways in which the actions of one group enable or constrain opportunities and experiences of others. For example, gender relations denotes that changes affecting women necessarily have repercussions for men and vice versa. Process sociologists focus on shifts in balances of power within figurations, for example within gender relations, ethnic relations and other differential relations such as tutor/student. As George and Jones (1992) point out: although a tutor has more power in certain respects than students, no one is powerless. The entire qualitative research process in this study was dependent on the students, their contributions and commitment, and in that sense the students were very powerful.

Gender

Gender refers to ways in which the Muslim women's lives are affected by the socially constructed (some would argue divinely constructed) attitudes, values, beliefs, actions and behaviours expected, adopted and embodied because of their sex. For example, in the subject area of physical education, myths and assumptions exist about constraints surrounding participation, particularly of Muslim girls and women. This is partly fuelled by the fact that Muslim women do not feature prominently in major international sporting events such as the Olympic Games, and when they do they may suffer discrimination and exclusion from within their communities (Hargreaves, 1994; Scharenburg, 1999). As we see in later discussion, women's participation in sport and physical education is not anti-Islamic but is dependent on religious requirements being met in relation to issues such as modest dress, privacy for changing and single-sex environments.

Undoubtedly there is a rhetoric/reality gap between theory of Islam and lived-experiences for many Muslim women, as recognised by Sfeir (1985). Ahmed (1992) explains the difference in terms of 'ideological Islam' in which the equality of women in Islam is not disputed, and 'establishment Islam' where political/legal Islam fixes women's position as 'subordinate'. There is much that is misunderstood about the position of women in Islam, particularly when viewed from western feminist perspectives (Faruqi, 1991). This is not to deny that terrible abuses and constraints have been carried out on Muslim women in the name of Islam as described by Jawad (1998: 15):

> Women have, in many cases been deprived even of the basic human rights advocated by Islam itself. Forced marriages, arbitrary divorces, female mutilations and other abuses are sadly common in the Muslim world, as are restrictions on women's education and on their role in the labour force. In order to better their position as dignified human beings we

need to address these and other issues in the light of the contemporary position. I am not suggesting that we should abandon the tradition – only those aspects of cultural oppression that go under the name of tradition.

Jawad points to what she describes as 'authentic Islam' where, in the Qu'ran the role of women is respected and treated with justice and fairness as exemplified through the life of the Prophet, Muhammad and his family.

In England issues of racial, religious and sexist violence against Muslims and the media misrepresentation of gender and Islam are provided as evidence of prejudice and discrimination based on 'Islamophobia', that is, 'dread or hatred of Islam – and therefore . . . fear or dislike of all or most Muslims' (Runnymede Trust, 1997: 1). For women who adopt the dress code of Islam, the hijab or head-scarf and distinctive dress makes their religion visible. Evidence in the research indicated that this visibility can have positive and negative repercussions depending on context and the beliefs and values of those interacting with the Muslim women. There was no doubt that religious prejudice, related to the visibility of their Muslim dress code, created both the greatest source of tension between the respondents and their non-Muslim peers, colleagues, tutors, pupils and parents, as well as the greatest source of dignity and fellowship amongst other Muslims.

'Race', ethnicity and culture

Since the majority of British Muslims are of Asian heritage, issues of 'race' or prejudice and discrimination on the basis of skin-colour cannot be ignored (Coakley, 1994). The participants in the qualitative research were self-defined Muslims, of predominantly Asian heritage. That is, they perceived themselves as belonging to a particular group and were 'black' in the political sense used by Siraj-Blatchford (1991, 1993). We cannot and should not overlook the racialisation of religion in Britain. Acts of violence on these grounds are a reality, as evidenced in the Runnymede Trust report 1997, but not all Muslims are black. In the search for clarity of definitions, the term 'ethnic group' might be a more appropriate term indicating an element of choice in the way people define themselves (Jenkins, 1997). It is recognized that this suggestion is contentious and not yet supported in law and therefore offers no protection to Muslims as a distinct group under the Race Relations Act (as compared to, for example, that which is afforded to Jews and Sikhs).

'Culture' is used as a much broader term than 'race' or ethnicity, since it involves meanings and understandings passed on through processes of socialisation in everyday life. Culture can refer to social and institutional processes that reproduce systems of meanings, in an active way, using relational power within and between cultures to perpetuate and develop particular ways of living or cultural distinctiveness. Deciphering religious requirements from local cultural practices and influences adds to the challenge of any research in this area and has been brought about as a result of processes such as globalization and cultural assimilation. For example, the needs of all Muslims in one city would not be the same since some prefer to follow stricter traditions and practices than others. Simplistically, traditionalists advocate strict adherence to traditional and absolute truths, modernists use modern values as a starting point for interpretation, and revivalists seek a middle way, trying to understand tradition to sift and organise meaning in relation to modern values. An important issue for British Muslims of South Asian heritage is the overlay of South Asian patriarchal cultural custom with 'a veneer of Islamic culture . . . to lend it legitimacy' (Raza cited in Lewis, 1994: 194). Whilst opportunities to study Islam enabled respondents to study for themselves and decipher 'real Islam' from cultural practice claimed to be Islamic, challenging traditions within families or communities was difficult, particularly for women.

Previous related research

Recognising the tensions and dynamic interplay between such issues as gender, ethnicity, culture and religion is important in understanding the Muslim women's perceptions of themselves and their professional and personal development in higher education. As emphasised in chapter 1, much research in education and physical education has focused on gender as an isolated factor or concept. Similar observations can be made about work that has focused upon issues of 'race' in education, sport and physical education. Here the tendency has been to focus on prejudice and discrimination experienced predominantly by black youngsters of African–Caribbean heritage because of their skin-colour (Bayliss, 1989; Cashmore, 1982; Chappell 1995). Research tackling the complexity and significance of interaction between 'race' and gender has often grown out of investigations into Asian communities. It has been very evident that religious and cultural beliefs and practices have led to differences in life-experiences for boys and girls (Brah, 1992; Brah and Minas, 1985; Carrington and Williams, 1993; Griffiths and Troyna, 1995; Jarvie, 1991). However, there have also been some tendencies to conflate 'Asian' experiences and to deny complexities within this group and important individual differences in experiences in and of physical education and sport. Some researchers (see for example MacGuire and Collins, 1998) have failed to acknowledge the very different effects that religion might have on particular groups within 'Asian communities'. Religion has sometimes emerged within studies on education, sport and physical education as an influencing factor on the lives and opportunities of young people but it has not been a main focus for studies. Growing awareness of the particular needs of specific ethnic groups, for example Muslim pupils, has stimulated some specific research focusing on religion and has given rise to acknowledgement of the need for more work in this area.

In some research, therefore, the dynamics of 'race', culture, gender and religion have been addressed (De Knop *et al.*, 1996; Haw, 1991; 1995; 1998;

Parker-Jenkins, 1995). The particular requirements of Muslim pupils in physical education have been identified (Carroll and Hollinshead, 1993; De Knop *et al.*, 1996), but the needs of those Muslim pupils who then choose to enter careers in physical education, or enter higher education more generally, have remained largely unexplored and unaddressed. Neal (1995) has suggested that the 'whiteness' of gender has contributed to rendering the position of black women in higher education 'invisible'. However, exceptions to this invisibility can be found. In 1988 Singh focused attention upon ethnic minority student-teachers, including Muslims, and revealed that they often had stressful experiences in securing and maintaining jobs. They often felt 'exploited' for their bi-lingual skills, isolated, under tight scrutiny, facing different expectations from their white colleagues and with particular difficulties surrounding prayer and dress requirements. As we will see, similar findings emerged in my research into the early teaching careers of Muslim women a decade later (Benn, 1998).

Visible yet invisible: 'Islamophobia – a challenge to us all'

The experiences, opportunities and aspirations of Muslims in the UK are relatively invisible to large sectors of society. This is due to multiple factors such as geographical location ('there are no Muslims in our area'), minority status in ethnic and religious dimensions, and superficial efforts to value and respect 'cultural diversity' in any real or meaningful way. The 1997 Runnymede Trust report 'Islamophobia – a challenge to us all' documents serious difficulties suffered by some British Muslims in terms of prejudice and discrimination, exclusion and violence. At the start of the new millennium, violence between Christians and Muslims was described as 'at its worst for generations' (Binyon, 2000: 14). With such barriers to extending knowledge and understanding it is important to use education for positive change, for example through sharing research that begins to address questions of equity, of rights and responsibilities.

Muslims and physical education

Since this research focuses on the subject of physical education and many myths still exist about Muslim participation, it is necessary to state that participation in practical sport/physical education activities is acceptable and, in fact, desirable in Islam (Niciri, 1993; Daiman, 1995; Sawar, 1994). Islam supports the maintaining of a healthy body and encourages both genders to participate in physical activity. The tensions arise at the interface of certain principles and practices within the subject, which can therefore present difficulties for some Muslims. As Carroll and Hollinshead (1993) and Benn (2000) have stressed, wider understanding may lead to a more inclusive education. For example religious requirements could be met through flexible kit that allowed coverage of arms and legs, segregating lessons for boys and girls after adolescence with a teacher of the same sex, sensitive selection of dance themes and accompaniment, options on issues such as showers, understanding and accommodation of dietary changes during Ramadan, and flexible extra-curricular programmes.

Interestingly, the conflation of physical education and sport in current discourse (see for example, Penney and Evans, 1997) does not help children and young people in the Muslim community. The western cultural significance of sport does not have the same significance in the lives of all people and there are issues in Islam related to the display of the body and the demands of training for sporting success which can be problematic. For practising Muslims, religion is the most significant factor in their lives, and nothing can distract or come before commitment to following the path towards 'oneness with God'. But the importance of physical education in the development of all children is not disputed in Islam. Physical education in the school context is recognised as important in helping Muslim children to acquire healthy lifestyles and active participation (De Knop *et al.*, 1996). The inclusion statement in the statutory National Curriculum for Physical Education (DfEE/QCA, 1999) means that all teachers at primary level and specialists at secondary level need to respond to diverse learning needs. These include those of different cultural and ethnic groups, taking into account pupils' religious and cultural beliefs and practices, and the need to remove barriers to learning.

Addressing 'inclusion' for Muslims in higher education

The needs of Muslim students do not change as they move from secondary school to college or university. Following the path of Islam is a lifetime commitment. Are the rights of inclusion now embedded in the national curriculum present in higher education? Whilst understanding of the needs of Muslim children in schools is improving and research is contributing to knowledge about physical education and the participation of Muslim pupils, the picture nationally is not even. Despite political good-will to increase the numbers of ethnic minorities in the teaching profession, there are difficulties attracting and retaining these students in higher education. In my own institution the start of an Islamic studies variant within the religious education main subject studies of the Bachelor of Education (BEd) degree course encouraged Muslim students, predominantly women, to enter primary initial teacher training. Neither the institution nor the physical education department were ready for this. The following research charts the 'micro' learning process that ensued in terms of meeting the needs of these Muslim students. This is synthesised with survey data offering a more 'macro' picture of the position of other higher education institutions involved in initial teacher training in relation to meeting the needs of Muslim students. Specifically, the discussion and analysis that follows is structured around a number of themes that emerged through data analysis.

Emergent issues

Does higher education offer a compatible environment for Muslim students?

In my own institution the liberal thinking underpinning the launch of an Islamic studies route through the BEd degree succeeded in attracting Muslim students, predominantly of Pakistani or Bangladeshi heritage, into teacher training. The students found that the culture of the institution was not completely compatible with their religious requirements as Muslims. On reflection it is interesting that despite willingness to design courses for this specific group there was initially little 'institutional' understanding or provision for Islamic religious requirements. Staff, including the physical education department, were naïve and unprepared. What happened was a gradual process of increased awareness and an integration of changes that would enable Muslim students to feel more comfortable, and in physical education, to participate more fully, without fear or anxiety of transgressing their religious beliefs.

It is important to stress that the Muslim students were not homogeneous, with some choosing to distance themselves from those asking for change. In tracking the Muslim students' experiences it was interesting to note that the study of Islam had a positive effect on the women. They started to understand the place and opportunities for women in 'real Islam'. At the same time the religiosity of many strengthened, with some adopting hijab for the first time during their higher education period, and experiencing a growing group identity within the institution.

In terms of the basic needs of Muslim students, single-sex accommodation had to be 'reinstated'. Local houses represented one means of providing 'separate' living space for small groups. The catering department easily integrated the dietary needs of Muslim students but lack of space meant that the provision of a prayer room dedicated to Muslim students was more problematic. This issue gave rise to some resentment on the part of non-Muslim students, who viewed this as 'encroachment' in real terms on 'their space'. These early tensions have dissipated with the passage of time. Fareeda[2] recalled:

> there was uproar when we asked for a prayer room. Now this course has been going for three years and it took us two years to get a prayer room. In our eyes this is ridiculous because to us a prayer room is an essential item. We need somewhere to pray . . . obviously some students think this is preferential treatment.

Another issue that arose was that of honouring Muslim Festivals. This was raised at senior management level after difficulties during a school-experience. Muslim students had asked for permission to be able to spend Eid with their families to celebrate the end of Ramadan. Plans had been made for External Examiners to visit schools on that day and inevitable tensions arose between students, tutors and schools. Shortly after this it became policy that Muslim students would be free to celebrate this Festival as they chose.

The changes related above were notably reactive. Muslim students first raised issues, staff and managers learned and responded, seeking satisfactory solutions together. Some early tensions existed between Muslim and non-Muslim students. However, institutional intention was to enable the Muslim students to be as comfortable as possible during their time in higher education and, therefore, to meet their religious requirements wherever possible. An example of an incident that did not result in change was when requests were made by a student for long-term leave of absence to attend Hajj, one of the five pillars of faith, a duty for all Muslims. Senior managers negotiated with staff in the Islamic studies department and decided not to grant this request because the long absence would be detrimental to progress on the course. The Islamic studies staff supported the decision, suggesting that the religious requirement of Hajj needed to be undertaken only once during a lifetime and that the students would have time for this later in their lives.

During the Muslim women's time in higher education they were able to influence changes that enabled them to live their lives 'more comfortably', that is 'more Islamically', with greater consciousness in their daily lives of Islam and Islamic traditions (relating to dress and prayer practices but also underpinning thoughts, actions and interactions in everyday life). Increasing numbers of Muslim students brought opportunities to share values and beliefs. Tensions were greatest in this early period of change when decisions supporting Muslim students affected other groups. Incidents of religious prejudice did occur between some non-Muslim and Muslim students. The experiences of the Muslim women provided evidence that overt religious identity invoked more prejudice in the HEI context than racial prejudice. As Nadia explained, the vehemence of comments against those who had adopted Muslim dress, particularly the hijab, was greater than against those who were Asian but not visibly Muslim:

> other students think hijab girls are strict . . . extremists . . . they're not –
> they are just normal . . . I (a non hijab-wearer) am just Asian to them, not
> Muslim. Even though they might be a bit rude towards me they are not
> as rude as they are to the hijab girls, because they'd know I'd answer them
> back and the hijab girls would be more respectful and dignified.

By the end of their four-year initial teacher training course the women had a strong sense of belonging to the institution and a network of support within the HEI's community. They recognised the changes they had initiated and the gains they had made. Leaving this environment became a source of anxiety for some of the Muslim women as they reached the point of going into relatively 'isolating' school situations. As Rabiah explained: 'if you wanted to share something (at college/university) there was always somebody there but in schools you are alone'.

The questionnaire survey suggested that many Muslim students may be 'isolated' during training. The survey revealed that most institutions did not gather data on religious affiliation, but indicated that very few Muslim students are entering initial teacher training. Only four respondents had any direct experience of conversations with Muslim students about religious requirements and institutional practices. Awareness of Muslim students on ITT courses was therefore essentially limited to recognition by dress code or informally through informal conversations about religion. Fourteen of the thirty-five responding HEIs were aware of Muslim students who had been through their initial teacher training courses. Four were aware of men only, five of women only and five had experience of both Muslim men and women. Numbers were very small (typically one or two per year). Issues related to religious requirements had only been raised in four of these HEIs and involved dress, the provision of space for prayer and fasting.

In terms of providing environments where Muslim students were able to feel 'comfortable' (that is able to meet religious requirements on a daily basis) fourteen HEIs could offer single-sex accommodation, seventeen could meet 'dietary needs', ten honoured Muslim Festival days and ten offered a 'prayer room'. All of these requirements could be met in only six institutions. Some provision happened 'accidentally' rather than intentionally. For example single-sex accommodation was in some instances available or not on an ad hoc basis, determined by pragmatic issues rather than a concern for the needs of Muslim students. One response indicated that dietary require- ments would be met but added that halal meat was not provided. This indicated that there was general accommodation of difference in dietary needs rather than provision for the specific needs of Muslim students. The extent to which provision of prayer rooms was specifically for Muslim students was not clear. Some responses indicated that a 'general prayer room' was available which would be unlikely to meet the needs of different religions.

It was therefore clear from the survey data that the majority of HEIs would not be able to accommodate the general religious requirements of Muslim students. Some could address certain needs but provision was not, as yet, happening at an intentional 'conscious' level within many institutions. This research has suggested that a lack of understanding has and does abound within traditional higher education institutes, even those espousing liberal thinking and originality in course design, including my own.

Institutional ethos and the inclusion of Muslim students

Whilst the majority of questionnaire respondents thought that there would be no resistance to changes to accommodate the needs of Muslim students, the ethos of different HEIs was raised as an issue in some. Where there was already 'a strong religious tradition' (Christian) (HEI-30) it was thought that change would be more difficult. In geographical locations with 'few Muslim people per head of population' respondents felt 'unaware of major issues' and suggested that more educational materials would be helpful (HEI-19). Other respondents suggested that 'greater communication and understanding would be beneficial' adding 'compromises have to be made by both parties' (HEI-6). Some respondents thought that staff and students would be helpful and willing to learn. One predicted 'some resistance'. Another found this question 'difficult to predict', whilst others actively sought recruitment from ethnic minorities via local schools. This picture denotes variability of experiences and expectations across institutions of higher education. There is clearly a need to pursue greater equity in relation to readiness for cultural diversity if real opportunity is to be created for more students. Due to the specific needs of this particular group a number of institutions suggested having particular HEIs specializing in provision for Muslim students. In such institutions one would imagine provision for single sex groups (for men and women) in physical education with same-sex staffing, timetabling compatible to prayer requirements, private sports spaces, changing and showering facilities. Other needs, including appropriate accommodation, honouring of Festival days, prayer rooms and provision for dietary needs, would be standard provision. Partnership schools would be fully cognisant of the needs of Muslim student-teachers in training. Such provision does not yet exist.

Muslim students 'finding a voice' in higher education

It was interesting to note that the first cohort of Muslim students at my own institution (seven), were well into the second year of their course before any mention was made of incongruity between institutional practices and their religious requirements. The second cohort (ten) were more vociferous and within months of their arrival an Islamic society was set up in the institution at their request. This became the forum through which the Muslim women were able to 'find a voice', to make their views public. If the numbers of Muslim students had not increased it is probable that the first cohort would have moved through their four-year course 'suffering in silence' rather than speaking out. In relatively isolated situations the option of 'stasis' (Menter, 1989), staying silent in preference to confrontation, was used. This coping strategy was evident in much of my research (Benn, 1998) and involved an element of retreat in terms of identity. As the Muslim women progressed in their training they became more skilful in deciding when to adopt this 'identity stasis' in the process of survival: 'You learn when to speak and when to stay silent' (Rabiah). Islamophobia and the fear that they would be labelled as 'fundamentalists' and further oppressed, underpinned and exacerbated the need for this strategy. The humility taught through Islam was recognised by one questionnaire respondent who suggested that:

There is a need to encourage more Muslims into PE in order to challenge stereotypical attitudes towards Muslims and physical ability/activity. More Muslim staff would inevitably be self-perpetuating. My experience (minimal) with Muslims in UK and abroad (in the context of PE) is of a timid approach fuelled as much by their pre-conceptions about the demands that will be made upon them by staff as by their religious teaching regarding humility and codes of dress etc.

(HEI-10)

The fact that so few higher education institutions had intentionally made changes to accommodate the needs of Muslim students reflects both institutional 'blindness' and Muslim students' own preference for 'stasis' to avoid confrontation. The women in this research felt torn between seeing higher education as a means to 'get on' in the West whilst believing that the dominant view of Islam that prevails in the West was anti-Islamic. They recognised in particular that their dress made them a potential target for prejudice and discrimination: 'people judge us as fundamentalist if we wear hijab' (Nawar).

Although this chapter is particularly concerned with Muslim women, it is necessary to recognise that Muslim men also have needs which can be invisible in higher education. When discussing the issue of the needs of Muslim students at a guest lecture in a leading higher education institution specialising in physical education teacher training, two Muslim men approached me at the end of the session. They said that they had been suffering in silence for three years because they did not feel that they had the right to ask for changes to meet their religious requirements. They had been praying daily in the gymnasium store-cupboard! Their 'stasis' had led to misunderstandings of their behaviour, misinterpretations of actions and other tensions that could have been resolved with a more open sharing of difference. Fear of negative responses and anticipation of labelling prevented the Muslim men from raising issues relating to general or subject specific ways in which their experiences in higher education could have been more compatible with their preference to be practising Muslims. Clearly, there is a need to stress that all HEIs must strive to offer environments in which students feel able to raise issues and be open about their religious identities. Particular tensions for Muslim students that are associated with the subject of physical education are the focus of the next section.

Initial teacher training, physical education and Muslim students

The Muslim women who participated in the qualitative research were in many ways the instigators of change in their HEI environment. Physical education was no exception. The women in this research entered an environment where a number of traditional practices had not been questioned. For example, mixed-sex participation in physical education including swimming was the norm, subject spaces were very public and on occasions Muslim women had been asked to remove their hijab on the grounds of safety. There is no doubt that unintentional 'institutional racism', or more accurately religious discrimination, was happening which disadvantaged this particular group and which reflected a lack of knowledge about and little sensitivity to their religious needs.

Change was not straightforward, as pragmatic organisational issues arose which affected systems, staffing and other students. Decisions for changes requested by the Muslim students were largely made within the department, but a key issue, the provision of single-sex groups for women, had wider implications. The groups for professional studies in all subjects (including physical education) were traditionally mixed. In consultation with Islamic studies colleagues and students, it was agreed that the provision of single-sex groups for some of the Muslim women would be essential to facilitating their participation. The imbalance of male/female students in primary teacher training meant the predominance of women enabled one all-female group to be established. As this decision was made mid-year it entailed some movement of women between groups and the moving of one man out of his original group. He protested that this change was unfair and 'sexist', but at the time the needs of the Muslim women were the priority. Thereafter, Muslim women were able to choose whether they wanted to be in an all-female group from the start of the course, thereby avoiding the tensions of 'changing groups'.

Other ways of accommodating the religious requirements of Muslim women were easier. The physical education 'changing rooms' have become a private meeting place for some groups of Muslim women. The issue of changing for physical education was not problematic because the layout of the changing rooms meant that privacy was possible, although showering would not have been private if any had wanted to take advantage of this facility after exercise. Kit required for primary physical education students had always been 'liberal' in that students were invited to wear whatever was comfortable. Some Muslim students wanted reassurance that loose clothing was permissible, and that the hijab could be worn, if safely secured. Clothing for swimming was more difficult. Some Muslim women wanted to wear clothing over their swimming costumes, which made the activity harder and for weaker swimmers necessitated them staying in the shallow end. These students recognised that their efforts to make their bodies less conspicuous were actually making them more conspicuous and by the end of the course most had moved to swimming in only their costumes. This became largely a confidence issue, once an all-female environment was guaranteed. For the first cohort of Muslim students who had opted to stay in mixed-sex groups (when the option was given half way through their course), participating in mixed-sex swimming was impossible. Insistence on participation could have led to an explosive situation. Course teaching methods were adapted to involve the students from the pool-side, focusing on developing their observation and teaching skills. The course emphasis was on teaching, which in swimming is normally from the pool-side, so this adaptation was considered appropriate in the circumstances by staff and students.

Due to the lack of consensus over participation in dance within Islam (see Sawar's strong 'anti' position in his guidance to British Muslims and schools, 1994: 13), some of the Muslim women faced dilemmas when undertaking the compulsory 'dance in education' training course. One reason for tensions relates to the association of dance with discos and 'dance-halls' and the visible 'use' of the body in those contexts. Dance in those contexts may be interpreted as provocative and related to promoting sexual attraction between the sexes, behaviour which would be considered anti-islamic. The dilemmas that some of the Muslim students felt before participating in the dance course, their experiences and post-course reflections were captured in diaries. Early anxieties were evident but attitudes clearly changed in a positive direction during the course as students' confidence grew and the rationale, principles and practice of dance in education became clear. The shift was such that all the students finished the course believing that there was nothing anti-islamic about 'dance in education' and that any issues raised about the appropriateness of dance in education for young children were related to misconceptions of the activity. Zauda commented that:

> it's provocative dance that is problematic. The dance we do in PE is not that sort of dance, it's movement development . . . I don't see why there should be any difficulties. . . . There will be people who object to dance, but I think when they realise it's not *that* kind of dance, they should understand about dance in education.

One of the notable characteristics of dance courses is that themes can be selected to avoid contentious issues. Experiences on this course highlighted the way in which without adequate understanding of religious and cultural traditions and practices, we will be unable to make appropriate selections of content. In one instance I made the mistake of using a story as a starting point that involved representation of gods. Although symbolic, this caused some tension for one Muslim student. I was unaware of the possible interpretation and learnt by experience.

Other issues arose in training that again necessitated reactive strategies. In one instance a male teacher accompanied a class of children with whom the all-female group would be conducting a team-taught gymnastics lesson. A small number of Muslim women were inhibited by the presence of the male teacher. They asked if it would be possible to request a class with a female teacher next time, or for them to be warned in advance so they could be better prepared, for example in terms of dress. Their concerns and request relates to a reluctance of some Muslim women to move freely in front of adult males and the importance of modest dress in such situations. Again, staff were learning from the Muslim women students in the process of the course. In-depth knowledge of Islam and religious requirements of followers would have enabled us to anticipate and therefore avoid such tensions, but at the time we were relatively uninformed and unquestioning of traditional physical education practices and their possible effects.

The survey of HEIs revealed that only two institutions could offer Muslim women the opportunity to enter single-sex groups and only one of those could guarantee to provide a female member of staff. In primary teacher training nationally, a single-sex option for Muslim women may be considered feasible but because of numbers, it would seem impossible to provide this option for Muslim men. The imbalance of men and women entering primary teacher training, in favour of women, means that pragmatic and economic constraints may prohibit single-sex groupings. One questionnaire respondent commented:

> I would foresee the principal difficulty as one of 'numbers', i.e. single-sex classes for females would not generate problems but would leave inoperable groups of males. The knock-on effect for other teaching groups might be resisted by some staff.
>
> (HEI-10)

Many questionnaire responses located constraints in 'logistics' such as demands on timetabling, 'the timetable is so tight' and pressures on staff, for example in heavy teaching loads and expectations to maintain high research profiles, increasing annually. Small departments (one physical education lecturer in some cases) meant that equitable provision for Muslim men and women in terms of single-sex groups with same-sex staff was a product of chance: 'Single-sex physical education groups would not be possible – we have so few men and I am *the* member of staff!' (female) (HEI-6).

Ideally the kit or dress code for physical education would accommodate the needs of Muslim students. For example, allowing the hijab to be worn if preferred, arms and legs to be covered in a comfortable tracksuit, allowing men to wear knee length swimming shorts and women to negotiate a way to participate in swimming, would be helpful. Twenty of the responding HEIs regarded this area as less problematic than providing single-sex groups. The majority felt that their policy was relaxed, preferring all students to be comfortable and positive about participating, with safety being their only proviso. Of the rest, nine institutions stated that they did not have provision for accommodating to the dress code requirements of Muslim students, one did not understand the question and others did not indicate a response. Qualitative comments revealed that contrasting attitudes still prevail within training institutions. For example, while one respondent commented that 'It's about time this was laid to rest for good and not just from a Muslim viewpoint! . . . students wear whatever kit they wish, as long as it is safe' (HEI-31), another individual in a leading specialist University indicated a different perspective: 'I could foresee some resistance from some staff and non-Muslim students' (HEI-33). A reflective comment from a different

University suggested: 'It would be naïve and inaccurate to suggest "there ain't no problems here." We all bring prejudices and baggage of some sort or another to any teaching/learning encounter' (HEI-30).

The culture of the subject was an issue raised by another respondent who had spent some time with Muslims. He suggested that 'the Physical Education profession needs to shake off its harsh and coarse image in order to open up the franchise to a broader community and in so doing facilitate participation amongst diverse groups' (HEI-10). This is indicative of a deeper concern about particular ways of teaching, of gendered practices, a privileged position for 'sport', dominance of competitive team games, and of subject expectations, historically endowed and still existent, particularly for men and boys. Issues of inclusion for physical education are about recognising histories, legacies, cultural practices and meanings embedded, then confronting and challenging these in terms of their appropriateness for the next millennium.

Initial teacher training, school-based experiences and Muslim students

School-based experiences for the Muslim women in the qualitative research proved difficult times for a number of reasons. The women reported feelings of isolation, meeting incidents of religious prejudice from colleagues, senior managers, pupils and parents, misunderstandings of their Muslim identity, motivations, behaviour and lifestyle and confusions about their status as 'specialists' in religious education. Partnership schools in which the Muslim students were placed for their school-based experiences, were not always appropriate. The quality of the students' experience in part depended on how welcome they felt in the school situation. This bore little relationship to the ethnic diversity within the school but was more closely related to the management style and closed or open views of Islam (Runnymede Trust, 1997) held by colleagues, pupils and parents. Students who experienced religious prejudice in staffrooms again chose identity 'stasis' as a strategy for coping. That is, they preferred not to talk about anything related to Islam or being Muslim, not to answer questions or speak their mind, in order to avoid confrontation. The preference was to 'remain silent' (Asma), 'it's not worth challenging . . . the risk is too high' (Jamilah). These were comments made about staffroom experiences by hijab-wearing Muslim teachers. Feelings of loneliness and isolation in schools were high and some of this was related to religiosity 'the more practising you become the harder it is because your purpose is different to others – to live our lives Islamically' (Rabiah).

At the other end of the spectrum, a Muslim student went into an all-white school and on the first meeting with the head teacher was offered a room adjacent to the library, as a quiet room for prayer at lunch-time if she wanted to use it. This gesture made a difference to the student's confidence in the school and led to a very successful experience. The needs of Muslim teachers are not easily addressed in schools, particularly primary schools where space is at a premium. Privacy for hygiene rituals, for changing or for prayer are difficult issues as Nawar explained:

> I'd appreciate private washing facilities. I try to keep it secret and do my ablutions in the washbasins in the staff toilet. If anyone comes in I stop and continue when they go out. Some classrooms have their own sinks but mine doesn't. I don't mind praying in the classroom but obviously I would prefer privacy.

Incidents of religious prejudice happened at every level, indicating that schools did not represent the supportive environment that we endeavoured to ensure in the training institution. There were at least four occasions when head teachers telephoned the training institution to ask if students were allowed to wear the hijab into school and to discuss possible safety implications. In an interview one head teacher suggested that this practice might encourage the Muslim girls to wear head-scarves into school, something that they were trying to ban. Class teachers spent most time with the Muslim women students and there were many conversations that involved discussing Islam. Personal and prejudiced comments were made, leaving some of the women feeling as though they were 'defending their right to be Muslim'. Comments were made about the early marriage of Muslim girls, the house seclusion of many Muslim women, issues of equality and education. Initially the Muslim women treated the opportunity for discussion positively, despite the often coloured phrasing of questions, hoping to share knowledge of 'real Islam'. However, where 'closed' views of Islam were met (Runnymede Trust, 1997) they adopted 'identity stasis' choosing not to enter dialogue about being Muslim or about Islam.

Relationships with parents were both positive and negative. Sharing language skills, religious and cultural affinity with parents in particular schools helped some of the Muslim women to feel valued. At times this was in stark contrast to experiences with colleagues and senior managers in the same school. One student, Jamilah, left a school feeling undervalued, demoralised and unfulfilled, yet accompanied by gifts and cards from pupils (in a 98 per cent Asian, Muslim school) and parents indicating their appreciation of having her at the school.

Relationships with pupils were also varied. There were common problems of acceptance in the role of 'teacher'. The over-representation of Asian women as classroom assistants meant that the Muslim women students faced many questions about their role and were asked 'when is the real teacher coming?' Interactions with Asian children were largely very positive, with some student teachers experiencing real excitement from children enjoying having a 'teacher like them', but others encountered stereotyping from the Asian children as well. For example, Zahra was asked the same three questions on all three of her school-based experiences: 'Miss, are you Pakistani?', 'Miss, are you married?', 'Miss, have you got children?'. She was from Mozambique, of African-Asian heritage, spoke Portuguese as her first language and was single with no children. She was a challenge to the pupils' perception of a 'normal Asian woman' and used this opportunity to extend their views.

Physical education school-based experiences were often better than anticipated for the Muslim women. Unfortunately, this was more often attributable to the low status of the subject in the school and the small part that it played during their school experience, than about interrogating progress of teaching this aspect of the curriculum. The Muslim women were empathetic to Muslim pupils who experienced some difficulties with mixed-sex changing. They were sometimes incensed at the rigidity they witnessed in teachers' kit expectations and strict regimes, with Muslim pupils being refused the opportunity to wear tracksuits with excuses such as 'they are dangerous because they can get caught on apparatus in gymnastics'. The women saw themselves as role models and were positive about the importance of physical education. They quickly learned that for many pupils it was their favourite subject but that for many staff it was the first subject to be dropped at the sign of a crisis elsewhere. Being a teacher of physical education in a primary school was, for the Muslim women in this research, less problematic than participating in physical education as a student-teacher in higher education. They were in a more private situation and this became even more private once qualified, when they were not observed during lessons.

As indicated above, the difficulty of the presence of adult males arose on school experience. In one instance, a Muslim women changed her dance lesson to a different time when she knew her male tutor was coming in. For some Muslim women the actual experience of having a male class teacher or tutor was regarded as 'less problematic than expected'. For others 'we would change our teaching method, we would not be able to be as practically involved with the children as we would wish to be'. The response of the institution was to offer the Muslim students a choice of a male or female tutor for school-based experiences. The concerns raised by the Muslim women have clear implications for professional development. There is a need to address, for example, the effects of the presence of male inspectors or head teachers in physical education lessons taught by Muslim women and the procedures for monitoring and advancing the professional development for Muslim women who may prefer support from female senior colleagues.

Having religious education as a main subject with a specialism in Islamic studies proved particularly difficult for the Muslim women. They met responses from teachers which intimated that being so visibly Muslim they would be incapable of being objective about delivering a multi-faith religious education. No such questions or intimations would be made of Christian teachers. This adds to the weight of insidious Islamophobia that surrounded the Muslim women in this research. Accusations of indoctrination intentions were made at any suggestion that they might contribute to religious education. Although rare, there were some experiences of positive responses to the women's Muslim identities. One moved on to become subject co-ordinator for religious education when later employed by her final school-experience school. Another respondent enjoyed a very welcoming and open attitude to her visible Muslim identity and everything that she could offer to the school, but this was not the most common experience.

Educating for equity and initial teacher training (ITT)

The fact that the Muslim women in the qualitative research experienced racial and religious prejudice from some non-Muslim student trainees during their initial teacher training is a serious issue. If attitudes are not challenged and education is not provided to increase knowledge, awareness and understanding of equity issues in ITT then teachers' capabilities to respond to the needs of particular pupils, and colleagues, will be limited and potentially dangerous.

The questionnaire asked about ways in which issues of equity were addressed within ITT courses, with partnership schools and mentors. Twenty-five out of thirty-five HEIs addressed issues of equity within their courses. Content details were not forthcoming but some indicated times from thirty minutes to six hours being spent on issues of equity. Whether and how equity issues were addressed with partnership schools and mentors was less clear. Three HEIs stated that they adopted a 'permeation' model. One addressed this 'where there was an ethnic mix', one provided a cross-LEA 'inner City' experience, and one addressed issues 'if they were raised'. Approaches suggest reaction rather than proactivity and a likelihood of patchy awareness of equity issues amongst trainees and the future teaching profession. Many respondents identified pressures of time reductions, competing subjects and increasing centralised pressures as constraining the opportunities to address equity issues, as illustrated in the following comment: 'We would like to spend more time on such issues with trainees but there are other serious demands on our time that currently have a higher profile (e.g. PGCEs covering the fifty-four standards!)' (HEI-29).

The research has indicated that the increased responsibility of schools in the process of teacher training in England and Wales necessitates the sharing of knowledge and awareness of equity issues within and between HEIs, partnership schools, mentors and all colleagues with the power to influence the training of any teacher. Whilst the Muslim women in this study eventually felt empowered within their ITT institution they felt powerless and unable to challenge religious prejudice encountered in school-based training, indicating the need for better understanding of issues of equity amongst educators and communication between training providers. Clearly it would be helpful if schools in which Muslim student-teachers are placed are aware of their needs and of the types of experiences faced by the Muslim women in this research, so that they may be better prepared to support students in their professional training.

Conclusion

This research set out to engage with the complexity of overlapping structures of disadvantage in a particular time and place. The socio-political UK context has shaped the struggles identified as political agendas in a plural but unequal society to pursue polices of inclusion and equity. Increasing knowledge and understanding of diversity is one way to remove fear and foster positive ways forward. There are no easy answers to issues raised. Traditional practices are deeply ingrained in training institutions and therefore hard to challenge. However, change in the training context may also have the greatest long-term effects, since the training process shapes teachers and teachers shape children. My work has shown that there is a need to challenge both institutional 'blindness' and to foster more open debate with Muslim students, where previously fear and relative isolation has deterred individuals from speaking out. If we are to strive towards greater respect of cultural difference in the school curriculum (McPherson Report, 1999) it needs to start in raising consciousness and taking action to address disadvantage in the process of training the next generation of teachers.

The survey of HEIs in England and Wales indicated the current 'invisibility' of the need to address the religious requirements of Muslim students in teacher training. Government policies are driving HEIs towards ever increasing 'widening access' and policies of inclusion. But at the same time the pressures on ITT institutions for economic efficiency in provision exacerbate the pragmatic dilemmas of addressing the needs of this group, for example in the provision of separate-sex classes in a primary teacher training course. Some institutions may experience tensions in wanting to accommodate difference yet having to count the cost of provision.

The Muslim women involved in this research will be rare but vital role models for growing numbers of Muslim children in Britain. I am indebted to them and to my HEI colleagues who so willingly responded to the questionnaire. Their responses have opened the door to a broader picture and further debate.

Notes

1 Religiosity is a term used to describe a person's degree of religious conviction.
2 Pseudonyms are used for all of the students involved in the research.

References

Ahmed, L. (1992) *Women and Gender in Islam*, London: Yale University Press.
Bayliss, T. (1989) PE and racism: making changes, *Multicultural Teaching*, 7(2): 19–22.
Benn, T. (1998) Exploring experiences of a group of British Muslim women in initial teacher training and their early teaching careers, PhD thesis, Loughborough University.

Benn, T. (2000) Towards inclusion in education and physical education, in A. Williams (ed) *Primary School Physical Education*, London: Falmer Press.

Binyon, (2000) *The Times*, 4 January: 14.

Brah, A. (1992) Women of South Asian origin in Britain – issues and concerns, in P. Brahum, A. Rattonsi and R. Skillington (eds) *Racism and Anti-racism, Inequalities, Opportunities and Policies*, London: Sage.

Brah, M. and Minas, R. (1985) Structural racism or cultural differences: schooling for Asian girls, in G. Weiner (ed.) *Just a Bunch of Girls*, Milton Keynes: Open University Press.

Carrington, B. and Williams, T. (1993) Patriarchy and ethnicity: the link between school and physical education and community leisure activities, in J. Evans (ed.) *Equality, Education and Physical Education*, London: Falmer Press.

Carroll, B. and Hollinshead, G. (1993) Equal opportunities: race and gender in physical education: a case study, in J. Evans (ed.) *Equality, Education and Physical Education*, London: Falmer Press.

Cashmore, E. (1982) *Black Sportsmen*, London: Routledge & Kegan Paul.

Chappell, R. (1995) Racial stereotyping in schools, *BAALPE Bulletin* 31(4): 22–8.

Coakley, J. (1994) *Sport in Society: Issues and Controversies*, London: Mosby.

Department for Education and Science (1989) *Circular 24/89 Initial Teacher Training: Approval for Courses*, London: HMSO.

Department for Education and Employment (DfEE)/Qualifications and Curriculum Authority (QCA) (1999) *Physical Education: The National Curriculum for England*, London: QCA.

Daiman, S. (1995) Women in sport in Islam, *Journal of the International Council for Health, Physical Education, Recreation, Sport and Dance* 32(1): 18–21.

De Knop, P., Theeboom, M., Wittock, H. and De Martelaer, K. (1996) Implications of Islam on Muslim girls' sports participation in Western Europe, *Sport, Education and Society* 1(2): 147–64.

Equal Opportunities Commission (1989) *Formal Investigation Report: Initial Teacher Training in England and Wales*, London: Equal Opportunities Commission.

Elias, N. (1991) *The Society of Individuals*, Oxford: Blackwell.

Essed, P. (1991) *Understanding Everyday Racism: An Interdisciplinary Theory*, London: Sage.

Faruqi, L.A. (1991) *Women, Muslim Society and Islam*, Indianapolis: American Trust Publication.

George, R. and Jones, M. (1992) The human element in fieldwork, in A. Giddens (ed.) *Human Societies: A Reader*, Cambridge: Polity Press.

Griffiths, M. and Troyna, B. (eds) (1995) *Antiracism, Culture and Social Justice in Education*, Stoke-on-Trent: Trentham Books.

Hargreaves, J. (1994) *Sporting Females*, London, Routledge.

Haw, K.F. (1991) Interactions of gender and race: a problem for teachers? – a review of emerging literature, *Educational Research* 33(1): 12–21.

Haw, K.F. (1995) Why Muslim girls are more feminist in Muslim schools, in M. Griffiths and B. Troyna (eds) *Antiracism, Culture and Social Justice in Education*, Stoke-on-Trent: Trentham Books.

Haw, K.F. (1996) Exploring the educational experiences of Muslim girls: tales told to tourists – should the white researcher stay at home? *British Educational Research Journal* 22(3): 319–30.

Haw, K.F. (1998) *Educating Muslim Girls: Shifting Discourses*, Buckingham, Open University Press.

Jarvie, G. (ed.) (1991) *Sport, Racism and Ethnicity*, London: Falmer Press.

Jawad, H.A. (1998) *The Rights of Women in Islam: An Authentic Approach*, London: Macmillan Press.

Jenkins, R. (1997) *Rethinking Ethnicity: Arguments and Explorations*, London: Sage.

Lewis, P. (1994) *Islamic Britain*, London: I.B. Tauris.

Macguire, B. and Collins, D. (1998) Sport, ethnicity and racism: the experience of Asian heritage boys, *Sport Education and Society* 3(1): 79–88.

Macpherson, W. (1999) *The Stephen Lawrence Inquiry: Report of an inquiry by Sir William Macpherson of Cluny*, London: HMSO.

Mennel, S. (1994) The formation of we-images: a process theory, in C. Calhoun (ed.) *Social Theory and the Politics of Identity*, Oxford: Blackwell Publications.

Mirza, M. (1995) Some ethical dilemmas in fieldwork: feminist and anti-racist methodologies, in M. Griffiths and B. Troyna (eds) *Antiracism, Culture and Social Justice in Education*, Stoke-on-Trent: Trentham Books.

Neal, S. (1995) A question of silence? Antiracist discourses and initiatives in higher education: two case studies, in M. Griffiths and B. Troyna (eds) *Antiracism, Culture and Social Justice in Education*, Stoke-on-Trent: Trentham Books.

Niciri, M. (1993) The Islamic position in sport, in *Sport in the Modern World – Chances and Problems*, Scientific Congress, Munich Olympics, Berlin, Springer Verlag.

Parker-Jenkins, M. (1995) *Children of Islam*, Stoke-on-Trent: Trentham Books.

Penney, D. and Evans, J. (1997) Naming the game: discourse and domination in physical education and sport in England and Wales, *European Physical Education Review* 3(1): 21–32.

Runnymede Trust (1997) *Islamophobia – a Challenge for All of Us*, London: Runnymede Trust.

Sawar, G. (1994) *British Muslims and Schools*, London: Muslim Education Trust.

Scharenburg, S. (1999) Religion and sport, in J. Riordan and A. Kruger (eds) *The International Politics of Sport in the Twentieth Century*, London: E & FN Spon.

Sfeir, L. (1985) The status of Muslim women in sport: conflict between cultural traditions and modernisation, *International Review for Sociology of Sport* 20(4): 283–304.

Singh, R. (1988) *Asian and White Perceptions of the Teaching Profession*, West Yorkshire: Bradley and Ilkley Community College, UK.

Siraj-Blatchford, I. (1991) A study of black students' perceptions of racism in initial teacher education, *British Educational Research Journal* 17(1): 35–50.

Siraj-Blatchford, I. (1993) *Race, Gender and the Education of Teachers*, Buckinghamshire: Oxford University Press.

6 Gender positioning as pedagogical practice in teaching physical education

David Brown and Emma Rich

Introduction

In recent years a growing body of empirical work has helped develop our understandings of masculinities and femininities in education, physical education and school sports contexts (see for example, De Knop *et al.*, 1996; Tsolidis, 1996; Salisbury and Jackson, 1998; Wright, 1997; Hickey *et al.*, 1998; Ennis, 1999; Hargreaves, 2000). However, to date, rather less of this empirical work has considered the nature of gendered positions of Physical Education teachers themselves (see Evans *et al.*, 1996; Brown, 1999). In this chapter we consider some of the insights that are emerging from two studies that focus on the social significance of gendered physical education teacher identity. We present a view of teachers that acknowledges them not merely as the products of a brief period of initial teacher education, but as knowing subjects with lives and identities already strongly shaped by the time they enter the profession (Tabachnick *et al.*, 1984; Templin and Schempp, 1989; Grenfell and James, 1998). Our perspective also positions physical education teachers as key intermediaries in the social construction and transmission of what counts as 'gender legitimate' knowledge dispositions and practices. As such they can be considered as 'living links' (Brown, 1999) between generations of encultured gendered practice in the profession. We contend that a better understanding of this process of enculturation is crucial if we are to move towards more gender inclusive futures in physical education.

Our main concern in this chapter is to show the ways in which gendered student teacher identities, masculine and feminine, are 'positioned' and deployed as pedagogy, in response to the socio-cultural forces brought to bear on them during their period of Initial Teacher Education (ITT) and beyond. However, a point to note about our analysis is our concern to move from a critique that is essentially passive in its outlook, to one that engages with the possibilities for future practices that arise from our enhanced understandings. We therefore make the case that gender needs to be viewed as an integral part of the teacher's pedagogical repertoire (Gore, 1990; Luke and Gore, 1992) and that the positioned, gendered, self identity becomes a significant pedagogical resource. We are therefore viewing difference as a resource (see Evans, 1993) to be utilised in the further development of pedagogy in physical education.

A relational perspective of gender in physical education

Earlier chapters pay testimony to both the historical but also contemporary prevalence of gender inequities and exclusion within the fields of physical education and school sport (see also Kirk, 1992; Evans, 1993; Talbot, 1993). Following Messner and Sabo (1990) we contend that viewing this situation in terms of a relational 'Gender Order' provides a useful basis from which to gain insights into the issues of inclusion, exclusion, reproduction and change. They comment:

> A relational conception of gender necessarily includes a critical examin-
> ation of both femininity and masculinity as they develop in relation to
> each other within a system of structured social inequality.
>
> (Messner and Sabo, 1990: 13)

Humberstone (1990: 202) has highlighted that 'the complex web of inter-connections between cultural values, gender identity development and gender stereotypes surrounding sport are mediated through the PE curriculum'. Relational approaches attempt to gain insights into these interconnections and their implications for social reproduction and change. As Edley and Wetherell (1995) point out the relational nature of men and women (and similarly, other social categories) implies that changes to the position of one group will cause ripples, effecting the lives and positions of the others. These 'ripples' provide a key relational focus, as they are points of interconnections between masculinities and femininities. From a relational perspective, gender power relations operate in similar ways to Gramsci's (1971) observations on class hegemony, in that they are never total or absolute, but contested in social arenas such as schools and physical education classes. While we have to acknowledge that hegemonic forms of masculinity remain the dynamic ideological form around which western patriarchal relations are constructed, legitimised and defended (see for example, Brittan, 1989; Brod and Kaufman, 1994; Siedler, 1997; Pease, 2000; Whannel, 2000), we can also recognise multiple constructions of masculinities and femininities as men and women implicitly and explicitly are positioned and position themselves in relation to dominant ideological forms of hegemonic masculinity (Connell, 1995). Although it is necessary to clarify that women are *most* disadvantaged by a Gender Order dominated by hegemonic masculine ideology, it is equally vital to acknowledge that many men and boys are also marginalised and subordinated in and by this order. This prompts the deconstruction of over-simplified 'binary' male/ female gender boundaries from which categories of 'other' are constructed (Young, 1990). As Connell (1987) points out:

'Hegemonic masculinity' is always constructed in relation to various subordinated masculinities as well as in relation to women. The interplay between different forms of masculinity is an important part of how a patriarchal social order works.

(1987: 183)

In the analysis that follows we draw specifically on Connell's (1995) relational work on masculinities. Connell's work provides a useful heuristic that explores the dynamics of a patriarchy constructed around hegemonic masculine power and the ways in which individuals are positioned relative to it. We see hegemony, domination/subordination and complicity on the one hand and marginalisation/authorisation on the other (1995: 81). The former relations define the internal Gender Order with women, homosexual men and effeminacy being actively subordinated. A further position, complicity, refers to those who might not actively promote hegemonic masculinity but whose lives and dispositions benefit from the advantage men in general gain from the subordination of women (and of 'other' men). The second set of relations, marginalisation/ authorisation is caused by the, 'interplay of gender with other structures such as class and race' (ibid.: 80). These positions might be tentatively represented by the model below.

The ascendancy and 'logic' of this Gender Order also connects gender with sexuality through symbolic association. For example in physical education, where links between female/feminine and male/masculine are disrupted, sexuality is called into question. Men who do not demonstrate competitive, aggressive and dominant aspects of 'hegemonic' masculinity in contexts such as teaching physical education risk being positioned as 'effeminate' or 'gay'. Alternatively, women who do not act in 'appropriate feminine' ways might similarly be positioned outside the heterosexual other, which in physical education has historically meant 'lesbian', a powerful label and pejorative discourse that affects and limits all women, in terms of their gendered, sexual and professional identities (Griffin, 1992; see also Clarke in chapter 4). Neither this chapter, nor the studies that informed it, focus directly on issues of sexuality in teaching physical education. However, we acknowledge that the gender positioning that we identify in practice has implications for sexualities and their concomitant positions in a Gender Order based on heteronormativity. In short, the Gender Order constructs 'the other' through a series of oppositions that render dominant heterosexual forms of masculinity central but invisible and silent (Rutherford, 1988).

Notwithstanding the criticisms of Connell's model (see Peterson, 1997) for the way in which it might be interpreted as essentializing and reductionist in its categorization of masculinities and femininities, we sense nonetheless that, when viewed as a dynamic heuristic (i.e. context dependent, fluid and individualised rather than fixed and generalised), the framework offers a useful starting point in positioning the relative forms of gender that are in evidence in teaching physical education and sport. Moreover, it offers the

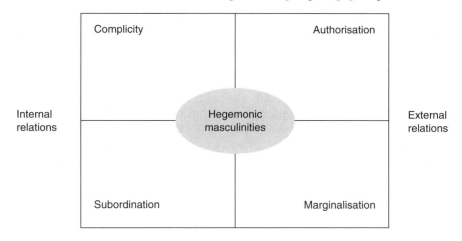

Figure 6.1 The Gender Order: internal and external relations

opportunity to expose the previously 'invisible centre' of the Gender Order that works relationally to legitimise certain gendered pedagogies, and render marginal or subordinated, the many possible alternatives.

Viewed through these relational lenses the domination of the contemporary social landscape of physical education and school sport in England and Wales by a particular European, elite middle class, heterosexual masculine ideology becomes more clearly visible. We begin to see an ideological ideal producing a series of discourses and practices which have long served as a benchmark for the legitimate uses of the body, standards of performance, modes of physical and emotional expression, patterns of interaction, curriculum organisation and so on (see for example Mangan, 1981; Hargreaves, 1986; Fletcher, 1987; Mangan and Walvin, 1987). Acknowledging such processes Connell (1995) stresses that:

> Any curriculum must address the diversity of masculinities, and the intersections of gender with race, class, and nationality, if it is not to fall into a sterile choice between celebration and negation of masculinity in general. The importance of education for masculinity politics follows from the onto-formativity of gender practices, the fact that our enactments of masculinity and femininity bring a social reality into being.
>
> (Connell, 1995: 239).

Locating the studies and the participants

The empirical data for this work have been drawn from two parallel studies that focus respectively on male and female student teachers as they progress towards becoming and being teachers of physical education on a

Postgraduate Certificate in Education (PGCE) course in an English university. The two studies have some important (and shared) methodological characteristics. Primarily the studies have utilised life history analysis of biographical data gathered from intensive semi-structured interviews conducted at intervals during and after their training. The constructions of gendered self-identity have been analysed from the positioned gendered stories that the participants reconstruct about themselves as a result of their previous, current, and future-anticipated life experiences. Here we cannot represent all of these stories. Instead we focus upon key moments and positions from the stories of four participants that are indicative of the dilemmas faced by all the participants.

In mapping masculinity and femininity onto identity we remain anxious to avoid falling into the essentialist trap mentioned above, by suggesting 'fixed' identities or types of men and women, however consistent they may appear. Femininities/masculinities can no longer be made sense of as unitary, static 'wholes'. Gendered multiplicity is a phenomenon observable across societies, cultures and history and it is also in evidence at the individual level. Finally, our use of the term 'positioning' as an active as well as passive verb is intentional. Analysis of the participants' life stories consistently indicates that positioning genders in teaching contexts has an active as well as passive dimension; it does involve agency. The student teachers are thus shown to draw on their own identities and experiences to make sense of gendered encounters and merge them with their developing pedagogies to *take, assign and receive* gendered positions.

Our participants here are two men and two women, whom we refer to by pseudonyms; Derek, Trevor, Christie, and Robin. While these participants talked explicitly about the 'positioning of their gender' within their teacher education, narratives of sexuality and sexual identity were either absent or silent. Participants made connections between gender-appropriate behaviour and sexual identities of others, acknowledging for example the myth of 'PE teacher as lesbian' (Griffin, 1992; Squires and Sparkes, 1996; Sparkes, 1997). The silences that we observed were largely indicative of culturally predominant discourses of heteronormativity, where perspectives of hetero-sexuality are considered implicit and taken for granted.

All of these individuals either were, or still are, active elite performers, involved respectively in athletics, semi-professional rugby union; county level badminton and netball, and elite level university football. In spite of these elite experiences, at the outset of their teaching careers all of these participants expressed a concern to be teachers who could provide equal opportunities for all pupils to access positive experiences of physical education and school sport. The following comments capture their beliefs:

> I'm going to be a teacher you know, who teaches PE, so I want to go into a school and be someone that kids can talk to, someone that they can

learn from, someone that they want to listen to, or maybe they can learn a few things about PE, about growing up, about handling themselves about respecting themselves, about doing what they want to do and about meeting challenges, which is, I mean, that's what it's all about. . . . So I want, I feel quite strongly that I could be a good teacher and then . . . because I love sport.

(Trevor)

I think what it needs to be is to be able to work with children. I always get a great buzz working with passing on all the knowledge and experiences I have had in PE . . . and you know, think about the sport for all especially . . . and I want everyone to have positive experiences in my classes.

(Derek)

PE is actually trying to show people the benefits of what they can get from it, whether it be physically, socially, success in something. It's something that can be available to anyone and there's so many different types of sports or activities. I am a games player and that is what I love, but there are so many types of being physically active that are beneficial and that is what PE should be about.

(Christie)

Robin made an explicit reference to masculinity and femininity, saying:

I think they are really important [the meanings of femininity/masculinity] because I am teaching PE, it's important to not have a stereotypical view of the body; so I am trying to get to grips with perhaps the correct terms to use. I haven't finalised anything definite. . . . I want to give other people the chance to realise their potential and to realise that they are individuals that can achieve things. . . . Enjoyment for everyone to feel safe, secure and happy.

(Robin)

All of these comments arguably reflect 'intellectual' and 'liberal' stances in relation to equal opportunities in physical education. The central perception of their role is to facilitate access and opportunity as key objectives, rather than to critically address the nature of the opportunities[1] themselves. As a cognitive, intellectual position a belief in gender equality and inclusion represents a very positive personal stance. However, as we shall see, the stance is not always retained when teaching. We see that how the student teachers position themselves, others, and how others position them, has implications for the reproduction of the Gender Order and reveals limitations in their shared liberal notions of equal opportunities.

The double bind of practice: gender positioning as pedagogy

Being positioned

The life histories indicate that 'gender positioning' is being practised and consolidated in these students' teaching placements and in subsequent teaching jobs. This pedagogical practice forms a part of what Templin and Schempp (1989) and others have referred to as 'professional socialisation' where the bringing together of personal and professional identities is a strongly gendered process. All of the participants reported *being in, taking and assigning* gendered positions according to the context in which they found themselves and fusing these positions with and within their teaching pedagogies. In spite of their intellectual intentions for equality, the participants experience forms of double bind or entrapment that forces them into positions complicit with dominant masculine norms. Derek experienced this early in his first teaching placement when he asked his head of department 'how much dance do you want me to do?' and received the answer, 'Oh none, I don't believe boys should do that.' Derek is implicated in this positioning and specifically, denied the experience and pedagogical practice of teaching dance. This is in spite of his own increasingly positive views about the value of dance in the physical education programme and its applicability to all pupils. Moreover, he was denied the opportunity to show and develop other dimensions to his own teaching identity and to forge alternative ways of fusing it with his practical pedagogies.

Trevor had similar experiences of being positioned at the outset of his teaching career. He explained the context that he encountered, saying:

> I mean the PE department that I was in was almost like the cadets you know, it was very structured, very rigid and very like, testosterone like, you know. You couldn't . . . it was charged, it was a charged atmosphere more than the second school . . . the first mentor at [school name], he was excellent, he was quite hard taskmaster, he was like old authoritarian schools, he was quite old fashioned . . . and he was good. . . . He always like said, oh you're too nice, you got to be this that and the other, do know what I mean? And I think part of that was it was just my first experience of teaching.
>
> (Trevor)

In this context Trevor's relaxed and friendly approach was immediately called into question, with the implication that being 'nice' was a sign of weakness and not the way that male physical education teachers should act. Trevor had to re-position his approach to teaching boys physical education towards something 'harder' and more authoritarian, and in line with the institutional culture. Consequently, Trevor's formative experiences of teaching boys physical education were based around dominant, authoritarian displays and pedagogies. He has 'learned' how to teach in these ways and they are the pedagogies that he continues to deploy, and that he is now comfortable with. Furthermore, as his judgement of 'excellent' above indicates, he has also come to value their 'effectiveness'.

In a similar but perhaps more oppressive way, Christie's and Robin's stories also feature the experiences of being positioned by other members of staff and pupils in their practice institutions:

> There was one bloke there [male physical education teacher] and he was very funny, and he was a good laugh but some of the comments that he made to the kids were very derogatory, you know one of the lads had a buckle on his shoe and he was calling him a, I can't remember what he called him now . . . a dancer. He was saying, oh you look like a . . . I don't know if he actually called him a poof, but it was some term along that line. And I'd think, I don't really think you should have quite put it like that, and they make some comments to me about, you know, football, of what do you know about football. And just I'd give as good as I got for a bit, and then I'd just be like, oh carry on.
>
> (Christie)

The comments made by Christie's male mentor are a good illustration of how the Gender Order operates to position everyone relationally in terms of an implicit dominant masculine norm, with femininity and homosexuality actively subordinated here. Furthermore, when the gendered positioning is direct and personal as in Christie's case, her response again demonstrates the double bind or entrapment experienced by those who would seek to challenge the Gender Order and work towards more inclusive perspectives and practices in education and physical education. If she challenges the Gender Order operating in this situation, Christie risks being stigmatized and actively subordinated as a non-complicit female and student teacher. But by not offering a challenge to the order, she accepts a complicit role and implicitly reinforces the established order. The following extract further illustrates her dilemma:

> To be honest I've been amazed by some of the stuff that I've heard at the school. I mean the other day, there is this one teacher, a male, and he is supposed to be one of the best teachers in the school. Anyway, we were all in the staff room and they've got exams on at the moment and this guy was talking about the fact that when the kids sat at their desks, during exams, the girls skirts like come up and he was going on about the fact that he could see the girls' knickers. They even call them slappers and things like that, and you know, it's just not appropriate, but everyone laughs, everyone joins in and that's it. How are you supposed to fight that? I really want to just walk out of the room, but then it would just be the

case that the tables would have been turned around onto me, and I would be the one to look bad, you know?

(Christie)

We can wonder how many other teachers in these staff rooms felt the same way as Christie, but also chose silence? What does it cost these young women to speak their minds, to challenge the status quo? The discourses within physical education and sport attempt to normalize heterosexuality for girls and women in ways which assert a heterosexuality that bonds sex and gender together (Sykes, 1998). Acting in 'female appropriate' ways therefore tacitly implicates 'sexuality'. Where female and feminine are not clearly linked, questions of sexuality are raised. Speaking up in these contexts means challenging the status quo, and those who disrupt gender binary logics run the risk of being positioned outside the heterosexual self as 'other'. Historically, this 'other' in physical education has meant 'lesbian'. These complex dilemmas of 'speaking up' and the dynamics of interaction illustrate the difficult if near impossible situation of exerting particular expressions of agency, in the face of potential stigma. Attempts to dispel the 'masculine' (read lesbian), stereotype which have haunted the profession not only compromises female teachers' actual identities but also dis-empowers them in terms of the Gender Order. Acting in ways that are gender appropriate, and that appear as safely heterosexual, positions them in the gender order as subordinate 'sexualised' females in these contexts. These dynamics further mediate the pedagogical advice offered by many teachers, wherein gender positioning features heavily. Robin recalls the following strong advice from her mentors about the way to behave and how to position herself when teaching physical education:

You've got to treat them like dogs. I talk to them like I do my own dog and that's the way that it has got to be because you've got to get them in a position whereby you've disciplined them, you've got control and they're ready to get on and learn. That's what they are there for. You have to remind them of the fact that we've all got to do things that we don't want to do but that's the way it is sometimes. You need to go right. You over there bang (points). You need to take a teacher-centred approach.

(Female teacher from Robin's teaching practice)

Here Robin is being prompted to develop a masculinized teaching identity, that in symbolic and practical terms draws on confrontational, authoritarian and didactic pedagogical approaches associated with dominant masculinities. Like her fellow student teachers, Robin is being denied the opportunities to adopt alternative gender positions and pedagogies. Moreover, these women are aware that to engage in particular pedagogical practices is to risk their personal identities, making the projection of a professional a process fraught with complexity and difficulty:

The lady that was there before [physical education teacher in school], I can't say she was stereotypical because she was married not single, and she wasn't particularly butch. She was hard and aggressive and a lot of the girls I remember used to call her a bitch and they thought she was very hard and aggressive, she wasn't butch looking but she was quite . . . well, you know.

(Christie)

Taking and assigning gender positions

As well as being positioned, participants in the study all had to engage in the practical *taking and assigning* of gendered positions themselves. Again, it is important to reiterate that these student teachers, like their more experienced mentors, are behaving reflexively in context, endeavouring to balance many priorities of their duties, such as trying to include, motivate, keep control, structure and deliver content knowledge in their classes. Such experiences, it would seem, again present a series of practical double bind situations, through which the gendered status quo remains unchallenged. Consider Derek's experiences of teaching girls:

It was different . . . I don't know, they tended not to go off tasks so easily, as much as mess around . . . and to motivate them, but yes, you had to deal with them a bit more sensitively I think – do it a bit quieter during your teaching . . . when you are talking to them, and plenty of praise for the ones that weren't so motivated, and teach in a slightly lower tone perhaps, I don't know. . . . I saw that with my mentor especially, the more caring side, with the girls you would tend to have to be a bit more, um, not so macho perhaps. . . . Especially in the mixed PE situation, they [the girls] challenge the boys and they adopt some of the characteristics that perhaps they [the boys] have got.

(Derek)

In this situation Derek positions both himself and his pupils in notably gendered ways and again inherent dilemmas are apparent. The basis for his differentiation is a gendered assumption, reinforced by his mentors, that the girls need a different approach to boys to make them participate and learn. However, in stating 'not so macho' Derek is also reflexively positioning himself, in order to offset the dominant masculine position which he accepts is also available to him and sometimes expected of him. His actions are likely to reconstruct the Gender Order. Derek also demonstrates how masculine discourses occupy an invisible centre through the use of this pedagogy; the girls will acquire some of the boys dispositions thereby showing how the boys' characteristics are implicitly being used as the benchmark against which others are judged.

Trevor's experiences are similar, as is the reflexive way in which he engages in positioning and specifically, the management of his own gendered teaching identity:

> Sometimes, I mean to be honest, in school it is quite handy as well because the kids [boys] that are a lot of trouble in a lot of other classes aren't trouble in PE because they look to do PE, and then if you have got them in other classes or other areas of the school you can take that with you, because you have got more control over them where they are prepared to at least listen to what you say, where they wouldn't listen to what the maths teacher or English teacher because they hate maths and English, so in a way that is useful.
>
> (Trevor)

Here we see Trevor actively gravitating towards a dominant position in response to his perception of the needs of the situation based around mentor and pupil expectations. Like Derek, Trevor is also caught in a double bind; while the need to keep control is not an exclusively masculine threat, it nevertheless represents a particularly acute threat to stereotypically dominant masculine assumptions of how 'strong men' and 'real male physical education teachers' should act in the face of challenges to their authority. This next extract seems indicative of a masculinity under threat, with Trevor drawing on dominant aspects of his own identity ('if you've got the tools') to position himself as a dominantly masculine teacher, in spite of his intentions to explore alternative pedagogies which reflect his preferred 'more laid back' masculine identity:

> Yes I think so, I think it does make it easier to teach and I think especially in a classroom if you've got those lads then you've got the class. You know what I mean, if you've got the tools, if you keep them quiet then everyone else is going to be quiet. . . . Well, I mean, a lot of young lads obviously, you know, that's what they look up to and that's what they lock onto.
>
> (Trevor)

Connell (1995) refers to such action as the 'patriarchal dividend'; the implicit strategy of many men to benefit from the Gender Order that they don't necessarily subscribe to in order to offset any chance of being marginalised or subordinated, that they would risk, should they engage in less obviously dominant displays of masculinity. The important lessons that these men are embedding through practice is that a fusion of their dominant masculine selves and their teaching pedagogy is not only a legitimate, but a necessary identity resource, as Trevor points out in the following comment:

> Everybody teaches differently, I think but it's like a continuum, I think, . . . and obviously you've got 'masculine of masculine' which would be

male, obviously wouldn't be a female, but there would be some women that maybe teach in a more masculine way than some men; you know there's a whole range. You know I put myself towards that end of it but not at that extreme.

(Trevor)

Explicit here is the firmly gendered view and apparent status and identity of particular pedagogies.

A similar series of positioning practices and gender relational binds is also in evidence in the experiences of the female student teachers represented here. The ways in which Christie and Robin take and assign positions are particularly significant since, of all the female student teachers studied, their educational philosophies were perhaps most strongly allied to a critical child-centred feminist approach. Their biographical narratives suggest that these women see themselves as having a particular form of agency for changing gendered practices, which they believed would form the basis of their pedagogical creativity. Despite this, they go on to describe situations during their teacher training in which they have failed to exercise any such agency. As a football player Christie found herself particularly caught up in relational dynamics of gender positioning by pupils when she taught boys football. Pedagogical positioning was made more problematic by the gendered institutional, structural features of Christie's teaching environment. Her positioning was clearly compromised by the need to gain credibility in male dominated arenas of physical activity:

This was core PE that was mixed, and this was just they had no experience of having been taught by women since Year 7 until they got to Year 10 and suddenly they had a female there and they had no respect for, I don't know whether they had no respect for women or whether it was women sports people, whether it was because I was female teacher or whether it was because I was a sporting female, but they had very little respect for me even though I probably could sort of, you know, in terms of skill-wise been a lot better than any of them.

(Christie)

Christie's natural reaction, to demonstrate herself as a competent performer, has consequences for the relational dynamics of this educational situation, and is typical of both the active positioning and the double bind that is central to this discussion. As a competent performer Christie implicitly challenges the masculine stereotypical orthodoxy of males play football better than females, if she does not – she reinforces it. But in challenging the orthodoxy in this way Christie has to demonstrate the very same set of values and practices that would qualify as a 'good' male performance, and thereby aligns herself with the dominant gender position and its associated values and practices that she wishes to play a part in changing:

> I took an all-boys football group, and it was quite interesting the way that they [the boys] reacted. One of the balls rolled over to me, and naturally I did take a flick and then a few keepie-ups and, you know, that was it, you know all the lads were like, 'Miss do you play football?' And I had my women's football top on, and then the lads started taking the mick out of one of the other boys in the group saying, 'Miss is better than you'.
>
> (Christie)

Here we see that Christie's feminine physicality is defined in *relation* to and *comparison* with male standards, while the boys compare themselves with a 'women' rather than 'a competent performer'. A similar situation arose in basketball:

> Yeah, the height thing can be a bit of a problem, like in basketball I had to do a couple of lay ups and a couple of three-pointers before I could even get them to listen and it was like, yeah, she can play basketball.

The demonstration of physical ability in these particular sports and contexts is in sharp contrast to the cultural conception of what it means to be stereotypically female. The disruption to the heterosexual logic of female/feminine brings sexual identity into question. Christie's competence as a woman is therefore positioned by the male pupils (and perhaps others) as an anomaly, as deviant, and she risks being defined as 'masculine' (read, lesbian). Consequently, Christie and doubtless other female teachers have the option of either taking a subordinated feminine position or a complicit position in a Gender Order, both of which ultimately suppress the alternative gendered identities that could be brought to teaching and learning physical education. In summary, while these women can position themselves in ways which allow them to access the masculine cultural project, significantly they have limited means to challenge its secular legitimacy, and in so doing embrace new ways of 'doing male things'. For the men, the fusion of their dominant masculine selves and their teaching pedagogy is a legitimate, expected and even demanded identity resource. For the women the expectation is that they become instrumental, dominant, authoritarian as teachers, whilst remaining stereotypically feminine women. In order to gain the available status and credibility, they have to fully embrace the symbolic gender dualisms, working towards a position of instrumental control, identifiable with a masculine tradition which has a disdain for that coded as feminine. Thus despite being female and challenging particular male orthodoxies, they also maintain the Gender Order through their paradoxical derogatory depictions of 'softer' forms of femininity. What we see in the next extract is the way in which Christie draws upon a segregation not only between the sexes but within, demonstrating a disdain for traditional subordinated forms of femininity. She comments that:

It's difficult to play games when there are only two out of a class of twenty-four, and ten are not doing it because they don't want to break their nails.

In addition, she makes sense of her own participation in sport through aligning herself more to masculinity than femininity:

We [her and her sister] are very different . . . can I say she is a typical girlie-girl? She is very, sort of, feminine with the short skirts and doing the hair. . . . The fact that I had a male friend growing up, I suppose I was a complete tomboy.

(Christie)

While Christie has taken important steps in gaining access to male ortho-doxies, her use of oppositional gendered criteria to position herself and pupils only serves to reproduce the polarised stereotypes currently predominant and that underpin the continued marginalisation of pupils that she and her fellow student teachers are so clearly committed to attempt to include and motivate.

Challenging the gender order: connecting the self, pedagogy and the politics of change

When considered as a heuristic device, the notion of gender positioning that emerges from this empirical work is useful for revealing the linkages between individuals and the gendered social worlds that they inhabit and consciously or subconsciously contribute to reconstructing. Particularly with the women here, it would be easy to regard these people, and many others like them, as merely victims of forms of oppression by what Brod and Kaufman (1994) refer to as the central invisible discourses of dominant masculine ideology in the field of education, physical education and sport. We would not entirely refute this interpretation. In many ways they all are victims. However, we would also suggest that the gendered positions taken might be viewed as the *unintentional consequences* of human agency (Giddens, 1984, 1990) as carried out by 'knowledgeable actors' behaving reflexively in the contexts of their lives. This latter view gives cause for some optimism about the potential for reconstructing alternative expressions of gender identity in teaching physical education that might facilitate a more gender inclusive future for the subject. Specifically, we argue that there a series of connections that need to be made between the gendered self, pedagogy and the politics of change in gender relations. We sense that these connections would offer these teachers a broader range of 'identity resources' that would help them become more 'active agents' in confronting the dilemmas of gender positioning in teaching physical education. These would seem to include:

1   An awareness of a socially constructed Gender Order in society, sport and physical education and its implications for positioning individuals within that order.
2   An awareness that challenging the Gender Order through teaching physical education involves taking a micro-political stance and developing carefully considered courses of action.
3   A broader range of personal practical and experiential identity 'resources' that can support intellectual commitments to develop alternative ways of teaching physical education.

An acknowledgement of the Gender Order in our society and its relational implications for everyone is crucial if change is to be initiated and sustained from the level of the individual teacher, cascading upwards and rippling outwards, through pupils, other teachers, future student teachers and so on.

The work of Sparkes (1991) on the subjective dimensions of educational change provides further qualitative insights into these connections and the means of exploring them. These participants and, we suspect, other similarly committed physical education teachers need assistance if they are to be aware of the micro-political nature of challenging the Gender Order in their teaching and its implications for their own self-identities. It is important to move beyond classic 'liberal' (equality of access) notions of political agency that is in evidence in Christie's aspirations to 'control' football in the school she teaches in:

> This other school, I would have been in charge of all the football, like boys and girls, all years and that would have been fantastic to have got that position as a female. To go in and just do that job. I mean it would be brilliant to go out onto the pitch, like at a league match, or something and you could just predict what would happen. I mean the other male teacher would come in with his lads and look at me and then look around and probably say to me 'Where is he then?' [referring to a male PE teacher]. And I'm just the sort of person to love that, to be able to go in and challenge that.
>
> (Christie)

While the success in gaining access to this arena would promote visibility and provide opportunity for change, ironically it will do little to challenge the Gender Order if Christie's own discourses and practices merely mimic dominant masculine pedagogies in evidence earlier. The opportunity here is for Christie to strategically challenge the status quo from within, by innovating with techniques and practices that challenge conventional dominant masculine positions and practices in this and other activity areas. Such action is far from easy and furthermore, requires considerable support and professional preparation.

Our third focus in pursuing notions of challenge relates to the nature of gender itself. Trevor's comments below show that 'lived' understandings of gender are necessary if articulate micro-political strategies are to be developed:

> It's quite . . . I think . . . I don't know, I try not to think of teaching girls and boys because I haven't got younger sisters or anything, also I haven't got any children, so, it's a bit difficult, sort of, this is how I teach girls as opposed to boys – I just try and teach them.
>
> (Trevor)

Trevor's position here as elsewhere in his biography is entirely laudable, but it is unlikely to sufficiently empower him to develop inclusive pedagogies without succumbing to positions complicit to hegemonic masculinity. A key resource here is reflection on one's own possible identities. These reflections can be used to inform the development of alternative pedagogies, but in order to do so they must extend beyond binary visions. This shift in thinking is crucial if we are to move towards the development of differentiation pedagogies and positions not based on assumptions of gender but on judgements of individual need. 'Difference' therefore, becomes a more situated, lived understanding of gender and physical education, in which Davies (1989) suggests:

> A first step is the conceptual separation of lived masculinities from the idea, and the idealisation of that idea, of hegemonic masculinity. A second is the realisation that males and females can equally take up what have been defined as masculine and feminine positioning without that being a moral blot on their character. A third and vital step is the recognition of multiple masculinities and femininities, most of which bear little or no relation to the genitals of the person taking them up.
>
> (Davies, 1989: 111)

Connecting the self, pedagogy and the Gender Order involves drawing on lived experience as a gender identity resource. The evidence emerging from these student teachers is that they do not always possess sufficient alternative gender identity resources, in the form of 'other' gendered experiences (including, internalised subject knowledge, communication skills and alternative narratives of the self, see Sparkes, 1999), to facilitate the transference of the inclusive cognitive beliefs into practical pedagogies. By way of example, Derek's comments pay testimony to the need for further 'lived' identity resources:

> No, my background was totally single sex, at the start it was slightly alien to me, but I totally came round to it, maybe gymnastics and dance

especially, if I was teaching in an all-boys group for both of those I just wouldn't have got the quality.

(Derek)

By 'quality' Derek was referring to the embodied physical expression of himself as a dance teacher, the movements, language and dispositions and ideas which come with involvement and experience. We agree with Kenway (1998) and Vertinsky (1992) who contend we should be encouraging a wide variety of ways of being female and develop and promote alternative and non-violent (or dominant) ways of being male, and we should expect students (and teachers) to take *risks* with their own gender identities. Relations of power operate in multiple directions, and through experimenting with gender identities we might begin to move outside, across and inside the gender divide. Given that dominant discourses within physical education assert a heterosexuality which bonds sex and gender together (Sykes, 1998), these qualifications might have implications for issues of sexuality in physical education. Specifically these practices may assist in challenging the silencing which has been central to the experiences of lesbian and gay physical education teachers (Khayatt, 1992; 1994; Sparkes, 1994a; 1994b; Squires and Sparkes, 1996; Clarke, 1998; Sykes, 1998).

Further, as Wright (1997) suggests, we should be concerned with finding ways of empowering women and girls, and men and boys, so that they feel confident and skilled in using their bodies in all aspects of life, rather than being restricted by narrow gendered forms of embodiment and practices. These are all embodied and experiential resources which lay much broader cross-gender foundations for what individuals feel comfortable doing and saying, and they facilitate the reconstruction of embodied agency (Shilling, 1999).[2] This also draws attention to the need for physical education (in schools' curriculum and in initial teacher training) to draw from a wider spectrum of activities and physical culture that is already represented in society (Kirk, 1999). As Penney and Chandler (2000) note, it also calls into question the current activity-based framework which dominates curriculum organisation and the subject matter of teaching and learning in physical education[3] in the United Kingdom.

In conclusion, our empirical work suggests that a vision for gender inclusive futures in physical education strongly implicates physical education teachers' gendered identities. While the quality and commitment of our participants' approach to their profession is not in doubt, the dimensions of their gendered identities which they drew upon during the difficult circumstances of teaching are implicitly strategic enactments that tend to fit into, rather than challenge the Gender Order in society, sport and physical education. In response, and in contribution to an inclusive agenda for change, we consider as imperatives, that the above connections between the Gender Order, the self, pedagogy and the politics of change should more explicitly underpin Initial and In-service teacher training. In addition, if the aggregate experiences of these teachers' biographies is indicative of wider patterns, subsequent generations of students, teachers and mentors will need to be encouraged to develop and internalize a greater range of practical, embodied and experiential gendered identity resources, including, alternative gendered modes of communication, movement skills, subject knowledge and narratives of the self. With these in place these teachers would be in a stronger and more flexible position to embrace their own and facilitate the development of their pupils' multiple masculine and feminine identities and in so doing take action to challenge the Gender Order.

Acknowledgement

We would like to thank the participants in this study, whose co-operation made this work possible. We would also like to thank Dr. Dawn Penney and Professor John Evans for their constructive comments on earlier drafts of this chapter.

Notes

1 The primary concern of liberal approaches to equal opportunities is with equality of access to valued social and cultural goods/opportunities – such approaches stop short of providing a critique of elements such as patriarchy, oppression or domination through which those goods are given value in the first place. By contrast critical approaches to equal opportunities retain the belief in equal access but question the nature of the opportunities we have access to.
2 Shilling argues that our understanding of an individual's ability to act in society has been based on cognitive-only models of 'rational' actors. But that the agency provided by the body is a crucial missing link – between agency and structure debates, and can help alter the way we think about human agency and its potential.
3 The specific reference here is to the NCPE in England and Wales but the activity-based model is also in evidence in many other physical education curricula around the world.

References

Brod, H. and Kaufman, M. (eds) (1994) *Theorizing Masculinities: Volume 5*, Thousand Oaks: Sage.
Brown, D. (1999) Complicity and reproduction in teaching physical education, *Sport, Education & Society* 4(2): 143–60.
Brittan, A. (1989) *Masculinity and Power*, Oxford: Basil Blackwell.
Clarke, G. (1998) Queering the pitch and coming out to play: lesbians in physical education and sport, *Sport, Education and Society* 3(2): 145–60.
Connell, R.W. (1987) *Gender and Power: Society, the Person and Sexual Politics*, Sydney: Allen & Unwin Pty Ltd.
Connell, R.W. (1995) *Masculinities*, London: Polity Press.
Davies, B. (1989) *Frogs and Snails and Feminist Tails: Preschool and Gender*, Sydney: Allen & Unwin Pty Ltd.

De Knop, P., Theeboom, M., Wittock, H. and De Martelaer, K. (1996) Implications of Islam on Muslim girls' sports participation in Western Europe, *Sport, Education and Society* 1(2): 147–64.

Dillabough, J.-A. (1999) Gender politics and conceptions of the modern teacher: women, identity and professionalism, *British Journal of Sociology of Education* 20(3): 373–94.

Ennis, C. (1999) Creating a culturally relevant curriculum for disengaged girls, *Sport, Education and Society* 4(1): 31–49.

Edley, N. and Wetherell, M. (1995) *Men in Perspective: Practice, Power and Identity*, London: Prentice Hall.

Evans, J. (ed.) (1993) *Equality, Education and Physical Education*, London: Falmer Press.

Evans, J., Davies, B. and Penney, D. (1996) Teachers, teaching and the social construction of gender relations, *Sport, Education and Society* 1(1): 165–84.

Fletcher, S. (1987) The making and breaking of a female tradition: women's physical education in England, 1880–(1980), in J. Mangan and R. Park (eds) *From the Fair Sex to Feminism*, London: Frank Cass.

Giddens, A. (1984) *The Constitution of Society: Outline of the Theory of Structuration*, Cambridge: Polity Press.

Giddens, A. (1990) *The Consequences of Modernity*, Cambridge: Polity Press.

Gramsci, A. (1971) *Selections from the Prison Notebooks*, London: Lawrence & Wishart.

Griffin, P. (1992) Lesbian and gay educators: opening the classroom closet, *Empathy* 3: 25–8.

Gore, J. (1990) *The Struggle for Pedagogies: Critical and Feminist Pedagogies as Regimes of Truth*, University of Wisconsin-Madison.

Grenfell, M. and James, D. (1998) *Bourdieu and Education: Acts of Practical Theory*, London: Falmer Press

Hargreaves, J. (1986) *Sport, Power and Culture: A Social and Historical Analysis of Popular Sports in Britain*, Cambridge: Polity Press.

Hargreaves, J. (2000) Gender, morality, and the National Physical Education Curriculum, in J. Nansen and N. Neilsen (eds) *Sports, Body and Health*, Odense University Press.

Hickey, C., Fitzclarence, L. and Mathews R. (eds) (1998) *Where the Boys Are: Masculinity, Sport and Education*, Geelong, Victoria: Deakin Centre for Education and Change, Deakin University.

Humberstone, B. (1990) Warriors or wimps? Creating alternative forms of physical education, in M. A. Messner and D. F. Sabo (eds) *Sport, Men and the Gender Order: Critical Feminist Perspectives*, Champaign, IL: Human Kinetics.

Kenway, J. (1998) Masculinity studies, sports and femininism: fair play or foul?, in C. Hickey, L. Fitzclarence and R. Mathews (eds) *Where the Boys Are: Masculinity, Sport and Education*, Geelong, Victoria: Deakin Centre for Education and Change, Deakin University.

Khayatt, D. (1992) *Lesbian Teachers: An Invisible Presence*, Albany, NY: State University Press of New York.

Kirk, D. (1992) *Defining Physical Education: The Social Construction of a School Subject in Postwar Britain*, London: Falmer Press.

Kirk, D. (1999) Physical culture, physical education and relational analysis, *Sport, Education and Society* 4(1): 63–73.

Luke, C. and Gore, J. (eds) (1992) *Feminisms and Critical Pedagogy*, London: Routledge.

Mangan, J.A. (1981) *Athleticism in the Victorian and Edwardian Public School: The Emergence and Consolidation of an Educational Ideology*, Cambridge: Cambridge University Press.

Mangan, J.A. and Walvin, J. (eds) (1987) *Manliness and Morality: Middle-class Masculinity in Britain and America, 1800–1940*, Manchester: Manchester University Press.

Messner, M. and Sabo, D. (eds) (1990) *Sport, Men and the Gender Order*, Champaign, IL: Human Kinetics Press.

Pease, B. (2000) *Recreating Men: Postmodern Masculinity Politics*, London: Sage.

Penney, D. and Chandler, T. (2000) Physical education: What future(s)?, *Sport, Education & Society* 5(1): 71–88.

Peterson, A. (1997) *Unmasking the Masculine: Men and Identity in a Sceptical Age*, London: Sage.

Rutherford, J. (1988) Who's that man?, in R. Chapman and J. Rutherford (eds) *Male Order: Unwrapping Masculinity*, London: Lawrence & Wishart, pp. 21–67.

Salisbury, J. and Jackson, D. (1998) *Challenging Macho Values: Practical Ways of Working with Adolescent Boys*, London: Falmer Press.

Shilling, C. (1999) Towards an embodied understanding of the structure/agency relationship, *British Journal of Sociology* 50(4): 543–62.

Sparkes, A. (1991) Exploring the subjective dimension of change, in Armstrong and A. Sparkes, (eds) *Issues in Physical Education*, London: Cassell Education.

Sparkes, A. (1994a) Life histories and the issue of voice: reflections on an emerging relationship, *International Journal of Qualitative Studies in Education* 7: 165–83.

Sparkes, A. (1994b) Self, silence and invisibility as a beginning teacher: a life history of lesbian experience, *British Journal of Sociology of Education* 15(1): 93–118.

Sparkes, A. (1997) Ethnographic fiction and representing the absent other, *Sport, Education and Society* 2(1): 25–40.

Sparkes, A.C. (1999) Exploring body narratives, *Sport, Education and Society* 4(1): 17–30.

Squires, S. and Sparkes, A. (1996) Circles of silence: sexual identity in physical education and sport, *Sport, Education and Society* 1(1): 77–102.

Sykes, H. (1998) *Teaching Bodies, Learning Desires: Feminist Post-structural Life Histories of Heterosexual and Lesbian Physical Education Teachers in Western Canada*, unpublished Doctoral thesis, Vancouver, BC: University of British Columbia.

Talbot, M. (1993) Gender and physical education, in J. Evans (ed.) *Equality, Education and Physical Education*, London: Falmer Press.

Tabachnick, B., Zeichner, R. and Kenneth, M. (1984) The impact of the student teaching experience on the development of teacher perspectives, *Journal of Teacher Education* 35(6): 28–36.

Templin, T. and Schempp, P. (eds) (1989) *Socialization into Physical Education: Learning to Teach*, Indianapolis: Benchmark Press.

Tsolidis, G. (1996) Feminist theorisations of identity and difference: a case study related to gender education policy, *British Journal of Sociology of Education* 17(3): 267–77.

Vertinsky, P.A. (1992) Reclaiming space, revisioning the body: the quest for a gender-sensitive physical education, *Quest* 44(3): 373–97.

Wright, J. (1988) Reconstructing gender in sport and physical education, in C. Hickey, L. Fitzclarence and R. Mathews (eds) *Where the Boys Are: Masculinity, Sport and Education*, Geelong, Victoria: Deakin Centre for Education and Change, Deakin University.

Whannel, G. (2000) Sport stars, narrativization and masculinities, *Leisure Studies* 18: 249–65.

Wright, J. (1997) The construction of gendered contexts in single sex and co-educational physical education lessons, *Sport, Education and Society* 2(1): 55–72.

Young, I.M. (1990) *Justice and the Politics of Difference*, Princeton, New Jersey: Princeton University Press.

Part III

Gender and physical education: policies and practice

7 Gendered policies

Dawn Penney

Introduction

This chapter focuses on what we conventionally regard as 'policy' in physical education; 'official texts' produced by governments or curriculum agencies that provide the reference point for the development of physical education in schools. However, it locates these texts as part of the complex process of policy development that we described in chapter 2. The discussion therefore highlights a number of important points in relation to investigations of the ways in which gender issues are represented in policies for physical education. In particular I stress that we need to look at physical education policy developments in the context of political influences and agendas, and in the light of pragmatic concerns relating to education and to physical education. Not for the first time we see that policy making always involves compromises and that these reflect the positions that particular people and particular interests either have or are denied in the policy process. In pursuing the representation of gender issues in physical education policies I also direct attention to what can *not* be said in policy debates and what is excluded from policy texts relating to physical education. I argue that silences can certainly speak louder than words and that neither silence, nor the use of 'neutral' language, is in any way neutral. In policy developments in education decisions to retain silences or to use particular language are conscious and political decisions that have important implications for future practice. These characteristics will influence the degree to which policies serve to demand or encourage that established and inequitable practices and beliefs are rendered a thing of the past, and new practices developed that signal a conscious commitment to better representation of individuals who are currently marginalised in and by physical education.

My discussion focuses upon texts associated with the development of the National Curriculum for Physical Education (NCPE) in England. However, the issues raised are ones that can be pursued in the investigation of other policies, at other times or in other places. The potential value of adopting a comparative perspective in policy studies is worthy of note. Often it takes a comparative perspective to reveal what could be different, or what is missing from the policies that we are most familiar with and may well have come to view unproblematically. In several respects an investigation of the progressive development of the NCPE in England through the 1990s illustrates the value of a comparative perspective. I deliberately focus attention upon an official text that has long since disappeared from view: the Interim Report produced by the original NCPE working group in 1991. It is a text that highlights what has not been said in relation to gender and equity in subsequent NCPE texts, but that also itself featured silences that it is important to pursue. I encourage readers to consider whether in implementation there is the scope for teachers and teacher educators to 'fill silences' that remain a feature of the official National Curriculum texts and to thereby extend the gender agendas inherent in physical education curricula and teaching. In 1993 Graham and Tytler expressed the view that 'The National Curriculum is a potent tool for change and for bringing about equality of opportunity. Its potential is largely unrealised as yet' (p. 132). This chapter provides some insights into that potential in the context of physical education. It also provides an important backdrop to the chapters that follow in this section. Harris and Penney (in chapter 8) and Williams and Bedward (in chapter 9) present data that illustrate the ways in which silences inherent in the official texts of the NCPE have been variously 'filled' and also overlooked by teachers. Both chapters show that policy texts issued by governments are far from finished and that they can and will be read and responded to in various ways, for better or worse in relation to gender equity.

My initial discussion comes in two parts. First I consider those instances in which equal opportunities, equity and/or specifically, gender equity, has been addressed explicitly within NCPE texts issued by the central government and/or curriculum agencies in England. In the second part of the chapter I turn to the ways in which other features of these texts have had important implicit messages in relation to gender issues in physical education. As many of the explicit references to equal opportunities, equity and gender have been removed as the development of the NCPE has progressed, this exploration of 'hidden messages' is particularly important. Recognising the ways in which particular requirements and particular language serve to legitimate inequities in gender relations in contexts of physical education and sport is crucial if we are to design policies that give different messages and/or encourage 'alternative readings' of notably conservative official texts.

A National Curriculum for Physical Education: the promise of progress

The development of a National Curriculum for all children in all state schools in England and Wales was heralded as securing 'an entitlement for all' (DES, 1989). It was a development that appeared to promise much in relation to equal opportunities in education. But since the launch of the National Curriculum several things have become clear about the 'entitlement' that was secured by the Education Reform Act of 1988. The relative absence of debates about the nature of the educational entitlement outlined in the National Curriculum, about whose and what interests the new statutory requirements were directed towards and set to provide for, or whose educational needs and interests may be being overlooked by the requirements, is not insignificant. In the rush of development and revision of the National Curriculum attention has invariably been fixed upon the practicalities of implementation rather than any need to pose critical questions of principles underlying requirements. Has it been a policy that has embraced the varied needs and interests of girls and boys, coming from different class, cultural and religious backgrounds, with different sexualities? Has it positioned those differences as a resource or a problem for the teachers charged with providing all children with their statutory entitlement? Have the official texts outlined an entitlement in physical education that would challenge long-established sex-differentiated patterns of curriculum provision and staffing in physical education and provide children with a physical education capable of reducing the dominance of gender stereotyped attitudes, beliefs and patterns of participation in physical activity and sport? It is these questions that underpin my exploration of various versions of the NCPE that have emerged throughout the 1990s in England. The discussion seeks to pursue the direction and/or encouragement that official texts (including non-statutory guidance materials issued by government agencies) have given teachers to engage with gender issues in contexts of physical education.

The Interim Report 1991: putting gender on the agenda

As others have noted, the Interim Report from the NCPE working group provided what has to now be seen as extensive commentary on 'equal opportunities in physical education' (Hargreaves, 1994; 2000; Talbot, 1993). Subsequent texts featured a dramatic loss of depth in discussion and a reduction in the strength of the messages being sent out to teachers about what action is expected of them in relation to equal opportunities in physical education. The Interim Report stood out for not only identifying equal opportunity as 'a leading and guiding principle for physical education' (DES/WO, 1991a: 16) but also clearly embracing a commitment to equity within this principle. The group specifically drew attention to the need for teachers to focus upon the individuality of pupils and furthermore, to view this positively. They explained that:

> All children will have their own individual gifts to contribute, some of which may be derived from or expressive of their backgrounds. These can be used to their own advantage and to enrich the experience of the group, but should never be used as a basis for restricting access to, or opportunity for, any learning experience in physical education.
>
> (ibid.: 16)

In addition, the group highlighted some of the complexities of gender and of pedagogical relations in physical education, and the challenges that engaging with these posed for schools and teachers within them. They stressed that:

> mere *access* cannot be equated with real *opportunity*. The distinction between access and opportunity is crucial. In some schools, girls and boys, able-bodied and disabled, from a range of cultures and ethnic background may be said to have the same *access* to the physical education curriculum: no children are prevented by virtue of their sex, religion, ability or race from taking part. But even when this desirable state of affairs exists, do children also have equal *opportunities* to learn and express themselves through and in physical education? The effects of attitudes and expectations of teachers, the preconditions of access, the interactions within mixed-sex, mixed-ability and multi-cultural groups, and the previous experiences and relative ranges and levels of the skills, knowledge and understanding of the children must also be considered.
>
> (ibid.: 17, original emphasis)

In a further move that openly questioned the legitimacy of common practices and perceptions in physical education, the group identified a number of issues that in their view, demanded 'particular thought and consideration' and upon which they would expand in their final report. These were:

(a) the public nature of success and failure in physical education;
(b) the competitive nature of many physical education activities;
(c) the legacy of single-sex teaching and teacher education in physical education;
(d) moves towards mixed-sex grouping, sometimes without an educational rationale, and without consideration of the conditions under which mixed-sex teaching and single-sex teaching might be more successful or appropriate;
(e) the biological and cultural effects of being female or male on the behaviour considered appropriate for girls and boys of different cultures;
(f) the physical nature of physical education, and the emergence of sexuality during key stages 2, 3, and 4, providing both problems and opportunities for physical education in challenging body images, sex stereotypes and other limited perspectives which constrain the choices and achievements of disabled children, and of both girls and boys;
(g) the effects of some culturally restricted interpretations of masculinity on the place and value of dance in the school curriculum, and on boys' opportunities for dance experience and education;
(h) the barriers to young people's involvement caused by the restrictive ways some sports and forms of dance are portrayed and practised;

(i) the rich potential for physical education to transcend categories of race, sex and learning need, through nurturing the value of individual contributions in group situations, and through presenting a wide range of cultural forms and experiences which reflect our multi-cultural society; and

(j) the treatment of physical education in sex discrimination legislation and the varied levels of understanding of its effects on curriculum physical education, extra-curricula activities and school sport.

(ibid.: 17)

The group acknowledged the complexity of these issues, but also stressed the need for teachers and teacher educators to engage with the complexity. They reiterated that 'mixed *grouping* (ability, sex, cultures) is not the same as mixed ability, multi-cultural or co-educational *teaching*' (ibid.: 18, original emphasis) and stated that:

Working towards equality of opportunity in physical education involves not only widening and ensuring access. It involves the understanding and appreciation of the range of pupils' responses to femininity, masculinity and sexuality, to the whole range of ability and disability, to ethnic and cultural diversity, and the ways these relate for children to physical education.

(ibid.: 18)

The limits of the existing understanding of these issues amongst both teachers and teacher educators was implicit in their comment that 'This will entail, both in initial and in-service training of teachers, the critical review of prevailing practice, rigorous and continuous appraisal and often the willingness to face up to long held beliefs and prejudices' (ibid.: 18).

True to their word, the working group further highlighted the importance and scope of equal opportunities in physical education in their final report (DES/WO, 1991b). They dedicated a chapter of the report to what they maintained was a 'guiding and leading principle' for the subject. They identified that the role of teachers should be 'to foster respect for fellow human beings; to question the stereotypes which limit children's behaviour and achievements; and to challenge, whenever necessary, instances of sexism and racism' (ibid.: 15). Once again they stressed the distinction between access and opportunity and the potential for enrichment by virtue of individuality, whilst also acknowledging the challenge that responding to these issues represented for the profession. They stated in no uncertain terms that legacies from the past continued to constitute a significant barrier to progress towards gender equity in physical education, saying that:

the different ideologies and content of programmes of the former single sex institutions, and commonly for men and women in mixed courses, continue to affect not only teachers' attitudes, but also the ability of both men and women teachers to teach across a balanced programme of physical activities. In-service training will need to address this issue to avoid future undesirable sex stereotyping of activities (for example, with women teaching all dance and men teaching all contact sports).

(ibid.: 57)

Returning to the matter of grouping, they explained that 'Choices of mixed- or single-sex groupings in physical education should be made for educational reasons, and after considering the conditions under which they might be most successful and appropriate' (ibid.: 57). Notably, they pointed to the need for moves to address gender in schools to also engage with experiences (and inequities) beyond them, with 'recognition of the different opportunities which are available for girls and boys to acquire particular sets of skills outside of the school curriculum' (ibid.: 57). The report thus made it clear that different grouping would be appropriate in different contexts and that a move away from sex-differentiated curricula should not be interpreted as demanding wholesale adoption of mixed-sex grouping. However, they also warned of the tensions that may arise between policies adopted within schools and those beyond them, specifically in relation to 'the exclusionary practices and rules of some sports governing bodies on competitive school sport' (ibid.: 58). If not part of the education service, competitive sport may be exempted from the Sex Discrimination Act of 1974, with provision outside of the curriculum thereby potentially giving rise to contradictory messages for pupils. As O'Sullivan and colleagues note in chapter 10 of this text, competitive sport in the USA has, in contrast, been legally required to engage with sex discrimination issues.

On the matter of 'kit' for physical education, the report prompted further challenges to stereotypical conventions. The group stated that 'Considerations of safety, comfort and freedom of movement should override conventions associated with being male or female' (ibid.: 58). In later discussion of 'cultural diversity' the report also identified the need for negotiation to facilitate participation and enjoyment within particular religious conventions and drew attention to the need for teachers to be sensitive to the costs of clothing and equipment for physical education. Here the text thus acknowledged the importance of the constant interplay of issues of gender, ethnicity and class in relation to equal opportunities in physical education.

In a further effort to extend understandings of gender issues and counter stereotypical images and understandings, the group linked the breadth of experiences incorporated in the curriculum with the potential for the subject to extend current (and limited) perceptions of masculinity and femininity in relation to physical activity and sport. They stressed the need for schools to 'include equal opportunities considerations among the criteria by which they select the content of the physical education programmes, so that all children have the opportunity to experience a range of physical activities within both

National Curriculum physical education and extra-curricula school sport' (ibid.: 58) and stated that 'In particular, a broad and balanced programme of physical education, sensitively delivered, can help to extend boys' restricted perceptions of masculinity and masculine behaviour' (ibid.: 58). While not denying this potential, there is a need to recognise that it is not only boys who may have notably narrow perceptions about these issues. We need to engage both girls and boys in efforts to extend understandings of both masculinities and femininities.

Obscuring the agenda?

As indicated, we need to value the extent of the group's commentary on equal opportunities and see its inclusion in an 'official text' issued by the government as a significant achievement on the part of the group. However, in celebrating the commentary we are in danger of overlooking some characteristics of the final report that are important in relation to the degree to which it would succeed in securing equal opportunities as a 'guiding and leading principle' in the implementation of the NCPE. Would the progressive intentions of writers be reflected in practice? In this respect several points are worthy of note, not least of which is the physical position of much of the above commentary within the final report. The status and potential impact of many of the points made by the group in relation to equal opportunity in physical education seemed compromised by what can only be seen as 'relegation' to an appendix of the report. This location appeared contradictory to the claimed lead status of the principle. Furthermore it was a position that undoubtedly placed in jeopardy the expression of equal opportunities in practice. The appendices of any text do not carry comparable weight to the main text and points raised in the group's discussion of, for example, 'sex and gender' and 'cultural diversity' may have simply never been read by many teachers. Understandably, attention would be upon the specifics of statutory requirements rather than accompanying commentary.

Separate or focused discussion on 'equal opportunities' has 'pros and cons' wherever positioned in the text. The separation can be seen as reflecting the importance of equal opportunities as an issue for the subject and the profession. However, it is also a position that may lead to the issue being totally overlooked or given limited attention amidst a focus upon what were perceived as more immediate concerns, such as the general requirements established for the subject,[1] the programmes of study[2] outlined for each of the identified areas of activity within the curriculum, or the assessment framework provided for the NCPE. It is when we explore these other sections of the NCPE that we can begin to appreciate the extent to which policy texts always feature compromises between different interests, not all of which have equal status in policy developments (Ball, 1990; Bowe *et al.*, 1992; Penney and Evans, 1999). In addition, we see the significance of omissions and the way in which they may give rise to contradictions or inconsistencies in the messages

being given out to readers. If we are concerned to promote equal opportunities within physical education, consistency and reinforcement of messages
seem crucial.

Before expanding upon some of these issues in relation to the NCPE texts,
I should acknowledge another important characteristic of the development of
the NCPE. The working group's final report was not a text that the group had
autonomy over, in relation to either form or content. Like similar documents
produced for other subjects and subsequent national curriculum texts
produced by other government agencies, it was instead a text that openly
reflected the politics of policy development in education and a process that
was far from neutral (Evans and Penney, 1995; Penney and Evans, 1999). The
demands for writers to produce documents that would be acceptable to civil
servants and ministers have been vividly described by the Chairman and Chief
Executive of the National Curriculum Council,[3] Duncan Graham. Graham's
commentary on the development of the National Curriculum makes it very
clear that government officials required a particular content in a particular
form from the groups that had been appointed to advise them on the National
Curriculum (Graham with Tytler, 1993). The compromises and contradictions that we see in texts such as the NCPE final report therefore need
to be acknowledged as not entirely of the group's own making, but as
nevertheless, significant characteristics of the text. The following discussion of
such characteristics is illustrative rather than exhaustive. Furthermore, it is a
critique applicable to other policy texts relating to physical education. Many
of the omissions and contradictions noted are ones that have been replicated
in more recent official publications. Certainly, there is a continued need to
explore silences, compromises and contradictions in physical education
policies. As Noble (1999) has explained, readers interpret silences as well as
words. They can have powerful meanings and important implications for
future practice.

Limiting and excluding agendas

Above, I identified sections of the NCPE official texts that for many teachers
would be their priority and hold their attention. One such section was the
'recommended programmes of study' for physical education. This section of
the working group's final report addressed the breadth and balance of the
curriculum. However, here the text failed to reinforce the commentary
incorporated within the sections specifically dedicated to 'equal opportunities
in physical education'. In outlining their recommendations regarding the
areas of activity to be incorporated within the various key stages of the
curriculum, the group made no reference to the need to consider issues of
gender or cultural diversity. Instead their attention focused on the practicality
of their recommendations and the flexibility that they accorded to schools, 'as
requested by the Secretaries of State' (DES/WO, 1991b: 26). The impression
was that pragmatic rather than educational or specifically, equal opportunities

issues, would be the first and legitimate point of reference in curriculum design.

The section of the text that addressed the programmes of study associated with each specific area of activity could similarly be viewed as 'full of omissions'. For example, given the emphasis above that dance could 'help to extend boys' restricted perceptions of masculinity and masculine behaviour' (DES/WO, 1991b: 58) we could expect the programme of study for dance to feature explicit prompts to teachers to explore this potential. The absence of reference to gender and sexuality in recommendations such as those below has to be seen as not only an omission, but also a loss – in the status accorded to equal opportunities and of an opportunity to prompt its expression in practice. For key stage 3 dance (for pupils aged 11–14), it was recommended that pupils should:

- be taught to perform set dances showing an understanding of style;
- develop and use appropriate techniques and styles to communicate meanings and ideas;
- be guided to create and perform short dances showing sensitivity to the style of accompaniment;
- be taught to describe, analyse and interpret dances recognising stylistic differences, aspects of production and cultural/historical contexts; and
- be taught to support their own dance compositions with independently researched material, and, where appropriate, record dance in words and symbols.

(DES/WO, 1991b: 33)

The text relating to identified 'general requirements' that were applicable to all of the key stages and relevant to all of the areas of activity, was a further section devoid of mention of equal opportunities. The need for pupils to be physically active, to understand safety issues, to 'be taught to cope with both success and failure', to 'observe the conventions of fair play', engage in problem solving, 'be given the opportunity to consolidate their skills through repetition' and 'be made aware of the importance of good posture' were all matters that, unlike equal opportunities, gender or sexuality, were identified as 'general requirements' to be addressed in implementation of the programmes of study (DES/WO, 1991b: 28).

Requirements and guidance relating to assessment is another area in which there is both the opportunity and arguably a critical need for issues of equal opportunity to be addressed. Once again, there was a silence in the NCPE working group's text. The final report identified a number of 'issues in assessment'. Several of these could be seen as demanding that attention be directed to equal opportunities considerations. However, equal opportunities and/or gender issues did not feature in the discussion of criteria for assessment, or in the group's emphasis that the context of assessment needed to have meaning for pupils (DES/WO, 1991b: 42–3). Both the criteria for assessment and the context of assessment are important considerations if we wish to promote greater gender equity in physical education. The tendency may well be for a 'gender blind' or 'same for all' approach to be viewed as the desirable or defensible approach. However, it is an approach that ignores important differences between pupils that we should be actively responding to in teaching and assessment if we are to maximise opportunities for all pupils to progress and enjoy success in the subject.

Further absences in the text could be identified in the discussion of 'partnerships in provision'. Despite the group's stated belief that 'partnerships have a major role to play in furthering the aims of physical education' (DES/WO, 1991b: 49), the critical need for collective and co-ordinated action to challenge inequities in provision seemed underplayed (see also Macdonald, chapter 12 in this text). There was important recognition that ability can restrict pupils' access to extra-curricular physical education and sport and the need to use the extra-curricular arena to extend the breadth of pupils' experiences. But there was no prompt for teachers to move from the commonplace practice of male staff taking responsibility for organising extra-curricula activities for boys and female staff doing likewise for girls, with the result that extra-curricula programmes invariably promote stereo-typical images of masculinity and femininity and narrow perceptions of the range of physical activities that men and women can participate in (see Penney and Harris, 1997; Bass and Cale, 1999).

Sustained silence: the statutory orders for the NCPE

Absences such as those identified above have featured in texts that have superseded the NCPE working group's final report. The silences became progressively more obvious and more significant as cuts were made to the length of policy documents and the scope of discussion inherent in them. As the development of the NCPE progressed much of the commentary specifically directed to equal opportunities issues disappeared altogether, or was relegated to accompanying and notably *non*-statutory guidance texts. Far from being portrayed as a leading principal, equal opportunities and more specifically gender issues were hard to find in the consultation report issued in 1991 (NCC, 1991), the statutory order published in 1992 (DES/WO, 1992) and the revised order issued in 1995 (DfE/WO 1995). The bland impression was that equal opportunities and gender issues were simply not worthy of sustained commentary in the NCPE. Figueroa (1993: 100) reflected that 'The closest the National Curriculum Council Consultation Report – on which the statutory order, that is, the legal requirement, is based – gets to issues of multi-cultural and antiracist education is in mentioning, sparingly and in the broadest terms, such concepts as "fair play" and "cultural issues".' Meanwhile Evans and Davies (1993: 19) observed that 'there is little in the recommendations of the NC for PE to ensure that the practice of differentiating the curriculum for boys and girls will not continue' and Barton (1993) pointed to the relative lack of sophistication in the conceptualisation of 'disability' (and therefore, of equal opportunity) being presented by the text. Barton stressed the need for clearer engagement with the complex interaction of equal opportunities 'issues', explaining that 'the difficulties of and responses to being disabled are influenced by class, race, gender and age factors. These can cushion or compound the experience of discrimination and oppression' (p. 45). He was thus pointing to the clear failure of policy to promote sophisticated understandings of equal opportunities and equity. Such understandings are a crucial pre-requisite to the development of practices that respond to the individual needs of pupils. Later in the chapter I consider whether the latest version of the NCPE can be regarded as an advancement in relation to these concerns. First, however, I explore some of the less explicit gendered characteristics of the NCPE established as the entitlement for all children in state schools in England and Wales.

Gender off the agenda?

In the context of consistent gaps and omissions in the commentary on equal opportunities, equity and gender in the various versions of the NCPE, the implicit messages inherent in and portrayed by the official texts take on an enhanced significance. Following others (Hargreaves, 1994, 2000) I suggest that in its form and content the NCPE has been openly gendered and has repeatedly failed to prompt an extension of notably limited understandings of gender in physical education. The discussion below pursues some key characteristics of the NCPE in relation to these claims. The aim is to illustrate that even if apparently excluded from the texts, gender issues were very much embedded in them, and set to arise from them.

One of the issues that has consistently featured prominently in debates about the NCPE has been the breadth and balance of the curriculum outlined as a statutory entitlement. Previous commentaries have pointed to the progressively privileged position that was accorded to games following the government's response to the working group's Interim Report (see Evans and Penney, 1995; Penney and Evans, 1999) and the parallel reduction in requirements for other areas of activity to feature in the entitlement curriculum. The privileging of games is significant in relation to our interest in gender on at least two counts; curriculum content and organisation. Invariably the two issues are inextricably linked. Games remains an area of physical education frequently associated with sex-differentiated patterns of provision, with sports stereotypically regarded as exclusively 'men's' or 'women's' being provided for boys and girls respectively, and typically also staffed by male and female teachers respectively. The 'flexibility' of the NCPE requirements has enabled this practice to continue.

Many factors may contribute to the continuation of stereotypically gendered provision. Pragmatic issues of timetabling groups and staff (with differing expertise) may mean that patterns of provision that break with tradition are not regarded as a realistic possibility. Parent and pupil expectations may also be seen as a barrier to provision that deviates from stereotypical norms. The fundamental link between curriculum content and the established pattern of extra-curricula provision focusing upon the performances of school teams in stereotypically gendered sports (see Penney and Harris, 1997) may also be a driving force in curriculum design. However, there are opportunities to challenge these patterns of provision and the inequities inherent in them. Williams and Bedward (in chapter 9) illustrate that silences in the NCPE need to be seen as presenting important opportunities for change, not only barriers to progress. Silences may mean that texts fail to require or offer encouragement for progressive developments, but they certainly do not prevent such developments. The requirement for all children to experience invasion, striking/fielding and net/wall games can be fulfilled in ways that openly reproduce and legitimate stereotypically gendered patterns of provision and participation, or in ways that actively seek to challenge such practices and the perceptions about participation in particular activities and about masculinity and femininity that they generate amongst both girls and boys. Thus while Hargreaves (2000: 140) has stressed that:

> the 'hidden curriculum' of competitive team games, more than any other aspect of the physical education curriculum, replicates conventional notions of gender differences. Male bonding is encouraged, aggression and sexism are endemic, and boys quickly learn that the sporting man is a symbol of masculine character; those who are poor sportsmen are despised and ridiculed as 'less than male'

we need to balance this with recognition that games can be a context in which very different attitudes and behaviours are celebrated and encouraged. Not for the first time, the crucial role that initial teacher training has to play in the translation of policy 'into practice' is apparent. Initial teacher training remains the key forum in which 'alternative' readings of and responses to conservative policies can be encouraged and nurtured. However, as Flintoff (1993) has previously stressed and Rich and Brown reinforce in chapter 6, we cannot assume that there will be interest in or support for such action in initial teacher training. Notably, recent government policies relating to initial teacher training have served to openly dissuade deviations from conservative readings of the National Curriculum.

In addressing the breadth and balance of the curriculum, the privileging of games is only one dimension of debates. The marginalisation of other areas of activity, that in some instances are no longer a compulsory part of the entitlement curriculum, is equally important in relation to gender issues. Once again, we need to acknowledge that the absence of a requirement for coverage does not preclude schools extending provision in ways that will openly engage with gender equity concerns. The statutory order for the NCPE presented schools and teachers within them with some key choices in relation to these concerns. For many teachers, one of the most welcome features of the order issued in 1992 was the choice to include or alternatively omit dance from the curriculum at key stage 3, for girls, boys or both girls and boys. In Hargreaves' (1994, 2000) view the government's rejection of the NCPE working group's recommendation that dance should be a *compulsory* activity within the curriculum for all pupils signalled the loss of an opportunity to radically reshape many physical education curricula and specifically, to challenge the gender stereotyping inherent in them. Some teachers in some schools are challenging boys' and girls' perceptions about dance, about who can and should participate in what forms of dance. But in others, the picture of provision, the opportunities arising, and the attitudes promoted are very different and far less progressive. There is every potential for boys to be 'systematically shut off from an expressive movement experience and are schooled into physical robustness and aggressive competition, whilst girls are schooled into creativity and co-operation' (Hargreaves, 1994: 153).

Outdoor and adventurous activities is another area of activity worthy of note in relation to the flexibility of the NCPE requirements. There is the scope to include outdoor and adventurous activities within the NCPE, but not a requirement to do so. From a gender equity perspective the flexibility can be seen as a further loss of an opportunity to ensure experience of activities that may offer particular potential to extend understandings of and attitudes towards gender in physical education (Humberstone, 1993). However, in the case of both outdoor and adventurous activities and dance, we should avoid the temptation to assume that a different activity in and of itself, will signal greater gender equity in physical education. McFee and Smith (1997: 70) make the point that ' if we seek to make dance more accessible to males by ensuring ". . . masculinity through athletics in dance" (Hanna, 1988: p. 217) we are in danger of simply reinforcing traditional images of masculinity: thereby bringing about no more than the situated rebirth of ideology'.

One of the other characteristics of the NCPE that previous policy analyses have drawn attention to is the privileging of discourses of sport over discourses of health (Penney and Evans, 1997; 1999). With interests in gender equity in mind we need to critically reflect upon how sport is being defined and portrayed in the NCPE. The tendency for policies to feature a narrow conceptualisation of sport that openly celebrates stereotypically masculine values and behaviours is significant. However, as Harris and Penney illustrate in chapter 8, we cannot assume that discourses of health are any more equitable or progressive than those of sport.

The new NCPE: new principles; new prospects?

The year 1999 witnessed yet another revision to the NCPE, this time under a Labour rather than a Conservative government. The revision came at a time when it was widely acknowledged that teachers wanted stability in national requirements rather than further upheaval (QCA, 1998, 1999a). Thus, much that was familiar and established remained intact in the 'new' National Curriculum, and NCPE specifically. From a gender equity perspective the mix of 'old' and 'new' discourses inherent in the revised NCPE can certainly be seen as having 'pros and cons'. The new requirement for pupils at key stage 4 to follow programmes of study in at least two different areas of activity (as compared to two activities that could both be from the same area) may be celebrated as a direct challenge to the dominance of games in many curricula. However, as was emphasised early in the development of the NCPE, it is naïve to assume that extending the range of activities required will guarantee more equitable provision and experiences. Other areas of activity can reinforce narrow perceptions of masculinity and femininity in relation to physical activity and sport as much as games.

We also have to consider the dominant messages relating to gender issues that arise from the overlying frame of the NCPE. The retention of the six established areas of activity and the continued privileging of games through-out key stages 1–3, arguably reflect and portray a narrow (and culturally specific) conceptualisation of sport and physical activity. The framework does not embrace, for example, martial arts and nor does it provide a clear location for various activities (such as weight training, aerobics classes, recreational cycling) frequently associated with participation in physical activity primarily for health and/or social reasons. Exclusions such as these have important implications for the degree to which the NCPE can be seen as providing for the needs and interests of all girls and boys and it is notable that the new NCPE in Wales has recategorised activities at key stage 4 to embrace 'exercise activities' (National Assembly for Wales/Awdurdod Cymwysterau Cwricwlym Ac Asesu Cymru, 2000).

The programmes of study within the new NCPE in England, together with the accompanying non-statutory 'schemes of work' issued by the QCA (2000) have raised the profile of participation in 'other roles' in sporting contexts, such as the role of official or coach. The development of skills, knowledge and understanding in relation to these roles has thereby been formally established as 'legitimate knowledge' within the new NCPE. Diversifying teaching and learning to promote experience of 'other roles' may help to make physical education a subject that more girls and more boys may enjoy and experience success in. However, if those children (girls and boys) who have traditionally felt marginalised by the dominance of performance discourses are to now feel that they and their particular skills and interests are valued, there is a need to challenge the portrayal of the 'other roles' as the (inferior) 'other' to performance. Furthermore, we need to be aware that gender stereotyped images and understandings can be promoted amidst a focus on leadership or officiating as much as performance. How will boys react to a girl taking on a coaching role for their warm-up or skill-practice? Will girls feel that they can legitimately coach boys? Will boys be willing to undertake choreography for a dance performance and would girls accept a boy in this role? Questions such as these demonstrate the scope for the curricula developed from the new NCPE to either reinforce or alternatively, actively challenge and extend pupils' perceptions about who can legitimately 'do what' in physical education and sport.

In other respects discourses of elite performance have been privileged in new requirements, at times quite openly and on other occasions more subtly via 'hidden silences' in the text. For example, at a first glance the direct linkage between knowledge, skills and understanding relating to 'evaluation' and 'improving performance' that was written into the requirements may not seem problematic. That is, until we recognise the scope for notions of evaluation to be directed towards the social dynamics and relationships within learning contexts, and the gender inequities inherent in those dynamics and relationships. Thus, the particular definition of 'evaluation' presented in and promoted by the text of the NCPE and accompanying guidance material (QCA, 1999b) is important. The exclusion of 'other discourses', particularly of social justice, from notions of 'evaluation' is a far from neutral act. Physical education syllabus texts developed elsewhere and particularly in Australia and New Zealand (see Wright, chapter 11 in this text; Kirk *et al.*, 1998) demonstrate that in different political contexts, these 'other' discourses can come to the fore in the subject.

In some respects the influence of a change in government and new political agendas was very obvious in the new National Curriculum in England. The government made much of the fact that the new National Curriculum formally set in place an agenda for 'inclusion'. Specifically, it established that in all subject areas teachers must pay 'due regard' to the following three principles for inclusion:

- Setting suitable learning challenges
- Responding to pupils' diverse learning needs
- Overcoming barriers to learning and assessment for individuals and groups of pupils.

(DfEE/QCA, 1999: 28)

Each of these principles can be used as a focus for addressing gender equity issues in physical education, but currently there is little guarantee of such a response. Once again it is notable that the commentary on inclusion came after the detail of the programmes of study within the NCPE text and may be in danger of being overlooked. Silences on gender equity issues in other sections of the text seem to be echoed in early implementation. The principles of inclusion have been notably absent from discussions relating to the implementation of the NCPE order. The initial impression is that teachers have not regarded the principles as a priority in implementation (Penney, 2001). Professional development work seems essential if the opportunities inherent in the revised NCPE to promote greater understanding of the complexities of gender equity in physical education and to facilitate advancement of practice that embraces these complexities, are to be explored. Currently, the commentary on gender equity within the text is marginally positioned and provides very few insights into how teachers can respond to the complexities of gender in their teaching. It is explained that teachers should respond to pupils' diverse needs by creating effective learning environments in which:

- the contribution of all pupils is valued
- all pupils can feel secure and are able to contribute appropriately
- stereotypical views are challenged and pupils learn to appreciate and view positively differences in others, whether arising from race, gender, ability or disability.

(ibid.: 29)

As O'Sullivan and colleagues observe in chapter 10, such commentary leaves it to teachers and teacher educators to pursue the matters of how, when and where this can be achieved. Furthermore, we see a failure to embrace sexuality in the above guidance. In England education has mirrored the 'sports establishment' in failing to

> create a discourse to explain and deal with discrimination against homo-sexuals and, more specifically, against lesbians in sports. Silence implicitly condones taken-for-granted ways of thinking and behaving, which occur subtly and during informal activities, and which are hurtful and harmful to non-heterosexuals.
>
> (Hargreaves, 1994: 260; see also Clarke, chapter 4 in this book)

Conclusion: gendered policies; what prospects in practice?

The bottom line in the implementation of the National Curriculum for Physical Education and one that overseas observers may particularly view as contradictory, is that the statutory entitlement is different in different schools and may well be different for different pupils within the same school. The flexibility in the statutory requirements for the NCPE may be argued as essential given the very different school contexts in which implementation has to occur. Undoubtedly, if we are looking for openings for progressive practice that will further gender equity in physical education, it is an invaluable characteristic of the NCPE. However, as I have emphasised, it can also be seen as a further inherent weakness of the official texts, since by its very nature the flexibility does not ensure that all teachers or all teacher educators will engage with gender issues. There is extensive scope for 'slippage' (Bowe *et al.*, 1992) in the interpretation and implementation of the NCPE. It is a policy that was designed and destined to be interpreted differently in different schools, by different teachers, with varying resources and personal expertise to draw upon. The 1990s have clearly demonstrated that this has presented the potential for both conservativism and creativity in practice and this remains the case in the context of teacher's implementation of the 'new' NCPE. So what are the future prospects for gender equity in the context of the NCPE?

As Penney and Evans (1999) have emphasised, responses to policies need to be understood in relation to the political, economic and institutional contexts in which they occur. In important respects, contemporary contexts can be seen to offer limited support for creativity in implementation, and presenting instead considerable pressures for teachers to reinforce the dominance of established (and gendered) discourses, that promote and celebrate elite performance in a narrow range of games. In England, changes to the funding and structure of Local Education Authorities have considerably reduced the support available for teachers interested in innovation, while arrangements for inspection of schools discourage experimentalism. The direction of developments is towards teachers adopting a technicist approach within safe and clearly legitimate frames of reference. There seems little encouragement or support for risk-taking or deviations from texts that inspectors will recognise, or texts that parents (whose custom is to be attracted and nurtured in the education market, see Bowe *et al.*, 1992; Penney and Evans, 1999) will also recognise and value. In these circumstances the claimed 'spaces for action', freedom and flexibility in implementation may effectively be closed down. Space for action that will signal resistance to stereotypical patterns of provision, images and attitudes, that will enable masculinit*ies* and femininit*ies* to be expressed in and promoted via physical education and sport, and that will prompt various social, cultural and religious values to be embraced and celebrated, may regrettably be not merely unexplored, but unexplorable amidst other expectations and priorities. Mahony's (2000) observation of the absence of discourses of gender equity amidst discourses of effectiveness is important. The two need not be mutually exclusive, but regrettably:

> Conceptions of the 'effective teacher' and headteacher are being redefined in ways which render invisible the role of schools in contributing to the construction and maintenance of gender inequalities. Teachers' responsibilities to challenge these and other inequalities are being removed as the purposes of schooling are articulated around a narrow form of economic instrumentalism.
>
> (ibid.: 239)

Undoubtedly, there are pockets of progressive practice. But that is a far cry from what seemed promised with the introduction of 'entitlement for all'. As indicated above, initial teacher training remains the key arena in which readings of official texts are shaped and in which future teachers will develop opinions about the readings that are both possible and legitimate. It is a forum in which student teachers can be encouraged to actively explore the 'scope for slippage' and 'fill the silences' inherent in official texts in ways that serve to challenge the dominance of established gendered discourses and introduce and/or and raise the profile of alternative discourses. It is where boundaries to thinking and actions should be openly debated, challenged and extended if we are to succeed in establishing 'new gender agendas' in physical education in the years ahead – within and despite the constraints posed by a still largely conservative official National Curriculum text. Thus we can lament, but must also continue to actively oppose the degree to which requirements for initial teacher training in England serve to erode opportunities for creativity in the interpretation and implementation of the NCPE (Evans *et al.*, 1996).

Notes

1 General requirements applied to all key stages and were to be taught through all areas of activity. These requirements supplemented the general and activity specific programmes of study (DES/WO, 1992).
2 Programmes of study were designed to set out 'the matters, skills and processes which are required to be taught to pupils of different abilities and maturities during each key stage' (DES/WO, 1992: 4).
3 The National Curriculum Council was the agency established to advise the government on the original content of the National Curriculum in England and Wales.

References

Ball, S.J. (1990) *Politics and Policy Making in Education: Explorations in Policy Sociology*, London: Routledge.
Barton, L. (1993) Disability, empowerment and physical education, in J. Evans (ed.) *Equality, Education and Physical Education*, London: Falmer Press, pp. 43–54.
Bass, D. and Cale, L. (1999) Promoting physical activity through the extra-curricular programme, *European Journal of Physical Education* 4: 45–64.
Bowe, R. and Ball, S.J. with Gold, A. (1992) *Reforming Education and Changing Schools: Case Studies in Policy Sociology*, London: Routledge
Department for Education/Welsh Office (DfE/WO) (1995) *Physical Education in the National Curriculum*, London: HMSO.
Department for Education and Employment (DfEE)/Qualifications and Curriculum Authority (QCA) (1999) *Physical Education: The National Curriculum for England*, London: HMSO.
Department of Education and Science (DES) (1989) *National Curriculum: From Policy to Practice*, London: HMSO.
Department of Education and Science (DES)/Welsh Office (WO) (1991a) *National Curriculum Physical Education Working Group Interim Report*, London: DES.
Department of Education and Science (DES)/Welsh Office (WO) (1991b) *Physical Education for Ages 5–16: Proposals of the Secretary of State for Education and the Secretary of State for Wales*, London: DES.
Department of Education and Science (DES)/Welsh Office (WO) (1992) *Physical Education in the National Curriculum*, London: HMSO.
Evans, J. and Davies, B. (1993) Equality, equity and physical education, in J. Evans (ed.) *Equality, Education and Physical Education*, London: Falmer Press, pp. 11–27.

Evans, J. and Penney, D. (1995) The politics of pedagogy: making a National Curriculum physical education, *Journal of Education Policy* 10(1): 27–44.

Evans, J., Penney, D. and Davies, B. (1996) Back to the future? Education policy and physical education, in N. Armstrong (ed.) *New Directions in Physical Education. Change and Innovation*, London: Cassell Education, pp. 1–18.

Figueroa, P. (1993) Equality, multiculturalism, anti-racism and physical education in the National Curriculum, in J. Evans (ed.) *Equality, Education and Physical Education*, London: Falmer Press, pp. 90–104.

Flintoff, A. (1993) Gender, physical education and initial teacher education, in J. Evans (ed.) *Equality, Education and Physical Education*, London: Falmer Press, pp. 184–204.

Graham, D. with Tytler, D. (1993) *A Lesson for Us All: The Making of the National Curriculum*, London: Routledge.

Hargreaves, J. (1994) *Sporting Females*, London: Routledge.

Hargreaves, J. (2000) Gender, morality and the national physical education curriculum, in J. Hansen and N.K. Nielsen (eds) *Sports, Body and Health*, Odense, Denmark: Odense University Press, pp. 133–48.

Humberstone, B. (1993) Equality, physical education and outdoor education – ideological struggles and transformative structures?, in J. Evans (ed.) *Equality, Education and Physical Education*, London: Falmer Press, pp. 74–89.

Kirk, D., Burgess-Limerick, R., Kiss, M., Lahey, J. and Penney, D. (1998) *Senior Physical Education: An Integrated Approach*, Champaign, IL: Human Kinetics.

Mahony, P. (2000) Teacher education policy and gender, in J. Salisbury and S. Riddell (eds) *Gender, Policy and Educational Change: Shifting Agendas in the UK and Europe*, London: Routledge, pp. 229–42.

McFee, G. and Smith, F. (1997) Let's hear it for the boys: dance, gender and education, in A. Tomlinson (ed.) *Gender, Sport and Leisure: Continuities and Challenges*, Aachen: Meyer & Meyer, pp. 63–80.

National Assembly for Wales/Awdurdod Cymwysterau Cwricwlwm Ac Asesu Cymru (ACCAC) (2000) *Physical Education in the National Curriculum in Wales*, Cardiff: ACCAC.

National Curriculum Council (NCC) (1991) *Physical Education in the National Curriculum. A Report to the Secretary of State for Education and Science on the Statutory Consultation for the Attainment Target and Programmes of Study in Physical Education*, York: NCC.

Noble, C. (1999) Silence: absence and context, in I. Parker and the Bolton Discourse Network, *Critical Textwork. An Introduction to Varieties of Discourse and Analysis*, Buckingham: Open University Press, pp. 191–200.

Penney, D. (2001) The revision and initial implementation of the National Curriculum for Physical Education in England, *The Bulletin of Physical Education* (in press).

Penney, D. and Evans, J. (1997) Naming the game: discourse and domination in physical education and sport in England and Wales, *European Physical Education Review* 3(1): 21–32.

Penney, D. and Evans, J. (1999) *Politics, Policy and Practice in Physical Education*, London: Routledge.

Penney, D. and Harris, J. (1997) Extra-curricular physical education: more of the same for the more able ? *Sport, Education and Society* 2(1): 41–54.

Qualifications and Curriculum Authority (1998) *Developing the School Curriculum. Advice of the Secretary of State and his Response on the Broad Nature and Scope of the Review of the National Curriculum*, London: QCA.

Qualifications and Curriculum Authority (1999a) *The Review of the National Curriculum in England. The Secretary of State's Proposals*, London: QCA.

Qualifications and Curriculum Authority (1999b) *Terminology in Physical Education*, London, QCA.

Qualifications and Curriculum Authority (2000) *Physical Education: A Scheme of Work for Key Stages 3 and 4*, London: QCA.

Talbot, M. (1993) A gendered physical education: equality and sexism, in J. Evans (ed.) *Equality, Education and Physical Education*, London: Falmer Press, pp. 74–89.

8 Gender, health and physical education

Jo Harris and Dawn Penney

Introduction

This chapter explores the expression of gender in the context of policies and practices in physical education specifically directed towards health. Perhaps to the surprise of some readers we show that work within physical education curricula that is associated with health (and are therefore typically termed health-related exercise (HRE) or health-related fitness (HRF)) may be as likely to express and promote stereotypically gendered attitudes and images as sex differentiated games settings. Thus, while we are anxious to point to the potential for health-related work in physical education to extend pupils' understandings of gender issues, we stress that it cannot be assumed that either policies or practice will promote these progressive ideals. Research reported here has revealed the way in which teachers and the school and curriculum structures that they are working within, may act to reproduce and legitimate narrow and openly gender stereotyped understandings of health issues in contexts of physical education and physical activity. We therefore identify teacher training and continuing professional development as having a key role to play if health-related work is to contribute to the development of more equitable educational practices and learning environments in physical education.

Our analysis focuses on the National Curriculum for Physical Education in England.[1] As Penney (in chapter 7), we draw attention to a number of omissions in these texts. The significance of the omissions becomes vividly apparent in our accompanying presentation of data from research that has explored teachers' development of health-related work in the context of their implementation of the NCPE. The data demonstrates that in some instances this work openly legitimates and reinforces very narrow understandings of gender in relation to participation in physical activity and sport. We illustrate distinct differences in the respective approaches of male and female heads of physical education departments towards the development of health-related exercise in physical education, and in the curricula provided for girls as compared to boys. We see very clearly the centrality of teachers in policy and curriculum development and the ways in which their understandings and values will have a key role to play in determining the extent to which curricula advance gender equity in physical education. It is notable that the practices reported here occurred in the context of implementation of the National Curriculum for Physical Education in England: the provision of the 'entitlement curriculum' for *all* pupils in state schools. The entitlement is shown to be very different for different children, with gender issues playing a part in shaping those differences. The data thus reveals the way in which the gaps and flexibility that Penney (in chapter 7) identified as a key characteristic of the NCPE, may provide opportunities for creativity in curriculum design and teaching, but can equally present opportunities for the retention of openly inequitable practices. The notion of 'slippage' in the implementation of policy (Bowe *et al.*, 1992; Penney and Evans, 1999; chapter 2 in this text) is thus central to our analysis.

The concept of discourse (see chapter 2 in this text) also underpins our critical examination of the interests and values that are promoted or in contrast, marginalised or excluded in the policies and practices that we explore. We show that there are *many* discourses of health in physical education and that there are direct linkages between these and stereotypically gendered discourses of the body, of health and of physical activity 'for' men and women. Furthermore, there are clear associations between particular contemporary discourses of health in physical education and the gendered history of the profession and the subject (see Kirk, 1992; chapter 3 in this text). We therefore reaffirm the role that history has played in shaping both the policies and practices of the NCPE. The historical exploration of the gendered dimensions of health in the context of physical education in the United Kingdom serves to reveal the different discourses 'of health' that are variously expressed in physical education, the association of particular discourses with either 'men's' or 'women's' training, and with physical education for either boys or girls. Locating health amidst this historically gendered development of the subject is vital to understanding the contemporary policy developments and responses to them that we describe later in the chapter.

Health and physical education: historically gendered

An examination of the historical association of health and physical education reveals that it is an inherently gendered one. The post-war period witnessed the emergence of health education as a school subject in its own right and the development of two contrasting approaches to health within physical education; one developed by female physical education teachers for girls and the other by male physical education teachers for boys. The former version was developed within some private girls' schools and was expressed through a form of Swedish gymnastics which was strongly associated with the 'harmonious development of the whole body' (McIntosh, 1968: 120). The 'whole body' in question was a particular body, with the association between physical education and health clearly framed in terms of traditional images of femininity. The focus of the activities provided for girls was their capacity to develop elegance, poise and posture, and to provide physical preparation for child-bearing. In sharp contrast to this focus and these activities for girls, the approach developed by men centred on the role of exercise in developing strength and endurance as a basis for 'fitness'. Fitness in this instance, was fitness for engagement in activities that would demand muscular strength and endurance. This particular view of the exercise–health relationship was thus embedded in, and an expression of the 'new' scientific functionalist approach to physical education (see Kirk, 1992 and chapter 2 in this text). Within this approach, 'physical fitness' was linked to a mechanistic view of the body and development of its efficiency via circuit training and later weight training. Male physical education teachers were the pioneers of physical education with this orientation, while the sex-differentiated pattern of schooling meant that the practices that they developed only featured in physical education curricula for boys.

McNair (1985) has provided further insights into the very different orientation towards the body, health and fitness that was expressed in and pursued during the 1940s and 1950s by male and female teacher training colleges respectively. The protagonists of Ling's Swedish system of gymnastics, middle-class formally-trained young ladies, were looking to develop harmonious movement to enhance poise, posture and elegance. Male training colleges were in pursuit of very different notions of a physically fit body, and of fitness for very different purposes and aligned themselves with different practices. Tough experienced retired army officers from working-class backgrounds supported the more vigorous McLaren-based system of physical training. The Ling or Swedish system of gymnastics was invented by Per Henrick Ling in the early nineteenth century and consolidated into a system of physical training which involved mostly free-standing exercises that sought to systematically exercise each part of the body through intricate flexions and extensions (Kirk, 1992). The McLaren system of physical education was introduced by Archibald McLaren in the mid-1800s and comprised precise physical exercises that worked through the entire range of possible movements of the joints and actions of the muscles in a systematic way (Kirk, 1992).

Traditional stereotypical images of masculinity and femininity were thus both embedded in and openly promoted by the respective practices; the 'different knowledge' being defined as physical education 'for boys' as compared to that 'for girls', and the different knowledge respectively gained by future male and female teachers. Men and women positioned themselves and in turn, positioned boys and girls, as having distinct and furthermore, essentially homogeneous, educational needs. There was little acknowledgement of either the respective value of the practices developed by the two groups, or the need for either boys or girls to have access to 'the other' body of knowledge. As McNair (1985) recognised, the controversy between the two groups had the unfortunate effect of inhibiting 'the appreciation that each group had something to contribute to fitness and health' (p. 114).

The more recent history of health in physical education: health-related fitness and health-related exercise

As many readers will be aware, the 1980s saw a new wave of interest in health amongst physical educationalists in the United Kingdom. 'Health-related fitness' or HRF as it was commonly termed, became a new element of work in many physical education curricula. The terminology that was typically used in the early developments was significant in relation to our concern with gender issues. It is always vital to acknowledge that health-related work was developed in different ways in different schools. However, the critical commentary that followed much of the early development work clearly points to the tendency for HRF to be directed towards arguably narrow notions of 'fitness' that had many similarities to the notions inherent in the scientific functionalist approach previously pursued in the male training colleges. The focus of attention was invariably measurement of strength, speed and endurance, with improvement of these aspects of fitness portrayed as an individual responsibility to be instilled in children (Biddle, 1987).

It is only if we compare this focus with subsequent developments in the UK, and with developments overseas (see Wright, chapter 11 in this text), that some of the issues and interests effectively marginalised in early HRF become apparent. Circuit training, fitness testing and/or weight training were new activities introduced in many curricula, alongside activity-based units of work. The activities were directly linked to concerns for physical education to be promoting improvements in physical fitness, but we need to recognise these as particular aspects of fitness. They were aspects that clearly related to concerns to extend understanding of the importance of physical dimensions of fitness in relation to participation and performance in sport but that often had less obvious connections with interests in long-term health.

The association of particular activities with particular outcomes becomes clearer when we consider subsequent development of health-related work in physical education in the UK through the 1980s and into the 1990s. The adoption of a different terminology of health-related exercise (HRE) was symbolic of a different orientation in health-related work, with attention shifting towards the role that physical education may play in promoting regular participation in physical activity with interests in lifelong health uppermost in mind. Those advocating the development of HRE recognised the linkages between fitness and performance in sport, but sought to extend visions to make clear connections between aspects of fitness, involvement in physical activity and long-term health. With our interests in gender in mind, probably the most significant characteristic of the moves to develop HRE as compared to HRF, was the extended range of activities that HRE became associated with. Aerobics was by no means a feature of all HRE programmes developed in schools. Nevertheless, it became firmly linked with the growth in HRE in physical education. Several points need to be noted in relation to this association. First, it meant that HRE was associated with an activity that was widely regarded as primarily if not exclusively for girls and women, rather than boys and men. Aerobics was specifically seen as having important potential to regenerate interest in physical education and physical activity amongst teenage girls. Its popularity as a leisure time activity amongst young women was a key factor in relation to the perceived appeal to girls, providing important credibility for the activity. Second, we need to recognise that the different discourses (of fitness and health) that were being expressed and promoted via the introduction of aerobics were thus destined to themselves become viewed as inherently gendered. The version of health and fitness being promoted would be seen as primarily if not exclusively, one 'for women'. Finally, we have to acknowledge the criticisms that in some instances have been directed at the introduction of aerobics into curricula. Some lessons and by association, aerobics as an activity and in turn, HRE, have been deemed recreational and not educational, and described as a 'modern form of drill' involving repetitious, mindless, 'follow my leader' exercises' (Clay, cited in SCAA, 1997: 36). Practices and discourses that were particularly associated with the interests of girls, but that were also seen as contrasting to, rather than compatible with, a focus on performance in sport, were under fire here.

Several commentators have previously drawn attention to a mix of practices that were variously established in curricula under the banners of HRF and/or HRE during the 1980s (Biddle, 1987; Harris, 1997a). However, the stereotypically gendered dimension of the emerging practices and furthermore, the different discourses of fitness and health that were variously privileged, appears largely unexplored. The research that we report below leads us to the view that the gendered history of the subject of physical education and the profession has had a very significant influence on the emerging relationship between physical education and health in the context of contemporary policy and curriculum developments. Our data has prompted us to acknowledge the way in which HRF and HRE, together with their respective sets of interests and different foci, could quite neatly be accommodated within the sex-differentiated pattern of provision of physical education in many schools. Following Penney and Evans (1999) we therefore point to strong elements of accommodation of new policy requirements within largely unchanged practices in physical education. We suggest that in relation to the development of health-related work in physical education, this accommodation may have particular significance for gender equity.

HRE in the NCPE: policies and prospects

In now turning attention to policies and practices associated with the National Curriculum for Physical Education, we should first note a further important historical feature of developments within the subject relating to health. During the 1940s and 1950s the focus upon physical fitness that was dominant within the male training colleges became clearly linked with sports performance. Health, associated with the notion of 'fitness for sport', was tied with concerns over the national standing in international sport, focusing primarily on males (Kirk, 1992). In the development of a National Curriculum for Physical Education in England and Wales at the end of the 1980s, sport was the reference point for the structure and focus of curriculum requirements (Penney and Evans, 1999). As we explain below, from the outset 'health' was positioned in relation to the central focus on sport. Discourses of sport, not health, provided the foundation for the NCPE. Any analysis of the position and nature of health in the context of the NCPE needs to acknowledge this characteristic. The dominance of discourses of sport can be seen as not only setting a frame for the development of health in the NCPE, but as setting an openly gendered frame for development, that would have implications for the particular discourses of health that would be deemed (by policy-makers and by teachers) to have a legitimate place in the policies and practices of the NCPE.

In a similar way to which equal opportunities was identified as of central importance in the development of the NCPE and yet at the same time seemingly marginalised in the texts issued (see Penney, chapter 7 in this text), health-related exercise can be seen to have suffered a similar fate. The NCPE working group identified 'an urgent need for a coherent programme of education about exercise in order to establish its relevance and stimulate increased activity patterns' (DES/WO, 1991: 62). Yet, neither the working group's final report nor the statutory order that followed in 1992 provided an outline of such a programme. The commentary addressing implementation of requirements relating to health-related exercise remained at the level of broad guidance and pointers for prospective development. There was acknowledgement that there were many instances and different contexts in which health-related exercise could be incorporated in implementation of the NCPE. The need for 'reinforcement' of health-related concepts in the various areas of activity was also stressed, but as we explain below, the extent to which this need was pursued in the programmes of study for the respective areas of activity was limited. Health-related exercise was not *an* area of activity within the NCPE, but rather, was a matter that the working group acknowledged could and should be addressed in the context of requirements relating to the specified areas. We suggest that both this relational position and the lack of specificity about when, where and how teachers should develop health-related exercise work in the context of physical education, were key characteristics of the NCPE in relation to our interest in gender equity. In particular, we see these as characteristics that have meant that important potential for health-related work to extend the gender discourses expressed in physical education has not always been realised in practice. Furthermore, they have meant that health-related exercise could be developed in ways that reinforced stereotypical images and understandings relating to men's and women's participation in physical activity.

The working group noted that work focusing on health-related exercise shared with all other work in physical education the requirement for the experiences provided to 'respect pupils as individuals with different experiences, capabilities and preferences' and added that 'there is an important message that everyone can succeed in exercise' (DES/WO, 1991: 62). In the light of the data below, the absence of a comment to the effect that planning and teaching of health-related exercise work should also seek to challenge stereotypical attitudes and beliefs that may constitute a barrier to engagement in particular forms of exercise, was a notable omission.

Recalling our discussion of historical developments, the use of the term health-related *exercise* in the NCPE working group's final report was not insignificant. It signalled a privileging of particular discourses in preference to others. It appeared to legitimate and promote a focus upon holistic orientations towards health, acknowledging physical, affective and cognitive dimensions, and recognising the social and cultural construction of health (Stacey, 1988) in contexts of physical education. We contrast this orientation with the comparatively narrow orientation embraced in developments previously associated with health-related fitness (HRF). The focus on HRE can also be seen to reflect concerns about levels of physical activity in young people's lives and desires for education to be directed towards encouraging participation in regular exercise of moderate intensity (Blair and Connelly, 1994) as a feature of lifestyle (Armstrong and Welsman, 1997; Sports Council and Health Education Authority (HEA), 1992). The government's strategy for the health of the population of England (Department of Health, 1992) that was issued at the time of the introduction of the NCPE identified schools as key settings for health promotion and highlighted the role that physical education had to play in teaching the skills and understanding associated with adopting active lifestyles. Again, we can note the contrast with previous developments and specifically, tendencies for HRF to be associated with effective performance in high intensity activity in contexts of competitive sport. However, as we will see, the absence of detailed development of HRE requirements in the NCPE meant that there was no guarantee that the broader conceptualisation would be developed in practice. The flexibility inherent in the NCPE requirements relating to the development of health-related exercise (that can also be read as a lack of clarity) meant that there was the scope for discourses more aligned with HRF than HRE to come to the fore in implementation, and furthermore, be positioned alongside and in contrast to discourses of HRE in an openly gendered way.

As explained above, HRE was not identified as an area of activity in the NCPE. Instead, it was addressed in the context of general programmes of study outlined for each of the four key stages of teaching and learning[2] and also, within the statements developed to describe 'the knowledge, skills and understanding which pupils of different abilities and maturities can be expected to achieve at the end of the key stage in question' (DES/WO, 1992: 5). Programmes of study were designed to set out 'the matters, skills and processes which are required to be taught to pupils of different abilities and maturities during each key stage' (ibid.: 4). In physical education these comprised 'general' programmes of study for each key stage and activity-specific programmes of study for each key stage that related to the six areas of activity established within the NCPE (of athletic activities; dance; games; gymnastic activities; outdoor and adventurous activities; and swimming). The following requirements relating to key stage 3 illustrate the way in which HRE was positioned and articulated within the NCPE. Among the end of key stage statements for this key stage was the statement that pupils should be able to 'understand the short- and long-term effects of exercise on the body systems and decide where to focus their involvement in physical activity for a healthy and enjoyable lifestyle' (ibid.: 8). The following points were then incorporated in the general programme of study for this key stage; that pupils should:

- be given the opportunity to plan and undertake simple and safe health-related exercise in the context of different areas of activity, understanding the principles involved;
- be taught to understand the short- and long-term effects of exercise on the body systems;
- be made aware of the increasing need for personal hygiene in relation to vigorous activity;
- be taught how to prepare for and recover from specific activity.

(ibid.: 8)

When and where these points would be addressed in implementation of the NCPE, and specifically, fulfilment of the activity specific programmes of study, was a matter for teachers to decide upon. The activity specific programmes of study did not expand upon or make any clear linkages to the above points relating to HRE. Instead they focused upon the development of movement skills specific to the area of activity and understanding relating to particular aspects of performance in that area of activity (such as sequencing of movements in gymnastics, or tactical aspects of game play).

The data that we discuss below needs to be viewed in the context of this 'flexibility' (and arguably, lack of clear direction) relating to the implementation of HRE in the NCPE. Notably, the research that we draw upon did not set out to investigate gender issues in that implementation. Rather, it produced data that revealed them as 'an issue' in the implementation of HRE in the NCPE. After providing some key insights into the gendered patterns of development of HRE in contexts of implementation of the NCPE we return to our investigation of policy texts to examine the degree to which more recent NCPE texts have provided prompts to challenge the stereotypical practices that we describe.

Gendered PE: gendered HRE

Between 1993 and 1995 Harris undertook multi-method research addressing the implementation of HRE in the NCPE. This comprised a questionnaire survey of heads of physical education departments in 1000 secondary schools in England, and interviews, participant observation and documentary research in three selected case study schools. The survey aimed to provide data that would describe the provision of HRE in schools and explore factors potentially influencing this provision. Utilising focused interviews with physical education staff and documentary research, the case study investigations sought to provide further insights into teachers' views, approaches and practices relating to HRE in physical education. Three mixed-sex state secondary schools (11–16 age range) randomly selected in each of the South, Midlands and North of England were used for this phase of the research. Further details of the research methods are reported in Harris (1995, 1997a) and findings have been the subject of several previous publications (see for example Harris, 1995, 1997a, 1997b, 1998; Harris and Penney, 2000; Penney and Harris, 1997, 1998).

Scraton (1987) has described school physical education as overtly reinforcing gender differences in terms of the activities offered, and covertly through the attitudes of policy-makers and practitioners. Although it was not specifically directed towards the exploration of equity issues, Harris' research revealed the way in which implementation of the NCPE was occurring within clearly gendered patterns of curriculum organisation and gendered frames of reference. Overall, data supported Scraton's (1986) notion that separate and different physical education programmes remain a central and institutionalised feature of education in England, reflecting stereotypical assumptions about the respective educational needs, interests and abilities of girls and boys. Harris identified distinct differences in the curriculum provided for boys as compared to girls and found evidence to suggest that the NCPE was being developed differently by male and female staff respectively. The context of implementation of HRE within the NCPE was one in which sex-differentiated patterns of provision and staffing remained intact in physical education and in many instances, seemed destined to reinforce stereotypical images of masculinity and femininity and of the physical activities that men and women can participate in. For example, Harris' data revealed that boys had access to a broader and different range of games than girls, that girls and boys were introduced to different styles of gymnastics and that dance, if offered at all, was provided only, or predominantly for, girls and was usually delivered by female staff (see Harris, 1997a). Below we explore the ways in which sex-differentiated provision was evidenced in HRE specifically.

The first point to stress is the complex dynamic between staffing arrangements, grouping strategies and curriculum provision in physical education. The practicalities of timetabling (of staff, pupils and facilities) have very clear influences upon the provision that is deemed possible. However, when we address staffing arrangements in physical education and decisions relating to the activities that children will experience and the grouping strategies that will be employed in provision, we invariably encounter gender issues. Gender issues underpin and/or are inextricably bound up with decisions that are often described in relation to pragmatics of provision. For example, a teacher at one of Harris' case study schools explained that:

> The last couple of years there has been a problem – it's tended to be one man and two women. . . . Next year, we're going to have to go to mainly mixed groups . . . you can't have one member of staff being left with forty-odd. We'd quite like to keep it single sex – I think it suited both pairs of staff. We got on with what we had to do and they got on with what they had to do. We've got no real preference apart from, say, major games where we want single sex because you don't really want the girls around when you're doing rugby or football.
>
> (Male Head of Physical Education,
> State Comprehensive School, 1995)

The reference to games and the specific desire for this to be an area in which sex differentiated provision is retained, is important. In some schools, this desire may determine (and constrain) the grouping arrangements adopted for other aspects of the physical education curriculum. One head of department illustrated the way in which logistical issues associated with the privileging of games have these wider-reaching effects on the physical education curriculum:

> You can do them (health-related blocks) mixed and we'd be happy to do that but because of the structure of the timetable it would mean that we can't, we don't have the resources for everybody to do the health unit at the same time. So, that means that two groups can be doing the health module using the space that is required and two groups would be doing a games module. What that means, then, is the games module has to be a single sex module, then the health module has to be a single sex group. Once you've got a single sex module working with one group you can't mix it with the other group, you're tied in, as much as you might want to do it . . . I think I would prefer to have mixed lessons on that (health module), but . . . there are the practical problems.
>
> (Male Head of Physical Education,
> State Comprehensive School, 1995)

In the majority of mixed-sex schools, HRE was delivered in mixed-sex discrete units for the younger years and that over half of schools had mixed-sex units for the older years. Interestingly, Harris' research showed that more male than female heads of physical education organised HRE in mixed-sex groups for most year groups. This latter finding was consistent with that of Caldecott (1992) who reported that male teachers were in favour of mixing

Table 8.1 HRE theoretical content within the PE curriculum in secondary schools in England

HRE theoretical content	%
Stamina/Cardiovascular health	92.0
Suppleness/Flexibility/Stretching	87.4
Muscular strength and endurance	84.2
Fitness testing	61.0
Designing exercise programmes	46.6
Weight management	29.0
Relaxation/Stress management	21.4
Other	4.7

Percentage figures represent the proportion of the sample of secondary schools (N = 728) involved in the various activities. The sample comprised 41 per cent (299 out of 728) female and 59 per cent (429 out of 728) male responses.

boys with girls for health-related lessons whereas female teachers were of a more divided opinion. Harris' research suggests that there is also a link between teachers' grouping preferences and the age of pupils, with developmental issues being the key concern here. One teacher explained the thinking and subsequent grouping arrangements, saying that:

> I think keeping them (Year 9s) separate was a better idea with the fitness ... with the (Year) 9s I think, because, obviously, going through puberty and so on, I think that would work better single sex.
>
> (Female teacher responsible for Girls' Physical Education, State Comprehensive School, 1995)

Other data from Harris' work leads us to call for further investigation of the implications of sex differentiated staffing and/or grouping arrangements for HRE. Data relating to the theoretical aspects of HRE respectively developed by male and female teachers and the practical activity contexts that they respectively utilised in their teaching of HRE, indicates that if single sex grouping is adopted in the older years and if this is accompanied by sex differentiated staffing arrangements, girls and boys may receive very different versions of 'HRE'. More specifically, they may receive versions of HRE that openly legitimate and reinforce stereotypically gendered discourses of 'fitness', 'health' and 'exercise' in physical education.

With respect to the *theoretical content*[3] associated with HRE, table 8.1 illustrates the range of content variously featuring in the HRE developments within the schools in Harris' research.

The survey revealed statistically significant gender differences[4] in the theoretical content respectively addressed by female and male heads of physical education departments. More female heads of department included relaxation and stress management in HRE, while more male heads of department included strength work and fitness testing. Female teachers in two case study schools acknowledged that they were paying minimal attention to strength work within their HRE units and expressed the concern that 'formal' testing may adversely affect pupils' attitudes towards physical education. Questionnaire data showed that male heads of department included more fitness testing in curricula than their female counterparts, and revealed differences in the emphasis placed upon specific components of fitness by male and female teachers respectively. More female teachers incorporated flexibility tests and more males included upper body strength tests. Further, more males than females utilised measurement instruments such as flexibility testers, weighing scales, 'sit and reach' boxes, heart rate monitors, skinfold calipers and dynamometers.

Alongside these observed differences it is important to also register the overall privileging of particular content and the apparent marginalisation of other knowledge and understanding relating to HRE. The relatively few instances of teachers incorporating weight and stress management into HRE seem worthy of note. If physical education is concerned with lifelong issues, there are clearly arguments for raising the profile of both issues and further-more, to do so in the curricula provided for both girls and boys. In the case of weight management particularly, there are dangers that this may be regarded as something that is only relevant to girls and that therefore should only feature in the HRE provided for girls. While weight management may be a matter which has particular resonance with many girls, which features heavily in many women's involvement in physical activity, and which will demand particular sensitivity in the design of learning experiences, it is clearly an issue of relevance to all young people. If physical education (and HRE specifically) is to contribute towards the reduction of social pressures upon young people (both boys and girls) to be a particular shape, to challenge the tendencies that pupils themselves may have to accord very different social status to different bodies, and to extend understanding of the complex relationships between physical activity, fitness, health, weight and body shape, we need curricula for both girls and boys that actively engage them with these issues. We therefore see the predominance of content that appears to link with discourses of scientific functionalism as a concern for the education and lives of many girls, but also, many boys.

As indicated, statistically significant gender differences were also noted in the *practical activity focus* of HRE. The range of activities featuring in HRE within the schools in Harris' research are detailed in table 8.2.

In the compulsory physical education curriculum, more male than female heads of department included cross-country running, circuit-training, weight-training (both fixed and free weights) and keep fit in the compulsory physical education curriculum. More female heads of department included skipping in the curriculum. With respect to optional activities within curricula, more females offered aerobics and skipping, and more males offered cross-country running. Case study findings revealed similar differences in the

Table 8.2 HRE practical activities in the PE curriculum (compulsory and optional) and extra-curricular programme in secondary schools in England

HRE practical activity	Compulsory %	Optional %	Extra-curricular %
Cross country running	61.5	21.4	40.0
Circuit training	56.2	25.8	19.1
Aerobics	40.5	49.5	34.1
Skipping	29.1	10.2	5.6
Jogging	25.3	15.4	17.0
Weight training (fixed weights)	21.2	36.8	26.5
Keep fit	13.0	13.2	8.9
Weight training (free weights)	12.4	21.8	17.2
Step aerobics	6.2	17.4	12.1
Water exercise	6.2	7.4	4.3
Other	1.8	0.4	1.1

Percentage figures represent the proportion of the sample of secondary schools (N = 728) involved in the various activities. The sample comprised 41 per cent (299 out of 728) female and 59 per cent (429 out of 728) male responses.

activities respectively provided for girls and boys, pointing to the significance of underpinning sex differentiated patterns of staffing, whereby female staff take responsibility for developing a curriculum for girls, while men do likewise for boys. For example, in one school, at key stage four, the girls' HRF[5] course covered a range of aerobic-type activities while the boys' course focused on 'sporting activities'.[6]

Similar differences were observed in the content of extra-curricular programmes. The survey revealed that more female heads of department offered aerobics and step aerobics, while in contrast, more male heads of department included weight training (see Harris, 1997a for further detail of the data). Furthermore, in each case study school, aerobics and step aerobics were selected primarily if not exclusively by girls. The absence of boys participating in these activities can obviously be associated with the fact that the activities were only introduced in the curriculum for girls and were delivered only by female teachers.

Throughout Harris' data we see a tendency for girls and boys to be viewed as having quite distinct needs and interests, which, particularly as they get older, are deemed such that separate provision and/or different curricula are seen as appropriate. Further research is needed to pursue the degree to which single-sex grouping is accompanied by sex-differentiated staffing and/or curriculum provision. This needs to incorporate critical reflection upon the degree to which such provision may be limiting the educational experiences, knowledge and understanding, but also, future life chances, of some girls and some boys. There are certainly strong arguments for developments that raise the profile of activities that have particular appeal as leisure activities for women and that will appeal to many girls (see Flintoff and Scraton, 2001;

Markula, 1995; McDermott, 1996; Obel, 1996; Talbot, 1993; Whitson, 1994). However, issues of appeal and relevance in pupils' eyes need to considered within the context of concerns to introduce both girls and boys to a broad range of activities and in so doing, to be challenging narrow stereotypical preconceptions about who may legitimately participate in particular activities. In Wortley's (1994) view the elimination of gender bias in provision and developing a wide variety of activities for all pupils is a prerequisite to the successful development of healthy active lifestyles. In Harris' research girls and boys were talked about as homogenous groups and simplistic generalisations about, for example, the health-related activities that 'suit' girls or boys respectively, appeared to be informing planning. Thus, while HRE was an arena that at times clearly directed attention towards the individual (for example, with pupils developing personalised training programmes) it seemed to be largely failing to acknowledge some key individual differences. The data has prompted us to question whether teachers and pupils are engaging with the complexities of gender and with multiple femininities and masculinities within and via HRE, and how issues of ethnicity, sexuality and class are being addressed in HRE provided for either girls or boys. In the next section we explore whether revisions to the NCPE have provided any prompts for these issues to be addressed in the development of HRE. We explain how HRE has been repositioned in the context of two revisions of the NCPE and describe specific changes made to the requirements relating to HRE. Once again we pursue from a gender equity perspective, the particular discourses of health and fitness being privileged, or alternatively, subordinated, in the official texts.

HRE in the NCPE: repositioned; redefined?

The first revision of the NCPE (DfE/WO, 1995) saw few changes to the specific content of HRE. Instead, the changes were largely structural, with references to health-related work being repositioned as part of new 'introductory statements' for each key stage and within the 'End of Key Stage Descriptions' which summarised what pupils should know, understand and be able to do by the end of each key stage. The extract below, which again relates to requirements for key stage 3, shows that this change in position was not accompanied by notable changes in terminology or focus. Furthermore, the continued absence of comprehensive guidance relating to how teachers should develop HRE within their implementation of the NCPE meant that the re-positioning was likely to have very little effect upon established patterns of provision and approaches to teaching HRE.

The revised requirements for key stage 3 featured an introductory statement to the programmes of study that stated:

> Throughout the key stage, pupils should be given opportunities to engage in health-promoting physical activity, where possible within the local community. They should be taught: how to prepare for particular

activities and to recover afterwards; the short-term and long-term effects of exercise on the various body systems; the role of exercise in establishing and maintaining health.

(DfE/WO, 1995: 6)

The End of Key Stage Description identified that by the end of the key stage:

Pupils devise strategies and tactics for appropriate activities, and plan or compose more complex sequences of movements. They adapt and refine existing skills and apply these to new situations. Pupils show that they can use skills with precision, and perform sequences with greater clarity and fluency. Pupils recognise the importance of rules and apply them. They appreciate strengths and limitations in performance and use this information in co-operative team work as well as to outwit the opposition in competition. *They understand the short-term and long-term effects of exercise on the body systems, and demonstrate how to prepare for particular activities and how to recover after vigorous physical activity.*

(DfE/WO), 1995: 11, our emphasis)

Again, discourses that can be related back to the gendered history of the subject, that celebrate certain values, and certain bodies, were foregrounded in contemporary policy. Discourses relating to health-related exercise were also clearly positioned in a supporting relationship to discourses of performance in sport.

The more recent revision of the NCPE in 2000 (Department for Education and Employment (DfEE)/Qualifications and Curriculum Authority (QCA), 1999) has arguably further reinforced these characteristics. 'Knowledge and understanding of fitness and health' was one of four aspects of skills, knowledge and understanding that were established as a focus for the development of programmes of study relating to each of the key stages and to the various areas of activity. The other aspects identified were:

- acquiring and developing skills;
- selecting and applying skills, tactics and compositional ideas; and
- evaluating and improving performance.

(DfEE/QCA, 1999: 6)

In this revision of the NCPE, eight level descriptions replaced the previous end of key stage descriptions. By the end of key stage 3 the majority of pupils are expected to have reached or exceeded level 5, which was described in the following terms:

Pupils select and combine their skills, techniques and ideas and apply them accurately and appropriately, consistently showing precision, control and fluency. When performing, they draw on what they know about strategy, tactics and composition. They analyse and comment on skills and techniques and how these are applied in their own and others' work. They modify and redefine skills and techniques to improve their performance. *They explain how the body reacts during different types of exercise, and warm up and cool down in ways that suit the activity. They explain why regular, safe exercise is good for fitness and health.*

(DfEE/QCA, 1999: 42, our emphasis)

The changes in terminology here are important when we recall (from Harris' data) the language typically being used by male and female teachers respectively when talking about their health-related work within the NCPE. The predominantly male focus on physical fitness for performance in sport has been legitimated while other interests, expressed more often by female teachers, are absent. An accompanying text issued by the QCA, entitled 'Terminology in physical education' reinforces the specific focus being promoted in and via the NCPE. The QCA defined fitness as 'sufficient bodily function to carry out [a] specific task safely', and described 'fitness for purpose' via the following examples:

- Sufficient bodily capacity and function to carry out a task efficiently without strain;
- Strong enough to prop up a scrum;
- Strong enough to control or 'spot' a landing when jumping off apparatus;
- Enough stamina to maintain rapid pace for more than 30 seconds.

(QCA, 1999: 7)

Our interest here is in how these particular discourses of 'fitness and health' relate to established and stereotypical discourses of the body, of health, and of physical activity 'for' men and women – or HRE/F 'for' girls and boys. We question the degree to which the official texts can be regarded as promoting the development of practices in physical education (and health-related work specifically) that will be inclusive of all children's needs and interests, and specifically, their lifelong health interests. Recent research by Cale and colleagues[7] has reaffirmed that sex differentiation remains a characteristic of the NCPE in some schools and more specifically, that the new requirements relating to 'knowledge and understanding of fitness and health' are, in some instances, being expressed in ways that openly reinforce gender stereotyping. For example, a male head of physical education explained that:

We deliver a slightly different programme in KS3. Boys do not do dance. Boys do no gym in Year 9. KS4 choices operate, mainly restricted to football, basketball, cricket, athletics for boys; netball, aerobics, badminton, tennis, rounders, athletics for girls.

(Male Head of Department, State Comprehensive School, 2000)

In relation to health-related work specifically, teachers variously explained that

> the use of the multigym has a different emphasis for boys and girls generally – i.e. strength development *v.* toning and muscular endurance. In cardiovascular type work, the emphasis tends to be on running activities for the boys and aerobics type work for the girls.
>
> > (Male Head of Department, State Comprehensive School, 2000)

> Girls – aerobics and step aerobics. Boys – more work in multi-gym on strength and power.
>
> > (Female Head of Department, State Comprehensive School, 2000)

> Boys and girls taught separately but content is the same at KS3. At KS4 girls more towards aerobic type exercise than boys.
>
> > (Male Head of Department, State Comprehensive School, 2000)

These quotations illustrate the way in which the flexibility inherent in the NCPE requirements can result in continued gender inequity within and beyond physical education. In this context, guidance and training clearly has a key role to play in extending awareness and understandings in ways that will prompt the development of practices that challenge narrow and gender stereotyped images and understandings relating to men's and women's participation in physical activity and sport, what constitutes a healthy body, and what it is to 'be fit'. In the final section of our discussion we therefore turn our attention to guidance material that has been specifically developed to support teachers' development of health-related exercise in the context of their implementation of the revised NCPE.

Guidance and gaps: resistance and reproduction

The guidance material, authored by Harris (2000), was the product of a working group that included primary and secondary school teachers, lecturers, advisers/inspectors, consultants and representatives of national organisations relating to health, sport, exercise and the curriculum. Given the shift in terminology in the NCPE, the retention of a focus on health-related *exercise* is in itself notable. Definitions of terms further reinforce the way in which the guidance material has been designed to 'go beyond' the 'official discourses' of fitness and health. In contrast to the QCA's definition, Harris (2000) describes fitness as 'a capacity or a set of attributes that individuals have or achieve that enable them to participate in and benefit from physical activity' (p. 1) and adds that 'Fitness has physical and mental dimensions' (ibid.: 1). Harris also makes explicit that fitness can be associated with various interests, referring to 'fitness for life' and 'fitness for health' as well as 'fitness for performance' and 'skill-related fitness' (ibid.: 1). The concern to broaden thinking and to encourage the development of health-related work that extends beyond an exclusive focus upon a supporting function for performance in sport is evident throughout the materials. Encouraging and enabling all young people to participate in physical activity within and beyond schools, and ensuring that they enjoy doing so in the context of physical education, are principles underpinning the guidance offered to teachers about their approach to the development of HRE in the NCPE, their teaching approaches and assessment. Harris specifically addresses the need for teachers to consider notions of 'developmentally appropriate' and suitably differentiated physical activity. The guidance goes on to explicitly consider the ways in which health-related activities within physical education can be 'inclusive'. Harris (2000) states that:

> To promote current and future involvement in physical activity effectively, exercise experiences should be offered that meet individual needs and preferences. In practising and promoting the principle of equity, it is necessary to integrate all pupils including the least active, least competent and those with learning, physical or sensory impairments or specific health conditions.
>
> (p. 20)

Although Harris stresses that 'Often, the main barrier to participation in physical activity is not a specific medical condition or impairment but the attitudinal, economic and environmental barriers that society places in the way' (p. 21), the absence of any commentary on the way in which gender issues may be at the heart of much practice and many barriers seems a missed opportunity to raise awareness and prompt changes in practice. The silence on the issues that have emerged and continue to emerge from research, may be in danger of leaving a door open for stereotypical practices to continue in contexts of HRE within the NCPE.

Conclusion

Previously it has been proposed that a health-related approach to the development of physical education in schools is more likely to provide an equitable environment for pupils (Carrington and Leaman, 1986; McKenzie *et al.*, 1996; Williams, 1989) and that a health-based physical education programme can allow girls and less skilful students to feel more centrally involved in lessons (Velert and Devis, 1995). The findings from our research clearly call into question any assumed links between a focus on HRE and more equitable educational experiences. We stress that the practices that we have described should not be regarded as a feature of provision of HRE in *all* schools in England. Nevertheless, we regard it as noteworthy that our investigations have pointed to the existence of distinct 'female' and 'male' versions of HRE, considered appropriate 'for girls' and 'for boys' respectively. At least in some schools it seems that girls and boys are being given opportunities to develop quite *different* knowledge, understanding and skills in relation to health, fitness and physical activity. In these respects, the impression arising from the research is that the introduction of and subsequent revisions to the NCPE has had very little impact upon long-established beliefs and practices. The strength of the gendered divisions within health-related work in physical education and, more importantly, the absence of any prospect of change to this situation were highlighted by the following teacher who commented that:

> with regard to some areas such as HRF, we have different approaches to some of our work. This may not be politically correct but it has been discussed at length, without agreement, and the situation remains.
>
> (Male head of physical education,
> State Comprehensive School, 1993)

The extent and impact of the differences that we have identified in the respective approaches of male and female teachers and in the skills, knowledge and understanding that is being pursued by them in their development of HRE, are well worthy of further exploration. There is also a need to develop better understandings of what underpins the differences that we have observed. Clearly, the very conservative discursive frame (Penney and Evans, 1999) for curriculum development that has been set by the NCPE does not encourage the development of 'alternative' discourses of health, fitness and physical activity. Initial teacher training is an arena in which important foundations can be laid to enable and encourage teachers to explore the flexibility inherent in the NCPE (and specifically in its requirements relating to 'fitness and health') in ways that actively promote gender equity. However, the discursive frames shaping practices in initial teacher training in England are also extremely conservative (Evans *et al.*, 1996). HRE invariably remains marginalised in initial teacher training, subsumed within and subordinate to an overriding focus upon the development of skills, knowledge and understanding relating to particular areas of activity. The discourses of HRE that emerge from such contexts are likely to be ones that are compatible with and that serve to legitimate and reinforce the dominant discourses of elite sport performance.

Continuing professional development thus seems the key forum in which to promote alternative readings of policies and the development of practices that privilege discourses that are currently subordinated. If we are serious about gender equity, we cannot be content with the uncritical acceptance of the dominance of established discourses of fitness and health within the ongoing implementation of the NCPE. In failing to respond to the dominance, physical education teachers and teacher educators will be failing to respond to sustained inequities in schooling and in society and, furthermore, will be playing a part in the reproduction of those inequities. As others, we do not pretend that challenging and/or changing the dominance of particular discourses within and beyond the profession is easy. There are clearly many ideological, political and organisational barriers to overcome (Goodson, 1993, 1995; Penney and Evans, 1997). However, we also see a need to acknowledge that silence on these issues is by no means a neutral stance. We remain committed to a view that teaching and learning in HRE *can* be an arena in which we may actively challenge, deconstruct and reconstruct in new ways, views and images of the physical activities that girls and boys can legitimately pursue. Flintoff and Scraton (2001) have stressed the need for physical education to offer opportunities for young women to develop physical identities that are 'other than the antithesis of men – less able, less strong and less competitive' (p. 8). However, enabling and encouraging the development of a broader range of physical identities is important for the inclusion of many boys as well as many girls. It is a critical issue to address if physical education is to succeed in providing learning environments 'in which young people (girls and boys) acquire respect for themselves and each other' (Humberstone, 1993: 218) and in which we promote 'reciprocal under-standing and valuing between girls and boys' (ibid.: 218). We are very aware that training and ongoing support for teachers will be essential to such progress in physical education, and in HRE specifically. The relationship between difference in provision and equity in provision is far from straight-forward. The issues are complex and as we have seen, there appears at times 'remarkable resilience to change' (Williams and Bedward, 1999: 31) within physical education. But as Macdonald discusses in this text, the action required extends beyond physical education and beyond schools. We need change not only 'in the form and content of PE in schools but also a change in the deep structures of communication throughout education and society' (Humberstone, 1993: 219).

Acknowledgement

This paper draws on the following research project which is funded by the Nuffield Foundation: Cale, L. and Harris, J. (2001) *The Impact of Health-related Exercise Guidance Material on Secondary School Physical Education Teachers in England and Wales*. The support of the Nuffield Foundation is greatly appreciated.

Notes

1 The specific reference to England acknowledges that although early National Curriculum texts were developed for all state schools in England and Wales, subsequent separate documentation and requirements has been specific to each country.
2 The NC proposed a new nomenclature for the years of schooling comprising four key stages (KS): KS 1 (reception, Years 1 and 2, age 5–7 years); KS 2 (Years 3–6, age 7–11 years); KS 3 (Years 7–9, age 11–14 years; KS 4 (Years 10–11, age 14–16 years) (DES, 1989).

3 This term reflects an ongoing tendency within physical education in England and Wales, to disassociate disciplinary knowledge from practical activity, and thus to refer to 'theory' and 'practice' as distinct elements of curricula.

4 In this paper, only statistically significant differences (at the conventional 0.05 level) are reported from the research. See Harris (1997a) for more detailed information on the data.

5 It is notable that the term HRF was retained here, in preference to HRE.

6 Interview data did not indicate the specific activities referred to here.

7 Research by Cale, Harris and Leggett during 2000 examined the impact of the HRE guidance material on provision of HRE within secondary schools in England and Wales. A questionnaire was administered to a stratified sample of heads of PE departments in 500 state secondary schools in England and Wales. The questionnaire data were analysed using SPSS (Norusis/SPSS Inc., 1990; Cale and Harris, 2001).

References

Armstrong, N. and Welsman, J. (1997) *Young People and Physical Activity*, Oxford: Oxford University Press.

Biddle, S. (ed.) (1987) *Foundations of Health-Related Fitness in Physical Education*, London: Ling Publishing Company.

Bowe, R. and Ball, S.J. with Gold, A. (1992) *Reforming Education and Changing Schools: Case Studies in Policy Sociology*, London: Routledge.

Caldecott, S.W. (1992) A study of teachers' practices, perceptions and further intentions regarding health-related fitness, *Bulletin of Physical Education* 28(1): 33–9.

Cale, L. and Harris, J. (2001) *The Impact of Health-Related Exercise Guidance Material on Secondary School Physical Education Teachers in England and Wales*, Nuffield Foundation Research Project Report, Loughborough University.

Carrington, B. and Leaman, O. (1986) Equal opportunities and physical education, in J. Evans (ed.) *Physical Education, Sport and Schooling: Studies in the Sociology of Physical Education*, London: Falmer Press, pp. 215–26.

Department for Education/Welsh Office (DfE/WO) (1995) *Physical Education in the National Curriculum*, London: HMSO.

Department for Education and Employment (DfEE)/Qualifications and Curriculum Authority (QCA) (1999) *Physical Education: The National Curriculum for England*, London: HMSO.

Department of Education and Science (DES) (1989) *National Curriculum: From Policy to Practice*, London: HMSO.

Department of Education and Science (DES)/Welsh Office (WO) (1991) *Physical Education for Ages 5–16: Proposals of the Secretary of State for Education and the Secretary of State for Wales*, London: DES.

Department of Education and Science (DES)/Welsh Office (WO) (1992) *Physical Education in the National Curriculum*, London: HMSO.

Department of Health (1992) *The Health of the Nation: A Strategy for Health in England*, London: HMSO.

Flintoff, A. and Scraton, S. (2001) Stepping into active leisure? Young women's perceptions of active lifestyles and their experiences of school physical education, *Sport, Education and Society* 6(1): 5–21.

Goodson, I. (1993) *School Subjects and Curriculum Change. Studies in Curriculum History* (3rd edition), London: Falmer Press.

Goodson, I.F. (1995), *The Making of Curriculum: Collected Essays* (2nd edition), London: Falmer Press.

Harris, J. (1995) Physical education: a picture of health?, *British Journal of Physical Education* 26(4): 25–32.

Harris, J. (1997a) *Physical Education: A Picture of Health? The Implementation of Health-Related Exercise in the National Curriculum in Secondary Schools in England,* unpublished doctoral thesis, Loughborough University.

Harris, J. (1997b) Good practice guidelines for HRE, *British Journal of Physical Education* 28(4): 9–11.

Harris, J. (1998) Health-related exercise: rationale and recommendations', *British Journal of Physical Education* 29(3): 11–12.

Harris, J. (2000) *Health-Related Exercise in the National Curriculum: Key Stages 1 to 4.* Champaign, IL: Human Kinetics.

Harris, J. and Penney, D. (2000) Gender issues in health-related exercise, *European Physical Education Review* 6(3): 249–73.

Humberstone, B. (1993) Equality, physical education and outdoor education: ideological struggles and transformative structures?, in J. Evans (ed.) *Equality, Education and Physical Education,* London: Falmer Press, pp. 74–89.

Kirk, D. (1992) *Defining Physical Education: The Social Construction of a School Subject in Postwar Britain,* London: Falmer Press.

Markula, P. (1995) Firm but shapely, fit but sexy, strong but thin: the postmodern aerobicizing female bodies, *Sociology of Sport Journal* 12: 424–53.

McDermott, L. (1996) Towards a feminist understanding of physicality within the context of women's physically active and sporting lives, *Sociology of Sport Journal* 13: 12–30.

McIntosh, P. (1968) *Physical Education in England since 1800,* London: Bell & Sons.

McKenzie, T.L., Nader, P.R., Strikmiller, P.K., Yang, M., Stone, E. and Perry, C.L. (1996) School physical education: effect of the child and adolescent trial for cardiovascular health, *Preventive Medicine* 25: 423–31.

McNair, D. (1985) The historical concept of health and fitness: a review, in *British Universities Physical Education Association Conference Proceedings*, Belfast: Queens University, pp. 99–119.

Norusis, M. J./SPSS Inc. (1990) *SPSS Base System User's Guide: SPSS Statistical Data Analysis,* Chicago, IL: SPSS Inc.

Obel, C. (1996) Collapsing gender in competitive bodybuilding: researching contradictions and ambiguity in sport, *Review for the Sociology of Sport* 31(2): 185–200.

Penney, D. and Evans, J. (1997) Naming the game: discourse and domination in physical education and sport in England and Wales, *European Physical Education Review* 3(1): 21–32.

Penney, D. and Evans, J. (1999) *Politics, Policy and Practice in Physical Education,* London: E & FN Spon.

Penney, D. and Harris, J. (1997) Extra-curricular physical education: more of the same for the more able?, *Sport, Education and Society* 2(1): 41–54.

Penney, D. and Harris, J. (1998) The National Curriculum for Physical Education: have we got it right?, *British Journal of Physical Education* 29(1): 7–10.

Qualifications and Curriculum Authority (1999) *Terminology in Physical Education,* London: QCA.

School Curriculum and Assessment Authority (SCAA) (1997) Physical education and the health of the nation, in *Conference Proceedings: Full Conference Papers and Discussion Reports*, London: SCAA.

Scraton, S. (1986) Images of femininity and the teaching of girls' physical education, in J. Evans (ed.), *Physical Education, Sport and Schooling: Studies in the Sociology of Physical Education*, London: Falmer Press, pp. 71–94.

Scraton, S. (1987) 'Boys muscle in where angels fear to tread': girls' sub-cultures and physical activities, in J. Horne, D. Jary and A. Tomlinson (eds) *Sport, Leisure and Social Relations*, London: Routledge & Kegan Paul, pp. 160–86.

Sports Council and Health Education Authority (1992) *Allied Dunbar National Fitness Survey: Main Findings*, London: Author.

Stacey, M. (1988) *The Sociology of Health and Healing*, London: Routledge.

Talbot, M. (1993) A gendered physical education: equality and sexism, in J. Evans (ed.) *Equality, Education and Physical Education*, London: Falmer Press, pp. 74–89.

Velert, C.P. and Devis, J.D. (1995) Health-based physical education in Spain: the conception, implementation and evaluation of an innovation, *European Physical Education Review* 1(1): 37–54.

Whitson, D. (1994) The embodiment of gender: discipline, domination and empowerment, in S. Birrell and C. Cole (eds) *Women, Sport and Culture*, Champaign, IL: Human Kinetics.

Williams, A. (1989) Girls and boys come out to play (but mainly boys): gender and physical education, in A. Williams (ed.) *Issues in Physical Education for the Primary Years*, London: Falmer Press, pp. 145–59.

Williams, A. and Bedward, J. (1999) *Games for the Girls: The Impact of Recent Policy on the Provision of Physical Education and Sporting Opportunities for Female Adolescents*, Nuffield Foundation Study.

Wortley, A. (1994) Physical education, in J. Harrison and J. Edwards (eds) *Developing Health Education in the Curriculum*, London: David Fulton Publishers, pp. 110–14.

9 Understanding girls' experience of physical education: relational analysis and situated learning

Anne Williams and Julie Bedward

Introduction

In this chapter we use relational analysis as conceptualised by Apple (1979) and Giddens (1990) in the context of social science, and by Hall (1996) in the context of feminist critique, as a theoretical tool for the exploration of girls' perceptions and experiences of physical education and physical activity in England in the late 1990s. The concept of situated learning, as defined by Lave and Wenger (1991) and Kirk and Macdonald (1998), is also used as an aid to understanding what we conclude is the relative failure, to date, of policies purported to promote curricula which deliver entitlement for all. Our data reveal clear inadequacies in contemporary physical education in relation to the needs and interests of girls.

Relational analysis and situated learning

Kirk (1999) suggests that the value of relational analysis lies in its potential to reveal complexity and to act as an antidote to approaches that over-simplify educational issues through treating them as uni-dimensional. This seems consistent with Hall's (1996) view that relational analysis which acknowledges relationships between categories may be more fruitful than the analysis of categories in isolation. Hall's discussion of relational analysis focuses upon consideration of girls in relation to boys. That is, girls define themselves in relation to boys in different ways with different implications for those seeking to provide relevant physical education programmes for them. Relational analysis is equally useful as a tool for consideration of the experiences of other specific groups within societies, such as different cultural groups. Furthermore, it may provide insights into experiences in school relative to those within the wider community.

As Kirk and Macdonald (1998) have identified, Lave and Wenger's (1991) work on 'situated learning' appears to offer a useful framework for further explorations of this relationship. Although Lave and Wenger (1991) specifically exclude school learning from their discussion of legitimate peripheral participation as a part of situated learning, they nevertheless suggest that learning in the school context could benefit from the application of their thesis. Kirk and Macdonald (1998: 379–80) pursued this potential, explaining that 'Situated learning theories attempt to expand our attention from the learner as an "isolated" individual to include a focus on the social settings that construct and constitute the individual as a learner'. Here we are particularly concerned with inequities in those social settings and the ways in which they are expressed and legitimated via social relationships and within schools. With these interests in mind we pursue the notion (and later, representation in physical education contexts) of 'legitimate peripheral participation' (Lave and Wenger, 1991).

As part of the learning process 'legitimate peripheral participation' implies authentic involvement in the practices of a specific community and acknowledges that progress towards full participation may be affected adversely by denial of access to certain aspects of that community's practice; the social relationships that it promotes, permits and excludes; and who is allowed access to what resources (Kirk and Macdonald, 1998). This prompts us to question the relation of school practices to those of the communities in which schools are located and to investigate the relationship between the world of schooling and the world of adults more generally. While 'legitimate *peripheral* participation' does not preclude learning, an inability to move to *'full* participation', for whatever reason, is certainly relevant in considering the effectiveness of programmes which claim not only to promote learning, but also to interface with the world outside school. Central to the potential move to full participation (and therefore, barriers to realising this potential) are sets of relationships. Participation occurs within the relationships that shape experiences in powerful ways. As we see later, these matters have a particular applicability to our study which specifically sought to further our understanding of how female adolescents conceptualise their participation in physical activity and their participation and learning in physical education. This chapter thus aims to address the need that Kirk (1999) has highlighted, for analyses to go beyond simplistic formulations of participation in various forms of physical culture.

Forms of physical culture and communities of practice

Kirk alludes to the cultural forces within which the construction of identities is located, pointing to the influences of media and advertising as well as social institutions such as school and family. Drawing on Lave and Wenger's (1991) work, Kirk (1999) also proposes the use of the term physical culture to embrace three 'communities of practice' on which physical education draws: sport, physical recreation and exercise. He suggests that currently there is a disjunction between physical education and these associated communities of practice. Here we are concerned to pursue this disjunction in relation to the norms and values that physical educators embrace and then express in their curricula and teaching. Our study has specifically indicated a relative lack of change in physical education practice at a time of rapid and ongoing change in thinking about sport, recreation and exercise.

For Kirk (1999), this relative stability in the cultural practices and norms of the subject and the profession is not only highly problematic but also a critical issue in considering the current state and status of physical education. It may be that teachers insist upon sustaining and privileging the norms and values of their own, school-specific community of practice, rather than seeking to understand and incorporate those of related communities. As Penney and Evans' work has emphasised, it is neither accurate nor appropriate to portray teachers' decisions about these matters as exclusively their own. There are powerful and openly political frames to teachers' thinking and actions, not all of which are easily challenged or deconstructed (see for example, Penney and Evans, 1999). But whatever the collective influences, the situation that we have in many schools in England is that the norms and values of physical education continue to privilege team activities, a highly prescribed uniform chosen by those in authority, and conformity to particular codes of conduct which no longer play any significant part in recreation, exercise or many sports. Thus, disjunction may manifest itself in a variety of ways. Codes of conduct in elite sport may well be very different from those operating within the school context, with the former promoting and the latter dismissing, in some cases, particular behaviours relating for example, to professional fouls and sporting etiquette. The highly prescribed uniform for physical education which is retained by many schools as part of a policy which attempts to protect pupils from the pressures of conforming to transient fashion, not only differs but conflicts with recreational and exercise wear which values individual choice and which promotes such wear as part of the contemporary fashion scene. Individual choice and the scope to express youth, sporting and cultural identities are important issues for physical educationalists to pursue if they are concerned to facilitate engagement in cultures beyond schools. Are physical education and schools failing to provide significant numbers of boys and girls with the skills, knowledge, understanding and experiences that will enable and encourage them to become participants in the communities of practice identified by Kirk? How are they positioning pupils and directing learning in relation to these communities?

The study

The qualitative study from which data for this chapter is drawn aimed to improve understanding of some of the issues which underpin the gender differences which had emerged from earlier work (Williams and Woodhouse, 1996). Further details of the methodological aspects of the research can be found elsewhere (Williams and Bedward, 1999; 2000). Here we provide a brief outline of the focus and design of the study. Specifically, the study sought to pursue:

- the extent to which a 'common curriculum' was available to all pupils and was perceived by them to be equitable;
- the significance of issues such as teaching style, learning context and presentation in relation to these perceptions but also with likely future participation in physical activity and sport in mind;
- relationships between school curriculum experience and out-of-school participation; and
- girls' perceptions of their achievements in physical education.

The study involved the collection of data through interview and lesson observations over a period of half a term (six weeks during 1997 and 1998) in each of three schools, which we have named West Green, North Park and Southside. All three schools are located within a large conurbation. We aimed to achieve a varied sample that would reflect a broad range of experiences in relation to physical education and school sport. Our three schools therefore differed in catchment area, in the quality and quantity of the facilities available for physical education, in specialist staffing levels and staffing deployment. Two of the schools were co-educational, while the third is a single-sex girls' school. This variety was achieved by purposive sampling (Maykut and Morehouse, 1994).

We interviewed 91 students in total, mainly from Year 9 (45) and Year 11 (41). Five students were from Year 10. The student sample was self-selected in that the relevant year group students were invited to participate and volunteered to be interviewed. All students provided written parental consent to participate. Both the students and teachers involved in the research (see below) were given information about the project and about the use that would be made of the data collected. Interviews with the students were held on the school site either before school, during lunchtime and breaks, or after school. Students were given the option of being interviewed individually or in groups. Most (75) were interviewed individually. Group interviews were held with 16 students in seven groups of two or three. The interviews were semi-structured, using hierarchical focusing (Tomlinson, 1989) allowing issues to be explored in depth, and were tape recorded. The ethnic mix of the sample tended to reflect the ethnic mix of the research site. Thirty-three per cent of the students from West Green School and 35 per cent of students from North Park were from minority ethnic groups. At Southside, which served a predominantly white catchment area, just one interviewee was from a minority ethnic group.

Interviews were also held with the physical education teachers who taught the year group samples at each of the schools and again, interviews were conducted on a voluntary basis. Twelve teachers were interviewed all of whom were physical education specialists. All three physical education teachers at West Green were interviewed, one male and two female. Five out of the six physical education staff at North Park were interviewed, all of whom were female; and four out of seven at Southside were interviewed, one male and three female. Most (9) had been in their current posts for some considerable time, that is, between 13 and 24 years. One of the teachers at Southside was in her first year of teaching and two other teachers (one at Southside and one at North Park) were in their second year of teaching. The teacher interviews explored teacher perceptions of the National Curriculum for Physical Education and views on a range of issues relating to physical education provision. All the interview data was analysed using a thematic approach using constant comparative analysis which enabled us both to identify and compare data from different sources within and between schools, and to relate data to the theoretical themes which underpinned the study. Pseudonyms are used throughout our reporting of data.

Activity preferences

In relation to the matter of activity preference students' perceptions seemed largely ability- or context-driven. Our data suggests that we need to be wary of representing girls' attitudes towards different activity areas in over-generalised ways. In 1994 Hargreaves emphasised the gendered notions of sport, with the emphasis on team sports, which have characterised the development and implementation of the national curriculum in England and Wales. She suggested that this has produced a curriculum which stresses activities which girls tend to dislike, that is, team sports, and that diminishes the importance of activities such as dance and gymnastics which appeal more to girls than to boys. We drew similar conclusions from earlier work (Williams and Woodhouse, 1996), reporting that winter team games failed to attract female students. The research reported here leads us to suggest that we cannot make generalisations about girls' physical activity preferences. Specifically, it revealed that while winter team games were anathema to many of our sample, for others they were the highlight of the school week, played with obvious enjoyment and, for these students, their preferred activity choice. Gymnastics, dance and athletics generated equally polarised views. Not surprisingly, students tended to prefer those activities where they felt more competent.

> I'm not really very graceful, I wouldn't say. I'm just not very good at it (gymnastics) so . . . I got laughed at a bit which wasn't very good. I'm just not keen on it.
>
> (Sarah, Year 11 student[1])

> Basically I feel that you have to be good to play against people who actually enjoy them and I just haven't really got much interest in sports. . . . When you have to pick teams and stuff, you feel like, I'm not going to get picked for them and you have to be good.
>
> (Joanne, Year 11 student)

For other some students, these same activities constituted the highlight of their physical education experience.

When we did a performance of gymnastics . . . one person spotted me for this flip thing off the block, and she told everyone else. They were all, 'Watch Ursula in this performance!', and my head swelled. It was good.

(Ursula, Year 11 student)

You're not just relying on yourself, you're relying on other people, you're helping other people. You've got more momentum. You're not just running for yourself, you've got your team and they're shouting for you . . . and you're running a little faster, trying a little harder. And my friends are there.

(Simone, Year 11 student)

The negative view of some activities seemed to be exacerbated by being placed in situations where students felt publicly humiliated, particularly in activities or teaching contexts where individual public performance was demanded.

I did a bit of dance . . . And a couple of times I have had to do it in front of the whole class and it's really embarrassing. So I don't think I like that either.

(Tracey, Year 11 student)

[Gymnastics is Denise's least favourite activity because of] showing it in front of everybody, I suppose, and trying to jump on to those massive boxes that I can't do. It's really embarrassing.

(Denise, Year 9 student)

Nevertheless, it is important to note the gendered division of the curriculum and moreover, students' recognition and criticism of this characteristic. A key issue to emerge with respect to activities offered related to female students' views about the sexist nature of the curriculum offered, resulting from the division of games along traditional lines into boys' and girls' games. In particular most of the girls felt that it was unfair that they were denied the opportunity to play football. Many of the girls had played football at primary school and were critical of the fact that this was not offered to them at secondary school. One student had looked forward to continuing a game begun in primary school.

Well, I don't really like hockey and I enjoy football because I've done football a lot in my primary school. I was going to join a team but then, no. We were going to do a team in Year 7 but then Mr Jacques says you can't.

(Ravinder, Year 9 student)

Another notes the teacher's reaction.

> The teacher says, Oh that's for the boys, you can't play that. I don't think it's really fair because half of us in our year like football, but we don't get the chance to play it.
>
> (Judith, Year 9 student)

At North Park a girls' football club was available at lunchtimes which was extremely popular. However, the girls viewed this as a token gesture and still considered it unfair that football was not taught in physical education lessons.

Students' desire for the inclusion of football in physical education lessons were not limited to those who wished to play it. They saw the situation as a general matter of equal opportunity irrespective of the likely appeal. Similarly they felt that boys should have access to games, such as netball, which were currently restricted to girls. The students' comments may well reflect not merely concerns relating to equal opportunities but also and more specifically, power-relations inherent in physical education and in particular, the scope for them to exercise some power and make some decisions (Laws and Fisher, 1999). One student explained:

> I mean half of the boys probably wouldn't choose netball because they opt for basketball but I think it should be up to the boys, the school shouldn't decide for them and it should be their choice.
>
> (Natalie, Year 9 student)

Teachers appeared to be unaware of the level of interest amongst girls for football outside of school. Robert's belief that 'despite the growth of women's soccer, I still think that there are more girls playing netball when they leave school than are playing football' (Robert, white male head of physical education) is contrary to our evidence. He seemed to be unaware of the level of active interest in football among girls and of the opportunities which now exist for them, outside of school.

> I feel that it is in their interests for us to teach them games that they are actually more likely to be able to follow up after they leave school, so I actually feel that we're better sticking to the traditional range – that we teach rugby to boys and football to boys, basketball to boys, although we have done some mixed basketball, and netball and hockey to girls.
>
> (Robert)

On a reflective note he commented 'I don't think it (football) shouldn't be taught to girls, but I do have a little bit of a mental block about it to be honest, but it's something we may have to think about'.

Preferred teaching contexts

Our data clearly indicated the potential that the context (pedagogical and physical), as much as the activity, has to generate negative views amongst students.

> We have to have it (netball) outside and it's cold. When you've got the ball and you're passing it around it hurts our fingers and if you get caught or anything, the ball's hard and if it hits you it's sore.
>
> (Tracey, Year 9 student)

> I don't like it in the cold because I hate the cold and sometimes we can't wear jogging bottoms when it's really cold she makes us wear a skirt and we don't really like that because of how cold it is.
>
> (Natalie, Year 9 student)

Groupings used in physical education emerged as another critical contextual issue. Much discussion focused on mixed-sex teaching, where students expressed a range of views reflecting significant differences in the way in which they positioned themselves in relation to the boys. This positioning related to playing ability, to concerns about boys' perceptions of the girls' performance and to matters related to appearance. In general, girls who were competent games players welcomed the opportunity to play in mixed-sex teams as they saw playing with and against boys as increasing the competitive element of the game and providing them with more challenges.

> I think I prefer to do it mixed. Especially for tennis. I found that you probably get more competition through boys because of their pride.
>
> (Denise, Year 11 student).

Teachers generally demonstrated an awareness of the potential for other girls' self confidence to be undermined when playing competitive team games against boys, especially after Year 8 when gender differences in relation to physical strength were considered to be more pronounced. As one teacher explained, these differences could result in all but the most able female players being overwhelmed.

> I believe that for the girls who are perhaps not so able, they are disadvantaged mixing with the boys, because the boys are a lot stronger physically and mentally, a lot of the time. . . . I believe that the majority would be held back and they wouldn't want to perform in front of the lads. The lads would take the lead . . . the lads would hog the game, or the practice, or whatever you are doing and the girls would let them. They would stand back and they would rather let them get on with it. . . . Your stronger girls

will be fine; they will cope. Your weaker ones just wouldn't, and they will just cower in the corner somewhere.

(Michael, male head of physical education)

It was notable, however, that while aware of these issues, none of the teachers made any reference to the possibility of intervening to pre-empt such inequities being generated. Instead they appeared to regard particular male–female relationships as inevitable in mixed-sex group settings and as something to be managed rather than changed.

Gymnastics and dance were often identified as activities that students preferred to be offered in single-sex groups, because they considered that the performance aspect of these activities, and the clothing worn, would lead to embarrassment in the presence of the opposite sex. Male–female relationships in which boys were dominant and negative were cited by students as reasons for single-sex teaching and once again, reinforced the important influence of the pedagogical setting on the experiences of pupils.

You have to show the boys your dance and they just laugh. It's really embarrassing. They take the mick out of you. I think it would have been better with just girls in my class, because I would have done it properly, if you know what I mean.

(Teresa, Year 9 student)

A part of the experience of physical education still seems to be inadequately addressed, is that of 'kit' or uniform. Our research revealed significant differences between teacher and student perceptions about the issue of uniform for physical education. At least some of the students' concerns about mixed-sex activities could have been addressed through a different stance in relation to physical education kit. Most of the students accepted the need for a PE kit but felt that this should apply just to the colour of garments worn. They expressed a preference for shorts, jogging bottoms, T-shirts and sweatshirts; namely the type of clothing students would choose to wear for physical activities pursued outside school. The uniform required for physical education was quite different.

The PE skirts are really short, but you have to deal with it because that's the school uniform for PE. And you're not allowed to wear cycling shorts either. I don't think it's fair. . . . We have to wear PE pants. Even though it's not showing your other pants, it's still a bit revealing I think.

(Diane, Year 11 student)

This aspect of uniform rule was in force at all of the research schools. Many students expressed a preference for wearing cycling shorts, and many actually wore these for PE lessons despite being reprimanded.

If, say, you're chubby and you want to wear shorts under your skirt because you get picked on, they (the teachers) don't understand. They always tell you to take them off, but you can't. Like today, we had to stand up whoever didn't have the right PE kit, and I got a warning. . . . I thought it was embarrassing really because I wear shorts every PE lesson, and I get told off for that. I didn't do it. I didn't want to stand up, so I didn't do it.

(Teresa, Year 9 student)

Even where policy was applied consistently to all groups, teachers' arguments against particular choices of clothing seemed to demonstrate more about personal taste and a wish to impose their own definitions of appropriate dress than about sensitivity to adolescents' concerns about decency, and their developing body image. Here the students' preferences were clearly rejected and regarded as incompatible with appropriate dress for physical education.

We did go through a spate of them wanting to wear cycle shorts underneath rather than PE . . . they don't particularly like their PE knickers. It looks absolutely awful. We don't allow that.

(Kim, female head of physical education)

In addition to issues concerning body image, the students also drew attention to more pragmatic matters about what is appropriate and adequate dress for participating in physical activity. It was quite common to find students at one school playing netball during November and December in T-shirts and skirts.

It's just that when it's cold and, like, if you were at home you wouldn't go out in a short skirt and a T-shirt and jumper but for PE we have to. We sometimes can't wear our trousers and . . . It just puts you off totally.

(Helen, Year 9 student)

One of our sample schools had allowed changes to the uniform code that enabled all pupils to wear kit in which they felt comfortable. In another, it appeared that white pupils had to suffer the humiliation of being identified as unacceptably obese before they could access the policy which operated for Asian girls. Both white and Asian students felt that the school policy was unacceptable.

I've had problems this year with a Year 11 young lady who's quite weighty and she had problems trying to get a skirt that fitted her and to be fair to her she tried very hard to get one. And in fact I rang up the stockists for her and tried to get one. But in the end I agreed that she could wear a pair of joggers. That was no problem because as far as I was concerned as long as she was happy and participating I'd rather her be like that then embarrassed and, you know, not wanting to participate.

(Kim, female head of physical education)

Conclusions

In terms of activities within physical education, our findings both confirm the complexity of the issues involved in meeting individual needs (see also Kirk, 1999) and underline the difficulty of finding a common pattern of provision which would meet the needs of all. Our data supports Hargeaves' (1994) advocacy of the pursuit of multiple strategies for the advance of women's and girls' interests in sport and physical education. It has generated issues that are relevant to consider in relation to provision for both boys and girls and perhaps most importantly, has highlighted points of clear disjuncture between the norms and values of school physical education as articulated and reinforced by the teachers, and those of physical activity pursued in other contexts in which many students were involved and to which these students could relate. The disjunction is one that is expressed in various ways and that reflects differential power-relations in schooling. The activity priorities of the school and those of the adolescent girls expected to take part in them are at times openly contradictory, with the girls therefore seeing little relationship between the curriculum offered and their preferred leisure activities. Uniform policy provided one of the clearest examples of disjunction between school-based communities of practice and those related to other physical activity-focused communities. As far as our students were concerned, school expectations within physical education conflicted with out-of-school norms and values and even with school expectations outside the subject. The school concerns appear to prioritise conformity to a mode of dress which is, at best, probably only suitable for those who conform to the stereotypical ideal female body and for participation in a warm indoor environment. Uniform appears to remain as a significant mechanism for social control in many school settings. Students are concerned with warmth, comfort and decency and perceive these as essential prerequisites to enjoyable and meaningful participation in physical activity, regardless of its location.

If we further pursue the responses from the girls, we see that their views of physical education and physical activity are clearly related to ways in which they position themselves relative to boys and to 'male' activities. For some, more equitable provision is about opportunities to 'catch up with the men' (Dyer, 1982), an essentially pragmatic approach, rooted in liberal feminism. These girls want to be able to play 'boys' games' and point to the number of activities available to boys but not to girls, as compared with the single activity, netball, denied to the boys. They see the categorisation of activities along gender lines as anomalous in an education system which has given them equal access to all other areas of the curriculum. For others an inclusive curriculum would involve the opportunity to learn about and participate in more distinctively 'female' activities. These girls appear to locate themselves within a radical feminist paradigm which would support physical education organised by women for women. Such organisation would be on the basis of an equal valuing of activities or approaches which appealed to women and girls, and not on the basis of the assumed biological weaknesses which underpinned separatist developments in physical education earlier this century. It would liberate the girls from domination by boys in co-educational settings or from domination by essentially masculine constructions of activities within single-sex settings. These girls' concerns with their appearance and dress, especially in co-educational settings, and with boys' perceptions of their performance are consistent with radical feminist views about patriarchal power relations (see for example Weiss, 1997).

Our data seems consistent with a view of gender and culture as situated and transient. Our students seemed to position themselves differently, depending upon the context of the conversation. Football within the school context was discussed exclusively in relation to opportunities available to boys but denied to adolescent girls. Out-of-school activity, on the other hand (which included football for many of our sample), was often described in terms which were more culturally specific. That is, students talked of out-of-school opportunities as something which were governed by cultural expectations. These were sometimes related to ethnicity in that requirements to attend the Mosque or assumptions that out-of-school activities were home- and family-based because of a specific cultural affiliation were mentioned. They also relate to female participation more generally. Deem and Gilroy (1998) counsel against the development of strategies to promote sport which neglect the kinds of perceptions women in general have of sport and the negotiations they may need to engage in if they wish to participate in physical activity. They point out that a great deal of women's leisure activity takes place in the home. This is confirmed by the varied experiences of our sample which contrast with much narrower definitions of leisure opportunities suggested by some of the teachers.

Lave and Wenger seem to imply that participation in a particular community of practice beyond the stage of legitimate peripheral participation requires an acceptance of the norms and values of the specific community. Our data leads us to suggest that many girls remain at the peripheral stage for a variety of reasons, which, singly or in combination, serve as barriers to the sorts of full participation that are likely to maximise learning. This is not to say that learning cannot take place as a peripheral participant. Nevertheless, for some students, the activities themselves are associated with values to which they do not subscribe. Others' bodies fail to conform to the norm implied by school expectations of dress and public performance. For others, the context, particularly where activities take place outside in inclement weather, conflicts with their perceptions of physical activity as something to be enjoyed in warmth and comfort. Some of the comments made by our students resonate clearly with the three communities of practice identified by Kirk and indicate that some physical education teachers appear to be sustaining a separate and distinctive community of practice which is not compatible with associated communities. At times this leads to conflict, as girls bring to their physical education experience and expectations which are more consonant with the communities of sport, recreation or exercise. School requirements to exercise outside, in cold weather, dressed in minimal clothing conflict with the norms of exercise-based communities that stress the importance of warmth for effective and safe participation. Compulsory participation in activities which students dislike and for which they feel, rightly or wrongly, that they have no aptitude, conflicts with the values of recreational activity which emphasises choice, both of activity and of the form that participation will take.

We should conclude by noting that, for many of the students we interviewed, physical education is an enjoyable and rewarding experience. In order to extend this positive experience to all, a number of issues relating to inconsistency between school and out-of-school physical culture need to be addressed. Clearly, this inconsistency is not only an issue relevant to girls, but rather, to all young people. It challenges physical education to seek greater engagement with the body-cultures and lifestyles to which students can relate and aspire.

Acknowledgements

The authors would like to acknowledge the support of the Nuffield Foundation who provided funding for this study.

Note

1 The years specified for students refer to years within the National Curriculum framework in England and Wales. Years 9–11 therefore relate to the latter years of secondary schooling, for pupils aged 13–16 years.

References

Adams, N. (1997) Towards a curriculum of resiliency: gender, race, adolescence and schooling, in C. Marshall (ed.) *Feminist Critical Policy Analysis: A Perspective from Primary and Secondary Schooling*, London: Falmer Press.

Apple, M. (1979) *Ideology and the Curriculum*, London: Routledge & Kegan Paul.

Deem, R. and Gilroy, S. (1998) Physical activity, lifelong learning and empowerment: situating sport, *Women's Leisure, Sport Education and Society* 3(1): 89–104.

Dyer, K. (1982) *Catching up the Men: Women in Sport*, London: Junction Books.

Giddens, A. (1990) *The Consequences of Modernity*, Cambridge: Polity Press.

Hargreaves, J. (1994) *Sporting Females*, London: Routledge.

Hall, M.A. (1996) *Feminism and Sporting Bodies: Essays on Theory and Practice*, Champaign, IL: Human Kinetics.

Lave, J. and Wenger, E. (1991) *Situated Learning: Legitimate Peripheral Participation*, New York: Cambridge University Press.

Kirk, D. (1999) Physical culture, physical education and relational analysis, *Sport, Education and Society* 4(1): 63–73.

Kirk, D. and Macdonald, D. (1998) Situated learning in physical education, *Journal of Teaching in Physical Education* 17(3): 376–87.

Laws, C. and Fisher, R. (1999) Pupils' interpretations of physical education, in C. Hardy and M. Mawer (eds) *Learning and Teaching in Physical Education*, London: Falmer Press.

Maykut, P. and Morehouse, R. (1994) *Beginning Qualitative Research*, London: Falmer Press.

Penney, D. and Evans, J. (1999) *Politics, Policy and Practice in Physical Education*, London: E & FN Spon.

Tomlinson, P. (1989) Having it both ways: hierarchical focusing as research interview method, *British Educational Research Journal* 15(2): 155–75.

Weiss, L. (1997) Gender and the Reports, the case of the missing piece, in C. Marshall (ed.) *Feminist Critical Policy Analysis: A Perspective from Primary and Secondary Schooling*, London: Falmer Press.

Williams, E.A. and Bedward, J. (1999) *Games for the Girls: The Impact of Recent Policy on the Provision of Physical Education and Sporting Opportunities for Female Adolescents – a Report of a Study Funded by the Nuffield Foundation*, Winchester: King Alfred's College.

Williams, E.A. and Bedward, J. (2000) An inclusive national curriculum? The experience of adolescent girls, *European Journal of Physical Education* 5(1): 4–18

Williams, A. and Woodhouse, J. (1996) Delivering the discourse: urban adolescents' perceptions of physical education, *Sport, Education and Society* 1(2): 201–13.

Part IV

Extending gender agendas in physical education

10 Gender equity and physical education: a USA perspective

Mary O'Sullivan, Kim Bush and Margaret Gehring

Introduction

The struggles associated with a male-dominated sport curriculum in England (Kirk, 2001, chapter 3; Williams and Bedward, 2001, chapter 9) are also evident in the US (Chepyator-Thomson and Ennis, 1997). From the 1960s to the early 1970s a massive shift occurred in our profession, resulting in the unification of men's and women's physical education pedagogy programs and in boy's and girl's physical education classes. This shift led to the proliferation of a traditionally male model of physical education (Vertinsky, 1992). While curricular initiatives in the last fifteen years have made strides toward providing gender inclusive physical education, the traditional, male-based, multi-activity curriculum is still dominant in the US (Lawson, 1998). One of the biggest barriers to dissemination of new curricula initiatives in American schools is the lack of a national curriculum. The decentralized nature of the education system in the US means that widespread changes to curricula would require intensive, coordinated and sustained efforts with almost unanimous acceptance at the state and local levels.

There have been a plethora of educational reforms in the United States in the last twenty years. Efforts have been made to improve curriculum, bring greater accountability for teaching and learning, improve teacher preparation, provide induction programs for new teachers, and devote more money to support professional development for experienced teachers. In physical education, we have seen the development of national content standards for physical education (NASPE, 1995a) for the curriculum from kindergarten to grade 12[1] and the establishment of teacher preparation standards for beginning physical education teachers that align with the K–12 content standards (NASPE, 1995b). Most recently we have seen a national voluntary certification in physical education for experienced teachers established as one of over twenty such certifications administered by the National Board for Professional Teaching Standards (NBPTS, 1999). This is a system to recognize and reward accomplished teachers. In several states the legislature has agreed to pay enhancements of up to $5000 annually for upwards of ten years upon successful receipt of the Board certification.

There has been little if any attention in these reforms to gender and education (Nilges, 1998). Title IX is the only substantive piece of legislation that deals with gender and education and its most dramatic effect has been in relation to girls' participation rates in sport and physical education in American schools. We therefore begin with a review of some of the key policy documents dealing with sport and physical education and how they have addressed gender equity. We then identify some contemporary curricular trends and specifically consider the degree to which the curricula developed have attempted to address the physical education of *all* students. In the final part of the chapter, we draw some conclusions about gender equity in physical education and make some comparisons between developments in the US and in Great Britain.

Policy initiatives addressing physical education

Title IX

In 1972 the US Congress passed Title IX as part of the Educational Amendments of that year. Specifically, Title IX states 'No person in the US shall, on the basis of sex be excluded from participation in, or denied the benefits of, or be subjected to discrimination under any educational program or activity receiving federal aid' (20 U.S.C. §1681a, 1988).

The purpose of Title IX was to ensure that girls received the same educational opportunities as boys. Title IX applies to all educational institutions receiving federal support, ranging from preschools to post-graduate institutions. Since its inception, Title IX has been responsible for increasing the percentages of women graduating from college and graduating with degrees in mathematics and sciences (USDE, 1997). However, Title IX is perhaps most widely known for the dramatic increases in participation rates among girls and women in sport in the US. For example, in 1971 there were less than 300,000 girls participating in high school sports. This increased to 2.6 million girls by 2000 (NFHS, 2001). Title IX has also been responsible for a four-fold increase in the number of sports offered at the collegiate level since 1971 (Acosta and Carpenter, 2000). Additional benefits of Title IX in the sporting realm include increased funding for female sport programs at the high school and college level, increased numbers of collegiate athletic scholarships for women, and drastic improvements in facilities and equipment used by girls and women.

While the benefits of Title IX have been obvious in the sport arena there is growing concern about the declining physical activity and physical education participation rates, especially among girls. Almost half of the young people in the US aged 12–21 years are not active on a regular basis (USDHHS, 1996). Furthermore, adolescent girls are twice as likely to be inactive compared to adolescent boys (USDHHS, 1996), and African American girls have the lowest participation rates among all groups of US adolescents (USDHHS,

2000). Add to this the fact that in physical education classes girls have fewer opportunities to respond and lower participation rates in comparison to boys (Griffin, 1984) and one begins to wonder who is benefiting from Title IX. These findings suggest that while Title IX has afforded girls and women numerous formal sporting opportunities, the same is not true regarding physical activity and physical education opportunities. This quandary has prompted many teachers and scholars to examine the differential impact of Title IX on the physical education curriculum for boys and girls.

Coeducational ('coed') physical education

Prior to the passage of Title IX, most physical education classes were sex segregated. The largest influence of Title IX has been the mandate that physical education classes, like other disciplines, be offered on a coeducational basis. There are some exceptions to mandatory coeducational classes in physical education as Title IX does not prohibit sex-segregated classes when the purpose of the activity involves bodily contact (i.e. wrestling, boxing, rugby, ice hockey, football, basketball). However in sports not involving such contact (i.e. tennis, volleyball, track and field), classes must be coeducational. Students may also be grouped according to ability for instruction if objective standards of individual performance are applied without regard to sex and do not adversely effect members of one sex. An example would be if students were divided for archery instruction by their pre-test scores. In such cases, it is possible that classes could be comprised entirely of one sex. Finally, if students' religious beliefs prohibit them from participating in coeducational physical education, they may be excused from such classes or offered sex-segregated physical education (34CFR106.34). A rationale for such legislation was that boys and girls would have equitable opportunity for instruction and practice (Griffin, 1984). However, as other chapters in this collection have also noted, scholarly analyses of typical practices acknowledge a need for more careful distinctions between access and equity. Indeed access has not ensured gender equity. While coeducational physical education was originally mandated to ameliorate the conditions and quality of physical education for girls, researchers have found differential participation patterns and percep-tions when comparing boys and girls in coeducational environments, and when comparing coed PE to single-sex PE.

In studying participation patterns of girls in a coed middle school physical education unit, Griffin (1984) found that the majority of girls exhibited one of four nonassertive behavior types: giving up, giving away, hanging back, and acquiescing. Lirgg (1993) found that in comparison to single-sex classes, coed physical education classes can benefit boys more than girls. In a study comparing both class formats, Lirgg found that boys in single-sex classes had decreased self-confidence, while boys in the coeducational classes had increased self-confidence over the course of a ten-week basketball unit. Meanwhile girls in single-sex classes showed increased confidence levels but decreased levels in the coed classes. Lirgg (1993) maintained that boys' self-confidence may be influenced by social comparison and that their comparison reference group is likely to include more lower-skilled performers in coeducational classes than in single-sex settings. However, other data indicates that we need to be cautious in making connections between these effects on self-confidence and students' grouping preferences. In a study of 466 middle school students, Treanor, Graber, Housner and Wiegand (1998) found that 60 per cent of boys and 67 per cent of girls preferred single-sex to coed physical education. Both genders perceived that they had greater practice opportunities, performed skills and team sports better, and were less fearful of getting injured in single-sex classes. In addition, boys perceived that they competed harder, learned more, and behaved better in single-sex classes. The only significant preference for coeducation classes was that girls perceived that they competed harder in coed classes. The authors did not recommend single-sexed physical education but suggested that pre-service and in-service teacher education programs must acknowledge the challenges associated with administering coeducational physical education (Treanor *et al.*, 1998).

Other researchers have engaged with these challenges and gender equity debates more broadly in relation to physical education in the US. Siedentop (2001) asserted that grouping students according to interest and ability will make lessons more profitable for students. Vertinsky (1992) argued that coeducational physical education has led to the adoption of a male model of physical education. Coed programs 'implied that male standards would be the ones to emulate, reifying the values of competitive sport and further reinforcing masculine hegemony' (Vertinsky, 1992: 378). This is similar to gender equity concerns expressed by Talbot (1993) in the British context. Nilges (2000) contends that physical education curricula structured to focus primarily on team sports are likely to promote the traditional male model of movement. Meanwhile, some researchers believe the problems in physical education go beyond the content and relate to gender biases in how we evaluate students. Along these lines, Smeal, Carpenter and Tait (1994) argue that characteristics such as power, speed, strength, competitiveness, and aggression that are typically male dominated, are overemphasized in the content of physical education.

Vertinsky (1992) maintained that the major concern for most physical education teachers is to provide equal access for girls as opposed to questioning the relevance and consequences of a male dominated curriculum for all students. Referring to Title IX, the Holmes Report, and the Women's Educational Equity Act (Lock, Minarik and Omata, 1999: 403) stated, 'noticeably absent from the language of diversity is any reference to an educational system's moral and legal obligation to provide equality of opportunity, much less the equality of outcomes'. Recently researchers have challenged educators to move beyond 'equal opportunity' and focus on the power structures of the classroom. In studying a 4th grade (for students aged

9) physical education class over a 14-week period, Nilges (1998) found the physical education environment laden with 'patriarchal ideologies and patterns of gender differentiation' (ibid.: 189). This was evident in the trivialization of the physical performances of girls, and in the 'we–they dichotomy' that depicted boys as the privileged class members. Nilges (1998) called for physical educators to challenge gender-equitable teaching beyond the liberal definition of Title IX and move towards a feminist pedagogy. In Nilges' view physical educators and teacher educators should challenge the traditional norms of feminine and masculine movements and promote an atmosphere with which students can openly explore and understand all movement patterns (Nilges, 2000).

Although substantial research regarding participation rates in different physical education settings is lacking, many physical education teachers believe that participation rates for girls are higher when classes are single sex (Griffin, 1985; Lynn, 1999). They provide various reasons for the decline in mixed settings, including suggestions that sports and games are geared more toward boys' interests since physical education became coeducational; that girls are overly concerned about how they are perceived by boys; and that the physical, mental, emotional and social challenges of puberty are too overpowering in a coeducational setting to provide an environment conducive for optimal learning (Lynn, 1999). In response to these challenges and perhaps further complicating the issue, is that many physical education teachers 'get around' the coeducation stipulation by separating boys and girls for sport or fitness activities.

It is clear that Title IX has had differential effects on the experiences, opportunities and participation rates of girls and women in sport as compared to girls and women in physical education classes. Due to the lack of research and the multiple variables involved it is difficult to ascertain reasons for the differential effects between girls' and boys' participation rates in physical education, and between girls' sport opportunities and girls' physical education opportunities. Although Title IX is the only federal policy directly addressing gender in education, there are other federal policies that potentially impact the physical education and physical activity opportunities available to girls. Some might suggest that Title IX has unintentionally reinforced dichotomous images of gender and presented a shaky foundation from which to address the diverse educational needs of both boys and girls. In considering other policy developments since Title IX, we discuss the degree to which they have better addressed these complexities and the structural dimensions of inequity.

Healthy People 2010

Healthy People 2010 is a ten-year federal public health plan that was submitted by the United States to the World Health Organization (WHO) as part of a 'Health For All' strategy. The authors of the report presented two goals for the American public: to increase the quality and years of healthy life and to eliminate health disparities 'regardless of their age, race, ethnicity, gender, sexual orientation, disability status, income, educational level or geographic location' (USDHHS, 1996: 4). One of the twenty-eight areas of the report was devoted to physical activity and physical fitness among children and adults.

With the goals of Healthy People 2010 in mind, the US has devoted much time to collecting data relating to healthy lifestyles and physical activity levels of our society, to reset standards to improve the overall health and well-being of our country. One example of a massive data collection effort is The Youth Risk Behavior Surveillance (USDHHS, 1999). It concluded that only one half of young people aged 12–21 years and about one third of high school students participated in vigorous physical activity (activity that makes you sweat and breathe hard such as running) on at least three of the seven days preceding the survey. It also reported that male students were more likely than female students to report both vigorous and moderate physical activity, to participate in strength exercises, to play on sports teams and to exercise for longer than twenty minutes in an average physical education class. Several barriers to physical activity were identified: lack of time, lack of access to convenient facilities, lack of safe environments. Despite these barriers, the present goal is to have 85 per cent of adolescents and 30 per cent of adults participate in the recommended amounts of physical activity by 2010. Specifically, the goal is to increase the proportion of adolescents who engage in vigorous physical activity that promotes cardio-respiratory fitness three or more days per week for twenty or more minutes per occasion. Specific types of physical activity and exercise that young people might participate include 'walking, bicycling, playing actively (unstructured physical activity), participating in organized sports, dancing, doing active household chores, and working at a job that has physical demands' (Center for Disease Control and Prevention (CDC), 1997: 3).

Healthy People 2010 established seven objectives for physical activity among children and adolescents, of those, three are directly related to physical education in schools:

- Increase the proportion of the nation's public and private schools that require daily physical education for all students. The goal is a 47 per cent improvement for middle and junior high schools, and a 150 per cent improvement for high schools.
- Increase the proportion of adolescents who participate in daily school physical education. The suggested improvement is from 27 per cent to 50 per cent.
- Increase the proportion of adolescents who spend at least 50 per cent of school physical education class time being physically active from 32 per cent to 50 per cent.

(USDHHS, 1996)

These recommendations indicate goals for our country, but what is not addressed is how we may accomplish these goals or where gender fits into these goals.

The Center for Disease Control and Prevention (CDC) has responded to these recommendations by outlining ten strategies to promote health through lifelong participation in enjoyable and safe physical activity and sports. These guidelines address: Policy; Environment; Physical Education Curricula and Instruction; Extracurricular Activities; Family Involvement; Training; Health Services; Community Programs; and Evaluation. A specific example of one of the above guidelines would be the efforts that are being made to encourage communities to offer activities before and after school for our youth. The Prevention Institute provided a list of guidelines to promote physical activity in schools that require daily physical education for students in grades K–12. They indicated a need to provide a diverse range of age, developmentally and culturally appropriate activities that young people can enjoy throughout their lives, such as walking, running, swimming, cycling and dancing; and provide time and space during the day for unstructured physical activity (before or after school, and during break or lunch times). In addition the institute stated that adults should emphasize activity enjoyment more than competition for youth and form partnerships with businesses, community organizations, and parks and recreation, to provide diverse and quality programs in schools and neighborhoods. Although these recommendations appear to be reaching out to the needs of a diverse population, there was an absence of any objectives directly related to gender. Once again, we find ourselves with limited information; most notably about 'how' to implement policy recommendations. There seems to be a gap in policies that presents others, be they teacher educators, state departments officials, or state and local agencies, with a key role to play in advancing gender equitable practices.

On the state level, The Prevention Institute has developed a handbook titled 'Promoting Physical Activity Among Youth: It's Everyone's Business' (2001). This document explores 'why children, who appear to be in a state of perpetual motion from the day they are born, decrease or abandon physical activity as they progress through adolescence' (The Prevention Institute, 2001: 5). In addition to leading to overweight and obesity, physical inactivity can cause high blood pressure, poor self-concept, increased anxiety, stress, and depression (CDC, 1997). Long-term consequences often include 'chronic disease and conditions such as cardiovascular disease, diabetes, and colon cancer that affect quality of life and/or cause premature death' (The Prevention Institute, 2001: 6). Again, although a variety of topics such as why children are inactive and consequences of inactivity are addressed, the notion of how to get youth to be active is neglected.

It appears that although there are not direct strategies or recommendations as to *how* to promote and provide gender equitable physical activity programs, there is encouragement. The policy recommendations from the President's Council Report emphasized the fact that girls need safe and healthy environments within physical activity and sport that support them to excel and grow (USDHHS, 1997). In addition, this document stated that 'policies need to tap the power and potential of physical activity and sport to advance girls' health, physical and emotional development, social well-being and educational aspirations and achievements. Efforts must be directed towards increasing girls' participation in physical activity and sport' (USDHHS, 1997:1). This document provided three general realms of concern: the first was related to increasing participation among girls in physical activity and sport, the second related to better utilizing physical activity and sport as vehicles to promote girls' physical and mental health; and the third area focused on enhancing the contributions of physical activity and sport to girls' educational achievements and social development. It is vital to note that these recommendations are important for both sexes and could also enrich the experiences of boys as well.

National content standards for physical education (K–12)

Unlike most countries worldwide, education in America is mostly a state, not a federal, responsibility. The effect for any subject area is that adoption of a nationally deliberated set of standards or curriculum framework is voted on by each state level board of education (sometimes in conjunction with the state legislature) and often then by each school district. Thus there is little possibility for a national curriculum that would be similar to the National Curriculum for Physical Education in England and Wales. While such a decentralized system has some advantages, a key disadvantage is the difficulty of disseminating curricular innovations in any timely manner.

In the early 1990s, the National Association for Sport and Physical Education (NASPE) published a document that defined what it means to be a physically educated person following completion of a K–12 program of physical education (NASPE, 1992). This stated that a physically educated person is someone who:

- has learned skills necessary to perform a variety of physical activities;
- is physically fit;
- does participate regularly in physical activity;
- knows the implications of and the benefits from involvement in physical activities; and
- values physical activities and their contribution to a healthy lifestyle.

In 1995 NASPE (1995a) expanded the 'outcomes project' and developed a set of national content standards for physical education. The seven content standards established what a student should know and be able to do as a result of a quality physical education program and highlighted benchmarks for each standard for kindergarten, 2nd, 4th, 6th, 8th, 10th, and 12th grades. The content standards indicated that a physically educated person:

- demonstrates competency in many movement forms and proficiency in a few forms;
- applies movement concepts and principles to the learning and development of motor skills;
- exhibits a physically active lifestyle;
- achieves and maintains a health enhancing level of physical fitness;
- demonstrates responsible personal and social behavior in physical activity settings;
- demonstrates understandings and respect for differences among people in physical activity settings;
- understands that physical activity provides opportunities for enjoyment, challenge, self-expression, and social interaction.

From an equity perspective the content standards are a significant and positive development in that they attend to several components of physical education beyond psychomotor skill development and psychomotor skill competency. Only four of the seven content standards focus on fitness and psychomotor skill development. Two standards focus on personal responsibility for, and personal benefits of, physical activity and a seventh standard focuses on students respecting others and appreciating how their preferences and needs for physical activity may differ from others. The latter three standards clearly present the opportunity to engage with gender equity issues in the physical education curriculum. We would particularly anticipate that the assessments for Standard 6 (i.e. has respect for differences among people in physical activity settings) would address gender. In tenth grade, students are expected to complete an assignment that addresses the role of women in sport. In twelfth grade they might review offensive mascots from gender, ethnicity and cultural perspectives (see table 10.1).

The assessment of content has been presented to physical education teachers as an enhancement of learning. The assessment model is formative in nature and used to support instruction of physical education and student learning for all. Theoretically this approach encourages teachers to move away from a focus on psychomotor skill development and knowledge of the rules of the game/activity to a more diverse set of assessments that allow students to demonstrate the variety of ways they can be physically educated. Yet, of the examples provided to assess student learning, only four of 106 assessment examples focus directly on gender issues and the relationships between gender and sport. Despite their potential there is little in the sample assessments presented the NASPE Task Force that encourages discussion of differential access to physical activities and how gender (or race, sexual orientation, or class) might impact upon the ways in which sport is organized, structured and controlled in the students' school and community (NASPE, 1995a).

The national standards do encourage more student choice within the physical education curriculum but actual choice is still a local issue (i.e. school

Table 10.1 Selected physical education assessments by grade and standard*

Standard	6th grade	8th grade	10th grade	12th grade
1 Competency in many and proficiency in few movement forms	Design performance Routine	AAHPERD skill test	Skills test (Red Cross level 4)	Portfolio on three areas of personal skill competence
2 Applies concepts and principles to learning motor skill	Analyze HRF of physical activity	Develop training plan for a sport of interest	Self analysis of skill from video	Select PA for post graduation and res. Psychological factors of PA
3 Physically active lifestyle	Survey school and community physical activities	Join in a physical activity and journal the experience	*Survey community physical activity opportunities and develop plan to increase accessibility*	*Interviews of men/women in different age groups. *Engagement in PA (age/gender effects)*
4 Achieves and maintains health fitness levels	Log PA across weeks Design fitness plan	Record HR in different PAs and write of physiological responses	Assess fitness and plan program	Predict PA 10 years out and barriers to engagement Assess fitness levels
5 Demonstrate personal and social behavior in PA	Design a game with others	Reflect on engagement in PA and comment to improve for all	*Discuss influences on achieving personal PA goals*	Observe a peer mediation and comment on it
6 Has respect for differences among people in PA settings	Participate in a game with a 'disability', e.g. blindfolded	*Observe class for exclusionary behavior and suggest ways to improve*	*Role of women in sport*	*Factors that impact PA engagement across the life-span (gender, age, class)* *Review offensive mascots (gender, ethnicity, culture)*

Table 10.1 (continued)

Standard	6th grade	8th grade	10th grade	12th grade
7 Understands PA provides opportunities for enjoyment, challenge, self-expression	Feelings from adventure education experience	*Positive and negative feelings from sport involvement*	Write a dialogue to get a friend active Journal feelings on physical activity plan	Design camp experience for urban children

Source: Adapted from NASPE (1995a). *Moving into the Future: National Physical Education, Standards*. New York: Mosby.

Note The italicized assessments by standard and grade level indicate assessments that have direct or indirect potential to focus students' attention on the role of gender in developing and sustaining a physically active lifestyle.

by school more than state by state). Once again we see that policy guidance can be interpreted in several ways. Physical education is still required of students in most elementary and middle school and for two of eight semesters in high school. However, requirements and provision vary greatly nationwide and with curriculum overload there are fewer students opting for elective physical education if offered this beyond the 10th grade.

Curricular initiatives in physical education

There is a predominantly sport/games oriented curriculum in American middle and high school levels (Lawson, 1998). At the elementary grades physical education is focused on developing fundamental motor skills and movement, with some concern for a developmental approach to movement tasks and the integration of physical education with other content areas. In recent years there has been a growing interest in fitness and wellness programs with a move away from team sports especially at the high school level. Most physical education programs reflect a multi-activity program focus especially at the middle and secondary school. There is also some evidence that teachers are beginning to narrow their focus rather than trying to be all things to all students with limited time allocation. The major curricular initiatives that have gained the attention of physical education teachers in recent years are sport education (Siedentop, 1994 and below), teaching for responsibility (Hellison, 1995), and Fitness for Life curriculum (Corbin and Lindsey, 1997). Corbin's curriculum is quite prescriptive on content coverage while Hellison's model is prescriptive in terms of instructional goals and processes. Adventure education has also attracted attention, particularly in its focus upon conflict resolution and social skills content (Siedentop and Tannehill, 2000). Unlike in Britain (in examination program contexts) and in Australia and New Zealand, there has been little attention given to physical education as a 'content space' to study the theoretical aspects of physical education. The cultural studies approach (Kinchin and O'Sullivan, 1999) is one effort to develop students as literate and critical consumers of sport and has borrowed and adapted curricular ideas for classroom physical education in Australia and England for the American high school.

Focus on health-related physical activity: CATCH, SPARK and Fitness for Life

There are two nationally recognized school-based curricula found to be effective with regards to promoting physical activity: the *Child and Adolescent Trial For Cardiovascular Health* (*CATCH*) and *Sports, Play, and Active Recreation for Kids* (*SPARK*). CATCH was the first school-based multi-center randomized trial ever conducted, and was a national trial to educate elementary school children to develop healthy habits to prevent heart disease. The study involved more than 5000 ethnically diverse students in grades 3–8 from nearly 100 schools across four states. The goal of the study was to determine if health promotion efforts targeting the school environment and children's behaviors would reduce cardiovascular disease risk factors later in life. Significant increases in out-of-school moderate–vigorous physical activity were found and a three-year follow-up study indicated that students who participated in CATCH continued to pursue more vigorous physical activity levels than students in control groups. The data from CATCH were dis-aggregated by gender and it was found that boys were more active than girls. CATCH has since been replicated in other communities throughout the United States as a model of a comprehensive school-based approach to increasing physical activity. SPARK is an elementary (K–6) physical education curriculum and staff development program that offers materials and services to 'schools, university grants, recreation departments, after-school programs, hospital community outreach and health organizations on a non-profit basis, through San Diego State University Foundation' (The Prevention Institute, 2001: 16). Positive program effects have been found on variables such as physical activity, lesson context, teacher behavior, motor skill development, and long-term effects. SPARK indicated that trained classroom teachers improved children's physical activity levels compared to untrained teachers, but that physical education specialists produced even greater results (Sallis and Owen, 1999). The results of SPARK were also dis-aggregated by gender, but no suggestions were made as to how to address these gender differences.

At the secondary level Corbin's Fitness for Life curriculum focuses on important national health objectives from Healthy People 2000 and teaches students concepts of personal health and fitness. The purpose of the Fitness for Life program is to assist students in achieving three objectives: acquire knowledge about the benefits of physical activity, health and wellness and about the principles of fitness; become physically active while pursuing goals to become physically fit; and become an independent decision maker who can plan his or her own personal fitness program (Corbin and Lindsey, 1997). The program focuses on different aspects of health and fitness including: cardio-vascular fitness, strength, muscular endurance, flexibility, fat control and health-related/skill-related fitness. Although we did not read about any particular discussion on gender, gender concerns or gender differences in the Fitness for Life material, we did notice the following: there were pictures of both boys and girls throughout the sources, and there were occasional references to both girls and boys such as 'to better him or herself' but no explicit effort to discuss differential access to physical activity for girls was presented.

After reviewing health-related materials such as: CATCH, SPARK and Fitness for Life; and after reflecting back on statistics regarding the activity levels of boys versus the activity levels of girls, it is evident that our country has dis-aggregated data on boys and girls. However, there appears to be an aspect that is missing: what can we do to meet the varying needs of boys and girls to promote physical activity?

Trial of Activity for Adolescent Girls (TAAG)

As a consequence of the differential effects of physical activity programs on boys and girls, a multi-center study called a *Trial of Activity for Adolescent Girls (TAAG)* has begun in six centers around the country. These centers are responsible for designing, implementing, and monitoring a comprehensive, school-based, community-linked intervention to promote physical activity and physical fitness among middle-school girls. This is a six-year study with a 30 million dollar budget from the National Institute of Health (NIH) supporting six multi-trial sites with a goal of better understanding of how to prevent declines in physical activity levels among adolescent girls. The good news about this nationally funded project is that it is one of the few to focus directly on girls' physical activity levels. The intent is to design integrated in-school and after-school programs that are meaningful to young females lives. The sad news is that only a single pedagogy scholar is involved on the six research teams that will be studying these issues. There is not space in this chapter to discuss the politics of physical activity funding in the United States but we would argue that the absence of sport pedagogy faculty in these curricular innovations should be of serious concern to all interested in physical education experiences in schools for girls.

Restructuring games teaching in physical education: sport education

In the mid-1980s Daryl Siedentop introduced the sport education curriculum model in the United States. This model evolved from Siedentop's 'play education' theory which was premised on the notion that play, in the physical education sense, is 'central to a full and meaningful existence' (Siedentop, 1980: 266). Siedentop believed that by incorporating the most attractive features of institutionalized sport to a physical education context students would be more enthused about the subject matter, take greater ownership in their efforts and experiences and become well-rounded sports people.

The three main goals of sport education are to develop students who are competent, literate, and enthusiastic sports persons (Siedentop, 1995). These goals are achieved through incorporating characteristics traditionally associated with sport into the physical education context. For instance, rather than dividing the physical education curriculum into units, activities are presented within seasons, comparable to that of institutionalized sport. Seasons last longer than typical units, thereby providing students with a greater depth of experience within the sport and ultimately enhancing students' competence in the sport. Students are affiliated with teams and maintain their team membership throughout the season, thus promoting enthusiasm and teamwork among students. In addition to being affiliated with a team, each student has a role on the team (such as captain, referee, statistician, trainer). Team roles are intended to promote individual responsibility and engage students in all aspects of the sport. Teams are designed as equitably as possible to foster close competitions. Similar to traditional sporting settings, formal competitions take the form of dual competitions, round-robin tournaments, etc. Each season ends with a culminating event in which a championship team is determined. Finally, records specific to the sport are kept throughout the season and maintained over the years.

Siedentop (2001) contends that good competition engages students and is educationally useful. He maintains that sport education differs from institutionalized sport in three distinct ways. First, all students are involved in the planning, participation, and competition at all times. Second, games are modified to allow for developmentally appropriate competition. Finally, in addition to being performers, students have a wide variety of roles such as referees, record keepers, trainers, coaches, and managers. While the sport education model has an inherent competitive focus, if implemented properly it should promote cooperation; as team success is dependent upon maximizing the contribution of all team members. For example, it would behove the higher skilled students to assist and support their lower skilled teammates. A key issue here is the teachers' ability to provide such contingencies and to support captains and student leaders in their efforts to provide meaningful and plentiful opportunities for all students (D. Siedentop, personal communication, April 27, 2001).

While Siedentop (1995) maintains that long-term purpose of sport education is for sport involvement to benefit all participants regardless of gender, race, disability, or socioeconomic status, most of the research and literature on the sport education curriculum model does not address gender equity or girls' participation rates. Furthermore, traditionally male dominated sports are typically cited in the limited research examining sport education programs. The value of the sport education model as a means of promoting participation for all students needs further study. This is particularly important in light of research indicating that a major reason why girls opt not to participate in physical education is due to the excessively competitive environment (Browne, 1992; Carlson, 1995).

To date, few studies have compared the impact of the sport education model on both genders. Hastie (1998) examined the participation patterns and perceptions of middle school students participating in a twenty-lesson floor hockey season utilizing a sport education model. Results showed that boys had significantly more responses per minute and higher success levels than girls during the formal competition phase. No differences were found in participation patterns during the skill practice sessions or in the early season scrimmages. Girls preferred the sport education unit to previous experiences in physical education, indicating that it allowed them more opportunities to play. Girls preferred playing on mixed-sex teams rather than single-sex teams, with many indicating that they played harder on the mixed-sex teams. The finding that girls perceived they played harder on coed teams is consistent with Treanor *et al.* (1998).

In Hastie's (2000) study, positions of leadership (captains and referees) were overwhelmingly held by boys. Girls often commented that the boys were bossy and tended to dominate team decisions. These results suggest that the sport education model may not provide similar benefits to all participants. In particular, while girls enjoyed this experience more so that non-sport education experiences, they still had less opportunity to respond in a competitive setting or to engage in leadership roles when compared to boys, irrespective of skill level. Hastie (2000) suggests some problems with implementing the sport education model relate to the level of expertise of captains and student leaders. For instance, captains may be highly skilled players, however they may not have the skills to provide quality practices for all skill levels. Furthermore, it seems that practices are geared toward the higher skilled students. It would appear that girls might be at greater risk of not receiving beneficial practice opportunities. These research findings suggest that greater teacher involvement is needed in choosing leaders and in guiding leaders in their quest to administer effective practices.

The findings that were most encouraging from Hastie's (2000) study are that girls enjoyed their experiences more and perceived that they tried harder on coed teams as compared to single-sex teams. Yet, having studied a teacher implementing sport education for the first time Curnow and Macdonald (1995) questioned whether sport education could be inclusive of girls. It is clear that more research needs to be done to determine if the sport education is effective in promoting meaningful and active experiences for all girls. Some questions to consider in such inquiry are:

• How are teams chosen to ensure proper representation of both genders and all skill levels?

- How are captains and other student leaders chosen? And how do the genders of the captains or other leaders impact the experiences of all team members?
- How are games modified to promote active and meaningful participation among all team members regardless of skill level or gender?
- How does the type of sport impact upon the experiences of all students?
- What role should the teacher play in ensuring active and meaningful participation among all students?

A cultural studies approach to physical education

Physical education curricula that encourage students to question taken-for-granted assumptions about sport and physical education in today's society have received significant attention internationally (Kirk *et al.*, 1998; Kirk and Tinning, 1990; Macdonald and Tinning, 1995), but comparatively little attention in the United States (Kinchin and O'Sullivan, 1999; O'Sullivan *et al.*, 1996). Yet such curricula offer a potentially exciting complement to the practice of physical education in American high schools and furthermore, enhanced potential for addressing gender equity within and beyond physical education. Sport and physical activity play a central role in adolescents' lives (more boys than girls), yet all too many students (more girls than boys) are disenfranchised from the joys and benefits of physical activity. The cultural studies (CS) approach to high school physical education has been an attempt to help students appreciate and critique the role of physical activity and sport in their school, their community, and their own lives. The curriculum attempts to make meaningful connections between physical education in school and sport and physical activity, or lack thereof, in students' lives, and encourages intellectual engagement with what physical activity and sport experiences mean to young people. Time is allocated for discussions on the role and meanings of sport and physical activity in students' lives and in the wider community. Two key goals of the model are to assist students to develop as literate and critical sports persons who are cognizant of the 'structural and social inequities in their local, regional, and national sport culture' (Siedentop, 1994: 23).

Addressing issues of gender

Classroom experiences are designed to help students discuss factors that support or inhibit their own and others' opportunities for physical activity and sport. Gender equity in sport is one of several themes addressed in the curriculum. The historical and geographical roots of a sport are presented and students have opportunities to consider the role of sport (e.g. volleyball) in their lives and those of their family and friends. A key goal is the development of students as critical consumers. Students research the possibilities for sport and physical activity in their school and community and consider factors that influence access and interest in sport for themselves, their friends, and neighbors. Journal writing, student presentations and discussions are used to explore the role of gender, media, and body image in sport and society in relation to these issues. This approach to physical education has been tried in a number of urban high schools in Ohio (O'Sullivan *et al.*, 1996), with teachers and university staff working collaboratively to design the cultural studies curriculum. Following two pilot studies and subsequent revisions to the curriculum, we studied the curriculum and 9th and 10th grade students' reactions to it at a third high school.

Students were very positive about lessons on sport and the media, sport and gender, and gender and body image and they enjoyed the opportunities to debate and critique contemporary sports issues (Kinchin, 1997). One class session on body image began with students responding to a picture of a female beach volleyball player and a five-minute video segment of men's beach volleyball. Several students contributed to a lively and lengthy debate on the issue of clothing in sport. The following fieldnote provides an example of the issues that such activities can provoke among students:

> 'What do you notice about the picture and video you have just seen?' says
>   the teacher.
> 'The guys have tank-tops on' says Ray.
> 'The women have sport bras' adds Donnelle.
> 'They [women] need to get their shorts on' says Myshona.
> Tim says, 'Nobody would watch if they did not wear skimpy stuff' . . .
> 'Are you saying that women have to take their clothes off for us to watch?'
>   asks Genevieve.
> 'No that is not what I am saying' replies Tim. . . .
> 'What does this say about our society?' asks the teacher.
> 'Athletes knew when they decided to become pro-beach volleyball players
>   that they would wear this stuff,' says Jae.
> Tim adds, 'It is not them that is making that choice, the endorsers may
>   make those and determine what they wear.'
> 'Society views women as sex objects' Donnelle says.
>
> (Fieldnote, 9th grade lesson #9)

Other students spoke favorably of a lesson in which they investigated sport coverage in a local newspaper. Each student recorded the coverage of different sports, the types of advertisement, and differences amongst pictures of athletes in terms of race and gender. The teacher began the lesson distributing a journal page with an advertisement from a local university and community newspaper. The advertisement asked for male basketball players with prior high school varsity experiences to practice with a Women's Division 1 collegiate program. The advertisement was deemed sexist and discriminatory by some of the female students. Michelle referred to a heated discussion that took place with Jason during the class, on the issue of skill differences among men and women. She noted 'me and Jason got into it and he got into it with somebody else . . . that made us better people though' (Int. #3).

The unit also enabled students to make meaningful connections with each other. A highly skilled student, who initially was reluctant to help peers during practice sessions and was intent on winning volleyball games, learned to be more helpful to his classmates as the unit progressed. A low skilled female student wrote about the experience:

> I think I have learned something new about people. I mean that you can go up to a person and tell them that you are doing this wrong but you are doing a good job . . . you know just make it clear to them. I have a lot of people on my team who care about me . . . and you know I care about them. I have learned that people really do care about you.
>
> (Jnl. #15)

Addressing the interests of all students

While some students did not appreciate time taken from physical activity for discussions on sport, others favored this approach. The mixed reactions can be seen as reflecting the diversity of students in the two classes studied. A curricular approach that takes time from physical activity is problematic for many teachers given the continuing demise of mandated time for physical education in public high schools in the United States, and clearly, these are international concerns. However, given the central role that sport plays in our society, we need to provide opportunities to engage students not just in activity but as critical consumers of physical activity and sporting practices in their schools and communities. From this perspective the cultural studies approach was of particular interest to girls and to low skilled boys, and deserves further examination by teachers and by teacher educators who prepare teachers to teach a physical education for a contemporary time.

A more positive future?

Despite the dismal statistics regarding physical education and physical activity there is optimism in the United States with the approval of the Physical Education for Progress (PEP) Act on December 15, 2000 by the US Congress. This bill is a piece of legislation introduced by Senator Ted Stevens (Republican Senator from Alaska) that authorizes 400 million dollars to be spent over the next five years, with 5 million dollars being appropriated for the 2001 fiscal year. This program authorizes the Secretary of Education to award grants to help initiate, expand and improve physical education programs for grades kindergarten through to 12. Funds may be used for equipment

Table 10.2 National standards for beginning and experienced physical education teachers

Beginning teacher standards	National Board for Professional Teaching Standards
1 Content knowledge	Knowledge of subject matter
2 Growth and development	Knowledge of students
3 Diverse learners	Equity, fairness, and diversity
4 Management and motivation	Curricular choices
5 Communication	High expectations for learners
6 Planning and instruction	Sound teaching practice
7 Learner assessment	Assessment
8 Reflection	Reflective practice and professional growth
9 Collaboration	Collaboration with colleagues
	Family and community partnerships
	Learning environment
	Promoting an active lifestyle
	Engagement

Source: Adapted from NASPE (1995b) and NBPTS (1999).

purchases, to develop curriculum, hire and train physical education staff, and support other initiatives designed to help students participate in physical education activities. In addition, this legislation will require schools to provide 150 minutes of physical education by trained physical education teachers (NASPE, 2001). At the time of writing a section of the Elementary and Secondary School Act had been repealed by President Bush that includes the funding for the PEP Act. Passage of federal legislation could be a significant catalyst to focus attention and support on school physical education and appropriate distribution of the funding might encourage and support quality programs for children and youth. Increasing efforts to link federal spending on education to stricter accountability for students and teachers has been reflected in recent policy initiatives by the American Alliance for Health, Physical Education, Recreation and Dance.

Performance standards for novices and accomplished teachers

In the early 1990s NASPE established a task force of seven teacher educators to develop a set of standards for what beginning teachers should know and be able to do. The nine standards (see table 10.2) that were established represent teachers as 'reflective, inquiry oriented, professionals who are cognizant of equity and diversity issues, competent in their subject matter, and able to select instructional strategies best suited to the varying needs of their students' (NASPE, 1995b: 4). Each standard addresses what are considered central and specific dispositions, knowledge, and performance for beginning physical education teachers. They were designed with input from teachers and aligned with the content standards developed earlier for K–12 physical education curricula.

The standards represent what the profession believes is important for beginning teachers to know and learn. The task force argued that 'standards for beginning physical education teachers be congruent with those of teachers in other subjects' (NASPE, 1995b: 2) and so modeled the standards on the work of the Interstate New Teacher Assessment and Support Consortium (INTASC) (a collaboration of key stakeholders in teacher education).

One of the nine standards focuses specifically on diversity and how a beginning teacher must 'understand how individuals learn and develop, and can provide opportunities that support their physical, cognitive, and emotional development' (ibid.: 10). A number of the other standards address the importance of attending to all students' needs more indirectly (see standards 2, 4, 5, and 8 in particular). We found it quite interesting that in a thorough analysis of the document, gender equity was *never* mentioned. Indeed only one standard (Communication) suggests that the teacher be knowledgeable and communicate in ways that demonstrate sensitivity to gender. We would contend that much more direct, explicit, and frequent statements about gender equity in the curriculum, instruction, and assessment of physical education programs are critical if we are to design teacher education programs that prepare teachers to physically educate *all* students.

The National Board for Professional Teaching Standards does a somewhat better job of directly addressing gender equity (NBPTS, 1999). The standard on equity, fairness, and diversity indicates that accomplished physical education teachers must strive 'to eliminate gender-specific units or activities' (ibid.: 28) and teach content that transcend stereotypes with males teaching dance and females teaching wrestling units. Clearly there is much still to be done, as it is a long way from policy documents to the implementation of gender equity curriculum and instructional practices in US physical education programs. Encouragingly, there is a growing trend in larger high schools that support several physical education teachers to provide curricular choice within the program (Durante, 1997). In some cases, this allows girls to pursue activities that are of more interest and relevance to them. Student choice within units of work offer students options of cooperative and competitive practices, provide for greater student ownership of learning experiences and enable students to pursue various roles in physical education and sport settings. Instructional models such as Sport Education are making their way into physical education programs nationally as a consequence of better teacher preparation programs and in our view have the potential to provide more relevant and enjoyable physical activity experiences for all students, especially girls and less skilled boys. However, we are also aware that there are many programs that are overly teacher centered, lack student choice, and pay little attention to the needs/interests of students.

Where to go from here?

Policy perspectives

In the United States we have witnessed a tremendous amount of national attention on public health policy. We have gathered data to evaluate the health, fitness and physical activity levels of young and old alike, such as The Youth Risk Behavior Survey (YRBS). Federal agencies such as the National Institute for Health have supported clinical trials of in-school activity programs such as CATCH and SPARK. The data on the effectiveness of these programs when dis-aggregated by gender indicate that boys are more active than girls and in particular, African-American adolescent females are the least active of youth (CDC, 1997). Although our physical educators are being trained based on a set of national standards, it appears that a significant number of physical educators in our country are not familiar with the policy initiatives of our country. In addition, if we examine these policy documents closely, we observe an almost universal silence of gender, with the exception of the TAAG grant. There is a silence with regards to how to appropriately address the disparities that exist between genders within physical activity and physical education. We have had much policy in the United States, but what we are realizing is that policy is not driven by research. It is instead, driven by power. One of the two goals of Healthy People 2010 focuses on eliminating health disparities 'regardless of their age, race, ethnicity, gender, sexual orientation, disability status, income, educational level or geographic location' (USDHHS, 1996: 4). What is evident is that there have been great efforts to examine the activity levels of the American youth, but there continues to be a shortage of materials and policies that surround the specifics of this goal which address age, race, ethnicity, gender and sexual orientation, disability status, income, educational level or geographic location. In order for noticeable changes to be made regarding the activity levels of our youth, we need to begin to address boys and girls differently and meet their specific needs and not conglomerate our goals and methods into a patriarchal realm. With the great advances our society has made in developing programs and methods of collecting data, there is optimism that we can now incorporate this information into a game plan that will ensure success for all.

Instructional perspectives

Echoing the comments made by Penney in chapter 7, we conclude that the gender inequities in school physical education in the USA have as much to do with silences in state and national policy documents as with attitudes and practices of physical education teachers and teacher education training programs. There are still too many stereotypical unreconstructed PE programs. Perhaps one of the most significant differences between US and

Britain is that physical education programs in the USA are for the most part not sex differentiated. However, we still have a long way to go to convince some conservative physical educators of the value of alternative teaching strategies and curricular initiatives. In a recent opinion piece in the *Journal of Physical Education, Recreation and Dance* on the place of dodgeball[2] in physical education, the author noted that 'In this time of political correctness, adventure education, and cooperative games, dodgeball stands tall among them all' (Swartz, 2001: 55).

There have been some significant and meaningful efforts at gender equity in physical education in the United States when compared to some of the accounts presented in other chapters in this collection. There are now far fewer single-sexed classes, with more physical education classes being taught as legitimate co-educational classes than are not. While this is not in and of itself any guarantee of greater equity we do feel that significant and substantive progress has been made. Student choice in clothing for physical education is also commonplace and much less an issue than it seems to be in England. When uniforms are used teachers include policies that recognize various body types and gender. The physical education policies are likely to allow shorts and sweat pants while covering one's hair is a typical adjustment to religious customs. Showering is for the most part a non-issue in American physical education programs as physical education teachers no longer require that students shower following classes. Some critics might suggest that students don't work hard enough in PE to need a shower and the expectation was a moot one from a health and safety perspective. Many more teachers now group students on ability and not gender. While this too is problematic, it has focused teachers' attention on designing tasks that allow all to be successful. There has been a curricular shift from a dominance on psycho-motor skill development to other orientations that teachers, parents, and students value: taking responsibility for their learning, contributing to the sport in ways other than elite performance, and social interaction and peer support in physical activity settings (Ennis and Chen, 1993).

Federal rules and school policies have also established an agenda of social inclusion and equity in schools. In some instances physical education is one of the front line subjects in the implementation of this policy for children and youth with special needs. Most physical education teachers and teacher education programs have taken this task seriously. There are several studies that have looked at students' perceptions of inclusive classrooms from the perspectives of children with and without special needs (Murata *et al.*, 2000; Slininger *et al.*, 2000; Webb, 2000). The focus on teacher certification in adapted physical education may be a model for many other parts of the world.

While wanting to celebrate progress we are also aware of what is yet to be done and the areas of neglect in developments to date. We have not paid the same kind of attention to the inclusion of the physical cultures of the many different ethnic groups that populate our schools. There is a silence in our pedagogical research on these issues. Indeed there is much to be learned on this issue by American pedagogy scholars from a number of chapters in this book. We have a long way to go before we can refute the concern expressed by Penney (chapter 7 in this text) that all too often boys and girls will leave schools with their conceptions of femininity and masculinity and applications in contexts of physical activity and sport essentially intact and unchallenged.

Curricular perspectives

Recently there has been a concerted effort to respond to the needs and desires of all students through development and diversification of curricular perspectives in physical education. This is especially true for fitness activity models (TAAG, SPARK, CATCH). The cultural studies approach and recent adventure education/outdoor education initiatives appear promising in the quest to provide beneficial, meaningful and substantial opportunities for girls. The Sport Education model may have been founded on participation for all principles, but participation is not an automatic outcome of the model. Providing meaningful and plentiful opportunities for all is dependent upon teachers' cognizance of and ability to promote an appropriate environment for all to respond and achieve. Before implementing a curriculum, teachers must critically examine the impact such a curriculum is likely to have on all students, and then adapt as necessary to benefit all students in their classes. This may entail paying particular attention to girls and/or lower skilled students. Additionally, teachers need to extend the sporting and game opportunities beyond the traditionally male dominated sports; as gender and skill differences are diminished with novel sports and games. Some teachers have experimented with adopting the sport education model in a dance curriculum (Graves and Townsend, 2000). We need more teachers to not only experiment with different curricular models, but to also research the processes and outcomes associated with such initiatives.

Many students in the US have similar perceptions regarding physical education to those in England (Williams and Bedward, 2001, chapter 9). More girls than boys view themselves as marginalized in PE and girls seem to have fewer opportunities to participate in school sports (though their access to interscholastic activities seem to be significantly better than in Britain). However, moving forward on a gender equity agenda must not be done in isolation. The role of class, race and sexual orientation must be part of the conversations that shape new policies and practices to allow all boys and girls to gain the benefits of involvement in physical activity and sport in ways that are meaningful and relevant to their lives. We have much to learn from each other as we attempt to highlight and inform these agendas for physical education in our respective countries.

Notes

1 K–12 represents children aged 5–19 years.
2 Dodgeball is an elimination game (there are a variety of ways to play) where students are divided into teams. The objective of the game is to get points for your team. Points are accumulated by hitting players on the opposing team by kicking or throwing a ball at them. Most rules specify that hitting above the waist is a rule violation. See the issue section of *JOPERD* (April, 2001) for a discussion on the place for the game in PE. What has been amazing to watch in recent months is the interest of the media (with national editorials) on this game as an educational experience in contrast to what has been hyped as the New PE (student-centered, less sport-oriented, physical education programming).

References

Acosta, R.V. and Carpenter, L.J. (2000) Women in intercollegiate sport: A longitudinal study – twenty-three year update (1977–2000), unpublished manuscript, Brooklyn College, Brooklyn, NY.

Browne, J. (1992) Reasons for the selection or nonselection of physical education studies by year 12 girls, *Journal of Teaching in Physical Education* 11: 402–10.

Canadian Association for Health, Physical Education, Recreation and Dance (1995) *Gender Equity Through Physical Education and Sport*, Reston, VA: CAHPERD.

Carlson, T.B. (1995) We hate gym: student alienation from physical education, *Journal of Teaching in Physical Education* 14: 467–77.

Center for Disease Control and Prevention (CDC) (1997) *Guidelines for School and Community Programs to Promote Lifelong Physical Activity Among Young People, 1997*, 46, pp. 1–36.

Center for Disease Control and Prevention (CDC) (2000) Youth risk behavior surveillance: United States, 1999, *Morbidity and Mortality Weekly Report*, 49, SS–5.

34CFR106.34 (1999) Code of Federal Regulations. Title 34, Volume 1, Parts 1 to 299. Revised as of July 1, 1999 From the US Government Printing Office via GPO Access.

Chepyator-Thomson, J.R. and Ennis, C. (1997) Reproduction and resistance to the culture of femininity and masculinity in secondary school physical education, *Research Quarterly for Exercise and Sport* 68: 89–99.

Corbin, C.D. and Lindsey, R. (1997) *Fitness for Life*, Glenview, IL: Scott Foresman-Addison Wesley.

Curnow, J. and Macdonald, D. (1995) Can sport education be gender inclusive?: A case study in an upper primary school, *The ACHPER Healthy Lifestyles Journal* 42(4): 9–11.

Durante, F. (1997) Let your students choose! The PCAB method, *Runner Journal* 35: 3.

Ennis, C.D. and Chen, C. (1993). Domain specifications and content representativeness of the revised Value Orientation Inventory, *Research Quarterly for Exercise and Sport* 64: 436–46.

Graves, M.A. and Townsend, J.S. (2000). Applying the sport education curriculum model to dance, *The Journal of Physical Education, Recreation and Dance* 71(8): 50–4.

Griffin, L. (1984) Girls' participation patterns in a middle school team sports unit, *Journal of Teaching in Physical Education* 4: 30–8.

Griffin, P. (1985) Boys' participation styles in a middle school physical education team sports unit, *Journal of Teaching in Physical Education* 4(2): 100–10.

Hastie, P.A. (1998) The participation and perceptions of girls within a unit of sport education, *Journal of Teaching in Physical Education* 17(2): 157–71.

Hastie, P. (2000) An ecological analysis of a sport education season, *Journal of Teaching in Physical Education* 19(3): 355–73.

Hellison, D. (1995) *Teaching Responsibility Through Physical Activity*, Champaign, IL: Human Kinetics.

Henry, F.M. (1964) Physical education: an academic discipline, *Journal of Health, Physical Education and Recreation* 35: 32, 33, 69.

Kinchin, G.D. (1997) High school students' perceptions of and responses to curriculum change in physical education, unpublished doctoral dissertation, The Ohio State University.

Kinchin, G. and O'Sullivan, M. (1999) Making physical education meaningful for high school students, *Journal of Physical Education, Recreation and Dance* 70(5): 40–4, 54.

Kirk, D. (2001) Physical education: a gendered history, in D. Penney (ed.) *Gender and Physical Education: Contemporary Issues and Future Directions*, London: Routledge.

Kirk, D. and Tinning, R. (1990) *Physical Education, Curriculum and Culture: Critical Issues in Contemporary Crisis*, London: Falmer Press.

Kirk, D., Burgess-Limerick, R., Kiss, M., Lahey, J. and Penney, D. (1998) *Senior Physical Education: An Integrated Approach*, Champaign, IL: Human Kinetics.

Lawson, H. (1998) Rejuvenating, and transforming physical education to meet the needs of vulnerable children, youth, and families, *Journal of Teaching in Physical Education* 18: 2–25.

Lirgg, D.D. (1993) Effects of same-sex versus coeducational physical education on the self-perceptions of middle and high school students, *Research Quarterly for Exercise and Sport* 64(3): 324–34.

Lock, R.S., Minarik, L.T. and Omata, J. (1999) Gender and the problem of diversity: Action research in physical education, *Quest* 51: 393–407.

Lynn, S. (1999) *Should Physical Education Classes Return to Teaching Males and Females Separately?*, retrieved March 20, 2001 from the World Wide Web: http://mailer.fsu.edu/~slynn/issues1999.html

Macdonald, D. and Tinning, R. (1995) Physical education teacher education and the trend to proletarianization: a case study, *Journal of Teaching in Physical Education* 15(1): 98–118.

Murata, N.M., Hodge, S.R. and Little, J.R. (2000) Students' attitudes, experiences, and perspectives on their peers with disabilities, *Clinical Kinesiology* 54(3): 59–66.

National Association for Sport and Physical Education (NASPE) (1992) *Outcomes of Quality Physical Education Programs*, Reston, VA: NASPE.

National Association for Sport and Physical Education (NASPE) (1995a) *Moving into the Future. National Physical Education Standards: A Guide to Content and Assessment*, New York: Mosby.

National Association for Sport and Physical Education (NASPE) (1995b) *National Standards for Beginning Physical Education Teachers*. Reston, VA: NASPE.

National Association for Sport and Physical Education (NASPE) (2001) *Physical Education for Progress Bill Update*, retrieved May 4, 2001, from the World Wide Web: http://www.aahperd.org/naspe/whatsnew-pep.html

National Board for Professional Teaching Standards (NBPTS) (1999) *Physical Education Standards*, Arlington, VA: NBPTS.

National Federation of High Schools (NFHS) (2001) *National Federation of State High School Associations 1999–2000 Athletic Participation Summary*, retrieved March 20, 2001 from the World Wide Web: http://www.nfhs.org/part_survey99-00.htm

Nilges, L.M. (1998) I thought only fairy tales had supernatural power: a radical feminist analysis of Title IX in physical education, *Journal of Teaching in Physical Education* 17(2): 172–94.

Nilges, L.M. (2000) A nonverbal discourse analysis of gender in undergraduate educational gymnastics sequences using Laban effort analysis, *Journal of Teaching in Physical Education* 19(3): 287–310.

O'Sullivan, M., Kinchin, G., Dunaway, S., Kellum, S. and Dixon, S. (1996) High School physical education comes alive at your school: a unit on the culture of sport for your students, presented at *AAHPERD National Convention*, Atlanta, GA.

Sallis, J.F. and Owen, N. (1999) *Physical Activity and Behavioral Medicine*, Thousand Oaks, CA: Sage.

Siedentop, D. (1980) *Physical Education: Introductory Analysis*, Dubuque, IA: Wm. C. Brown.

Siedentop, D. (1994) *Sport Education: Quality PE Through Positive Sport Experiences*, Champaign, IL: Human Kinetics.

Siedentop, D. (1995) Improving sport education, *The ACHPER Healthy Lifestyles Journal* 42(4): 22–4.

Siedentop, D. (2001) *Introduction to Physical Education, Sport and Fitness* (4th edition), Mountain View, CA: Mayfield Publishing.

Siedentop, D. and Tannehill, D. (2000) *Developing Teaching Skills in Physical Education* (4th edition), Mountain View, CA: Mayfield Publishing.

Slininger, D., Sherrill C. and Jankowski, C.M. (2000) Children's attitudes toward classmates with severe disabilities: Revisiting contact theory, *Adapted Physical Activity Quarterly* 17: 176–96.

Slobogir, K. (2001) *New Physical Education Favors Fitness Over Sports*, retrieved May 18, 2001, from the World Wide Web: http://fyi.cnn.com/2001/fyi/teachers.ednews/o5/17/new.pe/index.html

Smeal, B., Carpetner, B. and Tait, G. (1994) Ideals and realities: articulating feminist perspectives in physical education, *Quest* 46: 410–24.

Swartz, M.J. (2001) Issues, *Journal of Physical Education, Recreation and Dance* 72(4): 54.

Talbot, M. (1993) Gender and physical education, in J. Evans (ed.) *Equality, Education and Physical Education*, London: Falmer Press.

The Prevention Institute (2001) *Promoting Physical Activity Among Youth: It's Everyone's Business*, Columbus, OH.

20 U.S.C. §1681a (1988) *Title IX, Education Amendments of 1972*, Public Law 92–318, 1972.

Treanor, L., Graber, K., Housner, L. and Wiegand, R. (1998) Middle school students' perceptions of coeducational and same-sex physical education classes, *Journal of Teaching in Physical Education* 18(1): 43–56.

US Department of Education (USDE) (1997) *Title IX: 25 Years of Progress*, Washington, DC.

US Department of Health and Human Services (USDHHS) (1996) *Physical Activity and Health: A Report of the Surgeon General*, Atlanta, GA: US Department of Health and Human Services, Centers for Disease Control and Prevention, National Center for Chronic Disease Prevention and Health Promotion.

US Department of Health and Human Services (USDHHS) (1997) President's Council on Physical Fitness and Sports Report *Physical Activity and Sport in the Lives of Girls: Physical and Mental Dimensions from an Interdisciplinary Approach*, Washington, DC.

US Department of Health and Human Services (USDHHS) (1999) Youth risk behavior surveillance, *Morbidity and Mortality Weekly Report*, 47, SS–3, Washington, DC.

US Department of Health and Human Services (USDHHS) (2000) *Healthy People 2010: Understanding and Improving Health*, Washington, DC: US Department of Health and Human Services, Governing Printing Office.

Vertinsky, P.A. (1992) Reclaiming space, revisioning the body: the quest for gender-sensitive physical education *Quest* 44: 373–96.

Webb, D. (2000) *An Attitudinal Analysis of Students with Orthopedic Disabilities Toward General Physical Education: A Pilot Study*, unpublished doctoral dissertation, The Ohio State University, Columbus, OH.

Williams, A. and Bedward, J. (2001) Understanding girls' experience of physical education: relational analysis and situated learning, in D. Penney (ed.) *Gender and Physical Education: Contemporary Issues and Future Directions*, London: Routledge.

11 Physical education teacher education: sites of progress or resistance

Jan Wright

Introduction

In chapter 6, Brown and Rich draw attention to the relative dearth of research in physical education teacher education which looks specifically at gender issues when compared to that addressing school-based physical education. They focus specifically on 'gendered student teacher identity', how this is constituted, and how it impacts on teaching practice. In this chapter I want to draw attention to the 'gender agendas' that have informed physical education teacher education (PETE) in Australia and the active role that research and researchers have played in this process. In the second part of the chapter I discuss how these agendas have been taken up and/or been resisted in contexts of initial physical education teacher education (IPETE) and teacher professional development. This chapter enables a comparison with the situation in England and Wales, which as Penney and Evans suggested in chapter 2, points to silences and absences in policy and practice in both contexts.

Ways of thinking and doing gender in PETE: a discursive history

Social practices are always embedded in the discourses circulating at a particular point in time. Some of these discourses will be more powerful in their effects than others. Earlier chapters in this book have pointed to the ways in which power has worked in the UK to shape policy and practice in relation to gender at all levels of education and schooling. Given the focus in this chapter on PETE in Australia, a useful starting point is to ask what ways of thinking about gender have been available to inform PETE curriculum, policy and practice.[1] In response to this question I will begin with a brief narrative of my own thirty years of experience in physical education secondary and tertiary institutions. My story is suggestive of the insularity that physical education has had for many years from feminist and social theory.

As a student at Sydney University in the late 1960s, I, together with the other students in my course, were oblivious to the feminist activity and writing around us. In my year there were ten women and one man. Our university education foundation subjects certainly never dealt with social issues or gender, except as a variable in education psychology. I attended single-sex classes in dance, gymnastics and games and I completed my practicum in a private girls' school. As far as I understood my own history at this stage, I had no personal experience of discrimination, nor had I much opportunity to witness it in my university or secondary practicum experiences. There was very little to draw gender issues to my attention until I began to teach, and even then in the 1970s, I mostly taught single-sex physical education classes. It was only when I took postgraduate courses at university, studied the sociology of education and met some 'radical women' in my subjects that feminism and gender issues began to be something that I read and thought about.

As a tertiary educator in physical education, my feminist position served for many years to marginalise me as a staff member, and my interpretation of physical education and sporting practices. However, national and state policies relating to gender equity eventually permeated to IPETE and teacher professional development, and gender issues are now much more widely researched and discussed in IPETE and to a certain extent, promoted as part of a teacher's professional development. While it would now be rare for an IPETE course coordinator not to be able to point to places in the course where gender issues are discussed, this does not necessarily mean that all is resolved. As so many point out (Dewar, 1990; Fernandez-Balboa, 1997; Flintoff, 1993; Kirk *et al.*, 1997), physical education teacher education and school-based physical education are still far from exemplary sites of gender practice (whatever these might look like), and to expect them to be so ignores the very complex interplay of institutional investments in particular forms of physical education practice, the discursive resources available to think differently about physical education, lecturer, student teacher and student identities, and the very structure and organization of IPETE programmes.

To understand why this might be so, I want to explore the discursive and institutional resources that have been available from the 1970s to the current day to inform the thinking about, and the doing of, gender reform in schools and tertiary institutions in Australia. What research, researchers, legislation and policy has been available to inform discussion and practice in relation to gender in physical education? In answering this question I do not intend to survey general and education-based feminist research and writing that would have been widely available during this period. As suggested above the insularity of physical education generally from feminist theory and activism suggests that for resources to have been drawn upon, they would need to be readily available and immediately relevant to teachers and academics. One of the main academic resources available to physical educators from the 1960s has been the *Australian Council for Health, Physical Education and Recreation (ACHPER) National Journal*. The national professional association ACHPER has provided the major forum for discussion and dissemination of information important to physical education policy and practice, through its state and national conferences and its journal. The journal, now called *The ACHPER Healthy Lifestyles Journal*, is the national professional and academic journal for physical educators in Australia. An analysis of articles in the journal provides a good indication of the interest or lack of it in gender issues.

Prior to the 1970s, there were no articles in the national journal which dealt with gender issues. A survey of the *ACHPER National Journal* in the 1970s and 1980s suggests that there was little written in the 1970s except for two notable exceptions: articles in 1975 by Geoffrey Watson and by Ponch Hawkes and her colleagues. These two exceptions were in their different ways informed by a liberal feminist approach which drew attention to the ways in which the practices associated with contemporary physical education and sport disadvantaged girls. Whereas Watson's (1975) article reported empirical research informed by psychological notions of sex role and sex role socialisation, the Hawkes *et al.* (1975) article documented inequalities in physical education and sport opportunities, resources and facilities for girls as compared to boys in Victorian and New South Wales schools. Watson (1975) was interested in asking how the dependent variable of measurable sex type attributes correlated with children's evaluation of Little Athletics. His prediction, which was confirmed by the study, was that girls would reveal a preference for 'more expressive activities such as the jumping events' and boys for 'the more challenging and aggressive activities such as throwing, hurdles and distance events' (p. 11). For Watson, writing in the context of social psychology, the issue was not so much about providing girls with the same opportunities as boys but about providing opportunities for girls and women to achieve and enjoy their participation in ways which fitted essential feminine characteristics. In contrast, for others like Hawkes *et al.*, the issue was more how particular sex role expectations led to assumptions about girls' lack of interest and ability in physical activity and how this argument in turn led to justifying inequalities in opportunities. Hawkes' and her colleagues' study demonstrated how girls were offered fewer sports and activity choices than the boys, and the boys had generally access to more and better facilities than the girls.

From the prevailing liberal feminist point of view, discriminatory practices based on sex stereotyping was the main issue. *The Girls' School and Society Report* (Schools Commission, 1975), for instance, was concerned to advise teachers that through the ways that they interacted with students, and particularly through their different expectations, they were at risk of socialising students into stereotypical sex roles which would disadvantage girls. This document recommended that teacher education should ensure that their students were 'at least correctly informed about the social basis of sex differences: we see these questions as being so fundamental as to warrant their inclusion in the main body of teacher education courses' (p. 97). On the basis of reports of discrimination the Report argues that:

The sex role socialisation in sport and physical education is particularly damaging for girls since it merely results in the self-fulfilling prophecy of weak and physically dependent females.

(p. 69)

In comparison to the two articles found in the ACHPER journal in the 1970s, the 1980s were characterised by considerable discussion and activitism beginning with the New South Wales (NSW) government sponsored 'Fit to Play' Conference in January 1980. This conference brought together leading British, North American and Australian feminist researchers from the human movement sciences, sociology of sport and physical education, to speak specifically on women and sport and physical education. At the time, the conference was a major source of inspiration to women working in sport, physical education and recreation. It was a catalyst for numerous actions to improve opportunities for women and to promote the recognition that the athlete and physical education student are not generically male. As part of its contribution to the conference, the Social Development Unit of the NSW Ministry of Education provided a 'discussion paper on the interrelationship between social attitudes and participation of girls in school sport' (Coles, 1980: 3). This paper and the conference sought to dispel the prevailing myths about women's participation in sport and the discussion paper in particular is clear that girls are discriminated against in school sport. Coles argues that '[o]nly by providing extra opportunities will the school be able to provide these students with "equal opportunities" ' (p. 42).

Given the importance attributed to the teacher as a role model and an agent of socialisation, Coles (1980) is very critical of the professional preparation programmes for physical education specialists of the time. She attributes physical education teachers' failure to impact on their students' quality of life to the recruitment of a particular kind of person to physical education, and to professional preparation which does nothing to sensitise student teachers to the needs of their students, especially students who are not like themselves. She is also critical of professional preparation that does nothing to develop an understanding of physical education and sport beyond the most technical details of teaching practical skills and games. She attributes the poor performance of girls in high school to the lack of skills and enthusiasm of their primary school (that is, female) teachers. This is a line of argument which has continued to receive considerable coverage to the present day (Senate Standing Committee on Environment, Recreation and the Arts, 1992).

Despite the growing coverage of gender issues, little attention seems to have been paid to issues of equity in the selection of keynote and plenary speakers for the ACHPER Commonwealth and International Conference associated with the Commonwealth Games in Brisbane in 1982. There were few female speakers and those who were invited presented mostly on dance and health. It was one of the men however, Richard Gruneau, the Canadian sociologist, who was the only speaker to directly address the topic of women in sport. In a radical move (for the time), in his abstract for the conference, he argued that:

> much of the literature on women in sport, while extremely provocative, is limited by its focus on women's involvement as an independent object of study rather than as a mediated set of practices constitutive of a whole social and material process. Related to this, I suggest (in my paper) how the focus which has developed in this literature on unequal opportunities in sport for women has tended to divert attention away from the more important questions about the role of sport as a contributor to the reproduction of patriarchal social relations.
>
> (Gruneau, 1982: 22)

In 1982 a Women in Sport and Recreation ACHPER Special Interest Group was established, but at the 1984 National Conference none of the abstracts in the Conference Issue of the journal (including my own) dealt with gender issues.

In 1984 the Anti Discrimination Act galvanised attention and action in education. It had very practical implications particularly for physical education where most schools had single-sex physical education classes except for social dance. In her paper in the *ACHPER National Journal*, Jennifer Browne interpreted the Act and its implications for the physical education and sport community, providing a detailed checklist of questions for teachers of physical education, as a means of determining whether they were implementing the intent as well as the letter of the law. The following extract provides a sense of the kinds of questions asked and some insights into the ways in which the Act was being interpreted:

> Are physical education requirements the same for boys and girls?
> Are all physical education and interschool sporting activities offered to both boys and girls?
> Are all facilities and equipment available equally to both sexes during breaks?
> Are the same events in track and field athletics championships offered to both boys and girls?
>
> (Browne, 1985: 7)

With gender issues clearly on the education agenda, funding followed policy, including funding for physical education projects. In 1984 a national project (Girls Achievement and Self-Esteem – the Contribution of Physical Education and Sport, also known as the GAPA project) was funded by a Commonwealth Schools Commission Grant for three years to address inequalities of opportunity for girls in physical education and sport (Oldenhove, 1989). Specifically, the project engaged schools across all states in action research projects designed to increase girls' involvement in physical activity – not so much for their 'fitness' as would be the case today but to improve their self-esteem, self-confidence and body image. The project tapped into the prevailing discourses and motivated considerable activity, particularly in South Australia where the project team was located. The project produced a number of resources that were distributed to schools and tertiary institutions around Australia, including a regular newsletter, a video and kits for classroom observations and for teaching about women in sport. The extent to which these were used is uncertain. The focus on girls meant that if used in tertiary settings it was likely to be by female physical educators who were still a small minority in colleges and universities. As I explain below, it is a question of what spaces were available in IPETE to discuss gender issues, by whom and with whom.

By the early 1990s, the other main sources of information on gender issues were North American (and some Australian) textbooks on the sociology of sport (e.g. Coakley, 1990; Leonard, 1993; and from Australia: Lawrence and Rowe, 1986; McKay, 1991; Stoddard, 1986) and an increasing collection of feminist texts on gender and sport (Birrell and Cole, 1994; Boutelier and San Giovanni, 1991; Messner and Sabo, 1990). The extent to which these were used as resources beyond undergraduate sociology of sport subjects is doubtful. However, with the growth of postgraduate courses, and particularly those informed by a critical pedagogy model such as the Master of Education programme at Deakin University, these resources were more likely to be taken up. As one notable example, the British feminist academic Sheila Scraton (1990) was invited to write and edit a Deakin distance education monograph which brought readily accessible ideas about gender to teacher education for both pre-service students and teachers undertaking professional development.

Until the 1990s the writing on gender which filtered through into PETE was primarily informed by liberal and radical feminist analyses of gender issues, although Tinning's (1985) paper on 'The cult of slenderness' looked forward to one of the main agenda items for the 1990s. In the 1990s, following trends in social and cultural theory which had gained prominence elsewhere in the decade before, the gender agenda shifted to engage with the notion of gender as socially constructed. This raised questions about the ways in which the practices associated with sport and physical education influenced gender construction, including the ways in which language in physical education lessons (Evans and Clarke, 1988; Evans, Davies and Penney, 1996; Wright and King, 1991; 1997) and in the media (Creedon, 1994; Lenskyj, 1998) promoted particular notions of femininity. This move away from discrimination to 'social construction' also provided a space in which researchers and educators could talk about the social construction of masculinity (Connell, 2000; Whitson, 1994).

There is now a wealth of accessible research drawing on social theories of the body and on the social constructions of femininity and masculinity to inform discussion of gender issues in physical education teacher education.

Again the impact that these are likely to have depends on the spaces available in IPETE programmes for their use. As will be discussed below there are organisational and curricula features of IPETE which continue to marginalise the discussion of social issues, including those concerning gender, and in this respect there are important similarities between training programmes in Australia and the UK. On the other hand, there are now national and state policies in Australia which are explicitly informed by the notion of gender as socially constructed. For instance the following statements are included in the 'Principles for Action' in the national document, *Gender Equity: A Framework for Australian Schools* (Gender Equity Taskforce for the Ministerial Council on Employment Education Training and Youth Affairs):

> Schools should acknowledge their active role in the construction of gender, and their responsibility to ensure that all organisational and management practices reflect [a] commitment to gender equity.
>
> (Gender Equity Taskforce, 1997: 9)

And in defining gender in the New South Wales Gender Equity Strategy, *Girls and Boys in Schools, 1996–2001* (Specific Focus Directorate, 1996) the following statement is included:

> A complex range of historical and social factors influence the ways in which girls and women, boys and men experience and express their femininity and masculinity. Current beliefs about feminine and masculine behaviours shape differences in educational and social outcomes for girls and boys.
>
> (Specific Focus Directorate 1996: 2)

As will be demonstrated below these policies have been important in motivating strategies for gender reform at the level of state Departments of Education. In addition, gender and sexuality have been more explicitly written into physical and health education syllabuses, particularly at the senior level of schooling. While this does not necessarily bring about changes in practices – in IPETE or in schools – it does provide a context within which it is possible to argue for some attention to gender issues and for changes to practices which bring more socially just outcomes for female and male students.

The potential of PETE programmes as institutional sites for gender reform

The first section of this chapter provided some indication of the discursive context in which IPETE programmes have been organised and taught. From the 1970s it is obvious that there was information, research, government policies and strategies to draw on for IPETE curricula. The question is to what extent have these resources been taken up and with what likely impact? What is there about IPETE programmes, the contexts in which they are produced, the lecturers who teach in them and the students who attend them which facilitate or work against a gender equity agenda?

Unlike England and Wales I would suggest that in Australia government policy specifically concerning curricula in physical education has far less impact on what is taught in IPETE, when compared to the traditional under- standings within IPETE programmes of what constitutes content knowledge in physical education. This has in turn been shaped by strong university traditions of what constitutes valued knowledge (that is scientific knowledge) and the long-standing dominance of sport and games in the Australian practice of physical education. To a great extent this is because universities are nationally funded, while government education systems are state based. University programmes are not directly accountable to state-based depart- ments of education. However, as employers of university trained teachers and through their development of school syllabi, state education systems indirectly affect what is taught as content. Yet at the time of writing, no state had produced explicit criteria for the characteristics necessary for teachers of physical education, beyond holding a degree with some physical education content knowledge (rarely made explicit) and a teacher education component with a specified amount of practical experience in schools. In most states it is also now a requirement that teachers of physical education have some content knowledge in health. This has had one of the more radical impacts on IPETE programmes in the recent past, as universities have adapted their syllabuses to meet this requirement. Subjects taken in the context of health range from broad public health issues to subjects such as 'drugs', 'nutrition', 'personal health' and 'community health', designed specifically to assist the teaching of health in schools. Thus the inclusion of Health provides a space to examine 'health discourses' such as those around exercise and fitness, sexuality and gender and other forms of difference. The resources and spaces to do this are now widely available. Whether they are utilised in this way depends on teachers' and students' choices of subjects and topics.

It follows that there is little accountability (and considerable flexibility) in what university programmes can do in producing physical education teachers. The constraints and the reshaping of programmes that have occurred in many universities in recent years are more an outcome of university economic and political decisions than choices made in the context of changing government policy about physical activity and sport. In this context it is competing interests within university IPETE programmes, budgetary constraints and teachers' and students' own investments that are likely to provide or shut down opportunities to address gender issues in the IPETE curriculum.

Although it is difficult to make many generalisations, there is enough evidence in Australia and elsewhere to suggest that physical education teacher education has not been one of the most responsive sites for the promotion of discussion and change in relation to gender issues. Indeed studies in the

UK (Flintoff, 1993, 1997), North America (Dewar, 1990) and Australia (Macdonald, 1993; Swan, 1995) suggest that PETE programmes have typically been underpinned by patriarchal discourses and practices which are recognisable in staff hierarchies, course organisation, the curriculum, the relationships between staff and students and in students' relationships with each other.

As Kirk points out in chapter 3 and elsewhere (Kirk, 1992), one of the most compelling explanations for this is the dominance within physical education since the 1950s of masculinist ways of thinking and doing movement. Despite their original pre-eminence, forms of physical activity and physical education pedagogy associated with a female tradition have been marginalised in UK, Australia and the US (Dewar, 1990; Kirk, 1992 and chapter 3; Wright 1996). Shifts to coeducational physical education and physical education teacher education have ensured that games and sports hold a privileged position over gymnastics and dance, and more recently aerobics, despite high levels of participation in these areas of physical activity outside of school (Australian Bureau of Statistics 1997; Williams and Woodhouse, 1996). As Kirk, Macdonald and Tinning (1997) argue, physical education teacher education in Australia is currently regulated by outmoded cultural imperatives which emerged in the 1940s and 1950s – that is, physical education centred on multi-activity sports based programmes. They go on to argue that:

> physical education teacher education regulated in part by a post-war form of physical culture is likely to be working within functionalist assumptions about gender, race and social class, if these are acknowledged at all, that may be culturally obsolete and certainly dangerously misleading.
>
> (p. 291)

In this context it becomes almost impossible to think and know physical education teacher education differently – to imagine other forms of pedagogy and knowledge. Change to the status quo becomes very difficult to argue, particularly when the social identity of some members of staff rests on the maintenance of a strong 'practical studies' component based on traditional sports and games. As I discuss below, challenging the place of team games also becomes difficult when students' pleasures and identities are bound up with sport.

The domination of PETE by a sports and games model of physical education has been complemented by the pre-eminence of the biophysical sciences in PETE curricula and a technocratic approach to the teaching of physical education (Tinning, 1991). The organisation of IPETE courses in Australia has helped to confirm the place of the biophysical sciences as the fundamental and essential basis for physical education teaching. In some cases an undergraduate education in human movement science and a background in sport, plus one year of professional preparation are taken as sufficient preparation for teaching physical (and sometimes health) education. With teacher shortages this form of preparation is likely to have more and more acceptance.

In Australia there are three broad models of professional preparation: integrated or concurrent degrees, e.g. Bachelor of Education (Physical and Health Education); parallel or double degrees, e.g. Bachelor of Teaching/ Bachelor of Applied Science; and an end-on model, with three years of an undergraduate degree plus one or two years of teacher education. In each of these models, if gender issues are to be discussed, it is in the context of educational foundation subject(s) and/or a specialist sociology subject on leisure, sport and/or physical education. Traditionally the most common programme has been the concurrent degree that usually involves a cohort of students studying a highly structured syllabus with few options. For some degrees a greater part of studies are shared with exercise science students preparing for work in areas other than teaching. Increasingly, numbers of students are completing end-on programmes with the professional component available through on-campus and distance modes. The first degree for most of these students is an exercise science/applied science degree.

There are few spaces in any of these courses for subjects which deal with social issues; and social issues are rarely integrated into science or pedagogy subjects. IPETE subjects tend to fall into strongly bounded or classified categories: biophysical sciences, pedagogy subjects tied to practicums which usually have a strong technical emphasis, practical studies (when these exist at all), educational foundations and one or two social science subjects. The inclusion of health education in state syllabuses in the last decade has led to the addition of health and health pedagogy subjects in most concurrent, parallel and the professional component of end-on degrees.

While it can be said that IPETE courses in Australia in general share a core curriculum of the human movement sciences, the degree to which broader education and sociocultural studies are included varies but only around a small range – that is, from none at all to one or two subjects in the core/mandatory component. The opportunities to study social or gender issues may be extended through elective subjects, though these often have to compete with practical and/or scientific subjects which many students may see as having more relevance to their future careers. Research in the UK, US and Australia on the concurrent model suggests that subjects that cover social issues including gender issues are not only marginalised in the programme – i.e. they receive little space, time and few resources – but are also regarded by students as irrelevant, soft options and where possible to be avoided, particularly when compared to the 'hard' sciences (Dewar, 1990; Macdonald, 1993; Swan, 1995). As Swan and others (Dewar, 1990) point out, the sociology subjects are often designed to challenge the taken-for-granted and thereby challenge the values and beliefs that are central at this stage to students' sense of identity as athletes and future physical educators who will encourage students to be more like themselves.

While it is in the education foundation subjects and in the sociocultural subjects that gender issues are most likely to be taken up, the other site with increasing potential for addressing these issues in IPETE is health/health education. Again health can be taught primarily from a bio-medical position and/or a position which emphasises individual responsibility for health outcomes. There is thus no guarantee that gender will become any more than a variable to be correlated with specific health dispositions. However, the expectation that senior (post-16) physical and health education will be taught from a sociocultural perspective has the potential to impact on IPETE curricula as well as school-based health and physical education and thereby provide a space for the discussion of issues concerning gender and sexuality.

At the time of writing, state and federal governments and professional teacher organisations in Australia had little control over what a physical and health education teacher might be expected to know in terms of content and pedagogical knowledge. Discussions are currently in progress to introduce a form of teacher registration which will recognise a wide range of attributes including those related to teaching diverse groups of students. However, until these deliberations produce results, the organisation and curriculum of IPETE in Australia continues to privilege the human movement sciences and sports performance, and thereby provide minimal spaces for the discussion of gender issues.

IPETE students

Swan (1995) and Macdonald (1993) in Australia and Hargreaves (1986) in the UK all describe a powerful 'normalising' process which both attracts students to, and then privileges certain kinds of students in physical education teacher education. As a profession physical education tends to attract students who themselves enjoy, are good at and identify with the values associated with sport and physical activity. As Hargreaves (1986) and others (Swan, 1995) point out, PETE students (and PETE lecturers) share a common interest, perhaps passion for recreational physical activity and/or sport. In addition or perhaps partly because of this, as many studies have suggested, PETE students as a group tend to be conservative. The IPETE student body is also not notable for its cultural diversity. In Australia this means students are primarily from a British heritage, with increasing numbers from second generation or later European families. There are very few Asian or Middle Eastern heritage students in physical and health education, despite the increasing proportion of these cultural minorities in Australia. Aboriginal students are underrepresented in Australia universities generally, but some students do take up scholarships in physical education teacher education. As a group, however, PETE students seem to have little experience of marginality or discrimination; students who do not identify within the majority cultural groups often bear an unrealistic burden to represent and articulate the experience of difference or else remain silent (and often extremely angry) as difference is either ignored, treated tokenistically or even pejoratively.

This is not a fruitful environment for radical change nor for the ready acceptance of values which are fundamental to gender reform in IPETE and in schools. The dominance of the human movement sciences, technocratic ways of working and thinking, the privileging of competitive games and sports all compound ways of thinking and being which have already been profoundly shaped by an immersion in a masculinist sports culture. In addition, for many students what will be important during their initial teacher education is survival – passing subjects and surviving their practicum, as well as enjoying their time at university or college and the companionship of their fellow students. What students value is the usefulness of knowledge, how it can be applied in, for example, a teaching, coaching or outdoor education context; that is, knowledge that can be applied to performance (Dewar, 1987). Such imperatives allow little room for critical reflection, particularly in the context of the teaching practicum unless explicitly required, which seems rare. As Luca, a very thoughtful mature age student, said on reading one of Juan-Miguel Fernandez-Balboa's papers challenging traditional practices in physical education:

> Reading Balboa, the impression that I have, and it is an excellent paper in terms of the way he mentions that as teachers we not only have to teach the PE content but be able to challenge the issues and bring that into our teaching and making that something that we are trying to get across – the Schulman categories. It is important that as teachers we are aware of the social issues, it is not easy, there are too much stigmas in society about what issues a teacher should not do and even the ways of talking, the ways of behaving, that, as a teacher – I am aware of those issues and it's interesting reading. In terms of thinking about that as a teacher, I am not at that stage. I am not at that stage of thinking about how my messages affect the boys or the girls. It's interesting reading and I enjoyed doing all those assignments and thinking about those issues but in terms of bringing that to my teaching it's going to take a while. I think it's probably easier to think than act and that's why research is probably so interesting in that area.
>
> (Interview with exiting student)

Not all students feel this way. However, experience suggests that these students are already identified in the programme as 'different', not necessarily in a pejorative way but as more academic, more likely to take a provocative position in relation to their peers and in some cases self-identified as different in terms of cultural background or sexual identity. For these students the opportunity to engage in questioning of the taken-for-granted is welcome. However, at times they seem to make up a very small minority of students and can be marginalised because of their different positioning.

Dealing with gender in the curriculum

At this point the outlook for influencing gender reform from physical education teacher education in Australia looks rather grim. However, there is room for optimism and spaces for change. In the first instance although they may often identify with conservative discourses associated with sport and/or fitness, like the students in Brown and Rich's study, most IPETE students are concerned to increase the participation and enjoyment of students in their classes. They often recognise the resistance of many girls and some boys to traditional physical education lessons and are ready to examine the reasons for this. But like many teachers (Wright, 1999) and the students interviewed by Brown and Rich, the kind of 'useful knowledge' that they wish to acquire is often a set of strategies which will increase participation in the forms of activity that they value.

I would want to argue that the kinds of resources that are needed are not a 'kit' of strategies which will have universal effectiveness. Indeed I would argue that no such strategies exist. Instead, an understanding of how the social practices associated with sport and physical education work to construct limiting notions of masculinity and femininity is required to assist teachers and students to interrogate their practice and to think about and practice physical education teaching differently. As Flintoff (1997: 164) suggests on the basis of her own ethnographic work in IPETE, 'without an understanding of gender relations and how they may be transmitted through schooling and PE, students will be unable to adopt strategies to challenge these in their own teaching'.

IPETE is clearly an important site to begin the process of gender reform through raising students' awareness, introducing the issues, current policy and the research on gender and physical education. Ideally such a process should be integrated throughout an IPETE course; it should become an important aspect of the way prospective teachers think about and evaluate their practice and the practices of others in physical education lessons. It should become part of what Tinning (1991) described as 'problematising practice' in physical education. In addition, gender issues need to be dealt with explicitly in a range of contexts. Given the structure of physical education teacher education this is most likely to be in educational foundation courses, sociology of sport and leisure subjects, and in physical education pedagogy subjects. In Australia and New Zealand gender and sexuality topics are also likely to be covered in the context of health education subjects. As indicated above, health as a 'content area' provides a space in which to examine 'health discourses' such as those relating to health and fitness and to examine problematic constructions of bodies. The spaces and resources to do this are usually available (students can take subjects as electives if they are not available as core subjects) but whether academic staff or students have the desire to do so depends very much on the kinds of identifications that they make with physical education as discussed above. Encouragingly there are increasing numbers of academics in IPETE interested in addressing gender issues explicitly in their teaching. However, most do not always find it an easy task. An informal survey of PETE practitioners working with gender issues in Australia and my own experience suggests that teaching through case studies, stories and media analysis provides a way of asking questions and of avoiding pronouncements. A hermeneutic approach – problematising practice during in-school observations, microteaching and practicum experiences through the use of video or critical friends – also provides ways of raising questions and seeking information from research and the practices of others (Wright, 1998).

How the knowledge and values produced in ITPETE programmes is taken up will vary considerably across programmes – depending on how important gender issues are across subjects and strands – and from one student to another. It will depend on the biographies of students and their investments in maintaining or discarding beliefs and practices which subscribe to dominant gender discourses. In the last few years the emergence of feminist informed masculinity studies in the area of sport has provided an important space to look more broadly at gender issues from a perspective which understand femininity and masculinity as constructed in ways which are limiting to both women and men. It helps to address the position so often taken by many male and quite a few female students that their female lecturers are all feminist extremists who hate men (Wright, 1998). A social construction position allows for a more nuanced understanding of traditional physical education practices as being potentially limiting and inappropriate not only for many girls but also for the many boys who do not conform or wish to conform to dominant notions of masculinity. It follows that if gender issues are dealt with across IPETE courses and/or in depth in some subjects in PETE courses most students will not leave the preservice education untouched whether they choose to reject, accept it, or simply put ideas about gender 'on file' until later.

Given the constraints that preservice education poses, it becomes obvious that educating about gender issues needs to go beyond initial teacher education to working with practising teachers. Postgraduate programmes such as those conducted at Deakin University, which promoted critical reflection through teacher engagement in action research in their own classrooms, provide another way in which practising teachers can become more aware of gender issues and work to address these. A promising approach, but one reliant on elusive government funding, has been taken in NSW. Prompted by the restitution of a 'gender agenda', derived in part by a focus on gender equity which included the 'education of boys', funding has followed State policy once again. In physical education this has taken the form of a professional development project for teachers and consultants. Following the national and state guidelines, this project was informed by an understanding that gender was socially constructed and that the social practices that are part of everyday school life have the potential to (re)produce narrow and limiting forms of femininity and masculinity or to challenge them. The Gender

Issues in Physical Activity (GIPA) Project initially involved Personal Development Health and Physical Education (PDHPE) teachers and consultants representing all Department of Education and Training districts in NSW in workshops and school-based initiatives (see Wright 1999, for a more detailed description).

Most recently the project has focused on involving and supporting the PDHPE faculties from four schools in contracted programmes of work addressing gender issues in the context of physical and health education. What has been important about this aspect of the project is the ways in which, through whole faculty involvement, it has raised awareness and promoted change in the practices of female and male teachers for whom gender was formerly not on their personal agendas. In addition most of the faculties have been involved in the planning and teaching of units of work which in their different ways take up the notion of the 'social construction' of gender. In undertaking this work the teachers have needed to clarify their own understanding and develop ways of communicating these to others.

What is particularly interesting about the GIPA initiative from a policy point of view is how strategic action was taken at a particular juncture when several government concerns intersected to provide an opportunity to apply for funding to work with teachers on gender reform in schools. To a very large extent this was also about the specific interest of key departmental officers in gender reform, their perceptions of the issues and their vision for change. Using the motivations provided by a government funded survey confirming (once again) the lower skill and fitness levels of girls and a renewed impetus in gender issues arising out of the 'boys education' push, the Department officials developed a notion of a project based on the current preferred model of professional development in the Department – one focused on whole school change to successfully attract funding in a context of economic constraint.

Conclusion

A reading of this chapter against others in this book suggests that in Australia, the constraints on gender reform do not come so much from national policy imperatives but through the discursive construction of IPETE programmes and the investments of those who teach and study in them. Indeed state government policies such as the integration of a broad notion of health with physical education in state syllabuses, and the move to a sociocultural perspective on physical activity and health in senior school physical and health education syllabuses provides opportunities to explicitly address gender issues in schools. This in turn provides an incentive to give more space to health and sociocultural perspectives in the IPETE curriculum. In addition, at least in NSW, government initiatives have promoted intensive professional development programmes addressing gender reform in physical education. The long-term potential of such initiatives will always depend on how their effects are promoted more widely, the lessons learned disseminated, and how this information finds its way into initial physical education teacher education.

Note

1 Following Penney and Evans (1999) policy is understood as a complex sociocultural and political process. Similarly curriculum is taken to be more than the content of specific syllabus documents; instead it is understood as a process of interaction between teacher, (IPETE) students and the content of their courses in the context of a particular social and cultural milieu. In this sense the boundaries between policy and curriculum are not fixed. Practice is the process by which policy and curriculum are constituted and enacted in time and space. Practice takes into account the specific biographies of participants, their investments and the social and cultural context which acts to constrain and make possible particular choices of action.

References

Australian Bureau of Statistics (1997) *Participation in Sport and Physical Activities 1995/96*, Canberra: ABS.

Birrell, S. and Cole, C. (1994) *Women, Sport and Culture*, Champaign, IL: Human Kinetics.

Boutelier, A. and San Giovanni, B. (1991) *The Sporting Woman*, Champaign, IL: Human Kinetics.

Browne, J. (1985) Equal opportunity in physical education and sport, *Australian Journal for Health Physical Education and Recreation* 110: 6–8.

Coakley, J. (1990) *Sport in Society: Issues and Controversies*, St Louis: Times/Mosby.

Coles, E. (1980) *Sport in Schools: The Participation of Girls*, Social Development Unit, Ministry of Education, NSW Government Printer.

Connell, R.W. (2000) *Men and Boys*, Sydney: Allen & Unwin.

Creedon, P.J. (ed.) (1994) *Women, Media and Sport: Challenging Gender Values*, Thousand Oaks, CA: Sage.

Dewar, A. (1990) Oppression and privilege in physical education: struggles in the negotiation of gender in a university programme, in D. Kirk and R. Tinning (eds) *Physical Education, Curriculum and Culture: Critical Issues in the Contemporary Crisis*, Basingstoke: Falmer Press, pp. 67–100.

Evans, J. and Clarke, G. (1988) Changing the face of physical education, in J. Evans (ed.) *Teachers, Teaching and Control in Physical Education*, Lewes: Falmer Press, pp. 125–43.

Evans, J., Davies, B. and Penney, D. (1996) Teachers, teaching and the social construction of gender relations, *Sport, Education and Society* 1(2): 165–84.

Fernandez-Balboa, J.-M. (1997) Knowledge base in physical education teacher education: a proposal for a new era, *Quest* 49(7): 161–81.

Flintoff, A. (1997) Gender relations in physical education initial teacher education, in G. Clarke and B. Humberstone (eds) *Researching Women and Sport*, Basingstoke: Macmillan.

Flintoff, A. (1993) Gender, physical education and initial teacher education, in J. Evans (ed.) *Equality, Education and Physical Education*, London: Falmer Press, pp. 184–204.

Gender Equity Taskforce (1997) *Gender Equity: A Framework for Australian Schools*, Canberra: Ministerial Council on Employment Education Training and Youth Affairs.

Gruneau, R. (1982) Class sport and patriarchy (an abstract), *Australian Journal for Health, Physical Education and Recreation* 96: 22.

Hargreaves, J. (1986) *Sport, Power and Culture*, Cambridge: Polity Press.

Hawkes, P., Dryen, R., Torsch, D. and Hannan, L. (1975) Sex roles in school sport and physical education – the state of play, *Australian Journal for Health Physical Education and Recreation*, March: 8–17.

Kirk, D. (1992) *Defining Physical Education: The Social Construction of a Subject in Postwar Britain*, Basingstoke: Falmer Press.

Kirk, D., Macdonald, D. and Tinning, R. (1997) The social construction of pedagogic discourse in physical education teacher education, *The Curriculum Journal* 8(2): 271–98.

Lawrence, G. and Rowe, D. (1986) *Powerplay*, Sydney: Hall & Iremonger.

Leonard, W.M. (1993) *A Sociological Perspective of Sport* (4th edition), New York: Macmillan.

Lenskyj, H.J. (1998) 'Inside sport' or 'On the margins'?: Australian women and the sport media, *International Review for the Sociology of Sport* 33(1): 19–32.

Macdonald, D. (1993) Knowledge, gender and power in physical education teacher education, *Australian Journal of Education* 37(3): 259–78.

McKay, J. (1991) *No Pain, No Gain*, Sydney: Prentice Hall.

Messner, M. and Sabo, D. (eds) (1990) *Sport, Men and the Gender Order*, Champaign, IL: Human Kinetics.

Oldenhove, H. (1989) Girls' PE and sports, in G. Leder and S. Sampson (eds) *Educating Girls: Practice and Research*, Sydney: Allen & Unwin, pp. 39–48.

Penney, D. and Evans, J. (1999) *Politics, Policy and Practice in Physical Education*, London, E & FN Spon.

Schools Commission (1975) *Girls, School and Society: Report by a Study Group to the Schools Commission*, Canberra: Schools Commission.

Scraton, S. (1990) *Gender and Physical Education*, Geelong: Deakin University Press.

Senate Standing Committee on Environment, Recreation and the Arts (1992) *Physical and Sport Education*, Canberra: AGPS.

Specific Focus Directorate (1996) *Girls and Boys in Schools, 1996–2001*, Sydney: NSW Department of School Education.

Stoddard, B. (1986) *Saturday Afternoon Fever: Sport in Australian Culture*, Sydney: Angus & Robertson.

Swan, P.A. (1995) *Studentship and Oppositional Behaviour within Physical Education Teacher Education: A Case Study*, unpublished Doctor of Education Thesis, Deakin University, Geelong, Australia.

Tinning, R. (1985) Physical education and the cult of slenderness, *The ACHPER National Journal* 107: 10–13.

Tinning, R. (1991) Teacher education pedagogy: dominant, discourses and the process of problem setting, *Journal of Teaching in Physical Education* 11(1): 1–20.

Watson, G. (1975) Sex role socialisation and the competitive process in Little Athletics, *Australian Journal for Health Physical Education and Recreation* 50: 10–22.

Whitson, D. (1994) The embodiment of gender: discipline, domination and empowerment, in S. Birrell and C.L. Cole (eds) *Women, Sport and Culture*, Champaign, IL: Human Kinetics, pp. 353–71.

Williams, A. and Woodhouse, J. (1996) Delivering the discourse: urban adolescents' perceptions of physical education, *Sport Education and Society* 1(2): 210–13.

Wright, J. (1996) Mapping the discourses in physical education, *Journal of Curriculum Studies* 28(3): 331–51.

Wright, J. (1997) The construction of gendered contexts in single sex and coeducational physical education lessons, *Sport, Education and Society* 2(1): 55–72.

Wright, J. (1998) Reconstructing gender in sport and physical education, in C. Hickey, L. Fitzclarence and R. Matthews (eds) *Where the Boys Are: Masculinity, Sport and Education*, Geelong: Deakin Centre for Education and Change, pp. 13–26.

Wright, J. (1999) Changing gendered practices in physical education: working with teachers, *European Physical Education Review* 5(3) 181–97.

Wright, J. and King, R.C. (1991). 'I say what I mean,' said Alice: an analysis of gendered discourse in physical education, *Journal of Teaching in Physical Education* 10(2) 210–25.

12 Extending agendas: physical culture research for the twenty-first century

Doune Macdonald

Introduction

The outcomes of gender research in physical education give us little cause for celebration. Despite many years of gender being on educators' agendas, practices in physical education lessons, school staff-rooms, community sport, and teacher education programmes, continue to be sexist. Meanwhile, gender research has become increasingly sophisticated, posing complex questions and drawing on contemporary feminist and poststructuralist theories. This chapter argues that there is a gulf between research and practice and provides some signposts for future gender research agendas that may attempt to address this gulf. These include moving beyond narrow conceptions of what is physical education, who are our partners, where learning occurs, narrow research paradigms, and the school/university divide.

Growing divides?

Recently I had the opportunity to teach physical education to years 8 and 9 students in a co-educational secondary school. In the twenty years since I last donned a tracksuit and whistle and agonised over lesson planning, I had developed my understanding of the gendering of physical education through academic reading and research. In doing so I also had become familiar with the wide-ranging strategies available to teachers and schools to promote equity. I therefore entered the school environment as a physical education teacher, curious to see how 'things had changed since my day'.

What did I find? In a student-led year 8 games-making unit the boys seized upon foam swords and devised a game with the aim of beating the opposition into submission. The girls crafted games with intricate rules using netballs, cones and ropes. When organising an associated mini-Olympics, the girls prepared the letters, posters and advertising materials while the boys chose to organise the equipment and prepare draws and score sheets on the computers. One girl wanted to help with the equipment but she was shunned by the boys and ostracised by the girls. Meanwhile, the year 9 unit focusing on physically active lifestyles revealed different student choices and interactions. Most boys and girls agreed that they would like to try indoor rock-climbing, judo, karate, and aerobics as part of their formal programme and participated enthusiastically. For their own fitness programmes, mixed-sex groups opted to play ball games, go walking or jogging, or do basic strengthening exercises together, appreciating the opportunity to engage in physical activities with which they felt most comfortable.

Why am I recounting these informal observations in this concluding chapter? They help remind me that many students' and teachers' experiences of physical education have not become more gender inclusive despite widespread awareness of equity issues and strategies. Indeed, Evans and Penney in the Introduction to this text ask 'Why has there been so little surface level, let alone deep structural, change?' (p. 3). This has been exemplified in previous chapters that have drawn our attention to continued exclusions and silences with respect to equity and social justice in contexts of physical education. Importantly, my school observations also remind me that many young people, and those who teach them, are looking for new versions of physical education where gender, body shape, sexuality, ethnicity, and physical ability do not limit individual involvement. Further, my experiences highlight that there is frequently a disjunction between research discourses and physical education practice. While the equity research that I was familiar with was concerned with bodies, subjectivities, sexualities, masculinities, policy analyses, and the like, it helped little in a school that was coping with an increasingly conservative and competitive marketplace, and the day to day stresses of students who felt alienated, harassed and bored. My intention here is not to blame teachers or researchers, or indeed reinforce any false dichotomy, but rather to highlight how the agendas have often grown apart.

A focus of this chapter is therefore this drift between the respective interests, questions, and language of those who practice physical education in universities and schools, typically researchers and teachers. I suggest that this has not always been so. In the 1970s and 1980s when gender equity was an explicit priority across various sites of physical education, research was largely concerned with questions such as student–teacher interaction and inclusive language, class organisation, and selection of activities (see for example Bischoff, 1982; Evans, Rosen and O'Brien, 1986; Griffin, 1985; Scraton, 1986; Vertinsky, 1984). Drawing on liberal, and less radical, feminist perspectives, this research conducted in university–school partnerships generated strategies in schools including inclusive language policies, single-sex classes, girl-friendly content, and girls' only spaces and facility usage. School communities themselves also initiated projects based upon this heightened consciousness and, using action research methodologies, addressed local questions such as the appropriateness of the physical education uniform and interventions for sex-based bullying and harassment. Since that time researchers have asked other questions, while in important respects the institution of schools and the above mentioned problems have remained the same. As modernist institutions, schools are still shaped by timetables, space allocation, bounded subject communities, industrial models of teachers' work, and frequently traditional syllabuses. Further, the physical education profession still attracts those who are middle class, heterosexual, able-bodied, and committed to sport and performance discourses (e.g. Armour and Jones, 1998; Macdonald and Tinning, 1995). While there have been some initiatives to shift curricula to more socially critical outcomes (e.g. Kirk and Macdonald, 1999; Wright, 1997), many position sporting performance as central (e.g. Penney and Evans, 1999). As what counts as research increasingly borrows from poststructuralist perspectives, it seems to have disengaged from the modernist and conservative institution of schooling which is still looking for strategies and practices that promote equity and justice.

The notion of a 'gender agenda for the twenty-first century' begs the question of 'for whom should agendas be'? All boys and girls? Schools? Teachers? Researchers? Policy-makers? Who, then, is this gender agenda for? It speaks to all those who might undertake physical education research – teachers, academics, students, professional associations, and policy-makers, wherever they might be located. Here, research is considered to be the systematic and empirical search for truth or truths. The following four signposts may be helpful across the spaces and places where gender equity is an issue. They may, it is to be hoped, play a part in reviving the gender debate, which in 1994, Ball argued was largely 'off the agenda' (p. 125).

Signposts for future gender agendas: moving beyond

Underpinning the research/practice disjunction have been dualistic discourses. For reasons such as interest, context, language and tradition, past and current physical education discourses have taken a dualistic position: female/ male; boys/girls; masculine/feminine; social structure/subjectivity; modern/ postmodern; homosexual/heterosexual; individual/societal; curricula/extra-curricula; Anglo-Saxon/Asian; curriculum/pedagogy; theory/practice; schools /universities – the list goes on (e.g. Layder, 1997). These binaries have been used differently depending upon the physical education context. For example, in schools, binaries have been used as a way of focusing 'problems', programmes and strategies, while in universities they have served to focus research perspectives and projects, academic territory and communities. Yet, as has been illustrated in earlier chapters, binaries, polarities and boundaries obscure differences within, and reproduce narrow and overly simplistic ways of thinking, talking and behaving. It is time to *move beyond* binaries and to establish some shared principles for how gender equity can be promoted across sites and by a variety of stakeholders who are concerned with physical education.

To move from overly narrow and singular/dualistic foci of research and account for complexity and interdependency of social practices, I am also arguing for the widespread use of relational analyses (Brown and Rich, chapter 6 in this text; Hall, 1996). Kirk (1999: 64) suggests the value of relational analysis lies in its potential to reveal complexity. It can:

> provide an important corrective to simplistic, one-dimensional analyses of education by revealing the interdependency of social practices across sites and . . . the complexities revealed by relational analysis may allow individuals and groups to transform unjust, inequitable and oppressive practices by providing powerful and sophisticated explanation of the practices constituting physical education that inform interventions for change.

Within this text, relational analysis has been associated with extending agendas (Chapter 2) and appreciating ripple effects (Chapter 6). The message for research is that it should frame questions of gender equity as complex, contextually-embedded, and potentially far reaching.

1 Beyond physical education

School and tertiary knowledge has tended to exist within highly bounded systems that we typically call subjects (e.g. physical education) and disciplines (e.g. sports science, human movement studies). The preceding chapters suggest that this arrangement of knowledge has not always served society well in terms of offering contexts that are inclusive, engaging, safe, or innovative. They have indicated that in schools, narrowly conceived, masculinized versions of physical education dominate, while PETE continues to alienate those who do not conform. The first signpost for all physical educators, whether they be located in schools, clubs or universities, is to think beyond physical education's boundaries in order to share, learn, dilute, and shift what have been discriminatory and sedimented discourses. Thinking beyond physical education may involve school curricula viewing physical education more broadly and establishing alliances that enrich the questions that are asked and the knowledge that is brought to bear on equity issues.

One way of viewing physical education more broadly and understanding the complexity of contextual influences shaping young people's involvement in physical activity is to work with the concept of physical culture. Kirk (1993: 340) uses the term physical culture to refer to:

> a range of practices concerned with the maintenance, representation and regulation of the body centred on three highly codified, institutionalised forms of physical activity: sport, physical recreation and exercise. Physical culture may be thought of, in turn, as one source of the production and reproduction of corporeal discourse, of a whole array of interconnecting symbol systems concerned with the meaning-making centred on the human body.

Preliminary work by Wright and Macdonald (in press) reveals that exploring not only students' perceptions of physical education but also the significance of symbol systems associated with clothes, friendship groups, music, and the media as they relate to physical culture, provides a richer understanding of inequity in physical education than would a focus upon the subject itself. Physical culture encourages a broader lens that helps to locate physical activity within the totality of young people's lives and thereby generate more impactful strategies for change.

Another way of moving beyond physical education is to recognise shifts in disciplinary knowledge and its representations in school subjects. The structure of the disciplines in universities and their translation into school subjects triumphed in the 1960s. Recently, in line with rapid growth in new and varied applications of knowledge (Bernstein, 1996), reconfigurations of disciplinary knowledge have occurred. Contemporary curriculum documents are not necessarily stories of 'the translation of an academic discipline, devised by "dominant" groups of scholars in universities, into a pedagogic version to be used as a school subject' (Goodson, 1988: 177). Particularly in the Australian context, middle schooling literature exploring the needs of 9 to 15 year olds has challenged the extent to which disciplinary and/or strongly collected knowledge meets the needs of young people. This knowledge has been shown to limit the possibilities for freedom or autonomy in learning and the opportunities for students to make meaningful connections across schooling (see for example Hargreaves and Earl, 1994). It is therefore argued that teachers should recognise and support new configurations of knowledge that encourage connectivity across subject matter, in order to produce well-rounded learners with economic, political, cultural and sociological understandings (Connell, 2000; Young, 1998). In response, in some contexts we are seeing the clustering of subject matter into learning *areas* that extend beyond subjects. In Australia and New Zealand this clustering has been reflected in the creation of 'key learning areas', with physical education re-positioned to sit with health education, outdoor education, home economics and religious education under the umbrella of Health and Physical Education (e.g. Glover and Macdonald, 1997; Macdonald *et al.*, 2000).

However, like Penney's observations in the UK context (chapter 7), my recent teaching experiences indicate that new curriculum documents may provide a platform for more equitable practices but do not necessarily ensure shifts in practices and relationships. What might this mean for research both within and beyond school? One possible response is to trial and monitor how best educators can work beyond their disciplines. More specifically, it generates questions concerning how teams of teachers can become 'cross-departmental' in their knowledge bases and justifications, traditions and practices, behavioural norms and priorities, and thereby possibly destabilize inequitable practices and promote new approaches to the study of physical activity. Accordingly, in universities, tertiary physical educators should be working with health professionals, social scientists, home economists, and academics in gender, cultural and leisure studies (Macdonald *et al.*, in press) to gain a fuller understanding of the complexities of inequity. The chapters by Benn, Brown and Rich, and Wright in this text suggest that tertiary physical education or human movement studies/science is still not adequately challenging gender inequity, extending understandings of gender equity, or providing clear insights into ways in which gender equity can be advanced in and via teaching and learning in physical education. Talbot (2000) argued that programmes have been gender blind and that critical issues and subjective experiences have been sidelined. It is important that researchers acknowledge that to continue to work within a bounded discipline is not helpful and that physical education would be well-advised to position itself with multi-disciplinary partners or teams. No one discipline has the intellectual resources to deal with the complexities of inequities. If physical educators considered themselves as part of a public health team alongside epidemiologists, nutritionists, psychologists, sociologists, health promotion professionals, school nurses, and social workers, the issues raised would take them (and their research) beyond their curriculum and pedagogical concerns to broader questions of access and opportunity to become physically educated.

Certainly, to research with partners beyond physical education is not easy. Bringing together professionals with different interests, priorities, knowledge and experience to set the parameters of equity issues, let alone address the issues, may be fraught. However, there are examples of positive progress in these respects. When physical educators have drawn upon feminist cultural studies they have been prompted to engage with a field in which different disciplines intersect in the analysis of culture defined as the 'social forms though which human beings live, become conscious, and sustain themselves subjectively' (Hall, 1996: 34). Feminist cultural studies draws upon sociology, political science, philosophy, semiotics, history, literature, and feminism to examine culture (or physical culture) in action. Work that stems from physical education with a feminist cultural studies perspective would thus include historically grounded studies, applications of feminist theory to the study of men, sport and masculinity, and deconstructions of the significance of the body. For some there may be a fear that with such approaches the theoretical and applied contributions of physical education may become lost in others' agendas. Yet, without broadening our focus beyond physical education to physical culture, key learning areas, and other sociocultural and biophysical sciences, we are likely to be asking questions and seeking solutions that are impotent.

2 Beyond school

Following the encouragement for equity research to move beyond physical education is the signpost for this research to account for factors or discourses both within and beyond school to more closely reflect young people's lives and learning. While several of the chapters in this text have addressed important questions relating to school curriculum and policy in terms of privileged discourses, I would argue that with the school as a bounded sphere of learning failing so many children, we need to recruit, recognise and understand new spaces and places for learning that are effective, inclusive and engaging, but are beyond formal school programmes (Tinning and Fitzclarence, 1992). We are increasingly aware that in any one space, such as a school system or school, there are multiple cultural identities (Ross, 2000). This has profound implications when we are asked to select a set of cultural attributes, knowledge bases, meanings, values, skills etc. for conscious transmission through the planned physical education curriculum. Increasingly, to make a selection and shape it into a physical education curriculum that suits the heterogeneity of young people is highly contentious if not impossible. Yet curriculum-makers continue to make selections, with assumptions and particular interests in mind (see Penney in Chapter 7). Therefore, the second signpost encourages researchers to recognise, trial, monitor, and analyse engagement in physical education or physical culture that is beyond the school. Work that seeks to understand people's multiple identities is already taking us beyond class-rooms, gymnasia, playgrounds, staffrooms, and school perimeters (see for example Benn, and Clarke, in this text). Meanwhile policy developments in England particularly are directly addressing the relationship between opportunities within physical education and those provided beyond it, in arenas of school, club and community sport (DCMS, 2000). Furthermore, young people are also actively extending the contexts of their learning. Many now have the motivation, lifestyle and resources to learn outside formal schooling given shifts in their access to money, the media, technology, and transport (Eisner, 2000; Young, 1998). What it means to be a school student is being reinvented through the interests of corporate capital. 'As culture becomes increasingly commercialised, the only type of citizenship that adult society offers to children is that of consumerism' (Giroux, 2000: 19). Young people's approach to learning is arguably now far more closely aligned to that of a consumer and a product. They may engage in physical education at school or, indeed, prefer options available through their families or communities. Further, the information revolution and the public pedagogies that it entails frees many learners to haphazardly explore as they wish, without boundaries and prescribed direction. 'Materials and means to construct personal projects of education and communication will be available . . . to us all' (Reid, 1998: 501) although we are warned that many girls are not engaging with information technology as readily as boys (Gilbert, 2001).

Wright and Macdonald's (in press) work with young people echoes other research (see, for example, Flintoff and Scraton, 2001) that has indicated that for girls particularly, activity out of school may have a far greater appeal than that within the curriculum and that for young people, there is often a lack of clear linkages between activity within and beyond schools. The indication is that for many girls and boys, their preferred engagement with physical activity outside school is at odds with what the formal school curriculum offers. As they become increasingly intolerant of curricula that are deemed irrelevant or inappropriate, and aware of alternative places and pathways for learning, as critical consumers they can bypass pre-selected, given, and inert curriculum and seek other products. In doing so, the learning/leisure binary conflates. Yet most of our equity research continues to focus narrowly upon the school as *the* site of meaningful learning for young people. In order to address inequity, research needs to include sites of learning outside schools and in particular, the meanings students make of 'on-line discourses' about lifestyle, diet, the body etc. This behoves researchers to account for the contemporary physical culture of different groups of young people and to explore these cultural spaces in terms of equity, access and responsible citizenship.

As all educators, physical educators need to recognise and work alongside not only the new spaces, places and technologies that now play a part in the physical education of young people, but also new people.

> If the school curriculum is to become an emancipatory experience for a much larger section of each cohort of students, this is going to require much greater involvement of many people who currently have no direct links with school, including parents and employers, and many activities by teachers and pupils which are not confined to the school nor, in conventional terms, are usually defined as 'educational' at all.
>
> (Young, 1998: 32).

This sentiment has also been expressed in much of the recent work of Hal Lawson (1998) who is arguing for attention to shift beyond the formal curriculum delivered by specialist physical education teachers to how coalitions of professionals and community members can become available to young people to enhance their learning.

Again, this signpost returns us to the question of what and how new spaces and places for equitable practices might be created and who might constitute partners in trialing and monitoring these. Also again, the new challenges bring potential hazards. The school environment can offer a relatively safe and supportive learning environment for the student-as-consumer compared to many options beyond school. Further, school–community links may not always see educational (and specifically equity) agendas remaining intact. For example, sporting organisations seeking to boost numbers could conceivably initiate a school–community programme with the aim of recruitment and not necessarily provide inclusive educational experiences for all students. If we are genuinely concerned with promoting greater equity in sport and in society it is arguably essential that more efforts are made to extend beyond binary relations. For researchers this demands the evaluation of the nature of engagements and transitions as young people move across sites of learning and physical activity.

3 *Beyond structuralism or poststructuralism*

The first two signposts are intended to encourage all those involved with researching gender questions related to physical education to set 'problems' in a broader, and I would argue, more contemporary framework, beyond the confines of the physical education subject, the school and its teachers. The second two signposts shift in their focus to questions of theoretical perspectives and approaches to gender equity research. More specifically, the third signpost gives some direction to the theoretical tension between structuralism and poststructuralism.

If the role of education systems is to assist all students to reach their individual potentials, then they have patently failed, as evidenced in this text and elsewhere (e.g. Apple, 1999; Morris, 2000; Young, 1998). We have seen ways in which equity policies and programmes have failed to override the influences of hegemonic masculinities, homophobia, and sportist discourses that are underpinned by power structures framed by gender, class and race and that social institutions such as schooling are generally *reproductive*; active in reproducing economic and cultural imbalances upon which a society is built (e.g. Bowles and Gintis, 1976). Bourdieu (1974) analysed cultural reproduction and the ways in which particular cultural capitals based upon language and values 'combine to create differential experiences for children of different social classes' (Bourdieu, 1974: 36). The point here is that structures relating to, for example, sex and class appear to still strongly shape students' experiences of schooling, and physical education within it, and therefore structuralism as a theoretical perspective has credence (Gilbert, 2001). Indeed, as Kirk *et al.* (1997) found in their studies of junior sport in Australia, socio-economic status had a strong bearing on the opportunities that children had to pursue club and representative sport. In the Introduction to this book, Evans and Penney also share my support for retaining a focus upon class, alongside other structural factors, to guide the research that we undertake. We agree that whether researching school physical education, club sport, recreational spaces, PETE, or physical culture, the intersection of structures such as gender, class and race remain significant but all too often are inadequately embraced.

However, there is a contrasting theoretical perspective, poststructuralism, that rejects the explanatory power of social structures as oversimplifying the complexity of social relationships and change. Rather, it focuses upon difference and diversity and views the self as socially and historically constructed and constantly changing with shifting contexts (Leistyna *et al.*, 1996). As reflected in several chapters in this text, this perspective shifts questions of gender equity from the experiences of all men, or all women, to differences within these categories. But as with any theoretical perspective, we should be circumspect in engaging in it wholeheartedly or exclusively. In a compelling paper, McLaren and Farahmandpur (2000) argue that post-structuralist positions are 'hyperindividualistic' with an overemphasis on identity politics, consumerism, pluralism and choice, and have lost sight of the reproductive structures. They do, however, acknowledge that post-structuralisms have drawn our attention to the complexity of circuits of power, the globalisation of knowledge and culture, shifts in time, space and boundaries, and how individuals may be active in constructing their life choices. Indeed, the first two signposts that I have outlined, draw on post-structuralist thinking with their encouragement to ask new questions that are beyond modernist curricular and institutional boundaries.

So where does this leave us in terms of gender agendas and theoretical perspectives that might shape our future research programmes? Here, we should return to the rejection of yet another dualism; structuralism versus poststructuralism. In the words of Apple (1999), we should retain our structuralist memory and when researching, trespass across structuralist and poststructuralist positions. Such a question might be, 'How does the socio-economic status of young people shape their engagement in physical culture? Furthermore, how does this class status articulate with gender, race, ethnicity and sexuality?' As Stanley (1997: 11) argues:

> The person missing is one who is complex and rounded, who is 'raced' and classed and gendered, who has a body and emotions and engages in sensible thought, and who inhabits space and place and time, and a person who may be a man but can be pathetic and weak, or who may be a woman but can be confidently powerful.

Connell's (2000) work with men and masculinity provides a good example of this type of research. In order to understand gender regimes, he encourages foci on globalization (e.g. technology, markets), bodies (e.g. sport, violence, health), symbolism (e.g. language, dress, sports), and power relations along-side their interface with practical issues and social problems that stem from differences within males and their widespread subordination of women. This call for plurality in theoretical perspectives brings us to the final signpost.

4 Beyond theory or practice

Signpost four returns to the opening of this chapter and the concern for the slippage between school/practitioner and university/theorist discourses together with questions of how policy-makers are positioned in the curriculum construction process. It directly aims to challenge the theory/practice binary. Physical education needs theory, policy and research that is grounded in practice or as Hall (1996: 30–1) wrote, research becomes 'prescriptive, exclusive and elitist'. Indeed, Connell (2000: 150) reflected that, 'Researchers have not done a great deal to help schools', predicated on the assumption that researchers are academics divorced from schools. It has also been claimed that schools and their teachers have become preoccupied with management and accountability issues and have not engaged with the intellectual dimension of their work (Smyth and Shacklock, 1998). We can reflect that in recent years, the imperatives of academics', policy-makers' and teachers' workplaces have undermined opportunities for educators across sites to engage with each others' perspectives and concerns. The slippage in the questions and language of research, policy and school practice is not unique to physical education gender research. In response to the 'crisis' in schooling, recent debates surrounding curriculum studies, theorizing and reform have been highly critical of the field with the use of descriptors such as 'disarray', 'blind', 'floundering' and 'schism' based upon the fragmentation of interests and the separation of concerns into theory and practice (e.g. McGinn, 1999; Morris, 2000; Reid, 1998). Might the same be said of gender research in physical education?

A way forward is to more closely link theorizing to action, to engage in praxis. Frequently the principle of praxis is best exemplified in research projects that entail partnerships that extend across the boundaries of schools, universities, clubs, teachers, parents and students (Fullan, 1999). For example, Ennis and her colleagues in the USA (1999) have worked with students, teachers, school administrators, and community leaders in a programme to increase physical activity participation amongst urban, African–American girls. In England, the Youth Sport Trust has brought together a multi-disciplinary team to work with a number of schools, their students and communities, to develop girl-friendly physical education (Kirk *et al.*, 2000). A strength of these examples of praxis is the breadth of voices which have had input. As both projects acknowledge, a weakness is school administrators' and teachers' difficulty in moving outside institutional constraints (e.g. showering policies, uniform) and conventional content (e.g. health-related fitness, sport, physical skill development). A number of curriculum projects in Australia would suggest that praxis is enriched when policy-makers and policy-making are integral to the change process preferably through all partners having a voice in policy creation (Kirk and Macdonald, 2001; Macdonald and Brooker, 1997).

The principle of praxis requires all potential stakeholders to also be involved in problem-setting. Transdisciplinary approaches to research take this further and suggest that problems are best defined by a community/group who 'lives' with the problem and that they recruit academics and other relevant professionals to come together with them, address the issue at hand, and move on (Johnston, 1998). Such an approach to knowledge production and problem-solving in equity research would be dynamic, share power and ownership, allow for a breadth of input, and be weakly institutionalised and bounded. Nevertheless, as with signpost two, there is a caution with this approach in the current climate. What the communities/groups 'set' as the problem might be framed within the discourses of the feminist backlash (e.g. Lingard and Douglas, 1999) and the pro-sport lobbies and thereby have a minimal or negative impact upon new ways of seeing gender equity in physical education.

Conclusion: what are we concerned about?

Why are we concerned about gender equity and physical education? Are we concerned that as a result of inequitable practices and programmes, fewer students are likely to lead a physically active lifestyle with health budget consequences? Or are we concerned about the emotional wellbeing of pupils and teachers who are oppressed, marginalised and harassed for their skills, interests, appearances, cultural practices or sexualities, that lie outside hegemonic discourses? Or are we concerned that unless physical education shifts to become more inclusive, that it will be considered anachronistic in schools, education systems, and universities? Or are we concerned that without drawing upon the skills and interests of all young people across a breadth of physical activities, the quality and success of elite sport performances will decline? The possibilities are many yet such positions shape academics', policy-makers', teachers', parents', community groups', and students' engagement with questions of gender equity.

Each reader will have her/his own position with respect to why gender equity in physical education may be important. With our own unique subjectivities, we identify with different politics, policies, imperatives, and strategies. However, as highlighted in the Introduction of this book and borne out in several chapters, while most physical educators claim a commitment to equity, there has been little surface level, let alone deep, change. It is hoped that the above-mentioned signposts may inform and strengthen your gender agendas as a physical educator in a school, bureaucracy, or university. Further, you might be encouraged to extend your networks to form partnerships with health professionals, 'classroom' teachers, youth workers, recreation officers, policy-makers, community organisations, parents, and, especially, students. It is important to remember that any strategies for change are frequently met with a mixture of resentment, anger, comfort, contempt, strength or relief (Fullan, 1999). Yet, taken alone or together, the signposts might generate new ways to add depth, breadth or relevance to the gender problem, challenge or task at hand.

While the literature in gender equity and physical education recognises the difficulty in creating meaningful change within current educational structures, the majority of analyses and innovations overlook the broader and more significant questions. Who are our young people, and what, where and how do they learn? For as long as gender reform focuses upon subjects, teachers, school-based lessons, and other modernist structures of schools that obfuscate difference, meaningful learning and the impact of technology, gender equity initiatives will fail to produce significant advances. Also, while physical education academics and teachers talk past each other, their gender agendas will be fractured and physical education will become more alienating for more students.

References

Apple, M. (1999) *Power, Meaning and Identity*, New York: Peter Lang.

Armour, K. and Jones, R. (1998) *Physical Education Teachers' Lives and Careers*, London: Falmer Press.

Ball, S. (1994) *Education Reform: A Critical and Post-structural Approach*, Buckingham: Open University Press.

Benn, T. (2001) Muslim women in teacher training: issues of gender, 'race' and religion, in D. Penney (ed.) *Gender and Physical Education: Contemporary Issues and Future Directions*, London: Routledge.

Bernstein, B. (1996) *Pedagogy, Symbolic Control and Identity: Theory, Research, Critique*, London: Taylor & Francis.

Bischoff, J. (1982) Equal opportunity, satisfaction and success: an exploratory study on co-educational volleyball, *Journal of Teaching in Physical Education* Fall: 3–12.

Bourdieu, P. (1974) The school as a conservative force: scholastic and cultural inequalities (trans. J. Whitehouse), in J. Eggleston (ed.) *Research in the Sociology of Education*, London: Methuen, pp. 32–46.

Bowles, S. and Gintis, H. (1976) *Schooling in Capitalist America: Educational Reform and the Contradictions of Economic Life*, London: Routledge.

Brown, D. and Rich, E. (2001) Gender positioning as pedagogical practice in teaching physical education, in D. Penney (ed.) *Gender and Physical Education. Contemporary Issues and Future Directions*, London: Routledge.

Clarke, G. (2001) Difference matters: sexuality and physical education, in D. Penney (ed.) *Gender and Physical Education: Contemporary Issues and Future Directions*, London: Routledge.

Connell, R. (2000) *The Men and the Boys*, Sydney: Allen & Unwin.

Department for Culture, Media and Sport (DCMS) (2000) *A Sporting Future for All*, London: DCMS.

Eisner, E. (2000) Those who ignore the past . . . : 12 'easy' lessons for the next millennium, *Journal of Curriculum Studies* 32(2): 343–57.

Ennis, C. (1999) Communicating the value of active, healthy lifestyles to urban students, *Quest* 51: 164–9.

Evans, J. and Penney, D. (2001) Introduction, in D. Penney (ed.) *Gender and Physical Education: Contemporary Issues and Future Directions*, London: Routledge.

Evans, M., Rosen, D. and O'Brien, D. (1986) Three teachers share their views on the teaching of mixed physical education, *British Journal of Physical Education* 17(4): 152 and 154.

Flintoff, A. and Scraton, S. (2001) Stepping into active leisure? Young women's perceptions of active lifestyles and their experiences of school physical education, *Sport, Education and Society* 6(1): 5–21.

Fullan, M. (1999) *Change Forces: The Sequel*, Lewes: Falmer Press.

Gilbert, P. (2001) Redefining gender issues for the twenty-first century: putting girls' education back on the agenda, *Curriculum Perspectives* 21(1): 1–8.

Giroux, H. (2000) *Stealing Innocence*, New York: St Martin's Press.

Glover, S. and Macdonald, D. (1997) Working with the health and physical education statement and profile in physical education teacher education, *The ACHPER Healthy Lifestyles Journal* 44(2): 21–5.

Goodson, I. (1988) *The Making of Curriculum*, London: Falmer Press.

Griffin, P. (1985) Teachers' perception of and responses to sex equity problems in a middle school physical education program, *Research Quarterly for Exercise and Sport* 56(2): 103–11.

Hall, M.A. (1996) *Feminism and Sporting Bodies*, Champaign, IL: Human Kinetics.

Hargreaves, A. and Earl, L. (1994) Triple transitions: educating early adolescents in the changing Canadian context, *Curriculum Perspectives* 14(3): 1–9.

Johnston, R. (1998) *The Changing Nature and Forms of Knowledge: A Review*, Canberra: Department of Employment, Education, Training and Youth Affairs.

Kirk, D. (1993) *The Body, Schooling and Culture*, Geelong, Vic: Deakin University Press.

Kirk, D. (1999) Physical culture, physical education and relational analysis, *Sport, Education and Society* 4(1): 63–73.

Kirk, D., Carlson, T., O'Connor, A., Burke, P., Davis, K. and Glover, S. (1997) The economic impact on families of children's participation in junior sport, *The Australian Journal of Science and Medicine in Sport* 29(2): 27–33.

Kirk, D., Fitzgerald, H., Wang, J., Biddle, S. and Claxton, C. (2000) Towards girl friendly physical education? A report on a large-scale, school-based intervention. Paper presented at the Pre-Olympic Congress, Brisbane, September.

Kirk, D. and Macdonald, D. (1999) Imagining beyond the present, *Teaching Elementary Physical Education*, November: 25–8.

Kirk, D. and Macdonald, D. (2001) Teacher voice and ownership of curriculum change, *Journal of Curriculum Studies* 33(5): 000–00.

Lawson, H. (1998) Here today, gone tomorrow? A framework for analyzing the development, transformation, and disappearance of helping fields, *Quest* 50: 225–37.

Layder, D. (1997) *Modern Social Theory*, London: UCL Press.

Leistyna, P., Woodrum, A. and Sherblom, S. (1996) *Breaking Free: The Transformative Power of Critical Pedagogy*, Cambridge: Harvard Educational Review.

Lingard, R. and Douglas, P. (1999) *Men Engaging Feminisms: Pro-feminism, Backlashes and Schooling*, Buckingham: Open University Press.

Macdonald, D. and Brooker, R. (1997) Moving beyond the crisis in secondary physical education: an Australian initiative, *Journal of Teaching in Physical Education* 16: 155–75.

Macdonald, D. and Tinning, R. (1995) Physical education teacher education and the trend to proletarianization: a case study, *Journal of Teaching in Physical Education* 15(1): 98–118.

Macdonald, D., Glasby, P. and Carlson, T. (2000) The health and physical education profile Queensland style, *The ACHPER Healthy Lifestyles Journal* 47(1): 5–8.

Macdonald, D., Penney, P., Hunter, L. and Carlson, T. (in press). Teacher knowledge and the disjunction between school curricula and teacher education, *Asia-Pacific Journal of Teacher Education*.

McGinn, N. (1999) What is required for successful education reform? Learning from errors, *Education Practice and Theory* 21(1): 7–21.

McLaren, P. and Farahmandpur, R. (2000) Reconsidering Marx in post-marxist times: a requiem for postmodernism, *Educational Researcher* 29(3): 25–33.

Morris, M. (2000) The pit and the pendulum: taking risks talking about the future of the curriculum, *Journal of Curriculum Theorizing* 16(3): 3–6.

O'Sullivan, M., Bush, K. and Gehring, M. (2001) Gender equity and physical education: a USA perspective, in D. Penney (ed.) *Gender and Physical Education: Contemporary Issues and Future Directions*, London: Routledge.

Penney, D. (2001) Gendered policies, in D. Penney (ed.) *Gender and Physical Education: Contemporary Issues and Future Directions*, London: Routledge.

Penney, D. and Evans, J. (1999) *Politics, Policy and Practice in Physical Education*, London: E & FN Spon.

Reid, W. (1998) Erasmus, gates, and the end of curriculum, *Journal of Curriculum Studies* 30(5): 499–501.

Ross, A. (2000) *Curriculum: Construction and Critique*, London: Falmer Press.

Scraton, S. (1986) Gender and girls' physical education, *British Journal of Physical Education* 17(4): 145–7.

Smyth, J. and Shacklock, G. (1998) *Re-making Teaching*, London: Routledge.

Stanley, E. (1997) *Knowing Feminisms*, London: Sage.

Talbot, M. (2000) Deconstruction – reconstruction of physical education: gender perspectives. Pre-Olympic Scientific Congress, Brisbane, September.

Tinning, R. and Fitzclarence, L. (1992) Postmodern youth culture and the crisis in Australian secondary school physical education, *Quest* 44: 287–303.

Vertinsky, P. (1984) In search of a gender dimension: an empirical investigation of teacher preferences for teaching strategies in physical education, *Journal of Curriculum Studies* 16(4): 425–30.

Wright, J. (1997) Fundamental motor skills testing as problematic practice: a feminist analysis, *The ACHPER Healthy Lifestyles Journal* 44(4): 18–20.

Wright, J. (2001) Physical education teacher education: sites of progress or resistance, in D. Penney (ed.) *Gender and Physical Education: Contemporary Issues and Future Directions*, London: Routledge.

Wright, J. and Macdonald, D. (in press) Young people and physical culture, *Leisure Studies*.

Young, M. (1998) *The Curriculum of the Future*, London: Falmer Press.

Index

Employment Law

CORE TEXT SERIES

Employment Law

Third Edition

ROBERT UPEX

Emeritus Professor of Law,
University of Surrey

RICHARD BENNY

Senior Lecturer in Law,
University of Surrey

STEPHEN HARDY

Barrister,
9 St John Street, Manchester

Series editor

NICOLA PADFIELD

Fitzwilliam College, Cambridge

OXFORD
UNIVERSITY PRESS

OXFORD
UNIVERSITY PRESS

Great Clarendon Street, Oxford OX2 6DP

Oxford University Press is a department of the University of Oxford.
It furthers the University's objective of excellence in research, scholarship,
and education by publishing worldwide in

Oxford New York

Auckland Cape Town Dar es Salaam Hong Kong Karachi
Kuala Lumpur Madrid Melbourne Mexico City Nairobi
New Delhi Shanghai Taipei Toronto

With offices in

Argentina Austria Brazil Chile Czech Republic France Greece
Guatemala Hungary Italy Japan Poland Portugal Singapore
South Korea Switzerland Thailand Turkey Ukraine Vietnam

Oxford is a registered trade mark of Oxford University Press
in the UK and in certain other countries

Published in the United States
by Oxford University Press Inc., New York

© Robert Upex, Richard Benny, and Stephen Hardy 2009

British Library Cataloguing in Publication Data

Data available

Library of Congress Cataloging in Publication Data

Upex, R. V.
    Employment law / Robert Upex, Richard Benny, Stephen Hardy.—3rd ed.
        p. cm.—(Core text series)
    Includes index.
    Previous ed.: Labour law, by Richard Benny, 2nd ed., 2006.
    ISBN 978–0–19–923286–4
    1. Labor laws and legislation—Great Britain.   2. Labor laws and
legislation—European Union countries.   I. Benny, Richard, solicitor.
II. Hardy, Stephen T.   III. Title.
    KD3009.B448 2009
    344.4101—dc22   2008051992

Typeset by Newgen Imaging Systems (P) Ltd., Chennai, India
Printed in Great Britain
on acid-free paper by
Ashford Colour Press Ltd, Gosport, Hampshire

ISBN 978–0–19–923286–4

10 9 8 7 6 5 4 3 2 1

Preface to the third edition

Since the first edition of this book, Employment Law has continued to flourish and change. At the time of publication of the last edition, the new TUPE Regulations 2006 had just come into force and the Age Discrimination Regulations were about to come into effect, on 1 October 2006. As this edition goes to press, we await the completion of the passage of the Employment Bill through the Parliamentary process. It is expected to come into effect in April 2009.

However, this much revised edition, like the last, seeks to summarise key principles and cases for the intellectual nourishment of students of employment law, both old and new. This new edition has benefited greatly from the kind comments of reviewers and readers of the previous editions.

We remain indebted to our publishers, and, of course, to our long-suffering families.

The law is stated as at 31 October 2008.

Robert Upex
Stephen Hardy
Richard Benny
London, October 2008

Contents

Table of Statutes

Table of Secondary Legislation

Table of European Legislation

Table of Cases

Decisions of the European Court of Justice are additionally listed below chronologically.

**Decisions of the European Court of
Human Rights are additionally listed
below chronologically.**

Introducing employment law

SUMMARY

This chapter introduces the whole field of employment law. It begins with definitions and terminology, eg 'employment law', 'labour law', 'industrial law', and then goes on to consider the key institutions in the field, from the courts and tribunals to government departments, the Equality and Human Rights Commission, and international organisations. It provides a very brief outline of employment tribunal procedure. Some of the most significant ideologies at work in employment law are then identified, in order to give the reader an idea of the various debates at play in this important area of law. The major sources of employment law are then outlined, followed by a brief overview of some of the key pieces of legislation. The topics covered are:

- definitions;
- institutions;
- ideologies;
- sources of employment law;
- key legislation.

1.1 Employment law is one of the most dynamic and interesting areas of the law. The study of this area offers an intellectually stimulating and challenging field for undergraduate students on law degrees and those following related programmes, such as business and management degrees. It is usually offered as an optional subject (sometimes called an 'elective') within degree programmes. In recent years the pace of change, both in terms of legislative and case-law developments, has been very fast indeed, and students of the subject should be aware that it is a demanding field of study, requiring diligence in keeping abreast of the continual deluge of developments.

1.2 As well as forming a discrete part of the law with its own specific case law and legislation, employment law also involves the study of several other, related areas of the law such as the law of tort, eg concerning the vicarious liability of employers; statutory torts under the discrimination statutes; and the duty of care placed upon employers, employees, and others in the tort of negligence. It also comprises a part of contract law, since the employment relationship is based upon a specialised contractual relationship, ie one with its own specific features, particularly with reference to implied terms (see Chapter 4).

Definitions

1.3 Essentially, employment law concerns the law of the workplace, ie those parts of the law dealing with: (1) the relationship between employees (and, in some cases, workers) on the one hand, and employers on the other; (2) the relationship between trade unions (or groups of trade unions) and employers (or employers' associations); and (3) the relationship between trade unions and their members, and trade unions *inter se*.

1.4 The first category of relationship identified above is often called 'individual employment law' or 'individual labour law', while the second and third categories are often termed 'collective labour law'. As indicated above, employment law is also known as labour law and, sometimes, industrial law (this latter term derives from the 1960s, although the phrase is still current, eg as embodied in the title of one of the leading journals in the field, the *Industrial Law Journal*, which was founded around that time, in 1971). Generally, these categorisations all mean the same thing, ie the relationships identified in (1), (2), and (3) in 1.3 above.

1.5 However, employment law covers a wide range of topics within these categories, including: the law of dismissal (both unfair and wrongful – see Chapters 8 and 9); discrimination law (sex (including equal pay), gender reassignment, race, disability, religion or belief, sexual orientation and, from 1 October 2006, age discrimination – see Chapter 5); 'family friendly' policies under which flexible working, parental leave, and enhanced maternity leave provisions have been introduced – see Chapter 7; working time and the national minimum wage – discussed in Chapter 4; enhanced protection of what was formerly called the 'atypical workforce', comprising a broad category of workers, including part-time workers (discussed in Chapter 7), and fixed-term employees (discussed in Chapter 7); and the protection of employees upon the transfers of a business or a part of one – see Chapter 11).

1.6 One particularly complex area concerns the basic division between employees who work under a contract *of* service, and the self-employed (sometimes called 'independent contractors'), who work under a contract *for* services. The categorisation of an individual as one or the other may be important, particularly for claims for personal injuries sustained in the workplace context, where employees may claim under the employer's compulsory liability insurance covering employees. The self-employed are not covered under this insurance. Somewhat confusingly, some rights are granted only to employees, eg the right to claim unfair dismissal, whereas other rights (such as those under the discrimination statutes, the Working Time Regulations 1999, and the National Minimum Wage Act 1999) cover both employees *and* 'workers', the latter being a broader category including employees *and* those working under a contract whereby they agree to provide their own services personally. These issues are discussed in Chapter 4.

1.7 Numerous other key definitions are dealt with in the following chapters, including those on the collective labour law side, eg the definition of a trade union (Chapter 12) and a strike (Chapter 14).

1.8 As in many other areas of the law, the significance of European Union (EU) law has been immense within the field of employment law. All lawyers within the UK are also European Union (EU) lawyers, since EU law not only forms an important part of our laws, but it has also had a major influence on employment law in this Member State. Several of the most important developments in domestic employment law have come about as a result of developments at EU level. These are discussed in more detail in Chapter 2.

1.9 Finally, students of employment law should be aware of the specialist publications in this area, not least the two main sets of specialist law reports, the Industrial Cases Reports (ICR), published by the Incorporated Council of Law Reporting, and the Industrial Relations Law Reports (IRLR), a privately published series containing, in addition to employment law reports, a very interesting *Highlights* section, written by the editor, Michael Rubinstein. It should be remembered that the most important employment law cases will also be reported in the general series of reports, such as the Law Reports, the Weekly Law Reports, and the All England Law Reports. Other important titles include the *Industrial Law Journal* (ILJ), the *Industrial Relations Law Bulletin* (IRLB), the *IDS Brief,* and the *International Journal of Comparative Labour Law and Industrial Relations* (IJCLLIR). Furthermore, many articles on employment law are published in the general law journals such as the *Modern Law Review* and the *Law Quarterly Review*. In addition to these sources, a wide range of relevant material is accessible on the internet from government bodies and other organisations.

Institutions

1.10 When studying employment law, it is essential to have knowledge of the key institutions (and, to some extent, the personnel working within them) comprising the institutional framework of the subject. The following section outlines these key institutions.

Advisory, Conciliation and Arbitration Service

1.11 The Advisory, Conciliation and Arbitration Service (ACAS) is a key organisation in employment law. It was established in 1974, and received statutory status under the Employment Protection Act 1975 (EPA 1975), although the main statutory provisions relating to ACAS are now contained within the Trade Union and Labour Relations (Consolidation) Act 1992 (TULRCA 1992). It has a head office in London and regional offices around the country, with offices in Scotland and Wales. It is an independent organisation and not a government body, although it receives government funding, since its functions are carried out on behalf of the Crown (see TULCRA 1992, s 247(3)), and it has close links with the Department for Business and Regulatory Reform (formerly the Department for Trade and Industry). It has the general duty 'to promote the improvement of industrial relations' (TULCRA 1992, s 209). Its constitution is specified in TULCRA 1992, ss 247–253: it is governed by a council, chaired by an appointee of the Secretary of State for Trade and Industry, with a tripartite structure. It has nine members in total, three representing employers, three representing trade unions, and three independent members.

Advice

1.12 ACAS' advisory function is one of the most important aspects of its work, providing free advice on a wide range of employment matters by way, inter alia, of telephone helplines and publications. It also publishes advisory handbooks (for example, *Discipline & Grievances at Work*) and booklets, and organises training events and seminars.

Conciliation

1.13 Conciliation is a way of resolving disputes without recourse to law. It involves bringing together the parties in dispute to help them reach an agreement by themselves. ACAS provides both individual and collective conciliation: on the individual level, it offers a conciliation service through its Conciliation Officers to employees in dispute with their employer or former employer, as is the case in unfair dismissal claims (the vast majority of employment tribunal applications are referred to a Conciliation Officer, who seeks to explore whether the dispute may be settled without the need for a tribunal hearing); on the collective level, ACAS offers a voluntary channel by which the parties (an employer and one or more trade unions) may resolve their dispute. Under TULCRA 1992, s 210, ACAS has the right to offer its conciliation services to the parties, or the parties may request them.

Arbitration

1.14 Arbitration is a voluntary process at the collective level whereby the parties to a dispute agree to submit to the decision of an arbitrator, although the decision itself is not legally binding (it is expected, however, that, having agreed to submit to this process, the parties will observe the terms of any decision arising from it). Under TULCRA 1992, s 212, 'Where a trade dispute exists or is apprehended ACAS may, at the request of one or more of the parties to the dispute and with the consent of all the parties to the dispute', refer the matters in dispute to arbitration. Arbitration should be considered by ACAS only after consideration has been given to whether conciliation or negotiation could resolve the dispute (these should be attempted before arbitration is offered). Arbitration is carried out through the Central Arbitration Committee (see below) or by an arbitrator selected from a panel of names kept by ACAS.

1.15 Under the Employment Rights (Dispute Resolution) Act 1998, a new section was inserted in TULCRA 1992, s 212A, which allowed ACAS to introduce a new voluntary arbitration scheme for certain *individual* disputes and, in 2001, ACAS introduced such a scheme for unfair dismissal disputes. This was intended to be speedier and less legalistic than going to the employment tribunal, and the hearing is held in private. The parties must waive their rights to have their case heard by an employment tribunal, and they must agree in writing to this process. However, there are severe limitations to the scheme: first, only disputes concerning whether the dismissal was unfair may be arbitrated in this way (ie if other issues arise, such as whether there was a dismissal in the first place, or whether the applicant qualified to make such a claim, the scheme cannot be used); second, there is no appeal from the arbitrator's decision; and third, arbitrators do not have to pay regard to legal principles, but rather to general principles of fairness, which may lead to uncertainty and a lack of trust in the whole process.

Codes of practice

1.16 ACAS has power to issue codes of practice giving practical guidance 'for the purpose of promoting the improvement of industrial relations' (TULCRA 1992, s 199). These codes are not legally binding but they may be taken into account by

Employment Tribunals (TULCRA 1992, s 207). ACAS has issued the following very important and useful codes of practice on: Disciplinary and Grievance Procedures (2003 edition, which came into force on 1 October 2004); Disclosure of Information to Trade Unions for Collective Bargaining Purposes (third edition, 2003); and Time Off for Union Duties and Activities (revised version issued April 2003).

Central Arbitration Committee

1.17 The Central Arbitration Committee (CAC) was established in 1975 under the Employment Protection Act 1975, although the relevant statutory provisions are now contained in TULCRA 1992, ss 259–265. It comprises ten members appointed by the Secretary of State for Trade and Industry, with a chair and a number of deputy chairs. Originally, the CAC's main roles were: (i) to provide arbitration in collective disputes referred to it by ACAS under TULCRA 1992, s 212(1)(b); and (ii) in relation to disputes where trade unions complained that an employer had failed to disclose information required for collective bargaining or selection for redundancy purposes. It also deals with disputes relating to the adequacy of information provided to employees to decide whether a Works Council (on the European model) is required. From 6 April 2005, its remit extended to the setting up of a regular system of information to and consultation with employees under the Transnational Information and Consultation of Employees Regulations 1999 (SI 1999/3323). However, since 6 June 2000 when the Employment Relations Act 1999, s 25 came into force, the CAC's most important role concerns the compulsory recognition of trade unions by employers for collective bargaining purposes, as set out in TULCRA 1992, Sch A1. This is considered further in Chapter 13.

Certification Officer

1.18 The office of Certification Officer (CO) was created in 1975. The office is now governed by TULCRA 1992, s 254. The CO is appointed by the Secretary of State after consultation with ACAS. One of the CO's main roles is to decide whether a trade union is independent, ie not associated with employers or employers' associations (see TULCRA 1992, s 5). If it is independent, the CO will issue a certificate of independence, from which a number of important things flow. For example, only members of an independent trade union are protected in law from dismissal or a detriment on grounds of their union activities. Among other duties of the CO is the maintenance of a list of independent trade unions, keeping records of the membership and financial returns of trade unions, and keeping copies of union rules. The CO also has powers, inter alia, to adjudicate complaints relating to the

election of trade union officials, and complaints concerning political exp
by unions.

The Equality and Human Rights Commission (EHRC) (originally entitled the Commission for Equality and Human Rights (CEHR))

1.19 Until October 2007, there were three commissions in the field of discrimination law: the Equal Opportunities Commission (EOC); the Commission on Racial Equality (CRE); and the Disability Rights Commission (DRC) (now referred to as 'the legacy Commissions'). The EOC's remit was within the field of sex discrimination and equal pay, while the CRE dealt with race discrimination and the DRC covered disability discrimination. An outline of the former powers of the legacy Commissions may be found in the second edition of this textbook. Some of the documents published by the legacy Commissions are also available on the website of the EHRC at: <http://www.equalityhumanrights.com>.

1.20 The idea of having three separate commissions covering discrimination law was reviewed in the years prior to 2004, following which the Government proposed a single commission in a White Paper of May 2004 (*Fairness for All: a New Commission for Equality and Human Rights*: Cm 6185). The White Paper proposed that a new body should be established – the Commission for Equality and Human Rights.

1.21 The Equality Act 2006, which received Royal Assent on 16 February 2006, contains provisions relating to the establishment of the Commission for Equality and Human Rights (as it was originally called: it changed its name, informally, to the Equality and Human Rights Commission (EHRC)) shortly before it became operational. It was formally established on 1 October 2007. The EOC, CRE, and DRC were merged into this Commission.

1.22 The initial proposal was to allow the CRE to remain independent until April 2009 or possibly longer, 'given the rise in Islamophobia, the increased activity of the Far Right, and the increasing lack of integration within our communities' (see 2004/11/18 – CRE Press Release re 'response to DTI statement on the Commission for Equality and Human Rights'). However, with the appointment of Trevor Phillips, the then chair of the CRE, to be the first chair of the EHRC (see 2006/09/08 – EHRC Press Release 'Trevor Phillips Appointed as Chair of New Equality and Human Rights Body') this postponement was reviewed and, on 8 November 2006, it was announced that the CRE, like the other equality bodies, would be subsumed under the new EHRC as from the proposed start-up date of 1 October 2007 (see 'CRE to Join Single Equality Commission at Start up' – Hansard col WA169 on 8 Nov 2006).

1.23 The EHRC has the duty to promote human rights and responsibility for the operation of the current discrimination statutes, the equality regulations on religion or belief, sexual orientation, and age.

1.24 In addition to the creation of the EHRC, the Equality Act 2006 also extends discrimination law to a number of fields outside employment. It:

- made unlawful discrimination on the grounds of religion or belief in the provision of goods, facilities and services, premises, education, and the exercise of public functions;
- created a duty on public authorities to promote equality of opportunity between women and men ('the Gender Duty'), and to prohibit sex discrimination in the exercise of public functions (s 84 of the Act, in force from 6 April 2007); and
- allowed regulations to be made prohibiting discrimination on grounds of sexual orientation in the provision of goods, facilities, and services.

1.25 The EHRC has improved powers (when compared with the three commissions it replaced) to promote equality and deal with discrimination. There was pressure on the Government to create a single discrimination statute, to replace the three main discrimination statutes and the various statutory instruments in the discrimination field, which led to a consultation paper, *Framework for Fairness* (consultation: 12 June 2007 to 4 September 2007). This was followed by a White Paper, published in June 2008, *Framework for a Fairer Future – The Equality Bill*. The consultation paper outlined proposals for a Single Equality Bill for Great Britain following on from the Discrimination Law Review of February 2005. The idea is to create '... a clearer and more streamlined discrimination legislative framework which produces better outcomes for those who currently experience disadvantage'. The Government's draft legislative programme for 2008–2009 contains a proposal to introduce this Bill in the 2008–2009 programme.

The general duty of the EHRC

1.26 The EHRC has a general duty (s 3 of the Equality Act 2006 – in force from 18 April 2006), which flows from the widening equality and diversity agenda of the current Government:

S 3 General Duty

The Commission shall exercise its functions under this Part with a view to encouraging and supporting the development of a society in which –

(a) people's ability to achieve their potential is not limited by prejudice or discrimination,

(b) there is respect for and protection of each individual's human rights,

(c) there is respect for the dignity and worth of each individual,

(d) each individual has an equal opportunity to participate in society, and

(e) there is mutual respect between groups based on understanding and valuing of diversity and on shared respect for equality and human rights.

Information Commissioner

1.27 The EC Data Protection Directive (95/46/EC of 24 October 1995) was implemented in the UK by the Data Protection Act 1998 ('the DPA'), which came into force on 1 March 2000. The DPA replaced the Data Protection Act 1984, which applied only to computerised records. The DPA applies to 'personal data', whether recorded manually or in print, as well as to computerised data.

1.28 The DPA gives 'subject access' to individuals, ie they have the right of access to information held about them and a right to have such information corrected or deleted if appropriate. This right is enforceable by a complaint to the Office of the Information Commissioner, who also has a statutory duty to ensure compliance with the DPA. The Information Commissioner was originally titled the Data Protection Registrar, and later the Data Protection Commissioner until 31 January 2001, when the title changed again to its current form, when further statutory responsibilities came within the remit of the role under the Freedom of Information Act 2000.

1.29 The Information Commissioner has issued a consolidated version of the Code of Practice on Data Protection in the Employment Field (June 2005). For the purposes of employment law, the DPA regulates the keeping of personnel records. These include data relating to recruitment and selection, employee records, monitoring of employees, and information about workers' health. Both the Directive and the DPA allow the processing of sensitive data in the field of employment, which is defined to include personal data indicating ethnic or racial origin, religion, political opinion, trade union membership, and health or sex life (DPA, s 2). This applies both where the data subject gives consent and also if it is 'necessary for the purposes of exercising or performing any obligation which is conferred or imposed by law on the data controller in connection with employment' (DPA, Sch 3, para 2 and the Data Protection (Processing of Sensitive Personal Data) Order 2000, SI 2000/417).

1.30 Individuals are entitled to copies of records containing personal data about them (DPA, s 7), although they do not have a right to copies of references supplied to a prospective employer (DPA, Sch 7, para 1(a)).

1.31 The Office of the Information Commissioner's website, which contains a wealth of relevant material, including guidance, the Code of Practice on Data Protection in the Employment Field, consultation documents, etc, may be found at: <http://www.informationcommissioner.gov.uk>.

International Labour Organisation

1.32 The International Labour Organisation (ILO) was created by the League of Nations under the Treaty of Versailles in 1919, although it is now a specialised agency of the United Nations. It seeks to promote social justice and the international recognition of human and labour rights. It has a tripartite structure, comprising representatives of employees, employers, and governments. It is a significant organisation in the field of employment law in that it seeks to promote the improvement of international labour standards by the adoption of fair working conditions through the Member States (MS) ratifying its Conventions, ie treaties. It also issues Recommendations. It has numerous Conventions, for example ILO Convention (No. 87) on freedom of association and protection of the right to organise (1948), and ILO Convention (No. 98) on the right to organise and collective bargaining (1949). Once an MS ratifies an ILO Convention, the normal obligations of international law apply, ie the MS has a duty to change its national law to ensure compliance with its international law obligations. It is possible for an MS to withdraw from its obligations under a Convention by denouncing it (a formal process whereby the MS gives notice, after which it is no longer bound by it). One of the weaknesses of the ILO Conventions is that there is no enforcement body to ensure an MS's compliance with any ILO Conventions. It is worth noting that ILO Convention No. 100 (1951) on equal pay for work of equal value was the precursor to our Equal Pay Act 1970 and to Article 141 (former Article 119) of the EC Treaty.

1.33 The ILO's website contains an on-line database of ILO legislation, together with other very useful resources. It may be found at <http://www.ilo.org>.

Employment tribunals

Introduction

1.34 Employment tribunals (ETs) were called industrial tribunals until 1 August 1998, when their name was changed under the Employment Rights (Dispute Resolution)

Act 1998. They were first established under the Industrial Training Act 1964 to consider employers' appeals against training levies, and their jurisdiction was extended under the Redundancy Payments Act 1965 to consider claims relating to redundancy payments. However, their workload has increased massively since 1972, when they were given jurisdiction in unfair dismissal claims, which account for a large part of their workload. Their jurisdiction covers both English and Scots law, as well as EU law.

1.35 Their jurisdiction extends, *inter alia*, to claims relating to: discrimination (ie sex, race, disability, sexual orientation, religion or belief and, from 1 October 2006, age discrimination), including equal pay; breach of contract claims arising out of or outstanding upon the termination of the employment relationship (up to £25,000); redundancy payments; unlawful deductions from wages; working time; the national minimum wage; infringement of the rights of part-time workers and fixed-term employees. They also have jurisdiction across a wide range of other matters, for example claims concerning a right to: written particulars of employment; guarantee payments; time off for public duties; written reasons for dismissal; and maternity, paternity, parental, and adoption leave.

1.36 The Annual Report of the Employment Tribunals Service (the ETS Report) reported that in the year 2006–2007 there were 132,577 applications to the ET. This figure represents a 15 per cent increase on the previous year's applications, which itself was higher than those for 2004–2005. Of these applications, approximately 34 per cent were for unfair dismissal. Unlawful deductions from wages claims accounted for approximately 26 per cent of applications, while breach of contract and all discrimination claims comprised approximately 21 per cent and 63 per cent of applications, respectively (with almost 53 per cent of the discrimination applications comprising equal pay claims). It should be noted that not all applications reach the hearing stage: the ETS Report recorded that, in the year 2005–2006, 26 per cent were settled with the assistance of an ACAS conciliator (see below), 34 per cent were withdrawn, 18 per cent were successful at the hearing, 6 per cent were unsuccessful and 10 per cent were 'disposed of otherwise', eg struck out, not at a hearing.

1.37 Although ET decisions do not create precedent, ETs are important as the first-instance forum in which an enormous range of employment-related matters are adjudicated. However, they are not courts of law, and at present they cannot enforce their orders: to do this, the successful party must take enforcement proceedings in the County Court or High Court by registering it with that court. (NB This will change from a date to be set: claimants will be able to proceed immediately to enforcement. These changes are made by s 27, Tribunals, Courts and Enforcement Act 2007, which amends the ETA, s 15(1): see Sch 8 para 43 and the Tribunals, Courts and Enforcement Act 2007 (Commencement No. 1) Order 2007, SI 2007/2709, which does not set a date for commencement). Originally, ETs were seen as a way of providing speedy, accessible, and relatively inexpensive resolutions of disputes, without the need for legal representation of the parties, in a hearing relatively free of the formal, legalistic approach of the courts. Despite this, over the years ETs have become rather more formal, ie like civil courts, with rules of procedure, rules and practices on the admissibility of evidence, fairly formal examination-in-chief and cross-examination of witnesses, etc. Legal representation of the parties is a feature of many hearings. The latter development could be explained by the fact that employment law has both proliferated and become increasingly complex over the years. However, ETs are still fairly inexpensive when compared to the cost of litigation in the ordinary civil courts, and hearings usually come on within a reasonably short time when compared to the listing times for cases in the courts: the ETS Report for 2005–2006 states that 79 per cent of single cases were heard within six months of the application being lodged. Many are heard within three to four months of this date.

Constitution and composition of ETs

1.38 The primary legislation governing ETs is the Employment Tribunals Act 1996 (ETA), although their constitution and rules of procedure are contained in the Employment Tribunals (Constitution and Rules of Procedure) Regulations 2004, SI 2004/1861 (the ET Regulations), in force from 1 October, 2004. ETs usually consist of a three-member panel, ie an Employment Tribunal judge (formerly Chairman), as they are now known (as from 1 December 2007, following the amendment to the Employment Tribunals Act 1996 (ETA) by the Tribunals, Courts and Enforcement Act 2007, Sch 8, paras 35–48: see ETA, s 3A), who is legally qualified, and two lay members (sometimes called 'wing members'), who are not legally qualified. The ET may sit with the ET Judge and one lay member if all parties consent (ETA, s 4(1)(b)). The ET Judge, who is appointed by the Lord Chancellor as either full-time or part-time, must be a barrister or solicitor of at least seven years' standing, while the lay members (who are all part-time) are chosen after consulting organisations representing employees and those representing employers. This means that the lay members have experience of each side of industry, ie management and labour, and together provide what is sometimes called an 'industrial jury'.

1.39 A challenge was mounted (see *Smith v Secretary of State for Trade and Industry* (2000)) against the composition of ETs and the method of appointment of lay members under the Human Rights Act 1998 (HRA 1998), arguing that these breached Article 6 of the European Convention on Human Rights (the Convention), which confers a right to a fair and public hearing before an independent and impartial tribunal in the determination of civil rights. As lay members were paid by the former

Department for Trade and Industry (DTI), whose responsibilites were transferred to the Department for Constitutional Affairs and then, from 9 May 2007, to the Ministry of Justice, the argument was that ETs did not have jurisdiction in cases where the DTI was one of the parties. The Employment Appeal Tribunal (EAT) in *Smith* did not reach a conclusion on this claim, but gave permission to appeal to the Court of Appeal (CA; no appeal was made).

1.40 However, following subsequent changes to the method of appointment of part-time Chairmen (as they were then called) and lay members in 2000, which meant that all such appointments are for a fixed term, renewable automatically except on specified grounds, the EAT has stated that these are sufficient to ensure the independence of lay members, so there is no breach of Article 6 of the Convention (see *Scanfuture UK Ltd v Secretary of State for Trade and Industry* (2001)).

1.41 Where there is a three-member panel, ET decisions are by a majority, which means that lay members may out-vote the ET Judge, although an ET may sit with only one lay member where both or all parties agree, in which case the ET Judge has the casting vote. Some ET proceedings may be heard by an ET Judge sitting alone in certain circumstances, for example where both or all parties have given their written consent to this, in breach of contract claims and on certain interlocutory matters.

Administration of Employment Tribunals

1.42 The President of the Employment Tribunals (a judicial officer appointed by the Lord Chancellor) is responsible for their running, assisted by a Central Office of Employment Tribunals (COET) in London (there is also one in Glasgow for Scotland, with a President of Employment Tribunals for Scotland), which keeps a public register of all ET applications and decisions. The system is divided into regions, with a number of Regional Offices of Employment Tribunals (ROETs), each with a Regional ET Judge, and ETs sit at these regional centres and at a number of permanent centres. Applications are lodged at the appropriate local ET.

1.43 The Employment Tribunal Service (ETS), which is now part of the Tribunals Service, which was an agency within the Department of Constitutional Affairs (whose functions were transferred to the Ministry of Justice, as indicated at para 1.39 above), has responsibility for the overall administration of ETs. It has a Director appointed by, and who reports to, the Secretary of State for Trade and Industry.

Procedure

1.44 Only an outline of the normal procedure of the ETs can be given here (a special procedure applies in certain claims, eg equal value claims and those involving national security). Essentially, ETs have an overriding objective which is 'to deal with cases justly' (ET Regulations, reg 3). This means dealing with cases, 'so far as practicable', so as to ensure that the parties are on an equal footing, saving expense (legal aid is not available in ETs), dealing with cases in ways proportionate to their complexity, ensuring that they are dealt with expeditiously and fairly. There is now a requirement to use a special form to commence proceedings in the ET (Form ET1) and to respond to such a claim (ET3): the use of these forms has been mandatory since 1 October 2005. The ET1 claim form must be lodged within the relevant time limit. In unfair dismissal and discrimination cases, for example, this is three months, whereas it is six months in redundancy payments claims and equal pay claims. The ET has discretion to extend this limit. There are a number of circumstances in which a claim will not be accepted by the ET, one of the most important being where the statutory grievance procedure has not been started by the employee under the Employment Act 2002, s 32, or, if it has, 28 days have not been allowed for attempts to settle the matter without a hearing (rule 3 of the Rules of Procedure). Other circumstances in which a claim will not be accepted are where it has not been submitted on form ET1, where it is incomplete, or where the ET does not have jurisdiction to hear it.

1.45 ETs have the power to strike out a claim (or response) on various grounds. These include: that it is scandalous, or vexatious, or has no reasonable prospect of success; that there has been non-compliance with an order or practice direction; and where the ET Judge or Tribunal considers that it is no longer possible to have a fair hearing in those proceedings. A copy of the claim is sent to the respondent employer, together with the response form on which the respondent may set out its response, which must be made within 28 days, although the ET may extend this limit where it is just and equitable to do so. Where the conciliation duty arises, a copy of the claim is also sent to ACAS, with a view to possible settlement before the hearing with the assistance of an ACAS conciliation officer.

1.46 For many ET claims, including unfair dismissal, there is now a fixed conciliation period within which the ACAS Conciliation Officer may operate: it is either seven or thirteen weeks (rule 22, Rules of Procedure). The former is 'the short conciliation period'; the latter is 'the standard conciliation period'. The short conciliation period applies to various claims such as breach of contract and unauthorised deductions from wages. The standard conciliation period applies to all other proceedings, including unfair dismissal. This fixed period of conciliation may be extended by up to two weeks by Tribunal Chairmen, if the parties agree and settlement looks probable. Once the fixed period has expired, ACAS no longer has a statutory duty to conciliate, but it retains the power to do so, although ACAS has indicated that it will only exercise this power in wholly exceptional circumstances.

1.47 ETs may make orders for disclosure and/or inspection of documents, further particulars of the claim or the Response, or to provide written answers to any question. They may also order a pre-hearing review (PHR), either on the application of one of the parties, or of their own motion, where it appears that an aspect of the claim or defence is unlikely to succeed. PHRs may be heard by an ET Judge sitting alone. Where the ET Judge decides that the aspect of the claim in question has 'little reasonable prospect of success' (rule 20(1) of the Rules of Procedure), it can impose a condition that a party pays a deposit of up to £500 within 21 days before being allowed to continue with the proceedings. Further, the party upon whom such a condition is imposed is warned that an order for costs could be made against them at the full hearing, together with forfeiture of the deposit.

The hearing

1.48 Although ETs are allowed to regulate their own procedure to some extent, their proceedings tend to be quite formal, akin to civil court proceedings, and the Rules of Procedure set out in the Schedules to the Employment Tribunals (Constitution and Rules of Procedure) Regulations 2004 (SI 2004/1861) must be followed. If possible, the parties should agree in advance of the hearing the documents to be used before the ET, usually contained within a Bundle of Documents, for ease of reference. The party with the burden of proof starts, eg in an unfair dismissal case where the employer accepts that a dismissal has taken place, this will be the employer. However, in a constructive unfair dismissal case, where the fact of dismissal is in dispute, it is the employee who starts. Witnesses give evidence on oath and undergo examination-in-chief and cross-examination. When all witnesses have given their evidence, closing submissions are made by each side, and the ET retires to consider its judgment (formerly known as a decision).

1.49 The ET may reserve its judgment until a later date or give it orally at the conclusion of the hearing. Where a judgment is reserved, it must be sent to the parties 'as soon as practicable', rule 29, Rules of Procedure). If an oral judgment is given, the parties may request written reasons either at the hearing or in writing within 14 days of the date on which the judgment was sent to the parties.

Costs

1.50 Although costs are not normally awarded by the ET, it does have power to make costs orders against a party (or a party's representative). There are three forms of costs orders available: (i) a costs order; (ii) a preparation time order; and (iii) a wasted costs order. A costs order will only be made if a party is legally represented, after taking into account the ability of the party to pay. A costs order is normally limited to a maximum of £10,000. It may be made in a number of circumstances, eg where in bringing the proceedings the party or the representative has 'acted vexatiously, abusively, disruptively or otherwise unreasonably, or the bringing or conducting of the proceedings by a party has been misconceived' (rule 40(3), Rules of Procedure). The ETS Report for 2006–2007 indicates that, in the year ended 31 March 2007, ETs awarded costs in 509 cases, comprising 166 awards to claimants and 343 awards to respondents. The average costs award was £2,078.

1.51 Preparation time orders may (or must) be made in the same cases as those in which a costs order may be made. However, a preparation time order may only be made when the receiving party has not been legally represented. They are limited to a maximum of £10,000, and the ability of the paying party to pay must be taken into account when such an order is being considered.

1.52 A wasted costs order may be made against a party's representative who has incurred unnecessary costs (including those to his or her own client), unless they are an employee of a party to the proceedings or are not 'acting in pursuit of profit with regard to those proceedings' (rule 48(4), Rules of Procedure). Wasted costs are defined as any costs incurred by a party 'as a result of any improper, unreasonable or negligent act or omission on the part of any representative', or where the ET 'considers it unreasonable to expect that party to apply' (rule 48(3), Rules of Procedure).

1.53 ETs may review their judgments, either of their own motion or upon the application of a party on certain specified grounds, within 14 days of promulgation. There are very limited grounds for review, eg a clerical error or that the decision was made in the absence of one party. An appeal may be made to the EAT on a point of law within 42 days of the promulgation of the decision.

Employment Appeal Tribunal

1.54 The Employment Appeal Tribunal (EAT) was established in 1975 under the Employment Protection Act 1975 (EPA 1975), although it is now regulated by the ETA and regulations made thereunder. The EAT hears appeals from the ETs on points of law (not fact). A President is appointed for a term of three years from the ranks of High Court judges. Its composition is similar to that of ETs, in that it has two lay members drawn from employers' and employees' organisations (although these tend to be fairly senior members with wide experience, compared to lay members of the ET), but the Chairman is a High Court judge or circuit judge.

Part-time recorders who also appear as counsel in the EAT are not allowed to sit as Chairmen of the EAT following the House of Lords decision in *Lawal v Northern*

Spirit Ltd (2003) that this practice tended to undermine public confidence in the judicial system. As in the ET, the judge may be outvoted by the lay members. A judge sitting alone in the EAT may hear appeals from a single-member ET (ETA 1975, s 28(4)), and the EAT may consist of the Chairman and one lay member where the parties agree to this. Unlike the ET, legal aid is available in the EAT. As appeals are made to the EAT on points of law, it is much more usual for the parties to have legal representation in this forum. Although proceedings are not quite as formal or legalistic as in the High Court, they are more formal than in the ETs.

1.55 The EAT is a court of record and, as such, its decisions must be followed by ETs and inferior courts. However, different divisions of the EAT are not obliged to follow their own decisions, which can lead to confusion at ET level about what is the correct legal analysis to be applied. The English EAT sits in London; the Scottish EAT sits in Edinburgh; the Welsh EAT sits in Cardiff. Appeals from the EAT are to the Court of Appeal and then to the House of Lords.

Court of Appeal and House of Lords

1.56 Once a case is appealed from the EAT to the Court of Appeal and beyond, it leaves the specialist tribunals set up to deal with employment law matters and moves into the ordinary civil court system. Clearly, cases reaching these higher courts are of wider public interest and, in appeals to the House of Lords, they must concern a matter of public importance.

European Court of Justice

1.57 The European Court of Justice (ECJ) has been immensely significant in the development of employment law within the UK, particularly in the field of sex discrimination and equal pay. Any court or tribunal, including ETs, from within the jurisdiction may refer a case to the ECJ under Article 234 for a ruling on the correct interpretation of EU law, or on its applicability within the domestic legal system. Although this topic is dealt with in more detail in Chapter 2, it should be noted here that the ECJ's rulings on, for example, whether directives have been correctly implemented by the Member States, or whether English employment law complies with our obligations under EU law, have been immensely significant in the field of employment law. The ECJ does not decide the issue before the domestic court or tribunal: it simply provides a ruling on the questions put to it by the domestic court, and it is for that court to decide the matter in the light of the ruling given by the ECJ.

Low Pay Commission

1.58 The Low Pay Commission (LPC) was set up in May 1997, although it was given statutory status by the National Minimum Wage Act 1998 (NMWA 1998), s 8, which came into force on 1 November 1998. Its main functions are (i) to monitor the national minimum wage (NMW) and evaluate its impact; and (ii) to make recommendations to the Government on changes of rates. With reference to (i) above, it carries out this function with particular reference to: the effect on pay, employment, and competitiveness in low-paying sectors of the economy and small firms; the effect of the NMW on different groups of workers; the effect on pay structures; and the interaction between the NMW and the tax and benefit systems. With reference to (ii) above, the LPC must consult such people and organisations as it thinks fit before making any recommendations. The LPC's recommendations, including the setting of NMW rates (of which there are currently three), are generally accepted by the Government, but not always: in 2001 and 2002 the LPC recommended that the adult rate be paid to 21-year-olds, but the Government rejected this recommendation on both occasions.

Ideologies

1.59 Employment law may be seen, at its simplest, as the legal rules regulating the workplace, but it may also be seen in a wider context: as *Deakin and Morris* (2001), p 1, comment:

> a broader perspective would see labour law as the normative framework for the existence and operation of all the institutions of the labour market: the business enterprise, trade unions, employers' associations and, in its capacity as regulator and as employer, the state.

1.60 A number of ideologies have been used to analyse this field. For example, one way of viewing employment law is to see it through the *conflictual* model, ie as a struggle between labour and capital (a broadly Marxist approach), while the theories of the current Labour Government underpin a 'partnership' approach to the subject (the *consensual* model), ie management and labour working together, the so-called 'third way', which is essentially an attempt to improve labour standards (including an encouragement to trade union recognition in the workplace) while maintaining a 'flexible and efficient labour market' (see the White Paper, *Fairness at Work*, Cmnd 3968, para 1.8). The 'labour *versus* capital' analysis of employment law is what is being described by *Collins, Ewing and McColgan* (2001), p 1, in the following passage:

> From a political perspective the employment relation lies at the centre of a fundamental conflict of interest that is intrinsic to capitalist societies. The conflict lies between the

owners of capital, who invest in productive activities, and the workers, who supply the necessary labour. Employers seek to maximise the return on their investments, whereas the workers seek the highest price available for their labour, which digs into the employer's profits. As in other contractual relations, however, the parties ultimately share a common interest in the successful achievement of production and profits through the combination of capital and labour.

1.61 Another way of analysing employment law is to see it as a balance between regulation and de-regulation, the former often associated with governments of the political left, the latter with Conservative administrations, such as that of former Prime Ministers Thatcher and Major in the 1980s and much of the 1990s. These approaches are a reflection of a deeper ideological debate on the labour market between, on the one hand, those holding the interventionists' stance and, on the other, those adhering to the abstentionists' (or non-interventionists') point of view (a classic example of the latter being the laissez-faire approach taken in the nineteenth century). The interplay of these approaches has been one of the characteristic features of employment law over the past few decades.

1.62 There are many other ways of analysing employment law. For example, it could be seen as the conflict between collectivist and individualistic approaches, ie between securing what is best for the majority of workers on the one hand, and ensuring the protection and enhancement of the rights of individual employees (as against the majority) on the other. It may also be subjected to a purely economic analysis, ie as an economic transaction between a worker and the employer. In this analysis, labour is simply a unit of production, to be bought and sold, and with a market value: this is to view labour as a commodity. This approach is fundamentally opposed to those who argue that workers have innate human rights, which is not reflected in the economic theory in which they are simply a commodity. (See the Declaration of Philadelphia (1944), which forms part of the ILO's Constitution, Article 1 of which states, 'Labour is not a commodity.' For an argument supporting this viewpoint, see P. O'Higgins, (1997) 'Labour is not a Commodity' *Industrial Law Journal*, Vol 26 (225)). Yet another approach would be to analyse employment law from the feminist perspective. This argues that employment law is gender-biased in that it is the product of largely male-dominated institutions such as the courts, tribunals, and Parliament. This perspective suggests that employment law fails adequately to represent, protect, or advance the interests of women (for an interesting text using this approach, see A. Morris and T. O'Donnell, *Feminist Perspectives on Employment Law* (1999)).

1.63 It will be seen from the above summary that the study of employment law will be enriched if one keeps in mind the various ideologies that may be employed to analyse this area of the law.

Sources of employment law

1.64 The sources of employment law are essentially legislation and case law. In terms of legislation, there is, at the national level, a body of both primary and secondary legislation comprising the statutory regulation of this area of law. At the European Union level, there are Treaty provisions, Directives, and Regulations regulating the employment law of the Member States. At the international level, there are, for example, ILO Conventions which the signatory states are expected to observe. The case law from both national courts and the ECJ is important in terms of the interpretation of this legislation. Case law is also important in that the employment relationship is based upon the contract of employment, so contract principles derived from the case law form an important part of the subject (in this sense, common law comprises a significant source). In employment law, the main sources of law derived from cases come from the decisions of the EAT, High Court, Court of Appeal, and House of Lords at domestic level, and the decisions of the ECJ and the European Court of Human Rights (ECHR) at the European level.

1.65 In addition to these two main sources of employment law there is a range of less formal 'sources', in the sense that these may have an influence on how the formal law is interpreted, applied, and changed. These informal sources include: the Codes of Practice and reports issued by the Equality and Human Rights Commission (and, formerly, the legacy Commissions, ie the EOC, CRE, DRC) and the Health and Safety Executive; EU Commission Recommendations; the Social Policy Agenda and the Social dialogue at EU level (see Chapter 2 for a discussion of this area); and ILO Recommendations. At the workplace level, informal, *voluntary* sources of law include collective and workforce agreements, works rules (ie the workplace rules, often contained in rule books or handbooks, issued by management to employees), and internal codes of practice and policies adopted by individual employers. However, although these sources form the 'core' of the subject, there is a whole raft of 'soft law' that may act as a source of law.

1.66 Students of employment law should be aware of these formal and informal sources of law, and of their interplay at the various levels, eg workplace, national, European, and international.

Key legislation

1.67 Students of employment law should have knowledge of the centrally important provisions contained in the key legislation which form the legislative backbone of the subject. The primary legislation is the main focus of this section, although secondary legislation, mainly in the form of statutory instruments, forms an important part of the regulation in this area. In the sphere of individual employment law, the Employment Rights Act 1996 is the primary legislation regulating, *inter alia*, the law relating to: unfair dismissal; redundancy; notice rights; protection of wages; 'whistle-blowing'; time off work; and maternity, adoption, and parental leave. At the collective level, the Trade Union and Labour Relations (Consolidation) Act 1992 concerns, *inter alia*, the law governing trade unions, their relationship with their members and employers, industrial action, and collective bargaining, including the important area of the statutory recognition of trade unions contained in Schedule A1 of the Act. Certain aspects of wages have been regulated by the National Minimum Wage Act 1998, which stipulates the minimum wage for certain categories of worker in any pay reference period.

1.68 Other important secondary legislation includes: (i) the Transfer of Undertakings (Protection of Employment) Regulations 2006 (SI 2006/246), which came into force on 6 April 2006. These Regulations replace the Transfer of Undertakings (Protection of Employment) Regulations 1981 (SI 1981/1794) (TUPE). The 2006 Regulations safeguard certain employment rights upon the transfer of a business (or part of a business) as a going concern. The 1981 Regulations were supposed to implement the Acquired Rights Directive (Directive 77/187/EC) (the ARD). The 1977 Directive was amended by Directive 98/59/EC, although both Directives have now been consolidated into Council Directive 2001/23/EC; (ii) the Working Time Regulations 1998 (SI 1998/1833), which regulate working time, daily and weekly rest periods and rest breaks, annual leave, and night work – these Regulations implement the Working Time Directive (Directive 93/104/EC, which was amended by Directive 2000/34/EC – the 'Horizontal Amending Directive': both of these Directives have been consolidated by Directive 2003/88/EC, in force from 2 August 2004) (the WTD); (iii) the Information and Consultation of Employees Regulations 2004 (SI 2004/3426), implementing the Information and Consultation Directive (Directive 2002/14/EC); and (iv) the National Minimum Wage Regulations 1999 (SI 1999/584), which contain detailed provisions concerning the minimum wage.

1.69 In the field of discrimination law, the key statutes are the Sex Discrimination Act 1975, the Race Relations Act 1976, and the Disability Discrimination Act 1995, covering sex, race, and disability discrimination, respectively. It should be noted that these statutes regulate a wider area than employment law as they include the provision of goods, services, and facilities. Generally, the student of employment law need only concentrate on the employment parts of these statutes. The Equal Pay Act 1970 should be considered alongside the SDA 1975 in any study of sex discrimination law, as this statute concerns the elimination of sex discrimination from pay structures. Important (and recent) secondary legislation in the discrimination field are the Employment Equality Regulations. There are three sets of these: the Employment Equality (Religion or Belief) Regulations 2003 (SI 2003/1660), the Employment Equality (Sexual Orientation) Regulations 2003 (SI 2003/1661), and the Employment Equality (Age) Regulations 2006 (SI 2006/1031), all of which implement various strands of the Equal Treatment Framework Directive (Directive 2000/78).

1.70 Other important pieces of legislation in employment law are: the Health and Safety at Work etc Act 1974; the Human Rights Act 1998; and the various Employment Acts.

1.71 At EU level, Article 141 (former Article 119) of the Treaty, the provision concerning equal pay for equal work or work of equal value, has been immensely significant in the development of equal pay law at the domestic level. Furthermore, several Directives have been centrally important in domestic law, eg:

- the Equal Treatment Directive (Directive 76/207/EC) (the ETD);
- the Equal Pay Directive (Directive 75/117/EC) (the EPD);
- the Parental Leave Directive (Directive 96/34/EC) (the PLD);
- the Part Time Workers Directive (Directive 98/2) (the PTWD);
- the Acquired Rights Directive and Working Time Directive (mentioned above);
- the Fixed-Term Contracts Directive (Directive 99/70) (the FTCD);
- the Equal Treatment Framework Directive (Directive 2000/78) (the ETFD);
- the Race Directive (Directive 2000/43/EC); and
- the Information and Consultation Directive (2002/14/EC).

1.72 It will be seen from the above list that EU law has had a major influence on the development of many aspects of domestic employment law. A detailed consideration of this aspect of the subject is contained in Chapter 2.

FURTHER READING

Davies, ACL, *Perspectives on Labour Law* (2004) Cambridge University Press.

Deakin, S, & Morris, G, *Labour Law* (4th ed, 2005) Hart Publishing (chapters 1 & 2).

Morris, A, & O'Donnell, T, *Feminist Perspectives on Employment Law* (1999), Cavendish Publishing.

Smith, I, & Thomas, G, *Smith & Wood's Employment Law* (9th ed, 2007) OUP (chapter 1).

ARTICLES

Craig, V, (2001) 'Employment Tribunals and the Human Rights Act: Part 1', *Employment Law Bulletin*, No 44 (August), pp 2–4.

Craig, V, (2001) 'Employment Tribunals and the Human Rights Act: Part 2', *Employment Law Bulletin*, No 45 (October), pp 2–4.

Earnshaw, J, & Hardy, S, (2001) 'Assessing an Arbitral Route for Unfair Dismissal', *Industrial Law Journal,* Vol 30, No 3, pp 289–304.

McKay, S, (2001) 'Dispute Resolution: Shifting the Focus from Tribunals to the Workplace', *Industrial Law Journal*, Vol 30, No 3, September, pp 331–333.

O'Higgins, P, (1997) 'Labour is not a Commodity', *Industrial Law Journal*, Vol 26, No 3 (September), pp 225–234.

USEFUL WEBSITES

ACAS:	www.acas.org.uk
CAC:	www.cac.gov.uk
Certification Officer:	www.certoffice.org
Courts Service:	www.hmcourts-service.gov.uk
DBERR	www.berr.gov.uk
EAT:	www.employmentappeals.gov.uk
ECHR	www.echr.coe.int/echr
ECJ	curia.europa.eu
Equality and Human Rights Commission:	www.equalityhumanrights.com
ETS:	www.employmenttribunals.gov.uk
House of Lords	www.parliament.uk/lords/index.cfm
ILO:	www.ilo.org
Information Commissioner:	www.informationcommissioner.gov.uk
Low Pay Commission:	www.lowpay.gov.uk
Ministry of Justice	www.justice.gov.uk

SELF-TEST QUESTIONS

1   What are the major employment law institutions at domestic, European, and international levels? What powers do they have?

2   Evaluate the role played by the Equality and Human Rights Commission in employment law.

3 List the sources of employment law and explain how each influences its development.

4 'ACAS offers more effective alternative methods to employment tribunals in terms of dispute resolution, but employers and employees alike still prefer a tribunal hearing.' Discuss.

5 Identify the various ideologies used to analyse employment law. Which do you think offers the most valuable insights into this field?

2

The European dimension

SUMMARY

This chapter considers the role and influence of European social law and policy on UK employment law. Furthermore, it examines the origins of EU input, its development, and its content, as well as its overall impact on UK law and practice. In addition, the EU's pervasive influence is examined and its application evaluated. EU remedies and state liability, such as *Francovich* actions, are explained.

The key points in this chapter are:

- EU social law as the result of a long historical path in which the point of departure was the Treaty of Rome;

- The Treaty on European Union ensuring under modest Articles 136–141, that the pursuit of economic objectives would carry as an automatic consequence an improvement in the quality of life and of work for workers;

- European legislation on social rights being now the great artifice of community social law;

- The importance of jurisprudence of the European Court of Justice as social law enforcer; and

- The European Social Model now covering a wide range of both living and working issues, such as social protection, health, education and environmental issues, public services, as well as all aspects of employment rights, social dialogue, direct participation, training, and non-discrimination issues.

Origins of the EU dimension

2.1 The European Economic Community (EEC) was formed as a result of the Spaak Report and established under the Treaty of Rome in 1957. The Treaty of Rome, as the foundational Treaty of the EU, sought to be the vehicle for economic integration. As the Treaty noted, its aim was to 'lay the foundations of an ever closer union among the peoples of Europe'. The Treaty of Rome observed the Monnet and Schumann view that economic integration will spill over into political and social union.

Foundation Treaty

2.2 Whilst the Treaty of Rome did not initially expound much social integration, it did have a Title on Social Policy, contained originally in Article 117 (now the heavily amended Art 136). Article 117 sought to 'promote improved working conditions and standards of living of workers'. The Spaak Report relied for direction on social policy upon the Ohlin Report of ILO experts of 1956, which argued for transnational harmonisation, favouring economic flexibility above social protection. However, Spaak remained concerned about market distortion, which social policy should act to eliminate.

2.3 Articles 136–141 (previously Arts 118–121) provide that the Community may perform social action, by setting down Directives adopted by special majority, in the fields of workers' health and safety, working conditions, the integration of those excluded from the labour market, of information and consultation of workers, and equality for men and women. Matters relating to pay, the right of association, the right to strike, and the right to impose lock-outs are still excluded from the provisions of Article 137. In contrast, Article 136, which refers to 'the Community and the Member States, having in mind fundamental social rights such as those set out in the European Charter of 1961 and in the 1989 Community Charter of Fundamental Social Rights', provides for extensive collective rights, including the rights of association and to strike. On the other hand, in *Kortner* (C-175/73) the Court has recognised freedom of association to be a fundamental right and in *Albany* (C-67/96) the Advocate-General suggested that the collective right to take action was a fundamental right.

Free movement of workers

2.4 Key social and employment principles:

- the promotion of employment;
- free movement of workers;
- employment protection/improvement of living and working conditions;
- health and safety;
- collective bargaining;

- information and consultation – dialogue between management and lat
- equal treatment of men and women;
- an equitable wage.

Some of the key measures that have been enacted under the protocol have been the Directives on:

- working time;
- European works councils;
- national works councils;
- the burden of proof in sex discrimination claims;
- part-time work;
- fixed-term contracts;
- parental leave;
- discrimination on the basis of sex, race and religion, age, or disability;
- the posting of workers.

2.5 The modest origins of European social law, which impacts upon all the EU Member States, arises from the Foundation Treaty's provisions on free movement of workers, guaranteed by Articles 39–42, which establish the principle that workers should enjoy the right to freedom of movement including the abolition of any discrimination based on nationality, as regards employment remuneration and any other conditions of work or employment. However, central to all the rights guaranteed under the fundamental freedom of movement is the key term 'worker', which is not defined by the Treaty or any other European legislation. Consequently, the European Court of Justice has interpreted this salient term: *Hoekstra* (75/63) defined the term 'worker' to also include job-seekers; *Levin* (53/81) and *Kempf* (139/85) accepted part-time workers; *Steymann* (196/87) noted that workers need not necessarily receive formal wages; and, *Bettray* (344/87) determined limits to the term 'worker' by requiring workers to be engaged in 'economic activities' or employment of a 'genuine nature'.

Notwithstanding these cases, the ECJ accepted that the term 'worker' generally refers to an employed person.

2.6 The rights given under the Treaty and Directives 68/360 and 64/221, as well as Regulation 1612/68 include:

- the right to exit, enter; and reside (C-2902/89 *Antonissen* allows job-seekers reasonable time to reside in order to job search; however, C-41/74 *Van Duyn*, disallows entry on public policy or national security grounds. But such restrictions must be proportionate (see C-36/75 *Rutili*, C-115 & 116/81 *Adoui and Cornuaille* and C-30/77 *Bouchereau*));

- the right to equal treatment (both Arts 12 and 39 of the Treaty and Regulation 1612/68, in terms of housing, social and tax advantages, access to training, and trade union membership (see C-39/86 *Lair* and C-197/86 *Brown* (education – tuition fees); C-316/85 *Lebon* (social advantages); C-379/87 *Groener* (linguistic knowledge));
- the right to remain (reg 1251/70);
- rights relating to workers' families (Regulation 1612/68, including spouses, children (see C-267/83 *Diatta*, C-131/85 *Gul*, C-59/85 *Reed* and C-370/90 *Singh*)).

Articles 43–55 provide similar rights and protections for self-employed persons under the right to establishment

Social Action Programmes

2.7 The EU Commission Employment, Social Affairs and Equal Opportunities Directorate is the EU institution which is responsible for setting out the Community Social Action Programmes (SAPs). These are its social priorities. SAPs seek to ensure that the social objectives are a constant concern of all EU policies. From 1974 to the present, SAPs have identified key legislative developments on: employment protection; the working environment; equality between men and women; employee participation; and employment creation. The Community's first SAP was in 1974, which proposed more substantive social policies than those in the original Treaty of Rome. The SAP was hailed as a 'human face' for the Community.

Social policy and 'social dumping'

2.8 With the enactment of the Treaty on European Union, the desire to combat unemployment, a high level of employment and social protection prevailed, seeking to raise the standard of living and solidarity amongst Member States, including additional activities under the new Article 3. These additional activities included 'a policy in the social sphere'. This marked the evolution of EC social policy. Both the EU Commission's Green and White Papers on social policy attempted to clarify the EU's social competences. Later these were set in Articles 136–139 of the Amsterdam Treaty.

2.9 The highly controversial '*Hoover Affair*', involving the decision by Hoover to close its factory in Dijon in France and move to Glasgow, UK, culminating in 600 job losses and the recruitment of some 400 fixed-term contract employees, clearly defines social dumping. In the Hoover case, the motive was clear – cheaper Scottish labour, given the UK's deregulatory style of employment regulation, which causes social, dumping. Whilst the concept of social dumping is easy to understand, the term itself is quite obscure. Social dumping in effect describes the behaviour designed to give a competitive advantage to companies due to low labour standards rather than productivity. Consequently, employers that move businesses to a location where there are lower labour standards are said to be engaged in social dumping. In addition, Member States who deregulate, in an attempt to capitalise from such practices, are equally guilty of such a charge.

2.10 Due to the prospect of social dumping within the EU, the EU Commission has committed itself to 'legislating for higher labour standards and employee rights across the EU in the social field', in order to ensure that social dumping is avoided. Yet the OECD denies that social dumping is widespread in European countries.

Social Europe?

2.11 The social objectives of the EU are broadly centred on the aspirations of social protection. COM(95) 466 defined social protection and its objectives as 'the collective transfer systems designed to protect people against social risks'. To that end, the EU Commission, whilst accepting the enormity in the variance between national systems, requires that all Member States provide specific laws relating to the protection of workers. The social objectives of the EU are set out in both the European Employment Strategy and the Social Action Programmes.

2.12 The new social policy agenda seeks to work towards core European objectives and increased co-ordination of social policies (COM(2000) 379). It was the Treaty of Amsterdam which moved social policy to the centre of EU policy. The strategic objectives 2006–2011 include:

- promoting new forms of European governance;
- a stable Europe with a stronger voice in the world;
- a new economic and social agenda; and
- better quality of life.

2.13 Taking up the subsequent Social Policy Agenda (COM(2000) 370), the EU Commission sought to further policies aimed at building a competitive and inclusive knowledge-based economy promoting social cohesion and full employment. Subsequently, the European Employment Strategy emerged as the new Social

Policy Agenda. More significantly, since the Lisbon Summit, an open method of co-ordination in terms of social policy agenda has emerged.

Social policy after Maastricht

2.14 The first substantive revision of the original Treaty, the Treaty of Rome 1957, took place in 1987 under the auspices of the 1986 Single European Act. First, the Act recognised and formalised the EU's relationship with the European Council (established in 1974 and composed of the Heads of State of each government member), providing for two meetings per year. More importantly, the Court of First Instance was created; the cooperation procedure for legislation was passed; the creation of the Single Market by 1992 was agreed; and, qualified majority voting was recognised as the norm.

2.15 The Treaty on European Union (TEU), more commonly known as the Maastricht Treaty, was agreed in 1992. The Maastricht Summit had two main aims: to sustain the pace of change captured by the earlier Single European Act; and to create the European Union, continuing to change the direction away from economic integration fully (under the EEC) and political union (under the EC) and towards social Europe (under the auspices of the EU). Consequently, the newly formed EU under the Treaty on European Union increased the Community's powers in the social sphere. The Community was supposed to not only work towards raising living standards but also to ensure a high level of social protection. The Social Fund's remit was widened and a whole new section was inserted on education and vocational training. The involvement of the European Parliament in the legislative process was again increased, by extending the cooperation procedure further and the introduction of the co-decision procedure. The TEU overall broadened the aims of the EU to include monetary union and social and environmental protection. The Court of Auditors and the creation of a European Central Bank were formally recognised.

2.16 Under the TEU three pillars were created: Pillar I (the EC); Pillar II (Common Foreign and Security Policy); and Pillar III (Justice and Home Affairs). Pillars II and III do not, unlike Pillar I, provide legally binding acts. As a consequence, the European Court of Justice has no role in Pillars II and III. Above all, under the TEU, all EU Member States' nationals became EU citizens under this distinctly newly created organisation – the EU.

The UK opt-out!

2.17 In an EU social policy context, the adoption of the Treaty meant that two sets of rules applied in the social area: the EC Treaty covering all (then) 15 Member States and the Agreement set out in the 'Protocol (No 14) on social policy' from which the UK opted out. The Agreement set out in Protocol No 14, which was annexed to the TEU, contained two significant innovations: a major boost for the role of management and labour, and extension of qualified majority voting in the Council in the following areas: improvements in the working environment to protect employees, working conditions, information and consultation of workers, equal opportunities for men and women in the labour market and equal treatment at work, and occupational integration of people excluded from the labour market. On the basis of the Agreement, the 14 Member States adopted four directives: Council Directive 94/45 on the introduction of European works councils; Council Directive 96/34 on the framework agreement on parental leave (a proposal on parental leave had been blocked in the Council for several years); Council Directive 97/80 on the burden of proof in cases of discrimination based on sex; and Council Directive 97/81 concerning the Framework Agreement on part-time work. The UK eventually opted into the Social Protocol on 7 June 1997.

EU social policy post-Amsterdam

2.18 The Treaty of Amsterdam (1998), which came into effect in May 1999, is essentially a consolidating Treaty. Its main purpose was to improve law-making, decision-making, and policy formulating processes. Consequently, greater openness in decision-making was brought about. The Treaty also transfers a number of areas formerly contained in Pillar III to Pillar I, including free movement of persons. As a result of such a transfer, much of the original Treaty was renumbered. Pillar III was also renamed Police and Judicial Cooperation. In addition to this, Article 136 (former Art 117) has been altered, thus now including references to the European Social Charter of Turin and the Community Charter of the Fundamental Rights of Workers. The Amsterdam Treaty also provides that the Council can act by unanimity, as before, but now in co-decision with the European Parliament on matters such as:

- implementing decisions relating to the European Social Fund;
- provisions for facilitating the exercise of a citizen's right to move and reside freely within the territory of the Member States;
- social security for Community migrant workers.

2.19 In particular, new additions to the Treaty included a new non-discrimination provision, which provided the authority to create legislation on gender, race, ethnic origin, religion or belief, disability, age, and sexual orientation. The usage of the co-decision procedure was expanded.

Nice Treaty 2002

2.20 Romano Prodi, the then EU President, described the aim of the Nice Summit in December 2000 as 'the reunification of Europe'. The outcome of the Summit was the Nice Treaty. This was eventually ratified in December 2002. This Treaty facilitates the enlargement of the EU. Since it was anticipated that 10 or more new Member States would in the future join the EU, including former Eastern European countries, institutional changes were proposed as follows:

- the number of Commissioners would increase to 26 (though larger Member States would lose their second Commissioner as a result, by 2005);
- qualified majority voting would be extended within the Council (a decline in unanimity is expected);
- the reweighting of votes in the Council in favour of the larger Member States would take place.

2.21 In addition to this institutional business vis-à-vis enlargement matters, the European Council agreed that the EU's Charter of Fundamental Rights should be viewed as a political document and therefore not necessarily legally binding in each Member State. The UK has tended to treat it as not legally binding. The EU now stands as the EU25, including new Member Accession States: the Czech Republic, Cyprus, Estonia, Hungary, Latvia, Lithuania, Malta, Poland, the Slovak Republic, and Slovenia.

2.22 PROGRESS is an EU-funded programme that runs from 2007 to 2013. Its goal is to support Europe's policy-makers as they strive to improve employment conditions and produce effective social protection initiatives. The programme will:

- help to strengthen Member States' knowledge and understanding of social and employment needs by funding analyses, evaluations, and monitoring exercises;
- support the implementation and monitoring of EU rules and regulations in the Member States while promoting networking across Europe – this will help nations and organisations to learn from each other and share best practice;
- provide funding for the development of statistical tools and indicators that can help governments and other bodies to assess the effectiveness of employment and social protection policies.

The European Commission hopes that PROGRESS will enhance cooperation so that Europeans can improve their social and employment policies together. It is about creating jobs while strengthening Europe's social dimension.

Every year, the Commission's Directorate-General for Employment, Social Affairs and Equal Opportunities sets priorities for PROGRESS through a work plan and their priorities include:

- supporting policy development: funding the collection of data on issues such as gender equality in employment and workplace accidents and diseases;
- helping Europe to share good practice and learning: this includes funding for training, events, and seminars;
- joining-up policy: funding studies to examine links between issues like gender, poverty, and discrimination;
- strengthening networks: especially those that support and promote policies and actions which are covered by the programme's remit.

EU social policy – its development

2.23 The EU Commission's White Paper on Social Policy (COM(94) 333) proposed the creation of the 'European Social Model', founded on individual rights, free collective bargaining, the market economy, equality of opportunity, social welfare, democracy, and solidarity (para 3). The ensuing Treaty of Amsterdam (1998) created the Employment Chapter – Title VIII. This Title was fast-tracked following an initiative by the Commission in 1997 (COM(97) 497), which sought to converge both labour market policy and employment levels within the EU. Subsequently, Member States were requested to draw up National Employment Action Plans (NAPs) by June 1998. The Title sought to promote the practice that NAPs be focused on employability, entrepreneurship, adaptability, and equal opportunities (the 'four pillars' of the Luxembourg Jobs Summit, 1997 (COM(99) 442)). The NAPs were discussed at the Cardiff Summit in 1998. The Employment Title is a remarkable achievement, demonstrating a commitment amongst all Member States.

The social partners

2.24 The social partners are organisations that represent different sides of industry at a European level. The three main organisations are:

- the European Trade Union Confederations (ETUC), which represent the labour force;
- the Union of Industries of the European Community (UNICE), which represents business and industry;

- the European Centre for Public Enterprise (CEEP), which represents public-sector employers.

The Confederation of British Industry (CBI) is a member of UNICE and the Trades Union Congress (TUC) a member of ETUC. As a result, both organisations respectively represent the interests of UK companies and employees in the drafting of EU legislation that then becomes legally binding in the UK, and applies equally to unionised and non-unionised companies and organisations alike.

2.25 The Social Protocol was approved by Member States at a 1989 summit, the UK dissenting. In 1997, the Labour Government renounced the UK's opt-out from the Social Protocol, and the Social Policy Agreement was signed in Maastricht on 7 February 1992.

Social dialogue

2.26 Under 118B (now Art 139) social dialogue was formalised, albeit voluntary and informal. This later developed into the role of the social partners. In fact, it was the former EU Commission President, Jacques Delors, who championed the concept of social dialogue. Yet Article 118B enabled the EU Commission in the first instance to promote social dialogue. Since the Treaty of Amsterdam, new Articles 138–139 ensure that social dialogue is an integral part of EU policy and its legal competence. It is often referred to as 'bargaining in the shadow of the law'. Such a methodology is often criticised for being outside the usual institutional law-making processes.

2.27 The European Commission is required to consult the social partners in relation to proposed EU legislation in the social and employment field. The social partners may also engage in negotiations on draft legislation on their own initiative. This process is known as social dialogue.

Typically the process is as follows:

> The European Commission asks the social partners whether they consider there is a need for EU legislation in a specific area. They usually have six weeks to submit their views.

↓

> If both the union and employers' confederations do not support a proposal, the process goes no further.

↓

> If either side supports it, the social partners have the option to try to formulate and agree a framework agreement on the scope and content of envisaged legislation. If they opt for this

route, they have nine months to negotiate a framework agreement. This agreement is then submitted to the Commission so that it can be put forward as a formal legislative proposal to be adopted by the Council of Ministers.

If the social partners fail to reach agreement on the shape of the legislation by the end of nine months, or if they simply decide they will not or cannot negotiate an agreement themselves, the Commission takes the drafting of the proposals forward itself.

2.28 The method of creating legislation through dialogue between the social partners is called the 'framework agreement' procedure. Social dialogue occurs where the two sides of industry, namely the employers and the workers, develop a dialogue which focuses upon a consensus on social policy objectives and policies. In 1991, the social partners, the ETUC, UNICE, and CEEP, reached a landmark agreement establishing a consultative, quasi-legislative role, whereby they should be consulted prior to the passing of any social policy. This agreement later became the ratified Concordat of the Social Partners of 1993 (COM(93) 600). Originally, Article 118B of the Treaty of Rome recognised 'relations based on agreement'. Now Article 138 promotes such consultation of 'management and labour'. Subsequently, the EU Commission must consult with the social partners and is obliged under Articles 136–145 to involve the social partners in a two-stage consultation process, the pre-legislative, as well as taking into consideration their opinion before concluding its proposal.

2.29 However, this social dialogue amongst the recognised social partners was challenged in 1996 by UEAPME (*Union Européenné de l'Artisant et des Petits et Moyennes Entreprises*), a group representing small and medium-sized businesses, arguing about the representativeness of the self-selected, designated social partners. UEAPME agued that their exclusion from consultation and negotiation created an unfair, unrepresentative closed shop. The Court ruled that UEAPME did not have a general right to be consulted. Consequently, the Council and the Commission must verify the representativeness of labour and management of the signatories to any agreement affecting labour and management. Since this ruling UEAPME has become an umbrella organisation of UNICE. Clearly, the social partners have a fundamental role to play in the development of social policy and labour law in the EU.

European Social Model (ESM)

2.30 The Essen Council, convened 9–10 December 1994, confirmed the EU's commitment to the promotion of employment objectives. This followed on from the contradictory proposals of the Commission's Green (COM(93) 551) and White

(COM(94) 333) Papers on the future of European social policy setting out conflicting arguments for and against the development of a European Social Model.

2.31 Following on from Essen, five emerging themes were identified:

- promoting employment;
- reorganising work;
- combating social exclusion;
- mainstreaming gender equality;
- consolidation, compliance, and enforcement of social legislation.

These co-ordinated priorities became known as the 'European Employment Strategy' (EES). Whilst these priorities, the so-called EES, were in the first instance without Treaty powers and are therefore a non-binding legal instrument, they were later formalised in Title VIII (Arts 125–130) of the Amsterdam Treaty. Under the EES, each Member State is responsible for ensuring the transposition of EU Directives and activity in key areas of action in their respective individual national employment policy.

EU labour law

2.32 The first pieces of EU labour law were the Directives on Equal Pay (75/117) and Equal Treatment (76/207). These were followed by collective redundancies (75/129) and business transfers (77/187), which emphasised the two-pronged aspirations of the evolving early social Europe project – that of equality and workers' rights to job security. In the 1980s, these aspirations sought to include health and safety under the 1989 Framework Directive.

2.33 Mainly EU social legislative initiatives have further promoted equality of treatment: Directive 76/207/EEC on equal treatment with regard to access to employment, vocational training, promotion, and working conditions, aimed at eliminating all discrimination, both direct and indirect, in the world of work and providing an opportunity for positive measures; and Directive 79/7/EEC on the progressive implementation of equal treatment with regard to statutory social security schemes. For example, during the 1980s, Directive 86/378/EEC sought to implement equal treatment in occupational schemes of social security, which was later amended by Directive 96/97/EC in light of the *Barber* decision (C-262/88 (1990) ECR I-1889). In addition, during that period, Directive 86/613/EEC on equal treatment for men and women carrying out a self-employed activity, including agriculture, was adopted.

2.34 More recently, the Treaty of Amsterdam explicitly introduced equality between men and women as one of the tasks (Art 2) and activities (Art 3) of the Community.

Article 13 also allows the Council, acting unanimously on a proposal from the Commission, to take action to combat any form of discrimination, including that based on sex. The principle of equal treatment is defined by Article 2(1) as 'there shall be no discrimination whatsoever on grounds of sex either directly or indirectly by reference in particular to marital or family status'. In the EU Charter of Fundamental Rights, Article 23 states that 'Equality between men and women must be ensured in all areas, including employment, work and pay. The principle of equality shall not prevent the maintenance or adoption of measures providing for specific advantages in favour of the under-represented sex.'

2.35 Gender equality, at EU level, became a mainstream phenomenon in 1995. The Fourth Action Programme (COM(95) 381) promoted that more should be done in this important legal area, since actual inequalities in employment persisted. Article 2 of Council Decision 95/593 defined 'mainstreaming' as the principle of integrating equal opportunities for women and men. Furthermore, the Commission (COM(94) 333) initiated the publication of an annual 'Equality Report', in order to review and monitor developments at both Member State and EU levels on equality policies.

2.36 The success of these initiatives led to gender equality becoming a priority task of the Community (COM(96) 67). Council Decision 95/593, which was to form the basis of this new, high-level, commitment to promoting equality in all areas, included:

- reconciling working and family life;
- promoting a gender balance in all EU decision-making;
- making conditions more conducive to exercising equality rights; and
- promoting equal opportunities for men and women in education, training, and the labour market.

2.37 In 1998 Articles 2 and 3(2) of the revised Treaty reinforced the EU's new commitment to gender equality and extended the provisions beyond the labour market. Council Directives 2000/43 (race equality) and 2000/78 (age, disability, and sexual orientation) are a result of such a legal change in legal competences under the Treaty.

The UK and the impact of EU social law

2.38 Historically, the Agreement on Social Policy (SPA) was enacted in order to enable the UK Government's opt-out from the processes which formalised the role of the social partners in decision-making at Community level. As noted above, in 1997 the newly elected UK Government ended the UK's opt-out under the Agreement on Social Policy. Later, the Amsterdam Treaty (1998) further strengthened the provisions formerly contained in Article 118B (now Articles 138–139) by providing an obligation on the part of the Commission to consult the social partners before making any labour law proposals (COM(96) 488). Overall, the SPA originally allowed 11 out of 12 (excluding the UK) Member States to utilise the EU institutions in an innovative way to establish a clearly defined legal basis for Community labour law. It also provided for the beginning of the development of the role of the social partners in creating an EU-wide collective agreement on social affairs and employment strategy.

2.39 From 1990 to 1997, the SPA formed a two-speed Europe. Latterly, post-Amsterdam, in EU Social Policy development terms, the SPA marked a paradoxical significant beginning in the broadening of the scope of Community competence in the social field. For instance, it extended the usage of qualified majority voting. In addition, the SPA envisaged a greater role for the social partners in being consulted and negotiating collective agreements on labour law.

Using EU labour law

2.40 Much of what EU legislators propose seeks, to some extent, to harmonise all existing EU measures and practices. However, positive harmonisation (ie the establishment of minimum standards) was recognised by the Social Action Programmes, the First Social Action Programme being an admission of such aims. Historically, ex Article 100 was therefore the appropriate legal base in providing direct affect. The need for a broad equivalence in labour standards emerges under the EU's banner of promoting a need for a 'level playing field' of competition. It should be noted that the ECJ in 1988 (C-324/86 *Foreningen af Arbejdsledere Danmark v Daddy's Dance Hall A/S*) defined 'harmonisation' as 'not intending to establish a uniform level of protection throughout the Community, but . . . extending the protection guaranteed to workers independently by the laws of the individual Member States'. Essentially, 'harmonisation' seeks to identify a common problem in Europe. However, it is the variance in EU Member States' employment relations and systems of labour law which prevents full harmonisation.

2.41 The EU is founded, like all Member States' legal systems, on the Rule of Law. To that end, Article 220 of the Treaty observes that the role of the European Court of Justice (ECJ) is 'to ensure that, in the interpretation and application of the Treaty, the law is observed'. Articles 220–245 of the Treaty explain the composition, structure, procedure, and function of the Court. The Court is located in Luxembourg. Since 1989, the ECJ has been assisted by the Court of First Instance (CFI). The CFI was belatedly created in order to relieve the ECJ of its excessively growing caseload.

2.42 The Court is currently composed of 25 judges. The ECJ is also assisted by eight Advocates General (AGs), whose role is to assist the judges by presenting a non-binding written opinion which provides advice prior to the Court's deliberations and ruling. Procedurally, the Court has two stages: the written, followed by the oral hearing, the emphasis being on the written stage. The matters brought before the Court are divided into either preliminary rulings or direct actions. Preliminary rulings are requests by Member States' national courts which ask the ECJ either to interpret Community law or rule on the validity of EU secondary legislation. Direct actions are those brought by the Commission against the various Member States which have failed to fulfil their obligations under Community law or individuals seeking to challenge the validity of certain EU legislation.

2.43 Overall, the ECJ has a specific role to ensure that EU law is observed. This broad general function allows the Court to adopt a purposive, or as it is known more commonly, a teleological approach to interpreting community law. As noted in the *CILFIT* case (C-283/81), such an approach allows the ECJ to 'fill the gaps' left by Community law. Such judicial activism has been both praised and criticised over the years. But it cannot be denied that the ECJ has created a 'new legal order' (see C-26/62, *Van Gend*).

2.44 The EU's doctrine of direct effect was established by the European Court of Justice to provide rights and obligations to individuals, enforceable in national courts. This principle was established in *Van Gend en Loos* (C-26/62). This case involved Dutch importers challenging the imposition of a duty, having imported chemicals from Germany. The ECJ, affirming its 'new legal order', observed that EU law conferred rights and obligations on individuals, as well as Member States, without the need for implementing legislation. Consequently, EU law was given direct effect, which means that both Member States and individuals are granted rights and obligations and that such rights and obligations are enforceable by individuals through their national courts.

2.45 Subsequently, the so-called *Van Gend* criteria emerged, suggesting when direct effect applied: the provision to comply must be clear and sufficiently precise (which could include only part of a provision – see *Defrenne v Sabena* (C-43/75)); the right relied upon must be unconditional (see *Van Duyn* (C-41/74)); and, not subject to any other implementing measure either at Community or national level (see *Reyners v Belgium* (C-2/74)). Following *Van Gend*, the doctrine of direct effect applied to Treaty Articles (Art 25), Regulations (Art 249), Decisions (see *Franz Grad* (C-9/70)), international agreements (see *Kupferberg* (C-104/81)), and Directives (but only where the date for implementation has passed (*Ratti* (C-148/78)).

2.46 The Doctrines of direct effect and direct applicability have given rise to an important question – what bodies are to be considered part of the State for the purposes of legal action under Community law? Consequently, the term 'emanations of the State' emerges. The European Court of Justice has been seen to adopt a rather liberal approach to the term 'State'; for example, a health authority in *Marshall* (C-152/84), local government in *Fratelli Constanzo* (C-103/88) and a Police Chief in *Johnston* (C-222/84).

2.47 However, the landmark case of *Foster v British Gas plc* (C-188/89) pushed wider the parameters. The ECJ ruled that a Directive could be relied upon against organisations or bodies which were subject to the authority or control of the State, or had special powers beyond those which result from the normal rules applicable. Such organisations and bodies are deemed to be 'emanations of State'.

2.48 Article 249 provides 'that a directive shall be binding, as to the result to be achieved, upon each member State to which it is addressed'. Directives are therefore not directly applicable; they require implementation before taking effect. Within the EU, such implementation is undertaken by the EU Member States. The *Von Colson* case (C-14/83) reminds EU Member States of their duty under Article 10 of the Treaty to 'ensure the fulfillment of the obligations...'. Consequently, not only do national governments have to transpose Directives into national law, but national courts are obliged to interpret and apply them in a manner which is consistent with the purpose and wording of the Directive concerned.

2.49 Due to the European Court of Justice's refusal to permit the horizontal direct effect of Directives, the principle of indirect effect has emerged. Indirect effect is also known as the 'interpretive obligation'. It was the *Von Colson* ruling (C-14/83) which was instrumental in creating a principle of indirect effect. Clearly, whilst Directives do not have direct effect, EU Member States have a duty to implement Directives. Yet post-*Colson*, Member States' courts also hold a duty to interpret national legislation in light of Community Directives. However, this principle is subject to three limitations:

- where to interpret national legislation in the light of a Directive would conflict with other general principles of EU law (see *Kolpinghuis Nijmegen* (C-80/86));
- only measures enacted prior to the Directive may be interpreted in this manner (see Marleasing (C-106/89));
- it does not apply where criminal proceedings could result (see Arcaro (C-168/95)).

2.50 In circumstances under which EU law places obligations on EU Member States only, such as through Directives, it may be possible for an individual to enforce those rights against the State. This concept is known as vertical direct effect:

Marshall (No 1) v Southampton and South West Hampshire Area Health Authority (C-152/84), in which Miss Helen Marshall wished to enforce her rights under the Equal Treatment Directive (Directive 76/297). The ECJ held that Miss Marshall could rely on the Directive against the State, the health authority being an emanation of State, the State being her employer. Hence, vertical direct effect permitted her to apply the rights and obligations under the Directive against her employer. Since Community law forms part of each EU Member State's domestic legal system, rights and obligations from EU law are normally enforced before the national courts. National courts can, however, utilise the preliminary reference procedure in order to seek the advice of the European Court of Justice. It has been left to the Member States' discretion to designate which national courts will hear actions founded on Community law, as well as the procedures to be adopted. As the ECJ ruled in *Comet* (C-45/76): 'It is for the domestic law of each Member State to designate the courts having jurisdiction and the procedural conditions governing actions at law intended to ensure the protection of the rights which subjects derive from the direct effects of Community law.'

2.51 Article 234 of the EC Treaty provides the European Court of Justice with the jurisdiction to give preliminary rulings on the interpretation of the Treaty and the validity of secondary legislation, when requested to do so by the national courts of the EU Member States. The purpose of a preliminary ruling is to ensure the uniform application and interpretation of Community law by national courts. Whilst the ECJ does not bind itself, it having no rule of precedent, it does ensure its own consistency (see C-28–30/62, Da Costa): a referring national court will be bound by the ECJ's ruling. Above all, the preliminary ruling procedures provide an important link between the national courts and the ECJ. The availability of such procedures also allows EU Member States' courts to familiarise themselves with EU law. Article 234 provides that 'any court or tribunal of a Member State may request a reference'. A national court will only make a reference where it considers that its decision rests upon a point of Community law. Notably, it is the court that decides to make the reference, not the parties to the case under scrutiny.

2.52 Whilst the right to refer is discretionary, it becomes an obligation where there is no remedy in national law. However, following the CILFIT (C-283/81) ruling it will not be necessary to refer the case to the ECJ where:

- the question of EC law is irrelevant to the case being heard by the national court;
- the question of EC law has already been interpreted by the ECJ in a previous ruling;
- the correct interpretation is so obvious as to leave no scope for doubt (acte clair).

The actual referral procedure requires the national court to formulate a question or questions to be addressed by the ECJ.

Francovich actions and State liability

2.53 The principle of State liability was introduced by the European Court of Justice under the *Francovich* ruling (C-6 & 9/90). This ruling allowed for damages to be awarded against a State where that Member State had failed correctly to implement the aims of a Directive. Consequently, damages flowed from the State due to the State's breach which had caused the ensuing losses.

2.54 This principle has since been refined in subsequent rulings. For instance, in *Brasserie du Pecheur and Factortame (No 3)* (C-46 & 48/93) serious breach as a concept was included. Serious breaches are considered those breaches which were intended (see *Dillenkofer*, C-178, 179, 188–190/94). Following *Brasserie du Pecheur*, a three-fold test applies:

- the law infringed must be intended to confer rights on individuals;
- the breach must be sufficiently serious;
- there must be a causal link established between the breach and the individual's damage being claimed.

2.55 The concept of State damages has developed under this principle. In *Rewe-Zentralfinanz* (C-33/76) the European Court of Justice was careful to ensure that appropriate remedies (ie compensation) should be available with regard to breaches of Community laws and rules. The ECJ ruled that it relied upon the national courts to ensure such remedies were available. Therefore, remedies available for similar breaches of national law should also be available for breaches of EC law. The remedy should therefore be an effective remedy. This was defined in *Von Colson* (C-14/83) where the ECJ explained that Article 10 of the Treaty (ex Art 5) provided that EU Member States' national courts should have remedies which act as a deterrent and be adequate to remedy the damage sustained, to be effective.

2.56 The ECJ later developed this principle based on proportionality in *Johnston v Chief Constable of the RUC* (C-222/84), highlighting the need for effective judicial protection for those who have sustained losses as a result of a breach of EU law. It was eventually *Marshall v Southampton and South West Hampshire Area Health Authority (No 2)* (C-271/91) which declared that not only did the remedy have to be comparable with that available for a similar national breach, but where such an effective remedy was not available then EU Member States should devise a new suitable remedy in those circumstances.

2.57 Such a legal situation seeks to promote uniformity amongst Community remedies. However, there is one exception to the rule, *Francovich* claims (see C-6 & 9/90, *Francovich*). With State damages, ie where a Member State has failed to correctly implement the aims of a Directive, compensation is available from the State due to the State's breach which caused the ensuing losses of those concerned. This right ensures that Member States do not benefit from their own breaches of Community law. In *Brasserie du Pecheur* (C-46/93) (see also *Factortame (No 3)*, C-49/93) serious breaches are included. Serious breaches are considered as those breaches which were intended (see *Dillenkofer*, C-178, 179, 188–190/94).

The influence and impact of EU law on social law

2.58 The Convention on the Future of Europe will have a major impact on the institutional framework and governance mechanisms of the Union. Issues of legitimacy and political authority are at the core of the reform process. The Convention is charged with four main tasks:

- division of competences: to clarify when and where competence lies, whether at the Community level, national or sub-national level (eg regional);

- institutional reform: should the EU have a 'federal' structure with the European Commission acting as government and the European Parliament as legislature; is a Europe of nation states with a stronger role for the Council more effective, or neither of these (whatever the choice the current 'Community method' has to change);

- simplification of the Treaties: presently, the legal basis of the EU rests on four treaties and assorted other constitutional acts. These should be integrated into a single text in a manner which makes them accessible to EU citizens;

- democratisation: throughout Europe national parliaments are losing power to their governments, while for those in EU countries the effect is greater due to the increasingly important role of the European Parliament as co-legislator.

The Future of an Enlarged EU – EU28 by 2010

2.59 The Treaty of Nice was ratified in December 2002, having been agreed in December 2000. It was intended to facilitate the enlargement of the EU. The Summit held on 16 April 2003 sought to confirm the commitment of the new acceding signatories to EU membership. The term 'enlargement' is used to describe the widening of membership to the EU. The six founding nations (Belgium, France, Germany, Italy, Luxembourg, and the Netherlands) established the EEC under the Treaty of Rome in 1957. The UK, Ireland and Denmark joined in 1973, Greece joined in 1981, Portugal and Spain acceded in 1986 and Austria, Finland, and Sweden in 1995.

2.60 The new EU25 Member States include, as already noted above, the Czech Republic, Cyprus, Estonia, Hungary, Latvia, Lithuania, Malta, Poland, the Slovak Republic, and Slovenia. By 2008, new EU28 includes Croatia, Romania, and Turkey.

FURTHER READING

Ashiagbor, D, *The European Employment Strategy: Labour Market Regulation and New Governance* (2005) Oxford.

Barnard, C, *EC Employment Law* (2nd ed, 2000) Oxford.

Barnard, C, *Substantive Law of the EU* (2004) Oxford.

Blanpain, R, *European Labour Law* (2006), Kluwer.

Kenner, J, *EU Employment Law from Rome to Amsterdam and Beyond* (2003) Hart Publishing.

ARTICLES

Bercusson, B, 'The European Social Model Comes to Britain', *Industrial Law Journal*, 2002, Vol 31, No 3, pp 209–244.

Dashwood, A, 'The Constitution of the EU After Nice: Law-making Procedures', *European Law Review*, 2001, Vol 26, pp 215–238.

SELF-TEST QUESTIONS

1   What recourse do UK citizens have for Governmental failure to adequately implement EU social laws?

2   To what extent does EU social law protect workers, whereas UK law does not? Give examples from various Directives.

3   'The European Court of Justice has become the most effective social law making institution in modern times.' Discuss with reference to recent decisions of the Court.

Human rights

SUMMARY

This chapter considers the role and influence of human rights at work. Furthermore, it examines the origins of human rights, its development and its content, as well as its overall impact on UK employment law and practice. In addition, the interface of EU law with human rights is also considered. Its key points are:

- EU social law as the result of a long historical association with international labour standards.

- the Human Rights Act 1998 and its applicability to employment rights;

- the importance of jurisprudence of the Court/Council of Human Rights; and

- the pervasive nature of the human rights issues at work.

Human rights in the work place

3.1 The objective of the member governments of the Council of Europe, under whose auspices the text of the European Convention on Human Rights (ECHR) was concluded in November 1950, was to secure the universal and effective recognition and observance of rights that had been proclaimed in the Universal Declaration of Human Rights on 10 December 1948 by the General Assembly of the United Nations. They 'resolved, as the Governments of European countries which are like-minded and have a common heritage of political traditions, ideals, freedom and the rule of law, to take the first step for the collective enforcement of certain of the rights stated in the Universal Declaration'. Originally, the rights chosen were civil and political in character, and so economic and social rights were left aside until later.

3.2 The Articles of the ECHR not only proclaimed fundamental rights but also laid down limitations and balancing safeguards. A European Commission of Human Rights and a European Court of Human Rights (situated in Strasbourg) were set up. States could choose to accept the competence of the Human Rights Commission to examine petitions from individuals claiming that they were victims of a violation of their human rights. The rights proclaimed in the ECHR and the procedures for their enforcement have had a substantial impact on the relationship between the individual and the State.

1950 ECHR

3.3 The 1950 European Convention on Human Rights (ECHR) established protection for basic human rights to: life; non-degrading treatment and slavery; liberty; punishment in accordance with law; fair hearing; privacy; freedom of conscience and expression; association; and non-discrimination. In Opinion 2/94 (Accession to the ECHR) the EU proposed that the 1950 ECHR should be incorporated into Community law. The European Court of Justice in *Rutili v Ministre de l'Interieur* (C-36/75) expressly confirmed that the Convention's rights are protected in Community law.

3.4 The European Convention on Human Rights ('the Convention') was drafted by the Member States of the Council of Europe, and signed in Rome on 4 November 1950, entering into force on 3 September 1953. It has now been ratified by 41 Member States of the Council of Europe (Albania, Andorra, Austria, Belgium, Bulgaria, Croatia, Cyprus, the Czech Republic, Denmark, Estonia, the Federal Yugoslav Republic of Macedonia, Finland, France, Germany, Georgia, Greece, Hungary, Iceland, Ireland, Italy, Latvia, Liechtenstein, Lithuania, Luxembourg, Macedonia, Malta, Moldova, the Netherlands, Norway, Poland, Portugal, Romania, San Marino, the Slovak Republic, Slovenia, Spain, Sweden, Switzerland, Turkey, Ukraine, and the United Kingdom).

3.5 The Convention mirrors the Universal Declaration in that it protects principally civil and political rights as opposed to social, cultural, and economic rights. Article 1 of the Convention provides that 'The High Contracting Parties shall secure to everyone within their jurisprudence the rights and freedoms defined in Section 1 of this Convention.'

3.6 Articles 2–18 list the relevant rights. In summary, these provisions of the Convention concern the right to life, freedom from inhuman or degrading treatment, slavery or servitude and forced labour, rights to liberty and security of the person, the right to a fair trial, freedom against retrospective criminal laws, rights to privacy, freedom of thought, conscience and religion, freedom of expression, freedom of assembly and association, and the right to marry and found a family.

The Human Rights Act

3.7 The Human Rights Act 1998 in effect incorporates Convention rights further into UK law. The White Paper, *Rights Brought Home; the Human Rights Bill* (October 1997), gave as the primary aims of this incorporation:

- to enable Convention rights to be enforced in the UK;
- to save time and money;
- to enable alleged breaches of rights in the UK to be decided by the UK courts and tribunals;
- to increase the influence of UK judges on European case law;
- to ensure closer scrutiny of human rights implications of new legislation.

3.8 Under s 3 of the HRA 1998, all courts and tribunals, in determining questions which arise in connection with a Convention right, must *take into account* judgments of the European Court of Human Rights, so far as relevant and so far as it is possible to do so.

3.9 Under ss 6–8, HRA 1998, all public authorities must act in compliance with the Convention. Indeed, 'It is unlawful for a public authority to act in a way which is incompatible with a Convention right' (s 6(1)). It is a defence, however, to show that the public authority was prevented from acting in accordance with the Convention as the result of UK legislation (s 6(2)).

3.10 If a public authority acts in a way which is inconsistent with Convention rights then a claim for a declaration, damages, or an injunction will lie against it. The following are clearly public authorities:

- courts;
- tribunals;
- central government;
- executive agencies;
- local government.

3.11 The European Court of Human Rights recognised that national authorities are better placed than an international court to evaluate local needs and conditions. This ignition had given rise to a doctrine with the jurisprudence of the Strasbourg institutions known as the 'margin of appreciation'. In broad terms, the doctrine is intended to grant to national authorities a degree of discretion in executive, legislative, and judicial action. It is primarily for national authorities, subject to European supervision, to assess whether restrictions on Convention rights are compatible with the Convention, whether such restrictions correspond to a 'pressing social need' and whether they are 'proportionate'.

3.12 A manner in which European supervision of the margin of appreciation is exercised is through the doctrine of proportionality. The European Court of Human Rights has observed that 'inherent in the whole of the Convention is a search for a fair balance between the demands of the general interest of the community and the requirement of the protection of the individual's fundamental rights'. In seeking to achieve this fair balance, the Court has stated the principle that any restriction on a freedom guaranteed by the Convention must be 'proportionate to the legitimate aim pursued'.

Human rights at work

3.13 The Articles of the European Convention on Human Rights which need to be considered in relation to employment law are:

- the right not to be subjected to inhuman or degrading treatment (**Article 3**);
- the right not to be required to perform forced or compulsory labour (**Article 4**);
- the right to a fair trial (**Article 6**);
- the right to respect for private life (**Article 8**);
- the right to freedom of thought (**Article 9**);
- the right to freedom of expression (**Article 10**);
- the right to freedom of peaceful assembly and to freedom of association with others, including the right to form and to join trade unions (**Article 11**);
- the right to enjoy the substantive rights and freedoms set forth in the Convention without discrimination (**Article 14**).

3.14 The ECHR has already had one major impact on employment law in the UK in that it was responsible for the end of the closed shop, whereby a trade union could enter into an agreement with an employer requiring the employer to employ only those who were already, or were willing to become, members of the trade union (see *Young, James and Webster v UK* (1982)).

Article 4 – slavery/forced labour

3.15 Article 4(1) of the Convention contains an absolute prohibition on slavery and servitude. Article 4(2) prohibits forced and compulsory labour, nor is derogation permitted from these provisions.

3.16 For example, in *Van der Mussele v Belgium*, a Belgian pupil advocate complained that he had been subjected to 'forced or compulsory labour' when he had been obliged under professional rules to represent a client without remuneration or reimbursement of his expenses. It was common ground between the parties, and was accepted by the Court, that his services amounted to 'labour' and that this concept is not restricted to manual work. As for 'forced' labour, the Court held that this refers to work extracted from a person under a physical or mental constraint.

Article 6 – fair trial

3.17 Under Article 6(1) of the Convention, everyone is entitled in the determination of his civil rights and obligations to a fair and public hearing within a reasonable time by an independent and impartial tribunal established by law.

3.18 Professional disciplinary and other regulatory proceedings have been held to involve determinations of 'civil' rights and obligations, so as to trigger the application of Article 6(1). In *Smith v Secretary of State for Trade and Industry* (2000), the Employment Appeal Tribunal held that there was a 'real and troubling' question as to whether employment tribunals satisfied the requirement of independence and impartiality in determination of claims brought by complainants against the Secretary of State for Trade and Industry, taking into account that lay members of tribunal were appointed and paid for by the Secretary of State. Consequently, Article 6(1) further guarantees the right to a fair hearing, which requires that everyone who is a party to proceedings must have a reasonable opportunity of presenting his case to the court or tribunal.

3.19 In *Dr Abegaze v Shrewsbury College of Arys* (2008) the EAT held, per HHJ McMullen QC, that an employment judge did not breach the European Convention on Human Rights 1950 Article 6 by striking out a claim which had not been actively pursued for a number of years, as the right to a fair hearing included the qualification that it should be within a reasonable time. In the circumstances, a fair trial was no longer possible.

Article 8 – privacy

3.20 Article 8(1) of the Convention guarantees the right to respect for private and family life, home, and correspondence. Under Article 8(2), no interference by a public authority with the exercise of this right is permitted except such as is in accordance with the law and is necessary in a democratic society in the interests of national security, public safety, or the economic well-being of the country, for the prevention of disorder or crime, for the protection of health or morals, or for the protection of the rights and freedoms of others.

3.21 In the employment law context, Article 8 may give rise to claims by employees that employers are infringing their rights to respect for private life, for example by acquiring and storing information about them, by intercepting their communications (including e-mail), by monitoring their use of the internet, by subjecting them to closed circuit television, drug testing, grooming and dress regulations, or by attempting to prohibit personal relationships between work colleagues.

3.22 For example, in *Fosh v Cardiff University* (2008) the EAT held that the employment tribunal had been entitled to conclude that a search of an employee's e-mail account did not breach her right to respect for private and family life or have any bearing on the fairness of her dismissal. The Tribunal had perceived conflict of interest and breach of confidentiality, which motivated the university consciously or subconsciously to treat Fosh as it did, not the protected act of representing the student. Assuming, without deciding the point, that the university was an emanation of the state, it had not breached Article 8. The search of Fosh's e-mails was authorised in accordance with the university's own internal rules, and the university was also entitled to rely on the provisions of the Regulation of Investigatory Powers Act 2000 and the regulations made thereunder.

Article 9 – freedom of conscience/religion

3.23 The values which underlie Article 9 are of fundamental importance in a modern democratic civil society based upon pluralism and tolerance. The European Court of Human Rights in its leading decision on Article 9 explained that (*Kokkinakis v Greece* (1993)):

> As enshrined in Article 9, freedom of thought, conscience and religion is one of the foundations of a 'democratic society' within the meaning of the Convention. It is, in its religious dimension, one of the most vital elements that go to make up the identity of believers and their conception of life, but it is also a precious asset for atheists, agnostics, sceptics and the unconcerned. The pluralism indissociable from a democratic society, which has clearly been won over the centuries, depends on it.

3.24 The Commission has not been sympathetic to employees who have claimed reduced hours or time off for religious practices. It is submitted that the reasoning of the Commission is open to question and if applied in the domestic courts it may deny

Article 9 of all potency in the employment field. In *X v UK*, the Commission ruled that a decision of the Inner London Education Authority not to release a Moslem school teacher to attend mosque on a Friday afternoon was not a breach of Article 9.

Article 10 – freedom of expression

3.25 The European Court of Human Rights has repeatedly emphasised that the freedom of expression guaranteed by Article 10 of the Convention is one of the essential foundations of a democratic society. All types of legal entity, including corporate persons, are capable of enjoying this right. Protection is ensured not only to 'information' or 'ideas' that are favourably received or regarded as inoffensive but also to those that offend, shock, or disturb the State or any sector of the population.

3.26 In the employment context, the relevance of Article 10 can be identified in three main areas: freedom to express views, dress codes, and duties of confidence and fidelity.

Article 11 – freedom of assembly/association

3.27 The rights guaranteed by Article 11 of the Convention protect freedom of peaceful assembly and freedom of association, both of which are closely related to freedom of thought, conscience, and religion.

3.28 Freedom of association with others expressly includes a right which is of central importance in the employment context, namely the right to form and join trade unions. Whilst recognising the importance of strike action to unions, the Court and the Commission have been restrictive in their approach. The right to strike does not appear to be an 'indispensable' element of rights of unions and members under Article 11.

3.29 For example, in *Young, James, and Webster v United Kingdom* (1981), the applicants complained that they had lost their jobs because they had refused to join any unions within a closed shop agreement. The Court held that the threat of dismissal for refusing to join a trade union following the conclusion of closed-shop agreements between unions and employers did contravene Article 11 of the convention.

3.30 For example, in *Sibson v United Kingdom* (1993), the applicant resigned from his union in circumstances where allegations of dishonesty had been made against him. His fellow employees voted in favour of a closed shop and threatened strike action unless he was transferred. The applicant refused, at the employer's invitation, to move to another depot and also refused to rejoin the union unless it provided him with a personal apology. The Court found no interference with Article 11 rights, which it held did not prohibit any form of compulsion to join a union but only such compulsion as strikes at the very substance of the freedom of association.

Article 14 – freedom from discrimination

3.31 Article 14 of the Convention provides that the rights and freedoms set forth in the Convention shall be secured without discrimination on any ground, such as sex, race, colour, language, religion, political or other opinion, national or social origin, association with a national minority, property, birth, or other status.

3.32 This provision is not a free-standing guarantee of equal treatment: it only prohibits discrimination in relation to the other rights and freedoms set out elsewhere in the Convention.

Social Charter

3.33 The 1989 Charter of Fundamental Social Rights of Workers (Social Charter) was a result of a Working Party of the Commission on Social Rights. Due to the UK opt-out of social policy at that time, 11 out of 12 of the then EU Member States approved the Charter. Consequently, the UK opt-out ensured that the Charter could not be integrated into the Treaty and therefore its legal status was that of a political declaration. This remained the case until 1997, when the UK opted in and the European Court of Justice (situated in Luxembourg) in the *Albany* case (C-67/96, para 137, per A-G Jacobs) confirmed its core set of social rights, as follows:

- free movement (**Articles 1–3**);
- remuneration (**Articles 4–6**);
- improved living and working conditions (**Articles 7–9**);
- social protection (**Article 10**);
- freedom of association (**Articles 11–14**);
- equal treatment between men and women (**Article 16**);
- information, consultation, and participation (**Articles 17–18**);
- health and safety (**Article 19**);
- protection of children (**Articles 20–23**);
- elderly persons (**Articles 24–25**);
- disabled persons (**Article 26**).

3.34 The Charter's focus was that of 'workers' rather than citizens. However, the 1989 Charter had similar intent to that of the 1972 Paris Declaration of the Council (COM (91) 511). Yet, the overall impact of the Charter was that it formed a legislative agenda which was useful in the refocusing of labour law issues across the EU. However, in particular it should be noted that notwithstanding its restrictive nature, the Charter did result in Directives on: Information (91/533); Collective Redundancies (92/56); Pregnant Women (92/85); Working Time (93/104); Young People (94/33); and Posted Workers (96/71). The Charter endorsed both individual employment rights, as well as collective rights. In any event, the Charter proved to be the impetus required for the development of social rights in the context of the social dimension, not the internal market. Above all, worker's rights were given special relevance under this Charter.

Charter of Fundamental Rights (2000)

3.35 The EU's Charter of Fundamental Rights was approved at the December 2000 Nice Summit and was ratified in late 2002. However, it remains a non-binding document (Chapter VII, Arts 51–54). Its origins go back to the 1975 Tindemans Report (COM(75) 481), which sought to promote citizenship. Whilst the Social Charter 1989 guaranteed fundamental social rights for workers, there were no references to social citizenship. The Comité des Sages of 1996 which pre-empted the Charter broke the deadlock and advanced the notion of social citizenship, the underlying idea of the Charter being to mould the embryonic EU citizenship into social citizenship. The ILO's 1998 Declaration on Fundamental Rights at Work also promoted social rights and therefore influenced EU thinking prior to the Charter.

3.36 The Charter itself is divided into three parts: Preamble; six chapters comprising over 50 rights, freedoms, and principles; and its scope. The Preamble reasserts the EU's proclamation of 'an ever closer union' with fundamental rights. The rights themselves are headed under six titles: dignity, freedoms, equality, solidarity, citizens' rights, and justice.

3.37 The Solidarity Chapter covers EU employment and social law. Chapter IV confers employment rights and social entitlements, including:

- **Article 27** – information and consultation;
- **Article 28** – collective bargaining and action;
- **Article 30** – protection from unfair dismissal;
- **Article 31** – fair and just working conditions;
- **Article 32** – prohibition of child labour and protection of young people;

- **Article 33** – family and professional life;
- **Article 34** – social security and assistance.

FURTHER READING

Allen, R, Crasnow, R, & Beale, A, *Employment Law and Human Rights* (2nd ed, 2007) Oxford.

Blanpain, R, *European Labour Law* (2006) Kluwer (esp. ch. 4 and Appendix 1).

ARTICLE

Ewing, K, 'The EU Charter of Fundamental Rights: A Waste of Time or Wasted Opportunity?', Institute of Employment Rights: London, 2002.

SELF-TEST QUESTIONS

1   How relevant are human rights to employment law?

2   List the Articles of the ECHR and find examples of potential areas/issues/concerns of interaction in the workplace.

3   Evaluate how the European Convention on Human Rights (1950) has impacted upon British employment law after 2000.

4

Contract of employment

SUMMARY

This chapter introduces the employment relationship, which is central to employment law. It is based on the notion of a 'contract of employment', which, like all contracts, contains both express and implied terms. The key points in this chapter are:

- general aspects of express and implied terms;
- specific terms;
- restrictive covenants; and
- the duty of trust and confidence.

It also considers how terms may be varied and concludes with a discussion of illegal contracts.

Parties to the contract

Employees

4.1 The following points should be noted here:

(1) Many statutory rights are given to employees and it is therefore important to identify who is an employee.

(2) The generality of the statutory definitions has led to a substantial body of case law in which the Courts have set out the tests for identifying an employee and the approach to be used.

(3) It is arguable that the scope of employment law should be widened and that ERA 1996, s 23 should be used to extend employment protection to all workers.

4.2 Many of the statutory rights discussed in this book are available only to 'employees', though there are some significant rights which are available to 'workers', a concept defined in the Employment Rights Act 1996, s 230(3) and considered later at paras 4.39 to 4.42. An employee is said to be employed under a 'contract of service' or a 'contract of employment'. This relationship is to be distinguished from that of independent contractor or self-employed person, who works under a 'contract for services'. The distinction between these two different types of relationship lies in the nature of the obligation undertaken. Both may be engaged to achieve a particular result, but the independent contractor may have far greater latitude than the employee in the way he or she achieves that result, for example in hours of work and use of sub-contractors; this relationship is considered below at para 4.46.

4.3 The Employment Rights Act 1996 (ERA 1996), s 230(1) defines an 'employee' as 'an individual who has entered into or works under . . . a contract of employment'. 'Contract of employment' means 'a contract of service or apprenticeship, whether express or implied, and (if it is express) whether it is oral or in writing': see s 230(2). There is no definition of 'self-employed person', 'independent contractor' or 'contract for services' in the Act.

4.4 The generality (or vagueness) of these statutory definitions has led to the courts laying down tests to enable a distinction to be made between employees and self-employed and contracts of service and contracts for services. Many of the older cases used what was called the 'control' test; some used the 'organisation' or 'integration' test. The test currently used is the 'multiple' test, which may take different forms. The fundamental problem is to identify correctly those who should fall within the embrace of employment law and to exclude those who have sufficient economic independence to make it unnecessary to protect them. It is arguable that the tests to be considered below too readily treat people as self-employed persons.

Employees: the tests

4.5 *Ready Mixed Concrete (South East) Ltd v Minister of Pensions and National Insurance* (1968) was the first case to formulate the 'multiple' test. In it MacKenna J set out the conditions to be fulfilled for a contract of employment to exist. He said: 'A contract of service exists if the following three conditions are fulfilled:

    (i) The servant agrees that in consideration of a wage or other remuneration he will provide his own work and skill in the performance of some service for his master.

    (ii) He agrees expressly or impliedly that in the performance of that service he will be subject to the other's control in sufficient degree to make that other master.

    (iii) The other provisions of the contract are consistent with its being a contract of service.

4.6 The judge reached his conclusion by asking whether the person in question was in business on his own account. A significant number of factors in the case suggested that the person concerned was an employee, but the judge concluded that he was self-employed, treating as the determinative factor what he called 'the ownership of the instrumentalities', ie the tools of the trade. It will also be noticed that he used the old-fashioned terms 'master' and 'servant'. Today, the parties are called 'employer' and 'employee'.

4.7 This case was followed soon after by *Market Investigations Ltd v Minister of Social Security* (1969). Cooke J's approach was similar to that of MacKenna J, but he refined the third part of that judge's test. He said that the fundamental test was: 'Is the person who has engaged himself to perform these services performing them as a person in business on his own account?' He went on:

> No exhaustive list has been compiled and perhaps no exhaustive list can be compiled of considerations which are relevant in determining that question, nor can strict rules be laid down as to the relative weight which the various considerations should carry in particular cases. The most that can be said is that control will no doubt always have to be considered, although it can no longer be regarded as the sole determining factor; and that factors, which may be of importance, are such matters as whether the man performing the services provides his own equipment, whether he hires his own helpers, what degree of financial risk he takes, what degree of responsibility for investment and management he has, and whether and how far he has an opportunity of profiting from sound management in the performance of his task.

See also *Lee Ting Sang v Chung Chi-Keung* (1990), in which the test was applied to a mason working mainly for a sub-contractor who was paid either a piece rate or a daily rate for his work, depending upon the nature of the work.

4.8 The most recent case in which the Court of Appeal has considered this issue is *Express and Echo Publications Ltd v Tanton* (1999). The facts of the case are similar to those of *Ready Mixed Concrete*. They involved a driver who was made redundant from his employment and who was later re-engaged under a contract which the company intended, and the driver agreed, should be a contract for services. Clause 3.3 of the agreement provided that should the driver be 'unable or unwilling to perform the services personally he shall arrange at his own expense entirely for another suitable person to perform the services'. The driver applied to the employment tribunal for a declaration that his status was that of employee. The tribunal determined that he was an employee and the Employment Appeal Tribunal (EAT) dismissed the company's appeal. The Court of Appeal, however, allowed the company's appeal, saying that as a matter of law where a person is not required to perform the contract personally the relationship is not one of employee and employer. Thus, clause 3.3 was wholly inconsistent with the contract being one of service. Peter Gibson LJ, with whom the other members of the Court agreed, said: '(I)t is necessary for a contract of employment to contain an obligation on the part of the employee to provide his services personally. Without such an irreducible minimum of obligation, it cannot be said that the contract is one of service...'

4.9 Thus it can be seen that the main elements which are necessary for there to be a contract of employment are personal service, mutuality of obligation, and control. There are also other factors, but these three elements are recurrent themes of the case law. Of the three, mutuality of obligation is of particular importance in cases which involve casual workers and is considered in more detail at para 4.21. The element of control has proved to be of particular significance in cases involving agency (or temporary workers) and is considered at para 4.25.

4.10 So far as the requirement of personal service is concerned, as has been seen, the Court of Appeal in *Tanton* said that the obligation to provide services personally is an 'irreducible minimum' of a contract of employment. The question is, however, what this means in reality. Clearly, if there is no obligation at all to provide personal service, that will negate the existence of an employment relationship. So it was in *Tanton*. The approach taken by the Court of Appeal in this case was followed by the EAT in *Staffordshire Sentinel Newspapers Ltd v Potter* (2004), which said that a clause expressly permitting the person concerned to provide a substitute was wholly inconsistent with a contract of employment. In *MacFarlane v Glasgow City Council* (2001), on the other hand, the EAT distinguished *Tanton*'s case. The case involved qualified gymnastic instructors working at sports centres operated by the Council. If an instructor could not take a class, she would arrange for a replacement from a register of coaches maintained by the council. The replacements were paid by the Council and not by the applicant. Lindsay J, President of the EAT, said that *Tanton* was distinguishable on the grounds, amongst others, that the applicant could not simply choose not to work in person and that she was not free to provide any substitute, but only someone from the Council's own register. Further, the Council paid the substitute direct. Of *Tanton* the EAT said: 'The individual there, at his own choice, need never turn up for work. He could, moreover, profit from his absence if he could find a cheaper substitute. He could choose the substitute and then in effect he would be the master.'

4.11 The approach set out above is not without its drawbacks, since the way the question is posed will tend to dictate the answer given. If one asks the question whether a given individual is in business on his or her own account, it is quite likely that the answer will be different from what it would have been had the question been whether the individual was economically dependent on the provider of labour. This is not, however, an argument which has commended itself to those making the decisions whose impact has been discussed above.

Employees: application of the tests

4.12 The process of deciding whether a person carries on business on his or her own account has been described by Mummery J in *Hall v Lorimer* (1992) in the following terms:

> [I]t is necessary to consider many different aspects of that person's work activity. This is not a mechanical exercise of running through items on a checklist to see whether they are present in, or absent from, a given situation. The object of the exercise is to paint a picture from the accumulation of detail. The overall effect can only be appreciated by standing back from the detailed picture which has been painted, by viewing it from a distance and by making an informed, considered, qualitative appreciation of the whole. It is a matter of evaluation of the overall effect of the detail, which is not necessarily the same as the sum total of the individual details. Not all details are of equal weight or importance in any given situation. The details may also vary in importance from one situation to another... The process involves painting a picture in each individual case.

4.13 The case was a tax case, but the judge accepted that the question whether or not there is a contract of employment is to be determined by reference to the general law of employment, as applied to all the facts of the particular case. The judge's decision was upheld by the Court of Appeal.

4.14 A recurrent question relates to the weight to be attached to a declaration by the parties that the person in question is to be treated as an independent contractor. MacKenna J, in the *Ready Mixed Concrete* case, stated it to be a question of law, irrespective of what the parties have declared it to be, though he went on to say that in cases of doubt, a declaration might help in resolving the doubt one way or the other. Subsequently, however, the Court of Appeal took the view that the label should be disregarded, even in cases of doubt: see *Ferguson v John Dawson and Partners (Contractors) Ltd* (1976) and *Young & Woods Ltd v West* (1980); contrast

Massey v Crown Life Insurance Co (1978). More recent case law suggests a tendency by the courts to hold the parties to the label they have used: see *Autoclenz Ltd v Belcher* (2008) UKEAT/0160/08. It is arguable that this might be an appropriate area in which to apply ERA 1996, s 203(1), since an agreement to provide work as a self-employed person is arguably an agreement which 'purports...to exclude or limit the operation of any provision of' the 1996 Act.

Employees: factors pointing towards employment

4.15 The following factors are the most important to evaluate in painting a picture of a person's work activity:

(1) the contractual provisions;

(2) the degree of control exercised by the 'employer';

(3) the obligation of the 'employer' to provide work;

(4) the obligation on the person to do the work;

(5) the provision of tools, equipment, instruments, and the like;

(6) the arrangements made for tax, National Insurance contributions, sick pay, and VAT;

(7) the opportunity to work for other employers;

(8) other contractual provisions, such as fees, expenses, and holiday pay;

(9) whether the relationship by which the person is a self-employed independent contractor is genuine or whether it is designed to avoid the employment protection legislation.

4.16 So far as the statutory provisions to be considered in this book are concerned, there is a clear divide between employees and self-employed: the former enjoy the benefit of the rights not to be unfairly dismissed and to receive a redundancy payment, whereas the latter do not. It may be noted, however, that, when the issue concerns health and safety rather than employment protection, particularly when a person has sustained injuries, the courts tend to treat as employees persons who might not be regarded otherwise as employees. This may be done in two ways: either by classifying the injured person as an employee, so that he or she is covered by the employer's common law duties, or by treating section 3 of the Health and Safety at Work Act 1974 as extending the employer's obligations so as to embrace the employees of subcontractors. Examples of the first approach are to be found in *Ferguson v John Dawson and Partners (Contractors) Ltd* (1976) and *Lane v Shire Roofing Company (Oxford) Ltd* (1995). In both cases, persons who were working 'on the lump' and who suffered serious personal injuries were classified as employees and were awarded large sums of damages, to which they would not have been entitled had they been classified as self-employed persons, since they would have been outside the employer's common law duty of care. Examples of the second approach are to be found in a series of cases involving injuries to employees of sub-contractors working on an 'employer's' site. In *R v Rhone-Poulenc Rorer Ltd* (1996), for example, three people were carrying out repairs at factory premises belonging to the company, two of whom were employees of a sub-contractor and one an employee of the company. One of the sub-contractor's employees fell and died. The Court of Appeal upheld the company's conviction under section 3 of the 1974 Act, saying that the proper discharge of an employer's obligations under that provision might well make it necessary to take the same precautions for the safety of a sub-contractor's employees as for that employer's own employees, if the sub-contractor's employees were under the employer's direction and control. The decision of the House of Lords in *R v Associated Octel Co Ltd* (1996) makes it clear, however, that for the purposes of section 3 it is necessary to determine whether the activity in question is part of the employer's undertaking.

Employees: homeworkers, casual workers, and temporary workers

4.17 It is not possible to consider all the various types of employment which have been considered in judicial decisions, and reference should be made to the relevant reference works, for example, Upex, *The Law of Termination of Employment* (7th ed, 2006), paras 1.21–1.57. The following categories have been considered:

(1) directors;

(2) partners;

(3) part-time workers;

(4) musicians;

(5) sub-postmasters;

(6) temporary workers;

(7) church ministers and priests;

(8) apprentices;

(9) barristers' clerks; and

(10) office-holders.

4.18 There have been significant developments in judicial thinking in relation to two groups over the last few years: (1) homeworkers and casual workers; and (2) so-called 'temporary workers'. Those who work for a person but do the work away from the premises are outworkers, and, if they do the work in their own domestic environment, are called homeworkers. Whether such persons are employees will depend upon the facts of any given case, as the cases have stressed. In *Airfix Footwear Ltd v Cope* (1978), for example, the decision that the homeworker in question was an employee was due to the fact that she had been working for Airfix Footwear five days a week for seven years. In *Nethermere (St Neots) Ltd v Taverna and Gardiner* (1984) both the homeworkers involved worked under flexible arrangements; they took as much work as they wanted and did not work when they wanted. They were held to be employees. The Court of Appeal stressed that the question is essentially one of fact and that an appellate court should be slow to interfere with the decision of the employment tribunal.

4.19 As the cases show, in this area the element of mutuality of obligation comes to the fore. This is usually expressed as an obligation on the part of the employer to provide work and a corresponding obligation of the employee to accept and perform any work offered. In cases of this kind, the individual carries out work on a casual or irregular basis over a period of time. The question which then arises is whether mutuality of obligation continues to subsist when the individual is not working. If there is, this will give rise to what is called a 'global' contract of employment spanning the separate engagements. If it does not, then the first question will be whether in relation to each individual assignment there was a contract of employment. If there was, then a further question will arise as to whether there is 'continuity of employment' between each period of work. In each case, the tribunal will look at the working periods themselves, and take into account their frequency and duration. Where there has been a regular pattern of work over a period, the tribunal is more likely to find the existence of a continuing overriding arrangement amounting to a contract of employment, as was found to be the case in *Nethermere (St Neots) Ltd v Gardiner* (above). In that case Dillon LJ said that a contract of employment could arise where a course of dealing between the parties continued over several years by which the individual's obligation to accept work implied an obligation on the employer to provide work. He also said that the fact that the individuals concerned could fix their own hours of work, take holidays and time off when they wished, and could vary how much work they were willing to take on in any day did not negative a contract of employment. Stephenson LJ quoted from MacKenna J's judgment in the *Ready Mixed Concrete* case:

> There must be a wage or other remuneration. Otherwise there will be no consideration, and without consideration no contract of any kind. The servant must be obliged to provide his own work and skill.

The judge went on to say:

> There must, in my judgement, be an irreducible minimum of obligation on each side to create a contract of service. I doubt if it can be reduced any lower than in the sentences I have just quoted ... [in the preceding quotation]

4.20   In *O'Kelly v Trusthouse Forte plc* (1983), which involved the question whether 'regular casuals' called in to work at banquets were employees, the decision of the employment tribunal was that they were not. The determinant factor was that there was no mutuality of obligation as they were effectively on 'standby' unless and until they were asked to come in and assist with a particular banquet. The Court of Appeal said that, as the tribunal had correctly weighed up all the factors involved in the case, there were no grounds for interfering with their decision. See also *Mailway (Southern) Ltd v Willsher* (1978).

4.21   The status of casual employee has received attention from both the Court of Appeal and House of Lords in recent years. In *Clark v Oxfordshire Health Authority* (1998) the issue was whether a nurse retained by a health authority on a casual basis to fill temporary vacancies in hospitals was an employee. She worked for the authority's 'nurse bank'; she had no fixed or regular hours of work but was offered work as and when a vacancy occurred at one of the authority's hospitals. When she did not work, she had no entitlement to pay, or to holiday pay or sick leave. She worked on this basis for some three years, during which there were various gaps. The only issue decided by the employment tribunal, and thus the subject of appeal, was whether there was a 'global contract of employment' between the parties. This was described by Sir Christopher Slade in the case under discussion as 'a continuing overriding arrangement which governed the whole of [the parties'] relationship and itself amounted to a contract of employment...' If a global contract of employment existed, the gaps in employment during the time she was on the nurse bank would have counted towards her length of employment and she would have had sufficient continuity; if there was not, each gap would have broken continuity and she would not accumulate sufficient continuity: continuity of employment is discussed in Chapter 9. Following its previous decisions in *Nethermere (St Neots) Ltd v Taverna and Gardiner*, above, and *Hellyer Brothers Ltd v McLeod* (1987), the Court of Appeal said that a contract of employment cannot exist in the absence of mutual obligations subsisting over the entire duration of the relevant period. They said that, although the mutual obligations required to found a global contract of employment need not necessarily consist of obligations to provide and perform work, some mutuality of obligation is required. In the present case, there was no mutuality of obligation: the authority was under no obligation to offer work, nor was she under any obligation to accept it. She had no entitlement to any pay when she did not work and no entitlement to holiday pay or sick leave. There was thus no global contract of employment. The Court of Appeal remitted the case, however, to the employment tribunal to consider other issues, such as whether there existed a specific engagement which could amount to a contract of employment and provide the basis for an unfair dismissal claim. This approach of considering individual assignments was again considered in *Cornwall CC v Prater* (2006). The case concerned a teacher who was engaged by Cornwall CC to teach children who were unable to attend school. Although Mrs Prater was not obliged to accept any particular assignment, once one was accepted she was personally obliged to fulfil her commitments for that particular student. The issue of employee status arose when claiming for a declaration of written particulars of her employment. The CA focused on each individual assignment and this personal obligation in finding that there was sufficient mutuality of obligations. This accordingly allowed the tribunal to find that the periods of time in between assignments were temporary cessations of work within section 212(3) of the Employment Rights Act 1996 (see Chapter 9) and that, accordingly, the claimant was to be regarded as an employee of the council continuously during the relevant period.

4.22　The issue of casual staff was again considered by the House of Lords, in *Carmichael v National Power plc* (1999). The case involved tour guides who were taken on by means of an exchange of letters on a 'casual as required basis' to act as guides taking parties on tours of power stations operated by the predecessor of the respondent company. As in the *Clark* case, they were not obliged to take work and the company did not guarantee that work would be available. They were paid only for the hours they worked. The employment tribunal and the EAT held that they were not employees, but the Court of Appeal allowed their appeal on the ground that the exchange of letters gave rise to a contract of employment. The majority of the Court of Appeal avoided the issue of absence of mutuality by implying terms relating to the performance of the guides' duties. The House of Lords rejected this approach and allowed the company's appeal. Lord Irvine of Lairg LC said that had the appeal turned exclusively on the construction of the exchange of letters he would have had no hesitation in holding as a matter of construction that there was no obligation on the company to provide work or the guides to accept it. He said that it was clear that the parties did not intend the letters to 'constitute an exclusive memorial of their relationship' and that, in looking at the documents, the surrounding circumstances and how the parties conducted themselves, the tribunal was correct to conclude that they did not intend that their relationship should be regulated by contract. See also *Stevedoring & Haulage Services Ltd v Fuller* (2001), *Wilson v Circular Distributors Ltd* (2006), and *Cornwall County Council v Prater* (2006).

4.23　The significance of both these cases is that those who have informal arrangements with their 'employers' are unlikely to be held to have a contract of employment and that the point on which their argument is likely to founder is absence of mutuality of obligation. Even if it is held that a particular engagement does give rise to a contract of employment, the gaps between the engagements may lead to the consequence that each time an engagement ends there is a break in continuity of employment, so that at the start of the next engagement the employee has to start accumulating continuity again. The termination of an engagement would only give rise to an unfair dismissal claim in such circumstances if the engagement had lasted more than a year, so as to give the person concerned sufficient qualifying employment to present a complaint.

4.24 Similar questions arise when considering whether part-time workers are employees as arose when considering the status of homeworkers and casual workers. It may be that a person may work for five different employers on five different days of the week, doing a full day's work for each employer. If that is so, then if the factors set out above point to employment, such a person's status is properly to be regarded as that of an employee. Equally, however, the very fact that such a person does work for five different 'employers' on five different days of the week must also raise the question whether he or she is more properly to be regarded as self-employed. As with casual workers and homeworkers, this question is very much a question of fact. All that can be said is that it should not be too readily assumed that the status of those who work for a number of different 'employers' is that of an employee. All the factors relevant to their work should be considered.

4.25 'Temporary' workers are those whose services are supplied by an intermediary (the labour supplier) for the benefit of a third party (the hirer or end user) for a limited period of time. Two relationships are involved – that between the worker and the agency and that between the worker and the hirer. Those covered here are workers whose services are supplied by an intermediary (the labour supplier) for the benefit of a third party (the hirer) for a period of time, which may be limited or, in some cases, of longer duration. Two relationships are involved – that between the worker and the agency and that between the worker and the hirer. Both types of relationship have been the subject of judicial scrutiny in recent years. It is in this area that the element of control has tended to be of significance, but the requirement of mutuality of obligation, mentioned earlier, may also lead to the conclusion in particular cases that no contract of employment existed. If it is shown that the agency or the hirer has control over the person whose status is in question, that will tend to lead to the conclusion that that person has become an employee. Finally, it should be noted that it is immaterial whether the individual supplying the services supplies them directly, or indirectly through a personal service (or other) company. The task of the tribunal is to ascertain whether there was a contractual relationship between the individual and the end user: see *Hewlett Packard Ltd v Murphy* (2002).

4.26 In *Construction Industry Training Board v Labour Force Ltd* (1970) the Divisional Court expressed the traditional view that the contractual relationship is that between the supplier/agency and the worker was not one of service but one *sui generis*. A similar decision was arrived at in *Wickens v Champion Employment* (1984), where temporaries were employed by an agency under a contract of service. Nevertheless, the court held that the other provisions of the contract were inconsistent with a contract of employment. The question in that case was whether the general terms of engagement of the agency's temporary workers gave rise to an employment relationship. As with the relationship between the worker and the hirer, there must be found in the relationship between worker and agency the irreducible minimum of mutuality of obligation to enable the tribunal to reach the conclusion that there was a contract of employment between them. This was emphasised by the Court of Appeal in *Montgomery v Johnson Underwood Ltd* (2001). It emphasised that mutuality of obligation and control are the irreducible minimum requirements for the existence of a contract of employment and said that, in determining whether a contract of employment exists, the guidance given by MacKenna J in the *Ready Mixed Concrete* case should be followed. The factor which caused the Court of Appeal to say that the tribunal had erred was the absence of control. The Court said that a contractual relationship concerning work to be carried out in which there is no control cannot sensibly be called a contract of employment. They said that it is not essential that there is control of how the work is done, but there must be some sufficient framework of control. They added that an offer of work by an agency could, in appropriate circumstances, satisfy the requirement of mutuality of obligation.

4.27 This area has received the attention of the Court of Appeal in four further decisions – *Dacas v Brook Street Bureau (UK) Ltd* (2004), *Bunce v Postworth Ltd t/a Skyblue* (2005), *James v London Borough of Greenwich* (2008), and *Consistent Group Ltd v Kalwak* (2008). The first case involved a worker who was supplied by the Brook Street Bureau to a local authority. She had a 'temporary worker agreement' with the agency which was expressly stated to be a contract for services and specifically excluded any contract of employment between them. The local authority exercised day-to-day control over her and supplied her with cleaning materials, equipment, and an overall. She was paid by the agency on the basis of time sheets supplied by the local authority. After an allegation that she had been rude, the local authority asked the agency not to send her to work there in the future. The agency told her that no further work would be found for her. She brought a complaint of unfair dismissal against both the agency and the local authority. The tribunal decided that she was employed by neither, but her appeal to the EAT was only against that part of the decision that she was not employed by the agency. This effectively precluded both the EAT and the Court of Appeal from dealing with that aspect of the tribunal's decision relating to her relationship with the local authority. The Court of Appeal upheld the tribunal's decision. They said that the agency was under no obligation to provide the applicant with work, nor was she under any obligation to accept work offered by the agency; nor did the agency exercise any relevant day-to-day control over her work for the local authority. In effect, therefore, both the necessary elements for a contract of employment were missing from the arrangements between Mrs Dacas and the agency. The judgment of the Court of Appeal in this case contains an extensive analysis of the relevant authorities and principles to be applied and used in such cases.

4.28 In the second of the two decisions mentioned in the preceding paragraph, the Court of Appeal had to deal with a situation very similar to that confronting it in the *Dacas* case. The worker concerned brought unfair dismissal proceedings against both the agency and the client but only appealed to the EAT against that part of the tribunal's decision dealing with his relationship with the agency. The agreement in question provided that its terms were not to give rise to a contract of employment. It made clear that there might be intervals between assignments when no work would be available and stated that there was no obligation on the worker to accept any assignment which was offered. The Court of Appeal upheld the decision of both the tribunal and the EAT that the claimant was not an employee of the agency. This was on the basis, as in the *Dacas* case, that there was no mutuality of obligation and an insufficient degree of control to establish a contract of employment.

4.29 In the third of the decisions mentioned in para 4.27, again a claim for unfair dismissal was brought when the end user brought an end to the engagement of the worker. In this case the Court of Appeal expressed the view that in order to question whether a contract of employment can be implied it must first be questioned whether the arrangement under consideration is a genuine agency arrangement or whether it is only consistent with an implied contract between the worker and the end user and would be inconsistent with there being no such contract. It is only where the arrangement is not genuine that one can question whether a contract can be implied. In the last of the four decisions above, the Court of Appeal emphasised that it is not for the court or tribunal to re-cast the parties' bargain and that they should be held to the agreement they have made.

4.30 It is clear that the same requirements of mutuality of obligation and a sufficient degree of control apply in the case of the relationship between the worker and the hirer or 'end user', as this person has come to be called; however, it is now equally clear in the light of *James v London Borough of Greenwich* (2008) that one must first determine whether a genuine agency arrangement is in place. In *Stephenson v Delphi Diesel Systems Ltd* (2003) Elias J said:

> The significance of mutuality is that it determines whether there is a contract in existence at all. The significance of control is that it determines whether, if there is a contract in place, it can properly be classified as a contract of service, rather than some other kind of contract.

In general, in view of these requirements, it is unlikely that a worker placed by an agency will become an employee of the hirer, although application of the tests already considered may lead to the conclusion that an employment relationship has arisen. In this context, as in the other considered, it is important to emphasise that each case depends on its own facts.

4.31 Examples of this general proposition are *Serco Ltd v Blair* (1998) and *Costain Building & Civil Engineering Ltd v Smith and Chanton Group plc* (2000). In both cases, employees were supplied by an employment agency to a customer of the agency in circumstances such that the EAT held that no employment relationship arose. In the second case, an engineer was supplied by an agency to Costain. There was an agreement between the agency and Costain for the supply of services by the engineer and the agreement stated that he would be under the strict supervision of Costain. There was no agreement between him and Costain, however, and he did not receive any disciplinary or grievance documentation, nor did he expect to receive sick pay or holiday pay, and there was no clause providing for notice of termination. The engineer raised a number of health and safety issues and eventually was appointed a health and safety representative for the site. After he had produced a number of reports critical of Costain's management of the site, Costain informed the agency that they did not want him to continue to work on the site. He claimed that he had been unfairly dismissed by Costain contrary to ERA 1996, s 100(1)(b). The EAT held that he did not become an employee of Costain and that therefore he could not complain of unfair dismissal. It followed that his appointment as a health and safety representative was ineffective. The EAT pointed out that when a health and safety representative is appointed, he or she should already be an employee. It rejected the argument that the appointment of the engineer as a representative had the effect of altering his status. These cases should be contrasted with the decision in *Motorola Ltd v Davidson and Melville Craig Group Ltd* (2001), a case where the worker was held to have become an employee of the end user.

4.32 In the present context, the significance of the Court of Appeal decision in *Dacas v Brook Street Bureau (UK) Ltd* (2004) should not be overlooked. Although that case was confined to a consideration of the relationship between the worker and the agency (simply because she had not appealed against that part of the tribunal's decision relating to her relationship with the end user), the observations of the Court of Appeal make it clear that in dealing with these kinds of cases tribunals should examine the facts very carefully to ascertain whether an employment relationship between the worker and the end user can be inferred. It is clear, at least from the judgment of Mummery LJ, that he regarded it as possible that there might have been an implied contract between Mrs Dacas and the authority, but that the case would have had to be remitted to the tribunal for it to determine the issue. Cases subsequently decided by the EAT suggest that there is a tendency to hold that the agency worker is an employee of the end user. Two subsequent decisions of the EAT – in *Cable and Wireless plc v Muscat* (2005) and *Royal National Lifeboat Institution v Bushaway* (2005) – both upheld the tribunal's decisions that the agency workers concerned were employees of the end user. In *James v London Borough of Greenwich* (2008) the Court of Appeal said that *Dacas* is not authority for the proposition that the implication of a contract of employment between the end user and the worker is inevitable in a long-term agency worker situation. If emphasised that the question whether an agency worker is an employee of an end user must be decided in accordance with the principles of implied contract.

4.33   The three most recent decisions of the EAT dealing with the position of agency workers are: *Heatherwood and Wexham Park Hospitals NHS Trust Limited v Kulubowlia & Others* (2007); *Astbury v Gist Limited* (2007); and *Cairns v Visteon UK Limited* (2006). The EAT, in the first two cases, favoured the restricted approach adopted in *James v London Borough of Greenwich* (2008) noted above. In *Cairns v Visteon UK Limited* (2006), the EAT held that an agency worker cannot be an employee of both the agency and the end user. Once a worker is deemed to be an employee of one, they cannot later argue to be an employee of the third party.

Employees: approach of the appellate courts

4.34   The final question which requires consideration here is the approach of the appellate courts to the question of whether a person is an employee or not. This depends upon whether or not the construction of a written contract or document is involved. If, exceptionally, the relationship is dependent solely upon the true construction of a written document, the question will be one of law, upon which an appeal will lie: see *Davies v Presbyterian Church of Wales* (1986), *Lee Ting Sang v Chung Chi-Keung* (1990), and *McMeechan v Secretary of State for Employment* (1997). For a discussion of the historical basis for this rule see Lord Hoffman's speech in *Carmichael v National Power plc* (1999) (at pp 1232–1233). In other cases, it has generally been regarded as a mixed question of fact and law. In *O'Kelly v Trusthouse Forte plc* (1983), the Court of Appeal affirmed that a question of law is involved. A majority, however, also held that the answer to the question whether a person is an employee or not involves questions of degree and fact which it is for the employment tribunal to determine. An appellate tribunal may not interfere with the employment tribunal's decision unless the employment tribunal has misdirected itself in law or its decision is one which no tribunal, properly directing itself on the relevant facts, could have reached. The effect is to place a heavy burden on an applicant who disagrees with a tribunal's decision and to restrict the scope for appeals to the EAT and the Court of Appeal.

4.35 In *Lee Ting Sang v Chung Chi-Keung* (1990), Lord Griffiths, who delivered the opinion of the Privy Council, pointed out that the decision whether or not a person is employed under a contract of employment will depend upon the evaluation of many facts and there will be many borderline cases in which similarly instructed minds may come to different conclusions. He said that in such situations an appeal court must not interfere. In *Hall v Lorimer* (1992), Mummery J applied *Lee Ting Sang*'s case and stated: 'The appellate court will not interfere with the conclusion of the fact finding tribunal where the decision... comes within what has been described as the "band of possible reasonable decisions". The appellate court realises that there are borderline or grey areas in which tribunals, properly instructed on the law and facts, can legitimately and reasonably arrive at different conclusions...'

4.36 More recently, the Court of Appeal appears to have modified the approach to dealing with appeals set out above. In *Express & Echo Publications Ltd v Tanton* (1999), Peter Gibson LJ said that he accepted that the correct approach to the determination of the question whether or not an applicant is an employee is as follows:

(1) The tribunal should establish what were the terms of the agreement between the parties. That is a question of fact.

(2) The tribunal should then consider whether any of the terms of the contract are inherently inconsistent with the existence of a contract of employment. That is plainly a question of law, and although this court, as indeed the Employment Appeal Tribunal before us, has no power to interfere with findings of fact (an appeal only lies on a point of law), if there were a term of the contract inherently inconsistent with a contract of employment and that has not been recognised by the tribunal's chairman, that would be a point of law on which this court, like the Employment Appeal Tribunal before us, would be entitled to interfere with the conclusion of the chairman.

(3) If there are no such inherently inconsistent terms, the tribunal should determine whether the contract is a contract of service or a contract for services, having regard to all the terms. That is a mixed question of law and fact.

4.37 In that case, the Court of Appeal treated as an error of law falling within the second part of the approach set out above the decision of the chairman of the employment tribunal that the relevant clause of the contract was one of many factors to be taken into account and did not preclude the relationship of employer and employee coming into existence. The Court of Appeal's view in *Tanton* appears to be at variance with the approach taken by that Court in *O'Kelly v Trusthouse Forte plc* and subsequent cases in its suggestion that the approach of a tribunal to individual terms rather than to the whole contract may be characterised as an error of law. In other words, the second stage of the three-stage approach accepted by Peter Gibson LJ appears to be an additional and arguable supernumerary gloss on the previous approach; see also *Consistent Group Ltd v Kalwak* (2008).

Employees: future developments

4.38 The Employment Relations Act 1999 (ERelA 1999), s 23 contains a provision which gives the Secretary of State power by order to extend employment protection rights to groups who currently do not enjoy them, including individuals expressly excluded from the rights. The order made may confer the rights on individuals who are of a 'specified description'; it may also provide that individuals are to be treated as parties to workers' contracts or contracts of employment and make provision as to who are to be regarded as the employers of individuals. The order may also modify the operation of any rights as conferred on individuals by the order. It is not clear what steps are intended to be taken under this provision. It may be that specific groups who are currently treated as excluded from the legislation will be included within the order, for example, clergy. Equally, there is no reason why the order should not be a general provision extending the relevant legislation to workers instead of employees, for example. In the latter case, the effect would be considerable and would, at least to some extent, reduce the problems involved in making a distinction between employees and self-employed persons.

4.39 In this context, it is worth observing that much of the legislation enacted in recent years has been expressly applied to a 'worker'. Before 1997, the only legislation to refer expressly to a worker was the Wages Act 1986, subsequently consolidated into the ERA 1996, Pt II. It may be noted, however, that the definition of 'employment' to be found in the discrimination legislation is wide enough to embrace self-employed persons and thus goes wider than the definition of employee in the ERA 1996: see, for example, section 82(1) of the Sex Discrimination Act 1975. The definition used there is replicated in all the other relevant Acts and Regulations.

4.40 The position of agency workers, as seen in the case-law considered above, is changing all the time. The future development of this area of the law is likely to be considerably affected by legislative changes at a European level. This is as a consequence of political agreement having been reached on the draft Agency Workers Directive at the European Employment Council on 9 June 2008. This Directive is now going through the EU legislative process. This is an important step as it brings an end to six years of deadlock and will result in all EU Member States being obligated to offer sufficient protections to agency workers. The UK appears to be meeting the requirements of the current draft, having implemented an agreement between the CBI and the TUC which entitles agency workers to equal treatment, covering pay and conditions once they have been engaged in a given job for at least 12 weeks, though the entitlement does not extend to sick pay and pensions.

Statutory definition of 'worker'

4.41 The ERA 1996, s 230(3) defines 'worker' as 'an individual who has entered into or works under:

(a) a contract of employment; or

(b) any other contract, whether express or implied and (if it is express) whether oral or in writing, whereby the individual undertakes to do or perform personally any work or services for another party to the contract whose status is not by virtue of the contract that of a client or customer of any profession or business undertaking carried on by the individual...

4.42 Clearly the definition embraces all employees; it also seems to be wide enough to embrace self-employed persons who offer consultancy services and thus are effectively sole traders. One of the apparent oddities of the legislation is that many of the recently introduced rights, for example under the Working Time Regulations (SI 1998/1833, as amended by the Working Time Regulations 1999 (SI 1999/3372)) or the National Minimum Wage Act 1998, apply to 'workers', but if such persons are dismissed for a reason connected with the Regulations or the Act they may only complain of unfair dismissal if they are employees. This seems to be anomalous.

Employer

4.43 Whilst in most cases there may be no problems in identifying who the employer is, nevertheless there may be cases where this proves to be a problem. The most obvious situation is where there appears to have been a 'relevant transfer' and where it is possible that the Transfer of Undertakings (Protection of Employment) Regulations (TUPE) apply. This matter is considered in Chapter 11. An example of the problem arising outside a TUPE context is to be found in *Andrews v King* (1991). The case involved the assessment to tax of a farm worker who organised a number of men together for picking or grading potatoes as and when they were required by potato merchants. The farm worker, Andrews, was assessed to tax on the basis that he was a self-employed gang-master who employed the members of the gang. He was therefore assessed to tax as a self-employed person and served with PAYE determinations of tax payable by an employer. The Vice-Chancellor held that he was not carrying on business on his own account and that all the members of the gang, including Andrews, were employed by the potato merchants.

4.44 The other matter which may be relevant here is employment by 'associated employers'. This is usually of more importance for calculating continuity of employment, but may also arise when it is necessary to decide who is a person's employer. An employee taken into the employment of a new employer associated with the previous employer may count the period of previous employment as employment with the associated employer: see ERA 1996, s 218(6). 'Associated employer' is defined in ERA 1996, s 231. The definition has two limbs. Under the first limb, two employers are to be treated as associated where 'one is a company of which the other (directly or indirectly) has control'; under the second limb, they will be treated as associated where 'both are companies of which a third person (directly or indirectly) has control'. In both cases, it should be noted that the controlling employer need not be a company and may, therefore, be a sole trader or a partnership. The Court of Appeal has held the definition to be exhaustive, which means that local authorities cannot be associated employers: see *Merton London Borough Council v Gardiner* (1981) and *Southwood Hostel Management Committee v Taylor* (1979).

4.45 The problem which has most frequently arisen in the context of this definition concerns the meaning of 'control'. In *Secretary of State for Employment v Newbold and Joint Liquidators of David Armstrong (Catering Services) Ltd* (1981) the EAT said that control means control by the majority of votes attaching to shares, exercised in general meetings; it is not how or by whom the enterprise is actually run. It is clear, however, that, where a number of companies is involved, one person must have a majority share in all the relevant companies for them to be treated as associated. In *Russell v Elmdon Freight Terminal Ltd* (1989), for example, one person held 55 per cent of the shares of the first company and 50 per cent of the shares of the second, and a second person held no shares in the first and 49 per cent of the shares in the second. There was thus no one person who had voting control over both companies. The EAT stressed that, where two companies are involved, there must be one or more persons who have voting control over both companies. See also *South West Launderettes Ltd v Laidler* (1986), *Secretary of State for Employment v Chapman* (1989), and *Tice v Cartwright* (1999).

Other relationships

4.46 As has been seen, the coverage of employment law embraces 'employees' and, in some contexts and for some purposes, 'workers'. There are, however, other relationships by which one person performs services for another. The most obvious of these is that of the self-employed provider of services. Such people have different names or titles depending on the sector in which they work. They may be called 'independent contractors', 'consultants' or 'freelancers'. It is important to ensure that, whatever title they are given, the substance of the relationship is clear. Put another way, it is no use giving a title which suggests self-employment to someone who is self-evidently an employee. An error of categorisation may be costly, particularly for an employer who finds that the Inland Revenue takes a different view. In every case of this kind, it is important to look at the substance rather than the label which has been attached to the relationship. Whilst it is well settled that tribunals will use the multiple test to determine whether a particular person is an employee or not, it is by no means axiomatic that this is the best test to use. As has already been pointed out, the form in which a question is asked will dictate the answer given. In view of the significant changes in working practices in recent decades, it is time to re-assess this test. A better test would be a test based on the economic dependence of the person doing the work. This is the approach taken by French law and is worthy of serious consideration.

Sources of contractual obligations

4.47 The following principles in relation to sources of a contract of employment should be noted:

(1) The main sources of an employment contract are express terms and implied terms.

(2) Express terms are to be found in the contract itself and/or documents expressly or impliedly incorporated into the contract, such as collective agreements or employers' handbooks.

(3) In cases where interpretation or construction of the contractual documentation is necessary, the court or tribunal will apply the ordinary rules of construction for contracts.

(4) In cases where there is no employment contract, the existence of a written statement of terms and conditions under section 1 of the Employment Rights Act 1996 will assist the determination of what terms were agreed.

(5) An express term may in appropriate cases be qualified by an implied term, such as the term not to behave in a way such as to undermine the relationship of trust and confidence between employer and employee.

(6) Implied terms will arise where the court or tribunal regards the implication of a term as necessary to give the contract business efficacy or reflect what the parties would have agreed had they addressed their minds to the issue.

(7) Terms may be implied from custom and practice, but such terms are of limited importance.

4.48 The main source of contractual obligations is the express terms of the contract. This process is assisted by the provisions of ERA 1996, s 1, which requires employers to give their employees written particulars of many of the more important terms of their contracts. Terms may be expressly incorporated by a reference in the contract to another document such as a collective agreement, but not all such terms are appropriate for incorporation; other documents may also be impliedly incorporated. A corollary of reducing a contract to writing is that the express terms (both in the contract and any incorporated document) should be clear and accurate so as to avoid the risk of a court interpreting the contract in a different way from what was originally intended. The construction of express terms is considered below.

4.49 Even if the employer complies with the requirements of section 1 and gives a written statement or decides to give an employee a full written contract of employment, there are likely to be areas in the contract which are not covered by express terms. In that case the court or tribunal will have to consider resorting to implied terms to fill the apparent gap. An example is in the context of mobility. If the contract contains no express term, and there is a dispute between the employer and the employee as to whether he or she may be required to move elsewhere, the court or tribunal will have to decide whether a mobility term should be implied. It is, however, a general feature of implied terms that the term implied will be no wider than is necessary. An employer who wants a wide term will need to insert an express clause into the contract. It is also noticeable that in recent years, implied terms have been used to qualify the apparent width of express term, as in *United Bank Ltd v Akhtar* (1989).

4.50 Finally, there is the possibility that custom and practice may be used either to interpret the contract or to fill a gap in the express terms of the contract. In contemporary conditions, the scope for custom and practice is considerably diminished.

Statutory written statements

4.51 The main statutory requirements are contained in ERA 1996, ss 1–7B. In effect, the main terms of the contract should be set out in the written statement, covering such matters as pay, hours of work, holidays and pay, sick pay, notice entitlement, and the like. It is not necessary to set out details relating to pensions and pension schemes if the employee's pension rights depend upon the terms of a pension scheme set up under a provision contained in or taking effect under a statute and the provision requires the relevant body or authority to give a new employee information concerning his or her pension rights: see s 1(5).

4.52 The statement may be given in instalments but the following particulars must all appear in a single document:

- the name of the employer and employee;
- the date of the start of employment with the employer;
- the date of the start of continuous employment; and
- the details relating to pay, hours of work, holiday entitlement, the employee's job title, and the employee's place of work: see ss 1(2) and 2(4).

4.53 The written statement must be given within two months (eight weeks) of the start of the employment; in the case of employees who are required within two months of the start of their employment to begin work outside the UK for more than one month, the statutory statement must be given to them no later than the time of their departure from the UK to start the work. Employers may use an alternative document, such as a contract of employment or a letter of engagement, to give employees the required particulars, but the document must contain the information set out in para 4.52 above: see ERA 1996, s 7A(1) and (2), inserted by the Employment Act 2002, s 37. The written statement given by the employer (but not, it appears, the alternative document) may refer to some other 'reasonably accessible' document for particulars of the employee's entitlement because of absence caused by sickness or injury and pensions and pension schemes applicable to him or her: s 2(2). For particulars of the notice provisions to which the employee is subject the statement may refer to the law or the provisions of a collective agreement which is 'reasonably accessible' to him or her: s 2(3). A reasonably accessible document is one which the employee has reasonable opportunities of reading in the course of employment or which is made reasonably accessible to him or her in some other way: see s 6.

4.54 There are specific provisions governing disciplinary and grievance procedures, which are set out in ERA 1996, s 3, as amended by the Employment Act 2002 (EA 2002). They do not apply to rules, disciplinary decisions, grievances, or procedures relaying to health or safety at work. As required by section 3 the statement must include a note:

(1) stating whether there is in force a contracting-out certificate stating that the employment is contracted-out employment;

(2) specifying any disciplinary rules applicable to the employee or referring the employee to a document containing the rules which is reasonably accessible to him or her;

(3) specifying any procedure applicable to the taking of disciplinary decisions relating to the employee, or to a decision to dismiss him or her, or referring him or her to the provisions of a reasonably accessible document;

(4) specifying a person to whom the employee can apply if dissatisfied with any disciplinary decision or decision to dismiss;

(5) specifying a person to whom the employee can apply for the purpose of asking for a grievance relating to his or her employment to be dealt with and the manner in which the application should be made;

(6) where there are further steps consequent on an application under (4) or (5) above, explain those steps or refer to the provisions of a reasonably accessible document which explains them.

The term 'reasonably accessible' is defined in section 6 and set out above.

4.55 In *W A Goold (Pearmak) Ltd v McConnell* (1995) the EAT used the existence of the statutory provisions relating to the provision of a note by employers relating to their grievance procedures as a basis for implying a term that an employer will 'reasonably and promptly afford a reasonable opportunity to their employees to obtain redress of any grievance they may have'.

4.56 ERA 1996, s 4 deals with changes in the terms and conditions covered by section 1. Any such changes must be notified to the employee by means of a written statement within one month. It should be noted, however, that this is a procedural requirement: it does not authorise an employer to change an employee's contractual terms simply by giving a notice of change. There must be a variation which is effective in law: see para 4.200. As with the original statement under section 1, the statement of change under section 4 may refer to other reasonably accessible documents for the same matters as those which may be referred to by the original statement. Similarly, in the case of changes in the notice provisions to which the employee is subject, the statement of change may refer to the law or the provisions of a collective agreement which is reasonably accessible to him or her. The term 'reasonably accessible' is defined in section 6 and set out above.

Legal effect of written statements

4.57 Despite confusions of terminology, particularly in the case law, it is clear that a written statement given by virtue of the requirements set out in ERA 1996, s 1 is not itself a contract of employment. It is, of course, evidence of the contract of employment and in many cases will probably be the best evidence available. The fact, however, that it is not the contract of employment means that it is open to an employee to argue in subsequent court or tribunal proceedings that the particulars contained in the statement did not represent what was agreed between the parties. In *System Floors (UK) Ltd v Daniel* (1982), approved by the Court of Appeal in *Robertson v British Gas Corporation* (1983), Browne-Wilkinson J said:

> [The statutory statement] provides very strong prima facie evidence of what were the terms of the contract between the parties, but does not constitute a written contract between the parties. Nor are the statements of the terms finally conclusive: at most, they place a heavy burden on the employer to show that the actual terms of contract are different from those which he has set out in the statutory statement.

4.58 The earlier decision of the Court of Appeal in *Gascol Conversions Ltd v Mercer* (1974) appears to suggest that a written statement is conclusive. Subsequent cases have distinguished *Gascol*, however, on the basis that in that case the employee signed the written particulars as constituting the new terms of his contract of employment, not merely the receipt for new particulars of employment. In such a case, therefore, care needs to be taken, since, if the written statement is converted into a written contract, the parties will be bound by what they have signed. The employee, in particular, should make sure that the terms contained in it are correct before signing it. Any change will require the agreement of both parties.

4.59 ERA 1996, s 11 provides for enforcement of the employee's right to be given a written statement. That is in addition to the employee's right to sue the employer for breach of contract before the ordinary courts or, where appropriate, the employment tribunal. Section 11 enables the employee to make a reference to the tribunal for it to decide what particulars ought to have been included, in cases where either no statement has been given or the statement does not comply with what is required. Where a statement has been given but there is a dispute as to what particulars ought to have been included or referred to in it, the employer or the employee may refer the matter to the tribunal. Section 12 gives the tribunal the power to determine what particulars ought to have been included, or whether any particulars which were included should be confirmed, amended, or substituted.

4.60 It is clear from the decided cases that the powers given by what is now section 12 are restricted and that the tribunal's role is effectively confined to declaring what the parties agreed to, on the basis of the evidence before it: see, for example, *Cuthbertson v AML Distributors Ltd* (1975) and *Construction Industry Training Board v Leighton* (1978). Thus, if there is a complaint that the written statement does not contain a term that was actually agreed, the tribunal's powers under section 12 are adequate to deal with it. If, however, the employee's complaint is that particulars of a term were not included in the situation where there had not in fact been any agreement, it is doubtful whether the tribunal has any power to deal with the matter. Despite suggestions by Stephenson LJ in *Mears v Safecar Security Ltd* (1982), the decision of another division of the Court of Appeal in *Eagland v British Telecommunications plc* (1993) makes it clear that the tribunal has no power to include in its determination terms which have not been agreed. Parker LJ observed at p 652:

> The wording of the section makes it perfectly plain…that there may be no such terms (*sc.* relating to pension, sick pay, holiday pay or disciplinary rules) and there is nothing in any section of the Act which empowers or requires the tribunal to impose upon the parties terms which had not been agreed when the statute recognises that it may be the case that no such terms have been agreed.

4.61 Leggatt LJ said, at p 654:

> If an essential term, such as a written statement must contain, has not been agreed, there will be no agreement. If it has, it is the duty of the employment tribunal, where necessary, to identify the term as having been agreed, whether expressly, by necessary implication, or by inference from all the circumstances, including in particular the conduct of the parties, without recourse to invention.

This firmly expressed decision of the Court of Appeal shows how limited are the powers of the employment tribunal under section 12.

4.62 The Employment Act 2002 has introduced a limited penalty which may be imposed on employers who fail to give a statement under ERA 1996, s 1 or 4. In the case of proceedings to which EA 2002, s 38 and Sch 5 apply (for example, sex discrimination claims or complaints of unfair dismissal), where the tribunal finds in favour of the employee, and the employer was in breach of its duty under s 1 or 4, the tribunal must make a minimum award of compensation in respect of the failure: see s 38(2)–(4). The minimum amount is two weeks' pay, but it may be increased to four weeks' pay.

Works rules

4.63 If an employer draws up works or company rules, it is possible that they may become terms of the employees' contracts. If all or any of the rules do become part of the employees' contracts, the consequence will be that they cannot be altered unilaterally by the employer, but only with the agreement of the employees, and the employees can insist on working those rules and refuse to operate any other rules. If, on the other hand, they are not contractual, they may be changed unilaterally by the employer and an employee who refuses to operate the rule in its changed form will be refusing to obey a lawful and reasonable order. Few cases have considered the position of works rules, but guidance may be obtained from cases involving other types of provision which are considered below. This issue is also important in relation to variation of contracts: an employer who unilaterally alters a provision or withdraws a facility will not be in breach of contract if the provision or facility is not contractual.

4.64 To determine whether a particular benefit or provision is contractual or not, much depends upon the intention of the parties. The question is whether it is reasonable to infer from the circumstances that the parties intended the provision to have contractual force. So, for example, if the contract specifies that a disciplinary procedure is to be incorporated into the employees' contracts, it will be incorporated; if it is stated not to be of contractual effect, it will not be incorporated. For an example of an incorporated disciplinary procedure, see *Dietmann v London Borough of Brent* (1988). In *Robertson v British Gas Corporation* (1983), the Court of Appeal held that an incentive bonus scheme had been incorporated into employees' contracts and could not, therefore, be unilaterally determined by the employer, despite the fact that no bonus scheme was in force at the time. On the other hand, in *Quinn v Calder Industrial Materials Ltd* (1996) the unilateral abandonment of a policy governing enhanced redundancy payments was held not to be in breach of the employees' contracts. This case is more fully discussed at para 4.81, below. A similar decision was reached in *Secretary of State for Employment v ASLEF (No 2)* (1972), where the Court of Appeal refused to hold that detailed works rules set out in a staff handbook were contractual; they were held to be collateral instructions to the employees as to how they were to carry out their work. It is clear, therefore, that not all works rules have contractual effect.

4.65 Similar considerations apply in the case of bonus schemes or share option schemes; if they are stated not to be contractual but capable of discontinuance at the employer's discretion, the employer will not be in breach of contract in exercising the discretion to discontinue. In *Cadoux v Central Regional Council* (1986), for example, the question was whether the employer was entitled to withdraw a non-contributory life assurance scheme. The employee's contract stipulated that his post was 'subject to the Conditions of Service laid down by the National Joint Council for Local Authorities Administrative, Professional, Technical and Clerical Services (Scottish Council) and as supplemented by the Authorities' Rules and as amended from time to time'. The Court held that this last phrase was sufficient to incorporate into the employment contract all the provisions of the Rules but went on to say that, as a matter of construction, the Rules were made unilaterally by the employers and could not be regarded as rules which were the subject of agreement between the employers and the unions. That being so, the Court concluded that the employers were entitled to vary, alter or cancel any of the provisions in the Rules and were entitled, therefore, to withdraw the scheme.

4.66 It is also possible that, in the case of a non-contractual provision, the employer will be at liberty to introduce a change which lies within the managerial prerogative. In that case, the employee will be bound to comply with it, if it amounts to a lawful and reasonable instruction. An example of a proposed change falling within the managerial prerogative is *Cresswell v Inland Revenue Board* (1984). There, the employees tried to argue that the Inland Revenue was in breach of their terms of service in requiring them to operate the proposed computerisation of the PAYE system. Walton J held that, although the proposed introduction of computerisation changed the way the employees performed their duties, they were still administering the PAYE system and performing the duties of tax officers. See para 4.207, where this case is more fully discussed. Similarly, in *Dryden v Greater Glasgow Health Board* (1992), the employee claimed to have been constructively dismissed when she resigned after the introduction by the employer of a no-smoking policy. The EAT held that this was within the employer's managerial prerogative, so that there was no breach of contract on the part of the employer.

Express terms

4.67 The following points in relation to express terms should be noted:

(1) Express terms are the principal sources of contractual obligations and the starting-point for a consideration of the respective rights and obligations of the parties is the contract or written statement of particulars.

(2) Express terms may be written or oral or partly written and partly oral.

(3) The best evidence of an express term is an express term contained in a written contract of employment, but, in the absence of such a written contract, the statutory written statement given to an employee under the Employment Rights Act 1996, s 1 is likely to provide the best evidence, though it is not conclusive as to the terms agreed.

(4) The express terms of the contract may also be found in documents expressly or impliedly incorporated into the contract, such as collective agreements or employers' handbooks.

(5) If the contract contains an express term covering a particular matter such as mobility, there will be no scope for the implication of a term in relation to that matter.

(6) An express term may in appropriate cases be qualified by an implied term, such as the term not to behave in a way such as to undermine the relationship of trust and confidence between employer and employee.

(7) Where interpretation or construction of the contractual documentation is necessary, the court or tribunal will apply the ordinary rules of construction for contracts.

(8) An apparently wide clause, such as a flexibility clause, will not always give the employer as free a hand as its terms suggest.

(9) Clauses which are apparently unreasonable may be subject to the Unfair Contract Terms Act 1977.

Incorporation of terms from other documents: collective agreements

4.68 As a general rule, if a contract expressly refers to some other document, that document will be incorporated into the contract: see, for example, *National Coal Board v Galley* (1958), where the contract was expressed to be 'subject to the collective agreement for the time being in force' and it was held that the collective agreement was incorporated. Other documents may be incorporated expressly, impliedly, or by custom and practice.

4.69 The main principles governing the incorporation of collective agreements are as follows:

(1) A collective agreement may be expressly incorporated into a contract of employment and thus become enforceable as between employer and employee, even though as between the collective parties, the employer and the trade unions, it is expressed to be binding in honour only and is thus not enforceable as between them.

(2) Even if a collective agreement is expressly incorporated into an individual employee's contract, the terms of the agreement will only be enforceable by an individual if they are apt for enforcement, such as terms fixing rates of pay and hours of work, but not terms setting up machinery for resolving disputes between the union and the employer.

(3) The terms of a collective agreement which has been incorporated into an individual employee's contract will remain enforceable despite the lapse of the agreement.

(4) A collective agreement which is not expressly incorporated may be incorporated by implication or by custom and practice, but only if its terms are appropriate for incorporation.

4.70 A convenient starting-point for a discussion of this issue is the decision of the Court of Appeal in *Robertson v British Gas Corporation* (1983), which involved the question whether an incentive bonus scheme in a collective agreement had been incorporated into an employee's contract. The Court of Appeal held that the scheme was incorporated into employees' contracts by virtue of their letters of appointment. Since the scheme gave no power to the employers to terminate it, the Court held that, when they tried to do so, they committed a breach of contract. Kerr LJ said, at p 358:

> It is true that collective agreements...create no legally enforceable obligation between the trade union and the employer. Either side can withdraw. But their terms are in this case incorporated into the individual contracts of employment, and it is only if and when those terms are varied collectively by agreement that the individual contracts of employment will also be varied. If the collective scheme is not varied by agreement, but by some unilateral abrogation or withdrawal or variation to which the other side does not agree, then...the individual contracts of employment remain unaffected.

4.71 The Court therefore held the employees to be entitled to the bonus payments to which they were contractually entitled. This case also makes it clear that the terms of a collective agreement which are incorporated into individual employees' contracts will survive the lapse of the collective agreement from which they originated.

4.72 The Court of Appeal followed this decision in *Marley v Forward Trust Group Ltd* (1986), in which the employee's contract of employment incorporated the employers' personnel manual, which included the terms of a collective agreement made between the employers and the union. The agreement was expressed to be binding in honour only and included a provision that, if a redundancy situation arose, an employee who accepted redeployment would have six months in which to assess its suitability without prejudicing his rights to redundancy compensation. This happened to the employee who, after two months, informed his employers that his new position was unsuitable and that he wished to exercise his 'redundancy option'. The employers took the view that the employee had been transferred under a mobility clause in his contract and not because of a redundancy situation. They therefore treated him as having resigned. The Court of Appeal held that the terms of the collective agreement had been incorporated into the individual employee's contract (even though the agreement itself was unenforceable) and that the employers could not rely upon the mobility clause when redeploying the employee.

4.73 The above two cases are examples of the well-established principle that a document referred to in the contract will be expressly incorporated into it and show the operation of the principle in relation to collective agreements. A further example is to be found in *Cadoux v Central Regional Council* (1986), which was considered above at para 4.65.

4.74 The *Alexander* litigation concerned terms in two separate collective agreements governing the procedure to be adopted in the event of a redundancy situation and whether those terms had become part of the employees' contracts. Both terms were to the effect that redundancy selection would be on the basis of 'last in first out'. In the first part of the *Alexander* litigation, *Alexander v Standard Telephones & Cables Ltd* (1990), the employees sought injunctions to restrain the employers from proceeding with the redundancies without applying this principle. The Court refused to grant an injunction. Aldous J said that the terms incorporated must be terms intended to govern the relationship between the employer and individual employees, and not the relationship between the employer and the trade union. He held that the employees had an arguable case that the provisions in the collective agreement providing for 'last in first out' in the event of a redundancy were part of their contracts of employment, although he refused them an injunction.

4.75 In *Alexander v Standard Telephones & Cables Ltd (No 2)* (1991), which was the trial of the action, the employees sought damages for breach of contract for the loss of their employment up to their respective retirement ages. Hobhouse J held that the seniority provisions in the collective agreements were not expressly or impliedly incorporated into the individual contracts of employment and the employees therefore had no contractual right not to be made redundant without LIFO being applied. So far as *express* incorporation was concerned, the judge held that as a matter of construction the agreement was not incorporated. The section 1 statement referred to 'the basic terms and conditions' and he held that it covered only those topics which are required by what is now the ERA 1996 to be dealt with in such a statement, and not redundancy matters. He also pointed out that 'even express general words of incorporation do not remove the need to consider whether all the contents of the incorporated document are apt to be terms of the actual contract of employment'. As regards *implied* or *inferred* incorporation, he said, at p 293:

> Where it is not a case of express incorporation, but a matter of inferring the contractual intent, the character of the document (ie the collective agreement) and the relevant part of it and whether it is apt to form part of the individual contract is central to whether or not the inference should be drawn.

4.76 He held that the relevant clauses were not apt for incorporation and remained part of the joint consultation scheme within a procedure agreement. Examining these clauses in the context in which they arose, particularly in view of the fact that none of the other clauses of the collective agreement were apt for incorporation, he said that it would require 'some cogent indication' in the clause 'that it was to have a different character and to be incorporated into the individual contracts of employment': see p 293.

4.77 This decision was approved by the Court of Appeal in *Kaur v MG Rover Group Ltd* (2005). At first instance, Judge Alton (sitting in the High Court) held that a provision in a collective agreement stating that there would be no compulsory redundancies was incorporated into the employee's employment contract so that the employer's right to dismiss the employee with notice for any reason had to be read subject to her contractual right not to be dismissed for redundancy. The judge held that the job security provision was apt for incorporation. In the Court of Appeal, Keene LJ, with whom the other Lords Justices agreed, allowed the company's appeal and held, following Hobhouse J's approach in *Alexander (No 2)*, that the words used in the collective agreement were not intended, and were not apt, to be incorporated into the employee's individual contract. For a further example of a collective agreement held not to be apt for incorporation, see *Griffiths v Buckinghamshire County Council* (1994), which related to the provisions of an early retirement and voluntary redundancy scheme. The judge held these to be primarily concerned with procedural matters such as consultation requirements and recommendations. The cases considered above suggest that terms in a collective agreement which are not obviously normative, for example those governing a redundancy procedure, are very unlikely to be held to be specifically incorporated, usually because the judges take the view that such terms are not apt for incorporation. There is no reason in principle, however, why this should not be so. Indeed, it does not seem unreasonable to suggest that an employer who has agreed a procedure with the unions should be held to it. On the other hand, terms which are normative, such as terms governing pay or working hours, are unlikely to pose such problems of incorporation.

4.78 Another question which arises relates to the incorporation of a collective agreement entered into by the employer *after* the start of the employee's employment. In *Hamilton v Futura Floors Ltd* (1990), the employers became members of the relevant employers' association after the employee started employment with them. Lord Kirkwood in the Court of Session (Outer House) in Scotland said that the fact that the employers joined the employers' association did not have the effect of altering, by necessary implication, the terms and conditions of the employee's contract, so that the provisions of the relevant collective agreement could be regarded as incorporated. He said that the terms of the association did not contain any reference to the agreement nor did it seek to impose any obligation on members of the association to introduce any particular term or condition into their employees' contracts. He also said that there was no evidence of a custom or trade by which the provisions of the agreement would be assumed to be incorporated.

4.79 The incorporation of collective agreements may be relevant in considering whether an employer has power to vary an employee's contract of employment. This aspect of collective agreements is considered later in this chapter: see para 4.218.

Incorporation of terms from other documents: documents other than collective agreements

4.80 Documents other than collective agreements may also be incorporated into the contract. A common example is disciplinary procedures. *Dietmann v London Borough of Brent* (1987), for example, involved the construction of a disciplinary procedure incorporated into an employee's contract, and is considered more fully below: see para 4.88. See also *Jones v Gwent County Council* (1992), in which the employee successfully sought an injunction against her employers to restrain them from dismissing her unless proper grounds for her dismissal existed and a proper procedure was carried out in accordance with her contract of employment.

4.81 *Quinn v Calder Industrial Materials Ltd* (1996) involved the unilateral abandonment of a policy governing enhanced redundancy payments and the question was whether this action was in breach of the employees' contracts. The policy was in a document containing guidelines on enhanced payments issued to companies in the group of which the employers were a part. The employers did not communicate the terms of the scheme to the employees or trade unions, although they became generally known. On the occasions when the need to make redundancies arose, the employers applied the guidelines and made enhanced payments. Payments were not made automatically, however, but required the managers to obtain instructions as to whether to pay the enhanced payments. The EAT said that the way the payments were introduced and handled did not warrant the inference that the employers intended to become contractually bound by the scheme. The relevant factors which were taken into account by the EAT in reaching this decision were the period of time over which the policy was applied, the way in which the policy became known to the employees and the fact that, when payments were made, the process was not automatic but required a decision on each occasion. The EAT applied the dictum of Browne-Wilkinson J in *Duke v Reliance Systems Ltd* (1982) (at p 452):

> A policy adopted by management unilaterally cannot become a term of the employees' contracts unless it is at least shown that the policy has been drawn to the attention of the employees or has been followed without exception for a substantial period.

4.82 In following this dictum, Lord Coulsfield pointed out that these factors are likely to be among the most important circumstances, 'but they have to be taken into account along with all the other circumstances of the case'. A similar decision was reached in *Secretary of State for Employment v ASLEF (No 2)* (1972), where the Court of Appeal refused to hold that detailed works rules set out in a staff handbook were contractual; they were held to be collateral instructions to the employees as to how they were to carry out their work.

Construction of express terms

4.83 The general principles governing construction of written documents are as follows:

(1) An offer which, upon acceptance, is relied upon as altering the legal relationship between the parties, must be construed objectively. Evidence to show what the offeror intended to be the meaning of the term is not admissible for that purpose.

(2) Evidence of the action of the parties to a contract is not admissible for the purpose of determining the proper construction of it, but such evidence will be admissible to prove the making of a new contract, whether by addition of a new term or variation of an existing term.

(3) When the agreed term has been proved, whether it is in writing or oral, the court in construing the term must have regard to the circumstances with reference to which the words were used and must have regard to the object, appearing from those circumstances, which the person using them had in view; and evidence of mutually known facts may be admitted to identify the meaning of a descriptive term.

(4) If one interpretation of the agreed term completely frustrates the object of the transaction, so as to render the contract futile, that may be a strong argument for an alternative interpretation, if that can be reasonably found; and if one interpretation is unreasonable it may properly cause the court to search for some other possible meaning of the contract.

(5) An agreement cannot be construed in the light of the subsequent action of the parties.

(6) If the words used in the contract are ambiguous they will be construed in the way least favourable to the party relying upon them.

(7) There is a general rule of construction that, in the absence of clear language to the contrary, it is not to be assumed that parties to a contract intended that one party could deprive the other of rights and benefits under the contract by relying on his or her own breach of contract.

4.84 In *Investors' Compensation Scheme Ltd v West Bromwich Building Society* (1998), Lord Hoffmann set out five principles by which contractual documents are nowadays construed. These are as follows:

(1) Interpretation is the ascertainment of the meaning which the document would convey to a reasonable person having all the background knowledge which would reasonably have been available to the parties in the situation in which they were at the time of the contract.

(2) The background was famously referred to by Lord Wilberforce as the 'matrix of fact', but this phrase is, if anything, an understated description of what the background may include. Subject to the requirement that it should have been reasonably available to the parties and to the exception to be mentioned next, it includes absolutely anything which would have affected the way in which the language of the document would have been understood by a reasonable man.

(3) The law excludes from the admissible background the previous negotiations of the parties and their declarations of subjective intent. They are admissible only in an action for rectification. The law makes this distinction for reasons of practical policy and, in this respect only, legal interpretation differs from the way we would interpret utterances in ordinary life. The boundaries of this exception are in some respects unclear. But this is not the occasion on which to explore them.

(4) The meaning which a document (or any other utterance) would convey to a reasonable man is not the same thing as the meaning of its words. The meaning of words is a matter of dictionaries and grammars; the meaning of the document is what the parties using those words against the relevant background would reasonably have been understood to mean. The background may not merely enable the reasonable man to choose between the possible meanings of words which are ambiguous but even (as occasionally happens in ordinary life) to conclude that the parties must, for whatever reason, have used the wrong words or syntax...

(5) The 'rule' that words should be given their 'natural and ordinary meaning' reflects the common sense proposition that we do not easily accept that people have made linguistic mistakes, particularly in formal documents. On the other hand, if one would nevertheless conclude from the background that something must have gone wrong with the language, the law does not require judges to attribute to the parties an intention which they plainly could not have had.

Although the case was not decided in the context of an employment dispute, it is clear that this approach should be followed in the construction of documents such as disciplinary procedures and collective agreements: see *Ackinclose v Gateshead Metropolitan Borough Council* (2005). The cases considered below were decided before the above decision, but they are helpful in showing the approach of the courts and relation to the construction of documents such as collective agreements.

4.85 In *Hooper v British Railways Board* (1988), for example, the question was whether the terms of a negotiated agreement were modified by the later actions of the employers and the trade unions. The original term involved a contractual right to full pay of a member of staff declared fit for work by his or her own doctor but who failed to meet the medical standards required by the railway medical officer. The term as drafted obliged the employers to pay such employees until resumption of work in their own post or in other suitable work. The question was whether the term operated so as to entitle an employee to be kept on full pay until he or she was redeployed or reached retirement age; in other words whether the term imposed no limitation on the right or whether it was only to be of short-term duration. The employers tried to argue that the term had been modified as a result of a later document in which they put forward their view that the original term was intended to provide for payment only for situations of a short-term duration. The Court of Appeal rejected this argument, applying the principle that an agreement cannot be construed in the light of the subsequent actions of the parties. They therefore upheld the employee's argument that the contractual right had not been modified. The employers were thus held to an interpretation of the term which they felt was not what had been agreed with the unions.

4.86   A similar view was taken in *Lee v GEC Plessey Telecommunications* (1993), considered in more detail at para 4.220, where the judge said that the employers' practice of issuing General Instructions and Notices did not have the effect of varying the employees' contracts. Much the same approach was taken by the EAT in *Johnson v Peabody Trust* (1996) in dealing with the question of redundancy in the context of an employee who was employed as a roofer but who was subject to a flexibility clause requiring him 'where possible...to carry out multi-trade operations'. The EAT said that the 'work of a particular kind', within the meaning of what is now ERA 1996, s 139(1)(b) (formerly section 81(2)(b) of the 1978 Act), was the work of a roofer and that the obligation to do work on multi-trade operations was 'very much a subsidiary obligation introduced to operate a degree of flexibility within the workforce in times of increasing economic difficulty': see p 389.

4.87   In *White v Reflecting Roadstuds Ltd* (1991), considered more fully at para 4.228, the EAT refused to construe a flexibility clause as being subject to an implied term that the employer would act reasonably when implementing the clause. They did add, however, that if there were no reasonable or sufficient grounds for the view that the employee should be required to move there would be a breach of the flexibility clause: see p 742. A similar view was expressed in *McClory v The Post Office* (1993), in which the court held that there is an implied term that an employer cannot exercise its power under a contractual provision on unreasonable grounds. It is important to bear in mind, therefore, that, even if an express clause is of apparently wide ambit, the court will either construe it narrowly or construe it subject to the implied term that the employer will not do anything to damage the relationship of trust and confidence between the parties. Flexibility clauses and clauses giving an employer the right to vary are considered in more detail at para 4.218.

4.88 Incorporated documents also give rise to problems of interpretation. In *Dietmann v London Borough of Brent* (1988), the document in question was a disciplinary procedure. The relevant clause read:

> Any breach of the disciplinary rules will render you liable to disciplinary action, which will normally include immediate suspension followed by dismissal, or instant dismissal, for offences of gross misconduct unless there are mitigating circumstances.

The employer's argument was as follows: (1) a breach of the disciplinary rules will lead to disciplinary action; (2) disciplinary action will normally include immediate suspension followed by dismissal; (3) for offences of gross misconduct, instant dismissal not preceded by suspension and without the need for a formal disciplinary meeting is permissible. The employee's argument was: (a) any breach will lead to disciplinary action; (b) if the alleged breach amounts to gross misconduct then this will normally mean immediate suspension pending the outcome of the disciplinary hearing; (c) in a case of gross misconduct the hearing may recommend (i) instant dismissal; or (ii) dismissal on proper notice. The Court of Appeal followed the employee's argument. See also *Honeyford v City of Bradford Metropolitan Council* (1986) and *McGoldrick v London Borough of Brent* (1987), which both involved the interpretation of a disciplinary procedure.

Specific express terms

4.89 Express terms relating to the following matters are considered here:

- mobility;
- working time;
- pay;
- benefits in kind;
- holidays;
- 'garden leave';
- notice and pay in lieu of notice.

Mobility

4.90 It is advisable to include an express mobility term in the employment contract; otherwise, a term will fall to be implied. Clearly, employers who want to save arguments later will be well advised to include an express clause. If a term is implied, there is the risk that the term will have a disproportionate effect which could have been avoided. In any case, ERA 1996, s 1(4)(h) requires the written statement to specify the place of work or 'where the employee is required or permitted to work at various places, an indication of that and of the address of the employer'. The provisions of section 1(4)(k) should also be noted. These come into operation for employees required to work outside the United Kingdom for more than one month. These statutory provisions are considered at para 4.51, above.

4.91 The Court of Appeal decision in *Meade-Hill v British Council* (1995) has led to suggestions that mobility clauses may be indirectly discriminatory and contrary to the provisions of the Sex Discrimination Act 1975. This is debatable, particularly as the Court of Appeal remitted to the county court for it to consider whether the term was justified. The observations of Millett LJ, at p 862, suggest that this should not be too difficult for an employer. As has already been mentioned, even a wide express clause does not entitle the employer to behave unreasonably in relying on it to require mobility from an employee. See, for example, *United Bank Ltd v Akhtar* (1989), which is discussed at para 4.132. In the light of that case, a mobility clause should provide for reasonable notice and financial assistance to be provided to employees affected. For examples of cases involving express terms, reference should be made to *United Kingdom Atomic Energy Authority v Claydon* (1974) and *Rank Xerox Ltd v Churchill* (1988). In the first case, the relevant clause read: 'The [employers] reserve the right to require any member of their staff to work at any of their establishments in Great Britain or in posts overseas.' In the *Rank Xerox* case, the relevant clause read: 'The company may require you to transfer to another location.' The EAT held that the words of the term were perfectly clear and simple and did not need to be qualified by words such as 'within a reasonable daily travelling distance of your home'. If the clause is ambiguous, it will be construed against the person seeking to rely upon it, ie in practice the employer. In the absence of an express mobility clause, a mobility term may fall to be implied, but it is likely that it will be of more restricted scope than could have been provided for by an express mobility clause. This matter is discussed at para 4.146, below.

Working time

4.92 The arrangements for working time will depend upon the nature of the employer's work. For example, the employer may operate a shift system for production staff and flexitime arrangements for administration staff; field sales staff and managers may have fixed hours. An employer may not generally vary the employees' hours of work without their agreement: see *International Packaging Corporation (UK) Ltd v Balfour* (2003). Although theoretically the employer might demand of the employee long working hours, it is possible that this might be subject to an implied restriction, arising from the decision of the Court of Appeal in *Johnstone v Bloomsbury Health Authority* (1991), which is considered more fully at para 4.135.

4.93 The effect of the Working Time Regulations 1998 (SI 1998/1833) should be noted. They were introduced to implement Council Directive 93/104/EC, which has now been consolidated into Council Directive 2003/88/EC. They apply to workers (as defined by reg 2(1)) and specify that working time, including overtime, should not exceed an average of 48 hours for each seven days in any 'reference period'. A reference period is usually a period of 17 weeks, though in certain circumstances it may be as long as 26 or, in some cases, 52 weeks: see Regulations 4(1), (3), and (5) and 23. 'Working time' is defined in Regulation 2(1); the main definition is 'any period during which (the worker) is working, at his employer's disposal and carrying out his activity or duties'. Whilst time spent commuting to work is clearly not covered by this definition, there are issues as to whether it covers time spent by doctors on call, for example, or similar waiting time. See *Sindicato de Médicos de Asistencia Pública (SIMAP) v Consellería de Sanidad y Consumo de la Generalidad Valenciana* (Case C-303/98) (2001) and *Landeshauptstadt Kiel v Jaeger* (Case C-151/02) (2004). The maximum weekly working time does not apply to workers whose agreement in writing has been previously obtained by their employer: see Regulation 4(1). However, due to a recent political agreement between the UK and the EU where an individual has opted out, an upper limit of a 60-hour maximum week will apply, calculated over the 17-week reference period. The agreement is terminable by seven days' notice in writing: Regulation 5(2)(b).

4.94 There are also provisions relating to night work, daily and weekly rest periods, and rest breaks: Regulations 6 and 10–12. The Regulations do not apply to those in 'domestic service' and workers in relation to whom 'on account of the specific characteristics of the activity in which he is engaged, the duration of his working time is not measured or predetermined or can be determined by the worker himself...'. See Regulation 20(1), which then goes on to give as an example 'managing executives or other persons with autonomous decision-taking powers'. In the early days of the Regulations, employers tried to designate those groups of workers who were covered by this Regulation, but the fact is that such attempts are pointless, since it is up to the courts or tribunals to decide who falls within this category. Although the 1993 Directive (and Regulations) originally exempted various sectors, such as the transport and maritime sectors and junior doctors, these exemptions have been removed or narrowed down by subsequent amending Directives: see EC Directive 2000/34 (now consolidated into Council Directive 2003/88/EC), transposed into domestic law by the Working Time (Amendment) Regulations 2003 (SI 2003/1684).

Pay and benefits in kind

4.95 Employees are usually either salaried or hourly paid and they are paid weekly or monthly (or at four-weekly intervals). The rate of pay may either be negotiated with the individual employee concerned or determined according to a collective agreement. In the latter case, the contract should cross-refer to the relevant agreement. The terms relating to pay may also make provision for profit-sharing, performance-related pay, bonuses, commission, and the like. The effect of the National Minimum Wage Act 1998 should be borne in mind.

4.96 An employee may be entitled to an increase in salary or to a bonus, but only if the relevant clause(s) in the contract can be construed as conferring that entitlement. In this connection, the cases of *Clark v BET plc* (1997) and *Clark v Nomura International plc* (2000) are relevant. In *Clark v BET plc*, the relevant clause stated as follows:

> The executive's salary shall be reviewed annually and be increased by such amount if any as the board shall in its absolute discretion decide. In making their decision the board shall consider a comparative group of companies similar to that used in section 4 of the report 'Review of Executive Remuneration' dated 14 December 1993 produced by William M. Mercer Ltd.

4.97 Timothy Walker J took the view that this clause was to be construed as obliging the employers to provide an annual upward adjustment in salary but leaving the amount (if any) of the increase to the absolute discretion of the board. In *Clark v Nomura International plc* the employee's contract provided for a 'discretionary bonus scheme which is not guaranteed in any way and is dependent on individual performance and after the first 12 months your remaining in our employment on the date of payment'. He was a senior proprietary equities trader who in the relevant period was responsible for profits for his employers of around £6.5 million. He was dismissed with three months' notice but, although he was still in employment at the date of payment of the bonus, he did not receive it. He made a claim for damages, alleging that the employers' failure to pay him any bonus amounted to a breach of contract. The judge upheld his claim. According to Burton J, an employer exercising a discretion which on the face of the contract of employment is unfettered or absolute, will be in breach of contract if no reasonable employer would have exercised the discretion in that way. The approach of the judges in the above cases was approved by the Court of Appeal in *Horkulak v Cantor Fitzgerald International* (2004). See also *Brand v Compro Computer Services Ltd* (2005) and *Peninsula Business Services Ltd v Sweeney* (2004).

4.98 It is common for employers to provide benefits in kind or 'fringe benefits' to their staff. Some, such as pensions or season ticket loans, may be provided to all staff who have been in the employer's employment long enough to qualify; some will be provided on the basis of the needs of the employee, for example company cars for salesmen; some will be provided on the basis of status, for example company cars, membership of a private medical expenses scheme and the like. In all cases, it is essential to make clear whether the benefit is discretionary or contractual. If it is contractual and the employee's employment is terminated in breach of the contract, the loss of the benefit will be included in the calculation of damages to be awarded to the employee: see, for example, *Shove v Downs Surgical plc* (1984). Even if the benefit is contractual, the employer may wish to retain some discretion, for example over the choice of company car or pension scheme. Benefits to which employees are contractually entitled are liable to be taxed. There are special provisions relating to the taxation of company cars.

4.99 Other benefits which an employer may wish to offer all or some of the employees are:

- health insurance (eg membership of BUPA);
- free or subsidised canteen;
- free or subsidised uniform or safety clothing;
- season ticket loan scheme;
- participation in a share option scheme.

4.100 In the case of an option scheme, the employer may wish to exclude the employee from benefit in certain circumstances, for example, cessation of employment or dismissal. In *Micklefield v SAC Technology Ltd* (1990), the relevant clause read:

> If any option holder ceases to be an executive for any reason he shall not be entitled, and by applying for an option an executive shall be deemed irrevocably to have waived any entitlement by way of compensation for loss of office or otherwise howsoever to any sum or other benefit to compensate him for the loss of any rights under the scheme.

For the purposes of the decision it was assumed that the employee was wrongfully dismissed and the question was whether he was entitled to recover damages for loss of the option to purchase shares. It was held that the clause was an exemption clause which exempted the employers from part of the liability for their wrong. The judge went on to say that if he was wrong in that conclusion, nevertheless as a matter of construction the clause had the effect of excluding the principle that a person cannot take advantage of their own wrong. He also held that the Unfair Contract Terms Act 1977 did not apply to invalidate the clause, since Schedule 1, paragraph 1(e) excludes any contract 'so far as it relates to the creation or transfer of securities or of any right or interest in securities'. See also *Levett v Biotrace International plc* (1999). In *Mallone v BPB Industries Ltd* (2002), the Court of Appeal made clear that where a scheme gives the directors of a company the discretion to cancel options, that discretion must be exercised properly and rationally.

Holidays

4.101 Until the advent of the Working Time Regulations (WTR) there was very limited statutory regulation of holiday rights and in practice an employee's entitlement to holiday depended upon the terms of the employment contract. Now Regulations 13 and 16 entitle workers to 4.8 weeks annual paid leave in each leave year (as defined by reg 13(2)). For a worker working a five-day working week this is equivalent to 24 days annual leave; this is calculated pro rata for part-time workers. As of 1 April 2009 workers will be entitled to 5.6 weeks annual leave, which is equivalent 28 days if one works a five-day week. There are detailed provisions dealing with the dates on which leave may be taken, which entail either party giving notice within prescribed time limits and containing prescribed information. An employer wishing to escape these provisions may do so by having a 'relevant agreement', in practice a collective agreement or employment contract: see the definition in Regulation 2(1). Leave may not be bought out unless the worker's employment is terminated: see Regulation 13(9).

4.102 It should be noted that ERA 1996, s 1(4)(d)(i) requires the written statement given to employees to contain particulars of terms and conditions relating to holidays, including public holidays, and holiday pay. The particulars must be sufficient to enable the employee's holiday entitlement, including any entitlement to accrued holiday pay on the termination of employment, to be precisely calculated. These particulars must be given in the written statement itself; it is not permissible to refer to another document which is reasonably accessible to the employee. This provision was considered by the Court of Appeal in *Morley v Heritage plc* (1993). The employee tried to argue that, on termination of his employment, he was entitled to accrued holiday pay in lieu of the unused holiday entitlement by virtue of a term which has to be implied to satisfy the requirements of s 1. The Court of Appeal said that s 1(4)(d)(i) merely recognises that a contract can include a provision relating to accrued holiday pay and that, if it does, the written statement should contain particulars of it. The Court also said that it was unnecessary, having regard to the terms of the particular contract and the status of the particular employee, to imply a term entitling the employee to accrued holiday pay to give the contract business efficacy. This suggests that there may be cases in which it may be possible to imply a term. See also *Thames Water Utilities v Reynolds* (1996), in which the issue was whether a clause entitling an employee to accrued holiday pay should be construed as entitling him to holiday calculated on the basis of calendar days or working days.

'Garden leave' clauses

4.103 A 'garden leave' clause is a clause found in employment contracts by which the employer reserves the right to require the employee not to perform his or her duties as an employee but agrees that he or she will continue to be paid. Such clauses have so far given rise to relatively little case-law and such case-law as there is has tended to be concerned with the principles upon which injunctions are granted.

4.104 The first case to consider a garden leave clause was *Provident Financial Group plc v Hayward* (1989). The employee's contract as financial director provided that, during the continuance of his employment, he would not 'undertake any other business or profession or be or become an employee or agent of any other person or persons or assist or have any financial interest in any other business or profession'. Another clause provided that the company was under no obligation to provide him with work but could suspend him from performance of his duties or exclude him from any premises of the company, but his salary was not to cease to be payable by reason only of the suspension or exclusion. During 1988 Mr Hayward tendered his resignation and continued working until 5 September when the employers decided that they did not want him to work out his notice. They were prepared to pay in full until the agreed termination date (31 December), provided that he did not work for anyone else. From 5 September, therefore, Mr Hayward was on 'garden leave'. On 13 October, he wrote to his employers announcing his intention to start work on the following Monday with another company. His employers were concerned about confidential information and applied for an injunction to stop him from doing so. The Court of Appeal upheld the judge's decision not to grant an injunction but their reasons for doing so had nothing to do with the validity or otherwise of the 'garden leave' clause. They really concerned the principles on which injunctions are granted. Although the Court of Appeal did not need to decide on the validity of the clause in question, Dillon LJ did comment on the fact that 'garden leave' clauses are capable of abuse, particularly as employers tend to have somewhat exaggerated views of what will or may affect their businesses. He also said that an employee is concerned to work and to exercise his or her skills. See also *Crédit Suisse Asset Management Ltd v Armstrong* (1996), *Symbian Ltd v Christensen* (2001), and *SG & R Valuation Service Co. v Boudrais* [2008] EWHC 1340. It is unlikely that in the absence of an express garden leave provision the court would be prepared to imply such a provision: see *William Hill Organisation Ltd v Tucker* (1999).

4.105 In the light of these decisions there are uncertainties surrounding garden leave clauses, since an excessively long period of notice linked with garden leave might be held to be in restraint of trade and thus void and unenforceable. A number of questions have yet to be fully considered:

(1) Can a garden leave clause be used to prevent an employee from working either at all or during the notice period?

(2) If so, does it conflict with the 'right to work'?

(3) Are there/should there be any limits on the period of garden leave? and

(4) In what circumstances will such a clause be enforceable by injunction?

It may be that the method of termination may affect the employer's chances of enforcing restraints against an ex-employee: see *General Billposting Co Ltd v Atkinson* (1909) and *Rex Stewart Jeffries Parker Ginsberg Ltd v Parker* (1988). It is clear from these cases that an employer who dismisses an employee in breach of contract will not be able to rely upon any restraints in the contract of employment. See further paras 4.107, 4.108, and 4.112 below.

Notice

4.106 At common law, the parties are free to choose whatever notice provision they like, though an employer who sought to impose an excessively long notice period on an employee might be prevented from doing so by the doctrine of restraint of trade. If the contract of employment does not specify a notice period a reasonable period of notice will be implied. In most cases where there are no express notice provisions, the situation is likely to be governed by ERA 1996, s 86, which gives a statutory right to a minimum period of notice. Employees continuously employed for one month or more but less than two years are entitled to at least one week's notice. After two years' employment, they are entitled to one week's notice for each year of continuous employment, but, if they have been employed for more than 12 years, their statutory entitlement will not exceed 12 weeks. Section 86(2) obliges an employee continuously employed for one month or more to give at least one week's notice. The notice must be definite and explicit and must specify the date of termination or give sufficient facts from which the date of termination can be ascertained: *Morton Sundour Fabrics Ltd v Shaw* (1967) and *Walker v Cotswold Chine Home School* (1977). Once a notice has been given, it cannot be withdrawn unilaterally, but only with the agreement of the other party: see *Riordan v War Office* (1959) and *Harris and Russell Ltd v Slingsby* (1973). Although an attempt to provide for a shorter period will be ineffective, section 86(3) provides that either side may waive his or her right to notice or accept a payment in lieu of notice. It is open to an employee and employer to agree upon longer periods of notice than those set out in section 86.

4.107 In the absence of an express clause the employee might seek to argue that he or she was impliedly entitled to a longer period of notice than the one week provided for by section 86(2). The length of notice afforded by an implied term is unlikely to be as long as that which may be provided for by an express term and is unlikely to exceed a year, even for the most senior of employees; in most other cases, it is unlikely that it would exceed six months. In addition to terms governing notice, employment contracts sometimes contain a clause providing for the employee to receive pay in lieu of notice to avoid the risk of any post-termination restraints being held to be unenforceable. An example of such a clause, usually called an 'agreed damages clause', is to be found in *Rex Stewart Jeffries Parker Ginsberg Ltd v Parker* (1988). The employee's contract provided that his employment could be 'determined by the giving in writing of six calendar months' notice on either side or the payment of six months' salary in lieu thereof'. He was given one week's notice and six months' salary in lieu of notice. He claimed that this amounted to a breach of contract but the Court of Appeal rejected this argument. Had it succeeded, he would have been able to claim that he was no longer bound by a non-solicitation clause. This is because of the principle stated in *General Billposting Co Ltd v Atkinson* (1909), that an employer who wrongfully dismisses an employee cannot enforce a restrictive covenant against him or her. The method of termination of an employee's contract of employment may, therefore, affect the employer's chances of enforcing a restraint against an ex-employee.

4.108 There are suggestions in the later case of *Rock Refrigeration Ltd v Jones and Seward Refrigeration Ltd* (1996) that this principle is of less wide application than had previously been thought. In that case the Court of Appeal refused to strike down as unreasonable restrictive covenants expressed to operate upon termination of the contract 'howsoever arising' or 'howsoever occasioned' in the circumstances that the employee resigned from the company to join a competitor. A majority of the Court said that the *General Billposting* principle would apply if the employers wrongfully dismissed the employee, but said that it did not apply to the circumstances which had arisen. Phillips LJ went further and suggested that the rule 'accords neither with current legal principle nor with the requirements of business efficacy'. His view was that the parties should be at liberty to agree to a restraint which continues to operate even if one of them repudiates the contract. This would appear to give generous latitude to contract-breakers.

4.109 At common law, the parties are free to insert an agreed damages clause into the contract, provided that the clause is not in the nature of a penalty. In that case, the amount stipulated will not be recoverable and the plaintiff will have to prove what damages he or she can. See *Dunlop Pneumatic Tyre Co Ltd v New Garage and Motor Co Ltd* (1915), where the principles governing penalty clauses are set out. There Lord Dunedin summed up the law in the following propositions, at pp 86–88:

(1) Though the parties to a contract who use the words 'penalty' or 'liquidated damages' may prima facie be supposed to mean what they say, yet the expression is not conclusive. The court must find out whether the payment stipulated is in truth a penalty or liquidated damages...

(2) The essence of a penalty is a payment of money stipulated as *in terrorem* of the offending party; the essence of liquidated damages is a genuine pre-estimate of damage.

(3) The question whether a sum stipulated is a penalty or liquidated damages is a question of construction to be decided upon the terms and inherent circumstances of each particular contract, judged of at the time of the making of the contract, not as at the time of the breach.

(4) To assist this task of construction various tests have been suggested which, if applicable to the case under consideration, may prove helpful or even conclusive. Such are:

(a) It will be held to be a penalty if the sum stipulated for is extravagant and unconscionable in amount in comparison with the greatest loss which could conceivably be proved to have followed from the breach.

(b) It will be held to be a penalty if the breach consists only in not paying a sum of money, and the sum stipulated is a sum greater than the sum which ought to have been paid...

(c) there is a presumption (but no more) that it is a penalty when a single lump sum is made payable by way of compensation, on the occurrence of one or more or all of several events, some of which may occasion serious and others but trifling damage.

On the other hand:

(d) It is no obstacle to the sum stipulated being a genuine pre-estimate of damage, that the consequences of the breach are such as to make precise pre-estimation almost an impossibility. On the contrary, that is just the situation when it is probable that pre-estimated damage was the true bargain between the parties.

4.110 A more recent example of the application of this principle is to be found in *Neil v Strathclyde Borough Council* (1984), which involved a clause by which the employee agreed to refund to her employers a proportion of their outlays in respect of a period of leave of absence during which she took a training course if she left their service within two years of completion of the course. She tried to argue that the provision was a penalty and therefore unenforceable, but the Sheriff Principal upheld the employers' claim against her, applying the principles set out above. See also *Giraud UK Ltd v Smith* (2000) and *Murray v Leisureplay Ltd* (2005).

Restrictive covenants

4.111 For a restrictive covenant to be enforceable, it must protect the employer's legitimate business interests, either trade secrets or goodwill and trade connections. It is not possible to prevent competition as such. A restrictive covenant in a contract of employment will be prima facie void, but will be enforceable if it is reasonable:

reasonable, that is, in reference to the interests of the parties concerned and reasonable in reference to the interests of the public, so framed and so guarded as to afford adequate protection to the party in whose favour [they are] imposed, while at the same time . . . in no way injurious to the public.

See Lord MacNaghten in *Nordenfelt v Maxim Nordenfelt Guns and Ammunition Co Ltd* (1894).

4.112 The covenants most likely to be enforced are those which are reasonably necessary to protect the employer's trade secrets and trade connection. It is possible that employees and suppliers may also be legitimate interests, but they would need to be clearly defined. An employee who accepts employment in which he or she would be likely to damage these interests may be restrained. If, therefore, an employee would be likely to use the employer's trade secrets in new employment, he or she may be restrained. He or she may also be restrained from soliciting the ex-employer's customers or from setting up his or her own business or accepting a position with one of the ex-employer's competitors, if that is likely to damage the employer's trade connection by a misuse of his or her acquaintance with the employer's customers or clients. The factors to be taken into account include:

(1) the area of restraint;

(2) the period of restraint;

(3) the nature of the interest sought to be protected; and

(4) the subject-matter of the restraint.

As a general rule, an employer who breaches the contract of employment, for example by wrongfully dismissing the employee, will not be allowed to enforce any restrictive covenants contained in the contract. This was established by the House of Lords in *General Billposting Ltd v Atkinson* (1909), and reiterated by the majority of the Court of Appeal in *Rock Refrigeration Ltd v Jones and Seward Refrigeration Ltd* (1996). See also *Rex Stewart Jeffries Parker Ginsberg Ltd v Parker* (1988).

4.113 The following points should also be noted here:

(1) It is for the judge to decide, on the basis of the appropriate evidence, whether in the particular of the case a restraint is reasonable or not. This means that a decision in one case that a particular restraint is reasonable (for example, two years in the case of a milk roundsman) does not mean that in all subsequent cases involving the same type of employment a judge is bound by that decision: see *Dairy Crest Ltd v Pigott* (1989). The Court of Appeal said that the judge was wrong in considering that he was bound by principle to hold that in the case of a milk roundsman a two-year restraint was not unreasonable.

(2) If there is a change of employer, in circumstances such that the Transfer of Undertakings (Protection of Employment) Regulations 2006 apply, the transferee

employer may be able to enforce a restrictive covenant entered into between the transferor employer and the employee. But a transferee employer will not be able to enforce a restrictive covenant introduced into the transferring employees' contracts as a result of the transfer. See *Morris Angel & Son Ltd v Hollande* (1993) and *Credit Suisse First Boston (Europe) Ltd v Lister* (1999) and Regulation 4(4) of the 2006 Regulations.

(3) In appropriate cases, 'severance' may be possible.

(4) The fact that a restrictive covenant is not restricted to the United Kingdom will not necessarily make it unreasonable: see *Scully UK Ltd v Lee* (1998).

Non-solicitation covenants

4.114 These covenants are intended to prevent ex-employees from soliciting the business of clients or customers of their former employer in competition with their former employer for a period of time after the employment ends. It must be shown that the employee's contact with the customers is sufficiently direct or influential as to give rise to the real possibility of misuse of the employee's knowledge of the customers. A covenant not to solicit customers may be enforced so as to prevent the solicitation of those who were customers not only at the date of termination of the employment but at any other time during the period of employment (even if they had ceased to be customers before its termination); it will not be reasonable to restrain solicitation of persons who might become the employer's customers after termination, for example by a clause restraining an employee from soliciting anyone in the relevant trade in the area in which he or she used to operate for the employer. In *The Marley Tile Co Ltd v Johnson* (1982), the court refused to restrain the solicitation of those who were customers of the employer within the 12 months preceding the termination of the employee's employment, on the grounds that the number of customers involved (said to be some 2,500) was so large that he could not possibly have known of or come into contact with more than a small percentage of them. In *Office Angels Ltd v Rainer-Thomas* (1991), the covenant in question prohibited the employees from setting up or being employed in or otherwise engaged in the trade or business of an employment agency within 1,000 metres of the branch where they had previously worked for a period of six months after the termination of their employment. The employees involved worked in one of the employers' four branches in the City of London, at Bow Lane. After leaving the employers, they set up in an employment agency operating from premises within 1,000 metres of Bow Lane. The Court of Appeal refused to enforce the restrictive covenant. They noted that the effect of the restriction was to preclude the employees from opening an office anywhere within an area of about 1.2 square miles, including most of the City of London. They said that an area restriction was not appropriate because it would do little to protect the employers' connection with their clients. Client orders were placed over the telephone and it was of no concern to them where the office was located. They took the view that this was not an appropriate form of covenant for the protection of the employers' connection with its clients and was wider than was necessary, though they acknowledged that they were entitled to protect their goodwill.

4.115 A second type of non-solicitation covenant which is much less common is a covenant restricting the solicitation or employment of former colleagues. This type of covenant, which is sometimes called a 'non-poaching' covenant, was considered by the Court of Appeal in *Hanover Insurance Brokers v Schapiro* (1994). The Court refused to enforce the particular covenant. Although such covenants are not inherently unenforceable, it is clear that the courts are wary of enforcing them. Two cases in which non-poaching clauses have been upheld are *Ingham v ABC Contract Services Ltd* (unreported) and *Alliance Paper Group plc v Prestwich* (1996). To stand any chance of being enforced, they will have to be narrowly drawn and applicable only to employees who were colleagues of the ex-employees at the same time; probably, too, they will need to be applicable only to particular types of employees. In *TSC Europe (UK) Ltd v Massey* (1999), the judge refused to uphold a non-solicitation covenant involving employees of a company on the two grounds that (a) the covenant prohibited solicitation of any employee without reference to his or her importance in the business or technical knowledge or experience, and (b) that it applied to any employee who joined the company during the prohibited period, including those whose employment began after the employee sought to be restrained had ceased to be an employee.

Non-competition covenants

4.116 These types of covenants are used to protect employers where the employee has a close relationship with clients (as in *Marion White Ltd v Francis* (1972)) or has knowledge of the employer's trade secrets or confidential information (as in *Commercial Plastics Ltd v Vincent* (1964)). In both cases, the restraint must be restricted to activities connected with the goodwill or trade secrets the employer is trying to protect; duration and area limitations are particularly important. An example is *Littlewoods Organisation Ltd v Harris* (1997), in which the Court of Appeal construed a clause which, on its face, prevented an ex-employee from working for a rival organisation or any of its subsidiaries throughout the world, so as to prevent him from working for the rival in the United Kingdom. Lord Denning MR said: 'I think that limiting words ought to be read into the clause so as to limit it to the part of the business for which the (employers) are reasonably entitled to protection.' See also *Lansing Linde*

Ltd v Kerr (1991), *Turner v Commonwealth & British Minerals Ltd* (2000), and *TFS Derivatives Ltd v Morgan* (2005).

4.117 Another example of a covenant involving an attempt by an employer to protect trade secrets is to be found in the case of *FSS Travel and Leisure Systems Ltd v Johnson* (1998), in which the relevant clause read as follows:

> For a period of one year after termination of your employment hereunder (howsoever caused) you shall not:
>
>> either alone or jointly as a manager or agent for any person directly or indirectly carry on or be engaged or concerned in any business in the United Kingdom which competes with the business of the FSS Group in which you shall have been personally concerned at the date of such termination.

At first instance the judge held that the company had trade secrets which it was entitled to protect but that the duration of the restraint was not reasonable. The Court of Appeal dismissed the appeal, although they held that the judge had erred in holding that the employers had trade secrets which they were entitled to protect. They said that the critical question in deciding whether an employer has trade secrets which are legitimately protected by means of a restrictive covenant is whether there are trade secrets which can fairly be regarded as the employer's property, as distinct from the skill, experience, know-how, and general knowledge which can fairly be regarded as the property of the employee to use without restraint for his or her own benefit or in the services of a competitor. In each case, it is a question of examining closely the detailed evidence relating to the employer's claim for secrecy and deciding, as a matter of fact, on which side of the boundary line it falls. In the present case, the evidence adduced by the employers was not sufficiently specific, precise, or cogent to identify and establish a separate body of objective knowledge qualifying for protection as a trade secret by means of a restrictive covenant. Subsequently, in *SBJ Stephenson Ltd v Mandy* (2000), Bell J reiterated that the true distinction to be made is between 'objective knowledge', which is the property of the employer, and 'subjective knowledge', which is the employee's own property, following Lord Shaw's dictum in *Herbert Morris Ltd v Saxelby* (1916), at p 714.

Implied terms

4.118 The following points should be noted:

(1) even if the employer complies with the requirements of ERA 1996, s 1 and gives a written statement, or decides to give an employee a full written contract of employment, there are likely to be areas in the contract which are

not covered by express terms and where the court or tribunal will have to consider resorting to implied terms to fill the apparent gap;

(2) a term will only be implied where there is no express term governing the matter over which there is dispute;

(3) if a term is implied the term will be no wider than is necessary to give efficacy to the contract;

(4) an express term may in some cases be qualified by an implied term;

(5) there is a difference between terms such as mobility/flexibility terms which have to be determined according to the particular contract, and 'status' or 'legal incidents' terms which, where used, establish rules for contracts of employment as a class;

(6) if a term is not implied on the basis of the tests set out below, it may be possible to imply a term based upon custom and practice, if the custom is reasonable, certain, and notorious.

4.119 Although there are specific terms which are implied into the employment contract and which give rise to specific obligations, it is worth drawing attention to the observation of Edmund-Davies LJ in *Wilson v Racher* (1974) (at p 430):

> Reported decisions provide useful, but only general guides, each case turning upon its own facts. Many of the decisions which are customarily cited in these cases date from the last century and may be wholly out of accord with current social conditions. What would today be regarded as almost an attitude of Czar–serf, which is to be found in some of the older cases where a dismissed employee failed to recover damages, would, I venture to think, be decided differently today. We have by now come to realise that a contract of service imposes upon the parties a duty of mutual respect.

4.120 It is important, therefore, to bear in mind that the decision of the court in a particular case may well turn on its own facts and that a single action in one context may amount to a breach which is sufficiently serious to justify summary dismissal, whereas in another context it would not. A good example of this is the decisions in *Pepper v Webb* (1969) and *Wilson v Racher*, above. In both cases the employee used bad language to the employer, but in the first case the use of bad language was coupled with a history of disobedience and the use of bad language coupled with disobedience of an order was the 'final straw'; in the second, the employer provoked the employee into using the bad language. In the first case, the wrongful dismissal claim failed, whereas in the second it succeeded. At common law, a breach by either party of an implied term may give the other party the right to terminate the contract without notice. Thus, a breach of an implied term by the employer may give the employee the right to resign and argue that the breach was so significant as to amount to a repudiation and to entitle him or her to treat the contract as at an end. In the context of the statutory right not to be unfairly dismissed this is usually called a constructive dismissal. In other contexts, it is probably best called a wrongful repudiation or simply a breach of contract: see Chapter 8.

4.121 If the *employee* is in breach of an implied term, again the question is whether the breach by the employee amounts to a repudiation of the contract. In *Laws v London Chronicle (Indicator Newspapers) Ltd* (1959), Lord Evershed MR said:

> [T]he question must be – if summary dismissal is claimed to be justifiable – whether the conduct complained of is such as to show the servant to have disregarded the essential conditions of the contract of service.

The facts of each case must be looked at to see whether what has happened amounts to a repudiation of his or her contract by the employee (or, indeed, the employer). Thus, in one context a single act may warrant instant dismissal (as, for example, in *Sinclair v Neighbour* (1967)), whereas in another the case may involve a history of acts similar to the act which causes the dismissal and effectively constitutes the 'final straw': see *Pepper v Webb* (1969), which involved unsatisfactory work, and *Clouston v Corry* (1906), which involved drunkenness. Much therefore depends upon the type of reason involved and the context in which it arises. In *Jupiter General Insurance Co Ltd v Shroff* (1937), the Privy Council emphasised that 'the test to be applied must vary with the nature of the business and the position held by the employee, and that decisions in other cases are of little value'. They also pointed out that in such cases 'one must apply the standards of men, and not those of angels, and remember that men are apt to show temper when reprimanded'.

4.122 The case law in this area was summarised by Lord Jauncey of Tullichettle (Special Commissioner) in *Neary v Dean of Westminster* (1999) in the following terms:

> [C]onduct amounting to gross misconduct justifying dismissal must so undermine the trust and confidence which is inherent in the particular contract of employment that the master should no longer be required to retain the servant in his employment.

In *Briscoe v Lubrizol Ltd* (2002) the Court of Appeal adopted this statement as the test to apply in cases of this kind.

4.123 It should also be borne in mind that attitudes change as social conditions change, a fact commented upon by Edmund-Davies LJ in *Wilson v Racher*, above. A good example of the need to be responsive to change is the EAT's decision in *Denco Ltd v Joinson* (1991), which involved deliberate misuse of a computer during employment. The *Denco* case also makes clear that the categories of implied terms are not closed and that it will often fall to a court of tribunal to consider whether a term should be implied and, if appropriate, what its ambit should be. Examples of this are to be found in the cases of *W A Goold (Pearmak) Ltd v McConnell* (1995), *Spring v Guardian Assurance plc* (1994), and *Aspden v Webbs Poultry & Meat Group (Holdings) Ltd* (1996). In the first case, the EAT used the existence of the statutory provisions relating to the provision of a note by employers relating to their grievance procedures as a basis for implying a term that an employer will 'reasonably and promptly afford a reasonable opportunity to their employees to obtain redress of any grievance they may have'. The employers' failure to provide and implement a grievance procedure was held by the EAT to amount to a breach of contract sufficiently serious to entitle the employee to resign and complain that he had been unfairly constructively dismissed.

4.124 In *Spring v Guardian Assurance plc*, Lords Slynn of Hadley and Woolf said, *obiter*, that it was an implied term of the employee's contract of employment that an employer will ensure that reasonable care is taken in the compiling and giving of a reference to a prospective employer. The main issue in the case was whether the employers were negligent or not, but the approach of two of their Lordships shows the development of a contractual liability in this area. It is possible that a similar line of reasoning may emerge in relation to the employer's common law duty to provide a safe system of work for the employees. For example, in *Walker v Northumberland County Council* (1995), the employers were held to be in breach of their duty of care to an employee in respect of a second mental breakdown he suffered whilst working for them. Although their liability arose in tort, there seems to be no reason why the claim should not also be framed in contract, relying upon the existence of an implied term. This is echoed in the case of *Johnstone v Bloomsbury Health Authority* (1991), which is also considered more fully at para 4.135.

4.125 *Aspden v Webbs Poultry & Meat Group (Holdings) Ltd* involved an employee whose contract contained an express term allowing the employers to dismiss by reason of prolonged incapacity. At the time of entering into the contract (in early 1986), the employee was a member of a health insurance scheme which he had joined in early 1985. The scheme provided for an employee to receive three-quarters of his last payable annual salary, starting 26 weeks after the start of the incapacity and ending with his death, retirement date, or the date on which he ceased to be an eligible employee (which included dismissal on any ground). He was dismissed while on sick leave and claimed damages for wrongful dismissal. Sedley J held that a term should be implied into the contract that, in circumstances where the employee's entitlement to benefit under the employers' health insurance scheme was dependent upon the continuance of the employment relationship, the employers would not terminate the contract while the employee was incapacitated for work. He implied the term on the footing that both parties knew, or would have realised had they considered it, that the written terms were not comprehensive and that they required qualification. The contract was not drafted with the insurance scheme in mind, nor was its aptness in the light of the scheme considered or negotiated. The judge therefore held that the employers were in breach of contract in dismissing him while he was unable to work.

4.126 *Ali v Christian Salvesen Food Services Ltd* (1997), on the other hand, is an example of a case in which the Court of Appeal refused to imply a term. The issue was whether there should be implied into an 'annualised hours' agreement a term entitling employees whose employment was terminated by the employer before the end of the pay year to be paid the standard hourly rate for hours actually worked in excess of 40 per week. The Court of Appeal refused to imply such a term. It is an example of an established doctrine that 'where the parties have entered into a carefully written contract containing detailed terms agreed between them', the court will be reluctant to imply a term: see *Jones v St John's College, Oxford* (1870). Reference may also be made to *Stubbes v Trower, Still & Keeling* (1987), where the Court of Appeal refused to imply a term into the contract of an articled clerk in a firm of solicitors that at the start of articles he would either have passed the whole of the final examination or be awaiting the result of it.

4.127 It is important to be aware of the tendency of courts and tribunals to make express terms in the employment contract subject to the qualification that the employer will not rely upon an express term in such a way as to breach the implied duty not to undermine the relationship of trust and confidence between employer and employee: see para 4.132.

Basis for the implication of terms

4.128 The two tests used historically for the implication of terms are the 'business efficacy' test and the 'officious bystander' test. The first derives from *The Moorcock* (1889) and the second from *Shirlaw v Southern Foundries (1926) Ltd* (1939). A third basis for the implication of terms was developed by Viscount Simonds in *Lister v Romford Ice & Cold Storage Co Ltd* (1957). He said in that case that the existence of an implied term depended on general considerations relating to the nature of contracts of employment. This is sometimes called the 'status' test. This type of implied term was referred to by Lord Reid in *Sterling Engineering Co Ltd v Patchett* (1955) as 'a term inherent in the nature of the contract which the law will imply in every case unless the parties agree to vary or exclude it'.

4.129 The implication of terms was considered by the House of Lords in *Liverpool City Council v Irwin* (1977). Lord Wilberforce said:

> Where there is, on the face of it, a complete bilateral contract, the courts are sometimes willing to add terms to it, as implied terms: this is very common in mercantile contracts

> where there is an established usage: in that case the courts are spelling out what both parties know and would, if asked, unhesitatingly agree to be part of the bargain. In other cases, where there is an apparently complete bargain, the courts are willing to add a term on the ground that without it the contract will not work – this is the case, if not of *The Moorcock* . . . itself on its facts, at least of the doctrine of *The Moorcock* as usually applied. This is . . . a strict test.

4.130 Lord Wilberforce went on to disagree with Lord Denning's view about the implication of reasonable terms and said that the test was a test 'of necessity'. An example of this strict approach is to be found in *Stubbes v Trower, Still & Keeling* (1987), where the Court of Appeal refused to imply a term into the contract of an articled clerk in a firm of solicitors that at the start of articles he would either have passed the whole of the final examination or be awaiting the result of it. Similarly, in *Nelson v BBC* (1977), the Court of Appeal refused to imply a restriction to a term by virtue of which the employee could be required to work when and where the Corporation demanded. The employee worked in the Caribbean service and, when they closed it down, the BBC sought to argue that he was only employed in that service and that he was therefore redundant. The Court of Appeal said that it was impossible to imply a restriction of this sort.

4.131 In recent years, the court and tribunals have been more willing to imply terms which appear to them to be reasonable in all the circumstances, rather than relying upon the supposed intention of the parties or a notion such as business efficacy. An important example of this more objective approach is to be found in the Court of Appeal's decision in *Courtaulds Northern Spinning Ltd v Sibson* (1988). The facts were that the employee worked as a lorry driver at the same depot from the start of his employment in 1973. His contract had no express mobility term. All the drivers belonged to the same union, but in 1985 he resigned from the union. To avert strike action, the employer required him to rejoin the union or transfer to another depot. He resigned and claimed that he had been constructively dismissed. The Court of Appeal held that, in order to give the contract business efficacy a term had to be implied in the contract, as being a term which the parties, acting reasonably, would probably have agreed if they had considered the matter, that the employer could, for any reason, direct the employee to work at any place within reasonable daily reach of the employee's home. The employers had therefore acted within their contractual rights and the employee had not been constructively dismissed. The Court rejected the employment tribunal's qualification of the implied term that the employer's request to the employee should be reasonable or 'for genuine operational reasons' as being potentially uncertain and difficult in operation but agreed that the employee could reasonably have demanded that the mobility requirement should be reasonable daily travelling distance. This view of the basis for implying terms appears to be in conflict with Lord Wilberforce's views, as expressed above, and should, therefore, be viewed with some caution, as it was by the EAT in *Aparau v Iceland Frozen Foods plc* (1996) when considering whether to imply a mobility term. In *Aparau* the EAT was reluctant to hold that any mobility term should be implied into the employee's contract beyond a term as to the place of her employment. They went on to say, however, that, if they were wrong and some term as to mobility fell to be implied, there was no basis for implying a term that the employee could be transferred against her will.

Relationship between express terms and implied terms

4.132 The traditional common law view of the operation of an express term is that if the employer relies upon it, however unreasonably, the employee cannot complain. Thus, if the contract contains an unrestricted express mobility clause and the employer activates it with little or no warning, the traditional view is that the employee must comply with what he or she has agreed. Judicial decisions over the last 15 years or so have suggested, however, a tendency to qualify this position. *United Bank Ltd v Akhtar* (1999) concerned the employers' use of a mobility clause and the employee's right, in response to that, to resign and claim constructive dismissal. The terms of the mobility clause were:

> The bank may from time to time require an employee to be transferred temporarily or permanently to any place of business which the bank may have in the UK for which a relocation allowance or other allowances may be payable at the discretion of the bank.

4.133 The employee was a junior clerk in the Leeds branch of the bank and was given six days' notice that he was to be transferred to the Birmingham branch. He asked his manager for a postponement of the transfer for three months because of personal difficulties relating to his wife's ill-health and the impending sale of his house. His request was refused. He wrote another letter asking for 24 days' leave which was due to him in order to sort out his affairs and start work afterwards. His pay was stopped. He complained that he had been constructively dismissed. The EAT upheld the employment tribunal's decision that he had. They said that the tribunal was entitled to imply into the employee's contract a term that reasonable notice should be given in the exercise of the bank's powers to require mobility of its employees and that the employers' discretion under the mobility clause was one which they were bound to exercise in such a way as not to make it impossible for him to comply with his contractual obligation to move. They also upheld the tribunal's decision that the employers' conduct in relation to the employee's transfer amounted to a fundamental breach of the implied term that employers must not, without reasonable and proper cause, behave in a manner calculated or likely to destroy or seriously damage the relationship of trust and confidence between employer and employee. This decision suggests a tendency to erect certain implied terms, such as the implied term of mutual trust and confidence, into terms which effectively override the powers given to an employer by the express terms of the contract.

4.134 A similar approach may be detected in later cases. In *White v Reflecting Roadstuds Ltd* (1991), for example, considered more fully at para 4.228, the EAT refused to construe a flexibility clause as being subject to an implied term that the employer would act reasonably when implementing the clause. They did add, however, that if there were no reasonable or sufficient grounds for the view that the employee should be required to move, there would be a breach of the flexibility clause: see p 742. In *McLory v The Post Office* (1993) the court held that there is an implied term that an employer cannot exercise its power under a contractual provision on unreasonable grounds. See also *BPCC Purnell Ltd v Webb* (EAT 129/90), considered at para 4.227, below.

4.135 Another term which may fall into this category is the employer's obligation to ensure the employee's health and safety: see *Johnstone v Bloomsbury Health Authority* (1991), which concerned the legal challenge to the lengthy hours worked by junior hospital doctors. The relevant clause in their employment contracts stipulated that their hours of duty should consist of a standard working week of 40 hours and an additional availability on call up to an average of 48 hours per week over a specified period. The employee in question worked some weeks in excess of 88 hours and, as a result of working those hours with inadequate sleep, became ill. He brought an action asking for a declaration that he should not be required to work in excess of 72 hours a week and damages for personal injuries and loss allegedly suffered as a result of the employers' breach of their duty to take reasonable steps to ensure his safety. The case reached the Court of Appeal on an interlocutory point and the Court was not therefore called upon to reach a considered conclusion on the issues involved. A majority of the Court of Appeal (Leggatt LJ dissenting) held that the result of the interaction of the employee's express obligations and his employers' implied obligation to take care for his safety was that they were not entitled to require him to work for so many hours in excess of his standard working week as would foreseeably injure his health. Leggatt LJ's view was that reliance upon an express term cannot breach an implied term: see p 282. There is a difference between the judgments of the two judges who were in the majority, however. Stuart Smith LJ was prepared to make the express term subject to the requirement of health and safety, and thus appears to have mixed the employers' duties in contract and tort. Sir Nicolas Browne-Wilkinson V-C did not go that far, saying that 'where there is a contractual relationship between the parties their respective rights and duties have to be analysed wholly in contractual terms and not as a mixture of duties in contract and tort': see p 283. He said:

> Therefore, if there is a term of the contract which is in general terms (eg a general duty to take reasonable care not to injure the employee's health) and another term which is precise and detailed (eg an obligation to work on particular tasks notwithstanding that they may involve an obvious health risk expressly referred to in the contract) the ambit of the employer's duty of care for the employee's health will be narrower than it would be if there were no such express term ... The express and the implied terms of the contract have to be capable of co-existence without conflict.

4.136   Subject to these possible exceptions, the general rule is that there is no room for the implication of a term where the matter is already covered by an express term. The implied duty of trust and confidence and, possibly, the duty to take care of the employee's health and safety, however, are emerging as terms which the courts and tribunals regard as qualifying the powers given to employers by express terms. For a recent example of a case in which the Court has qualified the operation of an express term by the use of an implied term, see *Jenvey v Australian Broadcasting Corporation* (2003). In that case, Elias J implied a term the effect of which was to prohibit the employer from dismissing the employee for any reason other than redundancy once it had decided to terminate the contract for that reason.

Terms implied by custom and practice

4.137   A term may be implied on the basis of custom and practice, if it is reasonable, certain, and well-known. So, for example, in *Sagar v Ridehalgh & Son Ltd* (1931) the court accepted that it was part of the custom and practice of the Lancashire cotton industry that employers might make deductions from weavers' wages for bad work so that this became part of the individual weaver's contract. In *Marshall v English Electric Co Ltd* (1945) the established practice of using suspension as a disciplinary measure was held to be incorporated into the employees' contracts. It is not clear whether the custom needs to be known to and accepted by the employee, but it seems likely that the court or tribunal would treat a custom as applicable to an individual in cases where it is well known within the industry or where it is so well established that the employee must be taken to have accepted employment subject to it. In *Sagar v Ridehalgh & Son Ltd* (1931) Lawrence LJ said, at p 336:

> [I]t is clear that the [employee] accepted employment in the [employer's] mill on the same terms as the other weavers employed at that mill ... Although I entirely agree with the [trial judge] in finding it difficult to believe that the [employee] did not know of the existence of the practice at the mill, I think that it is immaterial whether he knew or not, as I am satisfied

that he accepted employment on the same terms as to deductions for bad work as the other weavers at the mill.

4.138 Even if the employee may be taken to have accepted the custom, the other requirements for incorporation need to be present also. A custom which is unreasonable may lead to the view that the employee would be unlikely to have accepted it and the mere fact that a practice has happened once before is not sufficient to lead to its incorporation. Such terms are less important than formerly because of the move towards increased formalisation of terms of employment and statutory regulation. For a recent case in which the implication of a term based on custom was rejected, see *Solectron Scotland Ltd v Roper* (2004).

Employees' obligations: good conduct

4.139 Although it is clear that an employee is under a duty not to commit acts of misconduct, the ambit of the duty is of necessity vague. As Lord James of Hereford observed in *Clouston & Co Ltd v Corry* (1906) (at p 129):

> There is no fixed rule of law defining the degree of misconduct which will justify dismissal. Of course there may be misconduct in a servant which will not justify the determination of the contract of service by one of the parties to it against the will of the other. On the other hand, misconduct inconsistent with the fulfilment of the express or implied conditions of service will justify dismissal... In such a case the question whether the misconduct proved establishes the right to dismiss the servant must depend upon facts – and is a question of fact.

4.140 In *Sinclair v Neighbour* (1967), for example, the employee, who was a manager of a betting shop, borrowed money from the till in the betting shop in the knowledge that permission would have been refused had he asked. The employer dismissed the employee summarily on learning of what had happened. The Court of Appeal held that the employee's dismissal was justified since, even though his conduct might not have been dishonest, it was nevertheless of such a grave and weighty character as to undermine the relationship of confidence which should exist between an employer and employee. This case is an example of a single relatively minor act justifying instant dismissal, since money was involved and, even if the employee was not dishonest, his behaviour undermined the employment relationship.

4.141 Employees are under no general duty to disclose their own misconduct, nor are they obliged to disclose misconduct of fellow employees: see *Bell v Lever Bros Ltd* (1932) and *Nottingham University v Fishel* (2000). In this last case, the court held that the employee was not obliged to disclose to his employers that he was doing outside work in breach of his contract, nor was he obliged to apply for consent, although his contract required him to do so. On the other hand, the terms and nature of a particular employment may be such, however, that there is a contractual duty to disclose the conduct of other employees, even if that disclosure will inevitably lead to disclosure of the employee's own conduct: see *Sybron Corporation v Rochem Ltd* (1983). This case was applied by Peter Smith J in *Tesco Stores Ltd v Pook* (2004). He held that a senior manager was under a positive obligation to disclose to his employer his own wrongdoings in accepting a bribe in breach of his fiduciary duty. One aspect of the duty of good conduct is obedience to reasonable instructions, which is considered in the next section.

Employees' obligations: obedience to instructions

4.142 An employee is under an obligation to obey lawful and reasonable instructions given by the employer. This is a fairly wide obligation, which in effect enshrines the employer's managerial prerogative. It extends beyond the normal situation of obedience to instructions given in the workplace to such issues as mobility and the need to adapt to changes in working practice, as in *Cresswell v Board of Inland Revenue* (1984), considered more fully at para 4.207. There, the employees tried to argue that the Inland Revenue was in breach of their terms of service in requiring them to operate the proposed computerisation of the PAYE system. Walton J held that, although the proposed introduction of computerisation changed the way the employees performed their duties, they were still administering the PAYE system and performing the duties of tax officers. He said, however, that this was subject to the proviso that the employer must provide any necessary training or re-training for them. If, however, the nature of the work alters so radically that it is outside their contractual obligations, it will not be reasonable to expect the employees to adapt.

4.143 In *Laws v London Chronicle (Indicator Newspapers) Ltd* (1959), the facts were that the employee disobeyed an instruction given to her by the managing director not to leave a meeting after a row had developed between him and her superior. She was summarily dismissed. The Court of Appeal upheld her wrongful dismissal claim. Lord Evershed MR said, at p 701:

> I think it is not right to say that one act of disobedience, to justify dismissal, must be of a grave and serious character. I do, however, think... that one act of disobedience or mis-conduct can justify dismissal only if it is of a nature which goes to show (in effect) that the servant is repudiating the contract, or one of its essential conditions; and for that reason, therefore,... the disobedience must at least have the quality that it is 'wilful': it does (in other words) connote a deliberate flouting of the essential contractual conditions.

4.144 In *Pepper v Webb* (para 4.121 above), on the other hand, the employee's wrongful dismissal claim failed. His disobedience of the order which led to his summary dismissal was the 'last straw' in a series of incidents and, although the single act of disobedience might not of itself have warranted summary dismissal, the cumulative effect of the previous incidents, taken together with the final act of disobedience and the use of bad language, was such as to warrant summary dismissal. The decision of the Court of Appeal in *Briscoe v Lubrizol Ltd* (2002) shows how difficult it can be to decide whether a particular set of facts can be said to amount to misconduct. The majority of the Court (Ward LJ and Bodey J) held that the employee had been guilty of repudiatory conduct in failing, without explanation or excuse, to attend a meeting with his employers to discuss his position and in subsequently failing to reply to his employers' requests to contact them. Potter LJ, on the other hand, said that these failures could not be regarded as gross misconduct and did not demonstrate an intention to repudiate the contract. The differences in the Court of Appeal in this case show how difficult it can be to decide whether a particular course of conduct amounts to gross misconduct and is thus repudiatory.

4.145 If the employer's instruction is unlawful or unreasonable, the employee is not obliged to obey it. Thus, for example, in *Ottoman Bank Ltd v Chakarian* (1930), it was held that an Armenian was within his rights to refuse to obey an order to stay in Constantinople, where he had previously been sentenced to death. Similarly, in *Bliss v South East Thames Regional Health Authority* (1987), the Court of Appeal held that an employee was entitled to refuse to comply with the employer's requirement to submit to a medical examination, taking the view that that requirement was a breach of the implied term of mutual trust and confidence.

4.146 Allied to obedience to reasonable instructions is compliance with mobility requirements. This is best dealt with by means of an express term in the employee's contract, as in *United Kingdom Atomic Energy Authority v Claydon* (1974), which contained a wide clause reserving to the employers 'the right to require any member of their staff to work at any of their establishments in Great Britain or in posts overseas'; see also *Nelson v BBC* (1977). If a mobility term falls to be implied the court or tribunal is likely to imply a term of restricted ambit, as happened in *O'Brien v Associated Fire Alarms Ltd* (1968). In that case, which involved an employee of a company with a country-wide operation who lived in Liverpool and generally worked within commutable distance of his home, the Court of Appeal implied a term that he should work within daily travelling distance of his home and no more. They rejected the employers' argument that there was an implied term in his contract that he would work anywhere in the north west and that he could be compelled to work 120 miles away in Barrow-in-Furness. In *Jones v Associated Tunnelling Co Ltd* (1981) Browne-Wilkinson J said, at p 480:

> The term to be implied must depend on the circumstances of each case. The authorities show that it may be relevant to consider the nature of the employer's business, whether

or not the employee has in fact been moved during the employment, what the employee was told when he was employed, and whether there are any provisions made to cover the employee's expenses when working away from daily reach of his home…[A]ll the circumstances have to be considered…

As in the *O'Brien* case, the EAT implied a term that the employee could be required to work within reasonable daily reach of his home.

4.147 On the other hand, in *Stevenson v Teesside Bridge and Engineering Ltd* (1971), the court implied a wider term, that he could be required to work at any site where he might be required to work as steel erector. The implication of this term depended on the nature of the work involved, the fact that before being taken on the employee stated that he was prepared to work away from home and the provisions of his contract, which envisaged the necessity of travelling and staying away from home. If the tribunal does imply a term relating to mobility, the term is likely to be subject to the implied qualification that reasonable notice must be given. This is particularly likely following the decision of the EAT in *United Bank Ltd v Akhtar* (1989). In *Prestwick Circuits Ltd v McAndrew* (1990) the employee was required to transfer to another site some fifteen miles away but was only given four days' notice of the transfer; he subsequently resigned. The employment tribunal decided that the employers' implied right to transfer the employee was subject to the implied qualification that reasonable notice of any transfer would be given to him and that the employers had breached this right. They therefore concluded that the employee had been constructively dismissed. The Court of Session upheld this decision. This decision represents an emerging trend, which shows that courts and tribunals are prepared to imply a term that an employer will not exercise its power under a contractual provision on unreasonable grounds.

4.148 In *Jones v Associated Tunnelling Co Ltd* (above) the EAT said (at p 480) of mobility clauses:

> [A] contract of employment cannot simply be silent on the place of work: if there is no express term, there must be either some rule of law that in *all* contracts of employment the employer is (or alternatively is not) entitled to transfer the employee from his original place of work or some term regulating the matter must be implied into each contract…In order to give the contract business efficacy, it is necessary to imply *some* term into each contract of employment.

In the later case of *Aparau v Iceland Frozen Foods plc* (1996), the EAT distinguished *Jones*'s case on the grounds that in the context of an employer with a chain of stores it is not necessary to imply a term entitling the employer to move employees around, whereas in the context of an employer who carries out specialist tunnelling work (as in *Jones*'s case) some term must be implied because the nature of the work is such that it cannot be expected to continue indefinitely at the same place. They conceded that it is necessary to have a term relating to the place of work, but refused to go any further and imply a term entitling the employer to move the employee around against her will.

Employees' obligations: exercise of care and skill

4.149 It is an implied term in a contract of employment that the employee is reasonably competent to do the job: see *Harmer v Cornelius* (1858). Thus, a serious act of incompetence may justify the employer in terminating the contract summarily at common law. Similarly, the employee impliedly agrees to take reasonable care in the performance of his or her duties under the contract. Although the employer will usually be vicariously liable for the employee's act of negligence, theoretically the employer may sue the employee for an indemnity for breach of the duty of care, as in *Lister v Romford Ice & Cold Storage Co Ltd* (1957). In appropriate circumstances, carelessness may justify summary dismissal at common law, though clearly it would have to satisfy the general principle that it was so serious as to amount to a repudiation on the employee's part of his or her contractual obligations: see *Power v British India Steam Navigation Co Ltd* (1930) and *Jupiter General Insurance Co Ltd v Shroff* (1937). In this last case, an act of negligence by a manager was held to amount to serious misconduct justifying the summary dismissal. So too in *Baster v London and County Printing Works* (1899) a single act of forgetfulness by an employee which caused damage to a valuable machine used in the employer's printing business was held to justify summary dismissal.

4.150 Negligence is sometimes given the epithet 'gross', but in *Wilson v Brett* (1843) Rolfe B said that he 'could see no difference between negligence and gross negligence – that it was the same thing, with the addition of a vituperative epithet'. Similarly, in *Dietmann v Brent London Borough Council* (1987) (at p 748), Hodgson J characterised this usage as unhelpful.

Employees' obligations: loyalty and fidelity

4.151 The following points should be noted:

(1) an employer may rely upon the implied duty of loyalty and fidelity as an alternative to an express restrictive covenant or in the absence of such a covenant;

(2) the implied term may be used against an employee during the currency of the employment or after it has ended;

(3) enforcement is likely to be by means of an injunction.

4.152 As an alternative to relying upon an express restrictive covenant (or in the absence of such a clause in the contract of employment), an employer may seek to rely upon the implied duty of loyalty and fidelity. The employer's argument will be that the ex-employee's contract contained an implied term obliging him or her to respect confidential information relating to the employer's trade secrets and trade connections acquired during the course of the employment. In an appropriate case an ex-employee who commits a breach of the implied duty of loyalty and fidelity may be restrained from committing or continuing to commit the breach. As the cases show, however, the implied duty is of fairly limited ambit. It is advisable for employers who are concerned about protecting their trade secrets and trade connection to make sure that their employees' contracts contain express restraints which can then be sought to be enforced after termination. A further point to note is that the contractual doctrine of repudiation may operate so as to affect the situation. In *Thomas Marshall (Exports) Ltd v Guinle* (1978), for example, the employee was subject to various express restraints, which, to differing extents, affected him both during and after his employment. He purported to resign when his service contract still had four-and-a-half years to run. Sir Robert Megarry V-C held that this repudiatory act did not automatically terminate the contract and that, although the court could not force him to work, it could restrain him from committing other breaches of his obligations during the continuance of his contract. The Vice-Chancellor then went on to restrain him from dealing with the company's customers and suppliers and from using confidential information belonging to the company, on the basis of the employee's breach of the implied duty of loyalty and fidelity. The clause expressly restraining him during his employment covered only the *disclosure*, not the *use* of confidential information, but the implied term was held to cover both. *Guinle*'s case shows the interaction of the implied duty and express restraints; it also suggests that the courts are more prepared to use the implied duty against employees during their employment and express restraints against them once their employment has ended. In an appropriate case, however, the implied duty may be invoked against an ex-employee. If it is, it should be noted that it will not be subject to any limitation of time; on the other hand, it is essential that an *express* restraint be limited in time, since it will otherwise be held to be unreasonable.

4.153 The implied duty of loyalty and fidelity may be invoked against an employee during the course of his or her employment. The duty covers:

(1) acceptance of bribes, inducements, or other payments from a third party;

(2) the use of information for the employee's own benefit, which is obtained during the performance of the contract;

(3) the disclosure to third parties of confidential information relating to the employer's undertaking;

(4) competition with the employer's business, or conduct likely to damage the employer's business.

4.154 An example of the first type of situation is *Boston Deep Sea Fishing & Ice Co v Ansell* (1888), in which the managing director of a company contracted for the construction of some fishing boats and took a commission from the shipbuilders on the contract, without the knowledge of the company. He also owned shares in an ice-making and fish-carrying company which paid bonuses to shareholders who used its services. He was held to have acted in breach of contract in relation to the receipt of the commission and bonuses. The payments were also held to be recoverable by the employer. See also *Reading v Attorney-General* (1951), in which the House of Lords held to be recoverable bribes which an Army sergeant had received. It should be noted in this last case that the money was recoverable by the employer (the Crown), despite the fact that it was earned by a criminal act and that the employer had suffered no loss. In effect, the payment was recoverable because of his abuse of his position.

4.155 It is well established that there is a duty lying on the employee not to disclose confidential information, but the courts have had difficulty in establishing what amounts to confidential information in any particular case. A distinction must be made between an individual employee's general knowledge or individual skill, which he or she may legitimately put to use in the future, and a trade secret which the employer is entitled to protect. In *Printers and Finishers Ltd v Holloway* (1964), at pp 735–736, Cross J said:

> The mere fact that the confidential information is not embodied in a document but is carried away by the employee in his head is not of itself a reason against the granting of an injunction to prevent its use or disclosure by him. If the information in question can fairly be regarded as a separate part of the employee's stock of knowledge which a man of ordinary honesty and intelligence would recognise to be the property of his old employer and not his own to do as he likes with, then the court, if it thinks that there is a danger of the information being used to the detriment of the old employer, will do what it can to prevent that result by granting an injunction. Thus an ex-employee will be restrained from using or disclosing a chemical formula or a list of customers which he has committed to memory.

4.156 Although the confidential information need not be of a complicated nature (as in *Cranleigh Precision Engineering Ltd v Bryant* (1965)), the question is whether, in any particular case, the information is confidential. In *Thomas Marshall (Exports) Ltd v Guinle*, Sir Robert Megarry, V-C suggested, *obiter*, a test containing four elements:

> First . . . the information must be information the release of which the owner believes would be injurious to him or of advantage to his rivals or others. Second . . . the owner must

believe that the information is confidential or secret, ie that it is not already in the public domain...Third, the owner's belief under the previous two heads must be reasonable. Fourth...the information must be judged in the light of the usage and practices of the particular industry or trade concerned. It may be that information which does not satisfy all these requirements may be entitled to protection as confidential information or trade secrets; but I think that any information which does not satisfy them must be of a type which is entitled to protection.

4.157　The Court of Appeal considered this issue fully in *Faccenda Chicken Ltd v Fowler* (1986) (see also *Balston Ltd v Headline Filters Ltd* (1987) and *Berkeley Administration Inc v McClelland* (1990), where the information sought to be protected was information derived from financial projections in an appendix to the employers' own business plan). They upheld the existence of an implied duty in relation to the use and disclosure of information, but in effect confined it to trade secrets or their equivalents, ie information which has a sufficiently high degree of confidentiality to warrant protection after the employment has ended by means of an implied term. At first instance, Goulding J identified three classes of information which an employee might acquire in the course of employment (pp 598–600):

First there is information which, because of its trivial character or its easy accessibility from public sources of information, cannot be regarded by reasonable persons or by the law as confidential at all. The servant is at liberty to impart it during his service or afterwards to anyone he pleases, even his master's competitor...Secondly, there is information which the servant must treat as confidential (either because he is expressly told it is confidential, or because from its character it obviously is so) but which once learned necessarily remains in the servant's head and becomes part of his own skill and knowledge applied in the course of his master's business. So long as the employment continues, he cannot otherwise use or disclose such information without infidelity and therefore breach of contract. But when he is no longer in the same service, the law allows him to use his full skill and knowledge for his own benefit in competition with his former master; and...there seems to be no established distinction between the use of such information where its possessor trades as a principal, and where he enters the employment of a new master, even though the latter case involves disclosure and not mere personal use of the information. If an employer wants to protect information of this kind, he can do so by an express stipulation restraining the servant from competing with him (within reasonable limits of time and space) after the termination of his employment...Thirdly, however, there are, to my mind, specific trade secrets so confidential that, even though they may necessarily have been learned by heart and even though the servant may have left the service, they cannot lawfully be used for anyone's benefit but the master's.

4.158 Neill LJ, giving the judgment of the Court of Appeal, said that the court must consider all the circumstances of a case, taking into account the following factors:

> (a) The nature of the employment. Thus employment in a capacity where 'confidential' material is habitually handled may impose a high obligation of confidentiality because the employee can be expected to realise its sensitive nature to a greater extent than if he were employed in a capacity where such material reaches him only occasionally or incidentally.
>
> (b) The nature of the information itself ... [T]he information will only be protected if it can be properly classed as a trade secret or as material which, while not properly to be regarded as a trade secret, is in all the circumstances of such a highly confidential nature as to require the same protection as a trade secret ...
>
> (c) Whether the employer impressed upon the employee the confidentiality of the information ... [T]hough an employer cannot prevent the use or disclosure merely by telling the employee that certain information is confidential, the attitude of the employer towards the information provides evidence which may assist in determining whether or not the information can properly be regarded as a trade secret ...
>
> (d) Whether the relevant information can be easily isolated from other information which the employee is free to use or disclose ... [W]e would not regard the separability of the information in question as being conclusive, but the fact that the alleged 'confidential' information is part of a package and that the remainder of the package is not confidential is likely to throw light on whether the information in question is really a trade secret.

4.159 In the *Faccenda* case, the information in issue was sales information which the employers were very anxious to keep confidential; there were no express restrictive covenants in the employees' contracts. The Court of Appeal concluded that the information fell into Goulding J's second category and not the third category but did not rule out the possibility that information relating to an employer's commercial interests could be protected in certain circumstances. On the facts in the instant case, the employers had not done enough, however, to be able to protect their business information. A similar conclusion was reached in *Wallace Bogan & Co v Cove* (1997), where the Court of Appeal refused to imply a term into the contracts of solicitors whose effect would be to restrain them from canvassing or doing business with clients of their former employees. The Court's view was that the way for employers to protect themselves in a case of this kind was for them to extract a restrictive covenant from the employees concerned. See also the Court of Appeal's decision in *Brooks v Olyslager OMS (UK) Ltd* (1998), and *A T Poeton (Gloucester Plating) Ltd v Horton* (2000), which involved the disclosure by a former employer of information relating to his former employers' financial position.

4.160 In *Lancashire Fires Ltd v SA Lyons & Co Ltd* (1997), on the other hand, the Court of Appeal said that for information to be a trade secret falling within Goulding J's third category (see above), it is not necessary for the employer to point out to the employee the precise limits of what is sought to be protected as confidential. In the instant case, the employee acquired information about the processes involved in producing artificial coals and logs for use in gas fires. Carnwath J at first instance said that the information did not fall within the third category, but the Court of Appeal reversed his decision on that point.

4.161 As was mentioned earlier, the implied duty also covers competition during the continuance of the employee's contract. It is important to define the ambit of this aspect of the duty, since the way an employee uses his or her spare time may be seriously affected by an overly wide interpretation of it. In general, employees are free to spend their spare time as they please and, if they engage in 'moonlighting', they are free to do so provided their activities do not affect the employer's business. In *Hivac v Park Royal Scientific Instruments Ltd* (1946), the facts were that two highly skilled employees who had access to all their employer's manufacturing data and who were engaged in the assembly of miniature valves for use in hearing aids, performed similar work for a competing company on Sundays. They were held to be in breach of the implied duty. Lord Greene MR said:

> It would be deplorable if... a workman could... knowingly, deliberately and secretly set himself to do in his spare time something which would inflict great harm on his employer's business.

4.162 This decision should be contrasted with the decision in *Nova Plastics Ltd v Froggatt* (1982), in which the employee was an odd-job man who worked for a rival business in his spare time. The EAT held that, even though the other business was in competition, the work which the employee did for the other company was not work which contributed seriously to any competition with the primary employer. He was not, therefore, in breach of the duty of fidelity. It is important to keep in mind the restricted ambit of the implied duty. It does not apply to employees who do work in their spare time which has no relationship with the work of their primary employer; nor does it extend to the situation where an employee's spare time work (or other activities) has an effect on his or her work for the primary employer. Inadequate performance or sub-standard work is not covered by the implied duty of loyalty and fidelity. An employer who wishes to rely upon the implied term *after* the employment relationship has ceased will probably only be able to do so where the breach is actually committed before the employment ceased: see *Robb v Green* (1895), *Worsley and Co Ltd v Cooper* (1939), and *Wessex Dairies Ltd v Smith* (1935). In addition, the courts are more likely to restrain the use of tangible, rather than intangible, information.

4.163 It is clear that the ex-employee will be restrained from using a list of the ex-employer's customers copied out before leaving the employment (as in *Robb v Green*) and from deliberately soliciting the employer's customers, before leaving, to transfer their custom after his or her departure: see *Wessex Dairies Ltd v Smith* see also *Adamson v B & L Cleaning Services Ltd* (1995)). But if there is no written list, the court will be reluctant to restrain the ex-employee who solicits those customers whose names he or she can remember, unless there is evidence to suggest that he or she has deliberately committed an entire list to memory: see *Hart v Colley* (1890) and *Baker v Gibbons* (1972). In this last situation, the case may be difficult to prove, as happened in *Baker v Gibbons*. A further requirement in cases of this kind is that the employee must not be allowed to acquire an unfair advantage. This rule particularly applies where he or she deliberately obtains, memorises, or copies lists of customers in breach of the implied duty. An example of this type of situation is *Robb v Green* (1895), in which an employee was restrained from using a list of his employers' customers which he had copied out before his departure after his employment had ended.

4.164 More recently, in *Roger Bullivant Ltd v Ellis* (1987), the Court of Appeal said that 'it is of the highest importance that the principle of *Robb v Green* ... which ... is one of no more than fair and honourable dealing, should be steadfastly maintained'. When he left his employment, the employee took with him a card index showing the names and addresses of his employer's customers. The Court of Appeal said that in such circumstances it was appropriate to grant an injunction, but that the injunction should be limited to the period during which the unfair advantage might be expected to continue. This was limited to 12 months, as there was an express restraint limited to this period. Nourse LJ said:

> Having made deliberate and unlawful use of the [employer's] property, [the employee] cannot complain if he finds that the eye of the law is unable to distinguish between those whom, had he so chosen, he could have lawfully contacted and those whom he could not.

4.165 The final point to note here is that the public interest may require the disclosure of confidential information to those who have a 'proper interest' to receive it. In *Gartside v Outram* (1856), Wood VC said: 'There is no confidence as to the disclosure of iniquity.' In *Initial Services Ltd v Putterill* (1968), the Court of Appeal held that an exception to the implied duty arises where the information relates to iniquity or misconduct on the part of the employer which is of such a nature that it ought in the public interest to be disclosed to someone who has a proper interest in receiving it. This was followed in *Re a Company's Application* (1989), in which an injunction was granted to restrain the disclosure of confidential information but was expressed not to cover disclosure to the appropriate regulatory body (FIMBRA), which had the power to investigate whether the employers were complying with the regulatory scheme, or information concerning fiscal matters to the Inland Revenue.

4.166 The remedies most likely to be sought by the employer are an injunction against the ex-employee to restrain him or her from continuing to disclose or use the trade secrets or confidential information, and damages for breaches of contract already committed. The employer may also seek injunctions and/or damages against third parties to whom the trade secrets or confidential information have been passed.

Employer's obligations: provision of work

4.167 The general rule at common law is that an employer is not obliged to provide work for the employee to do but only to pay the wages due under the contract. The classic statement of this rule is that of Asquith J in *Collier v Sunday Referee Publishing Co Ltd* (1940) (at p 650):

> It is true that a contract of employment does not necessarily, or perhaps normally, oblige the master to provide the servant with work. Provided I pay my cook her wages, she cannot complain if I choose to take any or all of my meals out.

4.168 So, for example, in *Turner v Sawdon & Co* (1901), which involved a salesman on a fixed-term contract who was given no work to do but whose salary was still paid, the Court of Appeal held that there was no obligation on the employers to provide him with work. AL Smith MR said:

> It is within the province of the master to say that he will go on paying the wages, but is under no obligation to provide work.

It was argued that a failure to give the employee employment would mean that he could not keep his hand in and would become a less efficient salesman. AL Smith MR said of this argument:

> To read in an obligation of that sort would be to convert the retainer at fixed wages into a contract to keep the servant in the service of his employer in such a manner as to enable the former to become au fait with his work. In my opinion, no such obligation arises under this contract ...

Thus, application of the general rule means that an employer who pays the employee but gives him or her no work to do will not be in breach of contract.

4.169 There are, however, exceptions to the general rule which have arisen in cases where the law has recognised that in certain types of contract it is essential to the contract that the employee is given the opportunity to work. So, for example, it will be a breach of contract to fail to provide work for an employee paid on a piecework or commission basis, as in *Devonald v Rosser & Sons* (1906) and *Turner v Goldsmith* (1891). In this last case, the Court of Appeal said that an agent paid on a commission basis was entitled to be sent a reasonable amount of work to enable him to earn his commission; see also *Bauman v Hulton Press Ltd* (1952).

4.170 Another group of exceptions arises in cases where the nature of the work is such that the opportunity for publicity is as important as the remuneration paid to the employee. This applies to actors, singers, and the like. Thus, for example, in *Marbé v George Edwardes (Daly's Theatre) Ltd* (1928), a well-known actress was engaged by the managers of a theatre to play a particular part in a play. There was also a collateral agreement by which the managers undertook to advertise her name in a prominent position. On the day of the dress rehearsal they refused to allow her to appear in the part. The Court of Appeal held that the contract imposed an express obligation upon the managers to allow her to appear in the part as agreed. They also held that damages for breach of that obligation might include compensation for loss of reputation. A similar decision was reached by the House of Lords in *Clayton and Waller Ltd v Oliver* (1930), which expressly approved *Marbé's* case. These cases concern the loss of opportunity for an actor or actress to enhance his or her reputation and arise in circumstances where the contract specifically contemplated such an enhancement of reputation. They show also that the obligation may be to provide work of a particular kind or standard (for example, a particular role or part), rather than any work. This exception was extended to authors in *Tolnay v Criterion Film Productions Ltd* (1936), but the Court of Appeal refused to extend it to a company director: see *Re Golomb* (1931).

4.171 Although there are no decided cases dealing with other classes of employees whose career depends upon their receiving publicity through the media, such as broadcasters, journalists, and the like, it is arguable that in their case too the enhancement of their reputation is contemplated by their contract. In this context it is worth noting the words of Goddard J in *Tolnay v Criterion Film Productions Ltd*, above, at p 1626:

> All persons who have to make a living by attracting the public to their works, be they . . . painters or . . . literary men . . . or . . . pianists, must live by getting known to the public.

In the light of this dictum, it must be likely that in appropriate cases, the reasoning of the cases discussed above would apply. In *Provident Financial Group plc v Hayward* (1989), Dillon LJ said:

> The employee has a concern to work and a concern to exercise his skills. That has been recognised in some circumstances concerned with artists and singers who depend upon

publicity, but it applies equally, I apprehend, to skilled workmen and even to chartered accountants.

4.172 It may be that there is a further exception in the case of employees engaged to fill a particular office, particularly if it is of a professional nature. For example, in *Collier v Sunday Referee Publishing Co Ltd* (1940), from which Asquith J's dictum was quoted above, the employee concerned was employed as the chief sub-editor of a newspaper. The owners sold the newspaper, thus putting it out of their power to continue to employ him. Asquith J held that when they sold the newspaper they destroyed the position to which they had appointed him and thereby committed a breach of contract. Although this may remain a correct proposition of law, it should be remembered that the position would now be likely to be governed by the Transfer of Undertakings (Protection of Employment) Regulations 2006.

4.173 A further possible area of exception arises in relation to cases where the employee arguably has an implied right to work. The possibility of such a right existing was canvassed in a robust judgment by Lord Denning MR in *Langston v Amalgamated Union of Engineering Workers* (1974). The case arose under long-repealed provisions of the Industrial Relations Act 1971. For the employee to succeed in his claim, he had to show that the union had induced a breach of contract in circumstances where the employers were continuing to pay his salary. He thus had to show that he had a contractual right to be provided with work. Lord Denning commented upon the age of the previous cases and said that the courts had repeatedly said that a person had the right to work. He went on, at p 190:

> To my mind, therefore, it is arguable that in these days a man has, by reason of an implication in the contract, a right to work. That is, he has a right to have the opportunity of doing his work when it is there to be done . . .

4.174 The other members of the Court were less emphatic than the Master of the Rolls. It should be noted, however, that this was an interlocutory decision, where the Court merely had to be satisfied that the employee *arguably* had the right. Further, even if such a right does or may exist, its existence only enjoys the status of an implied term. A further problem concerns the definition of the right. It is not clear whether the right as formulated by the Court of Appeal in *Langston*'s case is a right to be given work so as to maintain the employee's job satisfaction or whether it is a right for him or her to keep his or her hand in and remain au fait with developments. In either of the latter cases, the resignation by the employee as a result of a failure to provide work might amount to a constructive dismissal, as was argued in *Breach v Epsylon Industries Ltd* (1976). This case also is of limited utility, however, since the EAT remitted the case to the employment tribunal to consider whether there was an implied obligation to provide work suitable for a chief engineer. The EAT did suggest, however, at p 322, that the case fell within an exception 'which, as it were, is a blend of thought between *Collier v Sunday Referee Publishing Co Ltd* and the other cases where exceptions have been found, moderated by the changed climate of opinion ...'.

4.175 That is not the end of the matter, however. There is the question of whether the implied right to work can survive in cases where there is an express 'garden leave' clause. The nature of such a clause is that the employer expressly reserves the right to require the employee not to work but agrees to continue to pay the wages due under the contract during that time. The clause may also contain the limitation that it may only be invoked during a period of notice given by either party. This sort of clause was considered in *Provident Financial Group plc v Hayward* (1989). In this case, it gave power to the employer to suspend the employee from work 'at any time or from time to time'. Although the Court of Appeal upheld the judge's refusal to grant an injunction, on the grounds that the judge below had correctly exercised his discretion, there is nothing in the judgments of the Court to suggest that the clause itself was unenforceable. Taylor LJ said, at p 169: 'As a matter of principle I consider the court does have power to grant injunctive relief such as is claimed in the present case.' Dillon LJ recognised (at p 165) that garden leave clauses are capable of abuse, but the general tenor of the judgments of the Court of Appeal in the *Provident Financial* case is to suggest that the court would be unlikely to exercise its discretion to grant an injunction in a case where it considered that the employer was trying to insist on an excessively long period of garden leave. See also para 4.103, where garden leave clauses are discussed. See also *SG & R Valuation Service Co. v Boudrais* (2008) for an interesting discussion of the right to work and the question of whether the employer has an implied right to put an employee on garden leave.

Employers' obligations: remuneration

4.176 The obligation lying upon the employer to pay the employee the wages which are due is at the heart of the employment contract. Normally, the contract will contain express provisions dealing with remuneration, and it is a statutory requirement that details of the scale, rate, or method of calculation of the remuneration should be given to the employee in writing: see ERA 1996 s 1(4)(a) and (b). Employees also have a statutory right, under ERA 1996 s 8, to receive an itemised pay statement upon payment of wages or salary. In the event of there being no express term governing pay, the court or tribunal would imply a term, no doubt to the effect that the employee should receive 'the going rate for the job'. Alternatively, the employee would be able to recover on the basis of *quantum meruit*, as in *Way v Latilla* (1937), where there was an understanding that the employer would look after the employee's interests; see also *Powell v Braun* (1954).

4.177 An area which has given rise to problems is the question of whether an employee is impliedly entitled to be paid sick pay in cases where there is no express term in the contract of employment. Although Pilcher J accepted in *Orman v Saville Sportswear Ltd* (1960) that there is a rebuttable presumption that wages will continue to be paid during the employee's sickness, the Court of Appeal in *Mears v Safecar Security Ltd* (1982) disapproved that approach and said that the court or tribunal must look at all the facts and circumstances of the relationship between the parties, including their subsequent acts under the contract. In view of the facts that it was well known that the employer's practice was not to pay wages during sickness, that he did not ask about sick pay before taking on the job and that he took sick leave without pay for seven out of the 14 months his employment lasted and never asked for sick pay, the Court decided that nothing was payable. If sick pay is payable by virtue of an implied term, the question then arises as to how long it is payable for. In *Howman & Son v Blyth* (1983) the EAT said that the tribunal should imply a reasonable term as to its duration having regard to the normal practice in the industry concerned. In the case in question, they looked to the working rule agreement for the industry involved.

Employers' obligations: safety and care

4.178 This term embraces a number of different facets of the employment relationship, ranging from the common law duty to care for the employee's health and safety to a duty to take care in the compilation of references for the employee. The decision of the House of Lords in *Wilsons & Clyde Coal Co Ltd v English* (1938) established that the employer owes a duty to an employee to provide competent and safe fellow-employees, to provide adequate materials and to provide a safe system of working. It may be a corollary of the first aspect of this duty that an employer is under a duty to take steps to terminate the employment of a potentially dangerous employee. Although the duty is generally regarded as arising in the law of tort, it gives rise to a contractual obligation on the part of the employer to act reasonably in matters of safety. This means that an employee who resigns because of the employer's failure in this respect may claim to have been constructively dismissed. So, for example, in *British Aircraft Corporation Ltd v Austin* (1978) the employer's failure to investigate the employee's complaint about the protective eyewear provided was held by the EAT to amount to conduct entitling him to resign without notice. In such a case, however, the breach by the employer must be sufficiently serious as to amount to a repudiation of the contract: see *Graham Oxley Tool Steels Ltd v Firth* (1980).

4.179 There are suggestions in *Johnstone v Bloomsbury Health Authority* (1991) that the express terms in an employee's contract may be qualified by the implied duty of care owed by the employer. In the case in question, the employee's contract stipulated that his hours of duty should consist of a standard 40-hour week and an additional availability on call up to an average of 48 hours a week over a specified period. A majority of the Court of Appeal said that the employers were not entitled to require the employee to work so many hours in excess of his standard working week as would foreseeably injure his health. Stuart-Smith LJ suggested that the employers' power under this contractual provision had to be exercised in the light of their implied duty of care, but Sir Nicolas Browne-Wilkinson V-C merely said that they had the right, subject to their ordinary duty not to injure the employee, to call upon him to work those hours up to the stipulated maximum.

4.180 In *Reid v Rush & Tompkins Group plc* (1990) the facts were that an employee suffered a road accident whilst working for his employers in Ethiopia but, as a result of the law in that country, he received no compensation for his injuries. He therefore tried to argue that there was an implied term in his contract either that his employers would take out appropriate insurance cover indemnifying him against the risk of death or injury whilst driving in the course of his employment or that, before he left for Ethiopia, his employers would give him all necessary advice relating to work conditions there, including any special risks such as a road accident involving an uninsured driver (as happened) and would advise him to obtain appropriate cover himself. The Court of Appeal considered the various bases upon which terms may be implied and, in the light of them, refused to imply any such term. Another aspect of the duty to take care is that the employer may be under an obligation to indemnify the employee against expenses necessarily incurred in the course of employment (including the cost of defending legal proceedings): see *Burrows v Rhodes* (1899), *Re Famatina Development Corporation Ltd* (1914), and *Gregory v Ford* (1951).

4.181 Finally, there is the duty of the employer to take care in giving references in respect of an ex-employee. It is clear from *Hedley Byrne & Co Ltd v Heller & Partners Ltd* (1964) that the employer will be liable to the new employer in negligence, but the question is whether it is possible to incur liability to the ex-employee. In *Spring v Guardian Assurance plc* (1994) the House of Lords by a majority held that an employer has a duty of this sort. Lord Slynn of Hadley and Lord Woolf also took the view that the ex-employee's contract contained an implied term that his employers would take reasonable care in the compiling and giving of the reference. Lord Woolf based this view on the decision of the House of Lords in *Scally v Southern Health and Social Services Board* (1991). He said, at p 647:

> [I]t [the *Scally* case] recognises that, just as in the earlier authorities the courts were prepared to imply by necessary implication a term imposing a duty on an employer to exercise due care for the physical well-being of his employees, so in the appropriate circumstances would the court imply a like duty as to his economic well-being, the duty as to his economic well-being giving rise to an action for damages if it is breached.

4.182　Clearly, there is scope for further development of the implied term in this area. One area to comment upon is the developing case law in relation to stress claims. Such claims may be founded in tort – thus being a species of negligence claim – or they may be based upon the implied term to care for the employee's health and safety. The first case of any significance in this area was *Walker v Northumberland County Council* (1995). Subsequently, the principles underpinning these types of claims were reviewed by the Court of Appeal, in *Hatton v Sutherland* (2002). Although the Court of Appeal in this last case categorised the *Walker* claim as being based on the implied term and treated the claim in the instant case as falling within that category, the summary of principles set out by the Court in paragraph 43 of its judgment tends to suggest an approach based more upon tort than contract. The Court of Appeal reviewed these principles in *Pratley v Surrey County Council* (2003). In *Barber v Somerset County Council* (2004), the House of Lords said that the guidance given by the Court of Appeal in *Hatton v Sutherland* was a valuable contribution to the development of the law but should not be read as having anything like statutory force. They said that every case depends on its own facts.

Employers' obligations: reasonable notice

4.183　There may be circumstances in which it is necessary to imply a term into an employee's contract as to the amount of notice he or she is entitled to receive or obliged to give. In most cases, if the parties have not agreed upon a notice period, the effect of section 86 of the Employment Rights Act 1996 will be to insert a statutory term relating to notice. This comes into play in the case of employees who have been continuously employed for one month or more. In the case of employment of up to two years, the employee's entitlement is to one week's notice; after that, it increases by one week for each year of employment up to 12, which is the maximum statutory amount of notice. Under the statute, the employee is only obliged to give one week's notice of termination. In cases where there is no express term and either party wishes to argue that the other is obliged to give more notice than that provided for by the statutory provisions, it will be necessary to contend for the implication of a term relating to notice. In *Richardson v Koefod* (1969), Lord Denning MR said: 'In the absence of express stipulation, the rule is that every contract of service is determinable by reasonable notice. The length of the notice depends upon the circumstances of the case.'

4.184　It is not possible to set out any rules as to the amount of notice to be implied into any contract. Much depends upon the facts of each case and all the circumstances must be looked at, including:

- the type of employment;
- any local, trade, or professional customs;

- the intervals at which remuneration is paid; and
- the period in relation to which remuneration is stated.

4.185 A consideration of the case-law on this subject, much of it dating from the nineteenth century, suggests that the notice to which an employee is impliedly entitled will lengthen with seniority, but that only in exceptional cases will a term of notice longer than six months be implied. The cases tend to deal with the amount of notice to which an employee is *entitled* rather than *obliged to give*. Arguably, perhaps, an employee entitled to three months' notice may also be obliged to give the same notice, but the cases say little about this. The fact remains, of course, that, as with other contractual terms, the parties should deal with the matter expressly rather than rely upon the unpredictable operation of an implied term.

Mutual trust and confidence

4.186 Reference was made at the beginning of this chapter to Edmund-Davies LJ's observation in *Wilson v Racher* (1974) that 'a contract of service imposes upon the parties a duty of mutual respect'. This case was decided when the law relating to unfair dismissal was in its infancy. Since the decision of the Court of Appeal in *Western Excavating (ECC) Ltd v Sharp* (1978), however, which emphasised that a constructive dismissal will only take place where the employer is in breach of an express or implied term in the contract and the breach is so serious as to amount to a repudiation of the contract, this implied duty has been considerably refined and developed, particularly as far as the employer's behaviour is concerned. Subsequent case-law has shown that the duty is flexible and will tend to vary with the circumstances of any particular case. The courts have also used the implied term to impose limitations on the managerial prerogative given by express terms, as in the case of *United Bank Ltd v Akhtar* (1989) and *Johnstone v Bloomsbury Health Authority* (1991), considered at paras 4.132–4.135.

4.187 In the context of constructive dismissal cases, the implied term has been variously formulated as a term obliging the employer to maintain the relationship of trust between the parties, or as a term obliging the employer not to treat the employees arbitrarily, capriciously, and not in accordance with good industrial relations practice or, more simply, as 'the implied obligation of good faith'. So, for example, in *Woods v W M Car Services (Peterborough) Ltd* (1981), Browne-Wilkinson J said:

> [I]t is clearly established that there is implied in a contract of employment a term that the employers will not, without reasonable and proper cause, conduct themselves in a

manner calculated or likely to destroy or seriously damage the relationship of confidence and trust between employer and employee... To constitute a breach of this implied term it is not necessary to show that the employer intended any repudiation of the contract: the tribunal's function is to look at the employer's conduct as a whole and determine whether it is such that its effect, judged reasonably and sensibly, is such that the employee cannot be expected to put up with it...

4.188   The case went to the Court of Appeal, which upheld the EAT's decision. The same judge later followed this dictum in applying the implied term to an employer's exercise of its powers under a pension scheme, in *Imperial Group Pension Trust Ltd v Imperial Tobacco Ltd* (1991). The rules of the pension scheme enabled the committee of management of the scheme to amend it 'with the consent in writing of the company'. The question arose whether the exercise by the company of its power to grant or withhold consent was qualified by an obligation to act in good faith. Sir Nicolas Brown-Wilkinson V-C held that the power was subject to an implied obligation that it would not be exercised so as seriously to damage the relationship of confidence between employer and employee and that, if the company exercised its power in breach of that obligation, the exercise of the power would be invalid. He called the obligation simply 'the implied obligation of good faith'. In the subsequent House of Lords decision in *Eastwood v Magnox Electric plc* (2004), Lord Steyn suggested that it would help clarity if this description of the implied term was used: see para 50.

4.189   The scope of the term was examined by Lord Steyn in *Mahmud v Bank of Credit and Commerce International SA* (1997). He approved the formulation of the term as set out by Browne-Wilkinson J above. Subsequently, the Court of Appeal made it clear that tribunals should follow that formulation and not use language which may detract from the correct test or suggest that a different test has been applied: see *Transco plc v O'Brien* (2002). In this last case, the Court of Appeal held that the employer had been in breach of the implied term in failing to offer an employee a new contract when offering them to all other permanent employees, despite the employer's mistaken belief (arrived at in good faith) that he was not a permanent employee. As Hart J observed in *University of Nottingham v Eyett* (1999), the terms in which the duty have been expressed have been 'in the negative form of prohibiting conduct calculated or likely to produce destructive or damaging consequences, rather than as positively enjoining conduct which will avoid such consequences'. This analysis may be said to underpin the cases considered in this section.

4.190   The EAT has treated as a breach of the implied term a failure to deal with a female employee's complaint of alleged sexual harassment: see *Bracebridge Engineering Ltd v Darby* (1990). It has also treated as a breach of the implied term an employer's failure to make reasonable adjustments in the case of a disabled employee and the use of highly abusive language: see *Greenhof v Barnsley Metropolitan Borough Council* (2006) and *Ogilvie v Neyrfor-Weir Ltd* (EAT/0054/02). It has said that an employer may breach the implied duty of trust and confidence by failing to notify an employee absent on maternity leave of a job vacancy for which she would have applied had she been aware of it: *Visa International Service Association v Paul* (2004). In *Horkulak v Cantor Fitzgerald International* (2004) the High Court held that an employee who was subjected to a campaign of bullying and intimidation, accompanied by foul and abusive language, had been constructively dismissed. The judgment of Newman J contains a useful and helpful discussion of the recent cases in which the implied term of trust and confidence has been developed. (The Court of Appeal decision in this case, in 2005, only deals with the measure of damages, not the issue of liability.)

4.191 The EAT has also held that a failure by the employer to provide a grievance proce-dure for its employees is a breach of the implied term: see *W A Goold (Pearmak) Ltd v McConnell* (1995). In this last case the EAT used the existence of the statutory provisions relating to the provision of a note by employers relating to their griev-ance procedures as a basis for implying a term that an employer will 'reasonably and promptly afford a reasonable opportunity to their employees to obtain redress of any grievance they may have'. In cases where the employer does provide its employ-ees with a grievance procedure, there may be an issue as to whether the employer has investigated the employee's grievance properly. The EAT has held that a failure to do so may amount to a breach of contract: see *Hamilton v Tandberg Television Ltd* (2002). In the context of a disciplinary procedure, the imposition of a dispro-portionate penalty may be sufficient to found a claim of constructive dismissal: see *Stanley Cole (Wainfleet) Ltd v Sheridan* (2003). It is not relevant, however, when deciding whether the employer committed a fundamental breach of contract, that the employee failed to invoke the employer's grievance procedure. The conduct to be assessed is that of the employer: see *Tolson v Governing Body of Mixenden Community School* (2003).

4.192 In *TSB Bank plc v Harris* (2000) the EAT upheld the tribunal's decision that the employers were in fundamental breach of the implied term of trust and confi-dence by revealing, in a reference to a prospective employer, complaints against the employee of which she was unaware, thereby blocking her progress in the financial services sector. They rejected the argument that the employers were not in breach of the implied term because they were only doing what was required of them under regulations governing the financial services industry. They said that the obliga-tion of the employers to their regulators is not the measure of their obligation to their employees. In *Euro-Die (UK) Ltd v Skidmore* (EAT/1158/98) the EAT held that an employer's failure to assure an employee that his continuity of employment would be protected following a transfer of the business amounted to a fundamental breach of the term of trust and confidence. The consequence was that the employee was treated as constructively dismissed and the transferee was liable for the unfair dismissal.

4.193   On the other hand, the EAT has refused to treat the introduction of a non-smoking policy as a breach of the implied term, in *Dryden v Greater Glasgow Health Board* (1992), taking the view that the employer's action was within the scope of its managerial prerogative; see also *Sita (GB) Ltd v Burton* (1998).

4.194   Cases involving an alleged breach of the implied term are not, of course, confined to the context of unfair dismissal complaints; see, for example, *Bliss v South East Thames Regional Health Authority* (1987). In that case, during a dispute between the authority and a consultant surgeon, the authority required the surgeon to undergo a psychiatric examination when there was no mental or pathological illness and suspended him when he refused. In the context of the surgeon's claim for breach of contract, the Court of Appeal held that this behaviour amounted to a breach of the implied term which was so fundamental as to constitute a repudiation of the contract. The Court followed Browne-Wilkinson J's formulation of the term used in the *Woods* case (para 4.187, above).

4.195   It is clear that the implied obligation discussed in this section does not extend to the employer's decision to dismiss the employee. This means that, however unfair or unreasonable the employer's behaviour when dismissing the employee, he or she cannot claim damages in a wrongful dismissal action or compensation in an unfair dismissal claim for the manner of the dismissal: see *Johnson v Unisys Ltd* (2001) and *Dunnachie v Kingston upon Hull City Council* (2004). If, on the other hand, the employer's behaviour *before* dismissal is such as to give rise to a claim for a breach of the implied term which can be said to exist independently of his subsequent dismissal, and financial loss flows directly from that failure, the employee may bring an action in respect of that loss. Such an action will not be barred by the availability of a claim in the employment tribunal for unfair dismissal. Further, since the claim is not an unfair dismissal claim there will be no ceiling on the compensation that may be awarded, though the claim will be subject to the rule against double recovery. This is the outcome of the important House of Lords decision in *Eastwood v Magnox Electric plc* (2004).

4.196   The cases so far considered in this section have involved breaches by the *employer* of the implied duty of mutual trust and confidence, largely because it is in the context of an unfair dismissal or breach of contract claim that the issue arises. It is not confined, however, to employers, as is shown by the case of *British Telecommunications plc v Ticehurst* (1992). The case involved deductions from the employee's wages made as a result of her participation in industrial action. She claimed that the deductions had been made in breach of contract. The Court of Appeal held that, as the employee was in breach of the implied term, the employers were justified in withholding part of her wages. They formulated the term as 'an implied term to serve the employer faithfully within the requirements of the contract': see Ralph Gibson LJ at p 398, with whom the other two Lords Justices agreed. In doing so, he adopted the formulation of Buckley LJ in *Secretary of State for Employment v ASLEF (No 2)* (1972).

4.197 At the beginning of this section, mention was made of the flexible and variable nature of the implied term of mutual trust and confidence, which has been adapted to circumstances such as a failure to deal with a complaint of sexual harassment or to institute a grievance procedure. The question of whether to extend the scope of employers' obligations is regularly canvassed before courts and tribunals and it is clear that, over the years since the introduction of the concept of constructive dismissal, they have developed this implied term to cover a variety of different situations. This can be seen in cases such as *Imperial Group Pension Trust Ltd v Imperial Tobacco Ltd* (1991), above, at para 4.188, and in *Scally v Southern Health and Social Services Board* (1991), where the House of Lords held that an employer had an implied obligation to take reasonable steps to publicise to an employee his rights under a pension scheme. The question which arises, when considering the limits of the implied term, is whether and to what extent an employer has a positive obligation towards the employee.

4.198 The case of *University of Nottingham v Eyett* (1999) (see also para 4.189 above) suggests that the implied duty of mutual trust and confidence in a contract of employment does not extend so far as to include a positive obligation on the employer. In the case in question, the employer failed to warn an employee who was proposing to exercise important rights in connection with the contract of employment that the way he was proposing to exercise them might not be the most financially advantageous. Hart J said that, although the duty of mutual trust and confidence may in principle impose positive obligations, recognition of a duty to alert an employee to the possibility that he was making a financial mistake would have far-reaching consequences for the employment relationship and would not sit well with other default obligations implied by law in the employment context. In the later case of *Ibekwe v London General Transport Services Ltd* (2003), the Court of Appeal followed *Scally* when considering whether an employer had fulfilled the duty to inform an employee of proposed changes to his pension rights and the availability of an option to transfer his accrued rights with a special enhancement to a new pension scheme. They said that attaching letters detailing the changes and options to his pay slips was sufficient. There is no duty, however, to take care for the employee's general well-being by warning the employee of the detrimental effect of his proposed resignation on his rights under a contractual permanent health insurance scheme: see *Crossley v Faithful and Gould Holdings Ltd* (2004). This case illustrates the point made above, that the duty of trust and confidence does not involve positive steps such as that required in the case in question; see also *Hagen v ICI Chemicals and Polymers Ltd* (2002).

4.199　In this context, the decision in *McClory v The Post Office* (1993) should be noted. There, the court said that there is an implied term that an employer cannot exercise its power under a contractual provision (in the case in question, an express power to suspend) on unreasonable grounds.

Variation of contract

4.200　The main principles governing variations of an employment contract are as follows:

(1) For a variation of an employment contract to be effective the proposed change must be notified to the employee and the employee must consent to it.

(2) The employee's consent may be express or inferred and, if express, need not be in writing.

(3) Consent may be inferred from other contractual material, such as a collective agreement, a flexibility clause, or a clause in the employment contract giving the employer a power of unilateral variation.

(4) A unilateral notification by one party to the other of a change in the contract will not amount to a variation in the absence of agreement.

(5) The imposition of a unilateral change by the employer will give the employee the right to resign and claim breach of contract or to claim a constructive dismissal giving rise to liability on the part of the employer for unfair dismissal or a redundancy payment or to make a claim for an unlawful deduction of 'wages' under Part II of the Employment Rights Act 1996.

(6) An employer who is unable to obtain the employee's agreement to a proposed change and chooses not to impose the change unilaterally may in the alternative dismiss the employee with notice and offer re-employment under a contract containing the changed terms but risks claims for unfair dismissal and redundancy.

(7) A variation of contract in the context of a transfer of an undertaking falling within the Transfer of Undertakings (Protection of Employment) Regulations 2006 may be affected by those Regulations.

The main legal principles

4.201   The two main issues which arise in the context of a variation are (1) whether the proposed variation relates to a contractual or non-contractual provision; and (2) whether the employee consented to it. Both may raise difficult questions. In the first case, questions will arise as to whether the particular provision has become part of the contract or not. If not, it is open to the employer to make a unilateral variation by, for example, discontinuing or abandoning or altering the particular provision, for example a bonus scheme or enhanced redundancy payment scheme. A further question here will be whether the proposed change falls within the employer's managerial prerogative. If the proposed variation requires consent, the question will then be whether it has been given. It is a fundamental principle of contract law that, as it takes the agreement of both parties to enter into the contract, so it takes the agreement of both to vary it: see *Robinson v Page* (1826), *Goss v Lord Nugent* (1833), *British and Beningtons Ltd v North Western Cachar Tea Co Ltd* (1923), and *Royal Exchange Assurance v Hope* (1928).

4.202   If the proposed variation does not require consent, it may be imposed unilaterally by the employer. If, however, the variation requires consent and the employer imposes it unilaterally, that act will constitute a repudiatory breach of contract giving the employee the right to resign. He or she will then be able to make a claim for breach of contract based upon the employer's breach; it will also be possible to complain of unfair dismissal or claim a redundancy payment, arguing that the resignation caused by the breach amounts to a constructive dismissal. If the variation involves a reduction in the employee's wages, he or she may also make a claim under Part II of the Employment Rights Act 1996 (formerly the Wages Act 1986).

4.203   As an alternative to imposing the claim unilaterally, the employer may dismiss the employee with notice and offer re-employment under a contract containing the changed terms and conditions. The risk in following that strategy is that the employer will then be exposed to complaints of unfair dismissal and claims for redundancy payments, though it does not follow that the unfair dismissal complaints will necessarily succeed. These principles are considered in more detail in the sections which follow. Finally, at the end of the chapter, variations of contract in the context of transfers of undertakings will be considered: see para 4.241.

Requirements for an effective variation: contractual and non-contractual provisions

4.204   The first question to consider here is whether the proposed variation is one which requires consent at all. Obviously, if it is a variation of a contractual term, then consent is essential. If, however, the employer is proposing to vary a non-contractual benefit or provision or to introduce a change which lies within the managerial prerogative and amounts to a lawful and reasonable instruction, there will be no need for the employee's consent. In the first situation, he or she can do nothing about the proposed change, simply because it is non-contractual; in the second, the change will fall within the employee's implied duty to obey the employer's orders. If the proposed change amounts to a contractual variation, the employer must give the employee notice of it: see para 4.209, below. To determine whether a particular benefit or provision is contractual or not, much depends upon the intention of the parties. The question is whether it is reasonable to infer from the circumstances that the parties intended the provision to have contractual force. So, for example, if the contract specifies that a disciplinary procedure is to be incorporated into the employees' contracts, it will be incorporated; if it is stated not to be of contractual effect, it will not be incorporated. For an example of an incorporated disciplinary procedure, see *Dietmann v Brent London Borough Council* (1988).

4.205 In *Robertson v British Gas Corporation* (1983) the Court of Appeal held that an incentive bonus scheme had been incorporated into employees' contracts and could not, therefore, be unilaterally determined by the employer. In that case, the employee's letter of appointment to a new grade stated: 'Incentive bonus scheme conditions will apply to meter reading and collection work.' The statutory statement given to the employee stated: 'Any payment which may, from time to time, become due in respect of... incentive bonuses... will be calculated in accordance with the rules of the scheme in force at the time.' The Court of Appeal said that the words used in the letter clearly and expressly imported into the employee's contract an obligation to pay the bonus. Ackner LJ went on to say that he did not consider there to be an inconsistency between the words of the letter and those of the statement, but that, if that view was wrong, the letter took precedence over the statement, which provided strong prima facie evidence of the terms of the contract but did not constitute the contract: see pp 356–357. He added that the employer's statement given years after the contract was made could not be used as admissible evidence for the interpretation of the contract itself. This case is also considered in the context of the requirement of consent: see para 4.219, below.

4.206 This decision should be contrasted with *Quinn v Calder Industrial Materials Ltd*, considered more fully at para 4.81, in which the EAT held that the unilateral abandonment of a policy governing enhanced redundancy payments was not in breach of the employees' contracts. See also to similar effect *Secretary of State for Employment v ASLEF (No 2)* (1972), where the Court of Appeal refused to hold that detailed works rules set out in a staff handbook were contractual; they were held to be collateral instructions to the employees as to how they were to carry out their work. Similar considerations apply in the case of bonus schemes or share option schemes; if they are stated not to be contractual but capable of discontinuance at the employer's discretion, the employer will not be in breach of contract in exercising the discretion to discontinue. An example is *Cadoux v Central Regional Council* (1986), in which the question was whether the employer was entitled to withdraw a non-contributory life assurance scheme.

Changes within the managerial prerogative

4.207 An example of a proposed change falling within the managerial prerogative is *Cresswell v Board of Inland Revenue* (1984). There, the employees tried to argue that the Inland Revenue was in breach of their terms of service in requiring them to operate the proposed computerisation of the PAYE system. Walton J held that, although the proposed introduction of computerisation changed the way the employees performed their duties, they were still administering the PAYE system and performing the duties of tax officers. He said that an employee is expected to adapt to new methods and techniques in performing his or her duties provided that the employer arranges for training in the new skills and that the nature of the work does not alter so radically that it is outside the contractual obligations of the employee. He emphasised that it is a question of fact and degree whether the introduction of new methods and techniques alters the work that an employee has agreed to perform so much that it is no longer the work that the employee agreed to perform under the terms of his or her contract. His conclusion therefore was that the Inland Revenue could vary the duties of the tax officers as proposed.

4.208 More recently, in *Dryden v Greater Glasgow Health Board* (1992), the issue arose as to whether the introduction by an employer of a ban on smoking amounted to a significant breach in an employee's contract entitling her to resign and claim constructive dismissal. The EAT held that the introduction of the new policy fell into the category of a works rule and therefore did not amount to a repudiatory breach. Lord Coulsfield said, at pp 471–472:

> There can...be no doubt that an employer is entitled to make rules for the conduct of employees in their place of work, as he is entitled to give lawful orders, within the scope of the contract...Where a rule is introduced for a legitimate purpose, the fact that it bears hardly on a particular employee does not...justify an inference that the employer has acted in such a way as to repudiate the contract with that employee.

It is, however, possible for an employer to act in such a way that, albeit that the action is within the managerial prerogative or is expressly permitted by a contractual term, the implied term of mutual trust and confidence is breached: see *United Bank Ltd v Akhtar* (1989), discussed at para 4.132.

Requirements for an effective variation: notice of the proposed change

4.209 Once it is clear that the proposed change is a contractual variation, the next question is whether the employee has been given notice of the variation, since an employee can hardly be said to have agreed to something of which he or she was not informed. In *Cowey v Liberian Operations Ltd* (1966), the issue was whether the employee was bound by a variation that reduced his notice entitlement from three months to one month. The method used to change the term was an office memorandum passed round and initialled by the staff, including the employee in question. He took the view, in the light of discussions he had had with a superior at the time of his appointment, that it did not apply to him; but he initialled it and passed it on. The judge held that the method used to vary the contract was ineffective. A relevant factor was that the employee's attention was not drawn to the fact that the change was intended to apply to him.

The requirement of agreement: introduction

4.210 A variation will not be effective unless both parties agree. In the context of a variation of an employment contract, the main question is likely to be whether the *employee* consented to the proposed variation. The following types of consent are possible:

(a) express consent;

(b) tacit or inferred consent;

(c) consent arising by virtue of

– a provision in a collective agreement;

– a flexibility clause in the employment contract;

– a provision in the contract giving the employer power to vary the contract unilaterally.

The requirement of agreement: express consent

4.211 Although in many cases it will be clear whether or not the employee has agreed, as, for example, in *Burdett-Coutts v Hertfordshire County Council* (1984), questions may arise as to whether the employee's action amounts to express consent. In that case, Kenneth Jones J refused to accept that employees faced with a unilateral change in their pay who stayed on and accepted the lower pay whilst making it clear that they were not prepared to accept the new terms should be treated as having accepted the unilateral variation. He therefore held them to be entitled to recover the wages which they should have been paid under their original contract. This case is considered further below, at para 4.217. Similarly, in *Miller v Hamworthy Engineering Ltd* (1986), the question was whether the evidence established an agreement between the employer and the trade union entitling the employer to make deductions from his wages by putting the employee on a three-day week. The Court of Appeal held that the documentary evidence did not establish that negotiations between the employers and the employee's trade union had resulted in a variation of his contract entitling them to reduce his salary. The Court said that references to short-time working and work-sharing in the employee's written terms and conditions and in a redundancy agreement entered into between the unions and the employers did not point to an agreement that was capable of varying the existing contractual terms between the employee and the employers; see also *Gibbons v Associated British Ports* (1985). In that case, the trade union terminated the applicable collective agreement. The employers argued that the termination of the agreement removed from the employee's contract the existing rate of remuneration to which he was entitled and allowed them to substitute a lower rate. The High Court rejected that argument and said that the employers were in breach of contract in unilaterally varying the contract, whose terms remained unaffected by the termination of the collective agreement.

The requirement of agreement: tacit or inferred consent

4.212 Questions as to whether there has been tacit or inferred consent may arise in the following cases:

- where the employee makes no response to a variation which amounts to a repudiation but continues to work and accept wages;

- where the employee consents to a variation in circumstances where he or she is faced with the alternative of dismissal;

- where the employee is given notice of a change in the contractual terms and continues to work subject to the new terms but under protest.

4.213 In the absence of express agreement on the employee's part to a variation, he or she may be held to have consented impliedly, but the cases make it clear that a court or tribunal will be slow to infer consent. One type of situation which may give rise to an argument that consent is to be inferred if it is not express is that which arose in *Cowey v Liberian Operations Ltd* (above), where the employee initialled an internal office memorandum announcing changes to the employees' contracts. Because no steps were taken to explain to him that the document affected him and what those changes were, and because the changes conflicted with what he had been told on his appointment by a superior, the court was not prepared even to infer consent from the fact that he had initialled the office memorandum. In *Jones v Associated Tunnelling Co Ltd* (1981), the EAT said:

> If...there is no evidence of any oral discussion varying the original terms, the fact that a statement of terms and conditions containing different terms has been issued cannot be compelling evidence of an express oral variation. The most that can be said is that by continuing to work without objection after receiving such further statement, the employee may have impliedly agreed to the variation recorded in the second statement or be estopped from denying it...[T]o imply an agreement to vary or to raise an estoppel against an employee on the grounds that he has not objected to a false record by the employer of the terms actually agreed is a course which should be adopted with great caution. If the variation related to a matter which has immediate practical application (eg the rate of pay) and the employee continues to work without objection after effect has been given to the variation (eg his pay packet has been reduced) then obviously he may well be taken to have impliedly agreed. But where...the variation has no immediate practical effect the position is not the same...We would not be inclined to imply any assent to a variation from mere failure by the employee to object to the unilateral variation by the employer of the terms of employment contained in a statutory statement.

4.214 It is more likely that the employee will be taken to have consented impliedly where the employer proposes a change to the contract which amounts to a repudiation and the employee makes no response. In *Western Excavating (ECC) Ltd v Sharp* (1978), Lord Denning MR said, at p 226:

> [The employee] must make up his mind soon after the conduct of which he complains: for, if he continues for any length of time without leaving, he will lose his right to treat himself as discharged. He will be regarded as having elected to affirm the contract.

4.215 Thus an employee who continues to work and to accept reduced wages without making any protest is likely to be taken to have affirmed the contract. In *W E Cox Toner (International) Ltd v Crook* (1981), for example, the employee delayed for seven months after repudiatory conduct on the part of his employers. For the first six months, the employee made objections to the repudiatory conduct and it was arguable that during this time he had not affirmed the contract. His solicitors then wrote to his employers saying that he would resign unless the allegations constituting the repudiatory conduct were withdrawn. He resigned a month later. The EAT decided that, in view of the fact that six months had already elapsed, he should be held to have affirmed the contract by continuing to work after this ultimatum. Browne-Wilkinson J pointed out, however, at p 828, that 'mere delay by itself (unaccompanied by any express or implied affirmation of the contract) does not constitute affirmation of the contract; but if it is prolonged it may be evidence of an implied affirmation...' Thus, in the case in question, the employee was held to have affirmed the contract by staying on only one month after the ultimatum, but it is clear that the EAT arrived at this conclusion because of what had happened in the preceding six months. Had the employee stayed on for six months without making any protest, it is highly likely that he would have been taken to have affirmed the contract earlier than the expiry of the six months.

4.216 A court or tribunal will be reluctant to infer that an employee has consented to a variation of his or her contract in circumstances where he or she was faced with the alternative of dismissal. In *Sheet Metal Components Ltd v Plumridge* (1974), Sir John Donaldson said, at p 376:

> It is without doubt the law that there is no dismissal where both parties to a contract of employment freely and voluntarily agree to vary its terms…However, the courts have rightly been slow to find that there has been a consensual variation where an employee has been faced with the alternative of dismissal and where the variation has been adverse to his interests.

In that case, the employees were told that they were to be transferred to the employers' parent company some distance away and they reluctantly agreed. After two months they left. The employment tribunal decided that they had no option to move since, had they refused, they would have been dismissed and that their conditional acceptance of the move did not amount to a consensual variation of their contracts. The NIRC upheld that decision. This decision does not mean, however, that an employee who agrees under threat of dismissal to a change in the terms of his or her contract will never be held to have consented to the variation. Consistently with the principles already considered, the time must come when he or she will be taken to have consented impliedly. In the *Plumridge* case, the employees worked for two months before resigning. Had they remained for six months or more, it is likely that it would have been inferred that they had given their consent to the change.

4.217 A further possibility is that the employee given notice of a change to the contractual terms continues to work subject to the new terms but under protest. This is what happened in *Rigby v Ferodo Ltd* (1988), considered below. The basic principle was set out by Browne-Wilkinson J in *W E Cox Toner (International) Ltd v Crook* (1981). He said, at pp 828–829:

> [I]f the innocent party further performs the contract to a limited extent but at the same time makes it clear that he is reserving his rights to accept the repudiation or is only continuing so as to allow the guilty party to remedy the breach, such further performance does not prejudice his right subsequently to accept the repudiation…

Two possibilities arise from this statement of principle: (1) that the employee continues to work under protest; or (2) that, after a period of working under protest, he or she resigns. An example of the latter situation is to be found in the *Cox Toner* case itself. The employee continued to work for six months under protest after a repudiatory act on the part of his employers and then, having delivered an ultimatum, continued to work for another month. This last act caused the EAT to hold that he had affirmed the contract. Had he left at the end of the six months, the conclusion of the EAT would have been that his actions had not prejudiced his right to accept the repudiation and claim constructive dismissal. An example of the first situation is to be found in *Burdett-Coutts v Hertfordshire County Council* (1984), where the employers unilaterally imposed a reduction in the employees' wages; the employees continued to work under protest and started proceedings for breach of contract. The judge upheld their claim and granted a declaration that the employers were not entitled to impose the variation; he also ordered the employers to pay the arrears of pay. This was a decision at first instance, but is impliedly supported by the later decision of the House of Lords in *Rigby v Ferodo Ltd* (above). The facts in that case were that the employer imposed upon the employee a 5 per cent reduction in his wages because of severe financial pressures. The employee continued to work under protest for the employer at the reduced rate of pay but sued for the difference between the wages to which he was entitled under his contract and the wages actually paid to him. The House of Lords held that he had not accepted a variation in the terms of his contract and upheld his claim. They rejected the argument that the behaviour of the employers brought the contract to an automatic end and that the employee's only remedy was to sue for damages for the period of notice to which he was entitled under that contract (12 weeks). They also refused to hold that there was some sort of implied acceptance on his part of the employers' repudiation.

The requirement of agreement: consent by virtue of a contractual provision

4.218 In addition to the possibility of consent being inferred, there is the possibility that consent will be treated as having been given by virtue of one of the following mechanisms:

(a) a provision in a collective agreement; or

(b) a flexibility clause or similar provision in the employment contract giving the employer power to vary the contract unilaterally.

These mechanisms are in effect methods by which an employer may argue that the employee has abrogated his or her power to refuse to accept a proposed change in the contractual terms.

4.219 In the case of a collective agreement questions will arise as to whether the agreement itself or the relevant provisions were incorporated into individual employees' contracts. This issue was discussed at para 4.68. An example of a case in which a collective agreement was incorporated is *Robertson v British Gas Corporation* (1983), in which the Court of Appeal held that an incentive bonus scheme was incorporated into employees' contracts by virtue of their letters of appointment. Since the scheme gave no power to the employers to terminate it, the Court held that, when they tried to do so, they committed a breach of contract. Kerr LJ said, at p 358:

> It is true that collective agreements... create no legally enforceable obligation between the trade union and the employer. Either side can withdraw. But their terms are in this case incorporated into the individual contracts of employment, and it is only if and when those terms are varied collectively by agreement that the individual contracts of employment will also be varied. If the collective scheme is not varied by agreement, but by some unilateral abrogation or withdrawal or variation to which the other side does not agree, then... the individual contracts of employment remain unaffected.

The Court therefore held the employees to be entitled to the bonus payments to which they were contractually entitled. A similar conclusion was reached in *Miller v Hamworthy Engineering Ltd* (1986), which was considered at para 4.211, above, and *Gibbons v Associated British Ports* (1985), also considered at para 4.211, above. In the latter case, the court held that the terms of a lapsed collective agreement remained part of an individual employee's contract and could only be varied with the agreement of the employee and not unilaterally, as the employers tried to do.

4.220 The case of *Lee v GEC Plessey Telecommunications* (1993) involved the withdrawal of an enhanced redundancy payment scheme. The scheme which was in dispute in this case was introduced as the result of the conclusion of a collective agreement providing for a specified level of enhanced payments. After it had been concluded, the employers issued statutory statements in 1985 expressly incorporating 'general instructions and notices' and provisions of relevant collective agreements into individual contracts. The employers conceded that the collectively agreed terms became incorporated into the individual employees' contracts. A subsequent statement of terms and conditions issued in 1990 made no reference to the incorporation of general instructions and notices, or the provisions of collective agreements into individual contracts. Later, the employers, by means of a general instruction, purported to withdraw the scheme. The two arguments advanced on behalf of the employers before Connell J which are relevant for present purposes were: (1) the introduction of the enhanced terms into individual contracts in 1985 was unsupported by consideration and the terms were not therefore binding; and (2) the employers had reserved to themselves the power to alter individual contracts of employment unilaterally, via general instructions. So far as the first argument was concerned, the employees argued that the consideration for an improvement in terms and conditions in the context of a pay claim is (a) the employees continuing to work; and (b) not continuing with their pay claim so that the employer avoids industrial action and benefits from the services of a known employee. Connell J accepted this argument, saying at p 389:

> Where, in the context of pay negotiations, increased remuneration is paid and employees continue to work as before, there is plainly consideration for the increase by reason of the settlement of the pay claim and the continuation of the same employee in the same employment.

Otherwise, as the employees' counsel argued, a pay increase would be liable to be withdrawn unilaterally by the employer at any time on the basis that there was no consideration for the increased payment.

4.221   In relation to the second argument, Connell J said that the terms (which were conceded by the employers to have become incorporated into individual contracts) remained part of the contracts unless and until specifically removed, either by agreement or by virtue of a specific right found within the contract. He refused, however, to find that there was any agreement as to their removal, saying, at p 390: 'I do not find there (ie in the 1985 statutory statement) clearly set out the right to effect unilateral adverse variations to the contract for which the (employers) contend.' Further, the 1990 statutory statement contained no reference to the incorporation of collective agreements or general instructions and notices. At that point, therefore, there was certainly no right to effect a unilateral variation by means of a general instruction.

4.222   *Lee*'s case bears a superficial resemblance to the more recent case of *Quinn v Calder Industrial Materials Ltd* (1996), considered above at para 4.81, in that both cases involved the withdrawal of an enhanced redundancy payment scheme. The difference between the two cases, however, is that in *Lee* the question was whether the terms of the collective agreement had been incorporated and could be unilaterally revoked, whereas *Quinn* involved a policy unilaterally introduced by the management and the question was whether it had even become incorporated into individual contracts by dint of the fact that it had been acted upon over a period of time. A similar conclusion to that arrived at *Lee* and *Robertson* was reached in *Davies v Hotpoint Ltd* (1994), which involved a provision in a collective agreement incorporated into the employees' contracts. It said: 'Where approved short time is worked as an alternative to redundancy . . . the guarantee shall be reduced accordingly.' The issue was whether the employers could reduce the employees' guaranteed wages unilaterally during a period of short-time working introduced without the approval of the trade unions. The EAT held that they could not, taking the view that the correct construction of the quoted provision was that the approval of the unions on behalf of the employees was required before the employers were entitled to reduce the employees' wages. The EAT said (at p 540) that the use of the term 'approved' indicated 'as a matter of ordinary English, a requirement of the consent or agreement of someone other than the person making the decision to be approved'. They said that the term would be redundant if it meant 'approved by the employer'.

4.223 In *Airlie v City of Edinburgh District Council* (1996), by way of contrast, the EAT had to construe the provisions of an incentive bonus scheme, which were unilaterally varied by the employers without the agreement of the trade unions or the employees. The scheme was contained in a code of practice set out in an appendix to a collective agreement. The EAT upheld the employment tribunal's decision that the code was incorporated into the individual employees' contracts, by virtue of a provision expressly incorporating the collective agreement which itself expressly incorporated the code. They also said that an individual contract may be varied if it includes a provision allowing unilateral variation of its terms, whether such a provision is included directly or by the incorporation of other agreements. Construing the code as a whole, the EAT said that, although there was no express provision giving the employers a power to alter the bonus scheme in a wholesale and comprehensive way, there were a number of provisions which indicated that the employers had the right to control its operation and to make adjustments to it. In view of the code's emphasis of the employers' right to manage and the fact that they were entitled to terminate the whole scheme, the EAT concluded that the proper construction of the provisions was that, after a review of the scheme had been embarked upon, changes could be put into effect without agreement as to the terms. A consideration of the relevant clause of the scheme (para 16) raises the question whether the conclusion arrived at by the EAT is correct and suggests that it would have been open to them to have arrived at the opposite conclusion.

4.224 It is clear from the cases which have been examined in this section that provisions incorporated from collective agreements are unlikely to contain a clause providing for consent to any future changes in the employees' contracts, not least because a trade union would be unlikely to agree to such a provision. Thus, in both *Lee* and *Robertson* the court's conclusion was that the benefit provided for in the contract could not be withdrawn unilaterally; similarly, in *Davies v Hotpoint Ltd*, the EAT said that a unilateral change in the employees' wages could not be effected by the employers. Although the EAT's conclusion in *Airlie* was that the correct construction of the provisions of an incentive bonus scheme taken as a whole permitted the employers to make adjustments to the scheme, despite the absence of an express power to alter the scheme in a wholesale and comprehensive way, a close reading of the provisions of the scheme leads to the view that the EAT's conclusion in this case is arguably wrong.

4.225 As will be seen from a consideration of the relevant decisions, difficult questions of construction are often involved in these cases, whether or not a collective agreement is involved. The cases considered so far have involved provisions incorporated into individual employees' contracts from collective agreements, but the same problems of construction arise in relation to contractual provisions which are not imported from collective agreements. *Cadoux v Central Regional Council* (1986), for example, involved the withdrawal of a non-contributory life assurance scheme. Although the Court of Session held that the provisions relating to the scheme were incorporated into the individual employee's contract, it held that the correct construction of the Rules (which included a rule concerning the scheme) was that any of the rules, including that relating to the scheme, could be varied, altered, or cancelled by the employers. That case also shows that not all provisions which are incorporated into employees' contracts require agreement if they are to be changed. The point about the case, however, is that the relevant contractual provisions did not give the express power to the employer unilaterally to vary the contract; the power arose by virtue of the fact that the rules in question were made unilaterally by the employer and were, therefore, held to be capable of being changed unilaterally.

4.226 An employer may reserve the right to make changes in the employee's contract either by reserving an express power to make variations or by inserting a flexibility clause. In both cases, the court or tribunal is likely to construe the clause against the employer and, particularly in the case of a clause permitting variation, to construe it narrowly. Thus, if the clause states that it will only be invoked in an emergency or in certain circumstances, the court will look to see if the events contemplated by the clause have taken place. An example of an express clause permitting variations in an employment contract is:

> The [employer] reserves the right to make alterations to the contract of employment. Such changes will be notified to you either individually, by an amendment to this handbook or by announcement on Branch Notice Boards.

See *United Association for the Protection of Trade Ltd v Killairn* (EAT/787/84), where the employment tribunal construed the clause as giving the employers a free hand to re-write the contract and to introduce new terms of a substantial or fundamental character. The EAT rejected this view as erroneous and said that the power of unilateral variation was limited to changes of a minor and non-fundamental character. A similar view was taken in *Lee v GEC Plessey Telecommunications* (para 4.220 above), where the judge said that the employers' practice of issuing General Instructions and Notices did not have the effect of varying the employees' contracts.

4.227   An example of a flexibility clause is to be seen in *BPCC Purnell Ltd v Webb* (EAT/ 129/90), where the relevant clause provided:

> Subject only to the Company providing the necessary training there will be total flexibility between all pre-press departments and between NGA Chapels covering specified NGA occupations.

The employee resigned and claimed that he had been constructively dismissed as a result of the company's decision to move him to another department and its subsequent decision that he should work day hours only. The move to another department would have involved the loss of a shift premium because of a change to a different shift system; the subsequent decision would have involved a further loss of pay. The employment tribunal's view of the flexibility clause was that it entitled the company to move the employee to a different department involving different work subject to an implied term that he would not be transferred to a place where his health made it impossible to continue work. They also took the view, however, that the flexibility clause did not entitle the company to change the employee's hours substantially or to reduce his pay and that since both decisions would have involved a loss of pay, the company was in breach of contract. The EAT refused to accept this view, holding that it was not possible to infer the limitations suggested by the tribunal. They went on to say, however, that the cumulative effect of the two decisions was such as to involve a breach of the implied term that employers will not, without reasonable and proper cause, conduct themselves in a manner calculated or likely to destroy or seriously damage the relationship of trust and confidence between employer and employee. See also *Land Securities Trillium Ltd v Thornley* (2005), in which the employment tribunal held that the flexibility clause in the employee's contract of employment did not entitle the employers to change the content of her work so substantially as to change its nature or require her to discharge duties so different from those of her original contract that the effect would be to deskill her. The tribunal concluded that Ms Thornley was therefore entitled to resign and be treated as having been dismissed. The EAT upheld their decision.

4.228   These decisions may be contrasted with that of *White v Reflecting Roadstuds Ltd* (1991), in which the relevant clause was:

> The company reserves the right, when determined by requirements of operational efficiency, to transfer employees to alternative work and it is a condition of employment that they are willing to do so when requested.

The issue in the case was whether the employer's decision to move the employee from one department to another amounted to a breach of his contract which was sufficiently serious as to amount to a repudiation entitling him to resign and claim constructive dismissal within section 95(1)(c). The tribunal decided that this express clause should be qualified by an implied term requiring the employers to act reasonably when deciding to move an employee. They also said that the employers were in breach of contract in causing loss of income to the employee when acting within the scope of the flexibility clause. The EAT rejected this and said that the tribunal had erred and that it was not necessary to give the contract business efficacy to imply the terms. The employee's constructive dismissal claim therefore failed. The EAT distinguished *United Bank Ltd v Akhtar* (1989) on the grounds that the implied term used to qualify an express mobility term was to the effect that the employer should not exercise the discretion conferred by the contract in such a way as to prevent the employee from carrying out his or her part of the contract. In *Prestwick Circuits Ltd v McAndrew* (1990), the Court of Session implied a mobility term into an employee's contract but said that it was subject to the implied qualification that the employee should be given reasonable notice of any transfer.

4.229 A comparison of *Akhtar* and *McAndrew*, on the one hand, with *White*, *Webb*, and *Thornley*, on the other, tends to suggest that the court or tribunal may be more prepared to qualify an express mobility term than a flexibility term, though it must be regarded as unlikely that the EAT in *White* would have treated a substantial change which caused considerable financial loss to the employee as being permitted by the express term, a view confirmed by the attitude of the EAT in *Webb*. What is clear is that, in both types of case, it is unlikely that an employer will be allowed to act in a wholly unfettered way, despite the apparent width of a flexibility or mobility clause, and that the express power will be qualified, where appropriate, by the implication of a term such as that used in *Webb*.

Effect of a unilateral variation

4.230 On the assumptions (a) that the employer has no power to impose a unilateral variation; and (b) that the employee's consent has not been given, the following possibilities arise as a result of an attempt by an employer to impose a variation unilaterally:

(a) the employee may resign and make a claim for breach of contract;

(b) the employee may resign and make a complaint of unfair dismissal or a claim for a redundancy payment based on a 'constructive dismissal';

(c) the employee may make a claim under Part II of the Employment Rights Act 1996 alleging that the unilateral variation amounts to an unlawful deduction of 'wages';

(d) the employee may continue to work for the employer and claim damages for breach of contract or a declaration that the contract has been breached;

(e) the employee may seek an injunction against the employer to restrain the employer from implementing the variation, though it is unlikely that the Court will grant an application.

4.231 In the first situation, where the employee wishes to claim breach of contract, the claim will be that the employer's act amounted to a wrongful repudiation of the contract entitling the employee to claim damages for breach of contract. The breach may be actual or anticipatory. An example of an anticipatory breach is threatened changes to a pattern of shift working or a threat to take an employee off one type of work and transfer him or her to another, as in *BPCC Purnell Ltd v Webb* (EAT/129/90). Another example of an anticipatory breach is to be found in *Harrison v Norwest Holst Group Administration Ltd* (1985), which makes it clear that the employee must also accept a repudiation unequivocally. In the second situation, the first step in a claim will be to persuade the employment tribunal that the resignation in fact amounted to a constructive dismissal within section 95(1)(c) or 136(1)(c) of the Employment Rights Act 1996: see Chapter 9 and, for a recent example, *Land Securities Trillium Ltd v Thornley* (2005), considered at para 4.227 above. The third possibility – of a claim under Part II of the Employment Rights Act 1996 (formerly the Wages Act 1986) – may arise if the variation amounts to the unilateral withdrawal by the employer of a benefit which falls within the definition of 'wages' in section 27 of that Act. Thus, the withdrawal of an incentive bonus scheme or the unilateral introduction of short-time working with a consequent reduction in pay may trigger such a claim: see, for example, *Davies v Hotpoint Ltd* (1994) and *Airlie v City of Edinburgh District Council* (1996), considered at paras 4.222 and 4.223, above, and *International Packaging Corporation (UK) Ltd v Balfour* (2003). In the fourth situation, the employee may choose not to resign but to continue to work under protest and either claim a declaration that the employer has acted unlawfully or claim damages for breach of contract. Examples of the former type of claim are to be found in *Burdett-Coutts v Hertfordshire County Council* (1984), and *Lee v GEC Plessey Telecommunications* (1993); examples of the latter in *Rigby v Ferodo Ltd* (1988). In the latter type of case, it is unlikely that the damages should be limited to the employee's notice period, unless the employer has clearly given him or her notice of termination of employment. Otherwise, the breach will be effectively a continuing breach and the employee's loss of wages will accrue from day to day. So, for example, in *Miller v Hamworthy Engineering Ltd* (1986), the employee was awarded the difference between the amount of salary he would have received had he worked a five-day week and the amount he in fact received during the period of short-time working, which was held by the Court of Appeal to have been introduced in breach of contract. In *Gibbons v Associated British Ports* (1985), the employee was awarded both.

Alternatives to unilateral variation

4.232 An employer who decides not to vary the contract unilaterally, possibly because the consent of all the employees is not forthcoming, is left with little choice but to dismiss them and offer re-engagement on new terms. Clearly this course of action exposes the employer to various claims arising from dismissal, of which the most likely are claims for breach of contract (wrongful dismissal) and unfair dismissal. A claim for a redundancy payment is also possible, though less likely. For a more detailed discussion of these possible claims reference should be made to Chapters 8 and 9. What follows is an outline of the general considerations to be taken into account. An employer who clearly dismisses the employee but offers re-engagement on new terms will not risk claims for damages or an injunction provided that the correct notice of dismissal is given. In other words, a breach of contract action will not be possible. It is essential, however, that the communication to the employee makes clear that the contract is being terminated. In *Burdett–Coutts v Hertfordshire County Council* (1984), for example, the employer's letter gave 12 weeks' notice of the change in the employees' terms and conditions. Kenneth Jones J refused to treat this as a notice of termination of employment and said that it was merely notice of a change in their terms and conditions. A similar argument was advanced in *Rigby v Ferodo Ltd* (1988), but Lord Oliver of Aylmerton said that on the facts of the case the contention could not be sustained, observing, as had the trial judge, that 'the deliberate implementation of a policy preferred over others in order to keep the whole workforce in work cannot sensibly be construed as evincing an intention to terminate the contract of service': see p 33.

4.233 For the purposes of the statutory rights, there must be a dismissal, whether actual or constructive, before the employee may make a claim. The question is whether the unilateral imposition of new terms and conditions without an express dismissal amounts to a dismissal within the meaning of the statutory language. Applying the facts of a case such as *Burdett–Coutts v Hertfordshire County Council*, above, to the statutory provisions, the conclusion which would be likely to follow would be that there was no dismissal and that all an aggrieved employee could do would be to make a claim for damages for breach of contract or for unlawfully deducted wages, but that, since there had been no dismissal within the meaning of section 95 or 136 of the Employment Rights Act 1996, no claim under the unfair dismissal or redundancy payments provisions of the Act would be possible. If, however, the decision of the EAT in *Alcan Extrusions v Yates* (1996) is correct, then an employee affected by a unilateral variation could stay on and continue to work for the employer under protest but could also complain of unfair dismissal or, if appropriate, claim a redundancy payment. In that case, the facts were that a group of employers unilaterally imposed a variation on the employees, in circumstances which amounted to a repudiation of the contract. The employees chose not to resign but to continue to work the new terms under protest; they also complained of unfair dismissal. The EAT upheld the tribunal's decision that there had been a dismissal, taking the view that, where an employer unilaterally imposes radically different terms of employment, there is a dismissal if, on an objective construction of the relevant letters on the part of the employer, there is a withdrawal or removal of the old contract. They refused to accept that the imposition of changes in breach of the employees' contracts must always be characterised as a potential repudiatory breach giving the employee the choice of resigning and claiming constructive dismissal or remaining with the employer. It went on to say that whether the imposition of radically different terms has the effect of withdrawing and terminating the original contract is a question of fact for the tribunal to decide. They based themselves on a previous decision of the EAT in *Hogg v Dover College* (1990).

4.234 Although it is possible to imagine cases where one could say that the employer had terminated the old contract by departing radically from it, in most cases one would have thought that the correct analysis would be that the imposition of different terms amounted to a repudiatory breach by the employers and that it would require clear language to hold that the employer was in fact terminating the old contract and substituting a new contract. In view of the decision of the House of Lords in *Rigby v Ferodo Ltd* (1988) and the remarks of Lord Oliver of Aylmerton, it must be questioned whether the decision in *Alcan Extrusions v Yates* is correct. It may be noted that, although the EAT quoted from Lord Oliver's opinion, it made no attempt to deal with the case or to distinguish it.

4.235 The fact that a dismissal – whether actual or constructive – has been established does not necessarily mean that the dismissal is unfair. It is likely that the reason for the dismissal will be treated as 'some other substantial reason' within section 98(1)(b) of the Employment Rights Act 1996 and the main question will be whether the employer acted reasonably or unreasonably in treating that reason as a sufficient reason for dismissing the employee, within section 98(4): see below. A number of cases have considered the question whether and in what circumstances a dismissal caused by a change of contractual terms or operational changes will be fair, but cases such as *Hollister v National Farmers' Union* (1979) suggest that, provided that the employment tribunal has found that there was a substantial reason justifying dismissal, it is not necessary for the employers to show that the proposed changes are essential. All that needs to be shown is a sound commercial reason for making the changes. See also *RS Components Ltd v Irwin* (1973), which concerned the introduction into the employee's contract of a restraint of trade clause and *Horrigan v Lewisham London Borough Council* (1978), where the EAT regarded as fair the dismissal of an employee who refused to work regular overtime in circumstances where the effect of his refusal was to cause substantial disruption to the Council's services to the public. Similarly, in *St John of God (Care Services) Ltd v Brooks* (1992), in which the employees were dismissed for refusing to accept new, and less favourable, terms of employment, the employment tribunal held the dismissals to be unfair on the basis that the crucial question was whether the terms offered were those which a reasonable employer would offer. The EAT allowed the employers' appeal and said that to look only at the offer would necessarily exclude from consideration everything that happened between the time when the offer was made and the dismissal, and would be contrary to the wording of section 98(4), which points to the dismissal. '(W)hether it was fair or unfair must be judged in the light of the situation when it occurred and not when an earlier step was taken': see p 722.

4.236 In *Catamaran Cruisers Ltd v Williams* (1994) the EAT stressed that, in deciding whether a dismissal of an employee for refusing to accept a contractual change is fair, the tribunal should not only look at the advantage or disadvantage of the new contract from the employee's perspective but should also consider and take into account the benefit to the employer in imposing the changes. To some extent, this is a balancing exercise, though it is clear from this case, as well as from the others already cited, that an employer who can satisfy the tribunal of the need for the changes is likely to be held to have been dismissed fairly. See also *Chubb Fire Security Ltd v Harper* (1983), which involved an employee's refusal to accept a new contract as a sales representative in a new territory and under different pay arrangements, as he foresaw a sizeable drop in his income; again, the dismissal was held to be fair.

4.237 What these decisions suggest is that a dismissal for a refusal to accept new terms and conditions will not be of itself unfair. They are not to be taken, however, as authorities for the notion that an employer need not observe a fair procedure in arriving at the decision to dismiss. Thus, an employer who wishes to avoid the risk of an adverse tribunal decision should ensure that advance warning of the changes is given, together with a suitable lead-in period, that consultation with trade unions takes place, where appropriate, and that alternatives to dismissal have been considered, such as alternative jobs or locations, and that steps have been taken to accommodate an employee's reasonable grounds for refusing to agree to the change.

4.238 If the employee makes a claim for a redundancy payment, the main issues are likely to be (i) whether an employee who is subject to a flexibility clause can be said to be redundant; and (ii) whether an employee who refuses new terms and conditions of employment will be held to have unreasonably refused a suitable offer and thus be disentitled by section 141 of the 1996 Act from receiving a redundancy payment. So far as the first issue is concerned, it is clear from the case of *Johnson v Peabody Trust* (1996) that in looking to see whether an employee is redundant within the definition in section 139(1) an employment tribunal should look at the employee's contract in a commonsense manner to see what the basic task is that the employee was employed to do. In that case, the employee was employed as a roofer but was also subject to a flexibility clause stating: 'Where possible, tradespersons will be expected to carry out multi-trade operations.' By the time he was made redundant he was spending more time on multi-trade operations than on roofing. The EAT upheld the tribunal's decision that he was redundant and pointed out that otherwise an employer would never be able to establish that an employee subject to a flexibility clause was redundant unless it was possible to establish that there was a redundancy situation in every single trade encompassed by the flexibility clause. See also *Birds Eye Walls Ltd v Austin* (EAT/581/86), in which a similar conclusion was reached.

4.239 Cases such as the above are consistent with the general tenor of cases involving changes by employers of their employees' terms and conditions of employment. In *Lesney Products & Co Ltd v Nolan* (1981) Lord Denning stressed that 'it is important that nothing should be done to impair the ability of employers to reorganise their workforce and their terms and conditions of work so as to improve efficiency'. Similarly, in *Johnson v Nottinghamshire Combined Police Authority* (1974), he said, at p 176:

> [A]n employer is entitled to reorganise his business so as to improve its efficiency and, in doing so, to propose to his staff a change in the terms and conditions of their employment: and to dispense with their services if they do not agree. Such a change does not automatically give the staff a right to a redundancy payment. It only does so if the change in the terms and conditions is due to a redundancy situation.

4.240 So far as the second issue mentioned in para 4.238 is concerned, it is unlikely that an employee offered new terms and conditions involving a reduction in pay will be held to have been made a suitable offer of alternative employment and still less likely that his or her refusal would be considered reasonable; see *Taylor v Kent County Council* (1969).

Variations in the context of a transfer of an undertaking

4.241 The question which arises in the context of variations of contract concerns the extent, if any, to which the rules considered in this chapter are affected by the Transfer of Undertakings (Protection of Employment) Regulations 2006. The Regulations are considered in detail in Chapter 11, to which reference should be made. In the present context, the regulations which are relevant are Regulation 4 and, to a lesser extent, Regulation 7. The effect of the Regulations varies according to whether the employee is transferred without being dismissed or whether the employee is dismissed by the transferor employer with the termination payments to which he or she is entitled and is then re-employed by the transferee employer on different terms and conditions.

4.242   If the employee is transferred without being dismissed any purported variation of the contract will be void if the sole or main reason for the variation is the transfer itself or a reason connected with the transfer: see Regulation 4(4). If the reason for the variation is an economic, technical, or organisational reason entailing changes in the workforce, the variation will not be void. This provision gives effect to the Court of Appeal decision in *Crédit Suisse First Boston (Europe) Ltd v Lister* (1998), in which the Court of Appeal held that a variation of the employee's contract was made unenforceable by virtue of Regulation 5(1) of the 1981 Regulations. The facts were that CSFB bought part of an undertaking owned by BZW (the transferor) and entered into negotiations with the transferring employees, including L. He agreed, *inter alia*, to a restrictive covenant governing working for a competitor. When CSFB tried to enforce this, the Court of Appeal held that Regulation 5(1) made the agreement unenforceable on the grounds that he was not entitled to waive his rights under his contract with BZW even though under his new contract viewed as a whole he was better off than under his contract with BZW. The Court said that, since the transferor employer could not have prevented the employee from working for a competitor after the termination of his employment, the transferee could not do so either. It was irrelevant that the new contract also gave the employee a compensating benefit in return for agreeing to the imposition of the restriction. The decision followed the decision of the ECJ in *Foreningen af Arbedsledere I Danmark v Daddy's Dance Hall* (1988). It would seem that Regulation 4(4) would not affect any changes taking place some time after the transfer and unconnected with the transfer.

4.243   In the case of an employee dismissed by the transferor and re-engaged on different terms by the transferee, the position will be governed by the House of Lords' decision in *Wilson v St Helens Borough Council* and *Meade v British Fuels Ltd* (1998). If an employee is dismissed by the transferor and re-engaged by the transferee, he or she will not be able to insist on the observance by the transferee of his or her previous terms or conditions and will be bound by the terms and conditions agreed with the transferee.

Illegal contracts of employment

4.244   A contract of employment is illegal either if it is prohibited by statute or if its objects are forbidden by the common law on the grounds of public policy. The most significant impact which the doctrine of illegality has had upon this area of the law is in relation to contracts which involve the commission of a fraud on the Inland Revenue, and which may be made void at common law as being contrary to public policy. An example is *Miller v Karlinski* (1945), where the employee was employed under a contract which provided that he should receive a salary of £10 per week and should also recover from the employer the amount of income tax payable on that salary, by including it in an account for travelling expenses. Du Parcq LJ said, at p 86: 'I find it impossible to say that, where a man agrees to work and to be paid according to a scheme devised...so as to defraud the revenue, the whole agreement is not an illegal agreement which the courts will not enforce.' A similar view was taken by the Court of Appeal in *Napier v National Business Agency Ltd* (1951).

4.245 Illegal contracts fall into two distinct categories. In the first category are contracts which are illegal per se, or which cannot be performed by one or both of the parties otherwise than illegally, for example where employer and employee agree to defraud the Revenue. In such cases the state of knowledge of the parties is irrelevant and their ignorance of the illegality will not save them from the consequences: see *Miller v Karlinski* (1945), *Corby v Morrison* (1980), and *Newland v Simons & Willer (Hairdressers) Ltd* (1981). In these cases, as Lord Coulsfield explained in *Salvesen v Simons* (1994), the principle is that 'if a party knew what was being done, it is irrelevant that he did not know that it was illegal'. In this last case, the arrangement between the employee and his employer was that part of his wages should be paid as a management fee to a business operated by him and his wife in partnership. The EAT held that this arrangement involved a misrepresentation to the Inland Revenue in that there was no proper basis for the payment of a management fee to the partnership, since the payment was not for services provided but was a diversion of the employee's remuneration; to that extent it was a fraud on the Revenue. The employee's contract was therefore unenforceable. On the other hand, if the payments in question are irregular the employee's contract will not necessarily be rendered illegal: see *Annandale Engineering v Samson* (1994). It should be noted, however, that an arrangement will not necessarily be illegal if it is entered into in good faith and is a proper method of reducing tax, which is open and above board and either has been or will be disclosed to the Inland Revenue: see *Lightfoot v D & J Sporting Ltd* (1996).

4.246 In the second category are contracts which are ex facie legal but illegally performed; for example, where the employer defrauds the Revenue by failure to deduct tax from the employee's wages, or where performance of the contract by the employee involves acts for sexually immoral purposes, as in *Coral Leisure Group Ltd v Barnet* (1981), the facts of which were briefly that the employee's contract involved him in obtaining prostitutes for customers of his employers. In such cases, the employee's state of mind will be decisive. In *Newland v Simons and Willer (Hairdressers) Ltd* (1981) May J said:

> [W]here both employer and employee knowingly commit an illegality by way of a fraud on the revenue in the payment and receipt of remuneration..., which is an essential part of such a contract,...there can be doubt that this does turn it into a contract that is prohibited by statute or common law, and consequently the employee is precluded from enforcing any rights [he or] she might otherwise have against [the] employer.

4.247 In *Coral Leisure Group Ltd v Barnet* (1981) Browne-Wilkinson J drew a distinction between '(a) cases in which there is a contractual obligation to do an act which is unlawful and (b) cases where the contractual obligations are capable of being performed lawfully and were initially intended so to be performed, but which have in fact been performed by unlawful means'. In the former case, if it is possible to sever or separate the tainted contractual obligations from the untainted, the whole contract will not be unenforceable. In the latter case, the fact that the employee in the course of his or her employment has committed an unlawful or immoral act will not by itself prevent him or her from enforcing the contract unless the contract is entered into for the purpose of doing the unlawful or immoral act or the contract itself (as opposed to the mode of its performance) is prohibited by law; see also the later Court of Appeal decision in *Hewcastle Catering Ltd v Ahmed* (1992).

4.248 The cases set out above were subjected to a detailed analysis by Peter Gibson LJ in *Hall v Woolston Hall Leisure Ltd* (2001). The complaint in the case was one of sex discrimination, not of unfair dismissal, but, in the course of his judgment, Peter Gibson LJ set out clearly and helpfully the principles discussed in the antecedent case law. He summed up his views as follows:

> In cases where the contract of employment is neither entered into for an illegal purpose nor prohibited by statute, the illegal performance of the contract will not render the contract unenforceable unless in addition to knowledge of the facts which make the performance illegal the employee actively participates in the illegal performance. It is a question of fact in each case whether there has been a sufficient degree of participation by the employee.

This approach was followed by the Court of Appeal in the later case of *Wheeler v Quality Deep Ltd (trading as Thai Royale Restaurant)* (2005). The case involved an employee of Thai origin and with a limited knowledge of English and of the tax and national insurance provisions applicable in the United Kingdom. But for these circumstances, the Court of Appeal said that she might well not have succeeded.

4.249 The cases discussed in the preceding paragraphs were considered by the Court of Appeal in *Colen v Cebrian (UK) Ltd* (2004). The case involved payment of a commission which, according to the employer's contention, was made in such a way as to defraud the Inland Revenue. The Court of Appeal said that a contract which is lawful at its inception and was intended to be lawfully performed does not automatically become unlawful and unenforceable by any act of illegal performance. Waller LJ reviewed the cases mentioned above and said:

> [They] demonstrate that an analysis needs to be done as to what the party's intentions were from time to time. If the contract was unlawful at its formation or if there was an intention to perform the contract unlawfully as at the date of the contract, then the contract will be unenforceable. If at the date of the contract the contract was perfectly lawful and it was intended to perform it lawfully, the effect of some act of illegal performance is not automatically to render the contract unenforceable. If the contract is ultimately performed illegally and the party seeking to enforce takes part in the illegality, that *may* render the contract unenforceable at his instigation. But not every act of illegality in performance, even participated in by the enforcer, will have that effect. If the person seeking to enforce the contract has to rely on his illegal action in order to succeed then the court will not assist him. But if he does not have to do so, then . . . the question is whether the method of performance chosen and the degree of participation in that illegal performance is such as to 'turn the contract into an illegal contract' . . .

4.250   As can be seen from this discussion of the case-law, most of the cases in which illegality has been contended for have been cases which involved a method of payment of wages to an employee involving a fraud on the Inland Revenue. Another type of case which should be considered, however, is one where the employee enters employment whilst an illegal immigrant. Few cases have considered this question and those that have have done so fairly cursorily. In *Sharma v Hindu Temple* (EAT/253/90) the facts were that the employee was employed by the temple at a time when he had no visa relating to his stay in the United Kingdom or employment here. The employment tribunal dismissed his complaint on the ground of illegality. The EAT held that the tribunal had made insufficient findings of fact, particularly as to whether the employee was knowingly in breach of the conditions of his leave to enter the country, and remitted the case for a rehearing. In the course of the judgment, Wood J quoted from the judgment of Devlin J in *St John Shipping Corporation v Joseph Rank Ltd* (1957):

> [A] contract which is entered into with the object of committing an illegal act is unenforceable. The application of this principle depends upon proof of the intent, at the time when the contract was made, to break the law; if the intent is mutual the contract is not enforceable at all, and, if unilateral, it is unenforceable at the suit of the party who is proved to have it.

Wood J went on to say that if the employee was held knowingly to be in breach of the condition of his leave, the contract would be illegal in its formation.

4.251 This approach was followed by the EAT in the later case of *Bamgbose v The Royal Star and Garter Home*: EAT/841/95. It follows from the present state of the law that, if an employee is employed under a contract of employment tainted with illegality, no week of employment under that contract will count in computing continuous employment: see Chapter 9, for a discussion of continuity of employment.

The illegality or otherwise of a contract does not, however, affect the employment tribunal's jurisdiction to hear a case, but only concerns the parties' right to enforce the contract: see *Wilkinson v Lugg* (1990).

FURTHER READING

Deakin, S, & Morris, G, *Labour Law* (4th ed, 2005) Hart (chapters 3 & 4).

Smith, I, & Thomas, G, *Smith & Wood's Employment Law* (9th ed, 2007) Oxford University Press (chapters 3 & 4).

ARTICLES

Bowers, J, & Lewis, J, (2005) 'Recent Cases: Non-Economic Damage in Unfair Dismissal Cases: What's Left After Dunnachie?', *Industrial Law Journal*, Vol 34, pp 83–95.

Cabrelli, D, (2004) 'Post-Termination Covenants in the Spotlight Again', *Industrial Law Journal,* Vol 33, pp 167–179.

Cabrelli, D, (2005) 'The Implied Duty of Mutual Trust and Confidence: An Emerging Overarching Principle?', *Industrial Law Journal*, Vol 34, pp 284–307.

Davidov, G, (2005) 'Who is a Worker?', *Industrial Law Journal*, Vol 34, pp 57–71.

Lindsay, J, (2001) 'The Implied Term of Trust and Confidence', *Industrial Law Journal*, Vol 30, pp 1–18.

Mogridge, C, (1981) 'Illegal Employment Contracts: Loss of Statutory Protection', *Industrial Law Journal*, Vol 10, pp 23 et seq.

SELF-TEST QUESTIONS

1 Keith was registered with the Sorted Employment Agency. For seven years he has been assigned to Bullet Ltd, to work as a cleaner. Under the terms of his contract

with the Agency he agreed to cooperate with the client company to which he was assigned and to obey all reasonable orders. He was obliged to submit time sheets to the Agency at the end of every week to indicate the number of hours he had worked for Bullet Ltd during the preceding week and he was subject to any disciplinary measures the Agency might deem to be necessary. Two years ago Bullet Ltd redeployed Keith as a member of their catering staff 'as required', which resulted in his wages, still paid through Sorted Employment Agency, being increased.

Keith wishes to know if he has an employer and who it may be.

2 Explain the House of Lords decision in *Johnson v Unisys* (2001) and its implications for the implied term of mutual trust and confidence.

3 'Implied terms are dangerous in the hands of employers.' Discuss.

4 Illegal contracts should be enforceable, where they protect employees from bad employers. Put the case for or against.

5

Discrimination Law

SUMMARY

Discrimination law is assuming ever greater significance: in the employment field, this growth, whether from case law or legislation, is rapid. Recent changes to the law, which are outlined here, have been various and, often, immensely significant. This chapter assesses the prohibited grounds of discrimination: gender and transsexualism; race; disability; sexual orientation; religion or belief; and (from 1 October 2006) age. The significant recent amendments to the law in this field are considered, together with issues arising from the case law. The influence and importance of European Community law is identified at relevant points, together with the amendments introduced in domestic law, whether as a result of EC law or Government policy. The main forms of discrimination considered in each section are: direct; indirect; harassment; and victimization. The key areas of discrimination law examined are:

- sex and race discrimination: direct; indirect; harassment; victimisation; segregation (race only);
- disability discrimination;
- transsexualism;
- sexual orientation; religion or belief; age: the Employment Equality Regulations;
- age.

Introduction – the prohibited grounds of discrimination: sex and transsexualism; race; disability; sexual orientation; religion or belief; age

5.1 In the UK, there are a number of grounds on which discrimination is prohibited. They are sex (including sexual orientation and a change of sex, ie transsexualism), race, disability, religion or belief and, from 1 October 2006, age. Until recently, there were only three statutes covering discrimination: the Sex Discrimination Act 1975 (the 'SDA'), together with the Equal Pay Act 1970 (the 'EqPA'), which is considered in Chapter 6, comprising the legislation on sex discrimination (and discrimination on the ground of marital status), and the Race Relations Act 1976 (the 'RRA') covering discrimination on the ground of race. From 19 July 2003, the RRA has been amended to provide, *inter alia*, an extended definition of indirect discrimination on the grounds of race, ethnic or national origin (s 1(1), (1A), and a definition of harassment (s 3A)) (see the Race Relations Act 1976 (Amendment) Regulations 2003 SI 2003/1626 which introduced these and other changes, which were required to give effect to Council Directive 2000/43 of 29 June 2000 (the 'Race Directive')).

5.2 The SDA, too, has been significantly amended recently, as required by the Equal Treatment Framework Directive (Directive 2002/73/EC) (the 'ETFD'). Important changes have been made, *inter alia*, to the definition of indirect discrimination in the fields of employment and vocational training, and the inclusion of a separate ground of discrimination in the form of (i) harassment on the ground of sex; and (ii) harassment of a sexual nature. These amendments were introduced by the Employment Equality (Sex Discrimination) Regulations 2005 (SI 2005/2467) as from 1 October 2005. The 2005 Regulations were subsequently challenged successfully in the case of case of *Equal Opportunities Commission v DTI* (2007) EWHC 483 (Admin) (QBD) on 12 March 2007, (2007) ICR 1234, (2007) IRLR 327. Consequently, amendments were introduced with effect from 6 April 2008 to the definition of 'harassment' in section 4A of the SDA by the Sex Discrimination Act 1975 (Amendment) Regulations 2008 (SI 2008/656): under the amendment, it is necessary to establish that the harassing conduct is associated with sex, not caused by it. The 2008 Regulations also amended sections 3A (so that in pregnancy/maternity discrimination claims, there is no requirement for a comparator) and 6A (in general, there must be no differences between contractual benefits during compulsory, ordinary, and additional maternity leave).

5.3 Discrimination on the ground of disability was made unlawful (at least, in the field of employment) by the Disability Discrimination Act 1995, the employment provisions of which came into force on 2 December 1996. We will be considering these statutes from the employment law perspective, although it should be remembered that the scope of the SDA, RRA, and DDA is wider: these statutes also cover, for example, education and the provision of goods, services, and facilities.

5.4 Discrimination against transsexuals, which is discussed below, was initially rendered unlawful through a ruling of the European Court of Justice (the 'ECJ') in the case of *P v S and Cornwall County Council* (1996), but was put on a statutory footing from 1 May 1999 by the Sex Discrimination (Gender Reassignment) Regulations 1999 (SI 1999/1102), which amended the SDA by the insertion of section 2A (discrimination on the grounds of gender reassignment). Discrimination on the ground of sexual orientation and religion or belief was made unlawful in December 2003 by regulations implementing provisions of the Equal Treatment Framework Directive 2000 (Directive 2000/78/EC) (the 'ETFD'). These grounds of discrimination are discussed below.

5.5 The ETFD requires Member States to introduce legislation making age discrimination unlawful by 2006. The draft Employment Equality (Age) Regulations 2006, which implement this strand of the ETFD, were laid before Parliament on 9 March 2006. The Regulations came into force on 1 October 2006. The main provisions of the Regulations are considered below.

Gender equality duty

5.6 The Equality Act 2006, which received Royal Assent in February 2006, introduced new legal obligations on public authorities in respect of sex discrimination. A new section 21A is inserted into the SDA whereby it is unlawful for a public authority exercising a function to do any act that constitutes discrimination or harassment under the SDA. From April 2007, those authorities also have a gender equality duty (in addition to the race equality duty introduced by the Race Relations (Amendment) Act 2000, and the disability equality duty introduced by the Disability Discrimination Act 2005). The EOC at the time called this 'the most significant change in gender equality legislation for thirty years'. Section 84 inserts a new section 76A into the SDA to provide that public authorities shall, in carrying out their functions, have due regard to the need to perform a 'general duty' to eliminate unlawful discrimination and harassment and promote equality of opportunity between men and women. The Sex Discrimination Act 1975 (Public Authorities) (Statutory Duties) Order 2006, SI 2930, sets out the detail and required listed public authorities to prepare a 'Gender Equality Scheme' by 30 April 2007. In November 2006 the EOC issued a (draft) Gender Equality EOC Code of Practice (England and Wales), November 2006 for local authorities.

5.7 The measures summarised above go some way to fulfilling the obligation provided for by Article 2(5) in Directive 76/207 that requires Member States to 'encourage, in accordance with national law, collective agreements in practice, employers and those responsible for access to vocational training to take measures to prevent all forms of discrimination on grounds of sex, in particular harassment and sexual harassment in the workplace'. Article 8b(1) sets out various ways in which equality can be achieved, e.g., monitoring, codes of conduct, research, and under Article 8b(3) to do so in a 'planned, systematic way', with the provision of information and implementation of improvement measures. For employers, taking 'preventive *measures*' against discrimination, so-called 'equality plans' at an enterprise level are to be 'encouraged'.

Sex and race discrimination

5.8 There are distinct types of discrimination under both the SDA and the RRA, bearing similar definitions: direct discrimination; indirect discrimination; harassment; victimisation; and (under the RRA only) segregation. It is important to stress the fact that direct discrimination may not be justified under the SDA or the RRA, whereas indirect discrimination may be. The SDA and the RRA will be discussed together in this chapter, as many of the concepts and definitions used in these statutes are similar.

5.9 In terms of race discrimination, there have been two previous statutes, both of them largely ineffective: the Race Relations Act 1965 and the Race Relations Act 1968. The former, which was not applicable in the employment field, established the Race Relations Board, with powers of investigation and conciliation, while the latter prohibited discrimination in employment but was not really effective: there was no individual right of complaint to a tribunal. Complaints first had to be made to the Race Relations Board, which was the only body allowed to take proceedings concerning such complaints. In terms of eliminating race discrimination, these statutes failed.

Marital status and civil partners

5.10 The SDA makes unlawful discrimination (both direct and indirect) against married persons and civil partners in respect of employment (SDA, s 3(1), (2)). The provision relating to civil partners was inserted into the SDA by the Civil Partnerships Act 2004 (s 251(1), (2) as from 5 December 2005. In terms of discrimination on the ground of marital status, see the case of *Chief Constable of Bedfordshire Constabulary v Graham* (2002), EAT). However, under EU law, discrimination is prohibited against a person on grounds of 'marital or family status' (Equal Treatment Directive (Directive 76/207, Art 2(1)), which is wide enough to cover single as well as married persons.

Changes made to the SDA in 2005 and 2008

5.11 Significant changes have been made to the SDA as from 1 October 2005. These amendments implement the changes required by Equal Treatment Framework Directive (Directive 2002/73/EC) (see the Employment Equality (Sex Discrimination) Regulations 2005 (SI 2005/2467)). They include a new definition of indirect discrimination and a separate definition of harassment on the ground of sex and harassment of a sexual nature. The changes, which apply to employment and vocational training, align the SDA with the other legislation concerning unlawful discrimination in these fields. As noted above, significant changes were made to the SDA, particularly the definition of harassment (SDA, s 4A) with effect from 6 April 2008 by the Sex Discrimination Act 1975 (Amendment) Regulations 2008, SI 2008/656) as a result of the High Court's decision in *Equal Opportunities Commission v DTI* (2007) EWHC 483 (Admin) (QBD) on 12 March 2007, (2007) ICR 1234, (2007) IRLR 327. Consequential amendments were also made to SDA sections 3A and 6A (with effect from 6 April 2008).

Scope of the SDA and RRA

5.12 The territorial scope of both statutes is Great Britain (SDA, s 10; RRA s 8). The statutes do not apply where a person is employed wholly outside Great Britain. It should be noted that the SDA applies to men as well as women (SDA, s 2). Both statutes apply to: job applicants, employees and those working under 'a contract personally to execute any work or labour', ie independent contractors (SDA, ss 6 and 82; RRA, ss 4 and 78); agency workers (sometimes called 'contract workers'), who are protected from discrimination by both employment agencies and principals: SDA ss 9 and 15; RRA, ss 7 and 14, and see, for example, *Harrods Ltd v Remick* (1998). Former employees may claim for post-termination discrimination (see SDA, s 20A; RRA, s 27A). The range of possible respondents is wide and includes: employers; trade unions (SDA, s 12; RRA, s 11); qualification bodies for trades or professions (such as the Law Society) (SDA, s 13; RRA, s 12).

The prohibited grounds: sex, race, colour, nationality, ethnic or national origin

5.13 As has been mentioned above, the SDA extends to discrimination on grounds of sex, marital status, and civil partnership (ie it protects married persons and civil partners, as well as against discrimination that is gender-based). The RRA prohibits discrimination against a person on grounds of colour, race, nationality, and ethnic or national origin, although there is some difficulty determining what these terms mean.

5.14 In the well-known RRA case of *Mandla v Dowell Lee* (1983), HL, concerning a Sikh boy who was refused entrance to a private school because he could not comply with the school's uniform requirements as he wore a turban, the House of Lords defined 'ethnic group'. To be considered an ethnic group, the group had to regard itself, and be regarded by others, as a distinct community by virtue of certain characteristics. Two were essential: a long, shared history, and a cultural tradition of its own. Other relevant characteristics include either a common geographical origin or descent from a small number of common ancestors; a common language, literature, or religion; and/or a sense of being a minority (or oppressed or dominant) group. The House of Lords held, applying these tests, that Sikhs were indeed a distinct racial group.

5.15 Using these criteria, the courts have held that Jews (*Seide v Gillette Industries* (1980) and gypsies (*CRE v Dutton* (1989)) are ethnic groups but Rastafarians are not (*Crown Suppliers v Dawkins* (1993).

5.16 Nationality is not the same as national origins, so the English, Scots, and Welsh have different national origins, but the same nationality, ie British (*Northern Joint Police Board v Power* (1997)).

The Race Directive (Directive 2000/43/EC)

5.17 The Race Directive, which was issued to combat discrimination across a number of grounds, was implemented by the Race Relations Act 1976 (Amendment) Regulations 2000. Unfortunately, the scope of the Directive and that of the RRA is not the same: the Directive concerns discrimination on the ground of race, or ethnic or national origin, while the RRA extends to discrimination on the grounds of colour or nationality. Therefore, although the 2003 Regulations amend the RRA in a number of respects, these amendments do not apply to discrimination on the grounds of colour or nationality, which is unsatisfactory and seems to make the application of the RRA even more complex. However, it may be that the omission of 'colour' and 'nationality' will not present too many difficulties to complainants, on the basis that these two terms will usually be linked with race.

The burden of proof

5.18 It may be very difficult for a complainant under the SDA or the RRA to prove his or her case. The Burden of Proof Directive (Directive 97/80/EC) was intended to address this problem by changing the burden of proof in sex discrimination cases (it is sometimes erroneously stated that the Directive reverses the burden of proof, which it does not). The Sex Discrimination (Indirect Discrimination and Burden of Proof) Regulations 2001 implement the Directive by inserting a new section in the SDA – section 63A. This means that, if the complainant proves facts from which the ET could conclude, in the absence of an adequate explanation, that the respondent committed an act of discrimination against them, the ET will uphold the complaint, unless the respondent proves that he did not commit it. The same burden of proof provision applies in the RRA (s 54A). Although this might appear to be a significant change in the law, courts and tribunals had reached a similar position, ie they would take adverse inferences once the complainant had established a prima facie case (see *King v Great Britain China Centre* (1991), CA).

5.19 In *King v Great Britain-China Centre* CA [1991] IRLR 513, a case on the RRA (although it is generally accepted that the principles also apply to sex discrimination claims), Neill LJ said on how the burden of proof provision operates:

1. It is for the applicant who complains of [racial] discrimination to make out his or her case. Thus if the applicant does not prove the case on the balance of probabilities he or she will fail.

2. It is important to bear in mind that it is unusual to find direct evidence of [racial] discrimination. Few employers will be prepared to admit such discrimination even to themselves. In some cases the discrimination will not be ill-intentioned but merely based on an assumption that 'he or she would not have fitted in'.

3. The outcome of the case will therefore usually depend on what inferences it is proper to draw from the primary facts found by the tribunal. These inferences can include, in appropriate cases, any inferences that it is just and equitable to draw in accordance with [section 65(2)(b) of the Act of 1976] from an evasive or equivocal reply to a questionnaire.

4. Though there will be some cases where, for example, the non-selection of the applicant for a post or for promotion is clearly not on racial grounds, a finding of discrimination and a finding of a difference in race will often point to the possibility of racial discrimination. In such circumstances the tribunal will look to the employer for an explanation. If no explanation is then put forward or if the tribunal considers the explanation to be inadequate or unsatisfactory it will be legitimate for the tribunal to infer that the discrimination was on racial grounds.

(at p 518 of the IRLR report)

5.20 The EAT set out guidelines on how the burden of proof provisions should be applied in a sex discrimination case, *Barton v Investec Henderson Crosthwaite Securities Ltd*

(2003). The *Barton* guidelines have been approved by the Court of Appeal (with slight amendments) in *Igen Ltd and ors v Wong* (2005), CA.

5.21   In *Oyarce v Cheshire County Council* (2008), the Court of Appeal held that the reversal of the burden of proof does not apply to victimisation claims under Race Relations Act 1976, s 2. The 'reversal of the burden of proof' provision (Race Relations Act 1976 s 54A) applies only to direct and indirect discrimination on the grounds of race or ethnic or national origins and not to racial victimisation.

5.22   In *Appiah & Anor v Bishop Douglass Roman Catholic High School* (2007), CA and *Atabo v Kings College London & Ors* (2007), the Court of Appeal confirmed that if, after considering all the evidence, a court or tribunal comes to the conclusion that the facts do not establish a prima facie case of a difference in treatment on racial grounds, the burden of proof is not transferred. For the burden of proof to shift so that an employer is assumed to have committed discrimination unless he proves to the contrary, the employee must first show facts from which 'a reasonable tribunal could properly conclude' that there has been unlawful discrimination. It would be wrong to interpret the SDA 1975 section 63A to mean that the burden of proof shifts just because it is possible that a tribunal could make a finding of unlawful discrimination.

5.23   Note also that in *Okonu v G4S Security Services*, the EAT held that the 'reversal of the burden of proof' provisions in RRA s 54A apply to discrimination on grounds of race, ethnic, and national origin, but not to discrimination on grounds of colour or nationality.

5.24   In *Kuzel v Roche Products Ltd* (2008) on 17 April 2008, the Court of Appeal held that if a claim is for unfair dismissal under the Employment Rights Act 1996 then ERA 1996, s 98 applies in the normal way. The 'reversal of the burden' of proof rules applicable in the discrimination statutes are not relevant or necessary.

Direct discrimination

5.25   Direct discrimination is defined in the SDA and RRA as less favourable treatment on the ground of (under the SDA) sex, marital status, civil partnership, or gender reassignment (SDA, s 1(1)(a), 2A(1)(a)) and 3), or on racial grounds (RRA, s 1(1)(a)). (Gender reassignment is considered under the section on transsexualism below.) (For the purposes of the employment parts of the RRA, ie Part II, the definition of indirect discrimination differs from that for the other parts of the statute.) Direct discrimination is the most overt and explicit form of discrimination.

Direct discrimination and motive

5.26 The motive of the discriminator is irrelevant. In *James v Eastleigh Borough Council* (1990), which is not an employment case, the respondent council operated a concession to old age pensioners wishing to use its swimming pool, who were allowed entry free of charge. Others had to pay 35p. Both Mr and Mrs James were 61. However, Mrs James gained free entry, since the state pensionable age was 60 for women, while Mr James did not, because the pensionable age for men was 65. The council had no intention to discriminate in this case (in fact, just the opposite!) but the House of Lords held that the test in direct discrimination is objective: the 'but for' test was applied, ie but for the complainant's sex, would they have been treated less favourably. The answer here was 'no', so there had been direct discrimination. The intention or motive of the discriminator was irrelevant to that issue. The case also establishes that the application of a discriminatory criterion constitutes direct discrimination.

5.27 The employer's motive in *Ministry of Defence v Jeremiah* (1979) was also held to be irrelevant. In that case, the employer required men to work in a colour-bursting shop producing munitions, which was dirty work, but the women employees were not required to do so on the ground that it was necessary to shower after this work, which would ruin the women's hairdos. The men were paid an extra sum for this uncongenial work. They claimed that this was sex discrimination. The Court of Appeal held that a discriminator cannot buy the right to discriminate and that this was direct discrimination.

Comparators

5.28 Less favourable treatment requires a comparison to be carried out. The complainant must be treated less favourably than the way the employer treats *or would treat* a man (under the SDA) or a person not of the same race (under the RRA) (emphasis added). This means that an actual or a hypothetical comparator may be used. This requirement of finding an appropriate comparator has caused particular problems when considering pregnancy-related discrimination claims (see below). Pregnancy being a condition only experienced by females, no male comparator (either actual or hypothetical) is required where the woman claims sex discrimination for a reason related to her pregnancy or maternity. As from 1 October 2005, there are specific provisions relating to discrimination on the ground of pregnancy and maternity leave (see the SDA, s 3A, and the cases of *Dekker* and *Webb*, discussed below, paras 5.43 and 5.44). In direct discrimination claims, the less favourable treatment alone (in comparison to the treatment accorded to an actual or hypothetical comparator) is sufficient to found a claim, since it is clearly a detriment. However, it should be noted that in indirect discrimination cases in the employment field, the complainant must go on to show that they have been put at a particular disadvantage when compared to a comparator (SDA, s 1(2)(b); RRA, s 1(1A)), which cannot be shown to be a proportionate means of achieving a legitimate aim.

Dress codes

5.29 A number of cases have involved the application of rules concerning dress codes on employees. Clearly, if such codes are to be imposed on male and female employees, they would have to be different, to take into account the difference in sex and in compliance with convention. However, generally the courts have found that, provided such codes are applied in an even-handed way, such dress codes are not contrary to the SDA (although some interesting human rights points are raised on this issue). In *Smith v Safeway plc* (1996), a male delicatessen assistant wore his long hair in a ponytail. The dress code required men to wear their hair shorter, whereas women were allowed to have long hair provided it was tied back. The Court of Appeal held that there was no sex discrimination in this case. Such codes were not discriminatory provided they merely imposed general rules (with relevant changes to account for the difference in sex) enforcing a conventional or smart appearance: the question was whether, taken as a whole, there was less favourable treatment (see also *Schmidt v Austicks Bookshop* (1978), and *McConomy v Croft Inns* (1992)).

Harassment

5.30 Sexual and racial harassment constitutes direct discrimination, being a form of detriment based on the prohibited grounds. The Race Directive contains provisions relating to harassment, and changes have been made to the RRA by the Race Relations Act 1976 (Amendment) Regulations 2003 (SI 2003/1626) which insert a definition of harassment into the RRA. The SDA has also been amended (by the insertion of a new section, s 4A), so that it now contains an express reference to harassment as a discrete ground of discrimination (as is required by the Equal Treatment Amendment Directive (Directive 2002/73/EC). However, the harassment provisions in section 4A of the SDA were challenged (together with other challenges concerning pregnancy and maternity discrimination) by the EOC by way of judicial review proceedings before the Administrative Court of the High Court (see *EOC v Secretary of State for Trade and Industry* (2007), Admin Ct). The High Court held that section 4A(i)(a), which defines harassment of a woman by a person as where 'on *the ground of* her sex, he engages in unwanted conduct...' etc, does not correctly implement the Directive 2002/73/EC, which defines harassment as 'unwanted conduct related to the sex of a person...' etc. The phrase 'on the ground of her sex' impermissibly imports the notion of causation into the concept of harassment.

5.31 The High Court held that there can be conduct which is related to sex, but not of a sexual nature, which has the effect identified in the section, such as where there is denigratory treatment of a man related to sex. This would not be caught by section 4A(i)(a) because it would not be conduct on the ground of the woman's sex. Accordingly, section 4A(i)(a) needed to be recast so as to eliminate the issue of causation.

5.32 Section 4A(i)(a) was held to be incompatible with EU law and therefore needed to be recast so as to allow claims that an employer subjected an employee to harassment by knowingly failing to protect her from repetitive harassment by a third party, eg a customer or supplier. Since section 4A(i)(a) is cast in terms of unwanted conduct engaged in on the ground of a woman's sex by the employer, as the IRLR Highlights section on the case states, 'it is difficult to see how an employer could be held liable for the knowing failure to take steps to prevent harassment by others, since such knowing failure would have to amount to unwanted conduct by the employer on the ground of her sex'.

Amendments to the SDA in 2008

5.33 The SDA sections 4A(1)(a), 3A and 6A had to be amended following *Equal Opportunities Commission v DTI* because the changes to the SDA made by the Employment Equality (Sex Discrimination) Regulations 2005, SI 2005/2467 failed properly to implement the EC Equal Treatment Directive 76/207/EC as amended by 2002/73/EC. Regarding the harassment provision in section 4A(1)(a), the Court held that harassment arising from association with sex, not causation by it, should define harassment. Furthermore, as regards pregnancy and maternity, the wording of section 3A suggested that a comparator was needed: this is incorrect. Finally, as regards contractual benefits during maternity leave, the Court held that in general there must be no differences between contractual benefits during compulsory, ordinary, and additional maternity leave (SDA new s 6A must therefore be amended).

5.34 Amendments were therefore introduced with effect from 6 April 2008 (by Sex Discrimination Act 1975 (Amendment) Regulations 2008, SI 2008/656). The amended version of SDA 1975 s 4A provides that a person subjects a woman to harassment if 'he engages in unwanted conduct *that is related to her sex or that of another person and*' which has unwanted effects such as violating her dignity. The words in italics were introduced on 6 April 2008 replacing the previous wording (which was 'on the ground of her sex, he engages in unwanted conduct').

5.35 Also with effect from 6 April 2008 there is specific provision to make an employer liable for sexual harassment of employees by third parties such as customers, subject to important conditions (ie that the employee has been subject to third-party harassment at least twice before and that the employer had failed to take reasonably practicable steps to prevent such harassment). The new section 6(2B) provides that an employer is deemed to have subjected a woman to harassment where:

> (a) a third party subjects the woman to harassment in the course of her employment AND (b) the employer has failed to take such steps as would have been reasonably practicable to prevent the thrid party from doing so.

5.36 Section 6(2C) provides that this liability will apply only if 'the employer knows that the woman has been subject to harassment in the course of her employment on at least two other occasions by a third party'.

5.37 Before amendment, the definition of harassment in section 4A SDA was sufficiently similar to those in the other discrimination strands that the reasoning in this case is also likely to apply to the relevant provisions in those strands, which will mean that those definitions will also have to be amended.

5.38 Before these amendments to the SDA, complaints concerning sexual harassment were brought under sections 1(1)(a) and 6(2)(b), the latter concerning subjecting a person to a detriment. As sexual harassment is a form of direct discrimination, being less favourable treatment on the ground of sex, before the SDA was amended it was necessary to establish that (a) the treatment was on this ground (see *Porcelli v Strathclyde Regional Council* (1984)); and (b) that the complainant has suffered a detriment judged from the recipient's perspective (see *Wileman v Minilec Engineering* (1988)). Under the previous provisions, a single act of harassment, if it was sufficiently serious, could amount to harassment (see *Bracebridge Engineering Ltd v Darby* (1990) for an example of an outrageous act of discrimination). However, a series of incidents, no one of which taken on its own amounting to harassment, may not have been sufficiently serious to constitute harassment: see *Reed v Stedman* (1999). The hurdles facing complainants under the unamended version of the SDA are now removed under the amendments discussed above.

5.39 Downloading pornography from the internet by male colleagues may be harassment in that it creates an offensive and degrading environment to a female employee, even in circumstances where she cannot see what is being downloaded (see *Moonsar v Fiveways Express Transport Ltd* (2005), EAT). The employer may also be vicariously liable for this harassment (see the discussion below on vicarious liability).

Racial harassment

5.40   The Race Relations Act 1976 (Amendment) Regulations 2003 insert a new section 3A(1) into the RRA. Harassment occurs where, on the grounds of race or ethnic or national origins, a person engages in unwanted conduct which has the purpose or effect of (a) violating a person's dignity; or (b) creating an intimidating, hostile, degrading, humiliating, or offensive environment for him. There are both objective and subjective elements to the definition because conduct is to be regarded as having that effect 'only if, having regard to all the circumstances, including in particular the perception of that other person, it should reasonably be considered as having that effect'. The new definition applies only to harassment on grounds of race or ethnic or national origin.

Employers' liability for harassment

5.41   Employers may be liable for acts of harassment committed by employees in the course of their employment (SDA, s 41; RRA, 32). The test to determine whether an act was done 'in the course of employment' is not that used in the law of tort. In *Jones v Tower Boot Co Ltd* (1997), the Court of Appeal held that the statutory test was distinct from the common law one, ie the words 'in the course of employment'. This concept has been stretched to include acts of sexual harassment taking place outside working hours and away from the employer's premises in a social setting (drinks after work): see *Chief Constable of Lincolnshire Police v Stubbs* (1999), in which the EAT held that this was an 'extension' of employment. This would seem to stretch the scope of employers' liability under the statute in a way which leaves them very vulnerable.

5.42   The employer has a defence to liability for acts of harassment by employees, which is that he has taken reasonably practicable steps to prevent the acts (SDA, s 41(3); RRA, s 32(3)). This may be satisfied by employers having in place an equal opportunities policy, ensuring that all staff are aware of it, and have been given some instructions or guidance on it (see *Balgobin v Tower Hamlets* (1987)).

Pregnancy

5.43   Discrimination against a woman on ground of pregnancy is clearly discrimination on the ground of her sex (see the ECJ's ruling in *Dekker v Stichting Vormingscentrum voor Jong Volwassenen (VJV-Centrum) Plus* (1991), where the ECJ held that it was direct discrimination) but this area has caused some problems in the past because the SDA requires a comparator, actual or hypothetical, of the opposite to be identified.

Further, the relevant circumstances of the complainant and the comparator had to be 'the same or not materially different' (SDA, 5(3)). The courts and tribunals initially took the approach that a pregnant woman who was, for example, off work for a pregancy-related reason and who was then dismissed for her absence should be compared with a male employee who was off work with illness for a similar period (*Hayes v Malleable Working Men's Club* (1985)).

5.44 This approach was held to be incorrect by the ECJ ruling in *Webb v EMO Air Cargo (UK) Ltd* (1993). In *Webb* a female employee who was about to go on maternity leave was replaced by a woman taken on to cover the temporary absence of the pregnant employee, although the employer intended to keep the replacement on after the woman returned from maternity leave. When the replacement discovered that she too was pregnant, she was dismissed as she would not be able to provide the cover required, ie the employer argued, nothing to do with sex. The ECJ ruled that this was contrary to EC law. A pregnant woman should not be compared to a man who was off work through sickness: pregnancy is not an illness, and comparisons with illness are inappropriate. As pregnancy is gender-related, it is direct sex discrimination to dismiss a woman because she is pregnant (see also the House of Lord's decision in *Webb v EMO Air Cargo (UK) Ltd (No 2)* (1995)).

5.45 The ECJ has ruled that the period of pregnancy and maternity leave constitutes a protected period and dismissal of a woman for a pregnancy-related reason, including an illness related to childbirth, during this period will be unlawful sex discrimination (*Brown v Rentokil* (1998)). In *Brown*, the ECJ ruled that dismissal for absence caused by a pregnancy-related illness after this protected period has ended would only be unlawful if a man who was absent for a similar period through illness would not have been dismissed. However, the period of absence during the protected period itself should not be taken into account. Finally, it should be remembered that the ERA, s 99, provides that it is automatically unfair to dismiss a woman for a reason related to pregnancy (no qualifying period of continuous employment is required).

Indirect discrimination

5.46 Indirect discrimination is the application of an apparently gender-neutral or race-neutral requirement which places persons of one sex or persons of one colour, racial group, ethnic, or national origins at a disadvantage, and which cannot be objectively justified. Essentially, the indirect discrimination provisions concern disparate impact. The relevant provisions concerning the employment field are contained in the SDA, s 1(2)(b) and the RRA, s 1(1A). The SDA, s 1(2)(b) provides that:

a person discriminates against a woman if –

(b) he applies to her a provision, criterion or practice which he applies or would apply equally to a man but –

(i) which puts or would put women at a particular disadvantage when compared with men,

(ii) which puts her at that disadvantage, and

(iii) which he cannot show to be a proportionate means of achieving a legitimate aim.

5.47 Section 1(1A) of the RRA (which applies to the employment field) is now drafted in similar terms to the indirect discrimination provision in the SDA, as a result of the need to comply with the obligations imposed by the Race Directive. The RRA now requires the complainant to establish that the provision, criterion, or practice puts those of one racial group 'at a particular disadvantage' compared with others. Therefore, it would appear that there is no need to deal with pro-portions, it being enough merely to establish the disadvantage to a racial group (although this provision does not apply to discrimination on grounds of colour or nationality).

Provision, criterion, or practice

5.48 It should be noted that these provisions under the two statutes as originally drafted referred to a 'requirement or condition' rather than the current drafting which refers to a 'provision, criterion or practice'. This was introduced to comply with our obligations under the Burden of Proof Directive, which is applicable only in the employment field. It would seem that the new drafting is wider than the old 'requirement or condition' wording, which, as will be seen from the following dis-cussion, sometimes led to a rather restrictive analysis (see below). The new wording is likely to be broad enough to encompass, for example, job specifications that are divided into 'essential' and 'desirable' qualities or qualifications: the latter would probably not have been caught by the 'requirement or condition' provision, whereas the new wording would do so.

5.49 There are numerous cases under the old wording concerning what has been held to be a 'requirement or condition'. In *Price v Civil Service Commission (No 2)* (1983), for example, it was an age requirement for a Civil Service post (the successful applicant had to be between 17 and 28). The complainant, who was 32, succeeded in her claim that this was indirect sex discrimination as it disadvantaged women, who would be more likely to be over this age as they often took time out of their career for child-birth and child-rearing.

5.50 The limitations of the 'requirement or condition' wording may be illustrated by the decision in *Perera v Civil Service Commission (No 2)* (1983), in which the Court of Appeal held that only an absolute bar would constitute a requirement or condition under the RRA. This was followed in *Meer v Tower Hamlets LBC* (1988), brought under the RRA, where the requirement was that the applicant had previous experience working for the local authority, which the applicant contended screened him out as he was of Indian origin. As it was not an absolute bar (described as a 'must' in some of the cases) it did not constitute a requirement or condition. The new wording of RRA, s 1A should avoid these pitfalls.

5.51 Another important change is that the old wording of SDA, s 1 required the woman to establish that the requirement or condition was a detriment 'because she could not comply with it'. The new wording (relating to the employment field only) contained in section 1(2)(b)(iii) omits this phrase: if the 'provision, criterion or practice' puts a person at a particular disadvantage when compared with members of the opposite sex, it is prima facie sex discrimination, unless it can be shown to be 'a proportionate means of achieving a legitimate aim' (s 1(2)(b)(iii)).

Establishing adverse impact – SDA, s 1(2)(b)(i); RRA, s 1(1A)

5.52 Indirect discrimination claims under both statutes require disparate, adverse impact to be established. Under the old wording of the SDA, the indirect discrimination provision in the SDA called for a finding as to whether 'the proportion of women who can comply with' a particular requirement or condition was 'considerably smaller than the proportion of men who can comply with it'. Under the new wording, the provision, etc, must put women (or men) at a particular disadvantage, and put the complainant at that disadvantage. These amendments should lead to a move away from detailed examination of relevant statistics in order to determine disparate impact under the unamended version of the SDA. Under the previous provisions, complainants had to select the correct 'pool' of comparators (see *Jones v University of Manchester* (1993), CA – a case where the complainant failed because she had selected the wrong pool), and compare the ratio of male to female in it to establish that a 'considerably smaller' proportion of women could comply with the requirement.

5.53 It will be seen from this that many ET hearings were and are taken up with a close scrutiny of relevant statistics. There were no fixed guidelines as to what constituted a 'considerably smaller' or, now, a 'considerably larger' proportion. An example of the difficulties encountered by complainants facing this vague wording may be seen in *London Underground Ltd v Edwards (No 2)* (1998), CA. When the employer introduced new shift patterns for train drivers, Ms Edwards could not comply with them because of child-care responsibilities. The proportions established that 100 per cent of male train drivers could comply with the new shift patterns compared to 95 per cent of female drivers (but the male drivers numbered 2,033, and the female drivers only 21). The Court of Appeal held that there was indirect sex discrimination which the employer had to justify. Under the current provisions, Ms Edwards' task in proving indirect discrimination would have been somewhat easier because she would have had to establish only that women were put at a particular disadvantage (and that she was) by the new shift arrangements.

Justification

5.54 Under the SDA, it is a defence to an indirect discrimination claim if the employer can establish that the provision, criterion, or practice is justifiable, irrespective of the sex of the person to whom it is applied (SDA, s 1(2)(b)(ii)). However, under the amended RRA, the defence requires the employer to show that the provision, criterion, or practice is 'a proportionate means of achieving a legitimate aim' (NB this defence applies to discrimination on the ground of race or ethnic or national origins (RRA, s 1(1A)(c))).

5.55 These provisions are intended to ensure proper implementation of the EC Equal Treatment Directive 76/207/EEC (the 'ETD') (as amended). Article 2 of the ETD provides that indirect discrimination is where 'an apparently neutral provision, criterion or practice would put persons of one sex at a particular disadvantage compared with persons of the other sex, unless that provision, criterion or practice is objectively justified by a legitimate aim, and the means of achieving that aim are appropriate and necessary'.

5.56 These provisions are similar to the requirements of the objective justification set out by the ECJ in *Bilka-Kaufhaus v Weber von Hartz* (1987), concerning objective justification to be established under Article 141 of the Treaty. The ECJ ruled that the provision in question applied by the employer must:

(a) correspond to a real need on the part of the employer;

(b) be appropriate to that end; and

(c) be necessary to achieve that objective.

5.57 The objective approach in *Bilka* was followed in *Hampson v Dept of Education and Science* (1989), where the Court of Appeal rejected the employer's justification defence that the complainant's qualifications as a teacher in Hong Kong were not comparable to those required in the UK. The Court held that an objective balance needs to be struck between the discriminatory effect of the provision and the employer's legitimate business needs (the decision was reversed in the House of Lords but not on the justification ground) (see also the ECJ's ruling in *R v Secretary of State for Employment, ex p Seymour-Smith and Perez* (1999) and the House of Lords decision in *R v Secretary of State for Employement, ex p Seymour-Smith and Perez (No 2)* (2000), where the House of Lords held that the qualification period for unfair dismissal rights of part-timers, which was then two years, was objectively justifiable).

Genuine occupational qualification

5.58 Where sex or race is a genuine occupational qualification (GOQ) for the job, less favourable treatment will be allowed (SDA, s 7; RRA, s 5). This exception comprises a fairly narrow range of reasons, eg, under SDA, s 7(2):

(a) where the essential nature of the job calls for a man for reasons of physiology (excluding physical strength or stamina) or, in dramatic performances or other entertainment, for reasons of authenticity, so that the essential nature of the job would be materially different if carried out by a woman;

(b) where the job needs to be held by a man to preserve decency or privacy because:

(i) it is likely to involve physical contact with men in circumstances where they might reasonably object to its being carried out by a woman, or

(ii) the holder of the job is likely to do his work in circumstances where men might reasonably object to the presence of a woman because they are in a state of undress or are using sanitary facilities;

(c) the job is likely to involve the holder of the job doing his work, or living, in a private home and needs to be held by a man because objection might reasonably be taken to allowing a woman –

(i) the degree of physical or social contact with a person living in the home, or

(ii) the knowledge of intimate details of such a person's life, which is likely, because of the nature or circumstances of the job, or of the home, to be allowed to, or available to, the holder of the job.

5.59 There are corresponding GOQ provisions in the SDA relating to gender reassignment (ss 7A, 7B).

5.60 The number of GOQs permitted under the RRA, s 5 is fewer. The GOQs are to secure authenticity in (i) dramatic performances; (ii) as an artist's or photographer's model; (iii) work in a place where food or drink is provided for payment (sometimes called 'the Italian waiters' exception); and (iv) where the holder of the job is to provide personal services to persons of a particular racial group. See *Tottenham Green*

Under Fives' Centre v Marshall (1991) and *Lambeth v CRE* (1990). Implementing Race Directive obligations, a new section 4A was inserted into the RRA, extending the GOQ to situations where the nature of or the context in which the employment is carried out makes being of a particular race or of particular ethnic or national origin a genuine and determining occupational requirement, and it is proportionate to apply that requirement.

Transferred discrimination – RRA

5.61 It is possible for a person to claim under the RRA on the ground that they have been treated less favourably because of *another person's* race, colour, nationality, etc. In *Showboat v Owens* (1984) an employee was dismissed for refusing to carry out the instruction to exclude young blacks from an amusement arcade. He was successful in his claim that he had been discriminated against contrary to the RRA on the basis of another's colour (see also *Zarczynska v Levy* (1978), where a woman was dismissed for serving a black customer, against her employer's instructions; and *Weathersfield Ltd v Sargeant* (1999) where a female employee was dismissed for failing to comply with her employer's instructions not to allow Asians to rent vehicles). Such instructions to discriminate are unlawful under the RRA, s 30, but only the CRE may take enforcement action (see the similar provision in SDA, s 39, which only the EOR may enforce (s 72)).

Victimisation

5.62 Victimisation is a form of direct discrimination, ie it is less favourable treatment of a person by reason that they have brought proceedings, given evidence or information, or alleged a contravention of the SDA, RRA, or EqPA, (the 'protected acts') or where the discriminator knows or suspects that the person victimised intends to do any of those things, or suspects the person has done, or intends to do, any of them (SDA, s 4; RRA, s 2).

5.63 The allegation by the person victimised must be true and made in good faith. The alleged motive of the discriminator is not relevant – indeed, it may be unconscious or sub-conscious (*Nagarajan v London Regional Transport* (1999), HL: a case where the complainant was not appointed to a position because he had made claims against the employer before under the RRA). The House of Lords held that the protected act need not be the only reason for the treatment; it is sufficient if it is a substantial reason. In *Constable of West Yorkshire Police v Khan* (2001), HL, the House of Lords held that the correct comparison was with someone who had not performed a protected act. Victimisation is established if the person has been treated less favourably *by reason* that he has performed such an act. In *Khan*, their Lordships held that it was the existence of proceedings brought by Mr Khan which meant that they could not supply the reference he requested for the purpose of a job application he had made to another police force, as this might prejudice those proceedings. The decision in *Khan* seems difficult to reconcile with the House of Lords in *Nagarajan*.

5.64 The Court of Appeal held in *Oyarce v Cheshire County Council* (2008) that the 2003 amendment to the Race Relations Act (s 54A) adjusting the burden of proof in order to implement the EC Race Discrimination Directive applies only to cases where the claim is of discrimination on grounds of race, ethnic, or national origins. It does not extend to victimisation claims. The Burden of Proof Directive dealt with the burden of proof in discrimination cases in a separate article from that covering victimisation. The 2003 Regulations did not affect the provisions in respect of victimisation, as they were made under the European Communities Act and so could not go further than transposing the requirements of the Directive. Therefore, the Court held that the principles set out in *King v Great Britain-China Centre* continue to apply to race victimisation cases. This omission may be addressed by the single Equality Bill.

Segregation

5.65 It is unlawful under the RRA to segregate from other persons on racial grounds (RRA, s 1(2)). This is less favourable treatment, ie direct discrimination. There is no equivalent to this provision in the SDA. The concept of segregation does not loom large in the race discrimination field, and the only case on it, *Pel Ltd v Modgill* (1980), EAT, was unsuccessful, since the employer had not deliberately separated Asian employees on racial grounds, they had simply grouped themselves together in a particular part of the workplace, rather than there having been a deliberate and conscious policy on the part of the employer.

Code of practice

5.66 From 6 April 2006, a new Code of Practice came into force (the Race Relations Code of Practice on Racial Equality in Employment). As with the other Codes, this Code may be used in evidence in proceedings under the RRA.

Enforcement and remedies

5.67 An individual may make an application to an employment tribunal within three months of the alleged act of discrimination, although the tribunal may extend this where it considers it is just and equitable to do so (SDA, s 76; RRA, s 68). The

EOC and the CRE have powers to assist applicants where the case raises matters of principle or it is unreasonable to expect the applicant to deal with the case without support (SDA, s 75; RRA, s 66).

5.68 If the complaint is upheld, the tribunal may order (i) a declaration of the rights of the parties; (ii) compensation (which is unlimited); (iii) a recommendation that the employer takes action within a specified period to obviate or reduce the effect of the discrimination (SDA, s 65(1); RRA, s 56(1)(a)). On recommendations, see *British Gas v Sharma* (1991); *North West Thames RHA v Noone* (1988).

5.69 Compensation for injury to feelings may be awarded, and often comprises a major part of the compensation (SDA, s 66(4); RRA, s 57(4)). The statutory cap on compensation in discrimination was removed in 1993 following the ECJ's ruling in *Marshall Southampton & SW Hants AHA (No 2)* (1993) in which the statutory limits were held to be in breach of the Community law requirement that domestic remedies were adequate for a breach of Community law. The Sex Discrimination and Equal Pay (Remedies) Regulations 1993 (SI 1993/2798) removed the statutory cap on compensation for sex discrimination, and the RRA was amended by the Race Relations (Remedies) Act 1994 (SI 1994/1748), which abolished the statutory limit on compensation in race discrimination cases. The Court of Appeal gave guidance to tribunals on compensation awards in *Vento v Chief Constable of West Yorkshire Police (No 2)* (2003), and *Ministry of Defence v Cannock* (1994) indicates the size of awards that can be made by tribunals.

5.70 The Court of Appeal held in 2004 that, in discrimination cases, the appropriate test for deciding whether an employer is liable to pay compensation for psychiatric injury suffered by an employee is not whether the injury was reasonably foreseeable (the test in tort law) but is simply whether unlawful discrimination caused it (see *Essa v Laing Ltd* (2004)). This means that the complainant has an easier burden to discharge under the statutory tort (*Essa* was brought under the RRA) in respect of establishing a right to compensation than that applicable in the common law of tort.

The Equality and Human Rights Commission ('the EHRC')

5.71 As outlined in Chapter 1, the Equality Act 2006 established the EHRC, which has replaced the Equal Opportunities Commission (EOC), the Commission for Racial Equality (CRE), and the Disability Rights Commission (DRC). The statutory duties of the EHRC are similar to those of the three legacy Commissions, eg working towards the elimination of discrimination and promoting equality of opportunities.

5.72 The ECHR, which will also promote human rights, will have responsibility for the operation of the current discrimination statutes, the equality regulations on religion or belief, sexual orientation and, in due course, age. The CEHR is to have improved powers (when compared with the three Commissions it will replace) to promote equality and deal with discrimination.

Disability discrimination

5.73 Legislation concerning discrimination on the ground of disability has been on the statute books for some time. However, the Disabled Persons (Employment) Act 1944 required a person with sufficient degree of disability to register so that the quota system could operate, ie employers with 20 or more employees were required to employ a quota (3 per cent) of disabled persons. This scheme was not successful because there were no civil remedies for breach of the provisions; employers evaded the quota scheme by securing blanket permits allowing them to employ able-bodied employees (their argument was that there were no suitably qualified disabled persons for the job); and only about one-third of those disabled registered under the scheme. The Act was replaced by the Disability Discrimination Act 1995 (the 'DDA').

The Disability Discrimination Act 1995

5.74 The DDA covers discrimination against disabled persons in employment (Part II of the Act) and in relation to the provision of goods, services, and facilities (Part III), although this discussion considers the former. Part II of the DDA was brought into force on 1 December 1996. In 1996, in addition to the main statute, two sets of regulations were brought into force (the Disability Discrimination (Meaning of Disability) Regulations 1996 (SI 1996/1455), and the Disability Discrimination (Employment) Regulations 1996 (SI 1996/1456)). It should be noted that, since the coming into force of this legislation, significant amendments have been made to the DDA recently, which are discussed below.

5.75 The Secretary of State issued guidance in 1996, pursuant to powers under DDA, s 3: 'Guidance on matters to be taken into account in determining questions relating to the definition of disability'. New Official Guidance came into effect on 1 May 2006, which replaces the 1996 version. Although the Guidance does not have statutory force, Employment Tribunals are obliged to take it into account when considering 'whether an impairment has a substantial and long-term adverse effect on a person's ability to carry out normal day-to-day activities' (s 3(3)). The new Official Guidance takes into account changes made by the Disability Discrimination Act

2005, including a widening of the definition of disability to benefit those with Aids, cancer, or multiple sclerosis and the removal of the previous requirement that mental illnesses must be 'clinically well-recognised'. This latter provision extends the DDA's protection to those who would formerly not have come within the definition of disabled or having a disability.

5.76 The DRC has issued a new Code of Practice on employment and occupation, which came into force on 1 October 2004 and which replaces the original Code issued in 1996. Unlike the original Code, which was issued by the Secretary of State, the new Code is issued by the DRC under the DDA, s 53A (this new section giving the DRC power to issue Codes came into force on 5 December 2005). The EAT has stated (referring to the original Code) that ETs should make express reference to the Code in their decisions (see *Ridout v TC Group* (1998); *Goodwin v The Patent Office* (1999)). The Court of Appeal has held that, when determining whether there has been less favourable treatment, the relevant provisions of the Code should be taken into account (*Clark v Novacold* (1999)).

Comparison of the DDA with the SDA and RRA

5.77 As originally drafted, the DDA differed in some important respects from the two earlier discrimination statutes, the SDA and the RRA. Some of these differences have disappeared as a result of amendments to the DDA which came into force from October 2004 (see below). However, in the unamended version of the DDA, the main differences were: (i) there was no explicit distinction between direct and indirect forms of discrimination; (ii) the DDA used a different comparison for identifying discrimination; (iii) the justification defence was broader under the DDA; (iv) unlike the SDA and the RRA, the DDA imposes a positive duty upon employers to make reasonable adjustments to accommodate disabled persons; and (v) the DDA contained a small employer's exemption. The amendments referred to below substantially alter the DDA in respect of the differences identified above.

Amendment to the DDA – the Equal Treatment Framework Directive (ETFD)

5.78 The ETFD (Directive 2000/78/EC) contained provisions relating to disability discrimination as a result of which the DDA had to be amended by 2006. This has been done by the Disability Discrimination Act 1995 (Amendment) Regulations 2003 (SI 2003/1673) (the 'Amendment Regulations'). The amendments came into force on 1 October 2004. Some of the most important changes brought about by these amendments include a change in the meaning of discrimination. The amendments introduce an indirect discrimination provision (s 3A(1)), which is called disability-related discrimination in the Code, which is subject to a justification defence. Changes have been made to the justification defence (see below), and a definition of harassment has been inserted into the DDA (s 3B). (NB Much of the following discussion concerns case law decided prior to the coming into force of the amendments made to the DDA in the Amendment Regulations.)

Scope of the DDA

5.79 As is the case in the SDA and the RRA, the DDA applies to employees, ie those working under a contract of employment or apprenticeship, and those who work under 'a contract personally to do any work' (DDA, s 68). It includes contract workers (new ss 4 and 4B). The employment provisions of the DDA apply to work in an establishment in Great Britain. From 1 October 2004, employees currently not covered by the Act, eg police officers, fire-fighters, partnerships, barristers, and prison officers, are brought within the scope of the Act's employment provisions (armed forces' members will continue to be excluded) (DDA, ss 6A, 7A, 64, 64A).

Post-termination discrimination

5.80 The DDA, s 4(2), as originally drafted, did not cover discrimination against former employees: it concerned discrimination by employers against a person 'whom he employs'. From 1 October 2004, coverage is now extended to ex-employees (see the Amendment Regulations, regulation 15, which insert a new s 16A in DDA). This position had already been reached in the case law: see *Rhys-Harper v Relaxion Group plc* (2003), HL.

Small employer's exemption abolished

5.81 When it was first introduced, the DDA contained an exemption for small employers: those with fewer than 20 employees were outside the scope of the DDA. This exemption excluded the vast majority of employers. The limit was reduced in 1998, so that employers with fewer than 15 employees were excluded, although it is estimated that over 90 per cent were still outside the DDA. The Amendment Regulations removed this exemption altogether from 1 October 2004.

Meaning of disability

5.82 The relevant definitions relating to 'disability' and 'disabled person' are set out in DDA, s 1 and Sch 1. The DDA very largely takes the 'medical model' of disability, ie essentially, medical evidence determines whether a person is disabled, rather than the 'social model', in which a person may be seen as suffering discrimination because they are perceived to be disabled. A person has a disability for the purposes of the DDA if he has a physical or mental impairment which has a substantial and long-term adverse effect on his ability to carry out normal day-to-day activities. Section 2 includes in the definition of a 'disabled person' a person who has had a disability. This covers situations where someone with a past disability who is no longer suffering any effects may still be discriminated against (see *Greenwoood v British Airways* (1999), where the applicant was refused promotion because of his absenteeism record in the past, which was caused by his previous depression). The key points to note about this definition are:

A person has a disability if he or she has:

- a physical or mental impairment; and
- that impairment has an adverse effect on his or her ability to carry out normal day-to-day activities; and
- that effect is substantial; and
- that effect is long-term.

5.83   Addictions, eg alcoholism, drug addiction, and nicotine addiction, are outside the scope of the definition, although where these addictions cause other problems, eg liver damage, they will come within the definition (Sch 1, para 1(2)(a); Disability Discrimination (Meaning of Disability) Regulations 1996, regs 2 and 3(1)). However, the question is not what caused a condition but whether a particular condition constitutes a disability: see *Power v Panasonic UK Ltd* (2003), EAT, where alcoholism caused the applicant's depression.

5.84   Mental impairments include learning, psychiatric, and psychological impairments; the mental impairment which results from or consists of a mental illness no longer needs to be clinically well-recognised to come within the definition (Sch 1, para 1(1) has been amended by the Disability Discrimination Act 2005 (the 'DDA 2005'), s18(2) and Sch 2. In a pre-DDA 2005 case, the EAT had reached an interpretation which accords with this amended definition in holding (in June 2005) that general and non-clinically recognised 'learning difficulties' came within the DDA's definition of disability (see *Dunham v Ashford Windows* (2005)). However, psychopathic or anti-social disorders (eg kleptomania, pryomania, and paedophilia) are excluded (reg 4(1)). Spectacle wearers and hay-fever sufferers are also outside the definition of disability.

5.85   Under the DDA 2005, which inserts a new section into the DDA, s 6A, the meaning of 'disability' has been extended (from 5 December 2005) to include HIV (defined as 'infection by a virus capable of causing the Acquired Immune

Deficiency Syndrome'), cancer, and/or multiple sclerosis. Persons affected by any of these conditions are deemed to have a disability (and therefore to be a disabled person), so that they are protected under the DDA *from the point of diagnosis*, even if they do not come within the meaning of disability under the other DDA provisions because they can still carry out normal day-to-day activities.

5.86 'Normal day-to-day activities' (NB not necessarily those concerning the job the employee is or will be doing) must be affected ie:

  (a) mobility;

  (b) manual dexterity;

  (c) physical co-ordination;

  (d) continence;

  (e) ability to lift, carry or otherwise move everyday objects;

  (f) speech, hearing or eyesight;

  (g) memory or ability to concentrate, learn or understand; or

  (h) perception of the risk of physical danger.

(Sch 1, para 4(1))

5.87 The effect must be substantial and adverse. Whether an impairment has a substantial adverse effect upon a person is amplified by the Guidance, which indicates that factors relevant to this question will include: the time taken to carry out an activity; the way in which an activity is carried out; the cumulative effects of an impairment; and the effects of behaviour or environment (see the Guidance Part II, paras B2–A10). Some ETs were interpreting 'substantial' in the context of the DDA to mean very large, although this approach was corrected by the EAT in *Goodwin v The Patent Office* (1999), in which the ET had held that a paranoid schizophrenic was not disabled, despite clear evidence of the substantial effect his impairment had upon his ability to carry out day-to-day activities. The EAT held that he was disabled, and advised ETs to focus on the things the applicant in a DDA claim could not do, or could only do with difficulty, rather than on what he could do (see also *Leonard v Southern Derbyshire Chamber of Commerce* (2001), EAT).

5.88 Recurring effects are included, ie where the impairment has ceased to have a substantial adverse effect on a person's ability to carry out day-to-day activities, if that effect is likely to recur (Sch 1, para 2(2)). Severe disfigurements are also to be treated as having that effect (Sch 1, para 3). Progressive conditions such as cancer, multiple sclerosis, and HIV infection, which affects the person's ability to carry out day-to-day activities, are also to be taken as having a substantial adverse effect (even when that is not currently the case) if the condition is likely to result in such an impairment (Sch 1, para 8(1)). However, the applicant must establish that the effect is likely to become substantial (see *Mowat–Brown v University of Surrey* (2002), EAT). Applicants whose impairment results from the treatment for the condition, rather than the condition itself, are also covered (*Kirton v Tetrosyl Ltd* (2003), CA).

5.89 In *Richmond Adult Community College v McDougall* (2008) the Court of Appeal resolved the conflict in authorities in DDA case law as to the point in time for determining whether the effect of an impairment is likely to last for at least 12 months so as to be treated as having a 'long-term effect'. The question is whether it is at the date of the alleged discrimination, or, as the EAT held in this case, up to and including the ET hearing that any adverse effects of the claimant's condition are to be taken into account. The Court of Appeal held that it must be judged on the evidence available to it at the time of the decision complained of.

5.90 The claimant had her offer of a post withdrawn because she had not been given satisfactory medical clearance. The ET found that she had a mental illness, but that there was no evidence at the time the decision was taken that the illness was likely to recur, and therefore it did not have a long-term effect. In the event, subsequent to that, but prior to the tribunal hearing, she was admitted to hospital under the Mental Health Act. The EAT held that the ET should have taken this into account. The Court of Appeal held that the recurring conditions provision caters for the specific situation where the substantial adverse effects of the impairment have ceased. Pill LJ stated (at para 24) that:

> The central purpose of the Act is to prevent discriminatory decisions and to provide sanctions if such decisions are made. Whether an employer has committed a wrong must . . . be judged on the basis of the evidence available at the time of the decision complained of . . .

5.91 The effect of medical treatment, prostheses or aids is to be disregarded when considering whether the impairment is likely to have a substantial adverse effect (Sch 1, para 6(1)). This means that it is the 'deduced effects' that are considered. In *Kapadia v London Borough of Lambeth* (2000), the EAT held that the effects of an employee's clinical depression, which was attenuated by counselling, allowing him to continue work, should be judged as they would have been without the counselling. The evidence was that he would have had a breakdown without this counselling.

5.92 It is a matter for the ET to determine what constitutes day-to-day activities and whether the effect is substantial (*Vicary v BT plc* (1999), EAT). 'Substantial' in this context means more than minor or trivial (see the Guidance and Code of Practice).

5.93 The effect is a long-term adverse effect if the impairment lasts at least 12 months, or is likely to do so (or is likely to last for the rest of a person's life, in the case of a terminally ill person). Remissions and periods of good health are allowed for in the DDA, eg conditions such as arthritis and MS, and recurring conditions which cease to have a substantial effect are nevertheless to be treated as long term if they are likely to recur, but one recurrence must be (or be likely to be) at least 12 months after the first (Sch 1, para 2(1)).

5.94 A condition only occurring at work is to be taken into consideration when deciding whether it has a substantial adverse effect on an employee's ability to carry out normal day-to-day activities (*Cruickshank v VAW Motorcast Ltd* (2002), EAT: the applicant suffered from occupational asthma, which improved when he was not at work). *Cruickshank* is also authority for the principle that the impairment must be considered at the time of the alleged discrimination, and not only at the time of the hearing – this is particularly important for fluctuating conditions.

Meaning of 'discrimination'

5.95 The main forms of discrimination under the DDA, as amended are:

- **Direct discrimination** (s 3A(5)), ie where a person is treated less favourably, 'on the ground of the disabled person's disability'. This form of discrimination cannot be justified (s 3A(4)).

- **Discrimination for a disability-related reason** (s 3A(1)), ie less favourable treatment 'for a reason which relates to the disabled person's disability'. This form of discrimination is justifiable if 'the reason for it is both material to the circumstances of the particular case and substantial' (ss 3A(1)(b), (3)). Furthermore, no justification of this form of discrimination is possible where the employer 'is under a duty to make reasonable adjustments in relation to the disabled person but fails to comply with that duty...unless it would have been justified even if he had complied with that duty' (s 3A(6)).

- **Failure to make reasonable adjustments** (s 3A(2)). There is a free-standing statutory obligation to make reasonable adjustments and the failure to do so constitutes a discrete form of discrimination. However, as indicated above, the duty to make reasonable adjustments also arises as regards disability-related discrimination under s 3A(1).

One of the most interesting aspects of the DDA as originally drafted was that it contained a definition of direct discrimination (former s 5) which was similar to that in the SDA and RRA, ie less favourable treatment but, unlike those statutes, it was possible to justify such discrimination (under s 6 of the unamended DDA, which has been repealed). From 1 October 2004 the new definition in s 3A has applied, which means that it is no longer possible to justify direct discrimination (s 3A(4)and (5)).

5.96   The sequence of steps an ET should follow for determining whether there is a duty of reasonable adjustment was set out by the EAT in *Environment Agency v Rowan* (2008). According to Judge Serota QC (at para 27):

> an employment tribunal considering a claim that an employer has discriminated against an employee pursuant to s.3A(2) of the Act by failing to comply with the s.4A duty must identify:
>
> (a) the provision, criterion or practice applied by or on behalf of an employer, or
>
> (b) the physical feature of premises occupied by the employer,
>
> (c) the identity of non-disabled comparators (where appropriate) and
>
> (d) the nature and extent of the substantial disadvantage suffered by the claimant.

It should be borne in mind that identification of the substantial disadvantage suffered by the claimant may involve a consideration of the cumulative effect of both the 'provision, criterion or practice applied by or on behalf of an employer' and the 'physical feature of premises' so it would be necessary to look at the overall picture.

The EAT (at para 27) added that:

> an employment tribunal cannot properly make findings of a failure to make reasonable adjustments under ss.3A(2) and 4A(1) without going through that process. Unless the employment tribunal has identified the four matters we have set out above it cannot go on to judge if any proposed adjustment is reasonable. It is simply unable to say what adjustments were reasonable to prevent the provision, criterion or practice, or feature, placing the disabled person concerned at a substantial disadvantage.

5.97   Under s 4A, employers have a duty to 'take such steps as it is reasonable, in all the circumstances of the case, for [them] to have to take in order to prevent' a disabled person being put at a 'substantial disadvantage in comparison with persons who are not disabled'. This applies whenever '(a) a provision, criterion or practice applied by or on behalf of an employer or (b) any physical feature of premises occupied by the employer' puts the disabled person concerned at a substantial disadvantage (DDA, s 4A)(1)).

5.98   Section 18B stipulates the matters to which particular regard must be had in determining whether it is reasonable for a person to comply with the duty to make reasonable adjustments. These matters include, for example, the extent to which taking the step is practicable, the financial and other costs which would be incurred in taking the step, the financial and other resources available, and the nature and size of the undertaking.

Disability discrimination – 'associative discrimination'

5.99 Whether so-called 'associative' discrimination is within the scope of the DDA (or whether it should be, on a correct interpretation of EC law), is a question which was referred to the ECJ. In the context of the DDA, associative discrimination is discrimination suffered by a person who is not themselves disabled but suffers discrimination because of their association with a disabled person. In *Attridge Law & Anor v Coleman* (2007), EAT, a mother took time off work to look after her disabled son. She complained that her employers (a firm of solicitors) were acting unlawfully because they refused to allow her request for flexible working arrangements to look after her son. She complained that this refusal was a breach of the DDA. Mrs Coleman was claiming both direct discrimination and harassment under the DDA. In both instances, Ms Coleman claimed that the ground for the treatment was the fact that she was a carer for her disabled son. The case was referred to the ECJ.

5.100 The difficulty with the claim was that 'associative discrimination' is not unlawful under the DDA, although, arguably, it is prohibited by the relevant EC Equal Treatment Directive. The DDA provides for a claim being made by a disabled person but does not cover the position of a person who is discriminated against because of caring for a disabled person. The DDA on its face protects only those who are disabled themselves, but the ETFD prohibits direct discrimination on 'grounds' of disability, which is a wider concept than the DDA definition encompasses. The ECJ ruled (at para 48, see *Coleman v Attridge Law* (2008), ECJ) that the objectives and effectiveness of the Directive

> would be undermined if an employee in the claimant's situation cannot rely on the prohibition of direct discrimination...where it has been established that he has been treated less favourably than another employee is, has been or would be treated in a comparable situation, on the grounds of his child's disability, and this is the case even though that employee is not himself disabled.

This is because 'the fact remains that it is the disability which, according to Ms Coleman, is the ground for the less favourable treatment which she claims to have suffered' (para 48).

5.101 Although this case was concerned only with disability discrimination, it seems likely that this principle also applies to discrimination by reason of religion and belief, age, or sexual orientation.

5.102 • **Harassment**: This is a distinct form of discrimination, the statutory definition of which is in section 3B. This provision is discussed below.

• **Victimisation**: This is another separate form of discrimination, the statutory definition of which is in section 55. This provision is discussed below.

Comparators

5.103 The amendments to the DDA also clarify the position on comparators: section 3A(5) provides that the appropriate comparator in a direct discrimination case is a non-disabled person whose abilities are the same as (or not materially different from) the abilities of the disabled person.

5.104 The House of Lords' decision in *London Borough of Lewisham v Malcolm* (2008) IRLR 700 concerns the correct comparator in claims of disability-related discrimination. Although *Malcolm* is not an employment case (it concerned a secure tenancy), the principle identified applies to DDA claims in employment. The definition of disability-related discrimination in section 3A(1) of the DDA, which is the same throughout the DDA, provides that a person discriminates against a disabled person if 'for a reason which relates to the disabled person's disability, he treats him less favourably than he treats or would treat others to whom that reason does not or would not apply'. A majority of the House of Lords held that the correct comparison for disability-related discrimination was with how a person would have treated a non-disabled person to whom the same reason applied (in this case, a secure tenant who had sublet in breach of the rules). Since the local authority would have treated the non-disabled person the same way, the disabled person was not treated less favourably. In reaching this construction, the House of Lords overruled *Clark v TDG t/a Novacold*, which had been the leading case hitherto on disability-related discrimination: the House of Lords held that *Clark v TDG t/a Novacold* was wrongly decided because it held that the correct comparison is with a non-disabled person to whom the reason did not apply. *Novacold* concerned an employee who was absent from work because of a disability. On principle enunciated in *Malcolm*, the correct comparison in *Novacold* would have been with a non-disabled person with the same amount of absence. If that person would also be dismissed, there is no disability-related discrimination.

5.105 This construction is regarded as necessary because, as Lord Scott states, Parliament must have intended that the comparison should be 'meaningful'. Lord Scott asked, 'if a person has been dismissed because he will be absent from work for a year, what is the point of making the lawfulness of his dismissal dependent on whether those who will not be absent from work will be dismissed?'. Baroness Hale gave a robust dissenting speech, to the effect that the law has not been changed in its construction by any of the subsequent changes to the DDA. On the reasoning in *Malcolm*, if a non-disabled person would have been treated the same, there is no disability-related reason, and if a non-disabled person would have been treated more favourably, there will be direct discrimination 'on the ground of' disability, rather for a reason which relates to disability. The House of Lords' decision seems to have removed much of the content of this ground of discrimination, leaving complainants to take a different approach that is focused on the duty to make reasonable adjustments, where a difference in treatment is expressly recognised.

Knowledge of the disability

5.106 The question of whether an employer is liable where he does not have knowledge of the claimant's disability arises in the context of (i) direct discrimination; (ii) disability-related discrimination; and (iii) under the duty to make reasonable adjustments. As regards (i) and (ii) above, the House of Lords' decision in *Lewisham v Malcolm* overrules the previous case law of *London Borough of Hammersmith and Fulham v Farnsworth (2000)*, EAT and *H J Heinz Co Ltd v Kenrick (2000) ICR 491*, EAT which suggested the employer's knowledge of the disability was irrelevant for the purposes of disability-related discrimination. Since the fact of the employee's physical or mental condition (which amounts to the disability) must form part of the employer's reason for the less favourable treatment, an employer cannot be liable for disability-related discrimination unless it knows of the condition in question. According to *Malcolm*, it is not necessary for the employer to know that the condition amounts to a disability in law. The majority of the House of Lords (Lord Bingham, Lord Neuberger, and Baroness Hale) took the view that it would be sufficient to show 'imputed knowledge', ie that the discriminator knew or ought reasonably to have known about the condition.

5.107 The law concerning the knowledge of the employer in a reasonable adjustments claim remains the same: as regards the duty to make reasonable adjustments, the duty will not arise where the employer 'does not know and could not reasonably be expected to know' of the disability (in the case of employees) or that the disabled person was a job applicant, as the case may be (s 4A(3)).

Reasonable adjustments

5.108 There is a duty on employers to make reasonable adjustments where (under the new provisions, s 4A) any provision, criterion, or practice applied by him or any physical feature of premises occupied by the employer 'places the disabled person concerned at a substantial disadvantage in comparison with persons who are not disabled'. In such situations, it is the duty of the employer to take 'such steps as it is reasonable, in all the circumstances of the case, for him to have to take in order to prevent the provision, criterion or practice, or feature, having that effect'. The duty to make reasonable adjustments is a positive duty, ie the employer may be required to discriminate in favour of an employee (see *Archibald v Fife Council* (2004) and *Smith v Churchill's Stairlifts plc* (2006), CA).

5.109 Examples of reasonable adjustments are given in section 18B(2) and the Code, and may include: making adjustments to premises; allocating some of the disabled person's duties to another person; transferring the person to fill an existing vacancy; altering the person's working hours; or assigning the person to a different place of work. This is a non-exhaustive list, and the range of possible adjustments may be very wide indeed. For example, in *Archibald v Fife Council* (2004), HL, the House of Lords held (in a case on the previous provision on reasonable adjustment, ie s 6) that the duty might extend to transferring a female road-sweeper to a sedentary job at a higher grade without requiring her to compete with other applicants. However, the duty does not apply to the provision of a personal carer to attend to personal needs so as to enable a job applicant to work for the employer (*Kenny v Hampshire Constabulary* (1999), EAT).

5.110 The duty applies only when the employer knows, or could reasonably be expected to know, either (i) in the case of job applicants, that the disabled person is either an applicant for the job or a potential applicant; or (ii) in any case, 'that that person has a disability and is likely to be affected' by being put at a substantial disadvantage in comparison with persons who are not disabled (s 4A): see *Ridout v TC Group* (1998), EAT; *Mid-Staffordshire General Hospitals NHS Trust v Cambridge* (2003). This provision means that job applicants will have to disclose their disability for the duty to be engaged, and existing employees will have to make such disclosure if their disability is not apparent.

5.111 In determining what is reasonable in terms of adjustments, a number of factors may be taken into consideration, including: the extent to which a particular step would prevent the effect in relation to which the duty is imposed; the practicability of taking the step; and the financial and other costs incurred in taking it (s 18B).

5.112 An employer's failure to make reasonable adjustments for a disabled employee may give the employee the right to resign and claim constructive dismissal (see *Nottinghamshire County Council v Meikle* (2004), CA). This duty is wide enough to encompass a duty to consider paying employees full pay during sickness absence, regardless of their contractual sick pay entitlements (see

Nottinghamshire County Council v Meikle (2004), Court of Appeal on 8 July 2004 and *Greenhof v Barnsley MBC* (2005)).

Justification

5.113 The pre-amendment DDA allowed a justification defence for failure to make reasonable adjustments under s 5. The Amendment Regulations have amended the DDA in this regard by repealing that provision and substituting a new s 3A (in force from 1 October 2004), which provides that, apart from direct discrimination (see s 3A(4)), discriminatory treatment for a disability-related reason may be justified where the reason for it is both 'material to the circumstances of the particular case and substantial' (s 3A(1), (3)). In order to avoid liability, the employer would have to show that the adjustment was not reasonable. This imposes an objective standard (see *Smith v Churchills Stairlifts plc* (2006), CA). The ET must come to its own conclusion on the matter, ie on whether (under the amended DDA) reasonable adjustments could be made (NB the pre-amendment case law concerned direct discrimination (which cannot now be justified, following amendments to the DDA), ie less favourable treatment, as well as the duty to make reasonable adjustments). If it decides that there were reasonable adjustments that could be made, then it must consider whether the employer was reasonable in not carrying them out (see *Morse v Wiltshire CC* (1998), EAT).

Instructions and pressure to discriminate

5.114 It is unlawful for a person with authority over another (such as an employer) to instruct another person to commit an unlawful act of discrimination under Pts II or III of the DDA, ie employment and the provision of goods, services, and facilities, or to procure or attempt to procure such an act (s 16C).

Advertisements

5.115 Publishing or causing discriminatory advertisements to be published is unlawful (s 16B). Only the DRC may bring proceedings for this contravention (s 17B).

Aiding unlawful acts and liability of employers

5.116 It is a criminal offence to knowingly aid another person to do an unlawful act under the DDA (s 57), and employers and principals are liable for acts done by employees or agents, unless they took reasonably practicable steps to prevent the employee or agent from doing that act (s 59). Only the DRC may bring proceedings for this contravention (s 17B).

Harassment

5.117 From 1 October 2004 harassment is expressly covered. A person subjects a disabled person to harassment 'where, for a reason which relates to the disabled person's disability, he engages in unwanted conduct which has the purpose or effect of (a) violating the disabled person's dignity, or (b) creating an intimidating, hostile, degrading, humiliating or offensive environment for him'. Conduct is to be regarded as having that effect 'only if, having regard to all the circumstances, including in particular the perception of the disabled person, it should reasonably be considered as having that effect' (s 3B).

Victimisation

5.118 As in the SDA and RRA, it is unlawful to discriminate against a person by way of victimisation (s 55). The definition is similar to those in the other two statutes, ie less favourable treatment of a person who has engaged in the protected activities (or where the employer believes or suspects that the person has done so). These activities are: bringing proceedings under the DDA; giving evidence or information in relation to proceedings under the DDA; otherwise doing anything under the DDA; and alleging that another person has contravened the DDA (this allegation must be made in good faith).

Enforcement and remedies

5.119 Complaints under the DDA are made to the ET within three months of the act complained of (s 17A). The ET may make a declaration, or an order for compensation (which is unlimited, and may include a sum for injury to feelings), or a recommendation to the respondent. Compensation can be very high in disability cases. For example, over £100,000 was awarded to the complainant in *British Sugar v Kirker* (1998), EAT.

Remedies – Compensation and multiple discrimination

5.120 In *Al Jumard v Clywd Leisure Ltd & ors* (2008), the EAT held that where a case involves many discriminatory acts extending over a long period, some exclusively racial, some disability-related, and some both, it is wrong to take a general broad-brush approach to assessment of compensation. Compensation for the different types of discrimination should initially be separately assessed to the extent that is possible. At the end of the exercise a tribunal must stand back and have regard to the overall magnitude of the global sum to ensure that it is proportionate and that there is no double counting in the calculation.

Burden of proof

5.121   In line with amendments made to the SDA and the RRA as a result of Article 10 of the ETFD, a new provision is inserted into the DDA which establishes facts from which it may be presumed that discrimination has taken place, so the burden of proof is shifted to the employer to prove that there has been no discrimination (s 17A(1C), in force from 1 October 2004).

Transsexualism

5.122   Transsexuals are individuals who are born into one sex but believe that they should have been born into the other sex. In medical terms they are said to have gender identity disorder, and they often seek to reassign their gender by chemical and/ or surgical means. The case of *P v S* (1996) concerned a male employee who was dismissed because he intended to undergo gender reassignment surgery. The SDA, s 1, concerns discrimination 'on the ground of sex', and the terms used throughout the Act are 'man' and 'woman' (see s 5(2) for definitions of these terms). The Truro industrial tribunal (as they were then called) referred the case to the ECJ, which held that, taking a purposive interpretation of Article 5(1) of the Equal Treatment Directive (Directive No 76/207/EEC), which refers to discrimination 'on grounds of sex', and applying the equal treatment principle, it should be read to include discrimination that was based essentially on the sex of a person (the Advocate General's opinion interpreted Article 5(1) of the ETD as including discrimination based on grounds of *a change of* sex). The EAT held in the later transsexuals case of *Chessington World of Adventures Ltd v Reed* (1997) that the SDA could be read so as to be consistent with the ETD, although the SDA was amended on 1 May, 1999 by regulations (discussed below).

5.123   The SDA has now been amended by the Sex Discrimination (Gender Reassignment) Regulations 1999 (SI 1999/1102), which insert a new section 2A in the SDA. The section renders unlawful less favourable treatment (indirect discrimination is not included in the amendment) on the ground that a person 'intends to undergo, is undergoing or has undergone gender reassignment'. Section 82 of the SDA defines gender reassignment as 'a process which is undertaken under medical supervision for the purpose of reassigning a person's sex by changing physiological or other characteristics of sex, including any part of such process'. The protection only extends to employment and vocational training, ie Parts II (the employment field) and III (but only so far as they relate to vocational training), including sections 35A and 35B concerning discrimination by, or in relation to, barristers (or advocates in Scotland).

5.124   Under section 2A(3)(a), a person who is absent due to undergoing gender reassignment treatment must not be treated less favourably than someone who is off work through sickness or injury, although under section 2A(3)(b) they may be compared to employees absent due to some other cause, and it is reasonable in all the circumstances to treat them no less favourably than those employees.

5.125 The Court of Appeal held that, for the purposes of employment law, post-operative transsexuals should be treated as having their reassigned sex (*Chief Constable of West Yorkshire Police v A (No 2)* (2003), affirmed by the House of Lords in 2004). However, this principle does not mean that transsexuals should be regarded as having their reassigned sex for all purposes and at all stages of the process of gender reassignment: the Court of Appeal in *Croft v Royal Mail Group plc* (2003) held that a male-to-female *pre-operative* transsexual was not to be treated as of the sex to which they wished to reassign, so the complainant had not been treated less favourably when the employer refused to allow him to use the female lavatories. The employer had to exercise a judgement as to when a person in these circumstances was to be regarded as female for such a purpose.

5.126 In *Chief Constable of West Yorkshire Police v A* (2004), HL, it was held to be unlawful sex discrimination for a police force to refuse to accept a male-to-female transsexual as a police constable because he or she had had a sex change operation, unless such a refusal could be justified, eg by public interest considerations.

5.127 A causative link must be established between the discriminatory treatment and the transsexualism before liability will be imposed. In *Ashton v Chief Constable of West Mercia* (2001), the EAT held that the dismissal of a transsexual who was undergoing gender reassignment and who was taking medication as part of her treatment which caused her to be depressed and affected her work, had not been discriminated against. She had been dismissed fairly on the capability ground. The fact that her poor performance was caused by the depression brought about by the treatment was not sufficient to establish discrimination: the 'necessary causative link' had not been established.

5.128 As in the case of discrimination against men and women under the SDA, there are genuine occupational qualification exceptions applying to transsexuals (SDA, ss 7A and 7B), eg where a job might involve carrying out 'intimate physical searches pursuant to statutory powers' (s 7B(2)(a)).

Sexual orientation; religion or belief; age

5.129 Despite the fact that there has been discrimination legislation at domestic level concerning sex and race since the middle of the 1970s, there has been a gap concerning other grounds of discrimination, ie sexual orientation, religion or belief, and age (with disability not being addressed until 1995 under the DDA). Impetus for change came once again from the EU with the introduction under the Amsterdam Treaty in 1997 of a new Article 13 to be incorporated in the Treaty of Rome. This empowered the Council of Ministers to take action to combat discrimination across a wide range: sex, racial or ethnic origin, religion or belief, disability, age, or sexual orientation. The EU used this power to adopt the Equal Treatment Framework Directive (2000/78EC), which required Member States to legislate against these forms of discrimination by 2003, with the exception of age and disability, for which the implementation date is 2006.

5.130 As a result of the Directive, three sets of regulations were adopted: the Employment Equality (Sexual Orientation) Regulations 2003 (SI 2003/1661) (the 'SO Regs'), which came into force on 1 December 2003; the Employment Equality (Religion or Belief) Regulations (2003 SI 2003/1660) (the 'R or B Regs'), which came into force on 2 December 2003; and the Employment Equality (Age) Regulations 2006 (SI 2006/1031), which came into force on 1 October 2006.

5.131 There is very helpful guidance available on both sets of Regulations on the ACAS and DTI websites.

Sexual orientation

5.132 Until recently, there was no protection in Great Britain concerning discrimination on the ground of sexual orientation. The SDA renders unlawful discrimination 'on the ground of sex', whereas gay and lesbian complainants were bringing claims under the SDA on the ground of *sexual orientation*.

5.133 The courts and tribunals took a restrictive view: the SDA requires a comparison between the complainant and an actual or hypothetical comparator of the *opposite sex*, so the complainant would succeed only where it could be established that an actual or hypothetical person of the opposite sex but with the same sexual orientation, ie homosexuality, would not have been treated less favourably. Where such a comparator would have been treated in the same way as the complainant, ie badly, there was no contravention of the SDA. Thus, in *Pearce v Governing Body of Mayfield Secondary School* (2003), a case concerning homophobic abuse by pupils of a female teacher who was lesbian, the House of Lords held that this was not direct sex discrimination as a male homosexual teacher would have been subjected to such abuse (see also *Smith v Gardner Merchant Ltd* (1998)). The acts complained of in *Pearce* took place before the coming into force of the Human Rights Act 1998 on 2 October 1998, so no claim could be brought on the basis of an infringement of human rights (see below).

5.134 The ECJ took a similar view in *Grant v South West Trains* (1998), in which a lesbian employee brought a challenge under Article 119 (current Article 141) of the EC

Treaty against her employer's granting of travel concessions to spouses and live-in partners of the opposite sex but did not extend this to same-sex partners. The ECJ held that if a male homosexual would have been treated in the same way (which he would) there was no sex discrimination, since the Article did not cover sexuality but only discrimination on the ground of sex.

5.135 The only redress available until recently (before the European Convention on Human Rights was incorporated into English law by the Human Rights Act 1998), at least for employees of public authorities, was not to be found in domestic courts under the SDA but in the European Court of Human Rights (ECHR) through claims based on the European Convention on Human Rights (ECHR), on the basis that the complainants' Article 8 right to privacy had been breached, and therefore their Article 14 right had been breached. These claims succeeded before the European Court of Human Rights in two cases concerning members of the armed services who were subjected to questioning concerning their sexual orientation: *Smith and Grady v UK* (1999) and *Lustig-Prean and Beckett v UK* (2000).

The Employment Equality (Sexual Orientation) Regulations 2003

5.136 The Employment Equality (Sexual Orientation) Regulations 2003 (the 'SO Regs') now extend protection to persons who face discrimination on the ground of their sexual orientation. The legislation was introduced to implement the relevant strands of the Equal Treatment Framework Directive (ETFD), Directive 2000/78. Two sets of regulations implement the sexual orientation and religion or belief strands of the ETFD – the Employment Equality (Sexual Orientation) Regulations 2003 SI 2003/1661 (in force from 1 December 2003) and the Employment Equality (Religion or Belief) Regulations 2003 SI 2003/1660 (in force from 2 December 2003). This section considers the Employment Equality (Sexual Orientation) Regulations 2003.

5.137 Although not within the employment field, as they concern the provision of goods, services, and facilities, it should be noted that the Equality Act (Sexual Orientation) Regulations 2007, SI 2007/1263, which came in to force from 30 April 2007, include a provision (reg 30) to ensure that 'Anything done by a person in the course of his employment shall be treated for the purposes of these Regulations as done by the employer as well as by the person.'

5.138 There is very useful guidance on the SO Regs from ACAS and an Explanatory Note from the DBERR. The ACAS guide to *Sexual Orientation and the Workplace* (November 2005) may be found on the ACAS website: <http://www.acas.org.uk/media/pdf/e/n/sexual_1.pdf>; for the ACAS website generally, see <http://www.

acas.org.uk>. The DBERR (formerly DTI) Explanatory Note, which provides explanatory notes on both the SO Regs and those on Religion or Beliefsets of Regs, may be found on the DBERR website at <http://www.berr.gov.uk/employment/discrimination/emp-equality-regs-2003/page21856.html>.

5.139   Regulation 2 defines 'sexual orientation' as orientation towards persons of the same sex, the opposite sex, or both the same sex and the opposite sex. The legislation therefore covers homosexuals, heterosexuals, and bi-sexuals, making it unlawful to discriminate against a person in any one of these categories because of his or her sexual orientation. This definition does not cover asexuals, since an 'orientation' of some kind is required.

5.140   Under the regulations it is therefore unlawful to discriminate against:

- a heterosexual person because he or she is heterosexual;
- a homosexual person because he or she is homosexual; and
- a bi-sexual person because he or she is bi-sexual.

5.141   However, it should be noted that it is unlawful to discriminate 'on grounds of sexual orientation', rather than on the ground of the *applicant's* sexual orientation. This definition is wide enough to cover those who are discriminated against because, for example, they support or fraternise with others of a particular sexual orientation, even though they are not discriminated against on the ground of *their* own orientation. It is also wide enough to cover discrimination against a person where the employer *believes* that they are of a particular orientation, although they may not be.

5.142   The forms of discrimination covered are: direct, indirect, harassment, and victimisation.

Direct discrimination – Regulation 3(1)(a)

5.143   The SO Regs adopt the familiar division of discrimination into direct and indirect forms. Direct discrimination occurs where a person is treated less favourably than another on grounds of sexual orientation. It is always unlawful.

Indirect discrimination – reg 3(1)(b)

5.144   Indirect discrimination occurs where a provision, criterion, or practice which is applied generally to persons not of the same sexual orientation puts persons of a particular sexual orientation at a disadvantage. It is unlawful if it is not a proportionate means of achieving a legitimate aim (reg 3(1)(b)). The circumstances of the complainant and his/her comparator must be the same or not materially different (reg 3(2)).

Harassment on grounds of sexual orientation – Regulation 5

5.145 Harassment is defined as unwanted conduct which has either the purpose or the effect of violating another person's dignity or 'creating an intimidating, hostile, degrading, humiliating or offensive environment' for the other person. Conduct is to be regarded as having that effect only if it should reasonably be considered as having that effect taking into account the perception of the other person (reg 5(2)).

5.146 However, in *English v Thomas Sanderson Blinds Ltd* (2008), the EAT has held that the provisions of the Sexual Orientation Regulations relating to harassment are not compliant with EU law, ie Article 2 of Directive 2000/78/EC (the 'ETFD'). In *English* the claimant had been subjected to homophobic banter. This was because he had attended a boarding school and lived in Brighton. However, his work colleagues knew that he was not gay.

5.147 Regulation 5 of the Sexual Orientation Regulations prohibits harassment 'on grounds of' sexual orientation. This implements the harassment provisions of the ETFD, although the Directive refers to harassment *'related to'* any of the relevant grounds (Art 2(3)), including sexual orientation. The EAT upheld a tribunal finding that regulation 5 only protects a person who is homosexual, or is perceived by his harassers as homosexual, or who is harassed because of his failure to follow instructions to discriminate against another on grounds of sexual orientation. However, Judge Peter Clark held that regulation 5 'does not properly implement the Directive' (at para 21), on the basis of the differences between the 'related to' test and 'on grounds of'. The EAT stated that 'on grounds of', in the context of both race and sex discrimination, imports the 'reason why' question: why did the alleged discriminator act as he did? Therefore, the EAT held that, 'the protection afforded to Mr English by the domestic Regulations is narrower than that which the Directive provides'. However, Mr English could not rely upon the Directive against a private respondent. He therefore lost his claim.

5.148 A similar problem arose as regards the harassment provisions of the SDA. Following the decision in *Equal Opportunities Commission v Secretary of State for Trade & Industry Industry* (2007), HC, in which Burton J held that the words 'on the ground of her sex, he engages in unwanted conduct' in the amended Sex Discrimination Act's harassment provisions did not correctly implement the revised Equal Treatment Directive, the SDA was amended by the Sex Discrimination Act 1975 (Amendment) Regulations 2008, which came into force on 6 April 2008. The wording indicated above has now been replaced with 'he engages in unwanted conduct that is related to her sex or that of another person'. Clearly, similar changes will have to be made to the SO Regs (and the other legislation implementing the various strands of discrimination under the ETFD).

Harassment, sexual orientation, and religion

5.149 For an interesting, full, and detailed consideration of the balancing exercise to be undertaken where discrimination on the ground of a person's sexual orientation is motivated by religious belief, see the following case from the High Court of Northern Ireland: *Christian Institute and ors' application for judicial review, Re* (2008), which is discussed in the section on the GOR and Religious Discrimination.

Victimisation

5.150 Victimisation is less favourable treatment by a person (A) of another person (B) by reason that B has brought proceedings against A or any other person, given evidence or information in connection with proceedings, done anything under or by reference to the SO Regs, or alleged that A or any other person has committed an act which contravenes or would contravene the SO Regs (reg 4). This does not apply if the allegation, evidence, or information was false and not made or given in good faith (reg 4(2)).

Scope of the SO Regs

5.151 Protection is extended to: job applicants and employees, and ex-employees (regs 6 and 21); post-employment contract workers (reg 8); office-holders (including constables) (regs 10 and 11); barristers and advocates (regs 12 and 13); partnerships (reg 14); and civil servants and members of the armed forces (reg 36). A trade union (which includes any organisation of workers or of employers) is prohibited from discriminating against intending or actual members on grounds, *inter alia*, of sexual orientation (reg 15). Discrimination by employers is unlawful, as is discrimination by the following bodies: trade organisations (reg 15); bodies conferring professional and trade qualifications (reg 16); training providers (reg 17); employment agencies (reg 18); and further and higher education institutions (reg 20). Sexual orientation discrimination by trustees and managers of occupational pension schemes is also covered (reg 9A).

Contract terms or terms in collective agreements

5.152 A term of a contract or collective agreement or any rule made by a trade organisation will normally be either unenforceable or void if it purports to exclude or limit any provision of the regulations (Sch 4).

Genuine occupational requirements – regulation 7

5.153 As in the SDA and the RRA, there are genuine occupational requirement exceptions provided for in the SO Regs. These exceptions apply where: a particular sexual orientation is a genuine and determining occupational requirement, and it is proportionate to apply that requirement (reg 7); and where national security is at risk (reg 24). The exceptions include one concerning religious organisations with a doctrinal objection to particular sexual orientations (eg homosexuality, which is contrary to some religious doctrines) (reg 7(3)). This provision was introduced after lobbying from various religious groups. Regulation 7, together with the exception in reg 25, discussed below, was the subject of judicial review proceedings (see *R (on application of Amicus, NATFHE, UNISON, NASUWT, Public & Commercial Services Union, NURMTW and NUT) v Secretary of State for Trade and Industry* (2004)), as an improper implementation of the Framework Directive and an infringement of the Article 8 right in the ECHR. The unions argued that these exceptions could be used to discriminate against homosexual teachers in faith schools. The High Court rejected the unions' arguments, holding that, taking a purposive interpretation, the SO Regs properly implement the Framework Directive. However, the High Court gave leave to appeal to the Court of Appeal.

5.154 There is also a general exception in regulation 25 (as amended) which provides that it is not unlawful to prevent or restrict access to a benefit by reference to marital status or civil partnership.

5.155 This exemption would exclude, for example, retirement and occupational pension schemes providing pensions to surviving spouses and civil partners. As discussed above, this provision was unsuccessfully challenged in the High Court (and see the TUC Press Release 'Unions challenge gay law in High Court', 16 March 2004). However, under the Civil Partnership Act 2004 those individuals within 'civil partnerships' from 5 December 2005 have similar rights to those of married couples, including next-of-kin-entitlements such as surviving-spouse pensions (see the amended reg 25).

5.156 An interesting recent ruling from the ECJ on this issue is *Maruko v Versorgungsanstalt der deutschen Bühnen* (2008). It concerns the rights of same-sex couples. The case concerned a claim made by a German man who was denied a widower's pension from an occupational pension scheme after the death of his registered life partner (which is a similar status as the civil partner in the UK). The ECJ ruled that it is contrary to the prohibition on sexual orientation discrimination in the ETFD for same-sex civil partners not to have the same right to survivor's benefit under an occupational pension scheme as that provided for surviving spouses in a similar position.

The GOR and religious organisations

5.157 The GOR exceptions include one, similar to SDA, s 19, specifically for the benefit of religious organisations which have a doctrinal objection to homosexuality (reg 7(3)). On this aspect of the Regulations, it is interesting to note the decision of *Christian*

Institute and ors' application for judicial review, Re (2008), from Northern Ireland. This was a challenge by way of judicial review proceedings to the NI Regulations 2006 (see the Equality Act (Sexual Orientation) Regulations (Northern Ireland) 2006, SR 2006/439 (the 2006 Regulations)), concerning the harassment provisions in the 2006 Regulations. The applicants' argument was that the orthodox position of Christians was that homosexual practice was sinful, and that the 2006 Regulations imposed on those who hold such orthodox beliefs certain duties which were inconsistent with the practice of their religious beliefs. Although this is a case from Northern Ireland, it contains a close consideration by Weatherup J of the factors to be taken into account when balancing the legitimate rights of supporters of freedom of religious belief and practice on the one hand and opponents of sexual orientation discrimination on the other.

Questionnaire procedure

5.158　Employees who believe they may have been discriminated against or subjected to harassment contrary to the regulations may serve a questionnaire on their employers (reg 22 and schedules 2 and 3).

Vicarious liability of employers

5.159　As is usual under the discrimination legislation, employers are vicariously liable for the unlawful acts of their employees, unless they prove that they took reasonably practicable steps to prevent the employee committing such acts (reg 22).

Aiding unlawful acts

5.160　Anyone knowingly aiding another person to do an act rendered unlawful under the SO Regs is treated as doing the act themselves, unless they reasonably relied on a statement that such an act was not unlawful (reg 23).

ETs – claims, burden of proofs, and remedies

5.161　A complainant under the SO Regs may lodge a claim with an employment tribunal within three months of the act complained of. The burden of proof is the same as in the SDA and RRA, ie the complainant must establish facts from which the tribunal could conclude that an unlawful act of discrimination has taken place and the respondent must then prove that he did not commit any such act (reg 29). The usual remedies of a declaration, compensation, and a recommendation may be made (regs 27–30). There is no statutory maximum on the amount of compensation a tribunal can order to be paid to a person who brings a successful claim (reg 30).

ACAS guides and DBERR Explanatory Notes

5.162 As indicated above, ACAS have published two sets of guidelines on the SO Regs and the R or B Regs. The ACAS Guide on the R or B Regs is called *Religion or Belief and the Workplace* (November 2005). It is available on the ACAS website at <http:// www.acas.org.uk/media/pdf/f/l/religion_1.pdf>; for the ACAS website generally, see <http://www.acas.org.uk>. The ACAS Guide on the SO Regs is called *Sexual Orientation and the Workplace* (November 2005). It is also available on the ACAS website at: <http://www.acas.org.uk/media/pdf/e/n/sexual_1.pdf>.

5.163 The DBERR (former DTI) Explanatory Note on both sets of Regulations is available on the DTI website at <http://www.berr.gov.uk/whatwedo/employment/ discrimination/religion-belief/index.html>.

Employment Equality (Religion or Belief) Regulations 2003

5.164 The Employment Equality (Religion or Belief) Regulations 2003 SI 2003/1660 (the 'R or B Regs') came into force on 2 December 2003. The ETFD required all EU Member States to introduce legislation to outlaw religious discrimination by 2 December 2003, but with a possible extension to 2 December 2006 in some situations. This strand is implemented in Great Britain (not Northern Ireland) by the R or B Regs, which make it unlawful to discriminate on grounds of religion or belief in employment and vocational training.

5.165 The R or B Regs are drafted in similar terms to the SO Regs, with the relevant changes being made. The four forms of discrimination rendered unlawful are direct, indirect, harassment, and victimisation, with similar definitions, *mutatis mutandis*, as those in the SO Regs. Thus, for direct discrimination the definition is less favourable treatment on the grounds of religion or belief, while indirect discrimination involves (i) the application by A of a provision, criterion, or practice which he applies or would apply to persons not of the same religion or belief as B, but (ii) which puts or would put persons of the same religion or belief as B at a particular disadvantage when compared with other persons, (iii) which puts B at that disadvantage, and (iv) which cannot be shown to be a proportionate means of achieving a legitimate aim (reg 3). The religion or belief must not be that of A (reg 3(2)).

5.166 As originally drafted, the Regulations prohibit direct discrimination, indirect discrimination, victimisation, and harassment in the employment field (including vocational training) by reason of (under the original wording) 'any religion, religious belief, or similar philosophical belief' (emphasis added). However, an important amendment to the Regulations came into force on 30 April 2007. Section 77 of the Equality Act 2006 amends regulation 2(1) of the Regulations so as to replace the definition of 'religion or belief' with 'any religion, or religious or philosophical belief'.

5.167 Regulation 2(1) now reads:

> In these Regulations
>
> (a) 'religion' means any religion,
>
> (b) 'belief' means any religious or philosophical belief,
>
> (c) a reference to religion includes a reference to lack of religion, and
>
> (d) a reference to belief includes a reference to lack of belief.

5.168 The removal of the word 'similar' is important. This was previously interpreted as requiring that the philosophical belief be similar in nature to a religious belief (see *Baggs v Fudge* – the 2005 ET case (unreported) of the BNP member who claimed fascism was a 'similar philosophical belief': his claim was struck out). Thus this amendment re-opens the question of whether political belief can fall within the 2003 Regulations. It is interesting to note that, during the House of Lords' debate, it was suggested that a philosophical belief should cover a 'world view or life stance', which is broad enough to include political beliefs.

5.169 It is unclear whether 'fringe' religious beliefs, such as those of vegans and Rastafarians, are covered. A challenge under the European Convention on Human Rights, Article 9 (Freedom of thought, conscience, and religion) may be possible in such cases.

5.170 The explanatory notes accompanying the Regulations refer to belief systems or beliefs affecting world view or way of life, so it would seem that the legislation is wide enough to cover discrimination against atheists and humanists, as well as others holding beliefs that are not necessarily 'religious'. However, it is unlikely that they also cover *any* philosophical approach or system of analysis, such as political philosophy.

5.171 A recent and rather unusual case on the Regulations concerned section 79 of the Civil Partnership Act, which allows civil partners and same sex couples to adopt or foster children. In *McClintock v Department of Constitutional Affairs* (2008), EAT, a justice of the peace resigned from the family panel because he claimed that he could not in conscience, and compatibly with his philosophical and religious beliefs, agree to place children with same-sex couples. He argued that he strongly believed that the question of allowing same-sex couples to adopt had not been sufficiently researched and tested and that 'to send a child to a same sex household is to make him/her the subject of an experiment in social science'. He asked to be relieved from the duty to officiate in such cases, and claimed that the DCA discriminated indirectly against him on grounds of religion or belief by not doing so. His complaint failed on its facts. Mr McClintock could not show that he was disadvantaged as a consequence of holding a relevant 'belief' falling within the scope of the legislation. He had not put his objections on the basis of any religious or philosophical belief.

5.172 The EAT held that to constitute a belief 'there must be a religious or philosophical viewpoint in which one actually believes'. This was the case under the unamended Regulations, under which the claim was brought, as they required a philosophical belief to be 'similar' to a religious belief to fall within the scope of the Act. Elias, P, stated that 'the kind of objection which Mr McClintock voiced here, depending as it did on the lack of evidence to justify the approach adopted in the legislation towards same-sex parents, could not properly be described as a philosophical belief so as to fall within the scope of the Regulations, even after the amendment' (at para 47).

5.173 The first religious discrimination case brought under the Regulations to reach the EAT was *Mohmed v West Coast Trains Ltd* (UKEAT/0682/05/DA, judgment delivered on 30 August 2006). Mr Mohmed, a Sikh employed by West Coast Trains Ltd, wore a beard which he refused to keep tidy. Another Sikh employee did keep his beard tidy. Mr Mohmed was dismissed. The employer claimed this was because of his lack of enthusiasm, although Mr Mohmed maintained it was because of his beard and appearance. Mr Mohmed appealed against the ET's rejection of his claim of direct discrimination on the grounds of his religion or belief by way of dismissal. The EAT dismissed his claim, on the basis that the beard issue had no connection with religion: it related to tidiness of appearance only. The employer had adduced evidence (which was accepted) that it had no objection to beards or to Sikhs with beards, and no prima facie case of unlawful religious discrimination had been made out by Mr Mohmed. Therefore, there was no shifting of the burden of proof to require an explanation from the employer for the dismissal as provided for by regulation 29 of the Regulations.

Harassment – regulation 5

5.174 Under regulation 5, harassment is where a person is subjected to unwanted conduct on grounds of religion or belief with the purpose or effect of violating his dignity, or creating an intimidating, hostile, degrading, humiliating, or offensive environment for him.

Veil – requirement to remove – whether direct discrimination or indirect discrimination

5.175　In *Azmi v Kiklees BC* (2007), the EAT held that a female Muslim teaching assistant who was required to remove her full face veil while teaching had not been directly discriminated against. The correct comparator was a woman who, whether Muslim or not, wore a face covering for a reason other than religious belief. That comparator would have been issued with the same instruction and, if she had refused to comply with it, she would have been suspended. Furthermore, the EAT held that, although the instruction was a provision, criterion, or practice, any indirect discrimination was objectively justified as being a proportionate response to the legitimate aim of providing effective tuition to young children.

The test of proportionality

5.176　The Explanatory Note states (at para 41) that, for the provision, criterion, or practice to be 'proportionate', it must be an 'appropriate and necessary means of achieving the legitimate aim in question' (see C-222/84 *Johnston v RUC* (1986) and C-170/84 *Bilka-Kaufhaus GmbH v Karin Weber von Hartz* (1986)). The Explanatory Note points out that, although

> [p]roportionality will depend on the facts of each case . . . generally, an appropriate means is one which is suitable to achieve the aim in question, and which actually does so. A necessary means is one without which the aim could not be achieved; it is not simply a convenient means. This will include consideration of whether the aim could be achieved by other means which have lesser discriminatory effects.

5.177　The Explanatory Note further explains (para 42) that, '[p]roportionality thus requires courts and tribunals to weigh up the needs of the person applying the practice against its discriminatory effects' (see the House of Lords' decision in *Webb v EMOAir Cargo (UK) Ltd* (1987)).

5.178　It should be noted that, in direct discrimination, the less favourable treatment must be on grounds of religion or belief which does not necessarily have to be that of the complainant. For example, the definition could apply to an individual (X) who fraternises with or supports another person (Y), whether financially or in other ways, but who does not share Y's religion or belief, who is discriminated against because of that fraternisation or support of Y.

5.179　The Regulations cover, inter alia, job applicants and employees, terms of employment, opportunities afforded for promotion, transfer, training, or any other benefit, and dismissal (reg 6).

The 'religious organisations' GOR exception – regulation 7

5.180 There is an exception for a genuine occupational requirement (GOR), where, 'having regard to the nature of the employment or the context in which it is carried out being of a particular religion or belief is a genuine and determining occupational requirement', and it is proportionate to apply the requirement, and the person to whom it is applied does not meet it, or the employer is not satisfied that the person meets it (reg 7(2)). There is a specific GOR, in similar terms to that in regulation 7(2), where an employer 'has an ethos based on religion or belief'.

5.181 The most generally important exception is where being of a particular religion or belief is a genuine and determining occupational requirement for a post and it is proportionate to apply the requirement in the particular case. The Explanatory Note states that 'determining' in this context means 'the requirement must be crucial to the post, and not merely one of several important factors' (para 73).

5.182 A small but important gloss is that the requirement need not be a 'determining' requirement where an employer has an ethos based on religion or belief and 'having regard to that ethos and to the nature of the employment or the context in which it is carried out being of a particular religion or belief is a genuine occupational requirement for the job': this is referred to in the Explanatory Notes as the 'religious organisations GOR' (reg 7). Note that there is no specific 'domestic employment' exemption.

5.183 A 2007 case on regulation 7 is *Glasgow City Council v McNab* (2007), EAT, in which the EAT upheld an ET's decision that an atheist maths teacher had been subjected to unlawful discrimination contrary to the Regulations after he had applied but failed to get an interview for the temporary post of Acting Principal Teacher of Pastoral Care at a Roman Catholic state school. The EAT upheld the judgment of the ET that, on the facts of the case, the exception in regulation 7 'for genuine occupational requirement' did not apply.

5.184 A challenge being brought under the Regulations in 2008 is that of *Sheridan v Prospects Charity*. The Respondent is a Christian organisation which helps adults with learning difficulties. The complainant is arguing that in 2004, Prospects began recruiting only practising Christians for almost all posts, and told existing non-Christian staff that they were no longer eligible for promotion. Mr Sheridan, an ex-employee, is bringing an ET claim with the support of the British Humanist Association (the BHA). It is understood that Prospects considers that it should be protected by the religious organisations GOR exception in regulation 7 of the Regulations (see also the BHA website for December 2007, at <http://www.humanism.org.uk/site/cms/newsarticleview.asp?article=2400>).

Time off work for religious observance

5.185 There is nothing in the Regulations specifically requiring employers to provide time off or facilities at the workplace for religious worship or observance. However, in particular circumstances, employers will need to be careful to ensure that their policy with regard to refusing time off for religious observance does not constitute unjustified indirect discrimination.

5.186 There are provisions similar to the SO Regs in the R or B Regs relating to: vicarious liability (reg 22); aiding unlawful acts (reg 23); the questionnaire procedure (reg 33); and enforcement by way of a complaint to the employment tribunal, with the same burden of proof provision as in the SO Regs (regs 27–34), and the usual remedies available of a declaration, unlimited compensation, and a recommendation (reg 30).

The Employment Equality (Age) Regulations 2006

5.187 The Employment Equality (Age) Regulations (SI 2006/1031) were laid before Parliament on 9 March 2006 and came into force on 1 October 2006. They implement the age discrimination strand of the ETFD. The central provisions of these Regulations closely follow those of the two other sets of Employment Equality Regulations on sexual orientation and religion or belief, with the relevant changes being made. The following discussion provides a brief outline of the main provisions of the Regulations.

5.188 As regards the ETFD, the ECJ in *Mangold v Rudiger Helm* (2006) ruled that the Directive was concerned with practical measures to tackle age discrimination, but once approved by the Council of Ministers the Directive had already taken effect, ie before the implementation date. This means that any national laws that permitted age discrimination after this date would be contrary to EC law, subject to justification, which is that the aim behind the discriminatory act should not only be legitimate, but proportionate in that it must be shown that a less discriminatory measure was not available to the respondent. The case concerned the relatively poor protection afforded to workers aged 52 years or over engaged on fixed-term contracts.

Challenge to the Regulations

5.189 One interesting recent development is the challenge to the Regulations mounted by Heyday, a not-for-profit organisation linked to Age Concern. The Heyday challenge, which was by way of an application to the High Court in July 2006 for judicial review, concerned the default retirement age (DRA) of 65 and the associated mandatory retirement procedures (see *R (on the application of the Incorporated Trustees of the National Council on Ageing v Secretary of State for Trade and Industry* (2007)). The High Court has referred the issue to the ECJ; it is due to be heard by the EJC during 2008/2009.

5.190 Heyday argues that the DRA infringes the employment rights of those over 65 and is impermissible under the ETFD (further background information on the Heyday judicial review application may be found on its website: <http://www.heyday.org.uk/yoursay/campaigns/>).

5.191 The High Court has posed five questions for consideration by the ECJ, the basic one being:

> Does the scope of the Directive extend to national rules which permit employers to dismiss employees aged 65 or over by reason of retirement?

The case is listed in the ECJ as Case C-388/07 (see EC Official Journal 24 November 2007 re Heyday case, ECJ Case C-388/07). A final decision is not expected before 2009 but it seems unlikely that Heyday will win its challenge, largely because of the ECJ's ruling in Palacios (discussed below).

5.192 In *Palacios de la Villa v Cortefiel Servicios SA* (2007), ECJ, an employee who had reached the age of 65 was notified by his employer that, pursuant to a provision in a Spanish collective agreement, his contract of employment was automatically terminated on the ground that he had reached the compulsory retirement age. On a reference by the Spanish Social Court, the ECJ ruled that the ETFD does not preclude national legislation allowing collective agreements to provide for mandatory retirement at age 65, provided the measure is 'objectively and reasonably justified...by a legitimate aim relating to employment policy and the labour market, and the means put in place to achieve that aim of public interest do not appear to be inappropriate and unnecessary for the purpose'. The employment policy/labour market argument which satisfied the objective justification test here was that the mandatory retirement age adopted was to deal with unemployment. The ECJ said (at para 72):

> It does not appear unreasonable for the authorities of a Member State to take the view that a measure such as that at issue in the main proceedings may be appropriate and necessary in order to achieve a legitimate aim in the context of national employment policy, consisting in the promotion of full employment by facilitating access to the labour market.

5.193 The ruling in *Palacios* may have serious implications for the Heyday challenge, given that the ECJ has ruled that a mandatory retirement age falls within the scope of the ETFD's prohibition on discriminatory dismissal on age grounds. The ECJ has also ruled that there does not need to be a specific list of justifications for age discrimination. The Member State simply has to establish that discrimination was proportionate.

5.194 However, the labour market conditions, social policy objectives, etc in Spain are not the same as those in the UK, so it may be possible that the UK government's argument is susceptible to successful challenge. The essential question is whether the UK's default retirement age is proportionate, which will be for the High Court to determine, once the ECJ has made its ruling.

5.195 Meanwhile, all claims concerning the default retirement provisions which have been lodged with ETs have been stayed, pending the ECJ's ruling in the Heyday challenge (see the Practice Direction of HH Judge Meeran, the President of the ETs, dated 8 November 2007). Before the President's Practice Direction, the EAT had overturned an ET's decision to strike out a claim on the retirement provisions. The case has been stayed pending the ECJ ruling: see *Johns v Solent SD Ltd* (2008), EAT.

5.196 The Age Regulations apply to discrimination on the ground of age (at whatever age it may strike). The Regulations will have no effect upon the State Pension age, which will remain at 60 for women and 65 for men. However, all retirement ages under 65 (this default retirement age is to be reviewed in 2011) will be unlawful, unless objectively justified. Any such justification by the alleged discriminator must establish that the treatment or 'provision, criterion or practice' is a 'proportionate means of achieving a legitimate aim' (reg 3). This provision is intended to implement Article 6.1 of the ETFD.

Direct discrimination (reg 3(1)(a)) and indirect discrimination (reg 3(1)(b)) on the ground of age

5.197 The Age Regulations are unique in domestic discrimination law in that *direct* discrimination may be justified. Direct discrimination and indirect discrimination are defined as follows:

Reg 3(1)

For the purposes of these Regulations, a person (A) discriminates against another (B) if –

    (a) on grounds of B's age, A treats B less favourably than he treats or would treat other persons, or

    (b) A applies to B a provision, criterion or practice which he applies or would apply equally to persons not of the same age group as B, but –

        (i) which puts or would put persons of the same age group as B at a particular disadvantage when compared with other persons, and

(ii) which puts B at that disadvantage,

(c) and A cannot show the treatment or, as the case may be, provision, criterion or practice to be a proportionate means of achieving a legitimate aim.

5.198 Regulation 3(2) and 3(3) states:

(2) A comparison of B's case with that of another person under paragraph (1) must be such that the relevant circumstances in the one case are the same, or not materially different, in the other.

(3) In this regulation –

'age group' means a group of persons defined by reference to age, whether by reference to a particular age or range of ages; and

The reference in paragraph (1)(a) to B's age includes B's apparent age.

5.199 The objective justification defence is subject to a number of general exemptions, ie where justification is not required. These include: requiring retirement at age 65 or more (reg 29); benefits related to length of service, which are excepted unless the disadvantaged employee has more than five years' service, in which case the employer must establish that it 'reasonably appears' to him that the criterion of length of service 'fulfils a business need', eg encouraging loyalty or motivation, or rewarding experience (reg 32); pay related to the national minimum wage (this will apply only to those situations where the employees in the lower age groups (below age 22) are paid less than the adult minimum wage (reg 31)). This will not cover all pay differences based on the age bands used in the national minimum wage. Only those situations are covered where the employees in the lower age groups (below age 22) are paid less than the adult minimum wage (reg 32); age-related provisions in occupational pension schemes (sch 2).)

5.200 The exception in regulation 31 for the National Minimum Wage is permissible under the ETFD, since Article 6(1)(a) provides for such an exemption, as follows:

that differences of treatment on grounds of age shall not constitute discrimination, if, within the context of national law, they are objectively and reasonably justified...such differences...may include...(a) the setting of special conditions on access to employment...including dismissal and remuneration conditions for young people...in order to promote their vocational integration.

5.201 The differential rates and the flexibility provided for employers is therefore entirely consistent with the Directive and the Regulations, in that vocational integration is the legitimate objective at which the legislation is aimed.

5.202 The service-related benefit exception in regulation 32, which is, potentially, indirect discrimination on the ground of age, may be objectively justified in that the legitimate aim it seeks to secure is one of employment policy.

5.203 The service-related benefit exception in regulation 32, which is, potentially, indirect discrimination on the ground of age, may be objectively justified in that the legitimate aim it seeks to secure is one of employment policy: in the sex discrimination case of *Danfoss (C-109/88)* (1989), in which an employer was alleged to have indirectly discriminated against women by awarding pay based (in part) on length of service, the ECJ observed (para 117):

> since length of service goes hand-in-hand with experience and since experience generally enables the employee to perform his duties better, the employer is free to award him without having to establish the importance it has in the performance of specific tasks entrusted to the employee...the Equal Pay Directive must (therefore) be interpreted as meaning that where it appears that the application of criteria, such as the employee's mobility, training or length of service, for the award of pay...systematically works to the disadvantage of female employees...the employer does not have to provide special justification for recourse to the criterion of length of service.

5.204 The Danfoss principle was cited and approved by the ECH in *Cadman v Health & Safety Executive* (2006) concerning service-based pay scales as a defence to an equal pay claim. The ECJ ruled that such pay practices were permissible, but this was a rebuttable presumption, ie evidence could be adduced which would raise 'serious doubts' concerning the practice.

5.205 Positive action is lawful where it is to provide special help to persons of a particular age or age group in relation to particular work if this 'prevents or compensates for disadvantages linked to age suffered by persons of that age or age group doing that work or likely to take up that work' (reg 29).

5.206 The Age Regulations cover, among others, employees, workers, and job applicants. The prohibited forms of discrimination include harassment (reg 6) and victimisation (reg 4), which bear similar definitions to those in the other discrimination legislation. Instructions to discriminate are unlawful (reg 5), and employers and principals may be liable (reg 25), subject to the defence that the employer took reasonably practicable steps to prevent the unlawful act.

The duty to consider and related procedure (reg 47 and Sch 6)

5.207 The Age Regulations provide that not more than a year and not less than six months before an employee is dismissed by reason of retirement the employer must give a written notice to the employee concerned telling him (a) that he has the right to make a request not to retire on the intended retirement date; and (b) the date on which he intends the employee to retire (Sch 6, para 2). Failure to comply will entitle the employee to compensation of up to eight times a week's pay (subject to the same cap applying to the unfair dismissal basic award), provided the notice is given at least two weeks before the intended retirement date. If the notice is given later than that, or not at all, and if the employer still requires the employee to retire on that date, the retirement will be treated as automatically unfair dismissal (see below); in that case the normal unfair dismissal compensation rules will apply.

5.208 An employee can make only one, written request to his employer not to retire on the intended retirement date. The request must specify what the employee is requesting, ie that his employment continues indefinitely, or that it continues for a stated period, or that it continues until a stated date (Sch 6, para 5). The employer has a duty to consider the request in good faith within specified time limits, including (normally) a duty to 'hold a meeting to discuss the request with the employee'. If the request is rejected, the employee has a right to appeal, again within specified time limits (Sch 6, paras 5 to 7).

Age discrimination and unfair dismissal (retirement is the sixth potentially fair reason for dismissal)

5.209 Employees dismissed for an age-discriminatory reason are able to claim for both age discrimination and unfair dismissal, although employees over the age of 65 do not have a right to claim for unlawful age discrimination, since regulation 30 permits such a dismissal at or after 65 (but note that they are still able to claim unfair dismissal if the employer has failed to comply with the duty to consider a request for continued employment) (see ss 98ZA–98ZH, which have been inserted into the ERA: draft Sch 8, para 23 of the Age Regulations). This is potentially one of the most interesting areas in which case law developments may be expected, depending upon the outcome of the Heyday challenge.

5.210 The relevant parts of unfair dismissal and redundancy law which relate directly to age have been repealed, eg ERA s 109 (upper age limit for unfair dismissal), ss 156, 211 (upper and lower age limits for redundancy payments), s 119(4) (tapering provisions for the basic award).

FURTHER READING

McColgan, A, *Discrimination Law: Text, Cases and Materials* (2005) Hart Publishing (chapter 1).

Deakin, S & Morris, G, *Labour Law* (4th ed, 2005) Butterworths (chapter 6, pp 571–584).

Age regulations

Connolly, M, Discrimination Law (2006) Thomson (see the various, relevant sections on the Regulations, which are discussed at several points throughout the text).

Deakin, S, & Morris, G, Labour Law (4th ed, 2005) Hart Publishing (chapter 6).

McColgan, A., *Discrimination Law: Text, Cases and Materials* (2005) Hart Publishing (chapter 1), pp 1–14 (NB This is a very short section which was written before the Regulations were issued in final draft form).

Smith, I, & Thomas, G, Smith & Wood's Employment Law (9th ed, 2007) OUP (chapter 6, section 8).

The European Union has published a wide variety of research and policy documents on age discrimination: see http://publications.eu.int.

ARTICLES

Fredman, S, (2001) 'Equality: A New Generation?', *Industrial Law Journal*, Vol 30, No 2, pp 145–168.

McColgan, A, (2003) 'Principles of Equality and Protection from Discrimination in International Human Rights Law', *European Human Rights Law Review*, pp 157–175.

Disability discrimination

Hughes, P (2004) 'Disability Discrimination and the Duty to Make Reasonable Adjustments: Recent Developments', *Industrial Law Journal*, Vol 33, No 4, pp 358–366.

Age discrimination

The following article from the *Industrial Law Journal* provide very useful analysis of the Regulations:

Sargeant, M, 'The Employment Equality (Age) Regulations 2006: A Legitimisation of Age Discrimination in Employment', *Industrial Law Journal*, Vol 35, No 3, pp 209–227.

And for a very good article on the objective justification defence in the Regulations, see:

Swift, J., 'Justifying Age Discrimination', *Industrial Law Journal*, Vol 35, No 3, pp 228–44.

Sexual orientation

Manknell, D, 'Discrimination on Grounds of Sexual Orientation, Harassment, and Liability for Third Parties', *Industrial Law Journal*, Vol 32, No 4, pp 297–309.

Oliver, H, (2004) 'Sexual Orientation Discrimination: Perceptions, Definitions And Genuine OCCUPATIONAL requirement', *Industrial Law Journal*, Vol 33, No 1, pp 1–21.

Discrimination on the ground of religion or belief

Vickers, L, (2003) 'Freedom of Religion and the Workplace: The Draft Employment Equality (Religion or Belief) Regulations 2003', *Industrial Law Journal*, Vol 32, No 1, pp 23–36.

SELF-TEST QUESTIONS

1 Prakash and Hari are Sikhs: Winston, aged 27, is black, of West Indian origin and came to this country five years ago. Vacancies for jobs on the production line at Quick Snacks' factory are advertised in the local press. A written application and four passes at GCSE level are required for applicants. Prakash has difficulty writing English and asks a friend to complete the application form. Quick Snacks' board of directors decides as a matter of policy to reject all Sikh applicants: employees in the personnel office who process the application are duly informed of this and instructed to comply with the board's decision. Prakash and Hari's applications are rejected, as is Winston's on the ground that he does not have the required GCSE level passes. Robert, a clerical worker in the personnel department informs the EHRC about the board's policy: when his manager discovers this, Robert is summarily dismissed.

Advise Prakash, Hari, Winston, and Robert.

2 The following events occur on the premises of Fingals Ltd, a food-processing company:

(a) Fingals has advertised internally for a manager in the marketing office. Anne works part-time in the marketing office as an assistant, so as to fit in with her child-care responsibilities (she has two young children, aged four and two). She has seen the advertisement and wants to apply for the position. She is prepared to job-share, although she would consider working full-time. She applies for the job but is not interviewed because the company tells her the job is not open to part-time staff, nor can it be job-shared.

(b) Pippa, who has worked for Fingals for eight months, has been undergoing gender-reassignment, without Fingals' knowledge. After taking accumulated leave in order to complete female to male gender-reassignment surgery, Pippa returns to work as Philip. Upon his return to work, he informs the company that he intends to use the men's lavatory, and wishes to be known as Philip. At first, Fingals agrees to this but, following complaints from the male members of staff who object to Philip using their lavatory, Fingals dismisses him.

Advise Anne and Pippa/Philip of any claims they may have under discrimination law.

3 Peter, Charles, and Ruth work for Deejit Computing Services Ltd. Peter has worked as a computer programmer for six months. Charles has worked as an assistant programmer since 2002, apart from 28 weeks in 2003 when he was off work through illness, later diagnosed as chronic fatigue syndrome (CFS). Ruth has worked as a secretary since 1 October 2004.

(a) One month ago, Peter informed the company that he has been having counselling for depression. The counselling has controlled his depression, but he experiences relapses from time to time, during which he cannot function at work. He says that he finds the job too much during these relapses. Deejit has just secured a major contract which will require all programmers to work to very tight deadlines. Peter refused to work to these deadlines: he informed the company that he will not be able to do so as he has been experiencing relapses and cannot concentrate. Peter was dismissed last week because of this refusal.

(b) Charles had a further bout of CFS, which meant that he had to take six weeks off work. After that absence, he returned to work but was slow in carrying out his tasks and less productive than he was before his absence. One day last week, he failed to arrive for work without explanation. Later that day, the manager wrote to him dismissing him for breach of the rule requiring employees to report reasons for absence by 11.30 a.m. on the first day of absence. At the time, Charles was in fact visiting his GP for advice, as the CFS had worsened.

(c) Ruth suffers from severe claustrophobia. Upon the reorganisation of the company, all secretaries were relocated to other offices. Ruth was given a much smaller office to share with two other secretaries. She worked in the office for one week but, finding the working conditions brought on severe bouts of claustrophobia (for which she is being treated by her GP), she did not report for work for two weeks. She did not inform Deejit about the reason for her absence. Deejit, which Ruth has never informed of her problem, dismissed her last week for her unexplained absence.

Advise Peter, Charles, and Ruth, who wish to claim under the Disability Discrimination Act 1995 (DDA.).

6

Equal pay and wages

SUMMARY

This chapter provides an outline of equal pay law. It considers the three categories of claim, ie for like work, work rated as equivalent, and work of equal value and the problems of identifying appropriate comparators. It also explores the difficulties arising from the genuine material factor defence and identifies some of the arguments arising from case law as regards this defence. Finally, enforcement procedures and time limits for claims and claiming arrears of pay are outlined, including the use of the equal pay questionnaire. The key areas examined are:

- the scope of the Equal Pay Act 1970 and Article 141 of the Treaty;
- the equality clause in section 1 of the EqPA;
- comparators;
- like work, work rated as equivalent, and work of equal value;
- the genuine material factor defence;
- examples of genuine material factor defences;
- examples of genuine material factor defences;
- enforcement, time limits, claiming arrears, and remedies.

The final part of the chapter considers in outline the various statutory provisions regulating wages and the payment of or deductions from wages, including:

- the national minimum wage;
- guarantee payments;
- medical suspension pay;
- lay-off and short-time working;

- rights of employees to wages upon insolvency of employer;
- unauthorised deductions from wages.

Equal pay – introduction

6.1 Equal pay is essentially a form of sex discrimination, although a separate statute, the Equal Pay Act 1970 (the 'EqPA'), rather than the SDA, deals with this matter. There are proposals to introduce a single Equality Act in the near future, in which all discrimination legislation would be merged: this is likely to happen within the next few years. Equal pay legislation is necessary to eliminate sex discrimination from pay systems, and therefore to close the so-called 'gender pay gap', ie the difference in pay between men and women for equal work. Historically, women's earnings have been between approximately 80 per cent and 85 per cent of men's pay for equal work – see, for example, the Women and Equality Unit's (WEU) statistics: the WEU states that the median gender pay gap has reduced from 17.4 per cent in 1997 to 12.6 per cent in 2007. The mean figure has fallen from 20.7 per cent to 17.2 per cent in the same period. Interestingly, the WEU states that the 'median part-time gender pay gap has remained fairly static and has reduced from 43.5 per cent in 1997 to 39.1 per cent in 2007. The mean figure for 2007 is 35.6 per cent, compared with 41.9 per cent in 1997.'

6.2 Equal pay is governed by domestic legislation and Community law. The idea that men and women should receive equal pay for the same work of equal value is enshrined in Art 141 (ex Art 19) of the EC Treaty (which states that 'men and women should receive equal pay for equal work'), which is a directly enforceable Treaty provision (see *Defrenne v Sabena (No 2)* (1976)) and comes within the non-discrimination principle, which is one of the fundamental principles of Community law. The Equal Pay Directive (Directive 75/117/EEC) (the 'EPD') provides more detailed provisions relating to pay and concerns the application of Art 141, and the Equal Treatment Directive (Directive 76/207/EEC) (the 'ETD') may also be relevant in interpreting equal pay law. Article 1 of the Equal Pay Directive provides that the principle of equal pay 'means, for the same work or for work to which equal value is attributed, the elimination of all discrimination on grounds of sex with regard to all aspects and conditions of remuneration'.

Scope of the EqPA compared with that of Art 141

6.3 The EqPA covers all *contractual* benefits, whereas Art 141 applies to 'remuneration' an employee receives from her employer, including contractual benefits, gratuitous benefits, and any benefits which the employer is required to provide by statute. However, 'pay' has been given a very wide meaning under Art 141. The Article defines pay as 'the ordinary basic or minimum wage or salary and any other consideration, whether in cash or in kind, which the worker receives, directly or indirectly, in respect of his employment from his employer'. It has been held by the ECJ to include, for example: concessionary, non-contractual travel facilities (*Garland v British Rail Engineering Limited* (1982)); statutory redundancy payment and benefits paid under private, occupational pension schemes (*Barber v Guardian Royal Exchange Assurance Group* (1990), because it arises 'by reason of the existence of the employment relationship'); unfair dismissal compensation (*R v Secretary of State for Employment ex parte Seymour Smith and Perez* (1999)); and statutory sick pay (*Rinner-Kuhn v FWW Spezial-Gebaudereinigung GmbH & Co KG* (1989)).

The EqPA and the SDA

6.4 The Equal Pay Act 1970, which came into force at the same time as the SDA in 1975, is the domestic statute dealing with equal pay between men and women. The EqPA and the SDA together are supposed to form one homogeneous code of domestic legislation (*Shields v E Coomes (Holdings) Limited* (1978)). However, the EqPA covers only *contractual* terms which, despite its title, extends to *all* contractual benefits, not only pay, whereas the SDA covers discrimination *outside* contractual rights and benefits, eg appointment to a job, promotion, and transfer, where these are non-contractual. The EqPA applies equally to men as well as women (EqPA, s 1(13)), although the majority of cases under the Act concern claims brought by women (and the following discussion assumes a female applicant). The Act applies to employees, apprentices, and those engaged under a 'contract personally to execute any work or labour' (EqPA, s 1(6)(a)).

The objective of the EqPA

6.5 The objective of the EqPA is not to secure fair wages (see the remarks of Lord Browne-Wilkinson in *Strathclyde Regional Council v Wallace* (1998) at 149): its objective is to eliminate gender-based pay discrimination, so differences in pay between men and women are allowed, provided they are due to factors other than sex, eg performance-related pay, pay to reward qualifications achieved, or, arguably, pay based on seniority (see the discussion of the genuine material-factor defence below). Therefore it is a defence for the employer to show that the pay disparity is due to factors other than sex.

6.6 If successful in a claim under the EqPA, an equality clause is implied into the woman's contract of employment (s 1(1)). However, the woman must establish that she is in the same employment (or working for an associated employer) as the selected comparator(s) of the opposite sex, who is/are engaged on one of the following three situations: (i) like work; (ii) work rated as equivalent, ie work which has been given an equivalent rating under a job evaluation study ('JES'); or (iii) work which is of equal value (EqPA, s 1(2)(a), (b), (c): these requirements are discussed below. The equality clause operates where any term of the woman's contract is or becomes less favourable: the equality clause modifies the woman's contract of employment by raising the less favourable term in her contract so that it is not less favourable when compared to that of her male comparator.

6.7 If there is no corresponding term in the woman's contract, it will be deemed to include one (EqPA, s 1(2)). The House of Lords in *Hayward v Cammell Laird Shipbuilders Ltd* (1988) held that a term-by-term comparison is required under the EqPA, ie the individual contractual terms in the claimant's contract must be considered alongside individual terms in her comparator's contract, rather than looking at the contracts overall (when looked at overall, Mrs Hayward's terms were in fact more favourable than that of her male comparators). Upholding her equal value claim, their Lordships held that if there was any less favourable term in the woman's contract, the equality clause would operate to raise it so that it was not less favourable, ie there is upward equalisation. (See also *Redcar & Cleveland Borough Council and anor v Degnan and ors* (2005), CA, in which the Court of Appeal seemed to be departing from the principle enunciated in *Hayward*, ie of a term-by-term comparison, while affirming that the Court's decision was in line with *Hayward*.)

6.8 Unlike the SDA, where a hypothetical person may be selected, the claimant must (with one exception) choose an actual comparator (although more than one is permissible) of the opposite sex who is engaged on like work, work rated as equivalent, or work of equal value (EqPA, s 1(2)). The exception arises from *Alabaster v Woolwich plc* (2005), CA, in which a pregnant woman claimed discrimination in the calculation of her maternity pay: the Court held that no comparator (either actual or hypothetical) was necessary in such situations. This was necessary to give her an effective remedy under EC law. This is on the basis that pregnancy is a uniquely female condition, for which no direct male comparator is possible. This is consonant with the principle established under the SDA in *Webb v EMO Air Cargo(UK) Ltd* (1995).

6.9 As a result of this decision, appropriate amendments have been made to the EqPA, s 1 with effect from 1 October 2005 (see new sub-section 1(2)(d), inserted into Equal Pay Act by the Employment Equality (Sex Discrimination) Regulations 2005, SI 2005/2467, reg 36).

Choice of comparator and the pool of comparators – selection of the pool

6.10 The choice of comparator is left to the claimant, but selecting the wrong (ie inappropriate) comparator will prove fatal to the claim (see *Ainsworth v Glass Tubes and Components Limited* (1977): the EAT held that an industrial tribunal could not substitute for the applicant's choice of comparator another man whom it thought more appropriate).

6.11 More than one comparator may be selected, although the courts are alive to abuses of the equal value claims procedure process where the claimant might choose very many comparators, ie adopting a 'scatter-gun' approach (see *Leverton v Clwyd County Council* (1989), HL).

6.12 In *Grundy v British Airways plc* (2008), the Court of Appeal held that in equal pay cases there is no hard and fast rule for selecting which pool of employees is the appropriate pool for the purpose of making pay comparison. It is wrong to interpret case-law to suggest that the widest possible pool of comparators should always be chosen. What matters is that the pool must be one which suitably tests the particular discrimination complained of: it may be a wide pool in some cases and a narrow pool in others.

Predecessors and successors as comparators

6.13 Case law has established that permitted comparators may be predecessors or successors to the claimant, although evidential problems might arise if the time between when a predecessor left or a successor took up employment is too long. Thus, in *Macarthys Ltd v Smith* (1980) the ECJ held that Art 141 (ex Art 119) did not require contemporaneous employment, and it therefore could apply in a case where a female manageress was paid less than a man who was employed on equal work some four months prior to her period of employment. The EqPA must be read in the light of this ECJ decision.

6.14 Successors may be selected as comparators. In *Diocese of Hallam Trustee v Connaughton* (1996), EAT, Ms Connaughton selected as a comparator her male successor, who took up his post (on a higher salary) four months or so after she left her employment as Director of Music. The EAT allowed the comparison, but stated that such comparisons are likely to raise greater evidential problems than those involving a contemporary or immediate predecessor. However, the decision in *Hallam* has been held by another, later division of the EAT in *Bewley* (discussed below) to have been wrongly decided.

6.15 An issue arose in equal value claims concerning whether or not predecessor or successor employees can be used as comparators, as opposed to 'like work' cases. The argument is that in equal value claims there must be contemporaneous employment for the whole of the claim period, although that is not essential in 'like work' cases. The question was considered by the EAT in *Walton Neurological Centre v Bewley* (2008). In *Bewley*, an ET decided that a claimant in the NHS equal pay litigation can pursue a claim based on a comparison with a predecessor comparator who ceased to be employed by the Trust prior to the six-year back pay claim period. The Trust argued that predecessor or successor employee comparisons can only be brought in like work cases, and that equal value cases require contemporaneous employment for the whole of the claim period. In *Bewley*, Elias J held that 'the exercise of comparing with a successor is too hypothetical. The comparison requires asking what would have happened in the past, as opposed to the question in *Macarthys*, which is what did happen in the past' (para 52).

Same employment – common terms and conditions – EqPA, s 1(2) and (6)

6.16 The EqPA requires the claimant and her comparator to be in the 'same employment' (EqPA, s 1(2) and (6)). Under s 1(6), they are in the same employment if the comparator is employed by the same employer or an associated employer and either (i) the comparator is employed at the same establishment as the claimant; or (ii) he is employed at a different establishment of the employer (or an associated employer) but common terms and conditions of employment apply to both establishments.

6.17 Under s 1(6)(c), two employers are to be treated as associated if one is a company controlled, either directly or indirectly, by the other employer (which need not be a company), or if both are companies of which a third person has control, either directly or indirectly.

6.18 In *British Coal Corporation v Smith* (1996), over 1,200 female canteen workers and cleaners working in a number of different establishments chose as their equal value comparators 150 male workers who were either surface mineworkers or in clerical posts. Their terms and conditions were governed by a national agreement, although there were some local variations, ie their terms and conditions were not exactly the same. The House of Lords held the terms of the comparators did not need to be identical as the claimants', they had only to be 'on a broad basis, substantially comparable' (at p 410). In this case, the comparators were held to be in the same employment (see also *Leverton v Clwyd County Council*, HL (1989)). (See also *Dolphin and ors v Hartlepool Borough Council and ors*, EAT 2006, Appeal Nos UKEAT/0559/05/

LA and UKEAT/0684/05/ZT, August 2006. The EAT considered in detail the criteria to be satisfied when considering whether (male) comparators would be eligible to be selected by (female) equal pay claimants on the basis that they were all employed 'at the same establishment' or that they all were employed on 'common terms and conditions'.)

A single source of pay

6.19 A number of cases at domestic and ECJ level have clarified the scope of the comparison permitted under the EqPA or EU law. The ECJ has held that a claim under Art 141 will only succeed where the terms of the claimant and those of the comparator emanate from a single source. This is because it is only in such situations that the employer will be able to explain how the different pay rates arose and therefore establish a defence. In *Lawrence v Regent Office Care Ltd* (2002) the ECJ ruled that female employees employed by private companies who had successfully tendered for the catering and cleaning services in Yorkshire County Council schools could not use as comparators male employees employed directly by the same Council who were carrying out equivalent work (despite the fact that the female workers had been employed by the County Council a few years earlier, and their jobs had been rated as of equal value in a job evaluation study, but they were now working for a private employer on lower rates of pay than the Council had paid them). The ECJ ruled that Art 141 could not be relied upon where the pay conditions cannot be attributed to a single source, ie there was no single body which is responsible for the pay inequality, and which could restore equal treatment.

6.20 The ECJ gave the same ruling in *Allonby v Accrington & Rossendale College* (2004), where the applicant college lecturer who had been dismissed rejoined the college via an agency who placed her with the college. She was carrying out the same work (on lower pay) on a self-employed basis, and used as her comparator a male lecturer at the college. The ECJ ruled that such a comparison failed under Art 141, since pay could not be attributed to a 'single source': the college and the agency were separate sources.

6.21 Collective agreements may constitute a single source. In *Morton v South Ayrshire Council* (2002) the Court of Session held that a female primary head teacher who claimed equal pay with a male comparator who worked for a different local authority as a secondary school head teacher had selected an appropriate comparator, on the basis that the source of their contractual terms was a national collective agreement applying to all teachers in Scotland. Thus, pay emanated from a single source, and came within the interpretation of Art 141 given in the ECJ's ruling in *Defrenne v Sabena* (1976), ie it was a source of pay having its origin in a collective labour agreement. Lord Johnston stated that, despite the fact that each local authority decided how salary scales agreed by the Scottish Joint Negotiating Committee were to be implemented, there was a sufficient connection in a 'loose and non-technical sense', so that the applicant and her comparator could be said to be in the same 'service' of education in Scotland.

6.22 The principle that in claims under the EqPA there must be a single source responsible for setting pay continues to present difficulties to claimants. In *Armstrong v Newcastle upon Tyne NHS Hospital Trust* (2006) the Court of Appeal held that female workers in an NHT hospital could not use male workers in another NHT hospital as comparators for equal pay as there was no single source responsible for setting pay. It was held by the Court of Appeal in *Department for Environment Food and Rural Affairs v Robertson and ors* (2005) that state employees and civil servants could only use comparators from their own government departments, where those departments were responsible for setting pay (since that was the 'single source') and not from other government departments.

6.23 Contingent claims are also permitted under the EqPA. In *Milligan v South Ayrshire Council* (2003) the Court of Session held that a male primary school head teacher, who was unable to make an equal pay claim using secondary school head teachers as comparators because all of the latter were also male, was allowed to make a contingent claim by comparing himself to a female primary school head teacher, and to have his claim stayed until resolution of his comparator's equal pay claim against a male secondary school head teacher. The Court of Session stated that the claimant, unless permitted to bring such a contingent claim, 'would suffer real prejudice in relation to back pay since he could lodge a claim only after the comparator's claim succeeded' (per Lord Gill at p 156).

Like work – EqPA, ss 1(2)(a), (4)

6.24 One of the situations in which a woman may bring an equal pay action is where she is engaged on like work with her comparator. Section 1(4) defines 'like work' as work that is 'of the same or a broadly similar nature, and the differences (if any) between the things she does and the things they do are not of practical importance in relation to terms and conditions of employment'. When comparing the two jobs, 'regard shall be had to the frequency or otherwise with which any such differences occur in practice as well as to the nature and extent of the differences'.

6.25 A tribunal will take a fairly broad brush approach when looking at whether work is similar, focusing on the type of work, and the skill and knowledge required to do it. For example, in *Capper Pass Ltd v Lawton* (1976) a cook who prepared lunches for the company's directors (between 10 and 20) was held to be broadly similar to that of an assistant chef who worked in the canteen preparing meals for all the factory employees.

6.26 The question is whether the differences (if any) between the two jobs are of practical importance. If the employer claims a difference between the jobs, it is for the employer to establish that difference is of practical importance in relation to terms and conditions. For example, in *Shields v E Coomes (Holdings) Ltd* (1978), the employer claimed that male counter-staff at its betting shop were paid a higher hourly pay than female counter-workers because of risk of robbery, and the men were employed for security reasons. In fact, the men had never been called upon to perform any security function, and the Court of Appeal held that, as the men had never been required to deal with any disturbance or attempted violence, the jobs were essentially the same. However, a difference in the responsibilities between the woman and her comparator may be a difference of practical importance, as in *Eaton Limited v Nuttall* (1977), where an error by a female scheduler who dealt with items worth about £2.50 each, would have been less significant than those of a male scheduler (the comparator) who dealt with items worth between £5 and £1,000. The time the work is carried out is not necessarily a difference of practical importance (*Dugdale v Kraft Foods* (1977)), although the ECJ has held that a difference in qualifications, training and experience between the claimant and the comparator was a significant difference justifying a difference in pay (*Angestelltenbetriebsrat der Wiener Gebietskrankenkasse v Wiener Gebietskrankenkasse* (1999)).

Work rated as equivalent – EqPA, ss 1(2)(b), (4), and (5)

6.27 Where work has been rated as equivalent under a job evaluation study ('JES') under which the claimant's and the comparator's job have been rated as equivalent, an equality clause may be inserted under section 1(2). Claims under this provision depend upon the employer having carried out a JES, which is probably why so few claims are brought under this part of the EqPA.

6.28 Section 1(5) requires that the jobs of the comparator and the applicant have been given an equal value 'in terms of the demand made on a worker under various headings (for instance effort, skill, decision)', or where they would have been given equal values, but for the JES itself being discriminatory. There are a number of methods of job evaluation, although only the 'points assessment' and 'factor comparison' systems satisfy the requirements of section 1(5), since the JES must be analytical and objective (*Bromley and others v H & J Quick Ltd* (1988)). 'Analytical' means that the jobs of each worker covered by the JES must have been valued appropriately in terms of the demand made on the worker under various headings. 'Objectivity' means that the JES must be free from any subjective or discriminatory elements. The ECJ made this clear in *Rummler v Dato-Druck GmbH* (1987) (a case brought under Art 1(2) of the Equal Pay Directive), where a JES gave undue weight to muscular effort (which disadvantaged female employees) without being balanced by applying other criteria 'in relation to which women had a particular aptitude'. The employment tribunal may adjust the results of the JES to take into account any *direct* discrimination in its application. Finally, the JES, once accepted as valid by the parties, can be relied upon by the claimant, even if it has not been implemented (*O'Brien v Sim-Chem Ltd* (1980)).

Work of equal value – EqPA, s 1(2)(c)

6.29 A claimant may bring an equal value claim under section 1(2)(c) where her work does not come under either of the two other categories (an equal value claim may not be brought if her comparator is engaged on like work or work rated as equivalent). She must be engaged upon work of equal value in terms of the demand made on her.

6.30 The EqPA, as originally drafted, provided for equal pay claims in only two situations: where the man and the woman were engaged on like work or work rated as equivalent. Further, there was no requirement under the Act for the employer to conduct a JES, and one could not be conducted without the employer's consent. This meant that, if an employer refused to conduct a JES, a woman employee who was engaged on work of equal value to that of a man could not bring an equal pay claim. This was successfully challenged as being inconsistent with the principle of equal pay in Art 141 of the EC Treaty (ex Art 119) and the Equal Pay Directive (*Commission v United Kingdom* (1982)), and the EqPA was subsequently amended by the Equal Pay (Amendment) Regulations 1983 (SI 1983/1794) to allow a claim for equal pay to be made where work is of equal value, which is now contained in EqPA, s 1(2)(c).

6.31 Examples of the headings under which jobs considered under the equal value provisions may be assessed are given in section 1(2), eg 'effort, skill, decision'. The claimant may choose her comparator, even if there is a male employee working in the same job as her and on the same pay (*Pickstone v Freemans plc* (1988)). This prevents the employer blocking an equal value claim by having a 'token' male doing the same job as the woman. In *Pickstone*, a female warehouse operative chose as her comparator a male checker warehouse operative, although there was a male warehouse operative on the same pay as the claimant. The House of Lords, applying a purposive interpretation of section 1(2)(c) to ensure compliance with Art 119 (current Art 141) and the Equal Pay Directive, allowed the claim to proceed.

6.32 The employment tribunal procedure for equal value claims is complicated. Essentially, once an equal value claim is presented to the tribunal, it may appoint an independent expert from an independent panel to write a report on the issue within 42 days, which is also sent to the parties (s 2A(1)). However, the report is not binding on the tribunal. If the ET decides not to appoint an expert, the parties may appoint their own expert. An employer may conduct a JES after the presentation of an equal pay claim but before the final hearing, provided it considers the jobs as they were at the time of the complaint (*Dibro Ltd v Hore* (1990), EAT; EqPA, s 2A(2)).

6.33 In *Home Office v Bailey* (2005), the Court of Appeal held that a work of equal value claim could succeed where it was made by a group of employees who argued that there was a pay disparity between themselves and a group of higher paid fellow employees who were predominantly of one sex (male), which was contrary to the EqPA, even if the disadvantaged group is not predominantly of the other sex. This case establishes that, even if the disadvantaged group is neither predominantly male nor female (here the applicants' group was evenly split between men and women), a prima facie case of unlawful discrimination contrary to the EqPA arises, which requires objective justification. With respect, this decision seems to be a significant extension to the principles applicable in EqPA claims: it is questionable whether it will withstand closer critical scrutiny by the House of Lords in the future (leave to appeal in *Bailey* was granted on 28 July 2005, although no appeal was heard).

6.34 The ECJ has ruled that a difference in pay for two new employees of opposite sex relating to the same work or work of equal value cannot be justified by factors which become known only after they started work (see *Brunnhofer v Bank der österreichischen Postsparkasse AG* Case C-381/99 (2001)).

6.35 For the purposes of equal pay claims, when assessing whether the claimant and the comparator are receiving equal pay, it is normally their basic pay which must be compared. Any perks should not normally be taken into account in comparing the pay itself, although it may be relevant when considering whether a difference in pay is objectively justifiable (see *Jämställdhetsombudsmannen v Orebro* Case C-236/98 (2001), ECJ).

Procedure under the EqPA

6.36 New procedural rules have been introduced to simplify the previously complex procedure in equal value claims (see the Employment Tribunals (Constitution and Rules of Procedure) (Amendment) Regulations 2004 SI 2004/2351), which add a Sch 6 (rules for use in Equal Pay cases) to the Employment Tribunals (Constitution and Rules of Procedure) Regulations 2004 SI 2004/1861 with effect from 1 October 2004.

6.37   In *Amey Services Ltd v Cardigan & ors* (2008), EAT, it was held that EqPA claims must be taken in stages. First, a claimant must establish that her job was of like work, work rated as equivalent or work of equal value to a relevant comparator of the opposite sex. This then creates a rebuttable presumption of discrimination based on sex. It is only after this is established that the burden falls on the employer to show an appropriate defence. In this case, the ET wrongly ordered the employers to provide their defence, even though the claimant had not (yet) identified a comparator.

The genuine material factor defence – section 1(3)

6.38   If a claimant establishes that she is paid less than her male comparator who is engaged on like work, work rated as equivalent, or work of equal value, the employer may raise the defence that the difference in pay is not due to sex discrimination, and is a material difference between the claimant's case and the comparator's. This is the genuine material factor defence (GMF) under section 1(3). If the employer succeeds in this defence, the equality clause will not be implied to modify the claimant's contract. Where the complaint is based on like work or work rated as equivalent, the defence *must* be a material difference between the woman's case and the man's; where it is an equal value claim, it may be a material difference.

6.39   In the GMF defence, the employer must identify a factor which is (a) the genuine cause of the difference in pay; (b) is material; and (c) is not the difference of sex. The requirement of genuineness means that the reason put forward by the employer is not a sham or a pretence (*Strathclyde Regional Council v Wallace* (1998), HL). In *Wallace*, their Lordships held that a material factor must be 'significant and caus- ally relevant'. The employers argued that the pay disparities came about through different promotion structures of teachers and financial constraints. The House of Lords held that an employer is not required to justify its pay system in every case where unequal pay is alleged. The need to establish objective justification only arises where the factor relied upon is indirectly discriminatory.

6.40   A similar conclusion was reached in *Glasgow City Council and others v Marshall and others* (2000), HL, where the employers argued that the pay structure had been arrived at by different collectively bargained agreements, which were not tainted with sex discrimination. The House of Lords held that, where a pay system was not tainted with sex discrimination, the EqPA had no application, and the equal- ity clause would not operate. The employer was not required to go further and to provide an explanation of how the pay disparity had come about. Therefore, it is only where there is evidence of sex discrimination in the pay structure that the employer will be required to objectively justify the pay disparity.

6.41　However, pay disparities clearly tainted with sex discrimination will not satisfy the GMF defence (see *Ratcliffe v North Yorkshire County Council* (1995), HL (the 'Yorkshire Dinner ladies case')): where the claimants' jobs had been rated as equivalent to those of their male comparators under a JES, the reduction of their wages in order to compete with private contractor in a CCT exercise was not an adequate defence to meet the requirements of section 1(3).

Objective justification – recent case law (and problems arising therefrom)

6.42　The approach in *Wallace* and *Marshall* has recently been the subject of some controversy. One important (and rather contentious) issue concerning the GMF defence is whether, once the employer has established a GMF which is unrelated to sex, he has to go on to objectively justify it. Until 2005, the courts and tribunals had consistently ruled that the employer does not have to show that the factor relied upon is objectively justifiable, only that it was unrelated to sex, genuine, and not a sham. However in 2005, the EAT took a different view. It held that, where like work, or work rated as equivalent, or work of equal value has been established between a male and a female on different pay, then the difference will be unlawful unless it can be objectively justified (see *Sharp v Caledonia Group Services Ltd* (2006), EAT).

6.43　In *Sharp v Caledonia Group Services Ltd* (2006), the EAT held (following the ECJ ruling in *Brunnhofer v Bank der Österreichischen Postsparkasse* (2001), ECJ) that the 'European approach' differed from the domestic approach (as exemplified in these two cases).

6.44　Essentially, the domestic approach is that, where the employer establishes a genuine material difference which is not tainted by sex discrimination, there is no requirement to go on and objectively justify the pay disparity. Sharp held that the European approach, following *Brunnhofer*, required objective justification where there was a pay disparity between a claimant and her comparator, once it had been established that they were engaged upon like work, work rated as equivalent, or work of equal value. However, it is not clear that this is the correct interpretation of *Brunnhofer*. The EAT in *Villalba v Merrill Lynch & Co Inc* (2006) took the view that *Sharp* was incorrectly decided and that objective justification was not necessary. In the view of Elias J, the *Brunhoffer* ruling meant 'no more than that grounds which the employer relies upon to rebut discrimination do exist in fact' (para 175).

6.45 *Sharp* held that the tribunal erred in not following the European approach, which requires that the difference in pay has to be objectively justified, and instead following the approach laid down by the domestic line of authorities, which simply requires the employer to be able to account for the difference by reference to a factor which is material but is not the sex of the employee unless the factor relied upon by the employer is one which may itself indirectly discriminate against female employees, in which case the factor has to be objectively justified.

6.46 However, the 'conventional' approach was taken by the Court of Appeal in *Armstrong v Newcastle upon Tyne NHS Hospital Trust* (2006), shortly after the *Sharp* judgment was handed down. In *Armstrong* the Court of Appeal reinstated the position that if the reason for pay disparity between males and females was genuinely a material factor unrelated to sex then there is no need for the reason to be objectively justifiable, following *Glasgow City Council v Marshall* (2006), HL. In *Armstrong*, Lady Justice Arden found that there is no need for an employer to provide objective justification for the difference in pay if the 'genuine material factor' is not related to sex, saying (at para 33):

> It follows from the *Marshall* case... that there is no need for an employer to provide justification for a disparity unless the disparity is due to sex discrimination.

6.47 However, the conflicting approaches to these issues taken in *Sharp* and *Armstrong* indicate that this is far from settled law. Elias, P, stated in the EAT in 2007:

> We have no doubt that we are bound by the decision in *Armstrong*. It is not for the Employment Appeal Tribunal to act on the assumption that the Court of Appeal has misunderstood European law. Nor, in a case where that Court has sought to explain the effect of a decision of the House of Lords, at least in circumstances where that is part of the essential reasoning of the Court, is it open to the Employment Appeal Tribunal to say that the Court of Appeal has misinterpreted it and to adopt its own preferred construction of their Lordships' speeches. Whether right or wrong, the principle of precedent requires a loyal adherence to what is clearly the ratio of the decision of the Court of Appeal.

> (Elias P at para 45 in *Middlesbrough Borough Council v Surtees & ors* (2007), EAT)

6.48 The Court of Appeal was due to hear an appeal in *Sharp* in June 2006 but the case was settled out of court with Caledonia Group withdrawing their appeal upon payment of an undisclosed sum to Ms Sharp. It would appear that until the Court of Appeal or the House of Lords decides the issue, it is an open question as to which is the correct approach. It is interesting to note that the House of Lords refused the claimants' application for leave to appeal in the *Armstrong* case.

6.49 In the *Middlesbrough Borough Council* case, Elias, P, stated that 'that proof of a non-sex based reason will be a complete answer to any discrimination claim, direct or indirect' (Elias, P, at para 490).

Some GMF defences argued

6.50 Any factor argued under the GMF defence must be based on objectively justified factors which are unrelated to any discrimination on grounds of sex. The ECJ in *Bilka-Kaufhaus GmbH v Weber von Hartz* (1987) ruled that objective justification will be established where the practice: (a) corresponds to a real need on the part of the employer; (b) is necessary to achieve the objective in question; and (c) is proportionate to that objective ('the principle of proportionality'). The employer must balance the discriminatory impact of the practice against the reasonable needs of its business (see also *Hampson v Department of Education and Science* (1990)).

6.51 In Community law, the ECJ has ruled that where pay systems lack transparency (ie where employees do not know what criteria are involved or how they are applied), this is a potential breach of the Equal Pay Directive. The employer in such a case had to prove that pay differences were not discriminatory (see the *Danfoss* case (1989)).

6.52 It is not possible to provide an exhaustive list of factors which may satisfy the GMF defence requirements. Case law establishes that a number of grounds have been upheld, the following being some of the most significant ones:

Market forces

6.53 The 'market forces' defence may succeed: in *Rainey v Greater Glasgow Health Board* (1987), the House of Lords held that the pay difference between employees in the NHS prosthetic fitting service, which was facing staff shortages, and those recruited from the private sector had been objectively justified, since market forces meant that in order to recruit from the private sector commercial rates of pay had to be offered.

Productivity payments

6.54 In *Cumbria County Council v Dow (No 1)* (2008), EAT, the employer attempted to justify higher pay made by way of productivity payments and bonuses paid to predominantly male groups of employees. The employer sought to justify the pay differential partly by using the productivity argument and partly by using the market forces argument (see below for a discussion of productivity payments as a GMF). The EAT held that, when relying upon market forces as a GMF, the employer had to adduce evidence to establish whether market forces accounted for the whole differential or only part of it. This issue was remitted back to the ET to consider two issues afresh: firstly, whether the market forces GMF *might* justify the pay differential and, secondly, whether it *could* do so.

6.55 On productivity payments, the EAT held that, where an employer was using such a GMF, it had to adduce evidence to support this argument, ie to establish that productivity had increased as a result of improvements in the performance of the relevant employees. Here, the payments had become automatic, rather than being linked to the objective of improving productivity. Elias, P, stated 'It cannot be proportionate to pay bonuses to achieve a legitimate objective if that objective is not in any meaningful way being realised' (para 136).

'Red circling'

6.56 Red circling is a practice where an employee is placed on a lower grade but has his salary protected (or 'red circled'), while other employees on the same grade are paid at a lower rate (see *Snoxell and another v Vauxhall Motors Limited* (1978), where the argument did not succeed as it was based on past sex discrimination). In any event, this defence will not be available if the circumstances giving rise to the red circling come to an end (*Benveniste v University of Southampton* (1989)).

Collective bargaining

6.57 In *Enderby v Frenchay Health Authority and another* (1994), ECJ (the famous 'speech therapists' case') Dr Enderby and a number of other speech therapists claimed equal pay with male pharmacists and clinical psychologists. The employer argued that the pay disparity was the result of separate collective bargaining processes which were themselves indirectly discriminatory, on the basis that, although the speech therapy profession was predominantly female, pharmacists and clinical psychologists in the grades to which the claim related were overwhelmingly male. The ECJ ruled that a prima facie case of sex discrimination will be established where 'significant statistics' show that a job performed almost exclusively by women attracts an appreciably lower rate of pay than a job carried out predominantly by men. The ECJ also ruled that, although separate collective bargaining structures could provide justification, this was not sufficient to account for the pay disparity. Furthermore, the ECJ held that where only part of the pay disparity is justified, the defence would stand for such part of the difference as could be attributed to that reason.

Longer service and greater experience

6.58 Longer service and greater experience may be a genuine material factor justifying higher pay, even if it is indirectly sex discriminatory because those with longer service and greater experience are largely males (see *Health & Safety Executive v Cadman* (2004), EAT and CA, referred by the CA to the ECJ).

6.59 In *Cadman v HSE* (2006), ECJ, the ECJ held that length of service as a criterion upon which pay was based is permissible under EU law, unless the practice raised 'serious doubts'. The ECJ held:

Where there is a disparity in pay between men and women employed on equal work or work of equal value as a result of using the criterion of length of service as a determinant of pay, the employer does not have to establish specifically that recourse to that criterion is appropriate as regards a particular job to attain the legitimate objective of rewarding experience acquired which enables the worker to perform his duties better, *unless the worker provides evidence capable of raising serious doubts in that regard.*

(emphasis added)

Male comparators placed on lower grade in 'Single Status Agreement'

6.60 In *Redcar & Cleveland & borough Council v Bainbridge & ors* (2007), CA, some 1,400 women employed in manual jobs, for example as caterers and care workers, claimed parity with higher paid male comparators such as road sweepers, gardeners and refuse collectors. They won in the ET and the EAT and the Council appealed. The Council argued in the CA that the job evaluation process conducted under the Single Status Agreement (see below) had resulted in some cases in the men, even though they were higher paid, being in lower grades than the women. The Council's contention was that their jobs were therefore not 'equal' to the jobs of the women and that the women should therefore not be entitled to equal pay. The Court of Appeal rejected this argument.

'Single status agreements' and the EqPa

6.61 The equal pay legislation has been used with great success in recent years by public sector workers of local authorities who work under 'single status agreements'. In 1997, local authorities concluded agreements with trade unions for formal evaluation of jobs over the following ten years, to establish which council jobs should be regarded as at the same level as each other and which, therefore, should receive the same rate of pay. For example, cooks (who are mainly female in the relevant workforces) might be graded as equivalent to joiners (who are largely male). The pay differential between these two groups is about £3 to £4 per hour.

6.62 Under single status agreements which rated these two categories of jobs as being at the same level, the female employees could lodge valuable equal pay claims going back six years. There have been numerous successful claims through this route in recent years, leaving local authorities facing very large awards against them.

Trade unions as respondents in EqPA claims

6.63 There have been a number of EqPA claims brought by trade union members against their trade unions. These cases have very largely involved women who, having settled equal pay claims on their unions' advice, subsequently found that the settlements they had agreed were less favourable than they might have secured if they had taken their claims to tribunals.

6.64 These settlements were based on terms negotiated by unions which had adopted a 'reasonable, rather than maximum settlement, policy', on the basis that holding out for maximum compensation for equal pay claimants would inevitably have an adverse impact on other members, both men and women. The unions recognised that local authorities do not have unlimited funds, so that a deluge of successful EqPA claims against them would probably lead to redundancies, as well as difficulty in negotiating future pay rises generally.

6.65 They decided to bring ET claims rather than claims in the civil courts, so if they lost in the ET, the likelihood was that costs would not be awarded against them. Given that most of the beneficiaries of the 'reasonable settlement' policy adopted by trade unions were men and most, if not all, the losers were women, the specialist 'no win, no fee' advisers (operating under the conditional fee arrangement system) therefore recommended that the women should bring their claims against their union as sex discrimination claims in the ET, rather than, for example, as negligence claims.

6.66 In the leading case of *GMB Union v Allen* (2007), EAT, the EAT overturned an ET judgment which had held in favour of female members of the GMB trade union as regards indirect sex discrimination. The union, when negotiating over implementation of the local government single status agreement, had agreed to a low back-pay settlement for women with equal pay claims, as it wanted to ensure that there was as much money as possible for future pay increases for all its members and to give greater priority to pay protection for the (predominantly male) groups whose jobs had been assessed at a lower level under the local government single status scheme. The ET held that the union had not properly advised its members of the difference between what was being offered by the employers in terms of settling their equal pay claims and what the women could recover in an ET. The ET held that the union had manipulated the women by suggesting that the offer from the local authority was acceptable and by placing them in a position where they believed that if they pressed for more, it might lead to job losses.

6.67 The EAT, finding in favour of the GMB, held that, although the GMB had perpetrated indirect sex discrimination, it had used 'proportionate' means to achieve a 'legitimate aim', ie the justification defence applied, despite the fact that the union had acted unlawfully. However, the Court of Appeal (in a decision reported at [2008] IRLR 690) held that the means adopted to secure the objective were disproportionate.

Differences in contract terms between full-time and part-time employees

6.68 Differences in contract terms between full-time and part-time employees (such as the right of a part-timer to refuse work offered by the employer) can amount to a 'genuine material factor' with the result that the part-timers will not be entitled to claim equal treatment with the full-timers under the Equal Treatment Directive (Directive 76/207/EEC (see *Wippel v Peek & Cloppenburg Gmbh* Case C-313/02 (2005), ECJ).

TUPE transfer

6.69 A TUPE transfer (and the differences in pay which might arise from it) may be a valid GMF defence (see *Nelson v Carillion Services Ltd* (2003), CA). In that case, a contract for services was transferred under TUPE from Initial Healthcare Services to Carillion, along with Initial's employees, who transferred on their existing terms. The claimant was a female employee of Carillion, who had been taken on some 12 months after the transfer, who claimed equal pay with a Carillion employee engaged in comparable work and whose contract had been transferred from Initial. The male comparator was on a higher rate of pay, ie that applicable to the Initial employees at the time of the transfer. The Court of Appeal agrees with the EAT that the pay disparity was not tainted with sexual discrimination and that the TUPE factor satisfied the GMF defence under the EqPA.

6.70 Other examples of the GMF defence are London weighting, ie a pay system where employees working in more expensive areas of the country, such as London, are paid more than those living in less expensive areas (see *NAAFI v Varley* (1976)), and performance-related pay.

Enforcement and remedies – bringing a claim for equal pay

6.71 All equal pay claims must be brought in the ET (EqPA, 2(1)), and the claimant may rely upon EC law in the ET as well as the domestic legislation. It is not only employees who may make an application under the EqPA: under section 2(1A), employers may apply to the ET for a declaration where there is a dispute over the effect of an equality clause. The Secretary of State may also bring proceedings where it appears that the employer of any women is or has been in breach of a term modified or included by an equality clause, and it is not reasonable to expect the women themselves to bring proceedings (eg because they do not have a union to support their claim): section 2(2). The EOC is also empowered to seek a ruling from a tribunal as to whether an employer has infringed a term modified or included by an equality clause, to enable it to exercise its powers under SDA, ss 71 and 72 to apply for an injunction to restrain persistent discrimination (SDA, s 73).

6.72 Since the equality clause provision works by modifying the claimant's contract of employment, she may also bring an equal pay claim in the county court or High Court in the form of an action for breach of contract. However, the ordinary courts have the power to refuse to hear equal pay claims in two situations: (1) where it appears to the court that a claim or counterclaim in respect of the operation of an equality clause could more conveniently be disposed of by an ET, the court can strike the claim out in its entirety; and (2) where a question regarding the effect of an equality clause is part of a wider dispute which is before the court, the court may on the application of one of the parties or of its own motion refer that question to an ET (or direct one of the parties to do so) and stay proceedings in the meantime (s 2(3)).

Time limits

6.73 Equal pay claims must be brought within six months of leaving the employment to which the claim relates (s 2(4)). This time limit was challenged in *Preston and others v Wolverhampton Healthcare NHS Trust* (2000), ECJ, as being incompatible with EC law. The claimants were part-time teachers employed on fixed-term contracts who argued that the six months' limit applied to the entire employment relationship, rather than the particular fixed-term contracts. The ECJ held that the six months' rule was not incompatible with EC law, provided that the limitation period was no less favourable for actions based on Community law than for actions based on domestic law (see also *National Power plc v Young* (2001), CA, where the Court of Appeal held that the word 'employment' in section 2(4) does not refer to the particular job on which the woman bases her claim, but rather to the contract of employment).

6.74 The EqPA originally provided that a claimant could claim remuneration or damages in respect of the two years prior to the institution of proceedings. This was challenged in *Levez v T H Jennings (Harlow Pools) Ltd* (1999), and the ECJ ruled that the two-year limitation on claiming arrears of remuneration in EqPA, s 2(5) is precluded if the section infringes the Community law principle of 'equivalence'. This requires that a procedural rule must not discriminate as between community law rights and national law rights (eg breach of contract claims have a six-year limit for claiming arrears). In *Preston and others v Wolverhampton Healthcare NHS Trust*

(2000), ECJ, the ECJ ruled that the limitation of two years was incompatible with EC law, since it was a restriction on the right to have a full and effective remedy for breach of Art 141 (ex Art 119) and the Equal Pay Directive. The House of Lords followed this ruling in *Preston and others v Wolverhampton Healthcare NHS Trust (No 2)* (2001).

6.75 The EqPA has been amended in the light of these ECJ rulings. Although the time limit for bringing claims is still six months, there are special rules in certain cases where the employee and the employer had a stable employment relationship (even though one or more individual contracts of employment had ended). These are: (i) where the employer deliberately concealed relevant facts from the employee; or, (ii) where the employee was under a disability (meaning a legal incapacity), the time limit for bringing claims is six months from the date the woman discovered the concealed facts in (i) above, or six months from the time the woman ceased to be under a disability in (ii) (s 2ZA). There is now a six-year limit for claiming arrears of pay which is subject to similar rules on concealment and disability as discussed above, except that there is no time limit on claiming arrears, ie applicants may claim arrears back to the date of the contravention (s 2ZB).

Equal Pay Questionnaire

6.76 Obtaining information about the pay of potential comparators in order to bring an equal pay claim is often difficult. The recently introduced Equal Pay Questionnaire, based on questionnaires which have been used for some time under the SDA, RRA, and DDA, should assist claimants who wish to bring such claims (see EqPA, s 7(B) and the Equal Pay (Questions and Replies) Order 2003 (SI 2003/ 722)). Under the questionnaire provisions, a claimant (or proposed claimant) may ask the employer for relevant information which will assist them in establishing their complaint (or whether there are grounds to bring a complaint). The employer has eight weeks in which to respond. Although there is no statutory duty on employers to supply answers to the questionnaire, employment tribunals are entitled to draw inferences from a deliberate refusal to answer, or from a reply which is evasive or equivocal.

Code of Practice on Equal Pay

6.77 The EOC, using powers given by the SDA, s 56A, has issued a Code of Practice on Equal Pay (the 'Code') whose objective is 'to provide practical guidance and recommend good practice to those with responsibility for or interest in the pay arrangements within a particular organisation'. The Code is admissible in evidence in proceedings under the EqPA (SDA, s 56A).

Wages – statutory constraints and regulation

6.78 This section considers the statutory provisions concerning wages. It does not deal with any contractual terms (whether express or implied) concerning wages and the payment of wages, which are referred to in Chapter 4.

National Minimum Wage

6.79 The purpose of the National Minimum Wage Act 1998 (NMWA) has been to introduce a statutory minimum wage rate. The need for such a measure had been identified since the abolition of the various Wages Councils. Unlike many other measures in employment law, the NMWA was introduced as a result of purely UK Government domestic policy: there was no impetus from EC law.

6.80 While the NMWA sets out the essential legislative framework, the detailed provisions concerning the national minimum wage (NMW) are contained within the National Minimum Wage Regulations 1999 (SI 199/584). Section 5(4) NMWA provides that the NMW will apply to any 'worker' who 'as an individual has entered into or works under (or where employment has ceased worked under) a contract of employment; or any other contract, whether express or implied . . .'.

6.81 All employees, with a few exceptions, such as share fishermen or voluntary workers, irrespective of length of service or hours worked, have the right to be paid at a level no less than the applicable rate of the NMW. However, there are three rates: the adult rate the youth rate (or 'development rate'), and the young person's rate. The three rates applicable from 1 October 2008 (note that these rates usually change every October) are:

- **the adult rate** of £5.73 per hour, which is payable to those aged 22 or over (and those aged 22 or over who are within the first six months of their employment and in accredited training);
- **the Youth Rate (or 'development rate')** for 18–21-year-olds, which is currently £4.77 per hour;
- **the Young Persons' Rate**, ie the rate for 16–17-year-olds is £3.53 per hour (this rate was introduced from 1 October 2004, see below).

The Youth Rate – development rate

6.82 This reduced rate is payable to two groups of workers: those between 18 and 21, and those aged 22 or over who are within the first six months of their employment and who have agreed to take part in accredited training on at least 26 days between the start of employment (or of the agreement) and the end of the six-month period: NMWR, reg 13(2).

16–17 year olds – a note

6.83 From October 1 2004, 16- and 17-year-olds qualified for the national minimum wage (which was originally at the rate of £3 per hour (see National Minimum Wage Regulations 1999 (Amendment) (No. 2) Regulations 2004, SI 2004/1930, which introduced National Minimum Wage Regulations 1999, regulation 13(1A) and deleted National Minimum Wage Regulations 1999, regulation 12(1)).

6.84 The NMW applies to actual 'working time' determined by reference to the total remuneration over a 'relevant pay period' and the hours worked in that period, and is calculated on gross pay. Productivity and performance pay, commission, and other financial incentive pay is included, but the NMW does not include overtime or shift or other allowances or supplements.

6.85 Employers cannot avoid their obligation to pay the NMW by excluding certain work time from the relevant calculation, see: *British Nursing Association v Inland Revenue (National Minimum Wage Compliance Team)* (2002), CA, and *Scottbridge Construction Ltd v Wright* (2003), Ct Sess.

6.86 In *Nerva & ors v UK* (2002), ECHR, the European Court of Human Rights held that restaurant tips made by customers adding an amount to a payment by credit card or cheque can count towards the determination of the NMW because the applicants could not show that there was a legitimate expectation that the tips would not count towards their weekly pay in the absence of contractual rights, and so 'possession' of the money passed to the employer. There was no violation of Article 1 Protocol 1 to the European Convention which provides rights of access to private property. *NMW Guidance (URN 99/662)* states that tips paid to a worker through payroll should be counted as remuneration for the purposes of NMW, but cash tips paid either directly by a customer or through a pool do count towards the NMW.

6.87 HM Revenue and Customs (HMRC) guidance notes E24 (2006) on 'Tips, Gratuities, Service Charges and Troncs' outline the current law in relation to tips. The position is that if tips are collected as part of the customer's bill and then paid out by the employer to staff, they count as part of wages, but if they are paid direct to the worker by a satisfied customer, they do not. The government announced proposals at the end of July 2008 to change this and 'end the practice by which employers can use gratuities and service charges processed through the payroll to "top up" staff wages to meet the National Minimum Wage'.

6.88 Employees may bring a claim in respect of non-payment of the NMW under Part II ERA as an unlawful deduction of wages or under the NMWA. Workers not engaged under a contract of service may only bring an action under the latter. The burden of proof is on the employer who must prove that the NMW has been paid.

6.89 NMW (Inland Revenue) Compliance Officers are empowered to enforce the NMW by instigating legal action, gaining access to premises, inspecting records (which must be kept for all employees and workers).

Guarantee pay – ERA, ss 28–35

6.90 Guarantee pay is payable to employees who have been employed for one month or more but for whom there is no work because of a diminution in the employer's need for the kind of work the employee carries out, or any other occurrence affecting the normal working of the business in relation to such work (ss 28–35).

6.91 The statutory maximum daily amount of pay is currently £20.40 from 1 February 2008. The statutory maximum number of days for which payment is made is five days in any three-month period (ss 31(2)–(6)).

Medical suspension pay – ERA, s 65(1)

6.92 Medical suspension pay is payable to qualifying employees who have been suspended from work by their employer on medical grounds, eg for reasons relating to an unsafe working environment. Employees must be paid while suspended, up to a maximum period of 26 weeks.

6.93 To qualify, an employee must have at least one month's continuous employment: ERA, s 5(1). The statutory maximum for a week's pay applies, which is currently £330 (from 1 February 2008). This suspension (with medical suspension pay) is subject to a statutory maximum period of 26 weeks.

Lay-off and short-time working – ERA, ss 147 to 154

Definitions of 'lay-off' and 'short-time working'

6.94 A week of *lay-off* occurs when the employer provides no work for a particular week and the employee is therefore not entitled to any remuneration for that week (s 147(1), ERA). An employee is on *short time* if he receives less than half of his week's pay (as defined in s 221, ERA 1996 *et seq*) as a result of the diminution in work (s 147(2), ERA 1996).

6.95 The relevant scheme contained in sections 147 to 154 of ERA 1996 entitles an employee who is required to work short time or who is laid off in accordance with the terms of his employment contract to claim a redundancy payment. The scheme applies only where the employee has been laid off or kept on short time for a period of four consecutive weeks or for a series of six or more weeks within a 13-week period. The employee must comply strictly with the statutory procedure in order to claim the redundancy payment.

Insolvency – claiming unpaid wages upon insolvency of employer

6.96 Under the Insolvency Act 1986 (IA), in a winding up of a company 'preferential debts' must be paid in full, in priority to all other debts after the expenses of the winding up (IA, s 175). Similar rules apply in the case of an individual who is bankrupt (IA, s 328).

6.97 Debts which are 'preferential debts' are listed at IA, s 386 and Sched 6. As regards employees, preferential debts are money owing for remuneration (including holiday pay, guarantee payment, and pay for time off work if for trade union duties, ante-natal care or medical suspension required by statute). (Remuneration for the purposes of the IA (as amended by the Insolvency Act 1994) includes any sum of a type listed in Sched 6, para 13 to the 1986 Act.) In addition, PAYE, social security contributions and occupational pension scheme contributions also constitute 'remuneration'.

6.98 However, remuneration as a preferential debt is limited (except in regard to holiday pay) to pay for the last four months. It is subject to a maximum, which can be changed by order (IA, Sched 6, para 9). The current maximum is £800 (Insolvency Proceedings (Monetary Limits) Order 1986, SI 1986/1966).

Unlawful deductions from wages

6.99 Under the ERA, s 13:

> an employer shall not make a deduction from wages of a worker employed by him unless:
>
> (a) the deduction is required or authorised to be made by virtue of a statutory provision or a relevant provision of the worker's contract, or
>
> (b) the worker has previously signified in writing his agreement or consent to the making of the deduction.

6.100 Section 13 is inapplicable where the statutory exceptions apply. These are where the employer has made a deduction in reimbursement for either '(a) an overpayment of wages or (b) an overpayment of expenses incurred by the worker in carrying out his employment'.

6.101 'Wages' are defined in the ERA 1996, s 27 (formerly Wages Act 1986, s 7). The basic definition of 'wages' for the purposes of the unlawful deductions from wages provisions of the ERA is 'any sums payable to the worker by his employer in connection with his employment' (other than specified exceptions such as refund of expenses or pensions) and specifically including 'any fee, bonus, commission, holiday pay or other emolument referable to his employment, whether payable under his contractor otherwise' (ERA, s 27).

6.102 It should be noted that 'wages' includes statutory sick pay, statutory maternity, paternity, and adoption pay.

6.103 Clearly, contractual commission and bonuses constitute 'wages', while bonuses expressed to be 'ex gratia' and not under any contractual obligation (express or implied) are not likely to be wages. However, they may be classed as wages even if they are discretionary or ex gratia, particularly if they are regularly paid (see *Kent Management Services Ltd v Butterfield* (1992), EAT; contrast this case with *Diagonal Computer Services Ltd v Plews* (2003), EAT, 20 December 2002). Tips paid directly to waiters by customers are not 'wages' (see also the section on the National Minimum Wage Act).

6.104 Wages have been called 'sums to which the employee has some legal, but not necessarily contractual, entitlement' (see *New Century Cleaning Co Ltd v Church* (2000), CA). As soon as a non-contractual discretionary bonus has been declared and the employee has a legal entitlement to it, it counts as 'wages' for purposes of ERA 1996, s 27 (see *Farrell, Mathews & Weir v Hansen* (2005), EAT, in which the EAT rejected an employer's argument that the unpaid part of a discretionary bonus is not 'wages' for those purposes because ERA 1996, s 27(3)(b) provides that a non-contractual bonus is treated as payable 'on the day on which the payment is made'.

FURTHER READING

Collins, H, Ewing, KD, & McColgan, A, *Labour Law: Text and Materials* (2nd ed, 2005) Hart Publishing, pp 317–331.

Deakin, S, & Morris, G, *Labour Law*, (4th ed, 2005) Hart Publishing (chapter 6), pp 665–695.

McColgan, A, *Discrimination Law: Text, Cases and Materials* (2005) Hart Publishing (chapter 6), pp 420–471.

ARTICLES

Fredman, S, (2004) 'Marginalising Equal Pay Laws', *Industrial Law Journal*, Vol 31, No 3, pp 281–285.

Simpson, B, (1999) 'Implementing the National Minimum Wage – The 1999 Regulations', *Industrial Law Journal*, Vol 28, No 2, pp 171–182.

Simpson, B, (2004) 'The National Minimum Wage Five Years On: Reflections on Some General Issues', *Industrial Law Journal*, Vol 33, No 1, pp 22–41.

USEFUL WEBSITES

Commission for Equality and Human Rights (CEHR):	www.equalityhumanrights.com/pages/eocdrccre.aspx
Department for Business, Enterprise and Regulatory Reform:	www.berr.gov.uk/
Department for Work and Pensions:	www.dwp.gov.uk
European Union Commission Employment & Social Affairs:	www.europa.eu.int
Low Pay Commission:	www.lowpay.gov.uk/

National minimum wage : two of the most helpful websites on the NMW (apart from the Low Pay Commission's website) are:

HMRC;	www.hmrc.gov.uk/nmw/
DBERR:	www.berr.gov.uk/whatwedo/employment/pay/national-minimum-wage/index.html

SELF-TEST QUESTION

1   Jane, Rose, Emma, and Ruth are employees of Crocks & Things Ltd.

   (a)   Jane and Fred are production line operatives. Fred has been employed by Crocks for five years and Jane has worked for them for one year. Jane discovers that Fred earns £9 per hour, whereas she receives only £7 per hour. She also discovers that George, a former employee who previously carried out Jane's job, earned £8 per hour.

   (b)   Rose has worked as a personnel assistant for crocks for 12 years. She feels that her work is of equal value to that of male computer maintenance technicians who work on a different site to her. The technicians earn £800 per annum more than Rose, although Crocks provides free meals and free transport to work for her, benefits which the technicians do not receive. Crocks says that to increase her pay they would have to restructure the pay scales of all employees in the personnel section, and this would be too high an administrative burden to undertake.

(c) Emma is a cook paid £8 per hour. She works at the Reading site of the company. She believes that her job is of equal value to that of delivery van drivers employed by Fast Trak Services Ltd, a subsidiary of Crocks based in London. They are paid £10 per hour. Nine out of the ten delivery van drivers are men, but one is a woman.

(d) Ruth, who works as a packer, has been on maternity leave for the last eight weeks. Last month, the company awarded a bonus of £500 to all employees in the light of the excellent performance of all staff over the last twelve months. Ruth has not been awarded this bonus because she is on maternity leave.

Advise Jane, Rose, Emma, and Ruth, all of whom want to bring claims against Crocks concerning these pay discrepancies.

Work/life balance

SUMMARY

This chapter considers the raft of legislation and approaches to the issues of work/life balance and 'family-friendly' policies. The various extensions to the rights originally enacted are considered, together with the proposals to widen the scope of the relevant legislation. This chapter also considers related legislation which provides protection for part-time workers and fixed-term employees.

The topics covered in this chapter are:

- work/life balance and 'family-friendly' policies;
- parental leave;
- maternity rights;
- paternity leave;
- adoption leave;
- flexible working;
- time off to care for dependants;
- part-Time Workers Directive;
- fixed-term employees.

Work/life balance and 'family-friendly' policies

7.1 There have been a number of social policy developments at both EU and domestic level over the past few years which have the objective of allowing workers to achieve a better balance between work and family commitments. As with many developments in the social policy field, the impetus for the introduction of what have become known as 'family-friendly' polices in the UK came from the European Union.

7.2 The concern to achieve a better work/life balance for workers is articulated, *inter alia*, in the Community Charter of the Fundamental Social Rights of Workers (known as 'the Social Charter'): see, for example, para 16 which provides that 'measures should also be developed enabling men and women to reconcile their occupational and family obligations'. These objectives are incorporated in the Agreement on Social Policy annexed as a Protocol to the Treaty on European Union (TEU), and also underpin the Social Partners' Framework Agreement on Parental Leave, which is stated to be 'an important means of reconciling work and family life and promoting equal opportunities and treatment between men and women' (Preamble to the Framework Agreement).

7.3 Although the UK originally opted out of the Social Charter during the Conservative Government's term of office, the Labour Government, elected in 1997, pledged to opt in to it, which was done in the Treaty of Amsterdam in 1997, when the Agreement on Social Policy was incorporated into the Treaty of Rome (the TEU and the Treaty of Rome were merged by the Treaty of Nice in 2001, which came into force in February 2003).

7.4 Within the UK, the family-friendly policies (and legislation) flowing from these developments are those relating to: parental leave; maternity leave; paternity leave; adoption leave; and time off work to care for dependants in certain circumstances. The introduction of flexible working arrangements, discussed below, is also part of the family-friendly package of policies.

7.5 The DTI published a Green Paper in December 2000 entitled, 'Work and Parents: Competitiveness and Choice', concerning the entitlements identified above, and a Work and Parents Taskforce was established in 2001 to consider ways of introducing 'family-friendly' and 'business-friendly' flexible working practices. The Government published a document entitled 'Balancing Work and Family Life: Enhancing Choice and Support for Parents', in January 2003, which considers further developments to improve work/life balance for the future.

7.6 In late 2004, the Government announced its 'family-friendly strategy' for the following ten years. This contained a number of proposals, including:

- the introduction of a Childcare approval scheme from 6 April 2005, which provides families on incomes not exceeding £59,000 with Tax Credit support to help pay for home child care (this is now in place);
- the introduction of paid maternity leave of 12 months by the end of the next parliament, ie Spring 2010 (currently Statutory Maternity Pay ('SMP'),

statutory adoption pay, and maternity allowance are paid for 39 weeks (this was increased from 26 weeks (six months) to 39 weeks (nine months) in the period from April 2007;

- the introduction of legislation by the end of the next parliament to give mothers the right to transfer a proportion of their pay and leave to the child's father;

- consultation on extending the right to request flexible working to parents of older children;

- an out-of-school childcare place between the hours of 8am and 6pm each weekday by 2010 for all children aged 3 to 14;

- access to integrated services for every family through Children's Centres in their local community, with a goal of 3,500 centres by 2010.

7.7 In January 2006, the DTI published a consultation document, 'Work and Families: Choice and Flexibility', which puts forward for discussion the enhancement of rights for working parents, including extending the right to statutory maternity pay and statutory adoption pay from six months to nine months by April 2007, with the goal of one year's paid leave by the end of the next parliament (Spring 2010). These changes are implemented by the Work and Families Act 2006, which received Royal Assent on 21 June 2006 and came into force from 1 October 2006 (its provisions have full effect from 1 April 2007, together with the regulations indicated below).

Work and Families Act 2006 – main changes

7.8 The main changes introduced by the 2006 Act and relevant regulations which affect 'family-friendly' provisions are:

- **Statutory Maternity Pay**: an extension of statutory maternity pay ('SMP'), statutory adoption pay, and maternity allowance from the current six months (26 weeks) to nine months (39 weeks) from 1 April 2007, provided the woman has 26 weeks' continuous employment – see Social Security and Benefits Act 1992 (SSCBA), s 164(2)(a); the Work and Families Act 2006 s 2 and the Statutory Paternity Pay and Statutory Adoption Pay (General) and the Statutory Paternity Pay and Statutory Adoption Pay (Weekly Rates) (Amendment) Regulations 2006, reg 4).

- **Maternity Leave**: removing the need to have 26 weeks' service to qualify for a full 52 weeks maternity leave. Any employee whose expected week of childbirth begins on or after 1 April 2007 and who qualifies for ordinary maternity leave (26 weeks) will automatically also qualify for additional maternity leave (a further 26 weeks (the Maternity & Parental Leave etc Regs 1999, regulation

5 is revoked by the Maternity and Parental Leave etc and the Paternity and Adoption Leave (Amendment) Regulations 2006, SI 2006/2014, reg 6).

- **Notice of return**: the notice period of return from maternity or adoption leave from has been increased from four to eight weeks (amendments are made to the Maternity & Parental Leave etc Regs 1999 reg 11 by Maternity and Parental Leave etc and the Paternity and Adoption Leave (Amendment) Regulations 2006, SI 2006/2014, reg 8).

- **Small employer exemption removed – unfair dismissal**: the small employer exemption from automatic unfair dismissal if a new mother is not allowed to return to work has been removed. The exemption for employers with fewer than five employees from the normal rule that refusal to allow return to work after maternity leave is automatically unfair dismissal ended from 1 October 2006 in relation to employees whose expected week of childbirth began on or after 1 April 2007 (Maternity & Parental Leave etc Regs 1999 reg 20(6) is revoked by Maternity and Parental Leave etc and the Paternity and Adoption Leave (Amendment) Regulations 2006, SI 2006/2014 reg 11(b)). (NB A woman's right to return to work will still be determined according to whether she returns within 26 weeks or later, at any time up to the end of additional maternity leave at 52 weeks.)

- **Work during maternity or adoption leave**: apart from the two-week period of compulsory maternity leave, from 1 October 2006 an employee whose expected week of childbirth began on or after 1 April 2007 can carry out up to 10 days' work (known as 'Keeping in Touch' days or 'KIT days') for her employer during her statutory maternity leave period without bringing her maternity leave to an end. This will not extend the total duration of the statutory maternity leave period. In addition, reasonable contact from time to time between an employee and her employer which either party is entitled to make during a maternity leave period (for example, to discuss an employee's return to work) shall not bring the statutory maternity leave period to an end (Maternity & Parental Leave etc Regs 1999, reg 12A inserted by Maternity and Parental Leave etc. and the Paternity and Adoption Leave (Amendment) Regulations 2006, reg 9).

  A similar rule is introduced in respect of adoption (Paternity & Adoption Leave Regulations 2002, reg 21A inserted by Maternity and Parental Leave etc. and the Paternity and Adoption Leave (Amendment) Regulations 2006, reg 14).

- **New rights for carers to request flexible working**: there is a new right for carers to request flexible working (in force from 6 April 2007 under the Work and Families Act 2006). The definition of 'carer' covers any employee who is or expects to be caring for an adult who:

- is married to, or the partner or civil partner of the employee; or
- is a 'near relative' of the employee;
- falls into neither category but lives at the same address as the employee.

The 'near relative' definition includes parents, parent-in-law, adult child, adopted adult child, siblings (including those who are in-laws), uncles, aunts, or grandparents and step-relatives. The then DTI estimated that this definition would cover about 80 per cent of carers.

7.9 **Additional Paternity Leave consultation**: in 2007, the DTI launched a consultation on implementation of plans to provide new fathers with a legal entitlement to choose to take up to 26 weeks additional Paternity Leave, some of which can be paid if the child's mother has returned to work. This new provision will be available during the second six months of the child's life and will provide parents with the option of dividing a period of paid leave entitlement between them (see the *Additional Paternity Leave and Pay Administration Consultation, DTI Consultation 14th May 2007*).

Parental leave

7.10 The major impetus for the introduction of a right to parental leave came from the European Union. During the 1980s and early 1990s, the United Kingdom vetoed proposals from the Commission concerning parental leave (whether paid or unpaid). The other Member States adopted the procedure set out in the Social Policy Protocol under which they could adopt social policy legislation without the UK blocking such moves.

7.11 The Protocol requires consultation with the Social Partners (UNICE, CCEP, and the ETUC), representing management and labour, under Article 138 (ex Article 118a) of the Treaty of Rome before social policy proposals may be put forward. The Social Partners may themselves reach an agreement on social policy matters and request the Council to implement it (Article 139 (ex Article 118b) of the Treaty of Rome). The Social Partners reached a framework agreement on parental leave under this procedure on 14 December 1995, which was implemented by the Parental Leave Directive (Directive 96/34/EC). Having been adopted under the Protocol on Social Policy, from which the UK had opted out, the Directive did not apply to the UK, although the Labour Government which came into power in 1997 accepted the Agreement on Social Policy and the Directive was subsequently extended to the UK by Directive 97/75/EC. The transposition date was 15 December 1999, which was the date the Maternity and Parental Leave Regulations (MPLR) implementing the Directive came into force.

7.12 The Parental Leave Directive actually requires the implementation of two 'family-friendly' rights: (i) the right to leave to care for young children (up to eight years of age, according to Clause 2(1) of the Directive); and (ii) the right to time off work to care for dependants in family emergencies. This section deals with the former right, while the latter is considered in a subsequent section.

7.13 Under the MPLR, both male and female employees, whether full-time or part-time, are entitled to unpaid parental leave of up to 13 weeks (per parent, per child) if they have one year's continuous employment and have (or expect to have) responsibility for a child under five (MPLR, regs 2 and 13(1)(a)(b), 14(1)). An employee has responsibility for a child where he or she has 'parental responsibility' (as defined in the Children Act 1989, s 3) – a definition which is wide enough to include an adopted child – or where they have been registered as the parent on the child's birth certificate. There is a separate entitlement for each parent. The period of 13 weeks' leave must be taken in periods of a week or multiples of a week, except for parents of disabled children, who may take leave of a day or multiples of a day (the limitations of this provision are discussed below), during the first five years of the child's life or, in the case of an adopted child, within five years of the placement for adoption or the child's eighteenth birthday, whichever is the earlier (MPLR, regs 14(1), 15, Sch 2, para 7). This maximum leave period is extended to 18 weeks in the case of employees with a child who is entitled to disability living allowance (MPLR, reg 14(1A)). The leave is 'for the purpose of caring for that child' (MPLR, reg 13(1)).

7.14 When first brought into force, the MPLR gave a right to parental leave only where the child was born (or adopted) on or after 15 December 1999, although this restriction was removed after the Government was subjected to severe criticism from a number of quarters, including the TUC, on the ground that it was a breach of the Parental Leave Directive, arguing that parental leave should have been available to parents of children aged five at that date (see *R v Secretary of State for Trade and Industry, ex parte TUC* (2000); and the Maternity and Parental Leave (Amendment) Regulations 2001, SI 2001/4010). The right to parental leave now applies to employees whose children were under five on 15 December 1999.

7.15 Employers and employees may make their own agreements on how to implement the parental leave right by adopting individual, collective, or workforce agreements. This would allow them to agree, for example, that parental leave could be taken in units of less than one week, eg one day, which may be more convenient for the employee. In the absence of such an agreement, the default provisions of Schedule 2 apply.

7.16 Employers may require employees to provide evidence of their entitlement, including evidence of responsibility for the child and the child's date of birth (MPLR, Sch 2, paras 1(a) and 2). Failure to comply with these requirements means that the employee loses their entitlement to leave.

Notice requirements

7.17 Employees must give at least 21 days' notice of their intention to take parental leave (MPLR, Sch 2, para 1). In the case of employees giving this notice before the expected week of childbirth or placement for adoption, the employer must allow the leave. Apart from those two situations, the employer may postpone it for up to six months where he 'considers that the operation of his business would be unduly disrupted' if the employee took the leave, giving the employee seven days' notice in writing of the postponement (MPLR, Sch 2, para 6). An employee may complain to an employment tribunal that the employer has unreasonably postponed a period of parental leave or prevented or attempted him from taking it (ERA, s 80).

Terms and conditions of employment while on parental leave

7.18 Under regulation 17, the employee is entitled to certain terms and conditions of employment which apply during the period of parental leave, apart from the right to pay. These are: the implied term of trust and confidence; notice of termination of the contract; compensation upon redundancy; and the disciplinary and grievance procedures. During leave, the employee is bound by: the implied obligation of good faith and any terms relating to: notice of termination; disclosure of confidential information; the acceptance of gifts of other benefits; or participation in any business.

Right to return after parental leave

7.19 Employees returning after parental leave of four weeks or less are entitled to return to the job they were doing before going on leave. Employees taking longer periods of leave are entitled to return to the job they were doing before going on leave or, where that is not reasonably practicable, to a suitable and appropriate job (MPLR, reg 18). Upon return, the employee's rights to remuneration, seniority, pension rights, and other similar rights must be no less favourable than they were before taking leave (reg 18A).

Unfair dismissal and protection from detriment

7.20 It is automatically unfair to dismiss an employee for a reason connected with the fact that he took or sought to take parental leave (ERA 1996, s 99; MPLR, reg 20). The employee is also entitled not to be subjected to any detriment on the same grounds (ERA 1996, s 47C; MPLR, reg 19). The employee may make a complaint to an employment tribunal concerning such infringements by the employer (ERA 1996, s 48).

Maternity rights

7.21 Women have four rights in relation to pregnancy and childbirth. These are: the right to maternity leave; the right to maternity pay; time off for ante-natal care; and protection from detriment or dismissal on the grounds of pregnancy or childbirth.

Maternity leave

7.22 The Pregnant Workers Directive 92/85/EEC required Member States to provide women workers with at least 14 weeks' maternity leave. The relevant domestic law is now contained within ERA 1996, ss 71–75 and the MPLR, as amended by the Maternity and Parental Leave (Amendment) Regulations 2002, SI 2002/2789 (MPLAR 2002), which were further amended by the Maternity and Parental Leave etc and the Paternity and Adoption Leave (Amendment) Regulations 2006, SI 2006/2014, which apply to mothers of children born on or after 6 April 2003.

Ordinary maternity leave

7.23 Women are entitled to a period of ordinary maternity leave ('OML') of 26 weeks (extended from 18 weeks as from 24 November 2002), where the expected week of childbirth is on or after 1 April 2007, without the need to accrue a qualifying period of continuous employment): MPLR, reg 7. A woman is entitled to OML and any holiday leave: in *Merino Gomez v Continental Industrias del Caucho SA* (2004), the ECJ ruled that a woman is entitled to her statutory minimum annual holiday in addition to any maternity leave to which she may be entitled.

7.24 The right to OML was originally to a leave period of 14 weeks (in 1994), which was then increased to 18 weeks (as from 24 November 2002) and then to 26 weeks. OML was first introduced with effect from 10 June 1994 for the benefit of all employed women with babies born after 16 October 1994, as required by the Pregnant Workers Directive 92/85/EC.

7.25 NB Women who qualify for OML also qualify for Additional Maternity Leave (AML), which is a further period of 26 weeks. Therefore, women may take 52 weeks' maternity leave, without having to accrue any period of continuous employment.

7.26 However, note that Statutory Maternity Pay ('SMP'), which is now payable for 39 weeks (the period of payment was previously 26 weeks but was extended to 39 weeks for women whose expected week of confinement fell on or after 1 April 2007) is not payable for the whole 52 weeks' of maternity leave. The Government intends to extend SMP to 52 weeks for babies due on or after April 2010.

Notice requirements

7.27 There are detailed notification requirements to be followed, failing which the maternity leave may be lost. The employee must notify her employer no later than the end of the 15th week before the expected week of childbirth (EWC) – or as soon as reasonably practicable – of the fact that she is pregnant, the expected date of childbirth and the date on which she intends to commence her OML (reg 4). This date may be varied by notifying the employer at least 28 days before the date varied or before the new date, whichever is the earlier.

7.28 The employer must then give the woman notice of the date on which her OML will end (reg 8). If the employer fails to do this, she may return early and she is protected from detriment or dismissal if she does not return on that date (regs 10(c), 13 and 14).

Contractual terms during absence

7.29 With the exception of remuneration (see SDA s 6A: a woman is entitled only to statutory maternity pay while on maternity leave), certain other terms and conditions of employment continue to apply throughout the woman's absence (ERA 1996, s 71; MPLR, reg 17). This means that both parties are bound, *inter alia*, by the implied term relating to trust and confidence, notice provisions, and disciplinary and grievance procedures. However, a pro rata reduction of an annual bonus paid to a woman who had been on maternity leave under a provision in a scheme which allowed for reductions to the bonus through absence was held to be lawful in *Hoyland v Asda Stores Ltd* (2005), EAT.

Redundancy during OML

7.30 If the woman becomes redundant during her maternity leave, she has the right to be offered suitable alternative employment (if there is such a post) by the employer or an associated employer (reg 10).

Right to return to work after OML

7.31 After her OML, a woman has the right to return to the job in which she was employed before her absence, on terms no less favourable than she would have enjoyed had she not been absent (reg 18).

Unfair dismissal and protection from detriment

7.32 A woman is protected from detriment for exercising or seeking to exercise her rights to maternity leave, and it is an automatically unfair dismissal to dismiss a woman for a reason connected with pregnancy, childbirth, or maternity leave rights (regs 19 and 20). There is one exception to this provision on automatically unfair dismissals: it is not automatically unfair to dismiss a woman (for a reason other than redundancy) if it is not reasonably practicable to allow her to return to a suitable job and she has accepted or unreasonably refused the offer of such a job made by an associated employer (reg 20(7)).

Additional maternity leave

7.33 A woman who is entitled to OML and who has been continuously employed for a period of 26 weeks by the 14th week before the EWC is entitled to a period of additional maternity leave (AML) of 26 weeks (regs 5 and 7). This gives qualifying female employees a total maternity leave entitlement of one year. However, maternity leave only attracts statutory maternity pay for the first 26 weeks of leave (see the section on statutory maternity pay), which means that, in practice, women will only wish to take the full 52 weeks of leave if there is a contractual entitlement covering the last half of the leave year.

Contractual terms during absence

7.34 During AML a mother is entitled only to the benefit of her employer's implied obligation to her of trust and confidence and of any terms and conditions covering notice, contractual redundancy pay, and disciplinary or grievance procedures (see ERA s 73(4)(a) and Maternity and Parental Leave etc Regs 1999, regulation 17(a)). Any continuation of contractual terms and conditions will apply only if they are specifically agreed. Unlike OML, the AML period is not required to be counted for the purpose of assessing seniority, pension rights, and other payments based on an individual employee's length of service. A woman on AML therefore has fewer statutory rights than those to which she was entitled while on OML.

7.35 Under the amended SDA, s 6A (the 'maternity leave remuneration' provision, under which it is not sex discrimination for an employer to withhold remuneration from a woman during her maternity leave), the discrepancies of treatment between women on OML and AML as regards maternity leave remuneration have been removed for women whose expected week of childbirth begins on or after 5 October 2008. If her expected week of childbirth begins on or after that date it makes no difference whether the woman is taking OML, AML, or the two weeks' compulsory maternity leave. Under the amended SDA, s 6A (amended by the Sex Discrimination Act 1975 (Amendment) Regulations 2008, SI 2008/656) a woman must be paid: remuneration to which she is entitled as a result of being pregnant or being on maternity leave (called 'maternity-related remuneration'); remuneration in respect of times when she is not on maternity leave; and remuneration by way of bonus in respect of times when she is on compulsory maternity leave.

7.36 For the purposes of the basic provisions, 'remuneration' is defined as 'only sums payable to an employee by way of wages or salary are to be treated as remuneration' (see MPLR 1999, reg 9). Under the 2008-amended version of the SDA, s 6A, 'remuneration' means 'benefits (a) that consist of the payment of money to an employee by way of wages or salary, and (b) that are not benefits whose provision is regulated by the employee's contract of employment'.

Notice requirements

7.37 The same notice requirements apply concerning the taking of AML and dates of commencement and return as for OML.

Right to return to work after AML

7.38 The woman returning from AML has the same right as relates to OML to return to the job in which she was employed before her absence, on terms no less favourable than she would have enjoyed had she not been absent (reg 18), but there are two exceptions to this right to return (see the section on unfair dismissal below).

Unfair dismissal and protection from detriment

7.39 As in OML, a woman is protected from detriment for exercising or seeking to exercise her rights to AML, and it is an automatically unfair dismissal to dismiss a woman for a reason connected with pregnancy, childbirth, or maternity leave rights (regs 19 and 20).

7.40 The same exception also applies for AML, as set out in regulation 20(7), ie it is not automatically unfair to dismiss a woman (for a reason other than redundancy) if it is not reasonably practicable to allow her to return from AML to a suitable job and she has accepted or unreasonably refused the offer of such a job made by an associated employer (reg 20(7)). The small employer exception in the case of AML has been revoked as from 1 October 2006 in relation to women whose expected week of childbirth begins on or after 1 April 2007. This exception was to the effect that it was not an automatically unfair dismissal if the employer employed five or fewer employees, including employees of any associated employer, and it was not reasonably practicable for him to offer the woman a job 'which is both suitable for her and appropriate for her to do in the circumstances' (reg 20(6)).

Contractual and statutory maternity leave rights – OML and AML

7.41 Where an employee has both contractual and statutory maternity leave rights, she may not exercise the two rights separately but may choose whichever right is the more favourable (reg 21).

Compulsory maternity leave

7.42 A woman may not work during the period of two weeks after the birth (ERA 1996, s 72, MPLR, reg 8).

Statutory maternity pay

7.43 A woman with 26 weeks of continuous employment by the 15th week before the EWC with average earnings at or above the lower earnings limit (£87 per week for 2007–08 and £90 for 2008–09) for the payment of National Insurance contributions is entitled to statutory maternity pay (SMP): see the Social Security Contributions and Benefits Act 1992, ss 164–171. For the first six weeks, it is paid at the rate of 90 per cent of the woman's normal weekly earnings. For the remaining 20 or 33 weeks it is paid at the rate of statutory sick pay, which for 2007–08 is £117.18 per week. A woman must give 28 days' notice of the day SMP should start. In calculating the earnings-related part of SMP, any pay rise awarded during a woman's absence on maternity leave must be taken into account, even where it was not backdated (see *Alabaster v Woolwich plc* (2005), CA, following the ECJ ruling in the case).

Time off for ante-natal care

7.44 A pregnant employee may request paid time off work to attend an ante-natal appointment, which may not be unreasonably refused by the employer. The employer may request written proof of the pregnancy and the appointment (ERA 1996, ss 55 and

56). The amount of pay is the normal hourly rate. The employee may complain to an employment tribunal that her employer has unreasonably refused time off or has failed to pay her for the time off. The tribunal may make a declaration and order the amount of pay due. Dismissal or subjection to a detriment because the employee has exercised her rights under these provisions will give the right to claim under the MPLR, regs 19 and 20, as well as the right to claim unfair dismissal (as well as sex discrimination).

Protection from detriment or dismissal on grounds of pregnancy

7.45 It is automatically unfair to dismiss a woman (or select her for redundancy) for a pregnancy-related reason, or to subject her to a detriment for such a reason (ERA 1996, ss 99 and 47C; MPLR, regs 19 and 20). As well as pregnancy itself, pregnancy-related reasons include reasons related to: childbirth; suspension on maternity grounds under ERA 1996, s 66; taking or seeking to take OML or AML; parental leave; or time off for ante-natal care. An employee who is dismissed because she is pregnant or during or after OML or AML must be provided with a written statement of the reasons for her dismissal (ERA 1996, s 92(4)), for which there is no requirement of a qualifying period of employment.

Paternity leave

7.46 The Employment Act 2002 (EA, 2002), s 1, introduced new rights to paternity leave ('PL') by inserting new sections into the ERA 1996, ss 80A and 80B (in force from 8 December 2002). These concern the two categories of PL: one concerning the birth of a child (called 'paternity leave: birth'), and the other concerning adoption (called 'paternity leave: adoption'). Although the provisions relating to these two categories are similar, there are some differences and these two forms of PL are treated separately below. Under the ERA 1996, s 1, the Secretary of State was given power to make regulations concerning paternity leave, which was done by making the Paternity and Adoption Leave Regulations 2002, SI 2002/2788 (PALR), which came into force on 8 December 2002. Where there is also a contractual right to paternity leave, an employee may not operate both rights separately but may choose whichever right is more favourable, ie he may choose either the contractual right or the statutory one, but not both (PALR, reg 30). Furthermore, PL is in addition to the 13 weeks' parental leave entitlement, discussed above. The right to take PL also applies to civil partners as from 5 December 2005 (see the Civil Partnership Act 2004 (Amendments to Subordinate Legislation) Order 2005 (SI 2005/2114), Sch 17).

7.47 The Government proposes to extend parental leave to 26 weeks, some of it paid, following a consultation exercise.

Paternity leave – birth

7.48 The PALR apply to fathers of children born on or after 6 April 2003 and who have been continuously employed for not less than 26 weeks ending with the week immediately preceding the 14th week before the expected week of the child's birth. However, it should be noted that the interpretation of 'partner' in regulation 2, which defines a partner as, 'a person (whether of a different or the same sex) who lives with the mother...and the child in an enduring family relationship but is not a relative of the mother...' is clearly wide enough for the purposes of regulation 4(2) – discussed below – to apply to a woman, despite the fact that it is called paternity leave. This means, for example, the right to paternity leave could also apply (if the requirements set out in regs 2 and 4 are met) to the female partner of a woman in a lesbian relationship where that woman has had a child. However, the masculine form will be used in this description of the PALR, which should be read as also importing the feminine.

7.49 There are a number of other requirements to be satisfied under the PALR, reg 4(2), before a father is entitled to this right. These are that he is:

  (i) the father of the child; or

  (ii) married to or the partner of the child's mother, but not the child's father;

  (iii) and that he has (or expects to have) if he is the child's father, responsibility for the upbringing of the child; or

  (iv) if he is the mother's husband or partner but not the child's father, that he has the main responsibility for the child's upbringing.

7.50 The requirements in (ii) above are treated as satisfied in circumstances where the child's mother has died, and the requirements in (iii) and (iv) above are treated as satisfied even where the child has died.

7.51 The entitlement is for up to two weeks' paid leave, which must be taken together – there is no right to take separate days of leave, although an employee may choose to take either one week's leave or two consecutive weeks' leave – and it must be taken within 56 days (8 weeks) of the birth (PALR, reg 5(2)). The employee is entitled to Statutory Paternity Pay (SPP), which is paid at the same rate as SMP, ie for 2008–09, this is £1117.18 per week, or 90 per cent of average weekly earnings if this is less than that sum – these figures normally change every year (see: EA 2002, s 7;

Statutory Paternity Pay and Statutory Adoption Pay (General) Regulations 2002, SI 2002/2822, reg 3); and the Statutory Paternity Pay and Statutory Adoption Pay (Weekly Rates) Regulations 2002, SI 2002/2818, reg 2). As with SMP, there are recoupment provisions which mean that employers can recover SPP paid to employees.

7.52 Employees wishing to take paternity leave must comply with certain notice requirements. Under the PALR, the employee must give notice to their employer at least 15 weeks' notice before the child's expected week (or, if that is not possible, as soon as is reasonably practicable) specifying (i) that they intend taking paternity leave; and (ii) how much leave they intend to take (PALR, reg 6(1) and (2)). An employee may vary either or both (i) and (ii) above on giving at least eight weeks' notice: this was increased from 28 days' notice from 1 April 2007 (reg 6(4)). Interestingly, the employer may request that the employee provides 'a declaration, signed by the employee, to the effect that the purpose of his absence from work will be' for the purpose of caring for the child or supporting its mother and that he/she satisfies the entitlement conditions of regulation 6(3).

Paternity leave: adoption

7.53 The PALR also contains provisions on PL for employees on the adoption of a child, defined as a person who is under 18 when placed for adoption (it is important to note that this right is not to be confused with adoption leave, which is discussed below). Many of the provisions concerning paternity leave relating to adoption are similar to those governing paternity leave on the birth of a child, eg those on qualifying for the entitlement, the period of leave allowed and the requirement that it must be taken within 56 days of (in this case) the date on which the child is placed with the adopter (PALR, regs 8 and 9(2)). The declaration requirements are also similar. However, the notice requirements differ from those relating to paternity leave: birth. Employees must give their employer notice of their intention to take this form of PL no more than seven days after the date on which the adopter is notified of having been matched with the child.

Paternity leave – terms and conditions of employment while on leave

7.54 During the period of PL, employees are bound by all the obligations and entitled to the benefit of all the terms and conditions of their employment, apart from remuneration (ERA 1996, s 80C(5)(b)).

Right to return after paternity leave

7.55 Regulation 13 of the PALR confers a right to return to work after PL 'to the job in which he was employed before his absence' (PALR, reg 13(1)). This right applies whether the PL was (i) taken as an isolated period of leave; or (ii) whether it was the last of two or more consecutive periods of statutory leave. Employees returning after a period of PL not falling within these two categories has the right either to return to the job they were doing before their absence or, if that is not reasonably practicable, to another suitable and appropriate job. He or she is entitled to return to work on the same terms and conditions as if they had not been absent.

Unfair dismissal and protection from detriment

7.56 Employees who are dismissed because they took or are seeking to take PL (or are selected for redundancy for that reason) are to be regarded as having been unfairly dismissed, ie this is an automatically unfair dismissal (PALR, reg 29). Employees taking or seeking to take PL, or where the employer believed that they were likely to do so, also have the right not to be subjected to a detriment or any deliberate failure to act by the employer (PALR, reg 28).

Adoption leave

7.57 The EA 2002 inserted new sections 75A and 75B into the ERA 1996 concerning adoption leave (AL). The provisions concerning AL, as distinct from paternity leave on adoption, allow either adoptive parent of an adopted child born on or after 6 April 2003 to take paid AL. There are two categories of AL: ordinary adoption leave (OAL) of 26 weeks, and additional adoption leave (AAL) of a further 26 weeks: PALR, regs 18(1) and 20(2). OAL attracts statutory adoption pay (SAP), ie it is paid leave. SAP was increased from 25 weeks to 39 weeks from 1 April 2007. Note that there is no statutory payment for the element of AAL beyond the 39-week period (although there may be contractual provisions concerning payment during this leave). Employees with 26 weeks' continuous employment who have been matched with a child by an adoption agency with an agreement that the child should be placed with them are entitled to OAL. Employees completing a period of OAL are entitled to AAL, ie a total of 52 weeks of AL. The employee may choose when this is to begin (PALR, reg 16) and there are notice and documentary proof requirements similar to those applicable in PL (PALR, reg 17). Employees failing to comply with the requirements set out in reg 17 lose their right to take AL.

7.58   As in PL, during OAL an employee's terms and conditions (including obligations) of the contract of employment are preserved (PALR, reg 19), but only certain terms are preserved in AAL (PALR, reg 21).

Statutory adoption pay – ordinary adoption leave

7.59   An adoptive parent taking OAL is entitled to statutory adoption pay (SAP) for the 26-week period: Social Security Contributions and Benefits Act 1992, s 171ZN. This is paid at the standard SMP rate (£117.18 from 6 April 2008, although these rates are likely to change every year). Employees earning less than the lower earnings limit for National Insurance contributions (£90 per week from 6 April 2008 – again, this rate changes every year) are not entitled to SAP.

Notice requirements

7.60   There are detailed and important notice requirements concerning the intention to take AL and the intention to return to work after AL (PALR, regs 17 and 25).

Right to return after adoption leave

7.61   An employee is entitled to return to his old job at the end of AL, unless there is no job to which he can return due to redundancy, in which case the employer or associated employer must offer him suitable and appropriate alternative employment on terms that are not less favourable than those of his previous contract (PALR, reg 23).

Unfair dismissal and protection from detriment

7.62   It is automatically unfair to dismiss an employee because he took or sought to take AL, or is selected for redundancy for that reason (PALR, reg 29). This is subject to one exemption: this exemption applies where it is not reasonably practicable (for a reason other than redundancy) for the employer to permit the employee to return to his old job but an associated employer offers him a suitable and appropriate job and the employee accepts or unreasonably refuses the offer (PALR, reg 29(5)). (NB The exemption for employers with fewer than five employees from the normal rule that refusal to allow return to work after maternity leave is automatically unfair dismissal was ended from 1 October 2006 in relation to employees whose expected week of childbirth begins on or after 1st April 2007 (Maternity & Parental Leave etc Regs 1999, reg 20(6) is revoked by the Maternity and Parental Leave etc and the Paternity and Adoption Leave (Amendment) Regulations 2006, SI 2006/2014, reg 11(b)).

7.63 An employee is protected from detriment because he took or sought to take OAL or AAL, or the employer believed he was likely to do so, or the employee failed to return to work because of the employer's failure to satisfy him of the date on which the OAL or AAL period would end (PALR, reg 28).

Written reasons for dismissal

7.64 An employee who is dismissed while absent on OAL or AAL is entitled to a written statement of the reason or reasons for dismissal, without having to request it 'and irrespective of whether he has been continuously employed for any period if he is dismissed in circumstances in which that period ends by reason of the dismissal' (ERA 1996, s 92(4A)).

Flexible working

7.65 In November 2001, the Work and Parents Task Force delivered a report proposing that employees who were parents of children under six should be able to request flexible working arrangements, and that the employer should be required to take this request seriously. This was taken up by the Government, and a provision was inserted into the ERA 1996 by the Employment Act 2002 (see ERA 1996, ss 80F–80I), effective from 6 April 2003. There are two sets of regulations on flexible working: the Flexible Working (Procedural Requirements) Regulations 2002, SI 2002/3207 (the 'FE(PR) Regs'), and the Flexible Working (Eligibility, Complaints and Remedies) Regulations 2002, SI 2002/3236 (the 'FW(ECR) regs'). The right is to request to work flexibly (ie a right to request a contractual variation), rather than an automatic right to do so. The change must relate to hours or times and place of work (ERA 1996, s 80F(1)(a)).

7.66 The Government proposes to increase the age limit of children in respect of whom parents (and certain others) can request employers to allow flexible working arrangements. (A review took place, which was followed by a formal consultation. Following the consultation, a report was published, 'Flexible working: a review of how to extend the right to request flexible working to parents on older children' on 15 May 2008. On 26 August the Government launched a public consultation on implementing the recommendations of Imelda Walsh's independent review 'Amending and extending the right to request flexible working to parents of older children' (see also the national news item for 6 November 2007 on the DBERR website).)

Qualifying for the right

7.67 To qualify for this right, the employee must be:

- a qualifying employee, ie with at least 26 weeks' of continuous employment (FE(PR) Regs, reg 3(1)(a));

- having or expecting to have responsibility for the upbringing of a child aged under 6 (or under 18 if the child is disabled): ERA 1996, s 80F(3) and (7) (Note the Government's plans to increase this age, discussed above);

- either the parent, foster parent, guardian, or adopter of the child, or the husband, wife, or partner (including civil partner) of such a person (FE(PR) Regs, reg 3(1)(b));

- a carer: this new right is given to a 'carer' to request flexible working (this came into force on 6th April 2007 under the Work and Families Act 2006).

The definition of 'carer' covers any employee who is or expects to be caring for an adult who:

- is married to, or the partner or civil partner of the employee; or

- is a 'relative' of the employee;

- falls into neither category but lives at the same address as the employee.

The 'relative' definition includes parents, adopter, guardian, special guardian, parent-in-law, adult child, adopted adult child, siblings (including those who are in-laws), uncles, aunts or grandparents, and step-relatives. The then DTI (now DBERR) estimated that this definition will cover about 80 per cent of carers.

Procedure

7.68 The application to request the right must be made in writing, and must specify the change applied for, the date from which the employee wants it to be effective, and the effect (if any) the applicant thinks the change would have on the employer: FE(PR) Regs, reg 4; ERA 1996, s 80F. The application must be made before the 14th day before the day on which the child reaches the age of six (or 18 if disabled).

7.69 The employer must hold a meeting within 28 days of the request, and inform the employee of the decision within 14 days of the meeting (FE(PR) Regs, regs 3 and 4)). The employee may be accompanied by a fellow worker. The employee may appeal against the decision within 14 days and, if an appeal is made, an appeal meeting must be held within 14 days of the appeal being lodged, unless the appeal is upheld within 14 days of the appeal being lodged (FE(PR) Regs, regs 6 and 8)).

Grounds for refusal

7.70 The employer may only refuse the request on 'business grounds' (ERA 1996, s 80G(1)(b)). These are:

- burden of additional costs;
- detrimental effect of the ability to meet customer demand;
- inability to reorganise work among existing staff;
- inability to recruit additional staff;
- detrimental impact on quality or performance;
- insufficiency of work during periods that the employee proposes to work planned structural changes;
- any other ground that the Secretary of State may specify.

These grounds seem very wide, giving great scope to the employer to refuse the request.

7.71 Failure to follow these procedural requirements will mean that the employee may apply to an employment tribunal which can order the employer to reconsider its decision and award a maximum of eight weeks' pay (from February 2008 this is capped at the statutory maximum of £330 per week, ie a total award of £2,640 may be made): FE(PR) Regs, reg 15.

Unfair dismissal and protection from detriment

7.72 It is an automatically unfair dismissal if the reason is that the employee exercised or sought to exercise the rights to request flexible working (ERA 1996, s 104C). The employee is also protected from suffering a detriment on these grounds (ERA 1996, s 47E).

Time off to care for dependants

7.73 The Parental Leave Directive required Member States to introduce the right for workers to take time off for urgent family reasons. This was implemented by inserting a provision into the ERA 1996, s 57A (as amended by the Employment Relations Act 1999), giving employees a statutory right to request time off to care for dependants. No qualifying period of employment is necessary for entitlement to the right. A 'dependant' is the employee's wife, husband, child, parent, civil partner, or someone living in the same household (but is not his or her employee, tenant, lodger or boarder (ERA 1996, s 57A(3)). This is wide enough to include partners of the opposite or the same sex as the employee. The definition also includes a person who reasonably relies on the employee for assistance when they fall ill, are injured or assaulted, or who relies on the employee to make arrangements for the provision of care in the event of illness or injury (ERA 1996, s 57A(4)). Where there is unexpected disruption or termination of arrangements for the care of a dependant, the definition also includes any person who reasonably relies on the employee to make arrangements for care (ERA 1996, s 57A(5)).

7.74　The right is to 'reasonable' time off, ie it is intended to allow the employee to deal with unexpected crises or emergencies. This is reflected in the range of circumstances for which time off is allowed. It is time off to take action which is necessary:

- to provide assistance on an occasion when a dependant falls ill, gives birth, or is injured or assaulted;

- to make arrangements for the provision of care for a dependant who is ill or injured;

- in consequence of the death of a dependant;

- because of the unexpected disruption or termination of arrangements for the care of the dependant; or

- to deal with an incident which involves a child of the employee and which occurs unexpectedly in a period during which an educational establishment which the child attends is responsible for him (ERA 1996, s 57A(1)).

7.75　The employee must inform his employer as soon as is reasonably practicable of the reason for the absence and, if he is able to inform his employer in advance of the absence, state how long he will be absent (ERA 1996, s 57A(2)). The EAT in *Truelove v Safeway Stores plc* (2005) appears to indicate that the statutory requirements to be satisfied by an employee seeking time off to look after a dependant should be interpreted generously in the employee's favour.

7.76　There is no statutory entitlement to paid time off, so the absence will be unpaid unless there are contractual provisions relating to this in the employment contract.

7.77　The EAT in *Qua v John Ford Morrison Solicitors* (2003) gave guidance on the entitlement to time off under ERA 1996, s 57A. In determining what is a reasonable amount of time off, no account must be taken of operational disruption caused to the employer's business by the employee's absence. The employer should take account of the individual circumstances of the employee, including the number and length of previous absences and the dates on which they occurred. The EAT stated that the right is to allow the employee time off to deal with an unexpected event: they are allowed a reasonable amount of time off 'to deal with the immediate crisis' (per Mrs Recorder Cox QC at para 16).

7.78 The employee may complain that the employer unreasonably refused time off (ERA 1996, s 57B), for which the remedies are a declaration and such compensation as the tribunal considers to be just and equitable, having regard to the employer's default and the loss to the employee.

Unfair dismissal and protection from detriment

7.79 As with the other rights considered in this chapter, any dismissal is automatically unfair if it relates to entitlement to time off, and the employee may make a complaint to the ET if they have been subjected to a detriment for exercising their rights under ERA 1996, s 57A.

Part-Time Workers Directive

7.80 Encouraging part-time work and providing the opportunity to switch from full-time to part-time working, and ensuring adequate employment protection for those wishing to do so, is a very important aspect of achieving a better work/life balance across the labour market. The protections recently introduced for part-time workers may thus be seen as part of the package of family-friendly policies. The EC Part-Time Work Directive 97/81/EC of 5 December 1997 (which was extended to apply to the UK by the Part-Time Workers Directive 98/23EC) was implemented by the Part-Time Workers (Prevention of Less Favourable Treatment) Regulations 2000 (SI 2000/1551) (the 'PTWR') on 1 July 2000, some three months after the implementation date of 7 April 2000. The former DTI issued detailed guidance on the PTWR (Part-Time Workers – The Law and Best Practice), which encouraged employers to afford opportunities for allowing workers to switch to part-time work, and to consider more flexible working. This is in line with the objectives of the Directive, although the guidance does not have legal force.

Less favourable treatment of part-time workers

7.81 A part-time worker's main right under the Regulations is found in regulation 5(2), which provides that:

> A part-time worker has the right not to be treated by his employer less favourably than the employer treats a comparable full-time worker –
>
> - as regards the terms of his contract; or

- by being subjected to any other detriment by any act, or deliberate failure to act, of his employer.

7.82 This right applies only if:

(i) the treatment is on the ground that the worker is a part-time worker; and

(ii) the treatment is not justified on objective grounds.

7.83 There must be an actual comparable full-time worker with whom the part-timer can compare himself. One person can claim parity with another if (i) he is a part-time worker, ie he is not identifiable as a full-time worker, 'having regard to the custom and practice of the employer in relation to workers employed by the worker's employer under the same type of contract'; and (ii) the comparator is a comparable full-time worker (PTWR, reg 2(2)). Three conditions must be satisfied (reg 2(4)):

- the full-time worker is employed by the same employer under the same type of contract;

- both workers are engaged in the same or broadly similar work, having regard, where relevant, to qualification, skills and experience; and

- both workers are based at the same establishment (unless there is no full-time worker based at the same establishment as the part-time worker, but there is one based at another establishment).

7.84 The question of whether full-time workers were employed under the same type of contract as part-timers was considered in *Matthews v Kent and Medway Towns Fire Authority* (2006), in which the House of Lords held that retained (ie part-time) fire fighters could compare themselves to full-time, regular fire fighters as they were employed under the 'same type of contract' as whole-time fire fighters. This was on the basis that the main difference between the two categories was that full-timers worked extra hours and that the contracts of both must be treated as equivalent for the purposes of the Regulations.

7.85 According to Baroness Hale in *Matthews*, the court should consider (and give particular weight to) the extent to which the work of full-timers and part-timers is exactly the same and to the importance of that work to the enterprise as a whole. 'If a large component of their work is exactly the same, the question is whether any differences are of such importance as to prevent their work being regarded overall as the "same or broadly similar"' (para 44).

Pro rata principle

7.86 Part-time workers are entitled to the same treatment pro rata as full timers doing similar work unless the less favourable treatment can be objectively justified. For the purposes of this chapter, which focuses on family-friendly policies, it is important to note that part-timers must have the same entitlements to maternity leave (and maternity pay), parental leave, and time off for dependants, on a pro-rata basis, as comparable full-time workers (PTWR, reg 5).

Family-friendly policies and changing to part-time work

7.87 The PTWR may be particularly important in cases where a full-time worker's contract is varied, for example following a successful request under the flexible working provisions discussed above, so that they are working fewer weekly hours. In such a situation, the PTWR apply to them (reg 3). The PTWR also apply in situations where a full-time worker returns after a period of absence, eg parental leave or maternity leave, provided they are returning within a period of 12 months from the start of the absence to the same job or one at the same level (reg 4). The 'returning worker' is entitled not to be treated less favourably on the grounds of their part-time status (without objective justification) than they were before the contractual variation (PTWR, regs 4 and 5).

Objective justification

7.88 The right of a part-timer not to be treated less favourably than a comparable full-timer applies only if the treatment cannot be justified on objective grounds. Justification of the less favourable treatment on objective grounds means that it must be shown that it:

- is to achieve a legitimate objective, for example, a genuine business objective;
- is necessary to achieve that objective; and
- is an appropriate way to achieve the objective.

Written reasons for less favourable treatment

7.89 A part-time worker who considers that his employer may be treating him less favourably than a comparable full-time co-worker may require the employer to give written reasons for the difference (reg 6). If the employer fails to provide the statement within 21 days, a tribunal may draw an adverse inference that the employer has infringed the right in question.

Unfair dismissal and protection from detriment

7.90 It is automatically unfair dismissal to dismiss an employee for a reason relating to his rights under the PTWR (reg 7(1) and (3)), and a worker has the right not to be subjected to a detriment for a reason relating to his rights under the Regulations (reg 7(2)).

Complaint to an employment tribunal

7.91 A worker has the right to complain to an employment tribunal (reg 8), which may make a declaration, award compensation which the tribunal considers to be just and equitable, and make recommendations (regs 8(7) and 9). There is no statutory cap on the amount of compensation that a tribunal can award, but no award can be made for injury to feelings (reg 8(11)).

Fixed-term employees

7.92 While not strictly part of the work/life balance range of legislation, the law on fixed-term employees is discussed here because the relevant legislation forms part of the legal protection in place for those not on permanent, full-time contracts. In that sense, it sits with the Regulations on part-timer workers. In another sense, it represents the other side of the equation, ie fixed-term contracts are often used by employers for reasons of flexibility and business efficiency, while the objective of the work/life balance provisions is, partly at least, to allow individuals to secure flexibility in their working lives.

7.93 Employees on fixed-term contracts form part of what used to be called the 'atypical' or 'marginal' workforce, which is becoming more typical and far less marginal now that many more employers are striving to achieve a flexible workforce, in order to keep costs down and efficiency high.

7.94 Under common law, the expiry of a fixed-term contract terminates the contract 'by performance'. In such a situation, there is no dismissal at common law and therefore, without special rules, there would be no compensation for unfair dismissal or dismissal by reason of redundancy. For the purposes of unfair dismissal and redundancy law, statute provides that, if an employee is employed under a fixed-term contract and the term expires without the contract being renewed, he is treated as dismissed (see ERA, s 95(1)(b) for unfair dismissal and ERA, s 136(1)(b) for redundancy). However, these rules do not prevent the abuse of fixed-term contracts, for example by employers offering a series of short-term contracts (ie for less than one year), in an attempt to prevent the employee accruing unfair dismissal or redundancy rights. The legislative impetus to address such abuses and to afford fixed-term employees greater protection came from the EU.

Framework agreement

7.95 On 18 March 1999, a framework agreement was reached between the Social Partners in relation to fixed-term contracts (the definition of which extends to contracts for the duration of a particular task). The aims of the agreement were to:

(a) improve the quality of fixed-term work by ensuring the application of the principle of non-discrimination; and

(b) establish a framework to prevent abuse arising from the use of successive fixed-term employment contracts or relationships.

7.96 The principle of non-discrimination requires employers not to treat those employed on fixed-term contracts less favourably than those employed permanently unless the less favourable treatment can be objectively justified.

7.97 The agreement introduces rules requiring objective reasons for renewal, a maximum duration, and a limit on the number of times that a contract can be renewed. Employers are required to inform fixed-term workers about job vacancies in order to give them the same chance to gain permanent positions as other workers.

Fixed-Term Work Directive on fixed-term contracts (Directive 99/70/EC)

7.98 The Directive transposing the framework agreement into EU law was adopted by the European Council on 28 June 1999. It should have been adopted in the UK by 10 July 2001 (the implementing legislation came in to force in the UK on 1 October 2002). (NB The Directive covers 'workers', whereas the Regulations implementing them in the UK refer to 'employees'.)

Consultation paper

7.99 In March 2001, the Government published a consultation paper on implementing the Directive. The consultation period ended on 31 May 2001. The Government, relying on a provision in the Directive that permits a further period of up to 12 months for implementation in Member States that have 'specific difficulties', announced that regulations would not be in place by 10 July 2001.

Fixed-term Employees (Prevention of Less Favourable Treatment) Regulations 2002 (SI 2002/2034)

7.100 Section 45 of the Employment Act 2002 placed the Secretary of State under a duty to make regulations preventing less favourable treatment of fixed-term employees and preventing abuse arising from the use of successive periods of fixed-term employment. The Secretary of State made the Fixed-term Employees (Prevention of Less Favourable Treatment) Regulations 2002 (SI 2002/2034) to implement the Directive: the Regulations came into force on 1 October 2002.

7.101 The Regulations give fixed-term employees the right not to be treated less favourably than permanent employees doing similar work for the same employer. The right is exercisable by complaint to an ET and applies only if the less favourable treatment is not objectively justified. The Regulations also provide that where a fixed-term employee has been continuously employed on fixed-term contracts for four years or more, the next re-engagement of the contract will take effect as a permanent contract unless renewal as a fixed-term contract can be objectively justified.

Fixed-term employee

7.102 Regulation 1 provides that a fixed-term employee 'means an employee who is employed under a fixed-term contract'. A fixed-term contract is defined under regulation 1 as:

> a contract of employment that, under its provisions determining how it will terminate in the normal course, will terminate –
>
> > (a) on the expiry of a specific term,
> >
> > (b) on the completion of a particular task, or
> >
> > (c) on the occurrence or non-occurrence of any other specific event other than the attainment by the employee of any normal and bona fide retiring age in the establishment for an employee holding the position held by him ...

Exclusions

7.103 The following categories are excluded from the scope of the Regulations: employees engaged under government training schemes; students on work placements of up to one year; agency workers, ie people supplied by an employment business; employees on apprenticeships.

Right not to be treated less favourably (reg 3)

7.104 Regulation 3(1) provides that:

> A fixed-term employee has a right not to be treated less favourably than a comparable permanent employee –
>
> > (1)
> >
> > > (a) as regards the terms of his contract; or

(b) by being subjected to any other detriment by any act, or deliberate failure to act, of his employer.

Regulation 3(2) provides that:

the right conferred by paragraph (1) includes in particular the right of the fixed-term employee in question not to be treated less favourably than the employer treats a comparable permanent employee in relation to –

(a) any period of service qualification relating to any particular condition of service,

(b) the opportunity to receive training, or

(c) the opportunity to secure any permanent position in the establishment.

7.105 By virtue of regulation 3(3), this right applies only if '(a) the treatment is on the ground that the employee is a fixed-term employee, and (b) the treatment is not justified on objective grounds'.

7.106 A decision by the employer not to renew a fixed-term contract will not of itself constitute less favourable treatment. *Department for Work and Pensions v Webley* (2005), CA concerned a policy operated by the Department under which temporary employees in job centres had their contracts terminated after they had completed 51 weeks' service, whether or not there was a continuing requirement for their work. The Court of Appeal held that the non-renewal of a fixed-term contract, in itself, is not capable of involving less favourable treatment for the purpose of the Regulations. Ward LJ, who gave the leading judgment, stated (at para 36):

Once it is accepted, as it must be, that fixed-term contracts are not only lawful, but are recognised in the Preamble to the Directive as responding 'in certain circumstances, to the needs of both employers and workers', it seems to me inexorably to follow that the termination of such a contract by simple effluxion of time cannot, of itself, constitute less favourable treatment by comparison with a permanent employee. It is of the essence of a fixed-term contract that it comes to an end at the expiry of the fixed term.

Pro Rata Principle – regulation 3.5

7.107 The pro rata principle is used to determine whether a fixed-term employee has been treated less favourably than a comparable permanent employee – the pro rata principle shall be applied 'unless it is inappropriate'.

7.108 Regulation 1 defines 'pro rata principle':

'pro rata principle' means that where a comparable permanent employee receives or is entitled to pay or any other benefit, a fixed-term employee is to receive or be entitled to such proportion of that pay or other benefit as is reasonable in the circumstances having regard to the length of his contract of employment and to the terms on which the pay or other benefit is offered.

Comparable permanent employees

7.109 Under reg 2, an employee is defined as a comparable permanent employee in relation to a fixed-term employee if, at the time when the treatment that is alleged to be less favourable to the fixed-term employee takes place both employees are employed by the same employer; and

> engaged in the same or broadly similar work having regard, where relevant, to whether they have a similar level of qualification and skills; and
>
> > (b) the permanent employee works or is based at the same establishment as the fixed-term employee or, where there is no comparable permanent employee working or based at that establishment who satisfies the requirements of sub-paragraph (a), works or is based at a different establishment and satisfies those requirements.

Objective justification – regulation 4

7.110 Under regulation 4(1), where a fixed-term employee is treated by his employer less favourably than the employer treats a comparable permanent employee as regards any term of his contract, the treatment may be objectively justified 'if the terms of the fixed-term employee's contract of employment, taken as a whole, are at least as favourable as the terms of the comparable permanent employee's contract of employment'. Therefore, it is necessary to look at the whole package.

7.111 Explanatory Notes accompanying the Regulations state that less favourable treatment will only be objectively justified if its purpose is:

- to achieve a legitimate business or organisational objective;
- necessary for that purpose; and
- an appropriate means of doing so.

7.112 In *Adeneler v Ellinikos Organismos Galaktos* (2006), the ECJ gave guidance on what is required in order to establish objective justification under the Directive. In this case from Greece concerning the renewal of successive fixed-term contracts, the ECJ ruled that objective justification requires use of fixed-term contracts 'to be justified by the presence of specific factors relating in particular to the activity in question and the conditions under which it is carried out' (para 75). The ECJ stated that 'objective reasons' refers to (paras 69 and 70):

> precise and concrete circumstances characterising a given activity, which are therefore capable in that particular context of justifying the use of successive fixed-term

contracts . . . Those circumstances may result, in particular, from the specific nature of the tasks for the performance of which such contracts have been concluded and from the inherent characteristics of those tasks or, as the case may be, from pursuit of a legitimate social policy objective of a Member State.

Written statement

7.113 An employee who believes that he may have been subjected to less favourable treatment is entitled to request a written statement of the reasons for the suspected less favourable treatment (reg 5(1)). The statement must be produced by the employer within 21 days of the request.

Permanent vacancies

7.114 In order to ensure that a fixed-term employee may exercise the right conferred in regulation 3(2)(c), the employee has the right to be informed of available vacancies in the establishment.

Right to receive a written statement of reasons for less favourable treatment (reg 5)

7.115 Under regulation 5, where the employee requests one in writing, the employer must provide it within 21 days. Such a written statement under this regulation is admissible as evidence (reg 5(2))

Unfair dismissal and the right not to be subjected to detriment (reg 6)

7.116 Under regulation 6, the employee has the right not to be unfairly dismissed or to be subjected to detriment. The remedies available for unfair dismissal are the standard ones for this claim, ie a declaration; compensation; and a recommendation (reg 7(7)). No compensation is paid for injury to feelings (reg 7(10)).

Successive fixed-term contracts (reg 8)

7.117 Under regulation 8, where an employee is engaged on a fixed-term contract, and the contract has previously been renewed, or the employee has previously been employed on a fixed-term contract before the start of the contract, and the employee has been continuously employed under the contract (taken together with a previous fixed-term contract), for a period of four years or more, and the employment of the employee under a fixed-term contract was not justified on objective grounds, then any restriction as to duration of the contract is of no effect, and the employee shall be a permanent employee.

Modifying the provisions on successive fixed-term contracts by a collective agreement or a workforce agreement (reg 8(5))

7.118 Under regulation 8, a collective agreement or a workforce agreement may modify the application of certain provisions relating to one or more of the following:

(a) the maximum total period for which the employee may be continuously employed on a fixed-term contract or on successive fixed-term contracts;

(b) the maximum number of successive fixed-term contracts and renewals of such contracts under which the employee or employees of that description may be employed; or

(c) objective grounds justifying the renewal of fixed-term contracts, or the engagement of the employee or employees of that description under successive fixed-term contracts.

Right to receive written statement of variation (reg 9)

7.119 Under regulation 9, if an employee considers that he is a permanent employee, he may request in writing from his employer a written statement confirming that his contract is no longer fixed-term or that he is now a permanent employee. He is entitled to be provided with such a statement (or a statement giving reasons why his contract remains fixed-term) within 21 days of his request.

Liability of employers and principals (reg 12)

7.120 Vicarious liability applies to employers and principals for acts contravening the Regulations, if done 'in the course of employment', subject to the defence that 'he took such steps as were reasonably practicable to prevent the employee from (a) doing that act, or (b) doing in the course of his employment acts of that description'.

FURTHER READING

Deakin, S, & Morris, G, *Labour Law* (4th ed, 2005) Hart Publishing (chapter 6, pp 701–713).

EOC, 'Women and Men in Britain: The Work–Life Balance' (2002) EOC.

Smith, I, & Thomas, G, *Smith & Wood's Employment Law* (9th ed, 2007) OUP (chapter 6).

ARTICLES

Caracciolo di Torella, E, (2007) 'New Labour, New Dads: The Impact of Family Friendly Legislation on Fathers', *Industrial Law Journal*, Vol 36, No 3, pp 318–328.

Dickens, L, (2006) 'Equality and Work–Life Balance: What's Happening at the Workplace', *Industrial Law Journal*, Vol 35, No 4, pp 445–449 (NB This is in the Research and Reports section of the *ILJ* and is not a full article).

McColgan, A, (2000) 'Family-friendly Frolics? The Maternity and Parental Leave etc Regulations1999', *Industrial Law Journal*, Vol 29, No 2, pp 125–144.

McColgan, A, (2000) 'Missing the Point? The Part-time Workers (Prevention of Less Favourable Treatment) Regulations 2000', *Industrial Law Journal*, Vol 29, No 3, pp 260–267.

USEFUL WEBSITES

ACAS:	www.acas.org.uk
DBERR	www.berr.gov.uk
Equality and Human Rights Commission:	*www.equalityhumanrights.com*
ETS:	www.employmenttribunals.gov.uk
Government Equalities Office	www.equalities.gov.uk
House of Lords	www.parliament.uk/lords/index.cfm
ILO:	www.ilo.org
Ministry of Justice	www.justice.gov.uk
Personnel Today	www.personneltoday.com

SELF-TEST QUESTIONS

1   Annie has been employed for five years on a full-time basis as one of five designers for Poncho, a hat manufacturer. She has greatly benefited from Poncho's annual training programme in fashion trends, which includes travelling to fashion shows in Paris. Following the birth of her first child, Annie finds full-time work too exhausting.

Annie wishes to switch to working only three half-days per week for the next two years, but then resume full-time working. Advise Annie on any rights she may have.

2   'Reconciling "work/life balance" is not an issue which can be resolved by the principles of labour law.' Discuss.

3 Danny works as a solicitor. He and his wife, Mary, are about to adopt a four-year-old child.

   Advise Danny of his rights with regard to leave.

4 Are family-friendly policies working in Britain? Assess the impact of these policies on the UK labour market. Give examples from case law.

5 How effective is the law on requesting flexible working?

6 Does the legislation currently in place for part-time workers and fixed-term employees provide sufficient protection for those falling within these categories? How might it be extended?

8

Termination of employment

SUMMARY

This chapter considers what claims an employee whose contract is terminated by the employer may make. Central to all dismissal claims, whether based on the common law or upon the statutory provisions, is the question of whether the employee was dismissed. In addition, to be able to make a wrongful dismissal claim, the employee must show that the dismissal was in breach of contract. This chapter considers what amounts to a dismissal and the circumstances in which the dismissal will be wrongful.

Introduction

8.1 Those who are dismissed are likely to have two basic types of claim: they may either claim to have been dismissed in breach of contract, or they may claim to have been dismissed in breach of their statutory rights. A dismissal in breach of contract is usually called a 'wrongful dismissal'. A claim for breach of statutory rights will take the form of a complaint of unfair dismissal and/or a claim for a statutory redundancy payment. These two types of statutory claim are considered in Chapters 9 and 10. This chapter considers the concept of wrongful dismissal.

8.2 It is common to all forms of dismissal claim that the person making it must have been dismissed. Unless a dismissal (however defined) has taken place, no claim is possible. It is important to note, however, that the common law definition of a dismissal does not necessarily coincide with the statutory definition of dismissal. This is because the common law looks solely at the agreement between the parties. Statute, on the other hand, gives an extended meaning to dismissal, which means that a dismissal is deemed to have taken place for statutory purposes, even if it does not amount to a dismissal at common law. An example is the expiry of a fixed-term contract. So far as the common law is concerned, the expiry of a fixed-term contract represents what was agreed between the parties. Thus, when the contract expires, that is an event contemplated by them and cannot therefore give rise to any claim for breach of contract. The ERA 1996, however, treats the expiry of a fixed-term contract as a dismissal. On the other hand, if the contract is held to have been 'frustrated', neither the common law nor statute will treat the event that happened as amounting to a dismissal.

8.3   The critical distinction between a 'wrongful' and an 'unfair' dismissal lies in the limitations of the law of contract. If a person is dismissed in breach of contract – for example, without the notice to which he or she was entitled under the contract – then the common law is able to intervene and a claim may be made. If, however, the person is dismissed with the notice to which he or she was entitled, the common law can no longer deal with the matter since there has been no breach of contract. It is at this point that the law of unfair dismissal becomes important. The success or otherwise of a statutory claim to have been unfairly dismissed depends upon whether the employer has dismissed the employee in a way which infringes his or her statutory rights; in other words whether the dismissal was fair or unfair. Thus, it is perfectly feasible for an employee to be dismissed in accordance with the contract but in a way which contravenes his or her statutory rights. In such a case, a wrongful dismissal claim will fail, whereas an unfair dismissal claim will succeed. It is important to bear in mind that the terms 'unfair' and 'wrongful' cannot be used interchangeably. They are terms of art and embody different legal concepts.

What amounts to a dismissal?

8.4   This section considers various situations and examines whether they amount to a dismissal. In doing so, it compares and contrasts the position at common law and under the statutory provisions. The following situations are considered: expiry of a fixed-term contract; frustration; termination by mutual consent; dismissal with notice; dismissal without notice; resignation; resignation in breach of contract; and constructive dismissal.

Expiry of fixed-term contract

8.5   Fixed-term contracts may take a number of forms. The contract may specify that it is to continue for a stated period (eg five years from 1 January 2006). In that case, it cannot be terminated before the expiry of that period, unless its terms empower the parties to terminate it earlier or they agree to bring it to an end. See, for example, *Nelson v James Nelson & Sons Ltd* (1914). A second type of fixed-term contract is one which provides for a definite period of employment but specifies that it may be brought to a premature end by either party giving the other a stated period of notice of termination, for example six months or a year. In *Dixon v British Broadcasting Corporation* (1979) the Court of Appeal held that, in the context of employment protection legislation, such a contract is a contract for a fixed term even though it is terminable by notice on either side before the expiry of the term. Lord Denning, MR emphasised that a fixed-term contract must be for a specified period.

8.6 A third type of fixed-term contract is one which provides that it is to continue for a stated period (eg one year) and thereafter until determined by notice. The contract cannot be terminated before the stated period expires, but it is a matter of construction of the words used in the contract whether it can be terminated at the end of the period by notice given during that period, or whether it can only be determined after the expiry of the definite term by notice given after the end of the term. In *Costigan v Gray Bovier Engines Ltd* (1925) the contract was 'to continue for a period of 12 calendar months and thereafter until determined by three calendar months' notice in writing given by either party at any time to the other'. The court held that, although the contract could not be terminated before the expiration of the 12 months, it could be determined at the end of, or at any time after, the term by notice given either during or after the period of 12 months; see also *Morris Oddy & Co Ltd v Hayles* (1971).

8.7 It should be noted that limitations have been placed on the use of fixed-term contracts by the Fixed-Term Employees (Prevention of Less Favourable Treatment) Regulations 2002 (SI 2002/2034). The effect of these Regulations is, amongst other things, to prevent less favourable treatment of fixed-term employees by comparison with permanent employees and to convert fixed-term contracts into permanent contracts in the case of employees continuously employed for four years or more: see regs 3 and 8.

Frustration

8.8 Frustration occurs when circumstances beyond the control of either party to a contract make it incapable of being performed in the form which was undertaken by the contracting parties. In that case, the contract will terminate automatically and the frustrating event will not be treated as a dismissal either for the purposes of any dismissal claim, whether at common law or under the statute. In *Davis Contractors*

Ltd v Fareham District Council (1950) (at pp 728–729), Lord Radcliffe set out the basic principle of frustration as follows:

> [F]rustration occurs whenever the law recognises that without default of either party a contractual obligation has become incapable of being performed because the circumstances in which performance is called for would render it a thing radically different from that which was undertaken by the contract…[I]t is not hardship or inconvenience or material loss itself which calls the principle of frustration into play. There must be as well such a change in the significance of the obligation that the thing undertaken would, if performed, be a different thing from that contracted for.

8.9 The doctrine of frustration applies to a contract of employment, the most common examples being illness and imprisonment. The death of either party is also best treated as a frustrating event. The effect of frustration is to terminate the contract automatically without either party having to take steps to bring it to an end. Since the employee will not be treated as having been dismissed, a complaint of unfair dismissal or a claim for a redundancy payment will fail: see *Marshall v Harland & Wolff Ltd* (1972). It should be noted that ERA 1996, s 136(5) only protects an employee's right to a redundancy payment where the frustrating event relates to the employer, not the employee, though if the event affects both, it will be enough that some of the effect is upon the employer: see *Fenerty v British Airports Authority* (1976).

8.10 A permanent illness will probably frustrate the contract, as will one which is so prolonged as to prevent the employer from obtaining substantially what was bargained for. Theatrical and similar cases present peculiar problems. Cases to consider are: *Poussard v Spiers and Pond* (1876), *Bettini v Gye* (1876), *Storey v Fulham Steel Works Co* (1907), and *Condor v Barron Knights* (1966). Frustration through illness has come to be reconsidered in the past few years because of its operation in the context of the statutory rights. In *Marshall v Harland & Wolff Ltd* (1972) (at p 106), Sir John Donaldson set out the test as follows:

> Was the employee's incapacity, looked at before the purported dismissal, of such a nature, or did it appear likely to continue for such a period that further performance of his obligations in the future would either be impossible or would be a thing radically different from that undertaken by him and accepted by the employer under the agreed terms of his employment?

8.11 He outlined five factors to be taken into account in answering this question: the terms of the contract, including any provisions as to sick pay; how long the employment was likely to last in the absence of sickness; the nature of the employment; the nature of the illness or injury, how long it has already continued, and the prospects of recovery; and the period of past employment. In relation to short-term periodic contracts, the EAT has suggested four further factors to be taken into account: the risk to the employer of incurring obligations in respect of redundancy payments or compensation for unfair dismissal to a replacement employee; whether wages have continued to be paid; the acts and statements of the employer in relation to the employment, in particular the dismissal of, or failure to dismiss, the employee; and whether in all the circumstances a reasonable employer could be expected to wait longer. See *Egg Stores (Stamford Hill) Ltd v Leibovici* (1977); see also *Hart v AR Marshall & Sons (Bulwell) Ltd* (1977).

8.12 The EAT has returned more recently to the question of frustration of the employment contract by illness. In *Williams v Watsons Luxury Coaches Ltd* (1990) the EAT reviewed the case law and said that, in addition, two further factors should be added: the terms of the contract governing the provisions for sick pay and a consideration of the prospects for the employee's recovery. They made it clear that tribunals should be reluctant to decide that a contract of employment has been frustrated by an employee's illness and that the party alleging frustration should not be allowed to rely upon the frustrating event if that event was caused by the fault of that party. See also *Gryf-Lowczowski v Hinchinbrooke Healthcare NHS Trust* (2005). In *Collins v Secretary of State for Trade and Industry* (EAT/1460/99) the EAT held that a contract was frustrated as a result of long-term illness, even though both parties regarded the contract as continuing throughout the illness. When the employer subsequently became insolvent, the Secretary of State rejected his claim for a payment from the National Insurance Fund. The EAT upheld the tribunal's decision that, because of the frustration of his contract, he was not entitled to a payment.

8.13 It is clear the doctrine of frustration can in appropriate circumstances be applied to a periodic contract terminable by the employer by short notice: see *Notcutt v Universal Equipment Co (London) Ltd* (1986). The facts of that case were that the employee, a skilled workman, started working for the employers in 1957 under a contract which was terminable by one week's notice and which provided that no remuneration would be paid to him when he was absent from work because of sickness. In 1983 he suffered a coronary infarct and was absent from work from then on. By July 1984, when the employers were required to give him 12 weeks' notice under what is now ERA 1996, s 86, it had become apparent that he would never be able to work again. So the employers gave him the requisite 12 weeks' notice. The employee claimed sick pay during the period of his notice, but the county court judge dismissed his claim on the grounds that his contract had been frustrated by illness before the notice was given. The Court of Appeal upheld the decision. It is not clear, however, when the court regarded the contract as having ended. Dillon LJ seems to suggest that it was when the employee had the coronary; Sheldon J said that the latest moment when the frustration could have occurred was when the medical report was presented.

8.14 It seems to be settled law now that the imposition of a custodial sentence upon an employee frustrates the contract by making it impossible for the employee to perform his or her part of the contract. In *FC Shepherd & Co Ltd v Jerrom* (1986), the Court of Appeal decided that a sentence of borstal training was an event which was not foreseen or provided for by the parties at the time of contracting and that it rendered the performance of the contract radically different from that which the parties had contemplated when they entered into it. There had been no fault or default on the part of the employers and the employee was not entitled to rely on his own default. His criminal conduct, although deliberate, had no effect on the performance of the contract: the imposition of the custodial sentence was the act of the judge. The custodial sentence did frustrate the contract of apprenticeship in this case, since the imposition of the sentence meant that there would be a break in the period of training and at the end of the period of the agreement the employee would not be so well trained as the parties had contemplated he would be. Mustill LJ expressly dealt with the question of self-induced frustration and said that, by asserting that the frustration was self-induced, the employee 'asserts that he himself had repudiated the contract: and this is something which, in my judgement, he should not be allowed to do'. The Court of Appeal in *Shepherd v Jerrom* expressed the view that the previous decision of the Court of Appeal in *Hare v Murphy Brothers Ltd* (1984) was unsatisfactory.

Termination by mutual consent

8.15 At common law, the parties are free to enter into an agreement that the contract should terminate. They may also put a clause in the contract by which the employee agrees to accept a stipulated amount in satisfaction of any claims he or she may have in the event of specified events occurring, for example the premature termination of the contract. It is also open to them to agree in advance that, if certain events occur (eg a fixed-term contract being brought to a premature end by the employer), the employer will pay to the employee an agreed sum in satisfaction of any claims that he or she may have. Such clauses are called 'liquidated damages clauses' or 'PILON' (pay in lieu of notice) clauses. It should be noted that it is unlikely that a court or tribunal will find that there is a genuine bilateral agreement terminating the contract in cases where an employee's *statutory* rights are involved.

8.16 If the courts regard the clause as a liquidated damages clause, the amount recoverable will be as stipulated in the clause without the employee having the necessity of proving the actual loss suffered. If, however, the stipulated sum is not a genuine pre-estimate of the loss but is in the nature of a penalty intended to secure performance of the contract, then it is not recoverable and the claimant must prove what damages he or she can. The essential question for the court to decide is whether the stipulated sum is a genuine pre-estimate of the loss which is likely to flow from the breach. The principles to be used in dealing with this question are set out in the speech of Lord Dunedin in the leading case of *Dunlop Pneumatic Tyre Co Ltd v New Garage and Motor Co Ltd* (1915) (at pp 86–88: see para 4.109 above). See also the remarks of Lopes LJ in *Law v Local Board of Redditch* (1892) (at p 132), and *Neil v Strathclyde Regional Council* (1984), set out in para 4.110. For two very recent cases on this topic, see *Giraud Ltd v Smith* (2000) and *Murray v Leisureplay Ltd* (2005), which may usefully be contrasted with each other.

8.17 If the clause is treated as a liquidated damages clause, the sum stipulated will be recoverable. The employee may not disregard the sum and prove that he or she has suffered greater damages, nor may the employer prove that the employee has suffered less: see *Diestal v Stevenson* (1906) and *Cellulose Acetate Silk Co Ltd v Widnes Foundry Ltd* (1933). The employee may be able to recover additional damages in respect of a default which it was not within the parties' contemplation that the agreed damages should cover. If a dispute arises between the parties, it will fall to be dealt with by the County Court or the High Court: see, for example, *Gothard v Mirror Group Newspapers Ltd* (1988), in which the issue was whether the payment in lieu of notice which was agreed between the parties should be calculated on the basis of gross pay or net pay.

8.18 A further point to note is that a termination of employment which is within the scope of an agreed damages clause will not be a wrongful dismissal. In *Rex Stewart Jeffries Parker Ginsberg Ltd v Parker* (1988), for example, the employee's contract contained a provision that the employment could be 'determined by the giving in writing of six calendar months' notice on either side or the payment of six months' salary in lieu thereof'. He was informed that he was to be made redundant in a week's time and that he would be paid six months' salary in lieu of notice in accordance with the agreement. When he set up in competition to his former employers, they sought to enforce a non-solicitation clause against him. He argued that his dismissal was in breach of contract and that the clause was unenforceable. The Court of Appeal held that his contract entitled him to be dismissed with six months' notice or six months' salary in lieu of notice and, therefore, that his dismissal was not in breach of contract. A similar conclusion was reached by the Court of Appeal in *Abrahams v Performing Right Society Ltd* (1995). The employee was employed under a contract entitling him to two years' notice of termination, or salary in lieu of notice. The employers summarily terminated his employment. The Court of Appeal held that in doing so they were acting lawfully and were effectively electing to pay money in lieu of notice under the contract.

8.19 PILON clauses pose considerable problems and have led to a number of cases, which usually involve careful construction of the relevant clause. See, for example, *Skilton v T&K Home Improvements Ltd* (2000), in which the Court of Appeal said that a clause which said that the employee 'may be dismissed' with immediate effect for failing to meet sales targets did not terminate or exclude the employee's right under another clause in the contract to three months' notice or payment of salary in lieu of three month's notice. Similarly, the differences between the approach of the High Court and the Court of Appeal in *Gregory v Wallace* (1998) show how difficult this can sometimes be. It is not appropriate to examine these problems in detail but reference should be made to Upex, *The Law of Termination of Employment* (7th ed, 2006), paras 9.49–9.51.

8.20 The significance of the above discussion relates to the enforceability of restrictive covenants. As was noted in Chapter 4 (see para 4.105) an employer who breaks the contract by wrongfully dismissing an employee cannot enforce a restrictive covenant. If, however, a liquidated damages clause or PILON clause is upheld, that will mean that the employee's dismissal will not be wrongful and thus any restrictive covenant will be enforceable.

Dismissal with notice

8.21 Termination occurs when either party informs the other clearly and unequivocally that the contract is to end, or the circumstances are such that it is clear that termination was intended or that it can be inferred that termination was intended. The words used to terminate the contract must be capable of being construed as words of termination. The principles are the same whether the termination consists of a dismissal by the employer or a resignation by the employee.

8.22 A notice of dismissal by the employer must be definite and explicit and must state the date of termination (or enable it to be inferred); a mere warning of impending dismissal will not be enough. Once a notice of dismissal has been given, it cannot be withdrawn by the employer without the agreement of the employee; see *Morton Sundour Fabrics Ltd v Shaw* (1967), *Riordan v War Office* (1961), and *Harris and Russell Ltd v Slingsby* (1973). In the case of a dismissal by the employer, phrases such as 'I hereby give you notice of dismissal' are clear. Problems arise, however, where there is a row between the employer and the employee and words are used in the heat of the moment. If the words used by the employer are not ambiguous or could only be interpreted as amounting to words of dismissal, then the conclusion is clear. If, on the other hand, the words used are ambiguous and it is not clear whether they do amount to words of dismissal (eg 'You're finished with me'), it is necessary to look at all the circumstances of the case, particularly the intention with which the words were spoken, and consider how a reasonable employee would, in all the circumstances have understood them; see *BG Gale Ltd v Gilbert* (1978), *Tanner v DT Kean Ltd* (1978), *Sothern v Franks Charlesley & Co* (1981), and *J & J Stern v Simpson* (1983).

8.23 An example of the kind of problem which can occur is *Martin v Yeoman Aggregates Ltd* (1983). The employee obtained the wrong spare part for a broken-down car. There was an angry exchange between a director and the employee. He refused to collect the correct part and was dismissed by the director. A few minutes later the director realised that he had acted in anger and that he was in breach of the correct disciplinary procedure. So he told the employee he was suspended without pay for two days. The employee treated what had happened as instant dismissal. The EAT applied the test set out in *Tanner v DT Kean Ltd* (above) and held that there had been no dismissal, saying that it was a matter of common sense, vital to industrial relations, that either an employer or an employee should be given an opportunity of recanting from words spoken in the heat of the moment.

8.24 An employee may be treated as dismissed where the employer unilaterally imposes radically different terms of employment so that, on an objective construction of the employer's conduct, there is a removal or withdrawal of the old contract. This is what happened in *Alcan Extrusions v Yates* (1996), which involved the unilateral imposition of a new shift system on a group of employees. See, to similar effect, *Hogg v Dover College* (1990). The two cases are considered more fully at para 8.59 below.

8.25 A further requirement in the case of dismissals with notice is that, to be valid, the notice must specify the date of termination or contain material from which the date is ascertainable. If the employer utters a warning that the employee will be made redundant at some unspecified date in the future or that, if the employee does not resign, he or she will have to be dismissed at some future date, and the employee acts on that warning, finds another job and resigns, that action will be treated as a resignation only; he or she will not be treated as having been dismissed. In *Morton Sundour Fabrics Ltd v Shaw* (1967), for example, the employers told the employee that his employment would cease when the department in which he worked was closed down, but they did not specify when that would occur. The employee made arrangements to find another job, and duly gave notice. He later applied for a redundancy payment, but his claim was rejected. Widgery J said:

> As a matter of law an employer cannot dismiss his employee by saying 'I intend to dispense with your services at some time in the coming months.' In order to terminate the contract of employment the notice must either specify the date or contain material from which that date is positively ascertainable.

8.26 In *Rai v Somerfield Stores Ltd* (2004), the EAT said that a notice which enables an employer to terminate an employee's contract of employment only if the employee does or does not perform a particular act specified in the notice which only the employee can choose whether or not to perform is not an unequivocal notice to terminate the employment. In the case in question the employee was told that if he did not return to work by a specified date his contract would be regarded as terminated. The EAT said that this did not amount to a dismissal with notice.

8.27 A final point to be noted here is that a dismissal with notice may be converted into a summary dismissal if the employer dismisses the employee on the spot during his or her notice period. Such an action would amount to a wrongful dismissal. Reference should be made to paras 4.183–4.187, where notice provisions and the statutory provisions relating to notice are dealt with.

Dismissal without notice

8.28 A dismissal without notice – usually called 'summary dismissal' – is on the face of it a breach of contract, since the employee has been denied his or her contractual entitlement to termination of the contract by notice or to the unexpired part of a fixed-term contract. The employer's defence in such a case is that the employee had committed a repudiation of the contract sufficiently serious to justify dismissal without notice. In effect, therefore, the issue in a summary dismissal case is not whether the employee was dismissed but whether the dismissal was in breach of contract and thus 'wrongful'. This matter is considered more fully below: see para 8.48.

Resignation

8.29 The requirements in the case of a resignation by an employee are very similar to those for a dismissal. It is important for employers to know whether an employee has resigned, since if they treat the employee as having resigned when that is not in fact the case, they may be held to have dismissed the employee. If the employee's resignation is prompted by a repudiatory act or breach of contract by the employer, that may be treated as a constructive dismissal by the employer: see below, para 8.37. A resignation does not require acceptance by the employer and, if the employee wishes to change his or her mind and withdraw the resignation, the withdrawal requires the employer's agreement. Failure to give it does not amount to a constructive dismissal: see *Denham v United Glass Ltd* (EAT/581/98).

8.30 As in the case of dismissal, similar questions have arisen as to what amounts to a resignation, particularly where there has been a row between the employer and the employee and it is not clear from the language used whether the employee was in fact intending to resign. If the employee's words are not ambiguous (eg 'I am resigning') or, when construed, have a clear meaning, he or she will be treated as having resigned, irrespective of whether they were intended to bear that meaning, unless the words of resignation were uttered in the heat of the moment or as a result of pressure exerted by the employer; see *Sovereign House Security Services Ltd v Savage* (1989) (at p 116). In *Kwik-Fit (GB) Ltd v Lineham* (1992) the EAT said that there may be 'special circumstances' which may make it unreasonable for an employer to assume a resignation. The EAT said (at pp 191–192):

> Words may be spoken or actions expressed in temper or in the heat of the moment or under extreme pressure...and indeed the intellectual make-up of an employee may be relevant...These we refer to as 'special circumstances'. Where 'special circumstances' arise it may be unreasonable for an employer to assume a resignation and to accept it forthwith. A reasonable period of time should be allowed to lapse and if circumstances arise during that period which put the employer on notice that further inquiry is desirable to see whether that resignation was really intended and can properly be assumed, then such inquiry is ignored at the employer's risk...Thus where words or actions are unambiguous an employer is entitled to accept the repudiation at its face value at once, unless these special circumstances exist, in which case he should allow a reasonable time to elapse during which facts may arise which cast doubt upon that prima facie interpretation of the unambiguous words or action. If he does not investigate these facts, a tribunal may hold him disentitled to assume that the words or action did amount to a resignation...

8.31 On the other hand, if the words used are ambiguous, it becomes necessary to look at all the circumstances of the case, and, in particular, the intention with which the words were spoken, and to consider how a reasonable employer would, in all the circumstances, have understood the employee's words: see *Sothern v Franks Charlesly & Co* (1981) and *J & J Stern v Simpson* (1983); see also *Tanner v DT Kean* (1978) (in which the EAT suggested an approach to these kinds of cases), *Barclay v City of Glasgow District Council* (1983), and *Sovereign House Security Services Ltd v Savage* (1989).

8.32 A resignation will be treated as a dismissal if the employee is invited to resign and it is made clear that, unless he or she does so, he or she will be dismissed: see *East Sussex County Council v Walker* (1972) and *Jones v Mid Glamorgan County Council* (1997). In *Martin v Glynwed Distribution Ltd* (1983) (at p 519) Sir John Donaldson MR said of these kinds of cases:

> Whatever the respective actions of the employer and the employee at the time when the contract of employment is terminated, at the end of the day the question always remains the same, 'Who really terminated the contract of employment?' If the answer is the

employer, there was a dismissal within [section 95(2)(a)]...If the answer is the employee, a further question may then arise, namely, 'Did he do so in circumstances such that he was entitled to do so without notice by reason of the employer's conduct?'...

8.33 See also *Caledonian Mining Co Ltd v Bassett* (1987), in which the EAT held that the employers had dismissed employees whom they had inveigled into resigning with the intention of depriving them of their statutory rights. The EAT held that the employees had been dismissed within what is now ERA 1996, s 136(1)(a), applying Sir John Donaldson's dictum, above. There will be no dismissal, however, where the employee resigns and the employer invokes a contractual provision entitling him or her to terminate the contract early by making a payment in lieu of notice and, by doing so, brings the contract to an end before the expiry of the employee's notice: see *Marshall (Cambridge) Ltd v Hamblin* (1994).

Resignation in breach of contract

8.34 There are many cases where an employee resigns in breach of contract but it is not worth the employer's while to sue for the breach. There are also cases, however, where the employee is skilled and has been privy to confidential information. Here the failure to give the proper notice required by the contract may be significant. Employees of this type may often be subject to long notice periods of a year or more and may also have what are called 'garden leave' clauses in their contracts; such clauses are considered at paras 4.103 above and 8.35, below. If such an employee leaves without giving correct notice, the employer may wish to enforce the contractual notice period so as to prevent him or her utilising skills or confidential information whilst they are still fresh. The question whether it is possible to do so then becomes of acute importance, since an employer is likely to have more extensive powers of restraint against someone who is still an employee than against an ex-employee: see the discussion of *Thomas Marshall (Exports) Ltd v Guinle* (1978), at para 4.152 and para 8.61 below.

8.35 An example of this situation is the case of *Evening Standard Co Ltd v Henderson* (1987). The employee was employed as the production manager of the Evening Standard. His contract required one year's notice of termination and provided that, while it lasted, he was not to engage in work outside the company without special permission. He was offered a similar position with a competitor newspaper and gave his employers two months' notice of termination. The employers sought an injunction to restrain him from undertaking employment with or providing assistance to any competitor of theirs in breach of his contract of employment. The Court of Appeal said that there was no serious issue as to liability, since the employee's contract would continue until the expiration of the one-year notice period, unless his employers accepted his repudiation. If, during that time, he were to work for the competitor, he would be in breach of contract. The Court went on to hold that the balance of convenience favoured the granting of an injunction.

8.36 In *GFI Group Inc v Eaglestone* (1994), on the other hand, Holland J refused to hold an employee to his 20-week notice period, when he joined a competitor during the notice period. Instead, the judge granted an injunction to restrain him from joining the competitor for 13 out of the 20 weeks. The rationale for the decision was that two of the employee's colleagues, who were only on four weeks' notice, had already joined the competitor after the expiry of their notice.

Constructive dismissal

8.37 Different considerations arise where the employee's resignation is prompted by a breach of contract or repudiatory act committed by the employer. In that case, the resignation will be called a 'constructive dismissal'. It should be noted that this term has no statutory authority and is merely a convenient shorthand expression for a resignation on the part of the employee prompted by an action on the part of the employer which may be categorised as a repudiatory act or a breach of contract. In *Western Excavating (ECC) Ltd v Sharp* (1978) (at p 226), Lord Denning MR said:

> If the employer is guilty of conduct which is a significant breach going to the root of the contract of employment, or which shows that the employer no longer intends to be bound by one or more of the essential terms of contract, then the employee is entitled to treat himself as discharged from any further performance...[T]he conduct must...be sufficiently serious to entitle him to leave at once...

8.38 In cases of constructive dismissal, the first question to ask is whether the employer's action is in breach of its contractual obligations or is a repudiation of them. That will involve ascertaining the express terms of the contract and considering whether any terms should be implied. Once the breach or repudiation has been established, it must be serious enough to entitle the employee to leave without notice. Further, the employee's resignation must have been caused by the breach. Finally, there will be no constructive dismissal if the employee waived the right to terminate the contract, for example by affirming the contract. So far as the first issue is concerned, reference should be made to paras 4.67 and 4.118, where express and implied terms are considered. See also the decisions of the Court of Appeal in *Meikle v Nottinghamshire CC* (2004) and of the EAT in *Greenhof v Barnsley Metropolitan Borough Council* (2006). In both cases an employer's failure to make reasonable adjustments in the case of a disabled employee was treated as a breach of the implied duty of mutual trust and confidence. In *Horkaluk v Cantor Fitzgerald International*

(2004) the High Court held that an employee who was subjected to a campaign of bullying and intimidation, accompanied by foul and abusive language, had been constructively dismissed. For a more detailed consideration of these issues, reference should be made to Upex, *The Law of Termination of Employment* (7th ed, 2006), paras 3.49–3.81.

8.39   The court or tribunal must be satisfied also that he or she has not waived the right to terminate by staying on too long after the conduct in question. Otherwise he or she may be taken to have elected to affirm the contract. See paras 4.212–4.216, where this matter is considered in the context of variations of contract. In the event of a subsequent resignation, it will not be possible to claim constructive dismissal. In *WE Cox Toner (International) Ltd v Crook* (1981) (at pp 828–829), Browne-Wilkinson J said:

> Mere delay by itself (unaccompanied by any express or implied affirmation of the contract) does not constitute affirmation of the contract; but if it is prolonged it may be evidence of an implied affirmation . . . Affirmation of the contract can be implied. Thus, if the innocent party calls on the guilty party for further performance of the contract, he will normally be taken to have affirmed the contract since his conduct is only consistent with the continued existence of contractual obligation . . . However, if the innocent party further performs the contract to a limited extent but at the same time makes it clear that he is reserving his right to accept the repudiation . . . such further performance does not prejudice his rights subsequently to accept the repudiation.

8.40   The employee must also accept a repudiation unequivocally. An example of a failure to do so is *Harrison v Norwest Holst Group Administration Ltd* (1985). The employers wrote to the employee stating that he would lose his directorship in two weeks' time. The employee responded with a letter headed 'Without Prejudice'. The employers later withdrew their threat to deprive him of his directorship, but the employee left anyway. The Court of Appeal treated the original threat as an anticipatory breach but said that the employee's letter was not sufficiently unequivocal to amount to an acceptance of the repudiation. Because the repudiation had not been accepted, the contract continued to run and, during the continued currency of the contract, it was open to the employers to withdraw their threat of breach.

Wrongful dismissal

8.41   At common law, summary termination of the contract of employment by either party gives the innocent party the right to sue for breach of contract. The defendant may have a defence if the court is satisfied that the plaintiff was guilty of conduct which amounted to a serious breach of contract or to a repudiation of the contract.

This principle is an extension of the general rule of contract, that if a party to a contract breaches an important term of the contract or evinces an intention no longer to be bound by one or more of its essential terms, the innocent party has a choice: he or she may either waive the breach or repudiation and choose to treat the contract as continuing or may accept the breach or repudiation and treat himself or herself as discharged from the performance of any further obligations under the contract, which is thus at an end. As a general rule, the breach or repudiation, whether by employer or employee, requires to be accepted by the other party before the contract comes to an end. This issue has been the subject of considerable discussion and debate, particularly in relation to the summary dismissal of an employee by an employer, and is considered more fully below: see para 8.52.

8.42   A contract of employment is terminable by notice, express or implied, unless the contract is for a fixed term or for the completion of a specific task or contains an exhaustive enumeration of the grounds upon which it may be terminated. If, therefore, either party terminates the contract summarily, ie without notice, the other party has the right at common law to sue for breach of contract. If the defendant's summary termination of the contract was a response to an action on the part of the claimant, a defence may be available. But he or she must be able to show that the claimant's behaviour amounted to a breach of a serious term of the contract or a repudiation of the contract which entitled him or her to terminate the contract summarily. The plaintiff's breach need not have been known at the time of the summary dismissal: see *Boston Deep Sea Fishing & Ice Co v Ansell* (1888) and *Cyril Leonard & Co v Simo Securities Trust Ltd* (1972).

8.43   If the summary dismissal by the employer is not justified, the employee will be treated as having been wrongfully dismissed; if the employer's conduct causes the employee to resign and that conduct is held to be repudiatory or in breach of contract, the employee's contract will be treated as having been breached. An action for wrongful dismissal or breach of contract is heard in the County Court or High Court; the employment tribunals also have jurisdiction in such cases where damages are claimed.

Breach by employer

8.44   A summary dismissal takes place where the employer fails to observe the provisions in the contract relating to notice or a fixed term of employment. This type of case effectively brings the employment to an end and in practical terms does not give the employee the opportunity of choosing whether to affirm the contract or accept the repudiation. In such a case, the employer may be able to justify the action on the grounds of the employee's breach: see below at para 8.48. Otherwise, the question is principally one of how much the employee should receive by way of damages, since the remedies of injunction and specific performance are unlikely to be available.

8.45 The employer may also commit a breach of an express or implied term. For a fuller discussion, see Chapter 4. In the case of an alleged breach of an implied term, the term and its breach must be established. It must then be established that the breach was sufficiently serious to be repudiatory. Finally, the employee must have accepted the repudiation. The case-law, much of which has been considered in Chapter 4, shows the problems that can arise. An example is *Bliss v South East Thames Regional Health Authority* (1987), where the employers acted in a way which the Court of Appeal held to be a repudiation of the employee's contract, by requiring him to submit to a medical examination and suspending him when he refused. They held that the employer was in breach of contract by requiring the employee, without reasonable cause, to submit to the medical examination and, when he refused, suspending him. That was a breach of the implied term that they would not without reasonable cause conduct themselves in a manner likely to damage or destroy the relationship of trust and confidence between employer and employee. The breach was so serious as to go to the root of the contract and to entitle the employee to treat the contract as at an end. Further, the breach was a continuing breach until the employers lifted the suspension. After the employers withdrew the requirement and lifted the suspension, they offered to give him time to make up his mind about his future intentions and to pay him while he did so. They then tried to argue that his acceptance of his salary affirmed the contract so as to preclude him from accepting their repudiation, as he purported to do. The Court of Appeal held that he had not affirmed the contract by his conduct in accepting the salary payments and he was entitled to accept the repudiation. The Court took the view that the cardinal factor was that the employer was prepared to give the employee time to make up his mind and to pay while he was doing so.

8.46 The employee must accept the employer's breach or repudiation unequivocally. A failure to do so may lead to the consequence that the employer withdraws the repudiation before it has been unequivocally accepted. If the employee then purports to accept the repudiation after it has been withdrawn and resigns, he or she will not succeed in an action for breach of contract. An example of this is *Harrison v Norwest Holst Group Administration Ltd* (1985), considered at para 8.40 above. See also *Lewis v Motorworld Garages Ltd* (1986) and *Shook v London Borough of Ealing* (1986).

8.47 A problem associated with the foregoing discussion is the extent to which the employer may change the employee's job duties without committing a breach of contract. This matter has been discussed in Chapter 4. See, for example, *Cresswell v Board of Inland Revenue* (1984), which concerned the introduction of computerisation of the PAYE system within the Inland Revenue. The judge upheld this as a permissible change, despite the fact that considerable changes in the employees' jobs were entailed. In *Royle v Trafford Borough Council* (1984), on the other hand, an employee who continued to teach a class of pupils but refused to take extra pupils because of industrial action, was held to have had his breach of contract affirmed by his employers, who did not suspend or dismiss him. But, because of his imperfect performance of his contract, the judge held that there was no reason why he should receive his full salary. The Court was entitled to make a reduction from his salary representing the notional value of the services he did not render.

Breach by employee

8.48 A dismissal will be wrongful, if the employer dismisses the employee without giving him or her the notice he or she is entitled to, or, in the case of a fixed-term contract with no notice provision, allowing him or her to see out the fixed term. In this kind of case, the employer's defence will rest upon breaches of contract alleged to have been committed by the employee. There must be a breach by the employee of the express or implied terms of the contract, and the breach must amount to a repudiation or be sufficiently fundamental: see, for example, *Laws v London Chronicle (Indicator Newspapers) Ltd* (1959) (at p 700, Lord Evershed MR), considered at para 4.143, above. In this context, however, the remarks of Edmund-Davies LJ in *Wilson v Racher* (1974) (at p 430), should be noted:

> Reported decisions provide useful, but only general guides, each case turning upon its own facts...[A] contract of service imposes upon the parties a duty of mutual respect.

8.49 This means that opposite conclusions may be reached on similar facts, as in *Pepper v Webb* (1969) and *Wilson v Racher* (1974) and that, whilst in one context one single, relatively minor, breach may be sufficient to justify summary dismissal, the same will not be true of other, different contexts: see, for example, *Sinclair v Neighbour* (1967). The most common instances of breaches of contract giving rise to summary dismissals are misconduct, disobedience to lawful orders, and negligence. For cases involving misconduct or alleged misconduct, see *Clouston & Co Ltd v Corry* (1906), *Sinclair v Neighbour* (1967), and *Wilson v Racher* (1974). In *Laughton and Hawley v Bapp Industrial Supplies Ltd* (1986), the EAT held that an employee's expressed intention of setting up in competition with the employer was not in itself a breach of the implied duty of loyalty to the employer and did not amount to misconduct. For cases involving disobedience to lawful orders, see *Laws v London Chronicle (Indicator Newspapers) Ltd* (1959) and *Pepper v Webb* (1969); for cases involving negligence, see *Baster v London & County Printing Works* (1899), *Power v British India Steam Navigation Co Ltd* (1930), and *Jupiter General Insurance Co Ltd v Shroff* (1937). Most of the cases mentioned here have already been considered in detail in Chapter 4, to which reference should be made.

8.50 Although every case turns upon its own facts, a single act is less likely to justify summary dismissal than a series of actions; the quality of the breach is what counts, not the consequences flowing from it. The more serious the breach the more likely it is that it will be held to justify summary dismissal. The case law in this area was summarised by Lord Jauncey of Tullichettle (Special Commissioner) in *Neary v Dean of Westminster* (1999) in the following terms:

> [C]onduct amounting to gross misconduct justifying dismissal must so undermine the trust and confidence which is inherent in the particular contract of employment that the master should no longer be required to retain the servant in his employment.

In the later case of *Briscoe v Lubrizol Ltd* (2002) the Court of Appeal adopted this statement as the test to apply in cases of this kind. It is interesting to note, however, that the decision was a majority decision. Ward LJ, with whom Bodey J agreed, held that the employee had been guilty of repudiatory conduct in failing, without explanation or excuse, to attend a meeting with his employers to discuss his position and in subsequently failing to reply to his employers' requests to contact them. Potter LJ, on the other hand, said that these failures could not be regarded as gross misconduct and did not demonstrate an intention to repudiate the contract. The differences in the Court of Appeal in this case show how difficult it can be to decide whether a particular cause of conduct amounts to gross misconduct or is repudiatory. See also *Dietman v London Borough of Brent* (1988), which raised issues of construction of the employee's contract of employment and, in particular, whether she was guilty of gross misconduct, defined in the contract as 'misconduct of such a nature that the authority is justified in no longer tolerating the continued presence at the place of work of the employee who commits an offence of gross misconduct'.

8.51 At common law the employer is not obliged to give a reason for the dismissal, provided that grounds for dismissal exist: see *Ridgeway v Hungerford Market Co* (1835). It will be a complete defence in an action for wrongful dismissal if the employer can establish that, unknown to him or her at the time of dismissal, the employee had committed breaches of contract which, had they been known, would have justified summary dismissal: see *Boston Deep Sea Fishing and Ice Co Ltd v Ansell* (1888), approved in *Cyril Leonard & Co Ltd v Simo Securities Trust Ltd* (1972). The most likely remedy in a wrongful dismissal action is damages; the measure of damages will be the loss suffered by the employee until such time as the contract could have been lawfully terminated. Prima facie, therefore, the measure of damages will be the loss of earnings and other contractual benefits during the notice period to which the employee was entitled or for the unexpired part of a fixed-term contract. Injunctions are rarely available, except for the purpose of enforcing restrictive covenants or 'garden leave' clauses.

Effect of breach or repudiation on the contract

8.52 The question of the effect of a breach or repudiation on the contract of employment has given rise to considerable discussion. It has not always been clear whether a distinction should be drawn between a summary dismissal or termination, on the one hand, and breach or repudiation, on the other. It is arguable that a distinction should be made between conduct which actually terminates the contract and therefore amounts to a wrongful dismissal and conduct which amounts to a failure to observe a basic term of the employment relationship (eg a reduction by the employer of the employee's wages). In the former case, the conduct arguably terminates the contract without more. This question was left open by the House of Lords in *Rigby v Ferodo Ltd* (1988), considered at paras 4.217 and 4.232. Lord Oliver of Aylmerton said that the question did not arise on the facts of the case. In the latter case, where there is a failure to observe a basic term, the question is whether the conduct in question automatically terminates the contract or whether it gives the innocent party the choice of affirming the contract or accepting the breach as a repudiation and treating the contract as at an end.

8.53 A repudiation, or repudiatory breach, generally requires acceptance by the innocent party before there is a termination, but it has been argued that contracts of employment are an exception. The argument is often put on the basis that a contract of employment cannot be ordered by the courts to be performed, by means of an order of specific performance. In *Decro-Wall International S.A. v Practitioners in Marketing Ltd* (1971) (at p 369), Salmon LJ said:

> I doubt whether a wrongful dismissal brings a contract of service to an end in law, although no doubt in practice it does. Under such a contract a servant has a right to remuneration...in return for services. If the master, in breach of contract, refuses to employ the servant,...the contract will not be specifically enforced...[T]he only result is that the servant, albeit he has been prevented from rendering services by the master's breach, cannot recover remuneration under the contract because he has not earned it...His only money claim is for damages for being wrongfully prevented from earning his remuneration.

8.54 In the later case of *Gunton v Richmond-upon-Thames London Borough Council* (1980) (at p 771), Buckley LJ developed this view of wrongful dismissal further. He said:

> [C]ases of wrongful dismissal in breach of a contract of personal service have certain special features. In the first place, as the term 'wrongful dismissal' implies, they always occur after the employment has begun and so involve an immediate breach by the master of

his obligation to continue to employ the servant. Secondly, a wrongful dismissal is almost invariably repudiatory in character...Thirdly, the servant cannot sue in debt under the contract for remuneration in respect of any period after the wrongful dismissal, because the right to receive remuneration and the obligation to render services are mutually interdependent. Fourthly, the servant must come under an immediate duty to mitigate his damages and so must almost invariably be bound to seek other employment in fulfilment of that obligation...It follows...that at least as soon as the servant finds, and enters into, other employment he must put it out of his power to perform any continuing obligations on his part to serve his original employer. At this stage, if not earlier, the servant must...be taken to have accepted his wrongful dismissal as a repudiatory breach leading to a determination of the contract of service.

8.55 In the same case, Brightman LJ said, at p 778:

It is clear beyond argument that a wrongfully dismissed employee cannot sue for his salary or wages as such, but only for damages. It is also...equally clear that such an employee cannot assert that he still retains his employment under the contract. If a servant is dismissed and excluded from his employment, it is absurd to suppose that he still occupies the status of a servant.

8.56 These principles were followed in the later case of *Marsh v National Autistic Society* (1993), in which the principal of a school established by the Society was dismissed in breach of contract by them. The employee argued that, in the absence of any notice terminating his employment in accordance with his contract, the dismissal amounted to a repudiatory breach of contract, which was only capable of bringing his contract to an end if he accepted it, which he did not, and that the contract therefore remained in force until he either accepted the repudiation or was given proper notice by the Society. He sought an interlocutory injunction to restrain the Society from dismissing him or purporting to dismiss him otherwise than in accordance with the provisions of his contract of employment and an order that he should continue to be paid his remuneration. Both were refused by the judge. Ferris J reviewed the authorities quoted above, and went on to say, at p 459:

[T]hey [ie the authorities] show...that where...a contract of employment has been wrongfully terminated by the employer the ordinary contractual principles relating to acceptance of repudiatory breach apply and to some extent at least the authorities show that the contract continues to subsist...The very same authorities show, however,...that, although it is the employer who in those circumstances is in breach of contract by having committed a repudiatory breach, the employee is not thereafter entitled to remuneration as a matter of debt.

8.57 In *Boyo v Lambeth London Borough Council* (1994), the Court of Appeal reviewed the authorities dealing with this issue, particularly *Gunton*'s case and *Sanders v*

Ernest A Neale Ltd (1974). They felt constrained to follow *Gunton*, but it is clear, particularly from the judgments of Ralph Gibson and Staughton LJJ, that the majority would have preferred to decide the case unconstrained by the decision in that case. Ralph Gibson LJ's view was that a wrongful dismissal requires a real acceptance by the employee and that the court should not easily infer acceptance, as suggested by Buckley LJ in *Gunton*: see at p 743. Staughton LJ's view was that a direct repudiation, whether by employer or employee, determines a contract of employment and that, in that respect, such contracts are in a class of their own: see at p 747. More recently, in *Cerberus Software Ltd v Rowley* (2001), Sedley LJ in his dissenting judgment supported the elective theory but his remarks were obiter. For the moment, therefore, the principle is that a wrongful dismissal requires acceptance by the employee, but that acceptance will be easily inferred. Clearly, however, this area is ripe for re-examination by the House of Lords.

8.58 The alternative type of case is that in which the employer does not dismiss the employee but engages in actions which seek to change 'the nature of the work required to be done or the times of employment', as Shaw LJ said in *Gunton*'s case, above, at p 459. An example of such a case is the House of Lords' decision in *Rigby v Ferodo Ltd*, at para 8.52 above. The dispute arose from the unilateral imposition by the employers of wage reductions. The employee continued to work at the reduced rate but instituted proceedings for damages to recover the difference between the wages to which he was entitled under his contract and the wages actually paid to him by his employers. It was agreed that the employers' action amounted to a fundamental and repudiatory breach. The first point dealt with by the House of Lords was the employers' argument that the breach constituted the giving of the necessary 12 weeks' notice required under the contract to terminate the employment. The House of Lords rejected this, on the footing that it was an impossible contention on the facts of the case, since the employers were concerned to keep their workforce and never purported to give such a notice. The main argument was that contracts of employment are an exception to the general rule that an unaccepted repudiation leaves the contractual obligations of the parties unaffected and that the wrongful repudiation of the fundamental obligations of either party not only brings to an end the relationship of employer and employee but also terminates the contract immediately without the necessity of any acceptance by the party not in default. It followed, therefore, according to this argument, that the unilateral reduction in the employee's wages amounted to a termination of the contract, and his sole remedy was damages limited to the shortfall from his original contractual wage over a 12-week period. Lord Oliver of Aylmerton, who gave the main speech in the House of Lords, rejected this argument and said that there was no reason why a contract of employment should be on any different footing from any other contract. He did appear, however, to make a distinction between a repudiatory breach and a wrongful dismissal. Although he was at pains to point out that the case was not one of wrongful dismissal and said that it would not be appropriate to decide that question, which, on the facts, did not arise, he did say this, at p 34:

> Whatever may be the position under a contract of service where the repudiation takes the form either of a walk-out by the employee or of a refusal by the employer any longer to regard the employee as his servant, I know of no principle of law that any breach which the innocent party is entitled to treat as repudiatory of the other party's obligations brings the contract to an end automatically.

8.59 The decisions of the EAT in *Hogg v Dover College* (1990) and *Alcan Extrusions v Yates* (1996) are difficult to reconcile with this statement, however. In the first case, the employee was demoted and paid a reduced salary. The EAT held that the effect of this action was to dismiss him, despite the fact that he continued to work for the employers. In the second case, the facts were that a group of employers unilaterally imposed a variation on the employees, in circumstances which amounted to a repudiation of the contract. The employees chose not to resign but to continue to work the new terms under protest; they also complained of unfair dismissal. The EAT upheld the tribunal's decision that there had been a dismissal, taking the view that, where an employer unilaterally imposes radically different terms of employment, there is a dismissal if, on an objective construction of the relevant letters on the part of the employer, there is a withdrawal or removal of the old contract.

8.60 If these decisions are correct, then an employee affected by a unilateral variation could stay on and continue to work for the employer under protest but could also complain of unfair dismissal or, if appropriate, claim a redundancy payment. From a contractual point of view, however, they seem to fly in the face of Lord Oliver's statement above in suggesting that, where the employer commits a repudiatory act such that it can be said that there is a removal or withdrawal of the old contract, that contract ends automatically. If Lord Oliver's statement of the law is accepted as correct, it is possible to say that an employee who is a victim of a repudiatory act is effectively confined to a claim for damages (if the repudiation takes the form of a wrongful dismissal) or unpaid, or under-paid, wages (if the repudiation takes the form of a unilateral reduction in wages, as in *Rigby v Ferodo Ltd*). In other cases, such as a unilateral change in non-financial terms of the employee's contract, the choice is between waiving the breach and thus affirming the contract, or accepting the repudiation and resigning. In all these cases, it is highly unlikely that the court will grant injunctive relief.

8.61 On the other hand, if the act of termination or repudiatory act is the *employee's*, there are circumstances in which, despite the impossibility of forcing the employee to work in accordance with the contract, nevertheless the court is prepared to treat the contract as subsisting for the purposes of restraining him or her from committing breaches of the contract. The breaches in question are often breaches of a clause in the contract governing competition or the use of confidential information and the like. In *Thomas Marshall (Exports) Ltd v Guinle* (1978), for example, the employee purported to resign when his fixed-term contract still had four years to run. The contract had clauses in it dealing with competition and the use of confidential information. Megarry V-C held that the employee's wrongful termination of the contract required acceptance by the employer and did not automatically terminate it. He accepted that the court was powerless to compel the employee to continue to work in accordance with his contract, but said that his repudiation did not release him from his obligations. These were more extensive than they would have been had the repudiation been treated as effective to terminate the contract and had the employee been in the position of an ex-employee. The injunctions sought against the employee in this case were to restrain solicitation of the employer's customers and to restrain the disclosure or use of confidential information.

8.62 This may be contrasted with the later case of *Evening Standard Co Ltd v Henderson* (1987), which was considered at para 8.35 above. The employee was obliged to give one year's notice of termination, but purported to give two months' notice. There was a clause in his contract to the effect that, during its duration, he was not to engage in work outside the company without special permission. His purpose in giving shorter notice than he was obliged to was to enable him to accept a position on a rival newspaper which would be in competition with his employer's newspaper. In this case, the injunctions sought were to restrain him from undertaking or continuing employment with any competitor of the employers and from disclosing confidential information relating to them for the duration of the contractual notice period. The employers gave an undertaking to the trial judge to continue to pay the employee's salary until his contract lawfully expired but without requiring him to continue working for them, although in fact they were also willing to allow him to continue working for them. In those circumstances, the Court of Appeal granted the injunctions sought, on the footing that the employee would not be forced to work for the employers or be reduced to a condition of starvation or idleness.

8.63 Although there are perceptible differences between the two cases, the important point about both, at least for present purposes, is that the courts have held that there are circumstances in which, and purposes for which, an employer may be allowed to refuse to accept a repudiation. In the *Evening Standard* case, however, Lawton LJ stressed that the hearing of an interlocutory appeal is not the time to examine these issues in depth.

FURTHER READING

Deakin, S, & Morris, G, *Labour Law* (4th ed, 2005) Hart (chapters 4 & 5).

Smith, I, & Thomas, G, *Smith & Wood's Employment Law* (9th ed, 2007) Oxford University Press (chapter 8).

Upex, R, *The Law on Termination of Employment* (7th ed, 2006) Jordans.

ARTICLE

Brodie, D, (1998) 'Beyond Exchange: The New Contract of Employment', *Industrial Law Journal*, Vol 27, No 2, pp 79–102.

SELF-TEST QUESTIONS

1 Arnold, Bruce, and Clive work for Kings Ltd, which is in financial difficulties.

   A cheque for £1,000 has been fraudulently cashed by an employee of the company, and Mr P, the managing director, believes the employee to have been Arnold. When confronted by Mr P, Arnold denies the offence, but Mr P is convinced that only Arnold would have been in a position to do such a thing and dismisses him without consulting the other directors. Bruce, who is a senior foreman and has worked for the company's headquarters where he has always worked, is told that he will be moved to a small factory some 10 miles distant. When Bruce refuses to move, he too is dismissed. Clive is told that in order to effect economies, the company will not be giving him his annual pay rise to which he is contractually entitled. Clive remonstrates and two days later hands in his notice.

   Advise Arnold, Bruce, and Clive.

2 'The right to wrongful dismissal is no longer relevant in the twenty-first century.' Discuss.

3 Assess the impact of the term relating to mutual trust and confidence (see Chapter 4) on the termination of employment, with particular reference to remedies.

4 Colin alleges that he is being harassed at work by his line manger, Marlene. He has reported this to Marlene's manager, Bob. Bob has ignored Colin's grievance. Colin has complained to the managing Director, Linda, who has told Colin to 'grow up'. Marlene continues to harass Colin.

   Advise Colin.

9

Unfair dismissal

SUMMARY

One of the rights which arise when an employee is dismissed is the statutory right not to be unfairly dismissed. This chapter considers that right. The key points are that:

- the general rules of unfair dismissal apply to employees who have been continuously employed for one year; and

- certain types of dismissal have special rules and usually do not have a requirement of a minimum period of employment.

Overall, this statutory right provides a floor of protection for employees, but is it adequate?

9.1 Until the introduction of the right not to be unfairly dismissed in 1972, employees enjoyed limited statutory protection. Indeed, until the Contracts of Employment Act 1963 (now transformed into Part I of the Employment Rights Act 1996), employees had no statutory rights at all. The Redundancy Payments Act 1965 was the first attempt to provide a floor of rights and gave rise to a large volume of case law on the meaning of 'redundancy' but, looking back at it from the perspective of 2009, one can say that the level of protection it offered was limited. So it is fair to say that the introduction of the right not to be unfairly dismissed by the Industrial Relations Act 1971 – the only part of that controversial piece of legislation to survive – represents a significant advance for the rights of employees. The basic structure of the original legislation has been retained over the years of its life, albeit that there have been numerous additions and alterations. The qualifying length of employment has fluctuated according to political fashion, ranging from two years at the height of the Conservative era to six months during the life of the Labour

Government in the 1970s; the limitation period for presenting claims was originally one month and is now three. But what we have in 2009 is still recognisable as the creature which struggled to life in 1972.

9.2 As was mentioned in Chapter 8, those who are dismissed are likely to have two basic types of claim: a wrongful dismissal claim, in other words a claim that they have been dismissed in breach of contract, or a claim that they have been dismissed in breach of their statutory rights. The latter type of claim will either be an unfair dismissal claim – considered in this chapter – or a claim for a redundancy payment, considered in Chapter 10. In general, an employee who is dismissed by reason of redundancy is better advised to complain of unfair dismissal rather than to claim a redundancy payment, since he or she stands to be awarded a higher level of compensation if the claim is successful. Pure redundancy payments claims are for this reason fairly uncommon.

9.3 Potential claimants must fulfil certain requirements before being able to make a complaint of unfair dismissal. These are:

(1) they must be an employee;

(2) they must have been 'continuously employed' for one year;

(3) they should not be in one of the excluded classes;

(4) they must present their complaint of unfair dismissal within three months of the 'effective date of termination'; and

(5) they must have been 'dismissed'.

9.4 If the *special* rules apply, the requirement of one year's continuity of employment does not apply; nor does the rule that an employee must be under the age of 65. So, for an example, an employee claiming to have been dismissed for reasons related to trade union membership may be over 65 and may only have been continuously employed for three months. In the case of a dismissal to which the *general* rules apply, where the employee qualifies for the right and has been dismissed, the two main questions are (1) what was the reason for the dismissal; and (2) did the employer follow a fair procedure when deciding to dismiss? It is fair to say that in most cases of unfair dismissal, the main issue is whether the employer acted fairly.

Qualifications

Status of the claimant

9.5 ERA 1996, s 94(1) provides that an employee has the right not to be unfairly dismissed by his or her employer. This right is made subject to other provisions of the ERA 1996, such as the provision excluding those who have reached 'normal retiring age' or who are over 65: see s 109(1). Thus, the right not to be unfairly dismissed only extends to employees; it is not available to those who are self-employed. The distinction between employees and self-employed persons was examined in Chapter 4, to which reference should be made.

Excluded categories

9.6 The following categories of employee are excluded from the legislation:

(1) employees employed under illegal contracts;

(2) employees who do not work in the United Kingdom;

(3) those covered by diplomatic or state immunity;

(4) employees of international organisations or the Commonwealth Secretariat;

(5) Crown employees;

(6) Parliamentary staff;

(7) employees over retirement age;

(8) short-term and casual employees;

(9) employees affected by national security;

(10) share fishermen; and

(11) those in the police service and members of the armed forces.

9.7 It is not intended to go into most of these categories in any detail. Reference should be made to Upex, *The Law of Termination of Employment* (7th ed, 2006), paras 1.69–1.110. Illegal contracts have already been considered in Chapter 4.

9.8 Until 1 October 2006, when the Employment Equality (Age) Regulations 2006 came into operation, the effect of section 109 of the ERA was to exclude employees from the unfair dismissal right either if they had reached the 'normal retirement age' for an employee holding that position in that undertaking, or, if there was no normal retiring age, the age of 65. Section 109 was repealed by the Employment Equality (Age) Regulations. In its place, the Regulations inserted a series of specific provisions relating to retirement – sections 98(2)(ba), 98(3A) and 98ZA to 98ZH – whose effect is considered in the paragraphs which follow. The general provisions relating to the fairness or otherwise of the dismissal – the burden placed upon the employer to show the reason for the dismissal and the question whether the dismissal is fair or unfair – are considered later in this chapter: see paras. 9.68 *et seq.* and 9.82 *et seq.*

9.9 The new section 98(2)(ba) contains an additional 'potentially fair' reason for dismissal, called 'retirement of the employee'. Sections 98ZA to 98ZF contain provisions setting out in what circumstances the retirement of the employee is not to be taken to be the reason for the dismissal. If, by virtue of one of these provisions, retirement is not to be taken to be the reason for the dismissal, it will follow that the employer will have failed to show the reason for the dismissal, which will therefore be automatically unfair. So, for example, section 98ZA provides that, if the employee has no normal retirement age and the operative date of termination (i.e. the date when the termination takes effect) falls before the date when the employee reaches 65, retirement of the employee is not to be taken to be the reason for the dismissal. Section 98ZC is to similar effect but applies where there is a normal retirement age and the employee is dismissed before reaching it. Sections 98ZB and 98ZD mirror the previous two provisions but apply when the employee is dismissed at or after age 65 or at or after the normal retirement age. If the employee exercises the 'statutory right not to retire' (granted by Schedule 6 of the Regulations) and notifies the employer in accordance with Schedule 6, retirement of the employee will be taken to be the only reason for the dismissal by the employer. Section 98ZE applies where the employee has a normal retirement age below 65 and is dismissed at or after the retirement age. The relevant provisions are complex and can only be considered in outline here.

9.10 Section 98(3A) goes on to provide that in a case where the employer shows that the reason for the employee's dismissal is his or her retirement, the fairness or otherwise of the dismissal is to be determined in accordance with section 98ZG. Section 98ZG(1) only applies if the reason for the dismissal is retirement (and so, by parity of reasoning, does not apply if, by virtue of any of the above provisions, it is not). Section 98ZG(2) states that the dismissal is to be regarded as unfair if the employer has failed to comply with the obligations imposed by the relevant provisions of Schedule 6 of the Regulations. These impose a duty to inform the employee of his or her right to make a request not to retire and various duties in relation to a request made by the employee.

Continuity of employment

9.11 Continuity of employment is important in the present context because the statutory rights considered in this and the next chapter are available only to employees who have been 'continuously employed' for the requisite period of time. In the case of the unfair dismissal rights, that period is one year: see ERA 1996, s 108(1), as amended by the Unfair Dismissal and Statement of Reasons for Dismissal (Variation of Qualifying Period) Order 1999 (SI 1999/1436). Continuity of employment is also used to compute the amount of a redundancy payment and of a basic award of compensation for unfair dismissal.

9.12 The main rules for determining continuity are in sections 210–219. It should be noted that any week during which the employee has a contract of employment with the employer counts towards the period of continuous employment, irrespective of his or her weekly hours of work. Continuity of employment involves two elements: first, the existence of a continuous (ie unbroken) relationship between employer and employee; and secondly, an unbroken relationship which lasts the requisite length of time. The length of the employee's period of employment is normally computed in months and years, but if a question arises as to whether continuity has been broken, the employment must be looked at week by week in accordance with the statutory provisions: ERA 1996, s 219(3).

9.13 The date at which the employee must have the minimum period of employment is the 'effective date of termination', defined by ERA 1996, s 97 as either the date when the notice given to the employee expires or, in the case of a summary dismissal, the date of the summary dismissal. The starting date for the calculation is the day on which he or she started work: ERA 1996, s 211(1). That means the day on which the employment under the contract began, not the day on which the employee started to perform the duties: see *General of the Salvation Army v Dewsbury* (1984).

9.14 The effect of these rules is that the tribunal should decide the starting date of the employment and the effective date of termination. If the effective date of termination is less than one year after the starting date, the employee will have insufficient continuity. Thus, an employee whose contract starts on 1 September 2008 and whose effective date of termination is 26 August 2009 will not qualify for the right not to be unfairly dismissed. The provisions of sections 97(2) and 145(5) should be noted in this context, however. Their effect is to postpone the effective date of termination or relevant date in cases where the employer gives less notice than the employee is entitled to under section 86. The effect is that, if an employee on the verge of qualifying for the statutory rights is dismissed summarily, the effective date of termination or relevant date may be extended by one week, which may be sufficient to carry him or her over the threshold of the qualifying period. The one-year qualifying period does not apply, however, to the same groups of employees as were mentioned at para 9.6, above.

9.15 Provided that the employee is employed by the same employer, continuity of employment is not affected by the fact that he or she may have a number of consecutive contracts of employment with that employer involving different types of work or different terms of working in different places: see *Re Mack Trucks (Britain) Ltd* (1967), *Wood v York City Council* (1978) and *Bradford Metropolitan District Council v Dawson* (1999).

9.16 Sections 210–219 set out the rules for determining whether a week counts. The general rule is that a week which does not count under these provisions will break continuity: ERA 1996, s 210(4). If continuity is broken, the employee's period of previous employment will be destroyed, and the qualification process will have to start all over again. There are, however, specific provisions which prevent this result occurring, particularly in the case of strikes and lockouts: see para 9.31, below. If a period (a week or longer) does not count but does not break continuity (eg because the employee is on strike during that period), the beginning of the period of continuous employment will be treated as postponed by the length of the period which does not count; thus a month's strike will mean that the start of continuous employment will be taken to have been a month later: ERA 1996, s 211(3).

9.17 The following weeks count: (1) weeks 'during the whole or part of which an employee's relations with his employer are governed by a contract of employment'; and (2) weeks in which the employee is absent from work for certain specified reasons: see ss 212(1) and 210(4) and para 9.18, below. Employees who are absent may be covered either by section 212(1) or (3). Section 212(1) protects them during absence on holiday, for example, since their relations with their employer during their absence remain governed by a contract of employment. The weeks of absence will count under ERA 1996, s 212(1).

9.18 The question is when section 212(3) applies. A week of absence only counts under this provision if it is caused by the events specified in that paragraph and the employee's relations with the employer are not governed by a contract of employment. The events are: (1) absence because of sickness or injury; (2) absence on account of a temporary cessation of work; and (3) absence 'in circumstances such that by arrangement or custom, [the employee] is regarded as continuing in the employment of his employer for all or any purposes'. It is important to bear in mind that the employee's absence, and the fact that the contract may cease during the absence, will not break continuity, provided that the absence is covered by section 212(3).

9.19 The first situation, which falls within ERA 1996, s 212(3)(a), arises where the employee is incapable of work in consequence of sickness or injury, but only if the employee's relations with the employer are not governed by a contract of employment. The employee will be covered by section 212(1) if the contract continues during his or her absence, though there may come a stage when the illness causes the contract to be frustrated. An employee off sick for a long time may at some stage be dismissed, in which case both sections 212(1) and (3)(a) would apply. But section 212(3)(a) only applies to absence for up to 26 weeks by virtue of ERA 1996, s 212(4). After that, continuity is broken. Although the dismissal need not be expressly because of sickness or injury, there must be some causal connection between the two: see *Scarlett v Godfrey Abbott Group Ltd* (1978), *Green v Wavertree Heating and Plumbing Co Ltd* (1978), and *Pearson v Kent County Council* (1993).

9.20 The second situation, where the employee is absent from work on account of a temporary cessation of work, falls within ERA 1996, s 212(3)(b). The three main questions which arise here are: (1) whether there is a cessation of work; (2) whether the cessation is temporary; and (3) whether the employee is absent on account of that temporary cessation; see *Bentley Engineering Co Ltd v Crown and Miller* (1976).

9.21 The House of Lords held, in *Fitzgerald v Hall, Russell & Co Ltd* (1970), that the phrase 'cessation of work' means a cessation of work for the employee to do, because there is no longer any work for him or her to do; it is not necessary that the employer should cease operations in the factory or the section of it in which the employee works. On the other hand, the provisions of section 212(3)(b) will not apply in situations such as those where an employee is a member of a pool of workers amongst whom the employer distributes work and is not allocated work for some time, the work being given to another member of the pool: see *Byrne v Birmingham City District Council* (1987) and *Letheby & Christopher Ltd v Bond* (1988).

9.22 Arguably, the best approach to questions of this sort is to treat an employee's absence from work, whether caused by resignation or dismissal, as a cessation of work, so that the only question which then arises is whether the absence was temporary, looking at the matter with hindsight. The reported cases have not followed this simple approach, however. It has been held, for example, that an employee who leaves voluntarily and then returns, or is dismissed and then re-engaged, may not fall within section 212(3)(b): see *Bunt v Fishlow Products Ltd* (1970). In *Roach v CSB (Moulds) Ltd* (1991) the EAT decided that there was insufficient continuity of employment in the case of an employee who was dismissed by his employers, went to work for another employer for about 12 days, and then returned to his previous employers at a lower grade for some seven months before being finally dismissed by them; see also *Ryan v Shipboard Maintenance Ltd* (1980). On the other hand, it has been held that an employee who takes another job during the period of cessation may still be within section 212(3)(b), but the job must clearly be a stop-gap: see *Thompson v Bristol Channel Ship Repairers and Engineers Ltd* (1970). Absence caused by a resignation or by a dismissal regarded as permanent (for example, because the dismissal followed a row between employer and employee) has also been held not to count. It is difficult to see why such absences should not be regarded as temporary. It should be noted that an employee who works for the same employer in two successive weeks but with a gap between the two periods of work, for example because he or she resigned to go to work for another employer but then left and was re-engaged by the previous employer, will be held to fall within section 212(1): see *Carrington v Harwich Dock Co Ltd* (1998) and *Sweeney v J & S Henderson (Concessions) Ltd* (1999).

9.23 The cessation of work must also be temporary, a question which must be determined with hindsight, looking retrospectively at the circumstances of the absence from work. In doing so, the whole period of employment is relevant. Evidence of the intention of the parties at the time is relevant, but absence of such evidence is not conclusive. The test is objective. The question whether a cessation of work is temporary is one of fact and degree in each case. Although there is no limit on the length of the absence, if it is lengthy the question will arise whether it is to be regarded as temporary or permanent.

9.24 Attempts to decide whether any particular absence is or is not 'temporary' have given rise to an extensive body of cases which are not easy to reconcile with each other. The first question is what is meant by the word. In *Ford v Warwickshire County Council* (1983), Lord Diplock said: '(T)he whole scheme of the Act appears to me to show that it is in the sense of "transient", ie lasting only for a relatively short time, that the word "temporary" is used (in section 212(3)(b)) . . .'. Subsequently, the use of the word 'transient' has been deprecated and judges have preferred the phrase 'lasting only for a relatively short time': see Woolf LJ in *Flack v Kodak Ltd* (1986) and *Sillars v Charrington Fuels Ltd* (1989). What is a short time in one employment is not necessarily a short time in another employment. The whole matter is one of relativity.

9.25 The problems posed by section 212(3)(b) have led to two basic approaches: the 'mathematical' approach and the 'broad' approach. The first approach concentrates on comparing the length of the periods of employment with the length of the intervening gaps. The second approach involves looking at all the circumstances over the whole period of employment (including the intentions of the parties) to see whether the break in question is a temporary cessation. The decisions of the Court of Appeal mentioned above suggest that the mathematical approach is appropriate where there is a regular seasonal pattern of employment and non-employment and that the broad approach is preferable where the pattern of work is irregular. In this respect the two Court of Appeal decisions may usefully be contrasted with each other. The essential difference between the two approaches is that the mathematical approach is objective in its concentration upon comparing the periods during which the employee was in work and out of work. Because the broad approach, on the other hand, enables the tribunal to look at all the factors, including the intention of the parties, it gives far greater flexibility.

9.26 The third situation is catered for by ERA 1996, s 212(3)(c), where the employee is 'absent from work in circumstances such that, by arrangement or custom, he is regarded as continuing in the employment of his employer for all or any purposes'. It is necessary to establish both that there existed an arrangement or custom and that, by virtue of that arrangement or custom, the employee was regarded as continuing in the employment of the employer for all or any purposes; these should be regarded as strict requirements which cannot be made retrospectively: see *Wishart v National Coal Board* (1974), *Lane v Wolverhampton Die Testing Ltd* (1967), and *Rhodes v Pontins Ltd* (1971). But an agreement to reinstate a dismissed employee and, on reinstatement, to preserve accrued continuity appears to satisfy section 212(3)(c): see *Ingram v Foxon* (1984). More recently, the EAT has returned to this issue. In *London Probation Board v Kirkpatrick* (2005), the EAT said that it did not consider it to be necessary for there to be an arrangement in advance of the gap in service, thus suggesting that there could be a retrospective arrangement. It went on to say that, if that view was wrong, the existence of the discipline and appeal procedure in place in the instant case could be described as an arrangement in existence before the gap in the employee's employment.

9.27 In *Curr v Marks and Spencer plc* (2003), the Court of Appeal said that it cannot be said that an employee is regarded as 'continuing in the employment' where she participates in a child break scheme by which she is required resign with the option of re-employment at the end of the child break. They said that the arrangement in question could not be said to be one by which both parties regarded her as continuing in the employment of the employer for any purpose during the weeks of the child break.

9.28 In *Lloyds Bank Ltd v Secretary of State for Employment* (1979), the EAT held that ERA 1996, s 212(3)(c) covered an employee who worked on a 'week on, week off' basis, and said that the weeks when the employee did not work and was not required to work were periods not governed by her contract, and that, accordingly, she was absent by arrangement within section 212(3)(c). In the later case of *Corton House Ltd v Skipper* (1981), the EAT took the view that 'absent from work' has two possible meanings: either simply not working or not at the workplace, or absent from work when under the contract the employee should normally be present. Slynn J (as he then was) favoured the latter interpretation, on the basis of which section 212(3)(c) would not have been satisfied since the employee was not required to be there. Even if the former meaning were applied, as Slynn J felt bound to, in view of the *Lloyds Bank* decision, the provision would still have applied, since no special custom or arrangement had been established.

9.29 Arguably, however, the better way of interpreting section 212(3)(c) is that it only applies where an employee has no contract (where the contractual relationship has ceased temporarily or permanently) between two periods during which he or she works full-time under a contract of employment. It should not be used to protect employees whose hours fluctuate, nor should it be used as a safety net provision to catch hours of work, or periods of employment, which cannot be accommodated within the other paragraphs of Part XIV, Chapter I of the 1996 Act. This view is supported by some of the dicta of the House of Lords in *Ford v Warwickshire County Council*, above, albeit in the context of section 212(3)(b). If it is correct, the cases discussed above should be regarded as wrongly decided.

9.30 In *Letheby & Christopher Ltd v Bond* (1988), the EAT refused to apply the provisions of section 212(3)(c) to a casual worker who was absent from work for a week when she was on holiday. They said that the tribunal should have asked whether, when the absence took place, the parties regarded the employment as continuing. Since she was employed under single separate contracts, it was not possible to say that her employment was continuing after the cessation of the previous contract. A similar conclusion was reached in the later case of *Booth v United States of America* (1999). The employees worked under a series of fixed-term contracts, which in total exceeded the qualifying period of employment, but between each contract there was a gap of two weeks. At the end of the two-week gap the employees were re-engaged. The EAT upheld the tribunal's decisions that the employees were not protected by section 212(3)(c) as there was no arrangement.

9.31 Special rules operate for weeks during all or part of which an employee takes part in a strike or is absent from work because of a lockout by the employer. The two most important are: (1) the week will not count but the employee's continuity will not be broken; and (2) the beginning of the employee's period of continuous employment will be postponed by the amount of time the dispute lasts; ie a dispute lasting two months will cause the starting date of the period of continuous employment to be treated as two months later than it actually was: see ERA 1996, s 216(1)–(3). It is immaterial whether the strike is unlawful (ie without proper strike notice), unconstitutional (in breach of a procedure agreement), or unofficial (not given official union backing). A period of time after the end of the strike but before an employee returns to work will probably be treated as a 'temporary cessation of work' and covered by section 212(3)(b): see *Clarke Chapman-John Thompson Ltd v Walters* (1972). Employees laid off because of a strike or lockout at another plant will probably also be covered by section 212(3)(b).

Non-compliance by employees with the statutory dispute resolution procedures

9.32 The Employment Act 2002 introduced provisions whose aim is to improve the resolution of disputes in the workplace. The procedures are considered in more detail at paras 9.45–9.55, below. The important point for the purpose of this section is that an employee who fails to comply with the applicable procedure will not be able to present a complaint to the employment tribunal until the procedures have been complied with (subject to exceptions): see section 32. In addition, any award of compensation made in his or her favour by the tribunal is liable to be reduced by a minimum. This aspect of non-compliance is dealt with in the section on compensation: see para 9.195, below.

9.33 Section 32 of the Act applies to unfair dismissal cases and has the effect of depriving tribunals of jurisdiction in cases where the employee is obliged to go through a grievance. So an employee who is *dismissed* is not affected by that provision and will be able to present a complaint immediately. The 2004 Regulations also make provision for the time limit for presenting a complaint of unfair dismissal to be extended in certain circumstances: see para 9.36, below.

9.34 If the employee resigned and wishes to complain of *constructive dismissal* then the provisions of section 32 of the 2002 Act and reg 15 of the Dispute Resolution Regulations will apply. The first goes to the admissibility of the claim; the second provides for extension of the normal time limits. Section 32 applies in three sets of circumstances:

(1) the complaint of unfair dismissal concerns a matter to which the requirements of paragraph 6 or 9 of Schedule 2 applies and the requirement has not been complied with;

(2) the complaint concerns one of the above matters and the requirements of paragraph 6 or 9 have been complied *but* 28 days have not elapsed since the day on which the requirement was complied with;

(3) the complaint concerns one of the above matters and the requirements of paragraph 6 or 9 have been complied with and the day on which the requirement was complied with was more than one month after the end of the original time for making the complaint.

Paragraph 6, which is the first step in the standard procedure, requires the employee to set out the grievance in writing and send a copy of it to the employer. Paragraph 9 is the first step in the *modified* procedure: it requires the employee to set out the grievance in writing *and the basis for it*, and to send the statement or a copy of it to the employer. 'Grievance' is defined in reg 2 of the Dispute Resolution Regulations as 'a complaint by an employee about action which his employer has taken or is contemplating taking in relation to him'. Regulation 6 of the Dispute Resolution Regulations sets out the circumstances in which the standard or modified procedures apply; this is considered at para 9.52, below.

9.35 Decisions of the EAT concerning these provisions have now appeared. The first requirement of section 32 (above) has been considered in *Galaxy Showers Ltd v Wilson* (2006) and *Shergold v Fieldway Medical Centre* (2006). In both cases, the issue was whether the employee had raised a grievance and whether the tribunal had jurisdiction under section 32. The EAT in both cases made it clear that a grievance may be contained in a letter of resignation. In the latter case, Burton J said that the requirements of paragraph 6 of the Dispute Resolutions Regulations are 'simple' and 'minimal'. He also said that it is not necessary to make it plain in the written document that it is a grievance or is an invocation of a grievance procedure. He drew attention to reg 2(2), which states that it is irrelevant whether the written communication 'deals with any other matter'. It should be noted that, in both cases, the employee in question resigned with notice. It is not clear what would be the position if the employee resigned with immediate effect; see also *Mark Warner Ltd v Aspland* (2006).

9.36   The second aspect of the new legislation is the extension of the time limits, which is effected by reg 15(1) of the Dispute Resolution Regulations. If reg 15 applies, the time limit will be extended by three months from the day after the day on which the limitation period would otherwise have expired. Regulation 15(1)(a) comes into play where either of the dismissal and disciplinary procedures applies and the employee presents a complaint to the tribunal after the expiry of the normal time limit 'but had reasonable grounds for believing, when the limit expired, that a dismissal or disciplinary procedure was being followed in respect of matters that consisted of or included the substance of the tribunal complaint'. In *Piscitelli v Zilli Fish Ltd* (2006) the EAT held that a letter seeking a cash settlement of an employee's potential unfair dismissal claim did not raise an internal appeal against his dismissal. This meant that the time for presenting a complaint of unfair dismissal was not extended by regulation 15(1) and his complaint was therefore out of time. Regulation 15(1)(b) applies to constructive dismissals, amongst other things, and comes into play where 'the circumstances specified in paragraph (3) apply'. These are that the employee presents a complaint to the tribunal in one of two sets of circumstances: *either* within the normal time limit but in circumstances in which section 32(2) or (3) does not permit a complaint to be presented *or* after the expiry of the normal time limit but after compliance with the requirements of Schedule 2, paragraph 6 or 9 within the normal time limit. For an explanation of the circumstances in which section 32(2) or (3) applies see para 9.34, above. It should be noted that the procedures are to be repealed. See para 9.56 below.

Claims out of time

9.37   An employee will lose the right to complain of unfair dismissal if the complaint is presented out of time. ERA 1996, s 111(2) provides that an employment tribunal may not consider a complaint of unfair dismissal unless it is presented to the tribunal within three months of the 'effective date of termination' or such further period as the tribunal considers reasonable in a case where it is satisfied that it was not reasonably practicable for the complaint to be presented within three months. This provision goes to the tribunal's jurisdiction. This means that the tribunal cannot hear the complaint unless it has considered as a preliminary issue whether to allow the complaint to proceed: see *Porter v Bandridge Ltd* (1978).

9.38　The main question for the tribunal to consider in a case of this kind is whether it was reasonably practicable for the complaint to be presented within three months of the effective date of termination. If it concludes that it was reasonably practicable, the tribunal must go on to consider within what period it was reasonable for the complaint to have been presented. The approach of the Court of Appeal in *Dedman v British Building & Engineering Appliances Ltd* (1974) is still followed, although that case was decided under provisions whose relevant wording was 'practicable', and in the context of a 28-day limitation period. This approach has been affirmed in subsequent Court of Appeal decisions, and it has been stressed that employment tribunals should be fairly strict in enforcing the time limits and that questions of reasonable practicability are questions of fact: see *Wall's Meat Co Ltd v Khan* (1979). In *Palmer v Southend-on-Sea Borough Council* (1984), May LJ said that 'reasonably practicable' means more than what is reasonably capable physically of being done and that to construe the words as 'reasonable' would be to take a view too favourable to the employee. He also emphasised that, since the issue is pre-eminently one of fact, the EAT and the Court of Appeal should be slow to interfere with the employment tribunal's decision. See also *Consigna plc v Sealy* (2002), in which the Court of Appeal considered this issue in relation to a complaint delayed in the post; Brooke LJ set out guidelines for tribunals to follow when dealing with cases of this kind: see para 31 of the decision.

9.39　The decision that it was not reasonably practicable for a complaint to be presented within the time limit is not the end of the matter. The tribunal must go on to decide upon the period within which it was reasonable to present the complaint. In *James W Cook & Co (Wivenhoe) Ltd v Tipper* (1990), for example, which involved employees who delayed making applications because they were led to believe that work would pick up, the Court of Appeal took the view that it would not be right to fix a date earlier than two weeks after the expiry of the limitation period as the date when the employees should have realised that hope has gone; they then allowed a further two weeks after that as a reasonable period within which to make an application. Two employees, whose complaints were presented outside that period, had their complaints dismissed for want of jurisdiction. In *Schultz v Esso Petroleum Co Ltd* (1999) the Court of Appeal reversed the tribunal's decision that a complaint presented almost six months out of time was time-barred. This is a surprisingly long time outside the time limit, but the explanation for the Court of Appeal's decision probably lies in the unusual facts of the case.

9.40 The conclusion to be drawn from the above cases is that, in general, a tribunal should be careful about extending the time for presenting a complaint much beyond a month, except in exceptional circumstances. Clearly, too, the longer the period that elapses after the expiry of the limitation period, the less likely becomes an extension of time.

Dismissal

9.41 It is fundamental to a complaint of unfair dismissal or a claim for a redundancy payment that the employee should have been dismissed. Unless the tribunal is satisfied that there has been a dismissal, the case will fail. In the case of unfair dismissal complaints, ERA 1996, s 95 contains the definition of dismissal; the statutory provision is exhaustive. The combined effect of the statutory provisions and judicial interpretations of them is that some situations clearly fall within them, for example an actual dismissal; some situations are deemed to be a dismissal, for example a resignation prompted by a repudiatory breach on the employer's part or the expiry of a fixed-term contract. Some situations, for example a frustrating event or a voluntary resignation unprompted by action on the employer's part, are outside the definition.

9.42 It is important when determining whether an action falls within the definition of dismissal to start with the statutory language and then to examine the relevant judicial decisions. This is different from the common law position involving wrong-ful dismissal, to which the statutory definition does not apply. It is also important to bear in mind that an event which is treated as a dismissal by the statute may not be a dismissal at common law. For example, the expiry of a fixed-term contract is expressly treated as a dismissal by ERA 1996, s 95(2)(b). At common law, however, it will not amount to a dismissal.

9.43 The basic statutory definition of dismissal in ERA 1996, s 95(1) is as follows:

an employee is dismissed by his employer if (and . . . only if) –

(a) the contract under which he is employed is terminated by the employer (whether with or without notice),

(b) he is employed under a contract for a fixed term and that term expires without being renewed under the same contract, or

(c) the employee terminates the contract under which he is employed (with or without notice) in circumstances such that he is entitled to terminate it without notice by reason of the employer's conduct.

9.44 The statutory definition set out above is the basic definition used in both the unfair dismissal and (with a slight difference of wording) the redundancy payments provisions in the Employment Rights Act 1996. The third type of dismissal in the definition is usually called a 'constructive dismissal', but that is not a term to be found in the legislation. For a discussion of the first and third concepts – actual and 'constructive' dismissals – reference should be made to Chapter 8, where they are examined.

The statutory dispute resolution procedures

9.45 The Employment Act 2002 introduced provisions whose aim is to improve the resolution of disputes in the workplace. The relevant provisions of the Act (ss 29–33 and Sch 2) came into force on 1 October 2004. The Employment Act 2002 (Dispute Resolution) Regulations 2004 (SI 2004/752), which flesh out the statutory provisions, came into force at the same time. In this section they are referred to as 'the 2004 Regulations' and the Act as 'the 2002 Act'. Section 30(1) of the 2002 Act provides that every employer and employee must comply with the requirements of the procedure in relation to any matter to which the statutory procedure applies. Schedule 2 Pts 1 and 2 sets out the procedures which consist of (i) dismissal and disciplinary procedures; and (ii) grievance procedures. Each set of procedures consists of a standard procedure and a modified procedure. The Regulations set out the situations in which the procedures apply, and the exceptions to them. It should be noted that the statutory dismissal and disciplinary procedures apply where an employer is contemplating dismissing an employee. In the case of constructive dismissals by employees, the statutory *grievance* procedures apply.

9.46 Failure on the part of either the employer or the employee to observe the procedures will lead to certain consequences. In the case of the *employer*, a failure to complete the applicable procedure will mean that the dismissal is automatically unfair, provided that the non-completion of the procedure is 'wholly or mainly attributable' to the employer's failure to complete the requirements of the procedure: see ERA 1996, s 98A (inserted by EA 2002, s 34). In addition, any award of compensation made against the employer is subject to a minimum adjustment of 10 per cent and a maximum adjustment of 50 per cent: see EA 2002, s 31(3). The tribunal may make a lesser increase in cases where there are 'exceptional circumstances' and it considers that it would be 'unjust or inequitable' to make a smaller increase: see EA 2002, s 31(4). A failure by the *employee* to complete the applicable procedure will have two consequences. First, he or she will not be able to present a complaint of unfair dismissal to the tribunal (subject to exceptions) until the procedures have been complied with: see EA 2002, s 32. Second, as with the employer, any award of compensation made in his or her favour by the tribunal, is liable to be reduced by a minimum of 10 per cent and a maximum of 50 per cent, again subject to the possibility of a smaller reduction in 'exceptional circumstances': see EA 2002, s 31(2) and (4).

The disciplinary and dismissal procedures

9.47　These are to be found in Schedule 2 Part 1 of the Employment Act 2002, which provides for a 'standard' and a 'modified' procedure. The standard procedure comprises three steps: (i) the statement by the employer of the grounds for action and an invitation to a meeting to discuss the matter; (ii) the meeting itself; and (iii) appeals. The modified procedure consists of only *two* stages: (i) the statement by the employer of the grounds for action; and (ii) appeals. The difference between the two procedures lies in the nature of the statement which the employer must make. If the statement is the first stage in the standard procedure, the employer must set out in writing the employee's alleged conduct (or characteristics or other circumstances) which led the employer to contemplate dismissing, or taking disciplinary action against, him or her: see EA 2002 Sch 2, para 1(1). In the case of the *modified* procedure, the employer's statement of grounds for action must not only set out the employee's alleged misconduct which has led to the dismissal, but also the basis on which the employer took the view that at the time of the dismissal the employee was guilty of the alleged misconduct: see EA 2002, Sch 2, para 4(a). The modified procedure applies where the employee has already been dismissed, but he or she retains the right to appeal against the decision to dismiss. An employee has the statutory right to be accompanied at a meeting convened under the procedures: see para 9.100, below. In terms of content, the stage 1 letter need only state the issue in broad terms, without the need for specifics: see *Draper v Mears Ltd* (2006).

9.48　The standard procedure is intended to apply to all cases where the employer is contemplating dismissing, or taking 'relevant disciplinary action' against, an employee: see regulation 3(1) of the Regulations. The standard procedure applies to actual dismissals and dismissals arising on the expiry of a limited-term contract: see regulation 2(1). It does not apply to constructive dismissals, since they are not included within the definition of 'dismissed' given in regulation 2(1). Thus, an employee claiming to have been constructively dismissed falls within the provisions relating to grievance procedures. The modified dismissal procedure applies in the following circumstances: (a) the employer dismissed the employee by reason of his or her conduct without notice; (b) the dismissal took place at the time when the employer became aware of the conduct or immediately afterwards; (c) the employer was entitled, in the circumstances, to dismiss the employee without notice or pay in lieu of notice by reason of the conduct; and (c) it was reasonable for the employer, in the circumstances, to dismiss the employee before enquiring into the circumstances in which the conduct took place: regulation 3(2) of the Regulations. In effect, the modified procedure applies where there is a summary dismissal for gross misconduct. The DTI's Guidance suggests that this will only apply in a small number of cases, since 'it is almost always unfair to dismiss an employee instantly...even in a case of apparently obvious gross misconduct': para 15. However, it is clear that in order to fall within the jurisdiction of the modified procedure the summary dismissal must be an immediate response, with any delay in dismissing, even one day's delay, rendering the modified procedure inapplicable: see *O'Neil v Wooldridge Ecotec Ltd* (2007).

9.49 Schedule 2, Part 3 of the 2002 Act sets out what are called 'general requirements' in relation to the procedures. Paragraph 11 states that each step and action under the procedure must be taken without unreasonable delay. Paragraph 13 relates to meetings. It states that the timing and location of the meetings must be reasonable; the meetings must be conducted in a manner which enables both parties to explain their cases; and, finally, in the case of appeal meetings which are not the first meeting, the employer should be represented by a more senior manager than attended the first meeting (unless the most senior manager attended that meeting).

9.50 Where one party fails to comply with any requirement of the disciplinary procedure, including the general requirements set out in Schedule 2, Part 3 (relating to the timetable for taking steps and actions under the procedure and the meetings held), the procedure will in effect come to an end and the non-completion of the procedure will be attributable to the party in breach: see regulation 12(1).

9.51 The 2004 Regulations provide for a number of situations in which the statutory procedures do not apply. If a particular case falls within one of the exceptions the effect will be that the consequences (set out above) will not apply. A dismissal and disciplinary procedure will not apply, or, if it has started, will be treated as having been complied with, where the employer or employee's failure to start or complete the procedure is for one of the following reasons:

(a) the party has reasonable grounds for believing that starting or completing the procedure would result in a significant threat to the party or their property, or any other person or their property;

(b) the party has been subjected to harassment and has reasonable grounds to believe that following the procedure would result in further harassment;

(c) it is not practicable to start or complete the procedure within a reasonable period.

See regulation 11. The 2004 Regulations (reg 4) also provide that the dismissal and disciplinary procedures do not apply to the following types of dismissal, for example dismissals of a whole group of employees and dismissals of employees taking part in industrial action.

The statutory grievance procedures

9.52 The statutory grievance procedures are only relevant in the context of this chapter to the extent that they apply to constructive dismissals. They are clearly of much wider application, but the contexts in which they apply are not relevant here. As with the dismissal and disciplinary procedures, the grievance procedures are of two types: the 'standard' and the 'modified' procedure: see EA 2002, Sch 2, paras 6–10. The standard procedure comprises three steps: (i) the statement of grievance by the employee, which must be sent to the employer; (ii) the meeting itself; and (iii) an appeal: see EA 2002, Sch 2, paras 6–8. The modified procedure consists of only *two* stages: (i) the statement of grievance by the employee; and (ii) the employer's response: see EA 2002, Sch 2, para 9. It consists in effect of an exchange of letters. In the case of the standard procedure the employee is required to set out the grievance in writing and send the statement or a copy of it to the employer. If the modified procedure applies, the employee must not only set out the grievance in writing but must also set out the basis for it. It should be noted that an employee has the statutory right to be accompanied at a meeting convened under the procedures: see para 9.100, below.

9.53 Regulation 2(1) of the 2004 Regulations defines 'grievance' as: 'a complaint by an employee about action which his employer has taken or is contemplating taking in relation to him'. Regulation 2(2) goes on to say that, in determining whether a written communication fulfils a requirement of Schedule 2 of the 2002 Act, it is irrelevant whether it deals with any other matter. The EAT has said that it is not necessary for the employee *personally* to write the letter said to constitute the grievance and that such action may be taken on the employee's behalf by an agent, for example a solicitor: see *Mark Warner Ltd v Apsland* (2005).

9.54 The question which has caused most of the problems so far is what requirements are necessary for a communication written by an employer to constitute a 'grievance' for the purposes of the 2004 Regulations. In *Commotion Ltd v Rutty* (2005) the EAT said that a letter applying for a variation of an employee's working pattern (under ERA 1996, s 80) may fulfil the requirements of para 2(2) provided that it sets out a grievance. In the later case of *Shergold v Fieldway Medical Centre* (2005) the then President of the EAT, Burton J, dealt with the above issue and other questions arising under the 2004 Regulations. The facts of the case were that the employee resigned her employment and complained of unfair dismissal. Her resignation, which was with notice, was contained in a letter in which she set out at length her reasons for leaving. A meeting took place between the employee and the employer; she was advised to put in a formal grievance but her employment ended without her having done so. The EAT said that it was satisfied that the letter of resignation was sufficient to comply with section 32 and Schedule 2 of the EA 2002. Burton J observed that the requirements of paragraph 6 of the grievance procedure are 'simple' and 'minimal' and said that the requirement 'is simply that the grievance must be set out in writing'. It follows that it may be contained within a letter of resignation. The EAT also said that it is not necessary to make it plain in the writing that it is a grievance, or is an invocation of a grievance procedure. Nor is it necessary for the employee to comply with any company or contractual grievance procedure. The judge said, however, that 'different considerations might arise if the resignation is to have immediate effect' and added that there might be some argument in that case as to whether the Standard or Modified Procedure applies. The question would then be whether, at the time of submitting the resignation with immediate effect, the employee had ceased to be employed by the employer. In view of the fact that a resignation is the acceptance of the employer's alleged repudiation, it is arguable that the employee has not ceased to be employed by the employer until the letter of resignation is communicated to the employer. Clearly, however, an oral resignation would be insufficient, in view of the fact that the 2004 Regulations require a grievance to be *in writing*.

9.55 The 2004 Regulations provide for various situations in which the statutory procedures do not apply. A grievance procedure will not apply, or, if it has started, will be treated as having been complied with, where the employer or employee's failure to start or complete the procedure is for one of the following reasons:

(a) the party has reasonable grounds for believing that starting or completing the procedure would result in a significant threat to the party or their property, or any other person or their property;

(b) the party has been subjected to harassment and has reasonable grounds to believe that following the procedure would result in further harassment;

(c) it is not practicable to start or complete the procedure within a reasonable period.

See regulation 11. In addition, neither of the grievance procedures applies in the following circumstances: (i) where the employee has ceased to be employed by the employer and it is not reasonably practicable for him or her to write the grievance letter under step 1; (ii) where the grievance is about an *actual or contemplated* dismissal (but not a constructive dismissal); and (iii) where the grievance is about disciplinary action which the employer has taken or is contemplating; see regulation 6(4)–(6). Regulation 8(1) provides that where the standard procedure applies, the parties are to be treated as having complied with it if all of the following conditions apply: (i) the employee has ceased to be employed; (ii) the grievance letter has been sent; and (iii) since the end of the employment it has ceased to be reasonably practicable for either party to comply with the remaining requirements of the procedure. This is subject to reg 8(2), which states that the employer must nevertheless inform the employee in writing of its response to the grievance if the steps up to attendance at the meeting have been completed.

Statutory grievance and disciplinary procedures: reform

9.56 Michael Gibbons undertook a review of the Statutory Dismissal, Disciplinary, and Grievance procedures with a view to improving employment dispute resolution. The main criticism of the current system focused on the failure of the formal prescriptive system to deal with disputes, with Michael Gibbons indicating that: 'The key message from this Review is that inflexible, prescriptive regulation has been unsuccessful in this context and it follows that the measures to be used in future should be much simpler and more flexible – and therefore will offer rather less certainty and predictability in their operation.' In essence the Gibbons Review recommended a combination of clear, simple, non-prescriptive guidelines for employers on how to resolve disputes and the provision of an incentive for following the procedures. The principal aim is to enable a flexible approach to dispute resolution in the workplace.

9.57 Following on from the recommendations of the Gibbons Review, sections 1 and 2 of the Employment Act 2008 will repeal the current system and section 3 will replace it with a more flexible system. The current Statutory Dismissal, Disciplinary, and Grievance procedures will be repealed on 6 April 2009 and replaced with the new system through the Employment Act 2008 (Commencement No. 1 and Transitional and Savings Provisions) Order 2008. Section 3 amends the relevant provisions of the Trade Union and Labour Relations (Consolidation) Act 1992 that authorise ACAS to issue codes of practice to promote the improvement of industrial relations. The new provisions will empower a tribunal to increase or decrease any award made by up to 25 per cent where there has been a breach of the relevant code of practice. The fixed conciliation period that applies to ACAS will also be removed with a view to increasing the role of ACAS in resolving disputes.

Reason for dismissal

9.58 Once it has been established that the employee has been dismissed, an unfair dismissal claim will fall to be decided in two stages. The first stage consists of establishing what was the reason for the dismissal; at the second stage the tribunal must be satisfied that the employer acted reasonably in dismissing for the given reason.

9.59 Reasons may be divided into two categories: (1) what may be called 'potentially fair' reasons; and (2) reasons which, subject to certain exceptions, make a dismissal automatically unfair (eg dismissals for reasons relating to trade union membership or activities, or relating to leave for family reasons). The second category is discussed later in this chapter: see para 9.130. Where a dismissal falls within that category, it will be automatically unfair.

9.60 The 'potentially fair' reasons are so called because they can potentially justify dismissal, but they do not necessarily justify dismissal, since ERA 1996, s 98(4) obliges the tribunal to decide whether the employer acted reasonably or unreasonably in treating the reasons as sufficient for dismissing the employee. In a complaint of unfair dismissal involving the potentially fair reasons, ERA 1996, s 98(1) places the burden on the employer to show the reason (or, if there was more than one, the principal reason) for the dismissal. He or she must then show that the reason falls within one of the five specific categories set out in s 98(2) and (1)(b). These are set out below: see para 9.68.

9.61 As part of the process of establishing the reason for the dismissal ERA 1996, s 92 entitles an employee to be given a written statement of reasons for the dismissal by the employer. This right is considered first, after which the 'potentially fair' reasons will be considered.

Written statement of reasons under ERA 1996, s 92

9.62 ERA 1996, s 92 gives to a dismissed employee the right to be given a written statement giving particulars of the reasons for the dismissal by his or her employer. The employee's entitlement is to be provided with a written statement giving particulars of the reasons for the dismissal. But the employee must first ask for the written statement, which should be given by the employer within 14 days of the employee's request. In addition, an employee who is dismissed, either while she is pregnant, or after childbirth in circumstances in which her ordinary or additional maternity leave period ends by reason of her dismissal, will be entitled to be provided with a written statement. In such a case, her entitlement is irrespective of length of

... does not depend upon her first making a request: see ERA 1996,
... amended.

9.63 If the employer unreasonably fails to provide a written statement in either of the cases set out in the preceding paragraph or provides one containing inadequate or untrue particulars, the employee may present a complaint to the employment tribunal within three months of the date of termination: s 93. If the tribunal finds the complaint well-founded, it may make a declaration as to what it finds to have been the employer's reasons for dismissing the employee; it must also award the employee two weeks' pay: s 93(2).

9.64 The EAT has held that ERA 1996, s 93 should be rigidly construed and that there should be clear evidence that there has been an unreasonable failure: see *Charles Lang & Sons Ltd v Aubrey* (1978). A failure cannot be said to be unreasonable where it is based upon a conscientious belief that there has been no dismissal: see *Brown v Stuart Scott & Co* (1981). A statement of reasons is not untrue if the employer genuinely believes that the reason given is the reason for the dismissal. It is not necessary for the employment tribunal to embark upon a consideration of whether the reason was good or bad: see *Harvard Securities plc v Younghusband* (1990).

9.65 It is not enough merely to rely upon the answer put in to the employee's original application; the statute clearly contemplates an independent and separate document: see *Rowan v Machinery Installations (South Wales) Ltd* (1981). The document must be of such a kind that the employee, or anyone to whom he or she may wish to show it, can know from reading the document itself why the employee has been dismissed, and it may refer to other documents provided that the document the employee receives contains a simple statement of the essential reasons for the dismissal: see *Horsley Smith & Sherry Ltd v Dutton* (1977) and *Gilham v Kent County Council (No 1)* (1985).

9.66 The employment tribunal may only hear complaints relating to statements issued in response to an employee's request; if the employer voluntarily gives a written statement, the employee will not be able to complain about it unless the employer refers to it and effectively adopts it in response to the employee's request; see *Catherine Haigh Harlequin Hair Design v Seed* (1990) and *Marchant v Earley Town Council*, above.

9.67 Written statements are admissible in evidence in any proceedings, by virtue of ERA 1996, s 92(5). If the employer gives another reason in subsequent litigation, the tribunal would either ignore that other reason and hold the employer to the original statement or treat the change of reason as going to the employer's credibility.

General rules

9.68 In a complaint of unfair dismissal involving the so-called 'potentially fair' reasons, ERA 1996, s 98(1) places the burden on the employer not only to show the reason (or, if there was more than one, the principal reason) for the dismissal but also to show that the reason falls within one of the six categories set out in section 98(2) (as amended) and (1)(b), which are: (1) capability or qualifications; (2) the employee's conduct; (3) retirement of the employee; (4) redundancy; (5) statutory requirements; or (6) 'some other substantial reason of a kind such as to justify the dismissal of an employee holding the position which that employee held'. The burden of establishing the reason, or principal reason, for the dismissal lies upon the employer. If he or she fails to do so, the dismissal will be unfair. The third reason – retirement of the employee – is considered above at paras 9.8–9.10.

9.69 In *Abernethy v Mott, Hay, and Anderson* (1974) (at p 330), Cairns LJ said:

> A reason for the dismissal is a set of facts known to the employer, or it may be beliefs held by him, which cause him to dismiss the employee. If at the time of his dismissal the employer gives a reason for it, that is no doubt evidence, at any rate as against him, as to the real reason, but it does not necessarily constitute the real reason. He may knowingly give a reason different from the real reason out of kindness or because he might have difficulty in proving the facts which actually led him to dismiss; or he may describe his reasons wrongly through some mistake of language or of law.

9.70 So an incorrect label will not be fatal to the employer's case; see also *Clarke v Trimoco Motor Group Ltd* (1993) and *Ely v YKK Fasteners (UK) Ltd* (1994). In this last case, the Court of Appeal said that *Abernethy*'s case could be applied by analogy 'to enable resort to be had to a state of facts known to and relied upon by the employer, for the purpose of supplying him with a reason for dismissal, which, as a consequence of his misapprehension of the true nature of the circumstances, he was disabled from treating as such at the time'. The Court upheld the tribunal's decision that the employee's late notification to his employers that he had changed his mind about resigning could amount to 'some other substantial reason' within ERA 1996, s 98(1)(b).

9.71 If, however, the employer relies upon one particular reason and the reason is not established, it is not possible to try to rely upon an entirely different reason either at the tribunal hearing or upon appeal, though it may, of course, be possible to apply for leave to amend the notice of appearance: see *Nelson v BBC (No 1)* (1977), in which the reason given was redundancy, but the Court of Appeal held that the tribunal was wrong in deciding that he had been dismissed for redundancy, and that the EAT was not entitled to apply the facts found to a possible but unpleaded defence of 'some other substantial reason'. An error of characterisation of the reason for the dismissal by the tribunal is an error of law, since it is a question of legal analysis to determine under which part of section 98 the reason given by the employer falls: see *Wilson v Post Office* (2000) and *Burkett v Pendletons (Sweets) Ltd* (1992). The House of Lords' decision in *Smith v Glasgow City District Council* (1987) makes it clear that an employment tribunal must be careful in making its finding as to the reason or principal reason for the dismissal.

9.72 The House of Lords' decision in *W Devis & Sons Ltd v Atkins* (1977) (applied by the EAT in *Vauxhall Motors Ltd v Ghafoor* (1993)) established the principle that an employer may not bring in evidence of what happened after the dismissal or of events which occurred before the dismissal but which did not come to its knowledge until afterwards. In such a case, the consequence is likely to be a decision that the employee was unfairly dismissed, but the evidence of the misconduct will be relevant to the question of remedies.

9.73 Finally, it should be noted that ERA 1996, s 107 prevents a tribunal from taking into account any industrial pressure exerted on the employer to obtain the dismissal, when determining the reason for the dismissal: see para 9.186, below.

General rules: capability and qualifications

9.74 ERA 1996, s 98(3) defines 'capability' as 'capability assessed by reference to skill, aptitude, health or any other physical or mental quality', and 'qualifications' as 'any degree, diploma or other academic, technical or professional qualification relevant to the position which the employee held'. In *Shook v Ealing London Borough Council* (1986) the EAT stressed that under ERA 1996, s 98(2)(a) the reason for dismissal must relate to the employee's capacity and to the performance of his or her duties under the contract of employment. It is not necessary to show that the employee's incapacity (in this case disabilities caused by back trouble) would have affected the performance of all that he or she might be required to do under the contract.

9.75 This category of reason also embraces lack of capability. It should be viewed relatively narrowly as applying mainly to cases where the employee is incapable of satisfactory work; cases where a person has not come up to standard through his or her own carelessness, negligence, or idleness, are better dealt with as cases of conduct rather than capability. The difference is between 'sheer incapability due to an inherent incapacity to function' and 'a failure to exercise to the full such talent as is possessed': see *Sutton & Gates (Luton) Ltd v Boxall* (1978). See also *James v Waltham Holy Cross Urban District Council* (1973) and *Cook v Thomas Linnell & Sons Ltd* (1977). It should be noted that there is no distinction made for dismissal on capability grounds even where the incapability is due to the fault of the employer; however, if the incapability is caused by the employer then the employer is obliged to make concessions in retaining the employment of that employee, for example through considering alternative employment or accepting a longer period of sickness absence; see *McAdie v Royal Bank of Scotland* (2007).

General rules: conduct

9.76 There is no statutory definition of 'conduct'. Apart from the overlap between conduct and capability, conduct itself has been held to embrace a wide range of actions. Its scope includes gross misconduct, such as theft, violence, negligence, and working in competition with the employer, and lesser matters, such as clocking offences or swearing. What may be called 'off-duty' conduct will fall within this head, if it in some way bears upon the relationship between the employer and the employee, particularly where criminal offences are involved: see *Singh v London Country Bus Services Ltd* (1976), *Nottinghamshire County Council v Bowly* (1978), *Norfolk County Council v Bernard* (1978), *Moore v C & A Modes Ltd* (1981), and *P v Nottinghamshire County Council* (1992). See also *Perkins v St George's Healthcare HNS Trust* (2005).

General rules: redundancy

9.77 The definition of 'redundancy' is considered in Chapter 10, at para 10.5.

General rules: statutory requirements

9.78 ERA 1996, s 98(2)(d) provides that the fourth potentially fair reason is that 'the employee could not continue to work in the position which he held without contravention (either on his part or that of his employer) of a duty or restriction imposed by or under an enactment'. An example would be the loss of a driving licence in the case of a person employed as a driver, or a teacher declared unsuitable by the Department for Education and Skills: see *Sandhu v Department of Education and Science and London Borough of Hillingdon* (1978) and *Sutcliffe & Eaton Ltd v Pinney* (1977). The EAT has held, however, that the fact that the employers genuinely but erroneously believe that they will contravene a statutory requirement cannot be a reason falling within ERA 1996, s 98(2)(d), though it might be 'some other substantial reason': *Bouchaala v Trusthouse Forte Hotels Ltd* (1980). The fact that the continued employment of the employee contravenes a statutory requirement does not exonerate the employer from acting reasonably in accordance with ERA 1996, s 98(4).

General rules: some other substantial reason

9.79 The fifth category of reason is stated in ERA 1996, s 98(1)(b) to be 'some other substantial reason of a kind such as to justify the dismissal of an employee holding the position which the employee held'. This is a fairly wide category of reasons. The most common examples relate to the business needs of the employer and have tended to involve a refusal by the employee to agree to a change in contractual terms or a refusal to agree to a reorganisation falling short of redundancy: see *RS Components Ltd v Irwin* (1973) and *Hollister v National Farmers' Union* (1979). But this category is wide enough to embrace other reasons, for example the dismissal of one spouse as a result of the dismissal of the other; see *Kelman v Oran* (1983) and *Scottish and Newcastle Retail Ltd v Stanton and Durrant* (EAT 1126/96).

9.80   The Court of Appeal has considered this category of reason in a number of cases. It has held that it includes: dismissals instigated by a third party; the expiry and non-renewal of a fixed-term contract; the imposition of a sentence of imprisonment, a mistake as to the employee's intentions (brought about by his late notification to the employers that he had changed his mind about resigning); the lawful removal of the chief executive of a company from the board of the company following a takeover; and a breakdown in confidence between an employer and one of its senior executives: see *Dobie v Burns International Security Services (UK) Ltd* (1984), *North Yorkshire County Council v Fay* (1986), *Kingston v British Railways Board* (1984), *Ely v YKK Fasteners (UK) Ltd* (1994), *Cobley v Forward Technology Industries plc* (2003), and *Perkins v St George's Healthcare NHS Trust* (2005). In *Kent County Council v Gilham (No 2)* (1985), the Court of Appeal said the burden on the employer of showing a substantial reason is designed to deter employers from dismissing employees for some trivial or unworthy reason.

9.81   The Transfer of Undertakings (Protection of Employment) Regulations 2006 (TUPE), regulation 7(2) also provide that where, either before or after a relevant transfer, the employee is dismissed because of economic, technical, or organisational reasons entailing changes in the workforce of either the transferor or transferee, the dismissal will be treated as being for some other substantial reason; the tribunal will then have to consider section 98(4). Transfers of undertakings are considered more fully in Chapter 11.

Procedure leading to dismissal

9.82   Once a potentially fair reason under the ERA 1996 has been established, it is then necessary to consider whether the employer acted fairly in dismissing for that reason. Section 98(4) states as follows:

> the determination of the question whether the dismissal is fair or unfair (having regard to the reason shown by the employer) –

(a) depends on whether in the circumstances (including the size and administrative resources of the employer's undertaking) the employer acted reasonably or unreasonably in treating it as a sufficient reason for dismissing the employee, and

(b) shall be determined in accordance with equity and the substantial merits of the case.

9.83 The effect of section 98(4) is that there is no burden of proof on either the employer or the employee. It is therefore wrong for an employment tribunal to place the burden on the employer of satisfying them that he or she acted reasonably: *Post Office (Counters) Ltd v Heavey* (1990), *Boys and Girls Welfare Society v McDonald* (1996), and *Hackney LBC v Usher* (1997).

9.84 In this context it is worth reflecting upon what Aristotle had to say about the meaning of 'equity'.

> Equity, though just, is not legal justice, but a rectification of legal justice. The reason for this is that law is always a general statement, yet there are cases which it is not possible to cover in a general statement. In matters therefore where, while it is necessary to speak in general terms, it is not possible to do so correctly, the law takes into consideration the majority of cases, although it is not unaware of the error this involves. And this does not make it a wrong law; for the error is not in the law nor in the lawgiver, but in the nature of the case: the material of conduct is essentially irregular... This is the essential nature of the equitable: it is a rectification of law where law is defective because of its generality...
>
> (See Aristotle, *Nicomachean Ethics*, V.x.3 7)

The correct approach to reasonableness

9.85 The Court of Appeal has stressed that appeals to the EAT and beyond only lie on points of law and has discouraged attempts to dress up questions of fact as questions of law. But it is clear that the question of fairness cannot be considered solely as one of fact, and therefore unappealable. It is best described as a mixed question of fact and law. The tenor of the Court of Appeal decisions is to restrict considerably the circumstances in which appeals may be made to the EAT from employment tribunals' decisions and to discourage the EAT from reversing the tribunal's decisions because it would have reached a different conclusion. The case law in this area is extensive, but the main cases to be considered are: *Bailey v BP Oil (Kent Refinery) Ltd* (1980), *Thomas & Betts Manufacturing Ltd v Harding* (1980), *W & J Wass Ltd v Binns* (1982), *Woods v WM Car Services (Peterborough) Ltd* (1982), *O'Kelly v Trust-house Forte plc* (1983), *Martin v Glynwed Distribution Ltd* (1983), *Dobie v Burns International Security Services (UK) Ltd* (1984), *Gilham v Kent County Council (No 2)* (1985), and *Piggott Brothers & Co Ltd v Jackson* (1992).

9.86 In *Neale v Hereford and Worcester County Council* (1986) (at p 483) May LJ in the Court of Appeal said:

> Their [ie the employment tribunal's] job is to find the facts, and to apply the relevant law and to reach the conclusion to which their findings and their experience lead them. It will not...be often that when an employment tribunal has done just that, and with the care, clarity and thoroughness which the employment tribunal in the present case displayed, that one can legitimately say that their conclusion 'offends reason', or that their conclusion was one to which no reasonable employment tribunal could have come. Deciding these cases is the job of employment tribunals and when they have not erred in law neither the appeal tribunal nor this court should disturb their decision unless one can say in effect: 'My goodness, that was certainly wrong.'

9.87 This approach may be characterised as the 'reasonable decision' approach. It was summarised by Browne-Wilkinson J (as he then was) in *Iceland Frozen Foods Ltd v Jones* (1983) (at pp 24–25), in words quoted with approval by the Court of Appeal in *Neale's* case, above:

> The correct approach...is as follows:
>
> (1) the starting point should always be the words of section (98(4)) themselves;
>
> (2) in applying the section an employment tribunal must consider the reasonableness of the employer's conduct, not simply whether they (the members of the employment tribunal) consider the dismissal to be fair;
>
> (3) in judging the reasonableness of the employer's conduct an employment tribunal must not substitute its decision as to what was the right course to adopt for that of the employer;
>
> (4) in many, though not all, cases there is a band of reasonable responses to the employee's conduct within which one employer might take one view, another quite reasonably take another;
>
> (5) the function of the employment tribunal, as an industrial jury, is to determine whether in the particular circumstances of each case the decision to dismiss the employee fell within the band of reasonable responses which a reasonable employer might have adopted. If the dismissal falls within the band the dismissal is fair: if the dismissal falls outside the band, it is unfair.

9.88 In *Foley v Post Office* (2000), Mummery LJ robustly endorsed the *Iceland Frozen Foods* approach, saying that the decision itself, which had been approved and applied by the Court of Appeal, 'remains binding on this court, as well as on the employment tribunals and the Employment Appeal Tribunal'. He described the disapproval by the EAT of that approach as 'an unwarranted departure from authority'.

9.89 The tribunal must not substitute its own view for that of the employer. This point has been emphasised by decisions of the EAT, in *Beedell v West Ferry Printers Ltd* (2000), and the Court of Appeal, in *Foley v Post Office* (2000). This means that it is permissible for the tribunal to look at the employer's honest and genuine belief, but the belief must be upon reasonable grounds; see *St Anne's Board Mill Co Ltd v Brien;* (1973), *W Devis & Sons Ltd v Atkins* (1977), and *Alidair Ltd v Taylor* (1978).

9.90 The appellate courts have stressed that the relevant question is whether it was reasonable of the employer to dismiss the employee and that in many cases there may be a range of courses of action open to the employer, all of which fall within the band of reasonableness; for an employment tribunal to prefer one course of action to another will cause it to apply the test of what it would have done itself and not the test of what a reasonable employer would have done; see *British Leyland (UK) Ltd v Swift* (1981), *NC Watling & Co Ltd v Richardson* (1978), *Iceland Frozen Food Ltd v Jones* (1983), and *Neale v Hereford and Worcester County Council* (1986). See also *Whitbread & Co plc v Mills* (1988).

9.91 In deciding upon the fairness or otherwise of the dismissal, the tribunal must take into account any relevant provision of the Code of Practice on Disciplinary Practice and Procedures in Employment. In *W Devis & Sons Ltd v Atkins* (1977), Viscount Dilhorne said that non-compliance with the Code does not necessarily make a dismissal unfair, but that a failure to follow a procedure prescribed in the Code may lead to the conclusion that a dismissal was unfair, which, if that procedure had been followed, would have been held to have been fair. The decision of the EAT in *Lock v Cardiff Railway Company Ltd* (1998) appears to go further by suggesting that a failure by an employment tribunal to take into account the Code of Practice and to examine whether it has been complied with will vitiate the tribunal's decision. This cannot be right.

9.92 As the case law has developed over the years, adherence to the notion of procedural fairness has gained ground and considerable importance has been attached to it. It means that a dismissal may be made unfair by the use of an unfair procedure (eg lack of warnings or opportunity for the employee to state his or her side of the case), even where the reason is a perfectly good one. This was stressed by the House of Lords in its decision in *Polkey v AE Dayton Services Ltd* (1988), which has a particularly important bearing on the whole area of procedural fairness. The case involved the question whether a dismissal which would be unfair because of a failure to follow a fair procedure can be held to be fair if the employer is able to establish that following a fair procedure would have made no difference to the outcome. The House of Lords said that the correct question is whether the employer has been reasonable or unreasonable in deciding that the reason for dismissing the employee was a sufficient reason, not whether the employee would nevertheless have been dismissed even if there had been prior consultation or warning. Whether the employer could reasonably have concluded that consultation or warning would be useless so that the failure to consult or warn would not necessarily render the dismissal unfair was a matter for the employment tribunal to consider in the light of the circumstances known to the employer at the time of the decision to dismiss.

9.93 Lord Mackay of Clashfern LC, who gave the main speech, adopted the approach suggested by Browne-Wilkinson J in *Sillifant v Powell Duffryn Timber Ltd* (1983). In that case, the judge stressed that the only test of the fairness of a dismissal is the reasonableness of the employer's decision to dismiss, judged at the time at which the dismissal takes effect. He did suggest, however, that there may be rare cases 'where the offence is so heinous and the facts so manifestly clear that a reasonable employer could, on the facts known to him at the time of dismissal, take the view that whatever explanation the employee advanced it would make no difference...'. Browne-Wilkinson J went on to say that, if the decision to dismiss was unfair in the circumstances, but the observance of fair procedure would have made the dismissal fair, the correct approach would be for there to be a finding of unfair dismissal but a reduction in the employee's compensation.

9.94 The emphasis on procedural fairness, highlighted by this case, should not obscure the fact that it is as much about compensation as about procedural fairness. Effectively, the House of Lords is drawing attention to the fact that the observance of procedure is important but that, if the tribunal's judgment is that the outcome would have been a fair dismissal even had a fair procedure been observed, the issue becomes one of correctly reflecting that judgment in the measure of compensation.

9.95 This reflection makes one wonder whether the introduction of ERA 1996, s 98A(2) by the EA 2002, s 34(2), which was supposed to reverse the effect of the decision in *Polkey*, actually makes any difference. This new provision states that a failure by an employer to follow a procedure in relation to the dismissal of an employee 'shall not be regarded for the purposes of section 98(4) as by itself making the employer's action unreasonable if he shows that he would have decided to dismiss the employee if he had decided to follow the procedure'. This inelegant piece of drafting is largely meaningless and does not affect the position so far as compensation is concerned; see *Mason v Governing Body of Ward End Primary School* (2006) and *Alexander v Bridgen Enterprises Ltd* (2006). This provision is to be repealed by the EA 2008, with effect from 6 April 2009.

The effect of the incorporation of the European Convention on Human Rights

9.96 A question which has arisen in a number of cases in recent years is whether, and in what circumstances, the consideration of the fairness or otherwise of the dismissal requires the tribunal to take into account an employee's rights under the European Convention on Human Rights. In one of the earliest cases, *The Post Office v Liddiard* (2001), the Court of Appeal said, *obiter*, that it could see no reason why section 98(4) should be construed and applied in any way differently from the way it was before the Human Rights Act 1988 came into force. The incorporation of the European Convention took effect on 2 October 2000, when the Human Rights Act 1998 came into force. Since that decision, in 2001, the Court of Appeal has had the opportunity of considering this issue further.

9.97   The first case to consider this issue substantively was *X v Y* (2004). The facts, in brief, were that the employee worked for a charity which organised activities for young offenders. He was cautioned for an offence of gross indecency, but did not tell his employer. When some six months later the employer learned of the incident, he was dismissed for gross misconduct. Before the employment tribunal, the EAT and the Court of Appeal, he argued that his dismissal involved a breach of his rights under Articles 8 and 14. (Article 8 grants the right to respect for private and family life; Article 14 provides that the rights and freedoms set forth in the Convention 'shall be secured without discrimination'.) The tribunal concluded that his dismissal was fair; the EAT and the Court of Appeal dismissed his appeals. Mummery LJ said that the employee's conduct did not take place in his private life and was not within the scope of application of the right to respect for it. He said that Articles 8 and 14 were not, therefore, engaged and issues of incompatibility with the 1998 Act did not arise. He considered the interpretation of section 98 and said that, in general, a decision that a dismissal was fair would not be incompatible with Article 8 or 14. He went on to suggest that there may be cases, however, in which the 1998 Act point could make a difference to the reasoning of the tribunal. This would only arise where consideration of Article 8 might affect the outcome of the case. In that case, in accordance with section 3 of the 1998 Act, it would be necessary to read and give effect to section 98 of the 1996 Act so as to be compatible with Article 8. Mummery LJ's judgment is valuable for the guidance it gives in relation to cases containing a human rights element. See also the earlier EAT decision in *Pay v Lancashire Probation Service* (2004), whose facts are similar to those of *X v Y*, and *McGowan v Scottish Water* (2004).

9.98   The other Court of Appeal case to have considered the European Convention is *Copsey v WWB Devon Clays Ltd* (2005). The case involved a practising Christian who refused to agree to a change in his shift pattern which would involve Sunday working. He was offered a number of alternative jobs within the company but he refused because the company could not guarantee that he would not be required to work on a Sunday. He was eventually dismissed and claimed that he had been unfairly dismissed for exercising his right under Article 9 of the European

Convention (which gives the right to freedom of thought, conscience, and religion). The tribunal concluded that he had been fairly dismissed; the EAT and the Court of Appeal dismissed his appeals. Mummery LJ took the view that, in the light of decisions relating to Article 9, the Article was not engaged. Rix LJ, on the other hand, took the view that Article 9 was engaged, but that the employee's claim for unfair dismissal failed, whether or not viewed with reference to Article 9.

9.99 In the light of the cases considered above, it seems reasonable to conclude that, in general, even if an employee's rights under one or more of the Articles of the European Convention are engaged, the outcome of an unfair dismissal claim is unlikely to be affected. See Chapter 3 for a discussion of the European Convention on Human Rights and the Human Rights Act 1998.

Statutory right to be accompanied at disciplinary and grievance hearings

9.100 The Employment Relations Act 1999 (ERA 1999) gives a worker (as defined in s 13(1)–(3) of that Act) the right to be accompanied at a disciplinary or grievance hearing. It should be noted that this statutory right applies to meetings held under the statutory Dispute Resolution Procedures: see EA 2002, Sch 2, para 14.

9.101 Section 10 applies where a worker is 'required or invited' by the employer to attend a disciplinary or grievance hearing and 'reasonably requests' to be accompanied at the hearing. The employer must allow the worker to be accompanied by a single companion chosen by the worker. The companion must either be a trade union official, an official of a trade union reasonably certified in writing by the union as having experience of, or as having received training in, acting as a worker's companion at disciplinary or grievance hearings, or another of the employer's workers. In this last case, the employer should allow the fellow-worker reasonable time off during working hours to accompany the worker.

9.102 The employer must allow the companion to address the hearing (but not answer questions on the worker's behalf) and to confer with the worker during the hearing. ERA 1999, s 10(4) and (5) provide for the situation where the companion will not be available at the time chosen by the employer for the hearing. In that case the employer must postpone the hearing to the time proposed by the worker provided that it is reasonable and is within five working days beginning with the first working day after the day proposed by the employer. The definition of 'disciplinary hearing' has given rise to such case law as there is in relation to this right. Section 13(4) defines a disciplinary hearing as one which could result in 'the administration of a formal warning to a worker, . . . the taking of some other action in respect of a worker, or . . . the confirmation of warning issues or some other action taken'. In

London Underground Ltd v Ferenc-Batchelor (2003) the EAT said that sanctions in the form of training, coaching, or counselling did not amount to 'the taking of some other action...' within section 13(4). It went on to say that in certain circumstances an informal warning may amount to a formal warning. In that case, the hearing will be a disciplinary hearing and section 10 will come into play. In *Skiggs v South West Trains Ltd* (2005) the issue was whether a meeting held to investigate a formal grievance raised against an employee was a disciplinary hearing. The EAT held it was not, notwithstanding the fact that the matters to be discussed at the meeting could have led to some later disciplinary process against the employee; see also *Heathmill Multimedia ASP Ltd v Jones* (2003).

9.103 A worker who complains that the right has been infringed may present a complaint to an employment tribunal within three months of the date of the infringement or threatened infringement: ERA 1999, s 11(1) and (2). If the tribunal finds the complaint well-founded it must order the employer to pay compensation of up to two weeks' pay.

9.104 The final point to note is that the right not to be unfairly dismissed is extended to workers who exercise or seek to exercise their rights under section 10(2) or (4) and to workers who accompany or seek to accompany another worker: s 12(3). Further, the exclusions relating to length of employment and age (considered above at paras 9.3 and 9.7) do not apply. Section 12(6) specifically applies the unfair dismissal provisions to workers.

Procedural fairness: capability and qualifications

9.105 In cases involving unsatisfactory work performance, the employer must satisfy the employment tribunal that he or she honestly believed on reasonable grounds that the employee was incapable. A full and careful investigation of the facts should be undertaken; if, however, that is done, the employer does not have to satisfy the tribunal that he or she drew the correct conclusion, only that he or she had sufficient evidence upon which he or she could reach that conclusion; see *Alidair Ltd v Taylor* (1978) and *Cook v Thomas Linnell & Sons Ltd* (1977). It is necessary for the employer to follow a reasonable procedure, and, in particular, to give the employee a warning and an opportunity to improve, but a failure to do so will not automatically make the dismissal unfair, particularly if it can be shown that the employee is incapable of improving or already knows clearly what is expected, or that the giving of a warning would have made no difference to the result; see *Hollister v National Farmers' Union* (1979), *James v Waltham Holy Cross Urban District Council* (1973), and *AJ Dunning & Sons (Shopfitters) Ltd v Jacomb* (1973). In exceptional cases, it may not be necessary to follow a procedure, but that is only likely to be an option where the employee can be shown to be clearly incapable of improving or to know already what is expected: see *Cook v Thomas Linnell & Sons Ltd*, above.

9.106　When cases involving ill-health occur, particularly if the employee suffers from long-term or severe illness, the contract may be frustrated, in which case there will be no dismissal. This aspect has already been considered: see Chapter 4. The case law makes it clear that the employer must deal with ill employees carefully, particularly if the employee is suffering from mental illness, as in *O'Brien v Prudential Assurance Co Ltd* (1979). In cases of prolonged absence, the question is whether the employer can be expected to wait any longer, and, if so, how much longer: *Spencer v Paragon Wallpapers Ltd* (1977). Except in exceptional circumstances, the employee should be consulted and the employer should take reasonable steps to find out the true medical position, preferably by means of a sufficiently detailed medical report to enable an informed decision to be made: see *East Lindsey District Council v Daubney* (1977), *Williamson v Alcan (UK) Ltd* (1978), *A. Links & Co v Rose* (1991), and *Eclipse Blinds Ltd v Wright* (1992). The EAT has stressed that the decision to dismiss is managerial, not medical, but the employer should consider the possibility of offering alternative work within the employee's capabilities, if it is available: see *Merseyside and North Wales Electricity Board v Taylor* (1975).

9.107　In cases of persistent, intermittent absence for minor illness, the employer should conduct a fair review of the employee's attendance record and the reasons for it, and give the employee appropriate warnings and an opportunity to make representations. This type of situation was considered by the EAT in *Lynock v Cereal Packaging Ltd* (1988), in which the employee had a poor attendance record; see also *International Sports Co Ltd v Thomson* (1980).

9.108　A final point to note concerns claims made both under the Disability Discrimination Act 1995 and the unfair dismissal provisions. The EAT has pointed out that a tribunal should not hold a dismissal which is contrary to the DDA to be automatically unfair. They pointed out that it should be possible to have a disability-related dismissal which is not necessarily unfair, since the criteria applying under the DDA and the unfair dismissal provisions are different; see *HJ Heinz Co Ltd v Kenrick* (2000).

Procedural fairness: conduct

9.109　As with cases of unsatisfactory work performance, the employer must show that his or her view of the facts stemmed from an honest belief based upon reasonable grounds; it is also important to undertake a careful investigation which provides sufficient evidence for the conclusion reached: see *Trust House Forte Leisure Ltd v*

Aquilar (1976), *Cook v Thomas Linnell & Sons Ltd* (1977), and *Laughton and Hawley v Bapp Industrial Supplies Ltd* (1986). In *British Home Stores Ltd v Burchell* (1980) the EAT set out the following guidelines for tribunals to apply when dealing with cases of alleged misconduct:

> First . . . there must be established by the employer the fact of that belief; that the employer did believe it. Secondly, that the employer had in his mind reasonable grounds upon which to sustain that belief. And thirdly . . . that the employer at the stage at which he formed that belief on those grounds, had carried out as much investigation into the matter as was reasonable in all the circumstances of the case.

9.110   This approach was approved by the Court of Appeal in *W. Weddel & Co Ltd v Tepper* (1980). The *Burchell* case involved alleged dishonesty, but the test to which it has given its name is generally applied to those cases where the reason for the employee's dismissal is the employer's belief that there has been misconduct of some kind. The Court of Appeal has re-affirmed that the *Burchell* test 'remains binding on this court, as well as on employment tribunals and the Employment Appeal Tribunal. Any departure from that approach . . . is inconsistent with binding authority': see *Foley v Post Office* (2000).

9.111   It is particularly important to remember, when looking in detail at aspects of dismissal for conduct, that the overriding consideration for an employment tribunal is to decide whether the employer acted reasonably or unreasonably in dismissing the employee, within the requirements of ERA 1996, s 98(4). It is easy to allow decided cases and principles that are thought to be deducible from them to obscure the words used by the statute. It is also easy to forget that the decision in many cases depends on the facts as found by the tribunal. It is tempting to argue that, because a tribunal or another division of the EAT has decided a factual issue in a particular way, a subsequent tribunal should decide a similar factual issue in the same way. It is seldom that the facts of two different cases arising from different contexts are identical. It follows that two different tribunals may reach opposite conclusions on similar sets of facts, without either committing an error of law, simply because it is for each tribunal to decide, on the facts in front of it, whether that employer's decision to dismiss that employee in those circumstances was reasonable or unreasonable. It is essential to concentrate upon the necessarily general words of s 98(4) and the Code of Practice. A tribunal should not allow itself 'to be diverted into the channels created by judicial decisions' but should 'drink at the pure waters of the section': see Waite J in *Siggs and Chapman (Contractors) Ltd v Knight* (1984). In *Walls Meat Co Ltd v Khan* (1979), Lord Denning MR complained that 'if we are not careful, we shall find the [employment] tribunals bent down under the weight of the law books or, what is worse, asleep under them'.

9.112   In considering an employer's conduct of an investigation, an employment tribunal will generally follow the three-stage approach set out in *Burchell*'s case above, and widely followed. In *Scottish Daily Record & Sunday Mail (1986) Ltd v Laird* (1996) IRLR 665, for example, the Court of Session said that the employment tribunal had not erred in holding that the employee's dismissal was unfair because the employers had failed to satisfy the *Burchell* test. The Court pointed out that, although there is no burden on the employer to satisfy the tribunal that it acted reasonably, the employer is still required to produce some evidence to show that the requirements described at each of the three stages of the test were satisfied. In *Sainsbury's Supermarkets Ltd v Hitt* (2003) the Court of Appeal emphasised that the range of reasonable responses test applies as much to the question whether an investigation is reasonable in all the circumstances as it does to the reasonableness of the decision to dismiss. See also *Panama v London Borough of Hackney* (2003), in which the Court of Appeal held that the tribunal had not properly applied the second and third limbs of the *Burchell* test.

9.113   Problems of procedural fairness arise where an employer conducts an investigation but cannot identify the persons responsible for the acts in question. In such a case, the issue is whether it is reasonable for the employer to engage in 'blanket dismissals' and dismiss all the possible suspects even if some of them are innocent. The dismissal may be fair, but the employment tribunal must be satisfied that the employer conducted a proper investigation: see *Whitbread & Co plc v Thomas* (1988), in which the EAT applied *Monie v Coral Racing Ltd* (1981) (CA); see also *Parr v Whitbread plc, t/a Threshers Wine Merchants* (1990) and *Santamera v Express Cargo Forwarding t/a/ IEC Ltd* (2003).

9.114   Other issues which have arisen in the context of investigations have been the use of anonymous informants and the withholding of witness statements from the employee under threat of dismissal. In these, as in other types of case, the overriding consideration, which has been emphasised regularly by the higher courts, is that the employer must have acted reasonably. See, for examples, the following cases: *Morgan v Electrolux Ltd* (1991), *A v Company B Ltd* (1997) IRLR 405, and *Louies v Coventry Hood & Seating Co Ltd* (1990), distinguished by the Court of Appeal in the later case of *Hussain v Elonex plc* (1999). In *Louies* the substance of the case was contained in statements which the employee had asked to see but which had not been shown to him, with no good reason being shown, and on which substantial reliance had been placed by the employers in reaching the decision to dismiss him; in the *Hussain* case, on the other hand, although the employers failed to disclose to the employee the existence of statements obtained from independent witnesses in relation to the incident which led to his dismissal, nevertheless he was told of the accusations against him and given a full opportunity to respond to them.

Mummery LJ pointed out that 'there are no hard and fast rigid rules to be adopted in these cases...What matters is fairness and reasonableness.'

9.115 Issues of fairness also arise where the employer treats employees differently (eg by dismissing one and not another). In that case the dismissal will not be held to be unfair provided that the decision was one which a reasonable employer could reach. In such a case, however, the tribunal will commit an error of law if it substitutes its own view of the facts and the conclusions to be drawn from them for those of the employer: see *Securicor Ltd v Smith* (1989), which involved two employees one of whom was dismissed (his appeal being disallowed by the employers' appeal panel) whereas the other was reinstated by the appeal panel with a final warning, and *Cain v Leeds Western Health Authority* (1990), *Frames Snooker Centre v Boyce* (1992), and *London Borough of Harrow v Cunningham* (1996). Similar considerations arise where the employee in question is dismissed for an offence (eg assaulting another employee) but there is evidence that in the past other employees have not been dismissed for a similar offence: see *Procter v British Gypsum Ltd* (1991) and *Paul v East Surrey District Health Authority* (1995). In this last case the Court of Appeal stressed that in cases of this kind ultimately the question for the employer is whether in the particular case dismissal is a reasonable response to the misconduct; it warned that tribunals should scrutinise arguments based upon disparity of treatment with particular care.

9.116 These considerations do not only apply to disparate treatment between one individual and another; they may also apply to the treatment of a single individual. Thus, it is open to a tribunal to decide that the employer's response is disproportionate to the offence committed by the employee, with the consequence that the decision to dismiss falls outside the band of reasonable response of a reasonable employer: see *Strouthos v London Underground Ltd* (2004), in which the employee used a company car for private purposes without permission. The Court of Appeal said that it was relevant to take into account in this case the length of the employee's service in the circumstances, whilst acknowledging that there may be cases where the conduct is so serious that dismissal is appropriate irrespective of length of service.

9.117 Procedural fairness is particularly important in cases of conduct, though the requirements are not absolute. Generally, the employer should go through a procedure appropriate to the nature and size of the organisation and a failure to do so, except in the exceptional cases considered below, will cause the dismissal to be unfair. A failure to apply a procedure, however, will not cause the dismissal to be unfair, for example if the employee shows himself to be 'determined to go his own way' or has taken up a position which is unlikely to be altered by being given a hearing: see *Retarded Children's Aid Society Ltd v Day* (1978) and *James v Waltham*

Holy Cross Urban District Council (1973). But it is important to bear in mind that the decision in *Polkey*'s case means that in most cases such questions are not generally relevant.

9.118 The procedure will probably involve the application of the employer's disciplinary rules, which should make clear what amounts to an offence and what the result of a breach of the rules will be, and they should have been brought sufficiently to the employee's notice. If there are no rules, or the rules make no provision for the particular offence, the provisions of the Code of Practice will be relevant. In most cases (with the exception of a dismissal for a single act of gross misconduct), the employer should employ a warnings system, eg an oral warning followed by a written warning and then by a final written warning specifying that a further recurrence will lead to dismissal. The employee should also be interviewed and given the opportunity to state his or her case; he or she should also be told of any right to appeal.

9.119 In cases involving allegations of criminal offences, the employer does not have to prove the employee's guilt and, provided his or her belief is genuine and reasonable, the dismissal of the employee will not be made unfair by the latter's subsequent acquittal: see *Da Costa v Optolis Ltd* (1977). This is likely also to be the case where an employee accused of a crime pleads guilty and the employer refuses to accept the explanation that he or she was not guilty but had bowed to pressure to plead guilty to avoid a prison sentence. In such a case, the question is whether on the facts which were known or ought to have been known to the employers, they genuinely believed on reasonable grounds that the employee was guilty. If the procedure by which the employers reached their conclusion was faulty, they will have failed to act reasonably. In the absence of any lapse of procedure, it is an error of law for the employment tribunal to seek to reopen the factual issues on the basis of which the employers reached their conclusion: see *British Gas plc v McCarrick* (1991) and also *P v Nottinghamshire County Council* (1992) and *McLaren v National Coal Board* (1988).

Procedural fairness: redundancy

9.120 There are two possible types of complaints of unfair dismissal for redundancy. The first, and most common, type occurs where the employee complains that the way the redundancy dismissal was handled was unfair and therefore contrary to ERA 1996, s 98(4). The second type of complaint occurs where an employee dismissed for redundancy argues that he or she was selected for redundancy for one of the reasons which may cause a dismissal to be automatically unfair. These reasons are set out in para 9.131, below.

9.121 If the tribunal is satisfied that the reason was redundancy, it is likely that the dismissal will be held to be fair, unless the employer acts with blatant unfairness.

Although in recent years the EAT has shown greater preparedness to hold a dismissal for redundancy unfair, by emphasising standards of good industrial relations practice, it has expressed the view that, provided the selection process is fair, an employment tribunal should scrutinise critically a complaint that the dismissal was unfair on some other grounds: see *Williams v Compair Maxam Ltd* (1982), *Freud v Bentalls Ltd* (1983), *Grundy (Teddington) Ltd v Plummer and Salt* (1983), and *Stacey v Babcock Power Ltd (Construction Division)* (1986). Further, if the employee would still have been made redundant had the employer taken reasonable steps to consult with the employee or find him or her other employment, the tribunal may either find that the dismissal was fair or order that (if it was unfair) no compensation, other than the basic award, should be paid. In such a case, in view of the House of Lords' decision in *Polkey v A E Dayton Services Ltd*, para 9.92 above, the tribunal would normally find the dismissal unfair and award no compensation, though it is open to them to find that the employer could reasonably have concluded that consultation or warning would be useless so that the failure to consult or warn in the light of the circumstances known to the employer at the time the decision to dismiss was taken was not unreasonable. A tribunal may also conclude that, on the facts as found by it, the dismissal was unfair, but that, had a fair procedure been followed, the employee could have been fairly dismissed within a given period of time. In that case, it may confine the period of loss, for the purposes of assessing compensation, to that period of time.

9.122 A further alternative is that the tribunal may conclude that the dismissal was unfair, but that, had the employer gone through a fair procedure, the employee would have stood a chance of being fairly dismissed at the end of the procedure. If the tribunal reaches such a decision, it may go on to reduce the compensation by the relevant percentage. It is important, however, that the tribunal should consider what would have been the result if the proper procedure had been followed: see *Red Bank Manufacturing Co Ltd v Meadows* (1992).

9.123 The two main obligations laying upon an employer proposing to dismiss an employee for redundancy are to make reasonable efforts, where practicable, to find him or her suitable alternative employment in the undertaking, or, where appropriate, with an associated employer and to consult with him or her and give reasonable warning of impending redundancy: see *Vokes Ltd v Bear* (1974), *Thomas & Betts Manufacturing Ltd v Harding* (1980), and *Williams v Compair Maxam Ltd* (1982), which contains a particularly useful discussion of this area. In *Langston v Cranfield University* (1998) the EAT said that an employment tribunal should consider the two questions of failure to seek alternative employment on the part of the employee and lack of consultation; it should also consider the fairness of the selection. A failure to do so will amount to an error.

9.124 The important decision of the House of Lords in *Polkey v A E Dayton Services Ltd* is the general starting-point for a consideration of the employer's obligations when dismissing for redundancy. It was considered above, at para 9.92. The principles considered in *Polkey* were followed by the Court of Appeal in *Duffy v Yeomans & Partners Ltd* (1995). It said that the test of reasonableness under what is now section 98(4) is objective and it is not necessary for an employer to have applied his or her mind to the question of consultation for a dismissal without consultation to be within the range of reasonable responses under section 98(4). Although normally a dismissal will be unfair where there has been no consultation, the effect of a failure to consult is a matter of fact and degree for the employment tribunal. This view is consistent with the House of Lords' decision in *Polkey*'s case and, it is submitted, is correct in taking the view that each case must be decided on its own facts, bearing in mind the general proposition that normally an employer will not act reasonably unless he or she goes through the appropriate procedure.

9.125 The courts have thus continued to emphasise the need for prior consultation and warning, and have been reluctant to find exceptional circumstances which would obviate this requirement. These requirements are not avoided by the fact that the employers are a small company or that immediate decisions needed to be made: see *Heron v Citilink-Nottingham* (1993). More recently, in *Mugford v Midland Bank plc* (1997), the EAT reviewed the position regarding consultation and said this:

(1) Where no consultation about redundancy has taken place with either the trade union or the employee the dismissal will normally be unfair, unless the employment tribunal finds that a reasonable employer would have concluded that consultation would be an utterly futile exercise in the particular circumstances of the case.

(2) Consultation with the trade union over selection criteria does not of itself release the employer from considering with the employee individually his being identified for redundancy.

(3) It will be a question of fact and degree for the employment tribunal to consider whether consultation with the individual and/or his union was so inadequate as to render the dismissal unfair. A lack of consultation in any particular respect will not automatically lead to that result. The overall picture must be viewed by the tribunal up to the date of termination to ascertain whether the employer has or has not acted reasonably in dismissing the employee on the grounds of redundancy.

Procedural fairness rules: statutory requirements

9.126 The fact that the employer shows that it is not possible to continue to employ the employee in the particular job he or she does, without contravening a statutory requirement, does not mean that there is no need to go through a fair procedure before dismissing the employee: see *Sutcliffe and Eaton Ltd v Pinney* (1977) and *Sandhu v Department of Education and Science and London Borough of Hillingdon* (1978).

Procedural fairness: some other substantial reason

9.127   The two main areas which have evolved through the cases are reorganisations which fall short of redundancy, and changes in the employee's terms of employment, though this category of reason is wide enough to embrace other matters, for example the dismissal of one spouse as a result of the dismissal of the other: see *Kelman v Oram* (1983) and *Scottish and Newcastle Retail Ltd v Stanton and Durrant* (EAT 1126/96). They show the difficulty of drawing the line between fairness and unfairness where there is a clear conflict between the employer's legitimate business interests and the employee's contractual rights, since the employee's contract is static and, prima facie, he or she can insist upon continued performance of it as it stands.

9.128   In *Hollister v National Farmers' Union* (1979) the Court of Appeal said that, provided that the employment tribunal has found that there was a substantial reason justifying dismissal, it is not necessary for the employers to consult the employee about the reorganisation of the business. All that needs to be shown is a sound commercial reason for making the reorganisation. In *Labour Party v Oakley* (1988), by way of contrast, the Court of Appeal held that the dismissal of an employee because of a reorganisation was unfair. Although the reorganisation was a substantial reason of a kind to justify the dismissal, what made the dismissal unfair was that the employers used the reorganisation as a pretext for her dismissal when they had already decided not to renew her fixed-term contract; see also *Bowater Containers Ltd v McCormack* (1980), *Genower v Ealing, Hammersmith and Hounslow Area Health Authority* (1980), *Ladbroke Courage Holidays Ltd v Asten* (1981), and *Richmond Precision Engineering Ltd v Pearce* (1985).

9.129   Often, but not always, allied with reorganisations are unilateral changes in the terms of the employee's contract, which raise difficult issues of law and practice. It is clear that the rules of procedural fairness apply here too, despite the apparent tendency of the EAT and Court of Appeal to favour employers. See, for example, *RS Components Ltd v Irwin* (1973), *St John of God (Care Services) Ltd v Brooks* (1992), and *Willow Oak Developments Ltd (trading as Windsor Recruitment) v Silverwood* (2006).

Automatically unfair dismissals

9.130   In the preceding sections, the general rules of unfair dismissal were considered. These are the rules which generally apply to dismissals for what have been called the 'potentially fair' reasons. In this section, 'automatically unfair' dismissals are considered. They are so called because they are dismissals in circumstances such that statute has decreed that the ordinary considerations of fairness are overridden and thus do not arise. The cases where this happens are essentially cases where the legislature has taken the view that their importance is such as to justify treating them as special cases and to dispense with the usual qualifications of length of employment and age. It is interesting to note that the categories of automatically unfair dismissal have been regularly expanded over the years. In the early days of the unfair dismissal right, the only type of dismissal to be treated as automatically unfair was a dismissal in relation to trade union membership and activities. The thinking behind the development of these categories is not obvious.

9.131 The following types of dismissal are treated as automatically unfair:

(1) dismissals in connection with trade union membership and activities, or trade union recognition;

(2) dismissal for participation in official industrial action;

(3) dismissal of an employee in connection with leave for family reasons (including paternity and adoption leave);

(4) dismissal for reasons connected with health and safety;

(5) dismissal of a shop or betting worker for refusing Sunday work;

(6) dismissal in connection with an employee's rights under the Working Time Regulations;

(7) dismissal for reasons relating to an employee's performance of his or her duties as an occupational pension fund trustee;

(8) dismissal for reasons relating to an employee's performance of his or her duties as an employee representative;

(9) dismissal for making a 'protected disclosure';

(10) dismissal for assertion of a statutory right;

(11) dismissal of an employee in connection with the national minimum wage legislation;

(12) dismissal in connection with an employee's rights under the Tax Credits Act 1999;

(13) dismissals of employees arising under paragraph 28 of the Transnational Information and Consultation of Employees Regulations 1999;

(14) dismissals arising under regulation 7 of the Part-Time Workers (Prevention of Less Favourable Treatment) Regulations 2000;

(15) dismissals in connection with jury service;

(16) dismissals in connection with flexible working;

(17) dismissals arising under regulation 6 of the Fixed-Term Employees (Prevention of Less Favourable Treatment) Regulations 2002;

(18) dismissals of members of special negotiating bodies (and similar) of European public limited-liability companies under regulation 42 of the European Public Limited-Liability Company Regulations 2004;

(19) dismissals of information and consultation representatives under regulation 30 of the Information and Consultation of Employees Regulations 2004;

(20) dismissals of a worker in connection with the statutory right to be accompanied at a disciplinary or grievance hearing.

9.132 In cases (1)–(19), a selection for redundancy for one of those reasons may also make the dismissal for redundancy automatically unfair: see TULRCA 1992, s 153, and ERA 1996, s 105 (as amended). The first, fourth, ninth, and tenth cases will be considered in more detail since they have given rise to such case law as there is. Dismissals which are made automatically unfair by section 98A of the ERA 1996 because the employer has failed to comply with the requirements of a statutory disciplinary procedure are considered at paras 9.45–9.55, in the context of the discussion there of those procedures. It should be noted that employees to whom section 98A applies are not exempted from the requirement of one year's continuous service; they also remain subject to the requirement that they be below the normal retirement age. For a more detailed analysis of the statutory provisions relating to all the cases, reference should be made to Upex, *The Law of Termination of Employment* (7th ed, 2006), chapter 5.

Dismissals in connection with union membership or activities and recognition of unions

9.133 In this section two types of dismissal will be considered: (i) dismissals in connection with trade union membership and activities; and (ii) dismissals in connection with trade union recognition. This second type of dismissal arises as a result of the introduction of procedures relating to union recognition by the Employment Relations Act 1999.

9.134 Section 152(1) of the Trade Union and Labour Relations (Consolidation) Act 1992 (TULRCA) (as amended by the Employment Relations Act 2004) provides that a dismissal, or a selection for dismissal for redundancy, will be automatically unfair if the reason for it is one of the following:

(1) membership, or proposed membership, of an 'independent trade union';

(2) participation, or proposed participation, in its 'activities' at an 'appropriate time';

(3) making use of, or proposing to make use of trade union services (as defined) at an appropriate time;

(4) failing to accept an offer made in contravention of section 145A or 145B of TULRCA (which relate to inducements relating to trade union membership and activities and inducements relating to collective bargaining); and

(5) non-membership of any trade union, or of a particular trade union, or of one of a number of particular trade unions, or refusal or proposed refusal of such membership.

9.135 In the case of a dismissal, or a selection for redundancy, for one of these reasons, employees are protected whether or not they have been continuously employed for one year or have reached retirement age: TULRCA 1992, s 154(1). Further, they may be entitled to higher compensation and interim relief.

9.136 A trade union will be an 'independent trade union', and thus within section 152, if it satisfies the definition set out in section 235(1) of the ERA 1996. Two requirements need to be satisfied: (1) the trade union is not under the domination or control of an employer or a group of employers or of one or more employers' associations; and (2) the trade union 'is not liable to interference by an employer or any such group or association (arising out of the provision of financial or material support or by any other means whatsoever) tending towards such control'. See *Blue Circle Staff Association v Certification Officer* (1977), *Association of HSD (Hatfield) Employees v Certification Officer* (1978), *Squibb United Kingdom Staff Association v Certification Officer* (1979), and *Government Communications Staff Federation v Certification Officer* (1993) and see Chapter 10 for further detail.

9.137 Section 152(3) of the 1992 Act treats as falling within section 152(1)(c), above: (a) an employee's refusal, or proposed refusal, to comply with a requirement (whether or not imposed by the contract or in writing) that, in the event of a failure to become or ceasing to remain a member of a trade union or one of a number of trade unions, he or she must make one or more payments; and (b) an objection, or proposed objection, to the operation of a provision under which, in the event mentioned in (a), the employer is entitled to deduct one or more sums from his or her pay.

9.138 The Court of Appeal has said that section 152 is not concerned with an employer's reactions to a trade union's activities but with the employer's reactions to an individual employee's activities. If, therefore, a dismissal has nothing to do with anything the employee has personally done or proposed to do, section 152 will not apply: see *Carrington v Therm-a-Stor Ltd* (1983) and *Discount Tobacco & Confectionery Ltd v Armitage* (1990).

9.139 The provisions of section 152 apply only to dismissals for the reasons set out above. A distinction, not always easy to draw, needs to be made between such dismissals and dismissals for industrial action. In *Drew v St Edmundsbury Borough Council* (1980), for example, the employee, who was a trade union member, was dismissed after he had been employed for less than the qualifying period of continuous employment (at the material time, 26 weeks) for repeatedly complaining to his employers about health and safety matters. Although he purported to be following a trade union directive to go slow, the directive was not concerned with health and safety matters. The employment tribunal decided that he was not dismissed for taking part in trade union activities but for taking part in industrial action. He therefore had not been continuously employed for long enough. The EAT upheld their decision.

9.140 The first type of dismissal falling within section 152(1) is one where the reason for the dismissal is that the employee 'was...a member of an independent trade union'. In *Discount Tobacco & Confectionery Ltd v Armitage* (1990) Knox J said:

> [T]he activities of a trade union officer in negotiating and elucidating terms of employment is...the outward and visible manifestation of trade union membership. It is an incident of union membership which is, if not the primary one, at any rate, a very important one and we see no genuine distinction between membership of a union on the one hand and making use of the essential services of a union, on the other. Were it not so, the scope of section (152(1)(a)) would be reduced almost to vanishing point, since it would only be just the fact that a person was a member of a union, without regard to the consequences of that membership, that would be the subject matter of that statutory provision and, it seems to us, that to construe that paragraph so narrowly would really be to emasculate the provision altogether.

This approach was described by the Court of Appeal as 'unquestionably correct' in *Associated British Ports v Palmer* (1994); see also *Speciality Care plc v Pachela* (1996).

9.141 Section 152(1)(b) uses the phrase 'activities of an independent trade union'. This should not be interpreted restrictively but should be interpreted reasonably; it embraces an employee's participation in trade union activities during the course of his or her previous employment: see *Dixon v West Ella Developments Ltd* (1978) and *Fitzpatrick v British Railways Board* (1992). In *Britool Ltd v Roberts* (1993) the EAT said that actual participation in a strike, whether as a leader or otherwise, will rarely if ever constitute an activity within section 152(1)(b). But, since leading a strike involves not only leading the strike when it is in operation but a preliminary planning and consultation stage, those preliminary activities may be within the provision. In *Lyon v St James's Press* (1976), Phillips J said of acts claimed to come within the protection: 'wholly unreasonable, extraneous or malicious acts done in support of trade union activities might be a ground for a dismissal which might not be unfair'. See also *Bass Taverns Ltd v Burgess* (1995), which involved the dismissal of an employee who had made disparaging remarks about the company at an induction course for trainee managers, and *Chant v Aquaboats Ltd* (1978), in which the EAT said that 'activities of an independent trade union' do not include an individual's independent activities as a trade unionist and held that the organising of a petition about safety standards, which was vetted by the local branch of the union before being handed to the employers, was not a trade union activity within the Act.

9.142 TULRCA 1992, s 152(2) defines 'appropriate time' as a time which is either outside an employee's working hours or 'is a time within his working hours at which, in accordance with arrangements agreed with or consent given by his employer, it is permissible for him to take part' in the activities. 'Working hours' means any time at which an employee is required to be at work in accordance with the contract of employment; see *Marley Tile Co Ltd v Shaw* (1980) and *Zucker v Astrid Jewels Ltd* (1978). See Chapter 12 for further detail.

9.143 The second type of dismissal considered here is dismissal in connection with trade union recognition. Employees dismissed or selected for redundancy for one of the reasons set out below will be treated as automatically unfairly dismissed. Further, in the case of a dismissal, or a selection for redundancy, for one of these reasons, employees are protected whether or not they have been continuously employed for one year or have reached retirement age; see TULRCA 1992, Sch A1, paras 161 and 164. The reasons are as follows:

(a) the employee acted with a view to obtaining or preventing recognition of a union or unions by the employer under Schedule A1 of the TULRCA 1992;

(b) the employee indicated that he or she supported or did not support recognition of a union or unions;

(c) the employee acted with a view to securing or preventing the ending under the Schedule of bargaining arrangements;

(d) the employee indicated that he or she supported or did not support the ending of bargaining arrangements;

(e) the employee influenced or sought to influence the way in which votes were to be cast by other workers in a ballot arranged under Schedule A1;

(f) the employee influenced or sought to influence other workers to vote or abstain from voting in such a ballot;

(g) the employee voted in such a ballot;

(h) the employee proposed to do, failed to do, or proposed to decline to do, any of the things referred to above.

9.144　A reason will not fall within the above list if it constitutes an unreasonable act or omission by the employee: see TULRCA 1992, Sch A1, para 161(3). The dismissal of an employee selected for redundancy will be automatically unfair, by virtue of TULRCA 1992, Sch A1, para 162, if it is shown that:

> (a) the circumstances constituting the redundancy applied equally to one or more other employees in the same undertaking who held positions similar to that held by the employee and who have not been dismissed by the employer; and

> (b) the reason why the employee was selected was one of the reasons listed above.

Dismissals in health and safety cases

9.145　ERA 1996, s 100 governs these types of dismissal. As with the other types of automatically unfair dismissals, for employees covered by this provision there is no minimum qualifying period of continuous employment; nor are they excluded if they are over the normal retirement age: ERA 1996, ss 108(3) and 109(2). A preliminary point to note is that the person claiming unfair dismissal in these circumstances must be an employee of the employer: see *Costain Building & Civil Engineering Ltd v Smith and Chanton Group plc* (2000), considered at para 4.31. The claimant was an engineer who was supplied by an agency to Costain. He claimed that he had become an employee of Costain and, when his services were dispensed with, that he had been unfairly dismissed by them contrary to ERA 1996, s 100(1)(b). The EAT held that he did not become an employee of Costain and that therefore he could not complain of unfair dismissal.

9.146　It should be noted that selection for redundancy for any of the reasons set out in this section will also be automatically unfair: s 105(1) and (3). An employee dismissed for one of the reasons set out below may apply to the employment tribunal for interim relief under section 128. It should be noted that the statutory limit for a compensatory award of compensation does not apply to these types of unfair dismissal: s 124(1A).

9.147　Section 100(1) provides that the dismissal of an employee will be automatically unfair if the reason (or principal reason) for it is one of the six reasons specified in that subsection. The burden of proving that a dismissal was for health and safety reasons is on the employee: see *Tedeschi v Hosiden Besson Ltd* (EAT/959/95). Where there is more than one possible reason for the dismissal, the tribunal must determine what was the principal reason for the dismissal. The six reasons set out in section 100(1) are as follows:

(1) The employee carried out, or proposed to carry out activities in connection with preventing or reducing risks to health and safety at work, after being designated by the employer to do so.

(2) The employee, as a workers' representative on health and safety matters or member of a safety committee, performed, or proposed to perform, any functions as such a representative or committee member, in accordance with arrangements established under or by virtue of any enactment or by reason of being acknowledged as representative or committee member by the employer.

(3) The employee took part (or proposed to take part) in consultations with the employer pursuant to the Health and Safety (Consultation with Employees) Regulations 1996 or in the election of safety representatives (whether as a candidate or otherwise).

(4) In the case of employees at a place where there was no workers' representative or safety committee or, where there was a representative or a committee, but it was not reasonably practicable for the employees to raise the matter by those means, they brought to the employer's attention by reasonable means circumstances connected with their work which they reasonably believed were harmful or potentially harmful to health and safety.

(5) There were circumstances of danger which the employee reasonably believed to be serious and imminent, and which he or she could not reasonably be expected to avert, and he or she left, proposed to leave, or (while the danger persisted) refused to return to, the place of work or any dangerous part of it.

(6) There were circumstances of danger which the employee reasonably believed to be serious and imminent and he or she took, or proposed to take, appropriate steps to protect himself or herself or other persons from the danger. Whether the steps were appropriate is to be judged by reference to all the circumstances including, in particular, his or her knowledge and the facilities and advice available to him or her at the time: s 100(2). In the case of a dismissal for this reason, the dismissal will not be automatically unfair if the employer shows that it was (or would have been) so negligent for the employee to take the steps which he or she took, or proposed to take, that a reasonable employer might have dismissed him or her for taking, or proposing to take them: s 100(3).

9.148 The first two cases set out above relate only to the defined activities of safety representatives, employees with designated health and safety functions, and members of safety committees. An employee will only be protected by these provisions, however, if he or she is a representative in respect of the area where the health and safety complaint arises: see *Shillito v Van Leer (UK) Ltd* (1997). In *Goodwin v Cabletel Ltd* (1998), the EAT said that it is open to a tribunal to consider whether the manner in which the employee approached the health and safety problem took him or her outside the scope of his or her health and safety activities. They said:

The protection afforded to the way in which a designated employee carries out his health and safety activities must not be diluted by too easily finding acts done for that purpose to be a justification for dismissal; on the other hand, not every act, however malicious or irrelevant to the task in hand, must necessarily be treated as a protected act in circumstances where dismissal would be justified on legitimate grounds.

9.149 The fourth case covers any employee, provided that he or she has gone through any safety committee or representative where possible, unless it is not reasonably practicable to do so. Employees who take the issue into their own hands run the risk, therefore, of falling outside section 100(1)(c). In a case covered by this provision, the employee must show that he or she reasonably believed that the circumstances were harmful or potentially harmful to health or safety. In *Balfour Kilpatrick Ltd v Acheson* (2003) the EAT said that for this provision to come into play three conditions need to be satisfied: (1) it is necessary to show that it was not reasonably practicable for the employee to raise the health and safety matters through the safety representative or safety committee; (2) the employee must have brought to the employer's attention by reasonable means the circumstances that he or she believes are harmful or potentially harmful to health and safety; and (3) the reason for the dismissal must be the fact that the employee was exercising his or her rights. The EAT said that, in considering the first requirement, it would be artificial if, when drawing matters of serious and imminent concern to the employer, employees must concern themselves with the appropriate route by which that information is conveyed. The EAT said that the tribunal was entitled to find that it was reasonable for the employees to raise their concerns through their union representatives, even though it would have been practicable to use the safety representatives as the channel of communication. See also *Kerr v Nathan's Wastesavers Ltd* (EAT/91/95), which involved an employee who was dismissed for refusing to drive a vehicle which, in his opinion, might become overloaded by the end of the working day. The EAT said that the duty placed on the employee to show reasonable belief should not be too heavy, since the purpose of the legislation is to protect employees who raise matters of health and safety. The EAT nevertheless upheld the tribunal's decision that the case should be dismissed on the grounds that, although the employee's belief was genuine, it was not based on reasonable grounds.

9.150 *Harvest Press Ltd v McCaffrey* (1999) is a decision on the fifth type of health and safety dismissal above, under section 100 (1)(d). The employee left his workplace in the middle of a shift because of the abusive behaviour of a fellow-employee which made him fear for his safety. He was dismissed for walking out in the middle of a shift. The EAT upheld the employment tribunal's decision that the dismissal fell within section 100(1)(d) and said that dangers caused by fellow-employees are within the wider scope of that provision. They said that 'danger' is used in the provision without any limitation and is intended to cover any danger, however arising.

9.151 Employees who are tempted to report a health and safety matter to an outside body such as the Health and Safety Executive again run the risk of putting themselves outside section 100. In such a case, the question would be whether the case was covered by section 100(1)(e) and whether the steps taken by the employee were 'appropriate steps to protect himself or other persons from the danger'. Again, the question would arise as to whether the employee should have raised the issue internally with a safety official or the employer before taking more serious action. In *Masiak v City Restaurants (UK) Ltd* (1999), a chef who was dismissed for refusing to cook food which he considered unfit for human consumption complained of unfair dismissal under section 100(1)(e). The tribunal said that the phrase 'other persons' relates only to fellow-employees. The EAT allowed his appeal and said that the statutory provisions are not limited in this way.

Dismissals and protected disclosures ('whistleblowing')

9.152 Section 103A provides that a dismissal will be automatically unfair if the reason (or principal reason) is that the employee made a 'protected disclosure'. It is not necessary for employees covered by this provision to serve a minimum qualifying period of employment; nor are employees over the normal retiring age excluded: ss 108(3) and 109(2). Selection for redundancy on these grounds is also automatically unfair: s 105(1) and (6A). The present legislation derives from the Public Interest Disclosure Act 1998, which inserted the unfair dismissal provisions discussed in this section into the ERA 1996.

9.153 An employee dismissed for a reason set out above may apply to the employment tribunal for interim relief under s 128(1). It should be noted that the statutory limit for a compensatory award of compensation will not apply to this type of unfair dismissal, by virtue of s 124(1A).

9.154 The phrase 'protected disclosure' means 'a qualifying disclosure (as defined by section 43B) which is in accordance with any of sections 43C to 43H' of the ERA 1996. A disclosure made before the Public Interest Disclosure Act came into force may be a 'protected disclosure': see *Milaszawicz v Stolt Offshore Ltd* (2002).

9.155 An employee will be protected by the provisions of the Act if both the following requirements are satisfied:

(a) he or she makes a disclosure in relation to one of the specified categories of subject-matter; and

(b) he or she uses one of the specified manners of procedure to make the disclosure.

There are six categories of subject-matter and six procedures by means of which a disclosure may be made. Once the circumstances fall within one subject-matter category and one procedure, then the employee is protected.

9.156 A 'qualifying disclosure' is defined by ERA 1996, s 43B as 'any disclosure of information which, in the reasonable belief of the employee making the disclosure, tends to show one or more' of the following:

(a) that a criminal offence has been committed, is being committed or is likely to be committed;

(b) that a person has failed, is failing or is likely to fail to comply with any legal obligation to which he or she is subject;

(c) that a miscarriage of justice has occurred, is occurring, or is likely to occur;

(d) that the health or safety of any individual has been, is being or is likely to be endangered;

(e) that the environment has been, is being, or is likely to be damaged;

(f) that information tending to show any matter falling within any of the preceding paragraphs has been, is being or is likely to be deliberately concealed.

9.157 The following points should be noted, however:

(1) the employee's belief must be 'reasonable';

(2) a disclosure will not qualify for protection if the person making it commits an offence by doing so;

(3) a disclosure will not qualify if it is one in respect of which legal professional privilege would apply;

(4) it is irrelevant where the alleged failure takes place, eg that alleged environmental damage has taken place in Brazil.

9.158 In *ALM Medical Services Ltd v Bladon* (2002), the first case under these provisions to reach the Court of Appeal, Mummery LJ said that in cases of this kind the jurisdiction of the tribunal depends on the employee establishing, first, that he or she had made a protected disclosure and, second, that that was the reason for his or her treatment. He went on to say that the alleged unfairness of aspects of the employee's dismissal are 'of less importance' in a protected disclosure case. 'The critical issue is not substantive or procedural unfairness, but whether all the requirements of the protected disclosure provisions have been satisfied on the evidence.' He also said that it is the duty of the tribunal to hear and consider all the relevant evidence from the employer and to allow the employer to challenge the employee's evidence on the relevant issues.

9.159 The first issue which arises relates to the 'employee's reasonable belief'. This was considered by the EAT in *Darnton v University of Surrey* (2003). The facts were that the employee made a disclosure about his employer's management style, alleging that the employer's actions amounted to criminal harassment or a breach of the implied duty of trust and confidence. The employment tribunal found that the allegations were not proven and relied on this finding to conclude that the employee had not made a qualifying disclosure. The EAT said that the members of the tribunal had erred in departing from the statutory test by asking themselves whether the factual allegations were correct; instead, they should have asked whether the employee held the reasonable belief that what he was disclosing tended to show a relevant failure. The EAT said that reasonable belief must be based on facts as understood by the employee, not as actually found to be the case.

9.160 In relation to the second type of qualifying disclosure above, relating to a failure by a person to comply with a legal obligation, the EAT has said that section 43B(1) (b) is widely drafted and embraces a legal obligation arising from a contract of employment. There is no reason to distinguish a legal obligation which arises from a contract of employment from any other legal obligation: see *Parkins v Sodexho Ltd* (2002). The EAT has also said that the word 'likely' in s 43B(1)(b) requires more than a possibility or risk that an employer might fail to comply with a relevant legal obligation. The information disclosed should, in the reasonable belief of the worker at the time it was disclosed, tend to show that it is probable or more probable than not, that the employer will fail to comply with the relevant legal obligation; see also *Kraus v Penna plc* (2004).

9.161 The protection only applies to the employee if he or she follows one of the specified procedures to disclose the matter in question. The aim of the legislation is to encourage employees to disclose the information through the appropriate channels first, rather than going directly to an outsider. The Act makes it easier for employees to gain protection by making a disclosure to their employer rather than disclosing information to the press, for example.

9.162 Six procedures are specified: see ERA 1996, s 43C. It will be noticed that all of them except the second use the phrase 'in good faith'. This phrase is considered in para 9.166, below. The first procedure applies where the employee makes a qualifying disclosure in good faith to the employer or another responsible person. Disclosure may only be made to that other person, however, where the employee reasonably believes that the failure relates solely or mainly to the conduct of that person or any other matter for which that other person has legal responsibility. If the disclosure is made to another person in accordance with a procedure whose use by the employee is authorised by the employer, he or she will be treated as making the disclosure to the employer.

9.163 The second procedure applies to a qualifying disclosure made to a legal adviser; if it is made in the course of obtaining legal advice: s 43D. The third procedure applies where the qualifying disclosure is made in good faith to a Minister of the Crown. The procedure applies where the employee's employer is an individual appointed under an enactment by a Minister of the Crown or a member of the Scottish Executive or is a body any of whose members are appointed in this way: s 43E.

9.164 The fourth procedure applies to a qualifying disclosure made in good faith to a 'prescribed person': s 43F. A list of prescribed persons is to be found in the Public Interest Disclosure (Prescribed Persons) Order 1999 (SI 1999/1549). The disclosure will be protected if the employee reasonably believes that the relevant failure falls within any description of matters in respect of which the person to whom he or she makes disclosure is prescribed and that the information disclosed, and any allegation contained in it, are substantially true. It is not proposed to set out the complete list here, but it should be noted that the Schedule to the Order contains both a list of prescribed persons and a description of the matters which may be disclosed to them. Thus, for example, the Chief Executive of the Criminal Cases Review Commission is included and the description of matters in respect of which disclosure may be made is 'actual or potential miscarriages of justice'.

9.165 The fifth procedure, set out in section 43G, relates to qualifying disclosures in cases other than those set out above. Such disclosures must comply with the following conditions:

(a) the employee must make the disclosure in good faith;

(b) the employee must reasonably believe that the information disclosed, and any allegation contained in it, are substantially true;

(c) the employee must not make the disclosure for the purposes of personal gain;

(d) it must be reasonable in all the circumstances of the case for him or her to make the disclosure.

9.166 The first condition is that the disclosure must be made 'in good faith'. This phrase (which is also used in the first, third, fourth, and sixth procedures) was considered by the Court of Appeal in *Street v Derbyshire Unemployed Workers' Centre* (2004). It involved an employee who made disclosures alleging misconduct by her senior manager to one of the bodies providing funds to her employer. After an independent investigation the senior manager was exonerated. Subsequent disciplinary proceedings against the employee culminated in her dismissal; she claimed the protection of section 43G. The tribunal held that, whilst she reasonably believed in the substantial truth of the disclosures, she had been motivated to make them by her personal antagonism to the manager and, therefore, they were not made in good faith. The decision of the tribunal was upheld by the EAT and the Court of Appeal. The Court of Appeal said that it is for the employment tribunal to assess on a broad and common-sense basis whether in any particular case a disclosure fulfils all the requirements of section 43G(1). The Court said that 'good faith' requires more than a reasonable belief in the truth of the allegation made and, in considering good faith as distinct from reasonable belief, it is clearly open to a tribunal to consider whether the disclosure was not made in good faith because of some ulterior motive. It said that a tribunal should only find that the disclosure was not made in good faith when the dominant or predominant purpose of making it was for some ulterior motive unrelated to the statutory objectives. In view of the fact that the tribunal had found that personal antagonism was the employee's dominant motive for making the disclosures, they did not qualify for protection.

9.167　Section 43G(2) sets out a further list of conditions which must be satisfied and section 43G(3) sets out the factors which should be considered when determining whether it is reasonable for the employee to make the disclosure. The further conditions are as follows:

(1) at the time of making the disclosure the employee must reasonably believe that he or she will be subjected to a detriment by the employer if he or she makes a disclosure to the employer or to a prescribed person in accordance with section 43F;

(2) if there is no prescribed person in relation to the relevant failure, the employee must reasonably believe that it is likely that evidence relating to the relevant failure will be concealed or destroyed if he or she makes a disclosure to the employer;

(3) the employee must have previously made a disclosure of substantially the same information to the employer or in accordance with section 43F.

9.168　The factors relating to whether it is reasonable to make the disclosure are:

(a) the identity of the person to whom the disclosure is made;

(b) the seriousness of the failure;

(c) whether the failure is continuing or is likely to occur in the future;

(d) whether the disclosure is made in breach of a duty of confidentiality owed by the employer to any other person;

(e) any action which the employer or the person to whom the previous disclosure was made has taken or might reasonably be expected to have taken as a result of the disclosure; and

(f) whether in making the disclosure to the employer the employee complied with any procedure whose use was authorised by the employer.

The last two factors only come into play, if at all, in cases relating to previous disclosures under section 43G(2)(c).

9.169 The sixth procedure is available where the subject-matter of the disclosure is sufficiently serious to merit the employee bypassing the other procedures. For this to apply, ERA 1996, s 43H requires the employee to show that:

(i) the disclosure was made in good faith;

(ii) he or she reasonably believed that the information disclosed, and any allegation contained in it, were substantially true;

(iii) he or she did not make the disclosure for personal gain;

(iv) the matter disclosed was of an exceptionally serious nature;

(v) in all the circumstances, it was reasonable for him or her to make the disclosure.

Section 43H(2) provides that, in determining whether it is reasonable for the employee to make the disclosure, regard must be had to the identity of the person to whom the disclosure is made.

Dismissals for assertion of a statutory right

9.170 These types of dismissal are governed by ERA 1996, s 104. It is not necessary for employees covered by this provision to serve a minimum qualifying period of employment; nor are employees over the normal retiring age excluded: ss 108(3) and 109(2). Selection for redundancy on these grounds is also automatically unfair: s 105(1)(and (7).

9.171 The dismissal of an employee will be automatically unfair if the reason (or principal reason) for it was that the employee brought proceedings against the employer to enforce a 'relevant statutory right' or alleged that the employer had infringed a 'relevant statutory right', as defined by section 104(4). In both cases the right must be a right of the dismissed employee, but it is immaterial whether the employee has the right or not and whether it was infringed or not, provided that the claim to the right and its infringement are made in good faith: s 104(2). It is sufficient for this section to apply that the employee made it reasonably clear to the employer what the right claimed to have been infringed was; it is not necessary to specify the right: s 104(3).

9.172 The following statutory rights are stated by section 104(4) (as amended) to be 'relevant statutory rights':

(1) any right conferred by the 1996 Act, for which the remedy for its infringement is by way of a complaint or reference to an employment tribunal;

(2) the right conferred by section 86 to a minimum period of notice;

(3) the right conferred by sections 68, 86, 146, 168, 169, and 170 of the Trade Union and Labour Relations (Consolidation) Act 1992, relating to deductions of union dues, action short of dismissal on grounds related to trade union membership and activities, and time off for trade union duties and activities; and

(4) the rights conferred by the Working Time Regulations; and

(5) the rights given by the Transfer of Undertakings (Protection of Employment) Regulations 2006.

9.173 In *Mennell v Newell & Wright (Transport Contractors) Ltd* (1996) the EAT said that a dismissal of an employee because of his refusal to sign a new contract permitting his employer to make deductions from his wages could fall within section 104. They said that a threat of dismissal in order to impose a variation of the contract to enable the employer to make deductions from wages may amount to an infringement of the employee's statutory right under Part II of the ERA 1996 not to have deductions made from his or her wages without consent. It is not necessary for the employee to have brought proceedings; it is enough that he or she has alleged in good faith that the employer has infringed a relevant statutory right. When the case reached the Court of Appeal, however, that Court allowed the employers' appeal on the grounds that, on the facts, the reason for the employee's dismissal was his refusal to sign the new contract, not his allegation that a statutory right had been infringed. It is clearly important for tribunals hearing cases under this provision to make a clear finding of fact as to the reason for the dismissal. In *Armstrong v Walter Scott Motors (London) Ltd* (EAT/766/02), the EAT held that an employee had been unfairly dismissed for asserting his statutory right to paid holiday under the Working Time Regulations.

9.174 In the later case of *Elizabeth Claire Care Management Ltd v Francis* (2005), the EAT upheld the tribunal's decision that the employer's failure to pay the employee her salary constituted an unlawful deduction from her wages contrary to section 13(1) of the ERA 1996, that that was a relevant statutory right under section 104 and that she had asserted the right by making numerous telephone calls to her employer about the non-payment of her salary. The EAT said that a failure to pay any or all of an employee's wages on time amounts to an unlawful deduction under section 13(1).

Special cases

9.175 The types of dismissal discussed in this section are different from automatically unfair dismissals in that they do not share the two features common to that type of dismissal: that the dismissal was automatically unfair, and that the requirements relating to qualifying length of employment and age exclusion do not apply. These are cases which have special rules relating to the type of dismissal in question. Two cases are considered here: dismissal and industrial action and dismissals of replacement employees.

Dismissals and industrial action

9.176 Three types of dismissal fall to be considered here:

(1) dismissals of employees taking part in unofficial industrial action under TULRCA 1992, s 237;

(2) dismissals in connection with strikes and lockouts;

(3) dismissals caused by industrial pressure, under ERA 1996 s 107.

9.177 The first type of dismissal is governed by TULRCA 1992, s 237(1), whose general effect is to deprive of the right to complain of unfair dismissal employees who, at the time of dismissal, were taking part in an unofficial strike or other industrial action. The circumstances in which a strike will be considered to be unofficial are set out in TULRCA 1992, s 237(2). That provision operates in such a way as to place the burden of showing that the industrial action was not unofficial on the employee. The two circumstances in which industrial action is not unofficial are: (1) where the dismissed employee is a member of a trade union and the action is authorised or endorsed by that union; and (2) where the employee is not a member of a trade union but amongst those taking part in the industrial action are members of a trade union which has authorised or endorsed the action. The industrial action is not to be regarded as unofficial if none of those taking part in it are members of a trade union: see proviso to s 237(2) and also *Balfour Kilpatrick Ltd v Acheson* (2003).

9.178 Dismissals in connection with strikes and lockouts are covered by TULRCA 1992, s 238, which removes from the employment tribunal the jurisdiction to hear a complaint of unfair dismissal where, at the date of dismissal (as defined by s 238(5)), the employer was conducting or instituting a lockout, or the employee (complainant) was taking part in a strike or other industrial action. But its jurisdiction will be restored if one or more 'relevant employees' (as defined: see para 9.184 below) of the same employer either have not been dismissed or have been offered re-engagement within three months of their dismissal, but the complainant has not been offered re-engagement; see *Williams v National Theatre Board Ltd* (1982), *Highland Fabricators Ltd v McLaughlin* (1985), and *Bolton Roadways Ltd v Edwards* (1987).

9.179　The consequences of section 238 are that, if the employer dismisses all the strikers and re-engages none of them, the tribunal has no jurisdiction. Once, however, there is selectivity, either in dismissing or re-engaging, the saving provisions in section 238 will be triggered and the employer will have to beware of the various pitfalls they contain. If jurisdiction is given to the tribunal, it will proceed to hear the case in the ordinary way, subject to the amendments made to section 98(4) in cases of non-re-engagement. In such cases also, the limitation period for a complaint is extended to six months from the complainant's date of dismissal: TULRCA 1992, s 239(2).

9.180　There may be borderline cases in which the tribunal will have to decide whether the dismissal is for trade union membership or activities (and falls within TULRCA s 152) or is in connection with industrial action (and falls within s 238): see *Winnett v Seamarks Brothers Ltd* (1978) and *Drew v St Edmundsbury Borough Council* (1980). An employee dismissed for trade union membership or activities does not have to have been employed for the qualifying period, whereas an employee dismissed for industrial action does.

9.181　The Court of Appeal has stressed that the question as to the necessary elements of a lockout, strike, or other industrial action is not one of law, but of fact: see *Express & Star Ltd v Bunday* (1988). In *Tramp Shipping Corporation v Greenwich Marine Inc* (1975), Lord Denning MR said:

> [A] strike is a concerted stoppage of work by men done with a view to improving their wages or conditions, or giving vent to a grievance or making a protest about something or other. It is distinct from a stoppage which is brought about by an external event such as a bomb scare or by apprehension of danger.

9.182　In *Coates v Modern Methods & Materials Ltd* (1982) ICR 763 Eveleigh LJ said:

> [F]or a person to take part in a strike he must be acting jointly or in concert with others who withdraw their labour, and this means that he must withdraw his labour in support of their claim. The fact that a man stays away from work when a strike is on does not lead inevitably to the conclusion that he is taking part in a strike.

The main question in fact is whether a person was 'taking part' in the strike at the date of dismissal. This is part of the definition of 'relevant employees' and is considered below. See Chapter 14 for further detail.

9.183 Examples of 'other industrial action' have been held to be a refusal to work over-time, taking part in a decision to impose an overtime ban, a refusal to carry out a lawful instruction given by the employer without extra pay, and a threat of with-drawal of labour; see *Power Packing Casemakers Ltd v Faust* (1983), *Naylor v Orton & Smith Ltd* (1983), and *Lewis and Britton v E Mason & Sons Ltd* (1994). In *Rasool v Hepworth Pipe Co Ltd* (1980) the EAT held that attendance at an unauthor-ised mass meeting for the purpose of ascertaining the views of the workforce with regard to impending wage negotiations fell short of industrial action.

9.184 In relation to a lockout, 'relevant employees' means employees who were directly interested in the dispute in contemplation or furtherance of which the lockout occurred; in relation to a strike or other industrial action, it means those employees at the establishment who were taking part in the action at the complainant's date of dismissal: s 238(3). The provisions of section 237, which deal with the dismissal of those taking part in unofficial industrial action (considered above), do not affect the question of who are relevant employees for the purposes of section 238.

9.185 The main question which arises here is what constitutes 'taking part' in a strike or other industrial action. In *Coates v Modern Methods & Materials Ltd* (1982) the Court of Appeal stressed that the words 'taking part in a strike' are ordinary words the meaning of which the employment tribunal is best fitted to decide. It is the employee's actions, and not the reasons or motives behind the actions, that deter-mine whether an employee is taking part in a strike. So if an employee stops work when other employees come out on strike and neither says nor does anything to indicate disagreement with the strike or indicate a refusal to join the strike, the employee is taking part in a strike; see also *McCormick v Horsepower Ltd* (1981) and *Bolton Roadways Ltd v Edwards* (1987). In *Manifold Industries Ltd v Sims* (1991), the EAT emphasised that the question as to whether or not an employee is taking part in a strike is to be determined by what he or she was in fact doing; the employer's knowledge of the employee's actions is not a relevant consideration.

9.186 Finally, ERA 1996, s 107 requires the tribunal to ignore certain kinds of pressure from third parties and to decide upon the reason for the dismissal and its fairness as if there had been no pressure. 'Pressure' is defined as 'any pressure which, by calling, organising, procuring or financing a strike or other industrial action, or threatening to do so, was exercised on the employer to dismiss the employee'; see *Trend v Chiltern Hunt Ltd* (1977), *Hazells Offset Ltd v Luckett* (1977), *Ford Motor Co Ltd v Hudson* (1978), and *Colwyn Borough Council v Dutton* (1980). If the pressure was exercised because the employee was not a trade union member, the employer or the employee may ask the employment tribunal, under TULRCA 1992, s 160, to join as a party to the proceedings the person claimed to have exerted the pressure. That person may have to make a total or partial contribution to any compensation awarded against the employer.

Replacement employees

9.187 In view of the fact that the qualifying period for the right not to be unfairly dismissed is one year, the provisions of ERA 1996, s 106 are not likely to be needed very often. Section 106 specifically applies to employees engaged to replace employees absent because of pregnancy or childbirth or on adoption leave. The replacement must be told in writing that the employment will be ended when the absent employee returns. When he or she is dismissed, the dismissal will be treated as being for some other substantial reason, but the employer will still need to satisfy the requirements of section 98(4), which should not be difficult.

Remedies

9.188 The remedies available to an employee whose complaint of unfair dismissal succeeds are a re-employment order or compensation. In a limited number of cases, interim relief may be asked for. Employment tribunals do not have the power to grant injunctions, which in any case are most likely to be appropriate to enforce a restrictive covenant. It is worth bearing in mind that, at the end of the day, the only real question for an employer is how much it will be necessary to pay an employee, since non-compliance with a re-employment order or an order following on from an interim relief application will mean a larger compensation bill. For a full discussion of these remedies, see Upex, *The Law of Termination of Employment* (7th ed, 2006), chapters 7 and 8.

Reinstatement and re-engagement orders

9.189 The main remedies for unfair dismissal were intended to be reinstatement and re-engagement orders, and the whole tenor of the statutory provisions is to suggest that the employment tribunal should apply those remedies first: see ss 112–116. In reality, though, few re-employment orders are made.

9.190 A reinstatement order is an order to the employer to treat the applicant as if he or she had not been dismissed. In deciding whether to make an order, the tribunal must comply with the requirements of section 116(1), and take into account the following factors: the complainant's wishes; the practicability for the employer of compliance with the order; and, where the complainant caused or contributed to some extent to the dismissal, whether it would be just to order reinstatement.

9.191 If the tribunal decides not to order reinstatement, it should then consider whether to order re-engagement: s 116(2). A re-engagement order is an order that the employee should be engaged by the employer, or by a successor of the employer or an associated employer, in employment comparable to that from which he or she was dismissed, or 'other suitable employment': s 115(1). In deciding whether to make the order, the tribunal must have regard to the requirements of section 116(3). The three factors it must take into account are similar to those mentioned above in relation to reinstatement orders. In relation to the second factor (practicability), however, the tribunal must consider the practicability of re-engagement with a successor of the employer or an associated employer.

9.192 The first step the tribunal should take is to explain to the employee the re-employment orders it may make and to ask whether he or she wishes the tribunal to make an order; if the employee asks for a re-employment order to be made, the tribunal may then make an order, but is not obliged to do so: s 112(2) and (3). If the tribunal decides to consider making a re-employment order, it must first consider whether to make a reinstatement order; if it decides not to do so, it must then consider whether to make a re-engagement order. If it decides not to make any order, it must make an award of compensation: s 112(4).

9.193 The effect of an order of reinstatement is to give the employee his or her old job back; it will include an ancillary order for arrears of pay between the date of dismissal and the date of reinstatement. There is no statutory maximum to the amount which may be ordered to be paid under section 114(2)(a). The effect of a re-engagement order will be to give the employee a job similar to the one from which he or she was dismissed. Section 115(2) requires the tribunal when making the order to specify the terms of re-engagement, again including arrears of pay.

9.194 If the employer does not comply fully with the terms of a reinstatement or re-engagement order, the tribunal must award such an amount of compensation as it thinks fit having regard to the loss sustained by the employee, subject to the maximum permissible: s 117(1) and (2). If the employer totally fails to comply, then the tribunal must go on to award compensation in the usual way and it must also make an additional award of compensation in accordance with s 117(3)(b). In cases of total non-compliance, the employer may escape the consequences of non-compliance by showing that it was not 'practicable' to comply with the re-employment order: s 117(4).

Compensation

9.195 An employment tribunal will award compensation if it makes no order for re-employment, or if it makes such an order but the employer totally fails to comply with it. Compensation may consist of the following elements: a basic award; a compensatory award; and an additional award. The award of compensation is subject to an adjustment of up to 50 per cent in cases where the employer or employee has failed to comply with the statutory dispute resolution procedures. An employee who fails to comply is liable to have a *downward* adjustment; an employer who fails to comply is liable to have an *upwards* adjustment.

9.196 If the employment tribunal makes a finding of unfair dismissal, it must first consider whether to make an order for the re-employment of the applicant. If he or she does not wish such an order to be made or if the tribunal decides against making an order, it will proceed to award compensation. If it does make an order, but the employer totally fails to comply with it, the tribunal will make an additional award and then go on to award compensation in the usual way. In most cases, compensation usually consists of a basic award and a compensatory award.

9.197 The basic award is calculated in the same way as a redundancy payment. It is necessary to take the complainant's age, length of continuous employment on the effective date of termination, and the amount of gross weekly pay. The gross weekly pay is currently capped at a statutory maximum of £330 per week, which leads to a maximum basic award of £9,900 for the year commencing 1 February 2008 once the variable of age is taken into account. Reductions in the basic award may be made where the employee is near retirement, where the employee unreasonably refuses an offer of reinstatement, where the employee's conduct before dismissal makes it just and equitable to make a reduction, where the employee has already received a redundancy payment, and where the employee has received an *ex gratia* payment from the employer.

9.198 The compensatory award should be 'such amount as the tribunal considers just and equitable in all the circumstances having regard to the loss sustained by the complainant in consequence of the dismissal in so far as that loss is attributable to action taken by the employer': see s 123(1). The maximum amount of compensatory award that may be awarded is £63,000 as from 1 February 2008; it is usually increased annually on 1 February. The heads of loss which the compensatory award may cover were set out in *Norton Tool Co Ltd v Tewson* (1972) and are: (1) immediate loss of wages; (2) manner of dismissal; (3) future loss of wages; and (4) loss of protection in respect of unfair dismissal or dismissal by reason of redundancy. A fifth head of loss was subsequently added: loss of pension rights.

9.199 In two types of unfair dismissal the amount of the compensatory awards is unlimited. These are cases in which the dismissal is automatically unfair because it was a health and safety case and covered by section 100 or because the employee made a 'protected disclosure' and the dismissal fell within section 103A, or because the employee was selected for reasons falling within either of those provisions: see paras 9.145 and 9.152, above. This is an exception to the general rule that the compensatory award is subject to a limit.

9.200 The compensatory award is subject to deductions, the main ones being deductions in respect of mitigation and deductions for 'contributory fault' under section 123(4) and (6), respectively. Additional awards may also fall to be made.

FURTHER READING

Collins, H, *Justice in Dismissal* (1992) Oxford.

Deakin, S, & Morris, G, *Labour Law* (4th ed, 2005) Hart (chapter 5).

Smith, I, & Thomas, G, *Smith & Wood's Employment Law* (9th ed, 2007) Oxford University Press (chapters 8 & 9).

Upex, R, *The Law on Termination of Employment* (7th ed, 2006) Jordans, particularly chapters 4 and 5 and, in relation to time limit issues, chapter 11.

ARTICLE

Hepple, B, & Morris, G, (2002) 'The Employment Act 2002 and the Crisis of Individual Employment Rights', *Industrial Law Journal*, Vol 31, No 2, pp 245–269.

SELF-TEST QUESTIONS

1 Harry has worked for Speedy Co as an HGV driver for 10 years. Over the last six months Harry's attendance record has been poor; he has frequently been absent for at least one day each week and claims to have been suffering from back trouble. Speedy Co is suspicious about the absences and warns Harry that it cannot tolerate the situation indefinitely. In March 1994, Speedy's personnel manager, Graham, arranged for Harry to see Sheila, the company's medical officer, but Sheila is unable to confirm or deny whether the back trouble is genuine. On 1 April Harry failed to attend work and no explanation was received by the company. Graham thereupon telephoned Harry and told him that unless he apologised he need not turn up for work the next day. Harry retorted that he had no intention of apologising as he had left a message with Graham's secretary Flo, that his back was bad again. Flo denies this.

   Advise Speedy Co of the liabilities that arise in this scenario.

2 'The Employment Act 2002 does much to protect employers, but little for employees.' Explain this statement in relation to procedural fairness in unfair dismissal.

3 Emma is the owner of Posh's Garage. Robbie and Kylie are employed as mechanics and David is the petrol pump attendant. Recently Emma decided she was overdoing

things and has agreed to sell the garage to Geri, who already owns Spice Sports Cars Showroom. Geri tells Emma that David's services will not be required as his younger brother Liam is unemployed and looking for a job. Emma dismisses David two days before the sale is completed. One month after taking over Posh's Garage Geri decides there is not enough work there for two mechanics and asks Robbie to move to Spice Sports Cars Showroom. Robbie refuses since Spice Sports Cars Showroom is five miles further from his home than Posh's Garage, and he is therefore dismissed. The following week, Kylie is replaced by Noel, in order to service fuel-injection engines in high-performance motor cars.

Advise David, Robbie, and Kylie.

4 'There is no justice in dismissal.' Critically evaluate Collins' theory, using case-law examples to support your arguments.

Redundancy

SUMMARY

This chapter considers the law relating to redundancy. Employees dismissed for redundancy have two main statutory rights: (1) the right to complain of unfair dismissal; and (2) the right to claim a redundancy payment. The advent of the unfair dismissal right has meant that there are fewer claims for redundancy payments, for two main reasons: the qualifying period of employment is shorter, and the levels of compensation are potentially higher. In addition, the statutory provisions relating to unfair dismissal are less complex than those relating to redundancy payments.

This chapter will consider:

- the definition of redundancy; and

- redundancy payments claims.

At the end of this chapter, the right to time off during the notice period to look for new employment or make arrangements for training for further employment will be discussed briefly.

Introduction

10.1 The statutory provisions relating to redundancy payments originated in the Redundancy Payments Act 1965. That Act was the first attempt to provide a floor of rights and its provisions gave rise to a large number of cases, many of them trying to apply the definition of 'redundancy' to a variety of different situations. Much of that case law is now of historical interest only, but it gave rise to interesting and intricate discussions, for example, about the nature of pastry cooking. Nevertheless, looking back at the legislation, one can say that it was a notable milestone on the road to the creation of a floor of rights.

10.2 Employees are generally only entitled to the right not to be unfairly dismissed, as has been seen, if they have been continuously employed for one year, though that requirement is sometimes lifted: see ERA 1996, s 108, as amended by the Unfair Dismissal and Statement of Reasons for Dismissal (Variation of Qualifying Period) Order 1999 (SI 1999/1436) and Chapter 9. In the case of the right to claim a redundancy payment, the employee must have been continuously employed for *two* years: ERA 1996, s 155. In both cases, the employee must have been dismissed. The definition of 'dismiss' is considered in Chapter 7. It should be noted that, in the case of claims under Part XI (ie the provisions relating to redundancy payments claims), the definition is extended in cases where the employee is offered alternative employment: see ERA 1996, ss 136(5) and 139(1) and (4). The definition of 'redundancy', which is the first matter to be considered in this chapter, is common to both the unfair dismissal and redundancy payments rights. Apart from the definition of redundancy, however, the two Parts governing the separate rights are completely self-contained. This means that the provisions of Part XI are not applicable to unfair dismissal claims, nor are those of Part X applicable to redundancy payments claims. It will be an error of law if a tribunal applies the wrong provisions to the wrong type of claim: see *Hempell v WH Smith & Sons Ltd* (1986) and *Jones v Governing Body of Burdett Coutts School* (1997). See also *Shawkat v Nottingham City Hospital NHS Trust* (1999).

10.3 In general, an employee dismissed for redundancy will be advised to complain of unfair dismissal or make a dual claim. This is because a complaint under the unfair dismissal provisions enables the employment tribunal to decide whether the employer's decision to dismiss was reasonable in all the circumstances, whereas the redundancy payments provisions merely enable the tribunal to decide whether the statutory presumption of redundancy has or has not been rebutted. Further, the unfair dismissal provisions give an employee the possibility of receiving greater compensation, in the form of the basic award, which is calculated in the same way as a redundancy payment, plus a compensatory award, which is not available under the redundancy payments provisions. In the case of a dual claim, the successful employee will either receive a basic award or a redundancy payment, but not both, since ERA 1996, s 122(4) contains set-off provisions.

The definition of redundancy

10.4 As was mentioned above, the definition of redundancy serves a dual purpose: redundancy is one of the potentially fair reasons in unfair dismissal cases, and an employee who is dismissed by reason of redundancy is also entitled to a redundancy payment: ERA 1996, s 135(1).

10.5 Redundancy is defined in section 139(1) as follows:

> An employee who is dismissed shall be taken to be dismissed by reason of redundancy if the dismissal is wholly or mainly attributable to –
>
> (a) the fact that his employer has ceased or intends to cease
>> (i) to carry on the business for the purposes of which the employee was employed by him, or
>> (ii) to carry on that business in the place where the employee was so employed, or
>
> (b) the fact that the requirements of that business
>> (i) for employees to carry out work of a particular kind, or
>> (ii) for employees to carry out work of a particular kind in the place where the employee was employed by the employer,
>
> have ceased or diminished or are expected to cease or diminish.

10.6 Section 139(6) makes clear that 'cease' and 'diminish' mean cease and diminish either permanently or temporarily and for whatever reason.

10.7 In cases involving only a claim for a redundancy payment, section 163(2) enacts a presumption of redundancy. This means that the burden is on the employer who wishes to dispute liability to make the payment to prove that the employee was not redundant. In cases involving a complaint of unfair dismissal and a claim for a redundancy payment, however, the presumption will not operate in relation to the unfair dismissal complaint: see Employment Tribunals Act 1996, s 7(6). In unfair dismissal cases, the burden is on the employer to show what the reason (or principal reason) for the dismissal was. If an employer fails to discharge that burden, the dismissal will be automatically held to be unfair. It is therefore possible for an employer to fail to rebut the presumption of redundancy in the redundancy payment claim and thus become liable for a redundancy payment, and to fail to establish the reason for the dismissal in the unfair dismissal claim and thus be held to have dismissed the employee unfairly: see *Midland Foot Comfort Centre v Moppett* (1973).

10.8 The first question to determine is whether the dismissal is by reason of the particular circumstances which constitute a redundancy. In *Hindle v Percival Boats Ltd* (1969), the Court of Appeal held that, provided that the employer honestly believes that the dismissal of the employee is due to some reason other than redundancy (however mistaken the belief may be), the dismissal will not be by reason of redundancy. But it emphasised that employment tribunals must be wary of dishonest employers or employers who misdirect themselves into thinking that they were influenced by the employee's deficiencies, when the main factor was that the requirements of the business had declined.

Mobility and redundancy

10.9 The definition of redundancy in section 139(1) uses the phrase 'in the place where the employee was...employed'. In earlier cases, the issue was regarded as being one determined by reference to the employee's contract, in other words whether the employer had contractual authority, express or implied, to order the employee to move; or, put in another way, what degree of contractual mobility the employee was subject to. The effect was that if the employee was required to move to another factory within the radius of the mobility obligation because of the closure of the factory where he or she worked, it would not be possible to claim a redundancy payment, since there had not been a cessation of the business in the place where he or she was employed: see *United Kingdom Atomic Energy Authority v Claydon* (1974), *Sutcliffe v Hawker Siddeley Aviation Ltd* (1973), and *Rank Xerox Ltd v Churchill* (1988). This has been called the 'contractual test'.

10.10 In *Bass Leisure Ltd v Thomas* (1994), on the other hand, what has been called the 'factual' test was used. There, the EAT said that 'the place' where an employee is employed does not extend to any place where the employee may be contractually required to work; the question is primarily a factual one and the only relevant contractual terms are those which define the place of employment and its extent.

10.11 The question whether the 'contractual' or 'factual' test is to be preferred has been considered by the Court of Appeal, in *High Table Ltd v Horst* (1997). Peter Gibson LJ reviewed the case-law and distinguished the earlier cases on the ground that the issue considered there by the Court of Appeal was whether the employees in question were in breach of contract in refusing an instruction to work further afield than they had previously been accustomed to. He preferred the conclusion of the EAT in the later case of *Bass Leisure Ltd v Thomas* (above) that the place where the employee is employed 'is to be established by a factual inquiry, taking into account the employee's fixed or changing place or places of work and any contractual terms which go to evidence or define the place of employment and its extent, but not those (if any) which make provisions for the employee to be transferred to another'.

10.12 This is an important decision, but it should be remembered, however, that Peter Gibson LJ emphasises that it goes merely to the question whether the employee was redundant and not whether the employer acted reasonably. Equally it will not affect the question whether the employee should lose the entitlement to a redundancy payment because he or she is held to have unreasonably refused a suitable offer of alternative employment: see para 10.32, below.

Applying the definition

10.13 Of the two definitions of redundancy given in section 139(1), that relating to cessation of a business has caused little difficulty. It is not necessary to show that the employer is the legal owner of the business in question, only that that person is in control of the business: see *Thomas v Jones* (1978). The other definition, in section 139(1)(b), that there is a cessation or diminution in the requirements of a business for work of a particular kind, is by no means straightforward and has caused considerable difficulties. In a series of cases, the Court of Appeal has held that the fact that there has been a reorganisation of the business does not necessarily mean that there has been a redundancy; it is part of the factual background. The fundamental question is whether the requirement for employees to carry out work of a particular kind has ceased or diminished. So, for example, in *Carry All Motors Ltd v Pennington* (1980), the employee was dismissed from his job as a transport clerk when his employers decided that the work of the transport manager and transport clerk could be carried out by one employee only. The tribunal decided that he had not been dismissed by reason of redundancy because the same work remained. The EAT reversed their decision and held that the question was whether the requirement for employees to do that work had diminished. Since one employee was doing the work formerly done by two, there was a redundancy.

10.14 A reorganisation does not of itself mean that there is a redundancy situation, particularly if the amount of work remains the same or increases. In *Johnson v Nottinghamshire Combined Police Authority*, above, Lord Denning MR said:

> An employer is entitled to reorganise his business so as to improve its efficiency and, in doing so, to propose to his staff a change in the terms and conditions of their employment: and to dispense with their services if they do not agree. Such a change does not automatically give the staff a right to a redundancy payment. It only does so if the change in the terms and conditions is due to a redundancy situation.

10.15 Subsequent decisions have tended to espouse the idea that, in considering whether there has been a diminution in the requirements of the business for employees to carry out work of a particular kind, the tribunal must look at the terms of the employee's contract. This is called the 'contract test'. An example of this is *Cowen v Haden Ltd* (1983), where an employee was employed as a divisional contracts surveyor and was 'required to undertake, at the direction of the company, any and all duties which reasonably fall within the scope of his capabilities'. The Court of Appeal held that the requirement that the employee should perform the duties within the scope of his capabilities was restricted to the duties of a divisional contracts surveyor; the employers therefore had no right to require him to transfer from that work to assume the job of a quantity surveyor.

10.16 The authorities in this area were carefully and critically reviewed by the EAT in *Safeway Stores plc v Burrell* (1997), which contains a valuable analysis of the approaches propounded by the courts in recent years. The employee's dismissal arose from a reorganisation or 'delayering' of the employers' management structure, with the result that there were less management positions than before, which gave rise to redundancies. The tribunal decided that he had not been dismissed by reason of redundancy, since the work done by the employee still had to be done and, therefore, the requirements of the employers' business for employees to carry out work of a particular kind had not ceased or diminished. The EAT reversed this decision and said that he had been dismissed by reason of redundancy. They said that a three-stage process is involved in determining whether a dismissal for redundancy has taken place: (1) Was the employee dismissed? (2) Had the requirements of the employer's business for employees to carry out work of a particular kind ceased or diminished? If so, (3) Was the dismissal of the employee caused wholly or mainly by the state of affairs identified in stage 2? They said that at stage 2, the only question to be asked is whether there is a cessation or diminution in the employer's requirements for employees (not the applicant) to carry out work of a particular kind and that, at this stage, it is irrelevant to consider the terms of the employee's contract. At stage 3, the tribunal is concerned with causation.

10.17 The *Safeway* decision was approved by the House of Lords in *Murray v Foyle Meats Ltd* (1997). Lord Irivine of Lairg LC said:

> The language of s 139(1)(b)...asks two questions of fact. The first is whether one or other of various states of economic affairs exists. In this case, the relevant one is whether the requirements of the business for employees to carry out work of a particular kind have diminished. The second question is whether the dismissal is attributable, wholly or mainly, to that state of affairs. This is a question of causation...The key word in the statute is 'attributable' and there is no reason in law why the dismissal of an employee should not be attributable to a diminution in the employer's needs for employees irrespective of the terms of his contract or the function which he performed.

10.18 The Court of Appeal has looked at this issue again, in *Shawkat v Nottingham City Hospital NHS Trust* (2002). In that case, the employee was employed as a staff grade doctor in thoracic surgery. Following the establishment of a cardio-thoracic unit, he was required to perform both cardiac and thoracic surgery. He refused and was dismissed. The tribunal rejected his claim that his dismissal was for redundancy, but the EAT allowed his appeal and remitted the case to the tribunal, on the footing that it was not clear that a tribunal could only have reached one conclusion. On remission, the tribunal again concluded that there was no diminution in the employers' requirements for employees to carry out work of a particular kind, ie thoracic surgery. It said that there was no reduction in the amount of thoracic surgery or the number of employees required to do that work. It said that the reason why the employee's thoracic sessions was reduced was because they wanted him to do cardiac work in part of his time. It therefore concluded that he was not dismissed by reason of redundancy. The EAT dismissed the employee's appeal, as did the Court of Appeal, which said that the question whether the requirements of section 139 have been satisfied is a question of fact. Here, the tribunal's decision did not disclose an error of law and should not be disturbed.

10.19 In *Kingwell v Elizabeth Bradley Designs Ltd* (2002) the EAT said of these types of case:

> It appears to us that there is a fundamental misunderstanding about the question of redundancy. Redundancy does not only arise where there is a poor financial situation at the employers, although, as it happens, there was such in this case. It does not only arise where there is a diminution of work in the hands of an employer, although, as it happens, again, there was in this case. It can occur where there is a successful employer with plenty of work, but who, perfectly sensibly as far as commerce and economics is concerned, decides to reorganise his business because he concludes that he is overstaffed. Thus, even with the same amount of work and the same amount of income, the decision is taken that a lesser number of employees are required to perform the same functions. That too is a redundancy situation.

See also *Lambe v 186K Ltd* (2004), (CA). It should be borne in mind that a reorganisation which does not fall within the statutory definition of redundancy may amount to 'some other substantial reason', the fifth potentially fair reason in an unfair dismissal case: see para 9.79, above.

Redundancy consultation

10.20 Section 188 of the Trade Union and Labour Relations (Consolidation) Act 1992 (TULRCA) (as amended by the Collective Redundancies and Transfer of Undertakings (Protection of Employment) (Amendment) Regulations 1999 (SI 1999/1925)) provides for a duty to consult with employee representatives in respect of redundancy situations. This collective right arises from EU law, the Collective Redundancies Directive 75/129 (as amended by a further revising Directive (92/56)).

Duty to consult

10.21 Under the 1992 Act where an employer is 'proposing' to make 20 or more redundancies 'at one establishment', the consultation must begin 'in good time' and at least

30 days before the first of the dismissals takes effect. The consultation must be with the recognised trades unions (if there are any) or 'appropriate representatives' (usually elected representatives): see *Governing Body of the Northern Ireland Hotel and Catering College and North Eastern Education and Library Board v National Association of Teachers in Further and Higher Education* (1995). Where the employer is proposing to dismiss 100 or more employees within a 90-day period, the consultation must begin at least 90 days before the first of the dismissals takes effect: see *R v British Coal Corporation ex p Vardy* (1993) and *Irmtraud Junk v Wolfgang Kühnel* (2005). The obligation to consult remains in the situation where there is a proposal to dismiss 20 or more employees within a 90-day period, even if the employer intends to offer alternative employment to a number of those affected with a consequence of less than 20 dismissals being intended to take place: see *Hardy v Tourism South East* (2004).

Elected representatives

10.22 Where no trade unions are recognised (see Chapter 13), section 188A of the 1992 Act provides a set of default provisions, requiring the election of employee representatives for the purposes of consultation in relation to the proposed redundancies. Where nobody comes forward for election, then the consultation may be undertaken on an individual employee basis: see *R v Secretary of State for Trade and Industry ex p UNISON* (1996).

General duty to consult

10.23 TULRCA 1992, s 188(2) sets out the matters which should be included in the consultation with the appropriate representatives; s 188(4) sets out the information to be disclosed by the employer regarding the redundancies, including the methods of selection, the criteria for the redundancies and the consequences, including the redundancy payments.

Failure to consult

10.24 Where an employer fails to consult with the affected workforce, s 189(1) TULRCA 1992 provides for a complaint to be made to an employment tribunal on the grounds that the employer has failed to comply with the duty to consult or with the requirements for the election of employee representatives. Where a tribunal upholds a complaint, it must make a declaration to that effect and may also make a protective award.

10.25 Protective awards are defined in s 189(3). The effect of a protective award is to require the defaulting employer to pay remuneration to the employees affected, for no more than 90 days. The amount of the award is calculated on the basis of a week's pay of each employee for each week of the protected period.

10.26 Where 'special circumstances' exist which make it 'not reasonably practicable' for an employer to comply with the requirements of consultation, such as consequential immediate closure of the business on the death of the employer (*AEEU GMB v Clydesdale Group plc* (1995)), then the tribunal will take them into account when considering the length of the protected period during which remuneration is to be paid. But the tribunal would need to be persuaded that there were genuinely 'out of the ordinary' circumstances before allowing such a defence to succeed.

Mass redundancies

10.27 An employer proposing to dismiss a group of employees (more than 100 at one establishment within 90 days or less) must inform the Department of Trade & Industry (DTI) at least 90 days in advance of these redundancies taking place: see s 193 TULRCA 1992. Failure to notify the DTI is a criminal offence which is punishable on summary conviction by a fine not exceeding £5,000. In these situations, the Government may provide guarantee payments, as it does in insolvency redundancies.

Claim for redundancy payment

Offers of re-engagement or alternative employment

10.28 The provisions governing offers of re-engagement and alternative employment operate in two separate ways: either they affect the question whether or not the employee is to be treated as having been dismissed; or they operate to disentitle him or her from receiving a redundancy payment which would otherwise be payable.

10.29 There is the additional complicating factor of the trial period: this comes into operation in both cases where the offer of new employment differs at all from the terms of the previous employment. The trial period provisions are considered separately in the next section. The statutory provisions also apply where there is a change of employer: ss 141 and 146(1).

10.30 Section 138 deals with the situation where an employee who is under notice of redundancy (or who has been constructively dismissed) is offered alternative employment. As will be seen from the discussion below, there are circumstances in which an employee will be treated as not having been dismissed. In such circumstances, there will be no entitlement to a redundancy payment, simply because entitlement to a payment depends upon having been dismissed for redundancy and, therefore, if there is no dismissal, there can be no entitlement. Once, however, the employee is found to have been dismissed, he or she may be disentitled from receiving the payment which would otherwise be payable if there is held to have been an unreasonable refusal of a suitable offer: see ss 141 and 146. The trial period provisions in section 138 build on the basic structure of section 136 by setting out the circumstances in which a trial period will come into operation. If an employee unreasonably terminates the employment during the trial period, that act will disentitle him or her from the right to receive a payment. The basic definition of dismissal is to be found in s 136 and is considered in Chapter 8.

10.31 Section 138 caters for two alternative possibilities: either that the terms and conditions of the new employment are the same as those of the old, or that they are different. In both cases, there must be an offer of a renewal of the contract or of re-engagement under a new contract; an offer of re-engagement must be made before the ending of the employment under the previous contract. The renewal or re-engagement must take effect immediately on the ending of the previous employment, or within four weeks. If any of the conditions are not complied with, there will be a dismissal. Where the new contract is the same as the old, and all the conditions of section 138(1) are complied with, there will be no dismissal and section 213(2) will preserve continuity of employment. In *SI (Systems and Instruments) Ltd v Grist and Riley* (1983), the EAT said that, on a proper construction of what is now section 138(1), a distinction is to be drawn between cases of renewal and re-engagement. In cases of renewal, the offer need not be made before the termination of the contract of employment, but in cases of re-engagement under a new contract, the offer must be made before termination. 'Renewal' includes 'extension': ERA 1996, s 235(1).

10.32 The provisions of ERA 1996, s 141 affect an employee treated as dismissed for redundancy by virtue of section 138. An employee will be disentitled from receiving a redundancy payment where he or she unreasonably refuses an offer of suitable new employment. Section 141(1) applies to an offer made before the ending of the previous employment to renew the contract or re-engage him or her under a new one, the renewal or re-engagement taking effect no more than four weeks after the ending of the previous contract. If the provisions of the new contract are the same as those of the old, the employee will be disentitled, if he or she unreasonably refuses the offer: s 141(2) and (3)(a). Where the provisions of the new contract differ, the first question is whether the offer is an offer of 'suitable employment in relation to the employee', since section 141(2) will only disentitle the employee in the case of an unreasonable refusal of a suitable offer: see 141(3)(b). If he or she actually gives the new contract a try, the statutory trial period will come into operation; if he or she then leaves during it, entitlement will be lost if the new employment was suitable, and the termination of the employment during the trial period was unreasonable: s 141(4). Whether there has been an offer is essentially an issue of fact for the tribunal to decide.

10.33 The two significant questions here concern what is meant by 'suitable' and 'unreasonable'. They must be kept separate and dealt with separately by the tribunal: see *Carron Co v Robertson* (1967), *Hindes v Supersine Ltd* (1979), and *Taylor v Kent County Council* (1969). The suitability of the offer is to be looked at objectively by the employment tribunal and is regarded by the appellate courts as being a matter of fact and degree for it to decide. In *Taylor v Kent County Council* Lord Parker CJ said that suitability 'means employment which is substantially equivalent to the employment which has ceased', but there are suggestions in later cases that an objectively unsuitable offer may be made suitable (or vice versa) by the employee's attitude towards it: see, for example, *Hindes v Supersine Ltd* (1979) and *Executors of J F Everest v Cox* (1980). The employer's attitude is equally important; if an employer fails to discuss and clarify the new role being offered and this consequently has a disillusioning effect, this likewise can be taken into account in determining the suitability of a position: see *Commission for Healthcare Audit and Commission v Ward* (2008).

10.34 In the case of an offer found not to be suitable, it will not be necessary to go on to consider the reasonableness of the employee's refusal. If, however, the offer is found to be suitable, the tribunal must then consider the reasonableness of the refusal by looking at the personal reasons that relate to the employee. This is a subjective matter to be considered from the employee's point of view: see *Cambridge & District Co-operative Society Ltd v Ruse* (1993). This must be judged as at the time the offer is made and not with hindsight, taking account of the personal circumstances of the individual employee, and also his or her reaction in those circumstances; all the relevant factors should be considered as a whole: see *Thomas Wragg & Sons Ltd v Wood* (1976), *Paton Calvert & Co Ltd v Westerside* (1979), and *Executors of J F Everest v Cox*, above. In looking at the two separate factors of suitability and reasonableness, the employment tribunal is entitled to look at factors which may be common to both questions: see *Spencer v Gloucestershire County Council* (1985).

Trial period

10.35 Where the provisions of the new contract differ at all from the provisions of the previous contract, section 138(2) brings a trial period into operation. If the employee leaves or is dismissed during the trial period, he or she will be treated as having been dismissed under the previous contract. An employee whose termination of the contract during the trial period is held to be unreasonable will be disentitled from receiving a redundancy payment: see para 10.30, above.

10.36 The coming into operation of the trial period occurs in all cases whether the old contract is renewed or the employee is re-engaged under a new contract and where there is a difference between the terms and conditions of the new contract and the corresponding provisions of the previous contract. The trial period generally starts with the ending of the previous contract and ends four weeks from the date on which the employee starts work under the new contract: see s 138(3). In *Benton v Sanderson Kayser Ltd* (1989) the question arose as to the meaning of the phrase 'period of four weeks', used by section 138(3)(b). The Court of Appeal held that 'period of four weeks' means a period of four consecutive weeks calculated according to the calendar, rather than the period of time actually worked.

10.37 The trial period may only be extended, by agreement between the parties, for the purpose of retraining the employee and the agreement must comply with the requirements of section 138(6). An extension for any other reason will have no effect. This means that an employee who decides to leave during the period of the extension will be held to have resigned: see *Meek v J Allen Rubber Co Ltd and Secretary of State for Employment* (1980).

10.38 An employee who leaves during the trial period or who is dismissed by the employer (for a reason connected with or arising out of the change in the contract) will be treated as having been dismissed on the date on which the previous contract ended and for the reason for which that contract was ended: s 138(4). Similar considerations apply where there is more than one renewal of the original contract or the employee is again re-engaged under a new contract. Section 138 applies also to offers of re-engagement with associated employers: s 146(1). It may be noted that a refusal to offer an employee a trial period may cause the dismissal to be unfair: see *Elliot v Richard Stump Ltd* (1987).

10.39 In cases of constructive dismissal, the rules set out above will apply, but with the added complication that a so-called common law trial period will come into existence. This means that if, in breach of the contract, the employee is transferred to another department and takes the job there on trial, he or she has a reasonable period in which to decide whether to take the new job or leave (the 'common law' trial period). If he or she decides to take it, the statutory trial period then comes into operation: see *Air Canada v Lee* (1978) and *Turvey v C W Cheyney & Son Ltd* (1979). The difficulty with this is that, since the employee is granted a reasonable time under the common law trial period to make up his or her mind, it is not easy to know when the statutory trial period has started and whether, when the employee left the employment, the statutory period had ended or not. If it had, there will have been no dismissal and the employee will be held to have resigned.

10.40 If the employee leaves during the trial period, entitlement to a redundancy payment will be lost if the new employment was suitable, and the termination of the employment during the trial period was unreasonable: s 141(4). For a consideration of what is unreasonable, see para 10.34, above.

Change of employer

10.41 The statutory provisions discussed in the preceding sections apply equally to associated employers of the original employer. This means that an offer of employment made by an associated employer is as good as an offer made by the original employer and the provisions of section 141 apply in the same way to an employee who is offered employment by an associated employer: see s 146(1). Provided that the person offering employment is within the definition of 'associated employer', it does not matter that the associated employer has no employees at the time of the offer of employment and is a dormant company reactivated especially for the purpose of offering employment to the redundant employee(s): see *Lucas v Henry Johnson (Packers & Shippers) Ltd* (1986).

10.42 In other cases, the transferee of the business may incur liability. This will depend upon whether there has been a transfer of an undertaking within the Transfer of Undertakings Regulations 2006: see Chapter 11.

The effect of misconduct

10.43 If an employee is dismissed for misconduct, albeit in a redundancy situation, the presumption of redundancy will be rebutted and the dismissal will not have been by reason of redundancy. In such a case, the tribunal should scrutinise the employer's reason carefully, to ensure that it is not a reason trumped up to defeat a legitimate claim. If, on the other hand, the employer dismisses the employee for redundancy, but discovers misconduct on his or her part, ERA 1996, s 140(1) must be complied with. This provision operates so as to disentitle an employee where the employer, 'being entitled to terminate his contract of employment by reason of the employee's conduct', terminates it in one of three ways: (1) without notice; or (2) by giving shorter notice than the employee is entitled to; or (3) by giving the correct notice but also stating in writing that the employer would be entitled to terminate the contract summarily because of the employee's conduct.

10.44 The EAT has expressed the view that what is now section 140(1) applies where there is a single dismissal (ie a dismissal for redundancy and not explicitly for misconduct) as well as a double dismissal (ie a dismissal for redundancy followed by a dismissal for misconduct): see *Simmons v Hoover Ltd* (1977). So if, for example, the employer gives the employee less notice than he or she is entitled to and subsequently misconduct on the part of the employee comes to light, section 140(1) will relieve the employer of liability; if, on the other hand, the employer gives the correct notice, liability to pay a redundancy payment will not be extinguished unless the employee is dismissed a second time.

10.45 Section 140(1) uses the phrase 'where the employer, *being entitled* to terminate his contract...'. The effect of the italicised words was considered by the EAT in *Bonner v H Gilbert Ltd* (1989). It held that where the employer raises a defence to a redundancy payments claim based on section 140(1), the question of whether or not he or she is entitled to terminate the employee's contract must be determined according to the 'contractual' approach propounded in *Western Excavating (ECC) Ltd v Sharp* (1978). In other words, the employer must show that the employee was guilty of conduct which was a significant breach of contract or which showed that he or she no longer intended to be bound by one or more of the essential terms of the contract. A reasonable belief that the employee has committed a breach of contract will not be enough.

10.46 Section 140(3) gives the employment tribunal power to award all or part of the redundancy payment, where the employer terminates the contract in accordance with section 140(1) and the second dismissal takes place 'at any relevant time'. This phrase is defined in section 140(5) as 'any time within the obligatory period'; 'obligatory period' is defined in section 136(4). In *Simmons v Hoover Ltd* (1977) the EAT expressed the view that what is now section 140(3) applies only where there are two dismissals. If their analysis of section 140(1) and (3) is correct, the result is that some serious anomalies exist, which tend to favour employers who act wrongfully.

10.47 Special considerations apply in the case of strikes. The employee's action in taking part in a strike has been held to be 'employee's conduct' within section 140(1): see *Simmons v Hoover Ltd* (1977) above. If the dismissal provokes a strike, section 140(2) operates to negate the effect of section 140(1), so that the employee does not lose the entitlement to a redundancy payment. Section 140(2) will not operate, however, if the strike came first. In that case, section 140(1) will operate. It is a moot point whether section 140(3) will operate, but it would seem that it does not, since its terms exclude termination by reason of taking part in a strike.

Calculation of redundancy payment

10.48 The calculation of a redundancy payment is based on the following factors: the employee's age at the relevant date (in most cases, the same date as the effective date of termination in unfair dismissal cases); the number of years of continuous employment; and the amount of gross weekly pay (calculated in accordance with ss 220–229). The calculation is subject to the following limits: (1) the number of years used in the calculation may not exceed 20: s 162(3); and (2) the amount of a week's pay may not exceed a figure set annually by the Secretary of State, the amount being currently (from 1 February 2008) £330: s 227(1), as amended by the Employment Rights (Increase of Limits) Order 2008.

10.49 Redundancy payments are calculated in accordance with ERA 1996, s 162, and the total amount arrived at may be subject to a deduction in certain cases, mainly in the case of misconduct or where the employee is near retirement age. Social security benefits paid to the employee are not deductible.

10.50 The method of calculation is to take each year of continuous employment, working backwards from the relevant date. For each year of continuous employment the amount of the redundancy payment is assessed on the basis of the employee's age at the beginning of the year. For each year in which the employee was aged 41 or more (but not more than 64), one-and-a-half week's pay is payable; for each year in which he or she was between 22 and 41, one weeks' pay; for each year over the age of 18 between the time he or she started work and 22, half a week's pay: ss 162(2) and 211(2). Thus, an employee employed for 20 years and made redundant at 62 will receive a redundancy payment reckoned on the basis of the years of continuous employment from 62 going back to 42. The maximum redundancy payment that can be awarded at present is thus £9,900. Employment before the age of 18 may not be counted: s 211(2). The employee's period of continuous employment will be treated as starting on his or her 18th birthday if that date is later than the starting date. The employment tribunal may use its discretion to award all or part of a redundancy payment in cases involving misconduct by the employee: see para 10.46, above.

Right of employee to time off

10.51 Employees given notice of dismissal by reason of redundancy are entitled by section 52(1) to reasonable time off during the notice period to look for new employment or make arrangements for training for further employment. They must have been continuously employed for two years. They need not provide evidence that they have an appointment, though it may be relevant to the reasonableness of the employer's conduct to ask whether the employee has an appointment and to make some enquiries about it: see *Dutton v Hawker Siddeley Aviation Ltd* (1978). The amount of time off is not statutorily defined, but the employee is not entitled to be paid more than 40 per cent of a week's pay: s 53(1) and (5). That does not mean, however, that it would not be reasonable for the employer to allow more time off, though the employee would not be entitled to be paid. Disputes about this entitlement are heard by the employment tribunal: s 54.

10.52 It should be noted that only those made redundant are entitled to the right to time off, and not other employees who are dismissed, and that the entitlement to time off does not depend upon the employee's eventual entitlement, or otherwise, to a redundancy payment: see *Dutton v Hawker Siddeley Aviation Ltd*, above.

FURTHER READING

Deakin, S, & Morris, G, *Labour Law* (4th ed, 2005) Hart (chapter 5).

Smith, I, & Thomas, G, *Smith & Wood's Employment Law* (9th ed, 2007) Oxford University Press (chapters 9 & 10).

Upex, R, *The Law on Termination of Employment* (7th ed, 2006) Jordans.

ARTICLE

Hall, M, & Edwards, P, (1999) 'Reforming the Statutory Redundancy Consultation Procedure', *Industrial Law Journal*, Vol 28, No 4, pp 299–318.

SELF-TEST QUESTIONS

1   Violetta is a professional singer and is employed by Manc Operatics Company. Two weeks ago, Violetta overheard at a post-concert party that Aled, the Musical Director, would have to reorganise the Company due to financial pressures.

Last week, Violetta was offered a lead singing part in the next touring musical, to be played in the USA, Europe, and Australia. However, yesterday Violetta learnt that she is pregnant and decided that the travelling will be too much. When she informed the Company's managing director, Diana, of her news, Violetta was added to Aled's 'redundancy list'. The next day, Isolde was given Violetta's role on tour.

Figaro, the company's pianist does not like overseas travel and has asked if he might be found alternative work in the UK, whilst the others go on tour. Diana has informed him that 'it is part of your contract and if you don't go you are effectively resigning from your post'. Figaro formally resigned earlier today. However, the Management Team has today announced that it was intending to make all the Company's musicians redundant, since its future overseas tours would not require them any longer, as it would employ musicians in the various places during the tour.

Advise Violetta and Figaro.

2 'Redundancy payments fail to reflect an employee's loyalty to their employer.' Discuss.

3 Explain the legal significance of consultation in redundancy situations.

4 Talk-Francais, a French multinational company, makes mobile phones and has 70 per cent of the European market. Recently technological innovation in camera-mobiles has appeared and Talk-Francais is competing with its main market rival, Hellenic-Speak. Hellenic-Speak purchases the innovation and announces plans to manufacture camera-mobiles within the next six months. Consequently Talk-Francais' sales fall and as a result Talk-Francais announces the closure of its UK subsidiary and informs its French workforce that 20 per cent of the 1,100 workers will be dismissed and the remainder must accept a 30 per cent cut in pay. Simultaneously, Talk-Francais sells its Marketing Division to Hellenic-Speak.

Advise the employees of Talk-Francais of any dismissal and/or redundancy rights which they may have.

Transfers of undertakings

SUMMARY

Business reorganisations are widespread. To that end, the law seeks to regulate them under the Transfer of Undertakings (Protection of Employment) Regulations, usually known as TUPE. TUPE provides a complex blend of both EU and UK legal principles. This chapter considers the regulation of business transfers, the sale of the ownership of a business and the consequential changing from employer A to new employer B, and its effects upon the contract of employment and the employee subjected to the transfer.

This chapter will consider:

- the definition of a transfer;
- the concept of 'relevant transfer';
- what transfers and does not;
- whether unfair dismissal claims can be brought;
- what changes can be made to terms and conditions post-transfer; and
- the rights to consultation and information.

Introduction

11.1 The law relating to transfers of undertakings derived originally from EEC Council Directive 187 of 14 February 1977, on the Approximation of the Laws of the Member States relating to the Safeguarding of Employee's Rights in the Event of Transfers of Undertakings, Businesses or Parts of Businesses (77/187/EEC). The original 1977 Directive was subsequently amended by Directive 98/59/EC and both directives have now been consolidated into Council Directive 2001/23/EC, whose provisions are quoted in the text below. The original directive was transposed into domestic law by the Transfer of Undertakings (Protection of Employment) Regulations 1981 (as amended). The 2001 Directive has been transposed into UK Law by the Transfer of Undertakings (Protection of Employment) Regulations 2006, which came into effect on 6 April 2006.

Directive 2001/23/EC

11.2 The provisions of the Directive (which, as has been seen, derive from the 1977 Directive) have been considered in a considerable number of decisions in the European Court of Justice. In *Foreningen af Arbejdsledere i Danmark v Daddy's Dance Hall A/S* (1988), one of the cases of lasting significance in this area, the Court said:

> The objective of Directive 77/187 is to ensure as far as possible the safeguarding of employees' rights in the event of a change of proprietor of the undertaking and to allow them to remain in the service of the new proprietor on the same condition as those agreed with the vendor. The Directive therefore applies as soon as there is a change, resulting from a conventional sale or a merger, of the natural or legal person responsible for operating the undertaking who, consequently, enters into obligations as an employer towards employees working in the undertaking, and it is of no importance to know whether the ownership of the undertaking has been transferred.

11.3 Article 1(1)(a) of the Directive states that it is to apply to 'any transfer of an undertaking, business or part of an undertaking or business to another employer as a result of a legal transfer or merger'. Article 1(1) goes on to state:

> (b) ... there is a transfer within the meaning of this Directive where there is a transfer of an economic entity which retains its identity, meaning an organised grouping of resources which has the objective of pursuing an economic activity, whether or not that activity is central or ancillary.

> (c) This Directive shall apply to public and private undertakings engaged in economic activities whether or not they are operating for gain.

11.4 These new provisions were substituted by Council Directive 98/50/EC and are intended to clarify the legal concept of transfer in the light of the previous case-law of the ECJ.

11.5 Article 3 provides for the automatic transfer to the transferee of the transferor's rights and obligations arising from a contract of employment or from an employment relationship existing on the date of the transfer. In *CELTEC Ltd v Astley* (2005) the ECJ said that the phrase 'date of a transfer' is a particular point in time which cannot be postponed to another date at the will of the transferor or transferee and is the date on which responsibility as employer for carrying on the business of the unit transferred moved from the transferor to the transferee. It went on to hold that, for the purposes of applying Article 3(1), contracts of employment or employment relationships existing on the date of the transfer, as so defined, are deemed to be handed over on that date, regardless of what has been agreed between the parties. (See also the House of Lords decision in this case.) In *Katsikas v Konstantinidis* (1993) the ECJ held that Article 3 does not preclude an employee employed by the transferor from objecting to the transfer to the transferee of the contract of employment or employment relationship. It said that it is for the Member States to decide on the fate of the contract of employment or employment relationship with the transferor.

11.6 Article 4(1) (as substituted) states:

> The transfer of the undertaking, business or part of the undertaking or business shall not in itself constitute grounds for dismissal by the transferor or the transferee. This provision shall not stand in the way of dismissals that may take place for economic, technical or organisational reasons entailing changes in the work force.

11.7 Article 4(2) goes on to provide that if the contract of employment or the employment relationship is terminated because the transfer involves a substantial change in working conditions to the detriment of the employee, the employer is to be regarded as having been responsible for the termination. The relationship between Article 3(1) as interpreted in the *Katsikas* case (above) and Article 4(2) was considered by the ECJ in *Merckx and Neuhuys v Ford Motors Co Belgium SA* (1997). The distinction made by the Court is between the employee of his or her own accord deciding not to continue with the employment relationship with the transferee, in which case the *Katsikas* case will apply, and terminating the contract because the transfer involves a substantial change in working conditions, such as a change in the level of remuneration; in the latter case, Article 4(2) will apply. Much will depend upon the facts of any given case.

11.8 The following matters will be considered: (1) the meaning of 'undertaking' and 'business'; (2) what amounts to a 'transfer'; (3) the effect of Article 4 in relation to dismissals.

The meaning of 'undertaking' and 'business'

11.9 The question is important since it relates to the coverage of the Directive and the sorts of transfers which are embraced by it. In *Allen v Amalgamated Construction Co Ltd* (2000) the Court said:

> It is ... clear that the Directive is intended to cover any legal change in the person of the employer ... and ... it can, therefore, apply to a transfer between two subsidiary companies

in the same group, which are distinct legal persons each with specific employment relationships with their employees. The fact that the companies in question not only have the
same ownership but also the same management and the same premises and that they
are engaged in the same works makes no difference in this regard.

Thus a transfer between subsidiary companies in the same corporate group is covered by the Directive.

11.10 Decisions of the ECJ in the early 1990s suggested that the court was prepared to
take a broad view of activities which were to be treated as a business or part of a
business. In *Stichting v Bartol* (1992), the ECJ said that 'activities of a special nature'
may be regarded as comparable to a business or part of a business. The case arose
in the context of the switch of a grant from one foundation to another, neither
being profit-making organisations. In *Rask and Christensen v ISS Kantineservice
A/S* (1993), which involved the outsourcing of a staff canteen, the ECJ took the
matter a stage further and said that the Directive can apply to a situation where the
owner of an undertaking entrusts to the owner of another undertaking, by means
of a contract, the responsibility of providing a service for employees, which it had
previously operated directly, and which is ancillary to its economic activities. The
Court developed this view further in *Schmidt v Spar- und Leihkasse der Früheren
Ämter Bordesholm, Kiel und Cronshagen* (1995), when it decided that the Directive
may apply to an ancillary activity where the transfer involves a single employee
and does not involve the transfer of any tangible assets. See also *EC Commission v
United Kingdom* (1994), in which the ECJ said: 'The Court has already accepted,
at least implicitly, in the context of competition law ... or social law ... that a body
might be engaged in economic activities and be regarded as an "undertaking"
for the purposes of Community law even though it did not operate with a view
to profit.'

11.11 Recent decisions of the European Court of Justice suggest that the Court is taking
a more cautious approach to interpretation of the Directive. Thus, for example, in
*Ledernes Hovedorganisation (Acting on behalf of Rygaard) v Dansk Arbejdsgiverforening
(Acting on behalf of Strø Mølle Akustik A/S) (Rygaard's case)* (1996), which involved
the taking over by a sub-contractor of completion of a building contract, together
with the workers and materials assigned to it, the ECJ decided that the Directive
did not apply. The Court reiterated that the decisive criterion is whether the business in question retains its identity and went on to say that the transfer should relate
to 'a stable economic entity whose activity is not limited to performing one specific
works contract'. They said that the Directive does not apply where the transferor
undertaking merely makes available to the new contractor certain workers and
material for carrying out the works in question.

11.12 The decision in *Rygaard*'s case may be contrasted with the decision in *Merckx and Neuhuys v Ford Motors Co Belgium SA* (1997), decided some six months later. The case involved the transfer of a car dealership without a transfer of tangible assets from Ford dealers to independent dealers. More than three-quarters of the Ford dealer's staff were dismissed but the employees in question were told that they would be transferred to the new dealers; after the transfer the Ford dealers discontinued their activities. The ECJ ruled that Article 1(1) of the Directive applied to the transfer of the dealership, emphasising that the decisive criterion is whether the entity in question retains its economic identity. The Court reiterated its view that the transfer of tangible assets is not conclusive of whether the entity in question retains its economic identity and said: 'The purpose of an exclusive dealership for the sale of motor vehicles of a particular make in a certain sector remains the same even if it is carried on under a different name, from different premises and with different facilities.'

The meaning of 'transfer'

11.13 The starting-point for a consideration of this question is *Spijkers v Gebroeders Benedik Abattoir* (1986). In that case, the ECJ emphasised that the aim of the Directive is to ensure 'the continuity of employment relationships existing within a business, irrespective of a change of owner' and said that the decisive criterion is 'whether the business in question retains its identity'. It went on to say:

> It is necessary to consider all the facts characterising the transaction in question, including the type of undertaking or business, whether or not the business's tangible assets, such as buildings and movable property are transferred, the value of its intangible assets at the time of the transfer, whether or not the majority of its employees are taken over by the new employer, whether or not its customers are transferred and the degree of similarity between the activities carried on before and after the transfer and the period, if any, for which those activities were suspended. It should be noted, however, that all those circumstances are merely single factors in the overall assessment which must be made and cannot, therefore, be considered in isolation.

11.14 This approach has been articulated in very similar language in the cases which have followed this decision and the emphasis of the Court has been on whether an undertaking retains its identity: see *Schmidt v Spar- und Leihkasse der Früheren Ämter Bordesholm, Kiel und Cronshagen* (1995), *Ledernes Hovedorganisation (Acting on behalf of Rygaard) v Dansk Arbejdsgiverforening (Acting on behalf of Strø Mølle Akustik A/S) (Rygaard's case)* (1996), *Merckx and Neuhuys v Ford Motors Co Belgium SA* (1997), and *Süzen v Zehnacker Gebdudereinigung GmbH Krankenhausservice, Lefarth GmbH (Party joined)* (1997).

11.15 In *Dr Sophie Redmond Stichting v Bartol* (1992), the ECJ ruled that a transfer within Article 1(1) of the Directive may take place where a public body decides to terminate a subsidy paid to one legal person, as a result of which the activities of that legal person are terminated, and to transfer it to another legal person with similar aims. The Court said that the decision by a public body to alter its policy on subsidies is as much a unilateral decision as the decision of an owner to change its lessee.

11.16 In recent years, this issue has given rise to a number of significant cases. The first, *Merckx and Neuhuys v Ford Motors Co Belgium SA* (1997), involved the transfer of a car dealership without a transfer of tangible assets from Ford dealers to independent dealers. The employees advanced a number of arguments to the Court, saying that the transfer was outside the Directive: (1) because there had been no transfer of either tangible or intangible assets and no preservation of the undertaking's structure and organisation; (2) because the transferor dealer ceased trading and was put into liquidation after the transfer; (3) because the majority of the staff were dismissed upon the transfer; and (4) because the notion of a legal transfer within Article 1(1) of the Directive required the existence of a contractual link between the transferor and the transferee. The Court rejected all these arguments.

11.17 In *Süzen v Zehnacker Gebdudereinigung GmbH Krankenhausservice, Lefarth GmbH (Party joined)* (1997) the question was whether the termination of a cleaning contract with one contractor and the grant of the contract to another contractor amount to a transfer within the Directive. As in the *Merckx* case, there was no transfer of tangible or intangible assets. The Court reiterated what it had said in previous cases, that the decisive question is whether the entity in question retains its identity. It said that, although the absence of a contractual link between the transferor and the transferee or (as here) the two undertakings successively granted the cleaning contract might point to the absence of a transfer, it was not conclusive. It added the transfer may take place in two stages, through the intermediary of a third party such as the owner or the person putting up the capital, and stressed that the transfer must relate to a stable economic entity whose activity is not limited to performing one specific works contract (as in *Rygaard*'s case). It said, at pp 670–671:

> The term entity thus refers to an organised grouping of persons and assets facilitating the exercise of an economic activity which pursues a specific objective . . . The mere fact that the service provided by the old and the new awardees of a contract is similar does not therefore support the conclusion that an economic entity has been transferred. An entity cannot be reduced to the activity entrusted to it. Its identity also emerges from other factors, such as its workforce, its management staff, the way in which its work is organised, its operating methods or indeed, where appropriate, the operational resource available to it . . . The mere loss of a service contract to a competitor cannot therefore by itself indicate the existence of a transfer . . . In those circumstances, the service undertaking previously

entrusted with the contract does not, on losing a customer, thereby cease fully to exist, and a business or part of a business belonging to it cannot be considered to have been transferred to the new awardee of the contract.

11.18 The Court pointed out that the absence of a transfer of assets does not necessarily preclude the existence of a transfer and that, in considering the various criteria which have identified as relevant to the *question* whether the business has retained its identity, the degree of importance to be attached to each criterion 'will necessarily vary according to the activity carried on, or indeed the production or operating methods employed in the relevant undertaking'.

11.19 A similar approach may be detected in *Francisco Hernández Vidal SA v Gomez Perez* (1999) and *Sánchez Hidalgo v Asociacion de Servicios ASER* (1999). The first group of cases involved contracting-in, where cleaning work was brought back in-house after being contracted out; the second group involved a change of contractor. In both groups of cases, the ECJ concentrated on whether an 'economic entity' had been transferred and said it had.

11.20 This approach *was* followed in the later decision of *Allen v Amalgamated Construction Co Ltd* (2000), which involved the transfer of an employee between subsidiary companies in the same corporate group. Both companies shared the same management and premises and also shared administrative and support functions. The ECJ held that there was a transfer within Article 1 of the Directive. It is worth noting here that the Court approached this case on the basis that it was one involving an activity based essentially on manpower. This was because, although the activity in question (the driving of underground tunnels) required a significant amount of plant and equipment, the mine owner provided those assets and not the contractors. The ECJ pointed out that the fact that ownership of the assets required to run the undertaking do not pass to the new owner does not preclude a transfer.

11.21 Subsequent to this decision was the decision in *Oy Liikenne AB v Liskojärvi and Juntunen* (2001). The facts of the case were that the operation of seven bus routes was awarded to Oy Liikenne AB; they had previously been operated by Hakunilan Liikenne Oy. Hakunilan dismissed 45 drivers, of whom 33 were re-engaged by Oy Liikenne; no vehicles or other assets connected with the operation of the bus routes were transferred, although Oy Liikenne bought uniforms from Hakunilan for some of the drivers who entered its service. The applicants were amongst the 33 drivers who were taken on by Oy Liikenne. They claimed that there had been a transfer of an undertaking and that they were entitled to enjoy the more favourable terms and conditions applied by their previous employer. The Court said:

> In a sector such as scheduled public transport by bus, where the tangible assets contribute significantly to the performance of the activity, the absence of a transfer to a significant

extent from the old to the new contractor of such assets, which are necessary for the proper functioning of the entity, must lead to the conclusion that the entity does not retain its identity. Consequently, in a situation such as that in the main proceedings, Directive 77/187 does not apply in the absence of a transfer of significant tangible assets from the old to the new contractor.

11.22 This approach suggests that the decisive criterion in such cases is whether the tangible assets 'contribute *significantly*' to the activity and does not seem to take into account the possibility that there may be factors pointing towards the conclusion that the entity retains its identity.

11.23 The later case of *Abler v Sodexho MM Catering Gesellschaft mbH and Sanrest Großküchen Betribsgesellschaft mbH* (2004) involved a transfer of catering services, after a tendering process, to Sodexho. It refused to take over the materials, stock, and employees of the previous contractor, Sanrest. The ECJ said that in a sector such as catering, where the activity is based essentially on equipment, the failure of a new contractor to take over an essential part of the staff which the predecessor contractor employed to perform the same activity is not sufficient to preclude the existence of a transfer of an entity which retains its identity within the meaning of the Directive, whose main objective is to ensure the continuity, even against the wishes of the transferee, of the employment contracts of the employees of the transferor. The Court said that catering cannot be regarded as an activity based essentially on manpower since it requires a significant amount of equipment. Thus, the transfer of the premises and the equipment provided by the hospital was sufficient to make this a transfer of an economic entity. The Court added that the fact that the tangible assets taken over by the new contractor did not belong to its predecessor but were provided by the contracting authority could not preclude the existence of a transfer, since it is clear that the Directive applies whenever there is a change in the legal or natural person who is responsible for carrying on the business. See also *Temco Service Industries SA v Imzilyen* (2002), in which the ECJ held that there may be a transfer where the transferor is a sub-contractor of the original contractor, and *Güney-Görres v Securicor Aviation* (2006).

The effect of Article 4 in relation to dismissals

11.24 Article 4(1) contains two provisions relating to dismissals. The first is that a transfer of an *undertaking* 'shall not in itself constitute grounds for dismissal . . .'. The second is that the first provision 'shall not stand in the way of dismissals that may take place for economic, technical or organisational reasons entailing changes in the workforce'. The first is transposed into UK law by TUPE regulation 7(1), the second by regulation 7(2): see para 11.51 below.

11.25 The ECJ has made it clear that it is for national law to decide upon the appropriate remedy for a dismissal *which* contravenes Article 4(1), but that Article 4(1) of itself does not make a dismissal brought about by a transfer a nullity: see *Wendelboe v LJ Music APS* (1985) and *Foreningen af Arbedsledere I Danmark v A/S Danmols Inventar* (1985). The House of Lords has subsequently decided that what is now TUPE regulation 7(1) (formerly reg 8(1)), which declares a dismissal brought about by a transfer to be automatically unfair, gives effect to and is consistent with the Directive: see *Wilson v St Helens Borough Council* (1998). It is not therefore necessary to go so far as to say that a dismissal in such circumstances is a nullity.

The Transfer of Undertakings Regulations 2006 (TUPE)

11.26 The effect of the Regulations is that they afford protection to employees where there is a 'relevant transfer' of an 'undertaking'. Where there is a relevant transfer, an employee's contract will be automatically transferred to the person to whom the undertaking is transferred. The importance of the decisions of the ECJ considered above lies in the fact that courts and tribunals in the United Kingdom are required to interpret the Regulations so as to ensure that, so far as possible, they conform to the Directive.

11.27 The following matters are considered here: (1) the meaning of 'relevant transfer'; (2) the meaning of 'undertaking'; and (3) the effect of a relevant transfer.

11.28 It should be noted that, as a general rule, a tribunal considering whether there has been a relevant transfer of an *undertaking* should consider as separate issues, first, whether the entity in question was an undertaking and, second, whether there was a relevant transfer. The EAT has made it clear that these two issues should be considered as separate questions and has said that, although it is not invariably an error of law not to raise the two questions as separate questions or to fail to deal with them in that order, a tribunal which fails in this way runs a real risk of error: see *Cheesman v R Brewer Contracts Ltd* (2001) and *Whitewater Leisure Management Ltd v Barnes* (2000).

The meaning of 'relevant transfer'

11.29 In regulation 3 of the TUPE 2006 Regulations (which is headed 'A relevant transfer') two situations are treated as relevant transfers. The first is similar to the one found in the 1981 Regulations. Regulation 3(1)(a) of the 2006 Regulations defines this first type of transfer as:

> a transfer of an undertaking, business or part of an undertaking or business situated immediately before the transfer in the United Kingdom to another person where there is a transfer of an economic entity which retains its identity.

Regulation 3(2) defines the phrase 'economic entity'; this is considered in the next section, in the context of the discussion of the meaning of the words 'undertaking' and 'business': see para 11.38.

11.30 The second type of relevant transfer is what is called 'a service provision change'; it is defined in regulation 3(1)(b) as a situation in which:

(i) activities cease to be carried out by a person ('a client') on his own behalf and are carried out instead by another person on the client's behalf ('a contractor');

(ii) activities cease to be carried out by a contractor on a client's behalf (whether or not those activities had previously been carried out by the client on his own behalf) and are carried out instead by another person ('a subsequent contractor') on the client's behalf; or

(iii) activities cease to be carried out by a contractor or a subsequent contractor on a client's behalf (whether or not those activities had previously been carried out by the client on his own behalf) and are carried out instead by the client on his own behalf.

11.31 The conditions set out in regulation 3(3) must also be satisfied. These are:

(a) immediately before the service provision change –
  (i) there is an organised grouping of employees situated in Great Britain which has as its principal purpose the carrying out of the activities concerned on behalf of the client;
  (ii) the client intends that the activities will, following the service provision change, be carried out by the transferee other than in connection with a single specific event or task of short-term duration; and

(b) the activities concerned do not consist wholly or mainly of the supply of goods for the client's use.

11.32 The following points should be noted here:

(1) there must be 'an organised grouping of employees';

(2) such a grouping may consist of one person only;

(3) these provisions do not apply to situations where a contractor is engaged to organise a single specific event or task and the event or task is of short-term duration;

(4) the provisions do not apply where a client engages a contractor to supply goods for the client's use.

The above provisions are intended to apply to three situations: (1) contracting out or 'out-sourcing'; (2) assignment of a contract to a new contractor on subsequent retendering; and (3) contracting in or 'insourcing', ie where a contract with an outside contractor ends and the service is brought back 'in house' by the former client. In all cases, however, there must be 'an organised grouping of employees...which has as its principal purpose the carrying out of the activities concerned on behalf of the client'. This is intended to confine the coverage of the Regulations to cases where the transferor has in place a team of employees dedicated to carrying out the activities that are to transfer and would exclude cases where there was no identifiable grouping of employees. The DTI Guidance gives as an example the provision by a contractor of a courier service where the collections and deliveries are carried out each day by different couriers on an ad hoc basis rather than by an identifiable team of employees.

11.33　The starting-point of any discussion of whether there has been a transfer of an undertaking is the ECJ decisions in *Süzen v Zehnacker Gebdudereinigung GmbH Krankenhausservice, Lefarth GmbH (Party joined)* (1997), *Francisco Hernández Vidal SA v Gomez Perezi* (1999), and *Sánchez Hidalgo v Asociacion de Servicios ASER* (1999): see para 11.17, above. What falls to be considered here is how the Courts and tribunals in the United Kingdom have approached the ECJ's decisions.

11.34　Very soon after the decision in *Süzen*, the Court of Appeal heard the appeal from the High Court in *Betts v Brintel Helicopters Ltd* (1997). The case involved the loss by one company (Brintel) of a contract to provide helicopter services and its transfer to another (KLM). KLM only took over rights associated with the contract and engaged none of Brintel's employees. The main issue in the Court of Appeal was whether there was a transfer of an undertaking, in other words whether the undertaking had retained its identity in the hands of the transferee. Kennedy LJ reviewed the relevant case law of the European Court of Justice and said that the limited transfer of assets (the right to land on oil rigs and use oil rig facilities) could not lead to the conclusion that the undertaking had retained its identity. He said:

> The real distinction...is between (1) labour-intensive undertakings, in which if the staff combine to engage in a particular activity which continues or is resumed with substantially the same staff after the alleged transfer the court may well conclude that the undertaking has been transferred so that it has retained its identity in the hands of the transferee; and (2) other types of undertaking in relation to which the application of the Spijkers test involves a more wide-ranging inquiry.

11.35　This decision may be contrasted with the decision of another division of the Court of Appeal, about a year later, in *ECM (Vehicle Delivery Service) Ltd v Cox* (1999). A contract to distribute cars (the 'VAG contract') was lost by one contractor and awarded to ECM. They chose to organise the contracted service in a different way;

they dispensed with the previous contractor's base and refused to engage any of the staff employed on the vehicle delivery contract because they had asserted that their employment was protected by TUPE. The Court of Appeal upheld the decision of the tribunal and the EAT that there had been a relevant transfer. The argument of ECM in the Court of Appeal was that there was no transfer of an undertaking, although it accepted that there was an undertaking carried on by the previous contractor. The basis of their argument was that *Süzen* signalled a change of emphasis in the ECJ and that the position on transfers of undertakings following that decision was that, where the only continuing feature is the nature of the activity itself and all that continues is the service itself, it is impossible to find that an undertaking has been transferred. So in the case in question, it was argued, all that continued was the activity of delivering cars under the VAG contract. Mummery LJ, with whom the other lords justices agreed, rejected that argument and held that the employment tribunal had applied the correct test, as laid down in *Spijkers* and subsequent cases. He also observed that the tribunal was entitled to have regard, as a relevant circumstance, to the reason why the employees were not taken on by ECM. He suggested that the importance of *Süzen* had been overstated and pointed out that the ECJ had not overruled its previous interpretative rulings. He also observed that the criteria laid down by the ECJ still involve consideration of 'all the facts characterising the transaction in question' as identified in *Spijkers*.

11.36 In *ADI (UK) Ltd v Willer* (2001), a different division of the Court of Appeal returned to this issue. The case involved the provision of security services and thus involved a labour-intensive undertaking. The company which took over the contract from ADI took on none of its staff, two of whom made claims against ADI and the putative transferee. The employment tribunal decided that there had been no transfer of an undertaking. On appeal, the EAT held that there was no transfer of an undertaking when a contract to provide security services was awarded to a new contractor but none of the workforce transferred. The EAT said that this was a conclusion which was open to the tribunal. The Court of Appeal allowed the transferor's appeal and remitted the case to a tribunal to consider whether the reason for the transferees not taking on the employees was in order to avoid TUPE. The Court said that if the circumstances of an alleged transfer of an undertaking are such that an actual transfer of labour would be a relevant factor to be taken into account in deciding whether there has been a TUPE transfer, an employment tribunal is obliged to consider the reason why the labour was not transferred, in accordance with the Court of Appeal's decision in *ECM (Vehicle Delivery) Service Ltd v Cox* (above). If the economic entity is labour intensive such that, applying *Süzen*, there is no transfer if the workforce is not taken on, but there would be if they were, the tribunal is obliged to treat the case as if the labour had transferred if it is established that the reason or principal reason for this was in order to avoid the application of TUPE.

11.37 Following this decision was the EAT decision in *RCO Support Services and Aintree Hospital Trust v UNISON* (2002), which was upheld by the Court of Appeal. The case involved cleaners and caterers. The cleaners were employed by Initial Hospital Services Ltd at Walton Hospital, one of two hospitals run by the Aintree Hospitals NHS Trust. Initial tendered for the cleaning contract at Fazakerley, the other hospital run by the Trust, but it was won by RCO. None of the Walton cleaners applied for jobs with RCO and none were taken on. Subsequently the employment of cleaners at Walton ended and a number of them brought unfair dismissal proceedings. The catering staff were employed at Walton by the Trust itself. Three of the support staff were dismissed for redundancy. Applications were invited by RCO, who held the catering contract at Fazakerley. One applicant was not offered a job and another declined the job offered to her. The ET held that there was a relevant transfer from Initial to RCO in respect of the cleaners and from the Trust to RCO in respect of the caterers. The EAT dismissed the appeals. They said that the absence of movement of significant assets or of a major part of the workforce does not necessarily deny the existence of a relevant transfer and expressed the view that *Süzen* can no longer be safely relied upon. The Court of Appeal upheld the EAT's decision, favouring the approach taken by the Court of Appeal in *ECM* over that taken by the earlier CA in *Betts v Brintel*. The Court of Appeal's decision signals a preference for the *Spijkers* approach. Mummery LJ, with whom the other two members of the Court agreed, said that the mere fact that a putative transferee carries on the same activities or supplies the same services as the putative transferor is not by itself determinative in favour of a transfer, nor does it by itself support a conclusion that an entity retains its identity. Similarly, the fact that none of the workforce is taken on is not necessarily conclusive on the issue of retention of identity. He said that these matters are all factors to be considered in making an overall assessment of all the facts characterising the transaction, with no single factor being considered in isolation.

The meaning of 'undertaking' and 'business'

11.38 The 2006 TUPE Regulations contain no definition of the word 'undertaking', unlike their predecessor Regulations. It should be noted, however, that regulation 3 contains various phrases which clearly reflect the jurisprudence of the ECJ. In particular, regulation 3(1)(a) refers to the transfer of an economic entity which retains its identity; and regulation 3(2) defines 'economic entity' as 'an organised grouping of resources which has the objective of pursuing an economic activity, whether or not that activity is central or ancillary'. It should also be noted that, by virtue of regulation 3(4)(a) the Regulations apply to public and private undertakings engaged in economic activities 'whether or not they are operating for gain'. Regulation 3(5) provides that an administrative reorganisation of public administrative authorities or the transfer of administrative functions between public administrative authorities is not a relevant transfer.

11.39 The decisions of the Court of Appeal and the EAT have drawn heavily on the case law of the ECJ when considering whether a particular entity amounts to an undertaking. In *Whitewater Leisure Management Ltd v Barnes* (2000) the EAT said that there are two formulations which can be used to identify whether there is an economic entity. The first asks whether there is 'a stable and discrete economic entity'; the alternative version asks whether the entity is 'sufficiently structured and autonomous'. The EAT suggested that the expression 'distinct cost centre' might be helpful. Had the EAT considered the ECJ decision in *Allen v Amalgamated Construction Co Ltd*, above, it might have reached a different conclusion. That case, it will be recalled, said that there may be a transfer of an economic entity even where there is no transfer of the plant and equipment necessary to carry out the activity because they are supplied by the person granting the contract.

11.40 The Whitewater decision also appears to be inconsistent with the later decision of another division of the EAT, in *RCO Support Services and Aintree Hospital Trust v UNISON and others* (2000), which was upheld by the Court of Appeal. There, the EAT held that there may be an undertaking and a transfer of that undertaking despite the fact that neither significant assets nor a majority of the workforce moves over. He took a similar approach in *Argyll Training Ltd v Sinclair and Argyll & The Islands Enterprise Ltd* (2000) when deciding that a training contract and the arrangements made for its performance amounted to an undertaking. The Court of Appeal in *RCO Support Services and Aintree Hospital Trust v UNISON and others* (2002) upheld the EAT's decision, finding it not necessary for there to be a transfer of employees and/or assets in order for TUPE to apply; see also *Wynnwith Engineering v Bennett* (2002) and *P & O Transport European Ltd v Initial Transport Services Ltd* (2003).

11.41 In *Cheesman v R Brewer Contracts Ltd* (2001), which involved the loss of a maintenance contract, Lindsay J said:

(i) As to whether there is an undertaking, there needs to be found a stable economic entity whose activity is not limited to performing one specific works contract, an organised grouping of persons and of assets enabling (or facilitating) the exercise of an economic activity which pursues a specific objective...; (ii) In order to be such an undertaking it must be sufficiently structured and autonomous but will not necessarily have significant assets, tangible or intangible...; (iii) In certain sectors such as cleaning and surveillance the assets are often reduced to their most basic and the activity is essentially based on manpower...; (iv) An organised grouping of wage-earners who are specifically and permanently assigned to a common task may in the absence of other factors of production, amount to an economic entity...; (v) An activity of itself is not an entity; the identity of an entity emerges from other factors such as its workforce, management staff, the way in which its work is organised, its operating methods and, where appropriate, the operational resources available to it...

11.42 The approach taken in these cases by Lindsay J lays emphasis on the social objectives of the Directive, the safeguarding of employees' rights. That approach leads to the conclusion that tribunals should be ready to find that an entity is an undertaking and that that undertaking has been transferred.

11.43 A question which has become vexed, particularly since the ECJ decision in *Oy Liikenne AB v Liskojärvi and Juntunen* (see para 11.21 above), relates to changes of contractor in asset-intensive sectors. In *P&O Trans European Ltd v Initial Transport Services Ltd* (2003), the relevant facts were that, as part of the transfer to P&O from Shell of its delivery function, P&O took over from Initial (which had previously provided a back-up delivery service to Shell) its delivery drivers, but not the four administrators who had worked for Initial or any of Initial's vehicles. The question was whether the contract between Initial and Shell could be said to amount to an undertaking. The employment tribunal found that there was a discrete economic entity capable of being transferred. Despite the fact that the assets were not transferred from Initial to P&O, the tribunal concluded that there had been a transfer of an undertaking. It took into account the fact that there had been no transfer of assets but, whilst noting that this was an important factor, nevertheless held that Initial's activity of providing a back-up delivery service had retained its identity. The EAT upheld the tribunal's decision. The EAT said that all relevant factors have to be weighed in assessing whether or not a factor will vary in accordance with the facts of the case. The EAT emphasised that the approach to this issue remains the 'multifactorial' approach set out in the *Spijkers* case; see also the EAT decision in *NUMAST v P&O Scottish Ferries Ltd* (2005) and the Court of Session decision in *Scottish Coal Co Ltd v McCormack* (2005).

11.44 It is also clear, in line with the ECJ case of *Botzen v Rotterdamsche Droogdok Maatschappij BV* (1986), that the TUPE regulations also apply to situations where only a part of a business is transferred. However, in such circumstances it must be determined which employees are subject to the transfer. Guidance on this issue has been provided by the Scottish Court of Session in *Mowlem Technical Services (Scotland) Limited (Formerly Skillbase Services Limited) v King – Inner House of the*

Court of Session (2004). The Court of Session affirmed the EAT decision and expressed that there are four factors that need to be taken into account in determining whether an employee is to be transferred:

- how much time the employee spends on the business transferring as opposed to other businesses of the transferor;
- how much value the employee contributes to each part;
- what the employee's contract says in terms of what he can and can't be asked to do;
- how the cost of the employee's services is allocated between different parts of the business.

The effect of a 'relevant transfer'

11.45 The effect of regulation 4(1) is that a relevant transfer does not of itself terminate the employee's contract, so that the transferor will not be liable for a redundancy payment; the contract will be treated as if it had been made between him or her and the transferee (ie the new employer). It applies to the transfer of an undertaking or a part of an undertaking.

11.46 On the completion of the relevant transfer, regulation 4(2) provides that all the transferor's (ie old employer's) rights, powers, duties, and liabilities 'under or in connection with' the employee's contract of employment are transferred and 'any act or omission before the transfer is completed, of or in relation to the transferor in respect of that contract or a person assigned to that organised grouping of resources or employees' is treated as an act or omission of or in relation to the transferee. The wording of this regulation suggests that, when a relevant transfer takes place, liability passes to the transferee and the transferor drops out of the picture.

11.47 The predecessor of regulation 4(2) (reg 5(2) of the 1981 Regulations) has been held to embrace an employee's accrued right not to be unfairly dismissed, the transferor's right to enforce a restrictive covenant in an employment contract, and an employee's complaint of sex discrimination arising from an act of the transferor before the transfer: see *BSG Property Services v Tuck* (1996), *Morris Angel & Son Ltd v Hollande* (1993), and *DJM International Ltd v Nicholas* (1996). An employer's contractual obligations arising from a collective agreement incorporated into employees' individual contracts will also transfer under regulation 4: see *Whent v T Cartledge Ltd* (1997). In *Bernardone v Pall Mall Services, Martin v Lancashire County Council* (2001) the Court of Appeal held that what is now regulation 4(2) is wide enough to transfer to the transferee the transferor's tortious liability towards an employee injured at work and thus liability in negligence may pass to the transferee. The Court also held that the transferor's rights under an employer's liability insurance policy transferred to the transferee. In *Unicorn Consultancy Services Ltd v Westbrook* (2000) the EAT held that the payment of sums due to employees under the transferor's profit-related pay scheme was a liability which passed to the transferee on the transfer of the undertaking. Subsequently, in *MITIE Management Service Ltd v French* (2002) the EAT had to consider whether the benefits of a profit-sharing scheme, provided by the transferor, passed to the transferee. The EAT said that, since the transferee had no control of the transferor's scheme, it was impossible for it to provide any of the benefits to the transferred employees. It held that the entitlement of the employees under regulation 4(2) was to participate in a scheme of substantial equivalence to the transferor's scheme.

11.48 Regulation 4(4) and (5) now expressly protects rights which the employee has against the transferor so that they cannot be varied on a transfer to the transferee. Regulation 4(4) provides that any purported variation of the employee's contract will be void if the sole or principal reason is the transfer itself or a reason connected with the transfer that is not an economic, technical, or organisational reason entailing changes in the workforce. Regulation 4(5), however, permits the employer and employee to agree a variation if the sole or principal reason for the variation is a reason connected with the transfer that is an economic, technical, or organisational reason entailing changes in the workforce or is a reason unconnected with the transfer. These provisions effectively encapsulate the case law that had grown up in this area. However, the CA confirmed in *Regent Security Services Limited v Power* (2007) that in a situation where transferring employees are offered enhanced rights upon the transfer of the undertaking it is for the employee to elect either to enforce the rights that transferred with them or to rely on the new rights that were granted; it is not open for the transferee to argue that the changes were connected to the transfer and are consequently void.

11.49 The general position set out in regulation 4(1) is subject to three qualifications. First, regulation 4(7) provides that regulation 4(1) and (2) will not operate to transfer employees' contracts of employment and the rights, powers, duties, and liabilities under or in connection with them, if they inform the transferor or the transferee that they object to becoming employed by the transferee. The effect of an objection will be that the employees' contracts of employment will be terminated by the transfer but they will not be treated as having been dismissed by the transferor: see regulation 4(8). The effect will be the same, therefore, as if they had resigned before the transfer. Second, regulation 4(9) preserves the employee's right to resign and claim constructive dismissal where a substantial change is made in the working conditions to his or her 'material' detriment. In that case, the employee may treat the contract as having been terminated and will be treated as having been dismissed by the employer. Third, regulation 4(11) states that regulation 4(7), (8), and (9) are without prejudice to any right of the employee arising apart from the Regulations to terminate the contract of employment without notice in acceptance of a repudiatory breach of contract by the employer.

11.50 Regulation 4(3) applies to persons employed 'immediately before the transfer, or who would have been so employed if he had not been dismissed in the circumstances described in regulation 7(1)...'. The wording of this provision expands on the wording of regulation 5(3) of the 1981 Regulations and is clearly intended to give effect to the House of Lords' decision in *Litster v Forth Dry Dock & Engineering Co Ltd (in receivership)* (1989). In that case, the facts were that the transferor agreed to transfer the undertaking to the transferee and, as part of the agreement, agreed to dismiss the workforce before the completion of the transfer. One hour before the completion of the transfer, the workforce was dismissed. The House of Lords held that the Regulations should be given a purposive construction in a manner which would accord with the decisions of the ECJ on the 1977 Directive and, where necessary, words should be implied to achieve that effect. There should be implied into regulation 5(3) (as it then was) after the words 'immediately before the transfer' the words 'or would have been so employed if he had not been unfairly dismissed in the circumstances described by regulation 8(1)' (now reg 7(1)).

Dismissals – regulation 7

11.51 Dismissals on the transfer of an undertaking are governed by Regulation 7. Regulation 7(1) sets out the general rule, that an employee dismissed either before or after a relevant transfer will be treated as automatically unfairly dismissed, if the transfer or a reason connected with it is the reason or principal reason for the dismissal. The rule applies to employees both of the transferor and the transferee. The general rule does not apply, however, when there is an 'economic, technical or organisational reason entailing changes in the workforce or either the transferor or transferee either before or after a relevant transfer' and that is the reason or principal reason for dismissing the employee: regulation 7(2). In that case, the reason will be treated as 'some other substantial reason' within ERA 1996, s 98(1)(b) and the fairness of the reason must then be considered by the tribunal under section 98(4): see *McGrath v Rank Leisure Ltd* (1985). The correct approach is to consider first whether regulation 7(1) applies so as to make the dismissals automatically unfair; if it does not, then the tribunal should consider whether regulation 7(2) applies.

11.52 One issue which has now been resolved by the House of Lords concerned the effect of a dismissal which is brought about by the transfer of an undertaking. In *Wilson v St Helens Borough Council and Meade v British Fuels Ltd* (1998) two groups of dismissals were involved. The group involved in the *Wilson* case were dismissals for an economic or technical reason and thus within what is now regulation 7(2) (formerly reg 8(2)); the group involved in the *Meade* case were dismissals for a reason connected with the transfer and thus within what is now regulation 7(1). Lord Slynn of Hadley gave the main speech. It centred round the issue whether a dismissal of an employee brought about by a transfer of an undertaking is or is not a nullity. He took the view that the provisions of regulation 7(1) and (2) point to a dismissal being effective and not a nullity and do not create an automatic obligation on the part of the transferee to continue to employ employees who have been dismissed by the transferor. He then went on to consider whether TUPE complies with the Directive. Having considered the relevant case law of the ECJ, he concluded that the Directive does not create a community law right to continue in employment which does not exist in national law and that TUPE gives effect to and is consistent with the Directive. Thus, if an employee is dismissed by the transferor and re-engaged by the transferee, the latter will assume any liability for dismissals incurred by the transferor. The employee will not be able to insist on the observance by the transferee of his or her previous terms or conditions and will be bound by the terms and conditions agreed with the transferee. The dismissal will thus be unfair by virtue of regulation 7(1) but not ineffective.

11.53 The relationship between what is now regulation 7(1) and 7(2) was considered by the Court of Appeal in *Warner v Adnet Ltd* (1998). In that case, the argument on behalf of the employee was that the two paragraphs are mutually exclusive and that, if the tribunal concludes that the dismissal was for a reason falling within what is now regulation 7(1), it is precluded from considering the case under regulation 7(2). The Court of Appeal rejected that argument. Mummery LJ said that the Regulations must be read as a whole and that the drafting of what is now regulation 7(2) is such that it expressly contemplates circumstances in which regulation 7(1) will be disapplied and where a view formed by a tribunal under regulation 7(1) is not final or conclusive. This approach was followed by another division of the Court of Appeal in the later case of *Whitehouse v Charles A Blatchford & Sons Ltd* (2000).

11.54 The words 'economic, technical or organisational' in regulation 7(2) have been considered in a number of cases. The preferred approach now seems to be that of the EAT in *Wheeler v Patel* (1987). They said that the word 'economic' is to be construed *eiusdem generis* with the other two adjectives and is to be given a limited meaning relating to the conduct of the business. They said that it does not include broad economic reasons for a sale, such as the desire to obtain an enhanced price or a desire to achieve a sale. This approach was confirmed in the recent EAT decision

CAB Automotive Ltd v Blake and Others (2007), where it was held that if redundancies were made with the view of selling the undertaking, the principal reason for the dismissals could still be connected to the transfer even where a potential buyer had not yet been identified. See also *Gateway Hotels Ltd v Stewart* (1988) and *Ibex Trading Co Ltd v Walton* (1994). It should be noted, however, that the reason will not fall within regulation 7(2) unless it also entails changes in the workforce: see *Delabole Slate Ltd v Berriman* (1985). It has also been held that harmonization of terms post transfer will not be deemed to be an ETO reason, even where two years have passed since the transfer if there is evidence to suggest that the transferee always had harmonization in mind: see *London Metropolitan University v Sackur and others* (2006).

Consultation under TUPE

11.55 As with redundancy in Chapter 10, TUPE contains provisions which facilitate for consultation between employers (both transferor and transferee) and trade unions/ elected representatives. The effect of regulations 5 and 6 preserve the existing collective arrangements on sale of the business and to inform all of its happening, as well as consult on its consequences.

- Regulation 5 requires that any collective agreement made between the transferor and a trade union shall have effect as if it had been made with the transferee.
- Regulation 6 provides that any trade union which was recognised by the transferor shall be deemed to be recognised by the transferee.
- Regulation 13 obliges the transferor and transferee to consult with recognised trade unions or elected representatives (in the absence of a recognised trade union) for the purposes of collective consultation under TUPE.

11.56 Regulation 11 provides that the transferor shall provide employee liability information in respect of employees assigned to the organised grouping of resources or employees that is subject to a relevant transfer to the transferee in advance of a relevant transfer. Regulation 12 provides a remedy of £500 per employee for the failure of a transferor/transferee to comply with regulation 11.

11.57 Following the enactment of the Employment Relations Act 1999, as amended in 2004, and the establishment of trade union recognition, where there are sufficient members of the workforce who are trade union members, then regulation 6 may become more complex and may have to respond to the pace of change brought about by this new legal framework (see Chapter 13).

Information and consultation rights

11.58 Regulation 13 imposes a duty on an employer to provide information to appropriate representatives of affected employees about a relevant transfer and measures he envisages taking in respect of it, long enough before a relevant transfer to enable the employer to consult those representatives with a view to seeking their agreement to the intended measures. Regulation 14 makes provision for the election of employee representatives where there is no recognised independent trade union. Regulations 15 and 16 provide a remedy in the case of a failure to comply with the obligation imposed by regulation 13.

11.59 Under regulation 13 the transferor must inform and consult with 'appropriate representatives' of affected employees, ie those employees subjected to the transfer or by measures taken in connection with the transfer. This means that all those being transferred should be consulted/informed, but also other employees who are not transferring but are affected should be consulted. Regulation 13(3) makes provision as to who is to be consulted regarding a transfer. However, where no trade unions are recognised, then elected representatives must be in place.

11.60 Regulation 14 provides that the transferor should provide the elected representatives with information on: the facts of the transfer (date and reasons); the 'legal, social and economic' implications (as perceived by the transferee) for the affected employees; what measures are envisaged, post-transfer; and any other information provided or measures envisaged by the transferee. Regulation 14(2) requires the transferee to notify the transferor of any information appropriate to be given to the elected representatives.

11.61 The issue of consultation was considered by the EAT in *Baxter and Others v Marks & Spencer and Others* (2006). This case concerned the outsourcing of the Marks & Spencer loss prevention department, which affected some 200 employees. In recognition of this implication Marks & Spencer provided all those affected with the necessary information. However, election of employee representatives was somewhat delayed and subsequent consultation with the representatives did not occur. A number of employees appealed against the tribunal decisions, finding that consultation had occurred since the employee representatives received all the relevant information prior to the transfer, and that no compensation would be awarded since it was merely a technical breach that caused no detriment. The EAT confirmed the decision of the tribunal and expressed that the tribunal had a discretion whether to award compensation or not. The EAT offered some useful observations on the issue of consultation:

- there is no minimum consultation period for TUPE consultation, which contrasts with the 30/90 day requirement attached to collective redundancies;

- there is a distinction between a matter of principle and an inevitable administrative change. If an issue is deemed to be merely an inevitable administrative change then there is no obligation to consult on that particular issue. It is only matters of principle that require consultation.

Sanctions

11.62 Any breach of regulations 13 or 14 gives right to complain to an Employment Tribunal under regulation 15 on the grounds of failure to comply (ie electoral defects; no or lack of information; no, limited, or lack of consultation; lack of trade union recognition; or any other case affecting employees). Where an ET upholds the complaint, a Declaration is given and the transferor will be required to pay 13 weeks pay to each employee affected (regulation 16(3)). Note that the week's pay is *not* subject to the maximum limit of £290 per week for these purposes.

Transitional arrangements

11.63 Regulation 21 provides that these Regulations shall apply to a relevant transfer that takes place on or after 6 April 2006 whilst the 1981 Regulations will apply to a transfer to which the 1981 Regulations applied that took place before 6 April 2006.

FURTHER READING

Deakin, S, & Morris, G, *Labour Law* (4th ed, 2005) Hart (chapter 3).

Derbyshire, W, Hardy, S, & Maffey, S, *New TUPE 2006* (2006) Spiramus Publishing.

McMullen, J, *Business Transfers and Employee Rights* (2001) Butterworths.

ARTICLES

McMullen, J, (2006) 'Transfer of Undertakings (Protection of Employment) Regulations 2006', *Industrial Law Journal*, Vol 35, No 2, pp 113–139.

Sargeant, M, (2002) 'New Transfer Regulations', *Industrial Law Journal*, Vol 31, No 1, pp 35–54.

SELF-TEST QUESTIONS

1   Wessex County Council has decided to apply 'best value' tendering for its secretarial services. Dolly, Flo, Joe, and Bert are currently administrative staff providing secretarial services at Wessex County Council's offices. To improve service performance, a contracting-out exercise, with tenders from private contractors, to provide photocopying, typing, and filing were undertaken. Quicktype, a private provider, were awarded the contract. Dolly, Joe, and Bert were transferred. Flo, who was on maternity leave, was not transferred, as Quicktype claimed that she was not in the part of the business subject to the transfer. Dolly, due to her long service is paid more than the other staff, but Quicktype now wish to harmonise terms and are offering her a new contract on less pay. Joe has been told that he is to be dismissed due to his recent absence and Bert is complaining that his pension has not been transferred across.

Advise Dolly, Flo, Bert, and Joe.

2   'The Transfer of Undertaking (Protection of Employment) Regulations 1981 have provided a fertile source of litigation concerning their application. The revised 2006 Regulations seek to eradicate these difficulties.' Evaluate this statement, supporting your answer with case-law examples.

3   Explain the legal significance of consultation in TUPE situations.

4   The University of Dorchester has a dining room for its staff. Anna, Betty, Mark, and Henry are the kitchen staff employed to service the staff dining area room. Following complaints from lecturers, the University decides to provide them with an improved service and therefore invites tenders from private contractors to provide staff lunches. The University also realises that the service is overstaffed and makes Henry redundant. A week later a bid by a rival catering firm to run the staff dining room is accepted by the University. UK Catering interview the existing kitchen staff and tell the University that in view of his disciplinary record they do not wish Mark to work with them. Betty does not want to be transferred to the new catering company because she has heard that their overtime rates are less attractive then the University's. The new catering company has now told Anna, who does most of the cooking, that in view of the fact that there is to be a completely new menu, they will probably need to replace her with someone more experienced in vegetarian cooking.

Advise Anna, Betty, Mark, and Henry.

Trade unions and their members

SUMMARY

This chapter considers the legal definition of a trade union, how unions govern their internal affairs, the right to join a trade union, and trade union disciplinary matters (ie the rights not to be unjustifiably disciplined or expelled by a trade union).

In this chapter we show that:

- section 1 of TULRCA 1992 defines a trade union as 'an organisation wholly or mainly of workers... whose principal purposes include the regulation of relations between workers...';
- unions are *not* corporate bodies (s 10, TULRCA 1992);
- freedom of association protects trade unions from discrimination;
- the union contract of membership is set by the union's rules;
- statutory rules on exclusion, expulsion, and other disciplinary actions have existed since 1984. These rules protect union members from arbitrary action by their union's governing bodies and officials (ss 174, 64–66);
- political funds are expenditure for political objects (Osborne ruling (1911) and are subject to strict rules.

Employment Relations Act 2004

12.1 The Employment Relations Act 2004, in force since October 2005, is mainly concerned with collective labour law and trade union rights. Moreover, it implements the findings of the review of the Employment Relations Act 1999, announced by the Secretary of State in July 2002. The centrepiece of the revising 2004 Act was the provisions to increase the protections against the dismissal of employees taking official, lawfully organised industrial action by extending the 'protected period' from eight to 12 weeks; exempting 'lock-out' days from the 12-week protected period; and, defining more closely the actions which employers and unions should undertake when taking reasonable procedural steps to resolve industrial disputes. Furthermore, measures to simplify the law on industrial action ballots and ballot notices, as well as a power to make regulations to introduce information and consultation in the workplace (in Great Britain and Northern Ireland) by implementing the Directive on Information and Consultation Directive were introduced. Further, this Act clarifies the role of the companion in grievance and disciplinary proceedings. Finally, it grants greater powers to strike out weak and vexatious claims.

12.2 The Act is mainly concerned with collective rights and trade union rights:

- union recognition (**ss 1–21**);
- law relating to industrial action (**ss 22–28**);
- rights to trade union membership, workers, and employees (**ss 29–43**);
- enforcement of minimum wage legislation (**ss 44–47**);
- the Certification Officer (**ss 48–51**);
- miscellaneous (relating to internal affairs of trade unions) (**ss 52–55**);
- supplementary (eg consequential repeals, commencement date, etc) (**ss 56–59**).

12.3 Those sections that came into force on 1 October 2004 include the following:

- **sections 29–32**, which strengthen the protection of workers subjected to detrimental treatment as a result of union membership;
- **section 37**, which clarifies and extends the role of the companion in disciplinary and grievance hearings. The companion will now be permitted to put forward the worker's case, sum up the case, and respond on the worker's behalf to any views expressed in the hearing; and
- **section 38**, which gives the Employment Appeal Tribunal jurisdiction to hear disputes relating to the worker's right to be accompanied at disciplinary and grievance hearings.

12.4 Other important provisions brought in on 6 April 2005 include:

- **section 8**, which introduces postal voting for workers away from the workplace at the time of a workplace ballot;
- **section 20**: 'pay', for the purposes of collective bargaining, does not include occupational or personal pension schemes;
- provisions introduced to speed up the recognition or de-recognition process (**ss 2, 3 and 7**);

- **section 26**, which amends the protections which the 1992 Act provides for employees taking lawfully organised, official industrial action. The protected period is extended from eight to 12 weeks and 'locked-out' days are disregarded when calculating this period;

- **section 28**, which introduces new matters to which a tribunal is to have regard when assessing whether an employer has taken reasonable procedural steps to resolve a dispute with a union. The duty to have regard to these matters applies where the parties have accepted that the services of a conciliator or mediator will be used;

- **section 40**, which amends the Employment Rights Act 1996 (the '1996 Act') to provide that an employee has the right not to be dismissed or treated detrimentally because he serves on a jury or is summoned to do so. The 1996 Act is further amended to provide that selection for redundancy, where the reason or one of the principal reasons is connected to the employee's jury service, will be treated as an unfair dismissal. The right to bring a claim for unfair dismissal in relation to jury service is not subject to the requirement of one year's qualifying service, nor is it restricted to those who have not reached their employer's or the normal retirement age for their job or are otherwise below 65;

- **section 41**, which similarly extends certain protections to those taking advantage of the statutory provisions relating to flexible working. Thus, an employee dismissed for making a flexible working application can complain of unfair dismissal even when involved in official or unofficial industrial action. Flexible workers, those applying to be so or complaining in relation to some aspect of their treatment as such, are protected in respect of unfair dismissal and are not subject to the requirements as to length of service or age.

Employment Bill 2007–08

12.5 The Employment Bill, which received Royal Assent in November 2008 and therefore comes into force sometime in April 2009, intends to strengthen and clarify key aspects of employment law.

12.6 The aims of the Employment Bill are:

- to improve the effectiveness of employment law to the benefit of employers, trade unions, individuals, and the public sector;

- to bring together both elements of the Government's employment relations strategy: increasing protection for vulnerable workers and lightening the load for law-abiding business.

12.7 The Bill includes provisions on the following policy areas:

- **Dispute resolution**: makes changes to the law relating to dispute resolution in the workplace. In particular, the Bill repeals the existing statutory dispute resolution procedures and related provisions about procedural unfairness in dismissal cases; confers on employment tribunals discretionary powers to amend awards if parties have failed to comply with a relevant statutory code; makes changes to the law relating to conciliation by ACAS; amends tribunals' powers by which they may reach a determination without a hearing; and allows tribunals to award compensation for financial loss in certain types of monetary claim;

- **trade union membership**: amends trade union membership law to ensure UK compliance with the European Court of Human Rights ruling on *Aslef v UK*. The amendments enable trade unions to apply membership rules which prohibit individuals who belong or who have belonged to a particular political party from membership of the trade union.

Defining a trade union

12.8 It was the advent of the industrial revolution that produced organised labour. However, the initial reaction to trade unions in Britain was hostile. Strict measures resulted, including exile (eg the Tolpuddle Martyrs). Trade unions, or the combining of workers, remained illegal associations because they restricted the terms on which each member would sell his labour (*Hornby v Close* (1867)) until 1900. Since their creation and legal acceptance, trade unions have held a unique legal status in UK law.

12.9 A trade union is defined in section 1 of the Trade Union and Labour Relations (Consolidation) Act 1992 (hereinafter referred to as TULRCA 1992) as 'an organisation (whether temporary or permanent)...which consists wholly or mainly of workers of one or more descriptions and whose principal purposes include the regulation of relations between workers of that description or those descriptions and employers or employers' associations'.

Employers' associations

12.10 The same applies to employers' associations. Employers' associations are defined by s 122 TULRCA 1992 as organisations (whether or not they are temporary or permanent) consisting wholly or mainly of employers or individual owners of undertakings and having amongst their principal purposes the regulation of relations between those employers and workers or trade unions, though, unlike a trade union, an employers' association can be either an incorporated or unincorporated body. Where an association is unincorporated, it has the same rights and obligations as a trade union.

Trade unions and legal status

12.11 With regard to trade unions' legal status, at common law they are unincorporated associations (ie they are not corporate bodies with separate legal 'personality'), but they are given quasi-corporate status by s 10 TULRCA 1992. The effect of this is that unions are able to make contracts, sue and be sued in relation to contract, tort or other matters, hold property via trustees, and have criminal proceedings taken against them, but for all other purposes they are treated as unincorporated associations. It has been held by the High Court (somewhat controversially), that a union cannot be defamed because it does not have any legal personality beyond that of its members (*Electrical, Electronic Telecommunications and Plumbing Union v Times Newspapers Ltd* (1980)).

Independence

12.12 The grant of a certificate of independence is of fundamental importance to a trade union, because most statutory rights enjoyed by unions (eg those relating to disclosure of information, consultation, discrimination against union members, time off for union members and officials, and most recently, the right to use the statutory recognition procedures), require that the union must be independent. The requirement of independence as a precondition for the grant of union rights is to ensure that collective rights are exercised by bodies that are not mere staff associations over which an employer may have control.

12.13 The test of independence in s 5 TULRCA 1992 is in two parts: it requires that a union 'is not under the domination or control of an employer or group of employers or of one or more employers' associations, and is not liable to interference by an employer or any such group or association (arising out of the financial or material support or by any other means whatsoever) tending towards such control . . .'. Such requires no onerous control by their employer. This was considered in *Blue Circle Staff Association v The Certification Officer* (1977). Consequently, the Certification Officer must consider in respect of each application by a trade union the following:

(a) the history of the trade union/organisation;

(b) its membership base;

(c) its organisation and structure;

(d) its finance;

(e) employer-provided facilities; and

(f) its negotiating record.

12.14 In *News Group Newspapers Ltd v Society of Graphical and Allied Trades* (SOGAT 1982) the question to be determined was whether assets in the name of branches of the SOGAT 82 trade union belonged to the trade union or to the individual branches. Consequently, whilst each branch was not a separate trade union, the fact that it had the status of unincorporated association meant that its fund belonged to the branch rather than the union. The statutory definition also expressly includes federations or confederations of unions, 'an organisation which comprises wholly or mainly of employers or individual proprietors... and whose principal purposes include the regulation'.

Union amalgamations

12.15 There are two ways of proceeding under the 1992 Act, which also applies to unincorporated employers' associations (s 133); that is either:

(a) by amalgamation which must be supported by a separate ballot of both transferor and transferee union; or

(b) a transfer of engagements which requires approval only by a vote of the transferor's membership.

Certification

12.16 The Certification Officer certifies and makes periodic checks that a union is maintaining its independence since he may withdraw certificates if the characterisation of the union changes. An appeal from the Certification Officer to the EAT takes the form of a full re-hearing and 'the parties are not limited to the material presented to or considered by the Certification Officer in the course of his enquiries'.

Certification Officer

12.17 The role of Certification Officer (as previously defined in Chapter 1) is largely an adjudicative role on the political fund, trade union amalgamations, and principal executive committee elections. The Certification Officer is given specific power to regulate his own procedure. The Certification Officer may also make provision for expenses to be paid for the purpose of or in conjunction with their attendance at hearings before the Certification Officer. In addition, the Certification Officer has jurisdiction to hear complaints by members that their trade union (or any branch or section of the union) is in breach, or threatens to be in breach, of its own rules in respect of any of the following matters:

- regarding the appointment or election of a person to a union;
- union disciplinary proceedings;
- the constitution of proceedings of any executive committee;
- any such other matters as may be specified by the Secretary of State.

Employer interference

12.18 The second limb is forward-looking, and therefore more speculative. The test posed by the Act is whether the union is 'liable to interference' by an employer 'tending towards' control. In *The Certification Officer v Squibb UK Staff Association* (1979) it was decided that the phrase meant 'vulnerable to interference' or 'exposed to the risk of interference', eg the possibility of an employer withdrawing facilities that it might have granted to a union at some point in the future. The likelihood of such interference actually occurring is irrelevant.

Trade union registration

12.19 A list of trade unions is maintained by the Certification Officer, an independent office established in 1975, and now enjoying wide-ranging administrative and judicial functions in relation to trade unions. Listing is a voluntary and largely mechanical administrative process which nevertheless has significant advantages for a trade union. A body claiming to be a union may submit an application for listing (together with the appropriate fee, and a copy of its rules) to the Certification Officer. The Certification Officer is bound to list the body as a union provided it does not have the same name as an existing or de-listed body. The union will be entitled to tax benefits in respect of its provident benefits fund. It will also be allowed to take advantage of the special procedure for transferring property to the union's trustees. However, the most important advantage of being listed is that a union can apply for a certificate of independence. The decision in *Taff Vale Railway Company v Amalgamated Society of Railway Servants* (1901) concluded from the fact that they were registered under the Trade Union Acts 1871 and 1876 that unions could be sued in tort in their registered name. Yet a trade union cannot be sued for libel, as it lacks sufficient legal personality for those purposes in law (see *Electrical, Electronic Telecommunications and Plumbing Union v Times Newspapers* (1980)).

Listing of trade unions

12.20 A list of trade unions is maintained by the Certification Officer, an independent office established in 1975, and now enjoying wide-ranging administrative and judicial functions in relation to trade unions. Listing is a voluntary and largely mechanical administrative requirement. In *Bonsor v Musicians' Union* (1956), Lord Morton said that a union was 'a body distinct from the individuals who from time to time compose it'. At common law trade unionism itself is in unreasonable restraint of trade, since unions restrict the freedom of contract between employer and employee, most particularly in the taking of strike action and the closed shop; see EAT in *Blue Circle Staff Association v Certification Officer* (1977).

Bridlington principles

12.21 The Bridlington principles were adopted by the TUC in 1939 to govern inter-union disputes, so as to police the 'poaching' of members. The agreement is non-binding, yet all trade unions in the UK subscribe to them, although it establishes a strict regime. For instance, Regulation G of the principles allows the General Secretary of the TUC to appoint a legally qualified individual as Chair of the Committee (Professor Lord Wedderburn QC). Further, Principle 4 concerns the avoidance of inter-union disputes. This establishes a requirement that unions involve the TUC before any industrial action is taken. The TUC's Disputes Committee may also make an award with which the parties are obliged to comply (TUC Rule 12(b)). All of these principles set out basic rules to prevent inter-union rivalry and disputes.

Internal union governance

12.22 The basis for trade union governance is the rule book. Union rule books set out the terms of the contract to which membership must comply. To that end, the union's rule book allows its officials to work and provide power to them, in order to perform their function. For example, in *Heaton's (St Helens) Transport Ltd v Transport and General Workers' Union* (1973), the Court of Appeal construed that the respondent union was generally liable for its officials. Yet, on appeal, the House of Lords saw the union steward's authority as depending on the rule book and custom and practice. Consequently, whether union officials are liable for their actions depends on whether they complied with their own rule book or not.

The union rule book

12.23 The Court of Appeal in *Iwanuszezak v General Municipal Boilermakers and Allied Trades Union* (1988) stated that since unions exist, primarily, to promote the interests of the membership as a whole rather than the interests of individual members, it is permissible for a union to give priority to the collective interest of the membership as a whole over the individual interest. Consequently, union rule books exist to fulfil this task. In *Thomas v National Union of Mineworkers (South Wales Area)* (1985), it was established that it would be ultra vires for union officials to finance a form of picketing that would be bound to involve criminal acts; it was not ultra vires if the picketing were merely capable of involving criminal acts, as the union officials had acted within the agreed rules. Consequently, the union rule book provides the basis upon which the institutions that govern the union, can operate. In 1952, the Court of Appeal, in *Lee v Showmen's Guild of GB*, held that whilst the courts would normally not seek to interfere in the business of voluntary legal bodies, it was proper to protect the rights of trade union members. As a result, the courts hold certain grounds for judicial review against trade unions. This means that members can potentially complain to the courts about the processes adopted by any union, if they have grounds to believe that it breaches the union's own rule book and it is in the public interest. Yet Vinelott J summarised the situation in *Taylor v National Union of Mineworkers (Derbyshire Area)* (1985) when he stated:

> The courts are in principle reluctant to intervene in the internal affairs of any association, corporate or (otherwise). If they do intervene, they take the view that the affairs of the association should generally be conducted with the will of the majority, and they will decline to interfere if (the action being brought) could be overturned by a simple majority of the members.

Union funds

12.24 Duty to maintain accounts is found in s 28 TULRCA 1992, which sets down detailed rules for the carrying on of unions' and employers' associations' financial affairs, similar to those obligations imposed on companies. Trade unions accounts must be audited and submitted to the Certification Officer, s 32 TULRCA 1992. Furthermore, subject to s 32A TULRCA 1992 (inserted by TURERA 1993), every union member must receive a statement of the accounts submitted to the Certification Officer.

12.25 Section 15 of TULR(C)A 1992 renders it unlawful for a union's property to be applied for the purposes of indemnifying individuals for any penalty imposed by a court for:

(a) contempt of court; or

(b) a criminal offence.

Therefore, union officials in general owe a fiduciary duty to the member of their union. By s 16 of TULRCA 1992, members of trade unions have powers to act against trustees of the union's property in respect of unlawful application of such assets, or trustees who comply with any unlawful direction given to them under the rules of the union.

The political fund

12.26 The House of Lords in its landmark ruling in *Amalgamated Society of Railway Servants v Osborne* (1910), the '*Osborne* judgment' as it is more familiarly known, ruled that the use of union funds for political purposes was illegal, since they were only empowered to pursue those objects permitted in the Trade Union Act 1871 and this was not one of them (ie fund political parties). However, subsequently, the Trade Union Act of 1913 allowed trade unions to use trade union monies for 'political objects', where its members approved of it by ballot. The later 1984 Trade Union Act tightened up the rules, particularly allowing members to opt-out of this 'political levy'.

12.27 Under s 71 TULRCA 1992, unions must now seek approval for their 'political objects' and cannot expend on these without the consent of voting members, by majority. Section 72 TULRCA 1992, defines 'political objects' as:

- contributions to a political party;
- any service or property donated or provided to a political party;
- maintenance of a holder of political office;
- publication of materials persuading people to vote for a particular political party.

This ballot must take place every five years.

Union elections

12.28 By s 46 of TULRCA 1992, every member of the principal executive committee of a trade union has to be elected every five years by all members of the union. Unions are subject to strict rules in relation to elections, as follows:

- balloting must be held in secret and preferably by postal voting;
- there should be non-interference by 'the union or any of its members, officials or employees'; and
- unions should finance all elections.

As an alternative to a postal vote, a union used to be able to conduct a semi-postal ballot or workplace ballot if the union was satisfied that there were no reasonable grounds to believe that this would not result in a free election as required by sections 2 and 3 of the Trade Union Act 1984. Therefore, each union must appoint a qualified independent scrutineer, and give him the duties set out in sections 49(3) or 75(3). He may also be given 'additional functions'. The union should ensure that it would be unreasonable for any person to call the scrutineer's independence into question by reason of:

- anything in the terms of the scrutineer's appointment;
- interference with the carrying out of his function.

12.29 Any breach of these statutory election requirements can result in a complaint to the Certification Officer, seeking an enforcement order, requiring the trade union concerned to take remedial action and comply with the correct process. Should the Certification Officer fail to act, only thereafter can action be sought in the High Court.

12.30 In *Corrigan v GMB (No 1)* (2008) ICR 197, Elias J, held that a trade union had not breached the Trade Union and Labour Relations (Consolidation) Act 1992, s 46 by not electing a new general secretary within a year of a vacancy arising. Section 46 did not specify when an election had to be held, and the union was entitled to delay the election until the outcome of its internal inquiry into electoral malpractice. Moreover, section 46 did not specify when an election had to be held and did not oblige a union to fill a vacancy as soon as it became vacant. The purpose of section 46 was to ensure that anyone who in fact held the office of general secretary was elected. A person did not necessarily become the general secretary merely by exercising the functions of that office for a period of time together with the fact that the office was vacant unless the arrangement was a sham. It would be a breach of section 46 if the acting officer was in fact no longer considered by the union to be acting on a temporary basis but was holding the post in all but name. That would be an easy inference to draw if the union had no obvious or legitimate reason not to hold an election.

Discipline

12.31 All union rule books should set out clear rules in relation to disciplining its members. Therefore, any such disciplinary action must be carried out in accordance with the union's own rule book. As the Court of Human Rights in Strasbourg ruled in *Cheall v UK* (1986), unions should decide all matters in accordance with their own rules, particularly in relation to disciplinary proceedings. Clearly, the judges are reluctant to allow a domestic union tribunal to be final adjudicators of questions of fact on their own rule book, and also intervene if there is no evidence to support a finding of fact found by any disciplinary committee (*Lee v Showmen's Guild* (1952), also *Partington v National and Local Government Officers' Association* (1981)).

12.32 Consequently, trade unions must comply with the rules of natural justice because 'although the jurisdiction of a domestic tribunal is founded on contract, express or implied, nevertheless the parties are not free to make any contract they like' (*Breen v Amalgamated Engineering Union* (1971)). For example, in *Roebuck v National Union of Mineworkers (Yorkshire Area)* (1977), where the union president both brought the complaint and heard the complaint, it was held that such a situation breached the principles of natural justice, since it made no difference that the union rules generally required the president to chair the meeting since he could vacate it in special circumstances and should have done so here. A union is prohibited from disciplining a member for not taking part in industrial action notwithstanding that a majority of that member's colleagues voted in favour of the action in a properly held ballot, and this is naturally seen by the unions as a threat to traditional union concepts of solidarity.

Unjustifiable action

12.33 Section 64 TULRCA 1992 establishes the right of each trade union member not to be unjustifiably disciplined. To that end, the most important grounds (TULRCA 1992, s 65(2)) on which discipline of a trade union member is to be taken as unjustifiable are:

- failure to support a strike or industrial action;
- failure to participate in a strike or industrial action;
- indication of opposition to a strike;
- indication of lack of support for a strike;
- failure to contravene a contract of employment;
- the making of an assertion that the union, or any official, the representative or trustee thereof, has contravened or is proposing to contravene a requirement imposed;
- consulting the Certification Officer or asking him to provide advice or assistance;
- failure to agree to the making of a deduction of subscriptions arrangement;
- resigning from one union to join another.

12.34 The central term 'discipline' is given a broad definition. Section 64(2) TULRCA 1992 includes:

- expulsion;
- a sanction (usually, a fine);
- deprivation of benefits afforded to other members;
- union dues/subscriptions;
- subjecting the individual to any detriment (eg dissuading another union from allowing membership; see for example *National and Local Government Officers Association v Killorn and Simm* (1990)).

12.35 Aggrieved trade union members, claiming unjustifiable discipline, may complain to an ET and seek a declaration within three months of the date of the alleged act by the union. An order of compensation can be awarded, capped up to £61,300.

Expulsion

12.36 New sections 33 and 34 of the Employment Relations Act 2004 (the law governing the ability of trade unions to exclude or expel individuals wholly or mainly for taking part in activities of a political party) came into force on 31 December 2004. The House of Lords in *Cheall v Association of Professional, Executive, Clerical and Computer Staff* (1983) ruled that there was no right for an individual to associate with those who did not want to associate with them. The later Thatcher Government Employment Act 1980 enacted a right not to be unreasonably expelled or excluded from a trade union where a closed shop agreement was in operation. The provisions were modified by the Trade Union Reform and Employment Rights Act 1993, which removed the link with closed-shop employment. The modified right currently exists as s 174 TULRCA 1992.

12.37 Compensation can also be awarded, the amount depending upon whether the union has rescinded the decision to impose discipline. Damages can be recovered by a member where it is reasonably foreseeable that loss will flow as a result of breach of the contract of membership (*Bonsor v Musicians' Union* (1955)). In awarding damages, the court will not be required to take into account any injury to feelings that the member may have suffered. Further, a member will be required to take reasonable steps to mitigate losses (see *Edwards v Society of Graphical and Allied Trades* (1971)). Compensation is awarded on a just and equitable basis, subject to a statutory maximum of £62,600.

ASLEF v UK case – implications for trade union law

12.38 On 27 February 2007, the European Court of Human Rights issued a judgment in the case of *Aslef v the United Kingdom* (2008). The case concerns the freedom of trade unions under UK law to expel or exclude individuals on the grounds of their political party membership, and the Court concluded that the relevant part of British law violated Article 11 of the European Convention on Human Rights.

12.39 The summary findings from the consultation are:

- the Government reaffirms its view that the Trade Union and Labour Relations (Consolidation) Act 1992 must be amended;

- the consultation document put forward two options – A and B – to amend the 1992 Act. The Government has concluded that Option A should be pursued; and

- the Government does not consider that any other changes to the 1992 Act are required in order to achieve compliance with the European Convention on Human Rights in response to the judgment.

The right to join a trade union

12.40 With the repeal of the Combination Acts in 1824, trade unions were legalised and the freedom to associate prevailed. This right has long been protected under international and European law – ILO Conventions No 87 (Association and the Right to Organise) and 98 (Right to Organise and Bargain Collectively); Article 11, ECHR (1950); and, Article 5, European Social Charter. All of these labour standards provide the positive right to join a trade union.

Freedom of association

12.41 Notwithstanding these standards, the UK has been long troubled with this right. In the first instance, until relatively recently, unions were banned at GCHQ (a Government security intelligence unit) in Cheltenham. Furthermore, Lord Diplock in *Cheall v Association of Professional, Executive, Clerical and Computer Staff* (1983), regarded the positive nature of the right, to imply a mutuality of the negative: 'there can be no right of an individual to associate with others who are not willing to associate with him . . .'. In general terms, the freedom to associate means:

- the right to peaceful assembly and to freedom of association with others, including the right to join trade unions for the protection of their interests;

- no restrictions shall be placed on the exercise of these rights other than as are prescribed by law and are necessary in a democratic society, in the interests of national security or public safety, for the prevention of disorder or crime, for the protection of health or morals or for the protection of the rights and freedoms of others (Article 11, ECHR (1950)).

12.42 In *Wilson and Palmer* (2002) their respective employers had offered pay increases on the relinquishing of their trade union rights. The House of Lords held that such action did not deprive the employees, who desired to exercise their freedom of association and remain in their trade unions, of their statutory rights and protection. The European Court of Human Rights in Strasbourg, took a different view, upholding that the UK law had failed to protect trade union members and that the British employers concerned had violated the freedom to associate.

12.43 Section 2 of the Employment Relations Act 1999, contained a change of wording to s 146 TULRCA 1992, so as effectively to reverse the ruling in *Wilson and Palmer* (above). Section 2 ERelA 1999, makes it unlawful for an employee to be 'subjected to any detriment' for trade union reasons.

Refusal of employment

12.44 Where a person is refused employment because of a requirement to join a trade union or to cease to become a trade union member, s 137 TULRCA 1992 makes such conditions unlawful, although an important distinction must be made between trade union membership and activities (see *Harrison v Kent CC* (1995)), since section 137 provides protection in situations regarding membership only.

Closed shop

12.45 The 'closed shop' (a requirement to join a certain trade union to gain and/or retain employment) thrived in Britain between 1974 and 1980. It characterised some 1.8 million workplaces. Following the European Court of Human Rights ruling in the 'railwaymen's' case (*Young, James & Webster* (1981)), where the closed shop was declared a violation of the freedom to associate (Art 11) since it forced labour to join a trade union (thus enhancing the right to dissociation), Mrs Thatcher's first administration abolished it, making it almost an illegal practice, save where on religious grounds it was necessary and justifiable (Employment Act 1988, now s 152(1)(c) TULRCA 1992).

Action short of dismissal

12.46 Under s 146 TULRCA 1992, where a trade union member is subjected to any detriment attributable to such membership, for example where an employer prevents or deters membership of a trade union, whether by an act or omission of his employer, the employee (only regarding events during his employment) can complain to an employment tribunal on grounds of discrimination (see *Robb v Leon Motors Ltd* (1978), *National Coal Board v Ridgway* (1987), *Gallacher v Department of Transport* (1994), and *Wilson v United Kingdom* (2002), for examples).

Dismissal due to trade union association

12.47 Under s 152 TULRCA 1992, where a trade union member is dismissed because of his trade union membership, such a dismissal (as seen previously in Chapters 7 and 8) will be automatically deemed unfair (see *Fitzpatrick v British Railways Board* (1991)). Higher levels of compensation are also available in such cases with a minimum award of £3,500 being set and an additional award up to £13,500 being available in such cases. The special award was abolished in 1999.

Blacklisting

12.48 The Employment Relations Act 1999 gives the Secretary of State a power to make regulations prohibiting the compiling of blacklists of trade unions. Yet no regulations have been made to date.

Dissociation rights?

12.49 It was the Donovan Commission (1968) which observed that the right to dissociation must also exist, but that a negative right did not necessarily rely upon the existence of a positive right. To that end, the right to dissociate was reinforced in the early 1980s, by the then newly elected Conservative Government, so as to protect those individuals who did not desire to join a trade union.

12.50 The *Young, James and Webster* (1981) case highlights the case in favour of a parallel right of dissociation. These railway workers were being forced to join the railway union, then effectively a closed shop. They sought to challenge this requirement legally and succeeded in the European Court of Human Rights in Strasbourg. However, nowadays, s 152(1)(c) TULRCA 1992 provides the requisite protection for those individuals who do not wish to join a trade union and suffer a detriment as a result. Notably it will be automatically unfair to select a worker for dismissal due to non-membership of a particular trade union. Furthermore, section 146(1)(c) also protects the worker from discrimination for action short of dismissal.

FURTHER READING

Deakin, S, & Morris, G, *Labour Law* (4th ed, 2005) Hart (chapters 8 & 10).

Smith, I, & Thomas, G, *Smith & Wood's Employment Law* (9th ed, 2007) Oxford University Press (chapters 11 & 12).

ARTICLES

Davies, P, & Kilpatrick, C, (2004) 'UK Worker Representation after Single Channel', *Industrial Law Journal*, Vol 33, No 2, pp 95–120.

Ewing, K, (1999) 'Freedom of Association and the Employment Rights Act (1999)', Industrial *Law Journal*, Vol 28, No 4, pp 283–298.

Ewing, K, (2003) 'The Implications of Wilson and Palmer', *Industrial Law Journal*, Vol 32, No 1, pp 1–22.

SELF-TEST QUESTIONS

1 Statutorily define a British trade union and explain the legal implications of such a definition.

2 'Freedom of association is fundamental to collective organisation in the UK.' Discuss.

3 Arthur has been a member of his union, ACTNOW, since 1982 and has been a shop steward for the last four years. Two months ago, he stood for re-election and was beaten by Bill, a work colleague, losing by eight votes. However, a week after the election it transpired that Bill has stolen some ballot papers from the lockers of some colleagues and it is alleged that Bill used these votes to get elected. Arthur confronted Bill about this, and consequently a fight broke out. Subsequently, Arthur was disciplined by his union's regional representative, Colette, and it was decided that Arthur is banned from standing for a position in his union for the next five years. Arthur appealed to the union's National Executive, of which Colette is a member, but his appeal was dismissed. Apparently, at the appeal hearing Colette did not make any representations, but voted to dismiss Arthur's appeal.

Advise Arthur on any rights and remedies he may have with regard to his union's disciplinary action against him.

4 Assess the impact of the provisions of the Employment Bill 2007 on trade unions.

Collective bargaining

SUMMARY

This chapter considers trade union membership, rights and activities, voluntary and statutory recognition, and collective bargaining rights. In particular, this chapter considers the following points:

- Collective bargaining is the process by which a trade union negotiates with an employer on issues relating to the terms and conditions of employment.

- S 178(1) TULRCA 1992 defines collective bargaining as 'negotiations relating to...terms & conditions, physical conditions at work, engagement or non-engagement or suspension of employment, allocation of duties, matters of discipline and union membership or non-membership of a trade union'.

- Collective bargaining results in collective agreements and requires the duty to disclose information for collective bargaining (s 182 TULRCA 1992).

- The right of association is protected by UK law and ensures that workers are not refused employment on grounds of either trade union membership or non-membership.

- Trade union members are protected against dismissal on trade union grounds or are subjected to a detriment as a result of being a trade union member or involved in trade union action and/or activities.

- Recognition can be voluntary and statutory. The statutory basis is governed by the Employment Relations Act 1999, as amended by the Employment Relations Act 2004, and requires the CAC to adjudicate on applications. The voluntary system is underpinned by the common law, requiring the parties to intend such bargaining to take place. The statutory process requires compliance with a complicated set of rules, comprising the establishment of a level of support in an agreed bargaining unit. Following a ballot, should 50 per cent of the balloted bargaining unit support recognition, then recognition ensues and collective bargaining with the newly recognised trade union follows.

Trade union membership, rights, and activities

13.1 Collective bargaining evolved in the UK as a post-war initiative, as a means of regulating pay and other terms and conditions of employment. Following the success of Joint Industrial Councils, works councils, a growth in trade unions prevailed. Underpinned by International Labour Organisation (ILO) Conventions, these bodies became organised and collective bargaining began. ILO No 87 of 1948 provides for the freedom of association and the right to organise, and No 98 of 1949 provides for the right to bargain collectively. However, since 2000 under the 1998 Human Rights Act, the now incorporated European Convention on Human Rights (ECHR) of 1950, Article 11 ensures the right to freedom of peaceful assembly and to freedom of association with others.

Trade union membership

13.2 Article 1(1) of ILO Convention No 87 of 1948 secures that 'workers shall enjoy adequate protection against acts of anti-union activities'. In the context of the UK, since 1971 and now under the Trade Union & Labour Relations Consolidation Act 1992 (TULRCA) trade union rights are protected (see Chapter 12).

Trade union rights

13.3 The provisions of the TULRCA 1992 provide three distinct trade union rights:

- a trade union member has the right not to be subjected to any detriment (s 146, TULRCA 1992);

- dismissal of a trade union member is automatically regarded as unfair, particularly those affected employees who hold functions cognate to trade union duties (eg health and safety representatives or worker representatives) (s 152, TULRCA 1992); and,

- trade union officials and members are allowed 'reasonable' time off, without pay, to undertake their duties (s 168, TULRCA 1992). Note that trade union officials involved in collective bargaining receive paid time off to execute these duties.

Trade union activities

13.4 The exact scope of activities of trade unions is open to interpretation. Phillips J provides guidance in his judgment in *Lyon v St James Press* (1976), stating that: 'The special protection afforded to trade union activities must not be allowed to operate as a cloak for conduct which ordinarily justify dismissal.' The ACAS Code of Practice on Time Off for Trade Union Duties provides further advice, yet is more prescriptive in so far as it details 'voting in union elections, executive meetings and annual conferences' (paras 21–22) as union duties. However, case law has further expanded this rather narrow approach to include:

(a) seeking union recognition (*Taylor v Butler Machine Tool Ltd* (1976));

(b) discussing union matters (*Zucker v Astrid Jewels Ltd* (1978));

(c) seeking advice from union officials (*Stokes v Wheeler-Green Ltd* (1979)); and,

(d) seeking to recruit new members (*Bass Taverns Ltd v Burgess* (1995)).

Time off for trade union activities

13.5 Reasonable time should be given to such activities, including the holding of a meeting during the employers' time (see *Marley Tile Co Ltd v Shaw* (1980), per Goff LJ). The appropriate time for trade union activities is defined as not only occasions 'outside the employee's working hours' but also time 'within working hours at which, in accordance with arrangements agreed with, or consent given by his employer, it is permissible for him to take part in those activities' (TULRCA 1992, s 146(2), 170(2)). In *Post Office v Union of Post Office Workers* (1974), Lord Reid declared that, 'it does not include periods when in accordance with his contract the worker is on his employer's premises, but not actually working'. The time taken off must be reasonable as to amount and the circumstances when it is taken. For example, in *Wignall v British Gas Corporation* (1984) the applicant had already been granted 12 weeks' leave for union business when he sought a further 10 days for the preparation of a union district monthly magazine. The EAT upheld the tribunal's decision that it was reasonable for the employers to refuse the further time.

13.6 Yet the EAT in *Marley Tile Co Ltd v Shaw* (1980) held that a meeting of maintenance men to protest about the shop steward's lack of credentials during working hours was 'at an appropriate time', because the legislation had to be construed in the light of 'actual industrial practice'. On appeal, their Lordships took a more narrow view and agreed that whilst consent might be implied, it could not arise by way of extension from custom and practice elsewhere, only at the factory in question.

Time off by trade union officials

13.7 Where his union is recognised, an official is entitled to time off with pay 'to carry out those duties... which are concerned with industrial relations between his employer and any associated employer and their employees' (TULRCA 1992, s 168(1)), and this is in accordance with ILO Convention No 135. This is restricted to those duties concerned with negotiations about matters within s 244 TULRCA 1992 'in relation to which the trade union is recognised by the employer' or 'any functions related to or connected with any (such) matters…and the employer has agreed may be so performed by the trade union'. If the employer refuses, the official can complain to the employment tribunal and seek a declaration and compensation; however, he should not ignore the employer's refusal and take the time off regardless, since 'Official' is defined as any officer of the union or branch and any such other person elected under the union rules to represent the members or some of them (TULRCA 1992, s 119).

13.8 The ACAS Code of Practice on Time Off gives some indication of the duties for which time off should be granted:

(a) collective bargaining with the appropriate level of management;

(b) informing constituents about negotiations or consultations with management;

(c) meetings with other lay officials or with full-time officials;

(d) interviews with and on behalf of constituents on grievance and disciplinary matters;

(e) appearing on behalf of constituents before an outside body.

13.9 It may be argued, however, that 'duties' in s 168 TULRCA 1992 is used in the everyday sense of 'business, office or function', rather than inflexibly associating them with an official's duties.

Union learning representatives

13.10 By s 168A TULRCA 1993, introduced in 2002, an employer must permit an employee who is a union learning representative time off for the purposes of carrying on these activities in relation to qualifying members of the trade union: analysing learning or training needs; providing information and advice about learning or training matters; arranging learning or training and promoting the value of learning or training; consulting the employer about carrying on such activities, or preparing for these matters. The representative must have undergone sufficient training to enable him to carry on these activities and the union must give the employer notice of this fact. The amount of time off and the purposes for which it is taken are those that are reasonable in all the circumstances.

13.11 By s 170 TULRCA 1992, a trade union member is to be allowed reasonable time off during working hours without pay to take part in the activities of an independent trade union recognised by the employer for the purposes of collective bargaining.

The Employment Relations Act 1999 replaces the term 'action short of dismissal' with the broader term 'detriment', bringing this part of the TULRCA 1992 into line with other measures to protect union and employee representatives, who are not permitted reasonable time off by their employers. 'Detriment' can be suffered as a result of 'any act, or any deliberate failure to act, by his employer' (TULRCA 1992, s 146).

Time off for health and safety representatives

13.12 A duly appointed health and safety representative has a right to reasonable time off with pay to perform his function and to be trained (Safety Representatives and Safety Committee Regulations 1977 (SI 1977/1500, reg 4, para 2).

Strike action?

13.13 There is no general right to strike in Britain. In fact, strike action is positively discouraged by both the criminal and civil law. Essentially, the effect of industrial action impacts upon the contract of employment. As Donovan LJ said in *Rookes v Barnard* (1963), in the majority of strikes no such notice to terminate the contract is either given or expected. The law relating to industrial action is dealt with in detail in Chapter 14.

Collective bargaining and agreements

13.14 Collective agreements are contracts resulting from the process of collective bargaining between unions and employers, for the purposes of regulating the procedures that will be adopted by the union and employer, and/or determining the terms and conditions under which workers will work. Most collective agreements are likely to fall within the statutory definition of a collective agreement. Such collective agreements can either be legally enforceable as contracts or non-contractual, depending upon the intentions of the parties, as well as the content of the agreement. They are usually not legally enforceable. However, their provisions can become part of the contract of employment of individual employees.

13.15 The statutory definition of collective agreement can be found in s 178 TULRCA 1992. It defines a collective agreement as 'any agreement or arrangement made by or on behalf of one or more trade unions and one or more employers or employers' associations' and relating to one or more of the following matters:

- machinery for negotiation or consultation relating to the above, including recognition;

- terms and conditions of employment;
- engagement or non-engagement, or termination or suspension of employment or the duties of employment, of one or more workers;
- matters of discipline;
- a worker's membership or non-membership of a trade union;
- facilities for trade union officials;
- pay, including pensions, which has been emphasised and added to the list (see *UNIFI v Union Bank of Nigeria plc* (2001)).

13.16 Due to having such a wide scope, it is possible for most agreements to fall outside its parameters (see eg *Universe Tankships Inc of Monrovia v International Transport Workers Federation* (1982), which involved a dispute over a 'goodwill payment' to the union's welfare fund). Whilst collective agreements are unlikely to be legally binding, the legal position is complex. Traditionally, collective agreements can fall under one of three regimes: the first covers agreements concluded before 1 December 1971 (ie fall outside the statutory definition in s 178 TULRCA 1992); the second covers agreements concluded under the Industrial Relations Act 1971 regime; and, the third covers agreements made under the regime that replaced it.

Agreements prior to 1 December 1971
The common law governs these contracts. In particular the law focuses upon what was intended by the parties to the agreement and whether they intended that the agreement should be legally binding (see *Ford Motor Co Ltd v Amalgamated Union of Engineering and Foundry Workers* (1969), where it was held that the collective agreement was not intended by the parties to be legally binding).

Agreements under the Industrial Relations Act 1971
Agreements entered into between 30 November 1971 and 16 September 1974 fall under the Industrial Relations Act 1971. The Act requires that collective agreements entered into during this period should be automatically deemed to be binding on the parties to it, unless a clause stating the contrary exists, so making it non-binding. Most agreements entered into during that period routinely included such a clause, commonly known as the 'TINALEA' clause – 'This is not a legally enforceable agreement.'

Agreements made (after 16 September 1974) under TULRCA
Any collective agreements entered into after this date were governed by the provisions introduced by the Trade Union and Labour Relations Act 1974, now contained in s 179 TULRCA 1992. The new Act presumes that, unless an agreement is in writing and contains a clause stating that it is intended to be binding as between the parties to it, it is deemed not to be a legally enforceable contract. However, under

the 1999 Employment Relations Act, under the statutory recognition procedure any collective bargaining procedures imposed by the CAC will take effect as a legally binding contract enforceable before the courts.

13.17 It should be noted, even if a collective agreement is binding as between the parties, some clauses contained in it may not be enforceable by a court. Such clauses fall into two categories: 'no-strike' clauses, and clauses which are discriminatory. For instance, a clause in a collective agreement which prohibits or restricts the right of workers to engage in a strike or other industrial action will not be binding as between the employer and individual employees unless the following requirements under s 180 TULRCA 1992 are satisfied:

(a) the collective agreement which contains the clause must be in writing;

(b) the agreement must contain a provision expressly stating that the clause be incorporated into individual contracts;

(c) the agreement must be reasonably accessible to employees at their place of work and available for them to consult during working hours;

(d) the clause must in fact be incorporated into the individual contracts of employment.

13.18 Further, to the extent that a clause in a collective agreement discriminates against a person on grounds of sex, race or disability, it is void under the provisions of, respectively, s 77 Sex Discrimination Act 1975, s 72 Race Relations Act 1976, and s 9 Disability Discrimination Act 1995. As to when the provisions of a collective agreement become incorporated into individual contracts of employment, this is determined by fact. Incorporation may be express (as in *Robertson v British Gas Corporation* (1983), where the contract of employment stated that 'the collective agreement will apply to you'), or implied. In any event, procedural agreements (eg on recognition) are unlikely to be held appropriate for incorporation (see generally, *Cadoux v Central Regional Council* (1986), *Marley v Forward Trust Group Limited* (1986), *Whent v T Cartledge Limited* (1997), and *Burke v Royal Liverpool University Hospital NHS Trust* (1997)).

Trade union recognition

13.19 Recognition is accepting a trade union as the representative of the workforce. In effect, recognition is defined in s 178 TULRCA 1992 as meaning 'recognition of the union by an employer, or two or more associated employers, to any extent, for the purpose of collective bargaining…'. As noted already in Chapter 12, the Employment Relations Act 2004 amended how a bargaining unit is to be determined by the Central Arbitration Committee (CAC).

13.20　Clearly, the legal significance of recognition lies in the increased rights that a trade union derives as a result of recognition. Historically in the UK, union recognition has not been a compulsory process, but voluntary. The Employment Relations Act 1999 changed that and formally introduced a controversial new statutory recognition procedure, under which a union may claim recognition against the employer's wishes. However, the exception lies in situations relating to a transfer of an undertaking, where the former (transferor) employer recognised a union or unions, the new (transferee) employer is also bound to afford recognition to the union or unions (reg 6, Transfer of Undertakings (Protection of Employment) Regulations 2006). Yet, currently there is no legal provision which prevents the new employer from subsequently derecognising the union post-transfer, where recognition by the former employer was voluntary (ie not under the new statutory procedures).

Voluntary recognition

13.21　Under common law, recognition is an entirely voluntary process. In such circumstances, recognition occurs by agreement, as a matter of custom and practice and/or good employment relations, rather than through law. The established principles governing voluntary recognition are that pre-existing collective bargaining occurred expressly or impliedly, albeit evidenced (see *National Union of Tailors and Garment Workers v Charles Ingram & Co Ltd* (1977)). For example, in *National Union of Gold, Silver and Allied Trades v Albury Bros Ltd* (1978), the Court of Appeal held that recognition means negotiating with a view to striking a deal on an issue: a discussion over rates of pay was not sufficient to amount to representational rights or consultation (per Eveliegh LJ). Furthermore, once an employer is taken to have recognised a union, it cannot, in the absence of the formal withdrawal of recognition, argue that it did not intend to recognize it; such is supported in *Union of Shop, Distributive and Allied Workers v Sketchley Ltd* (1981). Finally, the recognising of a trade union by an employers' association does not bind all of its members to bargain with that union, as noted in *National Union of Gold, Silver and Allied Trades v Albury Bros Ltd* (1978), above.

13.22　Part II of the 1999 Act points out that in general the statutory provisions do not apply to voluntary recognition. However, where the employer and the union have previously reached a voluntary recognition agreement, but that agreement is not being honoured, or the parties have not been able to agree a method of collective bargaining, the union can apply to the CAC to determine a method of collective bargaining. The imposed method will be enforceable in the same way as if the CAC had declared the union to be recognised under the statutory procedures.

Statutory recognition

13.23 The Employment Relations Act 1999, which received Royal Assent on 27 July 1999, enacted a new statutory recognition procedure, whereby an employer has a legal duty to recognise an independent trade union (or trade unions) where a majority of the relevant workforce seeks it. The Employment Relations Act and its provisions (inserting a new s 70A and a Schedule A1 into the TULRCA 1992) on recognition came into force on 6 June 2000. These provisions are further amplified by a statutory instrument (the Trade Union Recognition (Method of Collective Bargaining) Order 2000 (SI 2000/1300)) which sets out the method by which collective bargaining might be carried out in the absence of any agreement between the union and the employer on the matter, and by a DTI Code of Practice on Access to Workers during Recognition and Derecognition Ballots, which gives practical guidance about the steps employers should take to allow unions reasonable access to workers during recognition ballots.

13.24 The review of the 1999 Employment Relations Act concluded that it was working well, yet identified a number of areas where recognition procedures could be improved and trade union law modernised. The amending law, Employment Relations Act 2004, provided for new sections 37 and 38 (Role of the companion at disciplinary or grievance hearings; Extension of jurisdiction at EAT), and sections 29 to 32 (Inducements and detriments in respect of membership etc of independent trade unions), which came into force on 1 October 2004, provide examples of how the 2004 Act has slightly modified the workings of the 1999 Act.

New process

13.25 Under the statutory procedure, a new process is born where an independent trade union may apply to an employer for recognition in relation to a particular group of workers (a 'bargaining unit'). If the employer does not agree to recognise the union, or disputes the appropriate bargaining unit for the purposes of recognition, the union may apply to the CAC to decide the appropriate bargaining unit and/or whether the union should be recognised. Subject to the circumstances, recognition can be automatic, or a ballot may need to be held. Where it is shown that a majority of the workers in the bargaining unit are members of the union, the CAC can declare the union recognised without a ballot; otherwise, a secret ballot of all the workers in the bargaining unit must be held. The recognition procedures do not apply where the employer employs fewer than 21 workers.

13.26 The scope of compulsory recognition under the new statutory procedures is restricted to collective bargaining over pay, hours of work, and holidays, although the parties are free to extend the scope of collective bargaining by agreement. The Act does not require collective bargaining over training, but instead imposes a separate obligation on the employer to consult union representatives periodically on the employer policy, actions, and plans on training. The statutory recognition procedures are intended for use only if attempts to reach a voluntary agreement have failed. Strong emphasis is placed on the desirability of reaching agreement. The procedures are subject to strict time limits, but additional time is permitted at every stage for the parties to negotiate. Where the parties fail to reach agreement and the CAC imposes a method of collective bargaining, the imposed method has effect as a legally binding contract between the employer and the union, enforceable in the courts. The new procedures also enable the employer or the workers to apply to the CAC for derecognition in certain circumstances. The procedures for derecognition are similar to those for recognition. In most circumstances, derecognition is not possible until at least three years from the time when recognition was awarded.

Applying for recognition

13.27 The statutory recognition procedure begins with a formal request for recognition to an employer. Two or more unions can apply jointly, but in such a case it must be shown that the unions will cooperate effectively in collective bargaining and, if the employer wishes, conduct single-table bargaining. The request must be in writing, must specify the union or unions and the bargaining unit in respect of which recognition is claimed, and must state that the request is made under Schedule A1 TULRCA 1992. The request will not be valid unless the union (or each of the unions) has a certificate of independence, and the employer (together with any associated employers) employs at least 21 workers on the day of the request, or an average of at least 21 workers in the 13 weeks leading up to that day.

13.28 Once an application has been received, the statutory procedure will end if, within 10 working days, the parties agree both the bargaining unit and that the union should be recognised for collective bargaining in respect of that bargaining unit. If the employer agrees to negotiate, either in relation to the bargaining unit or the union, the employer is then entitled to a further period of 28 days for negotiation, extendable by mutual agreement. If the parties subsequently reach agreement, the statutory procedure ceases to apply. If the employer rejects the application, or negotiations are unsuccessful, the union may apply to the CAC to decide the appropriate bargaining unit and/or whether there is majority support for recognition amongst the workers in the bargaining unit. No such application may be made where the employer has agreed to negotiate and the union has rejected or failed to respond to a timely proposal by the employer to seek the assistance of ACAS.

The CAC's test

13.29 Where an application is made to the CAC, the CAC has 10 days to decide whether the application is valid and admissible. The CAC cannot consider an application unless, in addition to the requirements already noted, it is satisfied that at least 10 per cent of the proposed bargaining units are members of the union, and that a majority of workers in the proposed bargaining unit would be likely to favour recognition. If the CAC receives more than one application, and the proposed bargaining units overlap (ie at least one worker is a member of all the bargaining units), then unless the unions agree to make a joint bid, or all but one of the unions withdraw, each application will be subject to the '10 per cent test' to see whether at least 10 per cent of the bargaining unit are members of the union. If only one application passes the test, it may proceed; if more than one application passes, or none of them passes, none of the applications will be allowed to proceed. Furthermore, the application must not cover any workers in respect of whom the CAC has already accepted an application, or in respect of whom an independent union is already recognised. No application may be made within three years of a previous unsuccessful application by that union in respect of the same (or substantially the same) bargaining unit, and an application must not be substantially the same as an application accepted by the CAC within the previous three years.

Bargaining unit?

13.30 If the CAC has been asked to decide on the appropriate bargaining unit, it must initially give the parties a further 28 days to agree the bargaining unit. If the parties are still deadlocked, the CAC must determine the appropriate bargaining unit within 10 days, taking into account the need for the bargaining unit to be compatible with effective management, and, so far as is consistent with that need, the following factors:

(a) the views of the employer and the union (or unions);

(b) existing national and local bargaining arrangements;

(c) the desirability of avoiding small fragmented bargaining units within an undertaking;

(d) the characteristics of the workers falling within the bargaining unit and of any other employees of the employer whom the CAC considers relevant;

(e) the location of the workers.

(paras 18–19 of CAC Guidance)

13.31 In *R v CAC ex p Kwik Fit (GB) Ltd* (2002), the Court of Appeal advised the CAC to take a 'light touch' approach, including a primary consideration of the geographical scope of the workers concerned. However, once the appropriate bargaining unit has been established, the CAC must consider whether there is majority support for recognition among the workers in the bargaining unit. If the CAC is satisfied that a majority of the workers in the bargaining unit are members of the union, the CAC must issue a declaration of recognition, without the need for a ballot, unless one of the following conditions is met:

(a) the CAC is satisfied that a ballot should be held in the interests of good industrial relations;

(b) a significant number of the union members within the bargaining unit inform the CAC that they do not want the union to conduct collective bargaining on their behalf;

(c) membership evidence is produced which leads the CAC to conclude that there are doubts whether a significant number of the union members within the bargaining unit want the union to conduct collective bargaining on their behalf. This evidence must either be evidence about the circumstances in which union members became members (eg were incentives provided to members to join?), or evidence about the length of time for which union members have been members (eg was there a membership drive prior to a recognition application?).

13.32 Further, in R (on the application of *Cable & Wireless Services UK Ltd) (claimant) v Central Arbitration Committee & Communication Workers Union (Interested Party)* (2008), Collins J held that there had been no error of law in a decision of the CAC that all field service employers in a company were an appropriate bargaining unit for the purposes of recognition under the Trade Union and Labour Relations (Consolidation) Act 1992; Sch A1. R *(on the application of Kwik-Fit Ltd) v Central Arbitration Committee* (2002) applied.

Ballots for recognition

13.33 If any of the above conditions is met, or if the CAC is not satisfied that a majority of the workers in the bargaining unit are members of the union, the CAC must arrange for the holding of a secret ballot of the workers in the bargaining unit. Detailed rules exist in connection with the conduct of a ballot on recognition. The ballot must be conducted by a qualified independent person appointed by the CAC. The ballot must normally be held within 20 working days of the appointment of the independent person. It must be secret, and may be held at the workplace or by post at the CAC's discretion (ie a postal ballot is not compulsory). The costs of the ballot are split equally between the union and the employer. The employer is under a legal duty to cooperate with the ballot, to give the union reasonable access to the workers in the bargaining unit to campaign for recognition, and to provide information to the CAC concerning the workers in the bargaining unit (eg their names and home addresses). If the employer does not cooperate with the ballot, the CAC may order the employer to take specific steps to remedy that failure, and if the employer still fails to cooperate, the CAC may cancel the ballot and declare the union recognised. Where the result of the ballot indicates that recognition is supported by the majority of those who vote and at least 40 per cent of all the workers in the bargaining unit, the CAC must declare the union to be recognised by the employer for collective bargaining over the pay, hours of work, and holidays of all the workers in the bargaining unit.

13.34 If the union is unsuccessful in the ballot, the CAC must declare that the union is not recognised. No further application for recognition may be made by the same union in respect of the same (or substantially the same) bargaining unit for the next three years.

CAC recognition

13.35 If the CAC declares a union to be recognised, and the employer and union cannot agree on a method for conducting collective bargaining over pay, hours, and holidays, either party can ask the CAC for assistance. The CAC must allow a 42-day negotiation period for the parties to try to reach a voluntary agreement before intervening. After that period has elapsed, the CAC will try for a further 28 days (or longer, if all agree) to help the parties reach agreement. If that attempt is unsuccessful, the CAC must impose the method of collective bargaining on the parties.

13.36 Where the CAC imposes a method of collective bargaining, the imposed method has effect as a legally binding contract between the employer and the union, enforceable in the courts by an order of specific performance ordering the other party to comply with the method. Failure to comply with such an order could constitute contempt of court. Once the CAC has imposed a bargaining method, the parties can vary it (including the fact that it is legally binding) by agreement in writing.

Changes affecting the bargaining unit

13.37 Part III of the Schedule, annexed to the 1999 Act contains provisions where bargaining arrangements may need to be varied over time to reflect changes in the employer's business (eg in its structure, scope, or size). Where recognition has been imposed under the statutory procedures, there is a further statutory procedure for altering the recognition arrangements. The employer or the union may apply to the CAC to determine whether the original bargaining unit is no longer appropriate because the organisation, structure, nature, or size of the business has changed.

13.38 On such an application, the parties have 10 working days in which to attempt to agree a new bargaining unit. If they do so, the CAC must declare the union recognised for the new bargaining unit. If they fail to agree, the CAC must decide whether the original bargaining unit is still appropriate, and if not, what other unit (if any) would be appropriate, applying the same criteria as in an original application. If the CAC decides that no unit is appropriate, the union will be derecognised. The employer may also seek derecognition on the grounds that the bargaining unit has ceased to exist. As before, the parties have 10 working days to agree a new bargaining unit, failing which the CAC must decide whether the original bargaining unit is still appropriate, and if not, what other unit (if any) would be appropriate. Again, if the CAC decides that no unit is appropriate, the union will be derecognised.

13.39 If the CAC decides that a new bargaining unit would be appropriate, it must then decide whether the union should be recognised for that unit. In particular, it must consider whether the difference between the original bargaining unit and the new bargaining unit is such that the level of support for recognition needs to be reassessed in a fresh ballot. If the changes are minor, the CAC may decide that support does not need to be reassessed, and will declare the union recognised for the new unit. If support does need to be reassessed, the same procedures apply as in an original application (ie the 10 per cent test, likelihood of majority support, automatic recognition if over 50 per cent membership, etc). If a ballot is required, it must follow the same procedures as the original ballot.

Derecognition?

13.40 As noted already above, the Employment Relations Act also contains procedures for derecognition which mirror those for recognition. Parts IV, V, and VII provide statutory derecognition procedures, where the CAC has made a declaration of recognition or has imposed a method of collective bargaining. Derecognition may not take place until at least three years after the CAC declared the union recognised or specified a method of collective bargaining. It is possible for an employer to apply to the CAC to derecognise where, after the three-year period has elapsed:

- the employer (together with any associated employers) has employed an average of fewer than 21 workers over a 13-week period;

- the employer believes that the majority of workers in the bargaining unit support the end of the bargaining arrangements;

- the employer applies for derecognition in relation to a union that was previously automatically recognised.

13.41 The detailed procedures differ according to the reason for derecognition. Where the basis for derecognition is the fact that the employer has fewer than 21 workers, the employer can give notice to the union that it is to be derecognised from a given date at least 35 working days after the notification. The union may appeal to the CAC if it wishes to contest the employer's claim. If the CAC finds that the employer still has 21 or more workers, the collective bargaining arrangements will remain in place; otherwise they will end on the date specified in the employer's notice.

13.42 Where the employer believes that the union is no longer representative of the bargaining unit, the employer must first write to the union requesting the end of the bargaining arrangements. The union has 10 working days in which to accept or reject the employer's notice or, if the union agrees to negotiate, a further 28 days to reach agreement. If no agreement is forthcoming, the employer may apply to the CAC to decide whether a majority of workers support derecognition. Just as with applications for recognition, a threshold '10 per cent test' must be satisfied before the CAC can consider an application for derecognition, ie there must be prima facie evidence that at least 10 per cent of the bargaining unit favour an end to the collective bargaining arrangements, and that a majority of the bargaining unit would be likely to do so. Where these requirements are satisfied, the CAC must hold a secret ballot to decide whether the majority of workers support derecognition. If the ending of the bargaining arrangements is supported by the majority of those who vote and at least 40 per cent of all the workers in the bargaining unit, the CAC must declare that the bargaining arrangements will cease to have effect from a specified date.

13.43 Similar requirements apply where workers in the bargaining unit request an end to the collective bargaining arrangements. Where the union was automatically recognised on the grounds of more than 50 per cent union membership in the bargaining unit, the employer may request the end of the bargaining arrangements on the grounds that fewer than half the workers in the bargaining unit are members of the union. Again, time is allowed for negotiation, and if no agreement is reached the CAC will hold a ballot of the workers in the bargaining unit. In addition to the above, workers may apply to the CAC for derecognition of a union which does not have a certificate of independence. Such an application may be made at any time after a non-independent union is recognised (ie the usual three-year limit does not apply). Again, the CAC cannot consider the application unless there is prima facie evidence that at least 10 per cent of the bargaining unit favour an end to the bargaining arrangements and a majority of them are likely to do so.

Recognition rights

13.44 The main rights accruing to an independent, recognised trade union in relation to consultation and the provision of information are:

(a) to receive relevant information for the purposes of collective bargaining;

(b) to be consulted in respect of collective (ie large-scale) redundancies; and

(c) to be consulted in relation to a transfer of an undertaking.

Disclosure of bargaining information

13.45 The duty to disclose information to a recognised trade union for the purposes of collective bargaining was introduced by the Industrial Relations Act 1971, and is now contained in ss 181–185 TULRCA 1992. Complaints of a failure to disclose information lie to the CAC. Prior to the Act, the duty to disclose information could be circumvented by an employer either refusing initially to recognise, or by subsequently derecognising, a union. This has changed following the introduction of the statutory recognition procedure by the Employment Relations Act 1999, although where recognition is voluntary the position is unchanged.

Extent of the duty to disclose information

13.46 The duty to disclose is contained in s 181(2) TULRCA 1992, which creates a two-limb test for deciding whether information needs to be disclosed. An employer must disclose to representatives of a recognised, independent trade union, on request, all information relating to the employer's undertaking which is in the employer's possession, and is information:

(a) without which the union would be impeded to a material extent in carrying on collective bargaining with the employer; and

(b) which it would be in accordance with good industrial relations practice for the employer to disclose.

13.47 Requests to an employer for information must be in writing, if the employer so requests (s 181(3)). The employer must disclose or confirm the requested information in writing, if the union representatives so request (s 181(5)). The duty is a duty to disclose information for the purposes of collective bargaining. It follows that an employer may only be required to disclose information under these provisions for collective bargaining about matters, and in relation to descriptions of workers, for which the union is in fact recognised by the employer. If recognition is partial, the employer need not provide information which falls outside the scope of that recognition. The CAC has indicated that what must be considered is whether the union would be significantly hampered without the provision of a particular type of information (ie would the absence of the information be a 'significant impediment' to the union in carrying on collective bargaining?).

13.48 The CAC must also consider whether it would be in accordance with good industrial relations practice to release the requested information. In considering this issue, s 181(4) states that regard must be had to the ACAS Code of Practice on Disclosure of Information (the 'Code'). The CAC has stated that 'good industrial relations practice' reflects the actual practice of good employers.

Exceptions to the duty

13.49 Whilst s 181 TULRCA 1992 creates a general duty to disclose collective bargaining information to independent recognised unions, the duty can be avoided in the circumstances set down in s 182(1), which lists seven categories of cases in which disclosure will not be ordered against an employer:

  (a) where it would be against the interests of national security to disclose;

  (b) where disclosure would contravene an enactment;

  (c) where the information requested was communicated to or obtained by the employer in confidence (eg tenders issued in confidence);

  (d) where the information requested relates specifically to an individual;

  (e) where disclosure of the requested information would cause substantial injury to the employer's undertaking (other than any effect which it might have on collective bargaining);

  (f) where the information has been obtained by the employer for the purpose of bringing, prosecuting, or defending any legal proceedings;

  (g) where the compiling or assembling of the information would involve an amount of work or expenditure out of reasonable proportion to the value of the information in the conduct of collective bargaining.

Complaints of failure to disclose information

13.50 If an employer fails to comply with the duty to disclose, a union can bring a complaint under the procedure set out in s 183 TULRCA 1992. A complaint lies to the

CAC. Upon receipt of a claim, the CAC is required to consider whether the complaint is reasonably likely to be settled by conciliation. If so, the CAC must refer the matter to ACAS and notify the union and the employer of the referral (s 183(2)). If ACAS cannot resolve the complaint, the dispute is referred back to the CAC. If the CAC is to deal with the claim, it proceeds to hear and determine the complaint, and makes a declaration stating whether or not the complaint is well-founded, in whole or in part, giving reasons for its findings (s 183(3)).

Central Arbitration Committee (CAC)

13.51   The Industrial Arbitration Board was replaced in 1975 by the Central Arbitration Committee (CAC). The newly constituted CAC has recently undertaken a review of its first five years. Its purpose is to act as independent machinery for arbitration, as well as to exercise its statutory jurisdiction under the 1999 Employment Relations Act (s 259 TULRCA 1992) to:

- review collective agreements;
- determine applications for statutory recognition/derecognition; and
- adjudicate on complaints under ss 183–186 TULRCA 1992 (failure to disclose information).

The CAC is headed by a Chairman and comprises of deputy chairmen, assisted by lay panel members, representing both employers and employees; see <http://www.cac.gov.uk>.

Remedies for non-cooperation in collective bargaining

13.52   The remedies for non-cooperation in collective bargaining include declaration and arbitration.

Declaration

13.53   If the CAC finds in favour of the union, s 183(5) requires that the CAC's declaration must specify the following matters:

(a)   the information which should have been disclosed;

(b)   date on which the employer refused to supply the requested information or refused to confirm the information in writing; and

(c) a period of time within which the employer is bound to make good the failure to disclose that information. In specifying a time limit, the CAC must allow a period of at least one week from the date of the declaration.

The CAC cannot specify what matters it thinks ought to be disclosed in the future as between the parties.

Arbitration

13.54 The ultimate remedy for a failure to disclose in accordance with the statutory provisions is unilateral arbitration. If the employer fails to comply with the terms of the declaration, the union may present a further complaint to the CAC under section 184. If the CAC finds wholly or partly in favour of the union, it must make a declaration to that effect. After such a declaration has been granted, it is possible for the union to make a further claim, in writing, that those employees specified in the claim should have their terms and conditions of employment modified in accordance with the claim (s 185(1)). The power of the CAC to award amended terms and conditions is restricted to employees and to terms and conditions which relate to matters within the scope of the employer's recognition of the union (s 185(4)). Therefore, if a union is only partially recognised by an employer, eg for the purposes of dealing with the employer's pension scheme, the union cannot seek an order modifying terms and conditions in respect of matters such as pay, hours of work, etc. Secondly, the CAC cannot impose an order in respect of terms fixed by statute (s 185(7)).

Information and consultation

13.55 At the EU Council of Ministers meeting on 17 December 2001, the Council's Directive on Information and Consultation (Council Directive 2002/14/EC) was agreed. The Information and Consultation Directive is based upon the social partnership approach. That is, workers should have the basic right to consultation, but a mechanism for bargaining should be agreed between the parties and utilised accordingly. This new law requires companies with 50 or more employees to regularly inform on an enterprises' economic situation and to consult with workers on key decisions regarding the organisation's future. These include situations where jobs are threatened and where any anticipatory measures, such as training, skill development, and other measures increasing the adaptability of employees are planned. Consultation is also compulsory for decisions that are likely to lead to substantial changes in work organisation or in contractual relations. National governments will enact their own implementing measures, with sanctions for breaches, and are free to extend further these minimal information and consultation rights. Since 2005, the Directive has applied to those organisations with more than 50 workers.

13.56 This new Directive was implemented in the UK by the Information and Consultation on Employees (ICE) Regulations 2004, which comply with the Directive's provisions. In the UK, since 2005 this law applies to those organisations with 150 or more workers, from 2007 for those businesses with over 100 workers and from 2008 for those with more than 50 workers.

National implementation

13.57 The UK Government opposed this Directive on the grounds of subsidiarity, in so far as it believes it to be an unnecessary measure. Under the new NIC Directive, consultation is required where an employer proposes to dismiss 20 or more workers as redundant at one establishment within 90 days or less. Where 100 or more redundancies are proposed, consultation must commence at least 90 days before the first dismissal. However, these rules duplicate existing legal arrangements required under the Collective Redundancy Directive, discussed in Chapter 10. The information that must be disclosed is a statement of the proposed dismissals and reasons for such, the numbers affected, and the proposed method of selection and what payments are available.

Worker involvement

13.58 After a record 31 years of EU negotiation, on 8 October 2001 the EU's Employment and Social Policy Council adopted a Regulation for a European Company Statute and a related Directive on Employee Involvement. Both these legal instruments took effect from 2004. This adoption arises after many years of controversy surrounding both the Fifth Directive, on Company Law, which proposed worker representatives on company boards, and the failed Vredling Directive, which proposed compulsory worker representatives in multinationals. The Regulation provides for companies located in the EU and operating in more than one Member State registering as a Societas Europea (SE) (a so-called 'European company') and to adopt one set of national rules and adopt a single management reporting system as a means of governance. More importantly, this Regulation permits an SE to trade within the EEA without having to register in each Member State in which they operate, on condition that it has a minimum capital of 120,000 euros. On the other hand, the Directive provides further regulation of information and consultation on matters concerning the SE itself and allows for employee participation in the supervisory or administrative body of the SE. The purpose of this Directive is to ensure that when an SE is established no reduction in employee involvement occurs. These additional workplace democracy provisions are modelled on those contained in the EWC Directive. They again include a 'default' set of rules whereby if no agreement on employee involvement can be reached, a consequential works council is established consisting of between three and 30 employees.

13.59 The passing of the European Company Statute Regulation, as well as the Employee Involvement and Information & Consultation Directives, with their potential impact to establish EU-wide frameworks for collective bargaining, are highly significant for the future development of a fully participative European social partnership model. However, the actual take-up rate of these new initiatives is uncertain, given the low level of establishment of European Works Councils since 1993. If such reluctance applies to EU-wide national bargaining, then it is clear that the Directive is also doomed to fail.

FURTHER READING

Deakin, S, & Morris, G, *Labour Law* (4th ed, 2005) Hart (chapters 7 & 9).

Smith, I, & Thomas, G, *Smith & Wood's Employment Law* (9th ed, 2007) Oxford University Press (chapter 3).

ARTICLES

Hardy, S, & Adnett, N, (2006) 'Breaking the ICE and Democracy at Work', *International Journal of Human Resource Management*, Vol 17, pp 1021–1036.

Simpson, B, (2000) 'Trade Union Recognition and the Law: A New Approach', *Industrial Law Journal*, Vol 29, No 3, pp 193–222.

SELF-TEST QUESTIONS

1   Outline the statutory procedure for trade union recognition, as enacted by the 1999 Employment Relations Act. What alternatives exist for trade union bargaining?

2   How has the Court's judgment in the *ASLEF* case changed the protection afforded to trade union members? And, is the law now adequate in dealing with potential discrimination against trade union officials, given the UK Government's response?

3   Vernon is the elected representative of TEACHU, the lecturers' union recognised at New Learn College. Last week, Vernon's manager, Mr Stickler, told him that he could not rearrange three lectures to attend a branch meeting and rejected his application for a day residential course on first aid.

Advise Vernon on his rights to time off as a trade union official.

4   EasyClean Ltd provide cleaning services throughout the UK, with eight branches nationwide, employing some 610 people. EasyClean does not recognise any trade union, nor does it desire to do so. Recently, Sweepers Unite, a UK union, has recruited new members at several of EasyClean's branches. Out of 165 staff at its Muncaster area branch office, some 83 staff have joined Sweepers Unite. Bob, the Muncaster Area Manager, has recently declined a request by Sweepers Unite, upon the advice of EasyClean's Head Office, for voluntary recognition.

Advise EasyClean Limited on the procedure to be followed, the potential outcomes, and likely result of Sweepers Unite's application for statutory recognition.

14

Industrial action

SUMMARY

This chapter considers the right to strike, the tortious liabilities of unions, trade unions' statutory immunities, as well as individual liability for industrial action. In particular this chapter considers the following:

- A trade dispute is defined as 'a dispute between workers and their employer which relates wholly or mainly to...: terms and conditions, engagement or otherwise of workers, matters of discipline and membership of trade unions' (s 244 TULRCA 1992).
- Strikes are defined as 'any concerted stoppage of work' (s 246 TULRCA 1992).
- The economic torts are: inducement to breach of contract, intimidation, conspiracy, and interference with trade or business.
- The 'golden formula' in 'contemplation and furtherance of a trade dispute', statutory immunity, prevails.
- Limitations on statutory immunity include secondary action and unlawful picketing.

Introduction

14.1 'Industrial action' is defined as a strike or withdrawal of labour. The basic principle in relation to industrial action is as Lord Watson puts it in *Allen v Flood* (1898): 'strikes are only effective when undertaken lawfully'.

14.2 Part III of the Employment Relations Act 2004 amended the law relating to industrial action, including measures to simplify the law relating to ballots for industrial action and ballot notices. Moreover, it strengthens the protection against the dismissal of workers taking official and lawful industrial action. The latter reform involves the exempting of employer 'lock-outs' for an 8-week period.

Strikes and contracts of employment

14.3 A 'strike' is defined in section 246 of TULRCA 1992 as 'any concerted stoppage of work'. In *Connex South Eastern Ltd v Rail Maritime and Transport Workers* (1999), the Court of Appeal held that the definition of 'strike' is wide enough to cover any refusal to work for periods when the workers would normally work. In most, if not all, strike action, contracts of employment are affected. However, no notice to terminate the contract is given. Even so, strike action amounts to a repudiation of contract. For instance, the EAT in *Simmons v Hoover Ltd* (1977) provided guidance: 'it seems to us to be plain that it was a repudiation for here there was a settled, confirmed continued intention on the part of the employee not to do any of the work which under contract he had been engaged to do; which was the whole purpose of his contract'. Consequently, the employer has a choice whether or not to accept the repudiation by the strikers. Such an acceptance results in dismissal. Yet some industrial action is non-contract based (see for example, *Secretary of State for Employment v Associated Society of Locomotive Engineers and Firemen (No 2)* (1972), *Cresswell v Board of Inland Revenue* (1984), *Miles v Wakefield Metropolitan District Council* (1987), and *Ticehurst v British Telecommunications plc* (1992)).

Pay and strike action

14.4 Action short of dismissing strikers is that the employer is clearly not obliged to pay the striking workers during the industrial action itself. Most notably, the employee must show that he/she is available and willing to work (*Henthorn and Taylor v Central Electricity Generating Board* (1980)). The general principle is that deductions from pay are regulated by agreement between parties and by a statutory exception under section 14(5) of ERA 1996.

14.5 Alternatively, an employer may take legal action and sue striking employees for damages instead on account of a breach of contract. However, the major legal dilemma in this scenario is how to calculate the damages concerned. For example, the courts have rejected a proportionate share of overhead expenses during lost days as the appropriate measure. Courts have a tendency to award only a proportional amount of the claim sought by the suing employers.

Forms of industrial action

14.6 Strike action is not the only form of industrial action. Other forms include work-to-rule and go-slow, as well as overtime bans. In addition, employees may work normally but refuse to perform the particular duty about which they are protesting. Sit-ins are another form of industrial action.

Industrial action by the employer

14.7 An employer may also resort to industrial action, since an employer holds the right to make changes in their business. Consequently, employers may have cause to 'lock-out' their workforce.

Legality of industrial action

14.8 Industrial action is lawful where it conforms to the well-enunciated two-fold test of Lord Diplock in *Dimbleby & Sons Ltd v National Union of Journalists* (1984):

(a) whether the employers have a cause of action at common law; and,

(b) whether those taking industrial action are acting in 'contemplation or furtherance of a trade dispute against the employer'. If so, section 219 of TULRCA 1992 gives immunity from action which:

- induced a person to breach a contract of employment;
- threatened that a contract of employment will be breached;
- interferes with the trade, business, or employment of a person; or
- constitutes an agreement by two or more persons to procure the doing of any such act.

This means that the normal torts are removed, where this test is satisfied.

The economic torts

14.9 As noted above (14.8), there are several different ways of committing this tort during industrial action:

(a) direct inducement;

(b) indirect inducement by unlawful means;

(c) procuring breach of contract by unlawful means.

14.10 Most commonly during industrial action, a relevant tort is committed when a trade union official directly persuades a worker to breach their contract of employment; similarly, where trade unions organise action against suppliers or distributors of the employer with whom it is in dispute and as a result induce a breach of the employer's commercial contracts. Alternatively, a tort is committed if the strikers unlawfully interfere with any contract by actually preventing performance.

Inducement

14.11 Inducement means more than the fact that a trade union official informs the workforce that the employer is intending to make redundancies and/or change working methods and the workforce goes on strike in protest. Now 219 of the TULRCA 1992 provides that an act done by a person in contemplation of furtherance of a trade dispute shall not be actionable in tort on the ground only:

(a) that it induces another person to breach a contract or interferes or induces any other person to interfere with its performance; or

(b) that it consists of his threatening that a contract (whether one to which he is a party or not) will be broken or its performance interfered with, or that he will induce another person to break a contract or to interfere with its performance.

The tort of direct inducement to breach a contract was recognized in *Lumley v Gye* (1853).

Interference

14.12 Lord Diplock in *Merkur Island Shipping Corporation v Laughton* (1983) regarded the tort of 'interfering with the trade or business of another person by doing unlawful acts' as a 'genus of torts' of which procuring breach of contract is a 'species'. Therefore, the tort of interference may include such interference with future contracts not yet in existence (*Stratford (J T) & Son Ltd v Lindley* (1965) and *Union Traffic Ltd v TGWU* (1989)). This was not made out by the distribution of leaflets outside supermarkets urging members of the public to boycott the employer's mushrooms (*Middlebrook Mushrooms Ltd v Transport and General Workers Union* (1993)). Consequently, to be tortious the persuasion had to be directed at one of the parties to the commercial contract in issue (see *Falconer v ASLEF & NUR* (1986)).

Breach of contract

14.13　The previous torts are required as a precondition to the commission of breach of contract, normally by unlawful means of indirect inducement and procuring breach of contract.

Intimidation

14.14　The tort of intimidation includes threat of a breach of contract or other unlawful act as well as threats of violence. Now according to s 219(1)(b) TULRCA 1992, 'where it consists in threatening that a contract (whether one to which he is a party or not) will be broken or its performance interfered with, or that he will induce another person to break a contract or interfere with its performance' immunity arises.

Conspiracy

14.15　A conspiracy to commit a crime or a tort is also included. A conspiracy to injure consists of an agreement to cause deliberate loss to another without cause or excuse with the intention of injuring the claimant (eg *Huntley v Thornton* (1957)). The unlawful means of pursuing the strike must, however, be integral to the aims of the conspirators and not peripheral to them. In most cases, immunity against liability for conspiracy is unnecessary because the cause if continued would amount to justification in itself at common law. Immunity is therefore provided by s 219(2) TULRCA 1992, where an 'agreement or combination by two or more persons to do or procure the doing of any act in contemplation or furtherance of a trade dispute shall not be actionable in tort if the act is one which, if done without any such agreement or combination, would not be actionable in tort'.

Trade dispute immunity

14.16　As noted above, when these torts emerged at common law and later statute, Parliament decided to provide protection to trade unions, so as to give them immunity from legal action against them. To that effect, it did not allow trade unions and their officials as well as members the right to break the law, but neutralised the normal effect of actions pursued for the torts listed above, when trade unions undertook legitimate industrial action (*Express Newspapers Ltd v McShane* (1980)). The latter immunity became known as the 'Golden Formula'.

The 'Golden Formula'

14.17　The 'Golden Formula' provides that to be protected and be given immunity from suit, the individual must be acting 'in contemplation or furtherance of a trade dispute' (s 219(2) TULRCA 1992). The words in 'contemplation' meant, according to Lord Loreburn in *Conway v Wade* (1909*):* 'that either a dispute is imminent and the act is done in expectation of and with a view to it, or that the dispute is already existing and the act is done in support of one side to it'. The formula has three parts to be satisfied:

(i) there must be a temporal relationship between the action to be taken and a trade dispute;

(ii) the trade dispute must be between workers and their employer; and

(iii) the dispute must be over one or more of the matters listed in s 244 TULRCA 1992, which defines a trade dispute.

Trade dispute

14.18 Section 244(1) TULRCA 1992 defines a trade dispute as:

> A dispute between workers and their employer, that is to say, which relates wholly or mainly to one of the following:
>
> (a) terms and conditions of employment, or the physical conditions in which any workers are required to work;
>
> (b) engagement or non-engagement, or termination of suspension of employment or the duties of employment, of one or more workers;
>
> (c) allocation of work or the duties of employment as between workers or groups of workers;
>
> (d) matters of discipline;
>
> (e) the membership or non-membership of a trade union on the part of a worker;
>
> (f) facilities for officials of trade unions; and
>
> (g) machinery for negotiation of consultation, and other procedures, relating to any of the foregoing matters, including the recognition by employer or employers' association of the right of a trade union to represent workers in any such negotiation or consultation or in the carrying out of such procedures.

14.19 Consequently, a trade dispute must relate wholly or mainly to one or more of the matters set out above in section 244 of TULRCA 1992. Yet, Lord Denning ruled in *Beetham v Trinidad Cement Ltd* (1960) that a dispute 'exists whenever a difference exists, and a difference can exist long before the parties become locked in combat . . . It is sufficient that they should be sparring for an opening.'

14.20 The Court of Appeal in *P v The National Association of School Masters/Union of Women Teachers* (2001) held that there was a trade dispute when employees refused to teach a particular pupil, who, it was claimed, was disruptive in class.

Losing immunity

14.21 The statutory immunities under section 219 will be removed in the following situations:

(a) secondary action;

(b) unlawful picketing;

(c) action to enforce union membership;

(d) action to impose union recognition;

(e) action in support of dismissed unofficial strikers;

(f) action without proper notice to an employer;

(g) action without a valid strike ballot.

Dismissal and post-termination protection

14.22 Section 244(5), TULRCA 1992, excludes a person who has ceased to be employed unless:

(a) his employment was terminated in connection with the dispute; or

(b) his employment was one of the circumstances giving rise to it.

14.23 The rules relating to the dismissal of employees during industrial action are set out in ss 237–238A TULRCA 1992. Section 238A(7B) of the Employment Relations Act 1999 (as amended by the Employment Relations Act 2004) amended the well-established principles on dismissal for industrial action by creating a 12-week 'protected period' during which a dismissal for taking part in industrial action will be automatically unfair. Consequently, employees are only protected if it is official action, and would be covered by the statutory immunities against liability in tort under s 219 TULRCA 1992, having complied with the relevant law.

14.24 Under s 237 TULRCA 1992, an employee cannot bring an unfair dismissal complaint if at the time of the dismissal the employee was taking part in an unofficial strike or other unofficial industrial action. Unofficial industrial action is when it is taken without the authorisation or endorsement of a union engaged in the action.

14.25 The Court of Appeal's conclusion in *University College London Hospital NHS Trust v UNISON* (1999) was that a dispute will relate to employees' terms and conditions only where it concerns their relationship with their current employer. Such might be fraught with difficulties when applied to TUPE situations. For example, in *Westminster City Council v UNISON* (2001), a dispute about a proposal to transfer an undertaking, including its employees, from the local authority to a private company was a trade dispute; the Court of Appeal held that the dispute was predominantly about the change in the identity of the employer and not about public policy issues.

Secondary action

14.26 Section 17(2) of EA 1980 first defined 'secondary action' as:

> when, and only when, a person –
>
> (a) induces another to break a contract of employment or interferes or induces another to interfere with its performance, or
>
> (b) threatens that a contract of employment under which he or another is employed will be broken or its performance interfered with, or that he will induce another to break a contract of employment or to interfere with its performance, if the employer under the contract of employment is not a party to the trade dispute.

14.27 Section 4 of the Employment Act 1990 finally removed all immunity for secondary action other than secondary picketing where it is peaceful.

Strike ballots

14.28 Sections 226–234, TULRCA 1992 removed the immunity of unions and individual strike organisers from certain actions in tort unless a majority of union members likely to be called out in industrial action have approved that action in a properly held ballot.

14.29 Typical industrial action timetable:

Day 1	Notice to employer of ballot
Days 2 to 4	
Day 5	Sample ballot paper to employer
Days 6 to 7	
Day 8	Opening day of ballot, ie ballot papers distributed
Days 9 to 14	
Day 15	(Earliest) date for return of ballot papers
Day 16	Result
Day 17	Notice to employer of the result
Day 18	Notification to the employer of the proposed action
Day 25	Action may start

14.30 A ballot is required only in respect of 'an act done by a trade union'; that is, if it is authorised or endorsed by the Principal Executive Committee, the President or General-Secretary of the trade union concerned. As a general rule, the first authorisation or endorsement of the strike or other industrial action must be given within four weeks from the date the ballot is taken. Since 1999, the union and the employer may extend this period by agreement for up to another four weeks. These ballot rules are strictly applied and a minor failure can negate industrial action and remove the relevant immunities. For example, in *National Union of Rail, Maritime and Transport Workers v Midland Mainline Ltd* (2001), it was held that this meant that the union had not accorded entitlement to vote in the ballot equally to members who it was reasonable, at the time of the ballot, for the union to believe would be induced to take part in the industrial action. A union intending to organise industrial action must conduct separate ballots for each place of work, subject to certain important exceptions. By s 228 TULRCA 1992, in so far as the union believes, and it is a reasonable belief, that the persons to be induced to take part in a strike or other industrial action are engaged at different places of work, it must hold a ballot at each such place of work.

14.31 For example, the High Court held, in *University of Central England v National and Local Government Officers' Association* (1993) that it is not necessary for entitlement to vote in a ballot to be restricted to employees of only one employer. Furthermore, in *British Telecommunications plc v Communication Workers Union* (2004), the High Court stated that not everyone balloted need be affected, where the union had mistakenly advised its members that strike action included action short of a strike. This too did not invalidate the ballot. But it had not given the information required under the TULRCA 1992 on the categories of workers who would be balloted, and this was grounds for an injunction.

14.32 Provisions contained in the Employment Relations Act 1999 established important exceptions to the above principles. The new section 228A of TULRCA 1992 provides that the union need not ballot different workplaces separately because of section 228 in any of the following situations:

(a) at least one union member in a workplace is directly affected by the dispute in question;

(b) entitlement to vote is restricted to union members who have an occupation (or occupations) of a particular kind and are employed by a particular employer (or any of a number of employers) with whom the union is in dispute;

(c) entitlement to vote is restricted to union members who, according to the union's reasonable belief, have an occupation (or occupations) of a particular kind and are employed by a particular employer (or any number of employers) with whom the union is in dispute.

14.33 By section 234A of TULRCA 1992, the union must give advance notice of industrial action to the affected employer(s). In fact, the trade union concerned must 'take such steps as are reasonably necessary to ensure that the employer receives' a specified notice of industrial action.

Ballot papers

14.34 Under s 229(3) TULRCA 1992, an industrial action ballot paper must specify who is authorised for the purposes of calling members to take part or continue to take part in industrial action. There will be no immunity for the trade union if action supported by a ballot is not in fact called by the person named in the ballot paper. The union must give the employer seven days' notice of its intention to hold a ballot. The Employment Relations Act 1999 removed the duty to 'name names', and replaced it with a duty to provide information to an employer so that the employer can make plans in relation to the industrial action. The union must also provide the employer, not less than three days before the ballot, with a sample voting paper (s 226A TULRCA 1992).

Picketing

14.35 The central justification of peaceful picketing lies in the right to freedom of speech and peaceful protest. Article 11 of the 1950 European Convention on Human Rights establishes the right to freedom of association and peaceful assembly, which applies to the law on picketing. The Employment Relations Act 2004 produced a new Code of Practice on Picketing, in force since October 2005.

14.36 Pickets may not commit the following crimes:

(a) Obstruction of the highway:
Subject to section 132 of the Highways Act 1980, 'if a person without lawful authority or excuse in any way wilfully obstructs the free passage along the highway, he shall be guilty of an offence . . .'. The illegality of an obstruction is a question of fact, and depends on 'the length of time the obstruction continues, the place where it occurs, the purpose for which it is done, and of course whether it does in fact cause an actual obstruction as opposed to a potential obstruction' (*Nagy v Weston* (1965)).

(b) Obstructing a police constable:

Section 51(3) of the Police Act 1964 makes it a criminal offence to obstruct a police constable in the execution of his duty and that duty is to prevent trouble where he reasonably apprehends a breach of the peace as a 'real possibility'.

(c) Assaults:

While assaults may be committed on a picket-line, there is no such crime or tort unless the capacity to carry into effect the intention to commit a battery is present at the time of the overt act indicating an immediate intention to commit a battery: *Thomas v National Union of Mineworkers (South Wales Area)* (1985), since the threats uttered by the picketing striking miners were made from the side of the road to working miners who were in vehicles which the pickets could not reach.

(d) Public Order Act Offences:

By section 4 of the Public Order Act 1986, a person is guilty of an offence if the picketeer:

(a) uses towards another person threatening, abusive, or insulting words or behaviour; or

(b) distributes or displays to another person any writing, sign, or other visible representation which is threatening, abusive, or insulting with intent to cause that person to believe that he will be subject to immediate unlawful violence.

(e) Unlawful assembly:

An unlawful assembly consists of the assembly of three or more persons with the intention of fulfilling a common purpose in such a manner as to endanger the public peace. It is an offence at common law to obstruct the public in the exercise or enjoyment of rights common to all, including free passage along the highway. In *J Lyons & Sons v Wilkins* (1899) Lindley LJ thought it did, since it constituted an attempt to persuade, regardless of any obstruction. Lord Denning MR in *Hubbard v Pitt* (1975) considered that this view 'has not stood the test of time . . .'.

(f) Harassment:

The Protection from Harassment Act 1997, s 1 establishes that it will be an offence for someone to pursue a course of conduct that amounts to harassment of another and which he knows, or ought to know, amounts to harassment. 'Harassment' is not defined in the Act, but can include 'alarming the person or causing the person distress' (s 7).

14.37 Picketing is not actionable per se but only if a tort is committed by the pickets (*News Group Newspapers Ltd v Society of Graphical Allied Trades* (1982)).

Nuisance

14.38 Private nuisance is an unlawful interference with an individual's enjoyment or use of his land. To sue for the tort, the claimant must have some proprietary interest in the land and this action is most likely to be relevant where pickets block an access route. Picketing accompanied by violence, or even merely noise, may be a private nuisance. Scott J in *Thomas v National Union of Mineworkers (South Wales Area)* (1985) held that mass picketing at the gates of five collieries in South Wales during the miners' strike of 1984/85 was tortuous and could be restrained at the suit of the plaintiffs who were working miners.

14.39 The immunity for picketing is found in s 220 of TULRCA 1992, which reads:

> It shall be lawful for a person in contemplation of furtherance of a trade dispute to attend
>
> (a) at or near his own place of work, or
>
> (b) if he is an official of a trade union, at or near the place of work of a member of that union whom he is accompanying and whom he represents.

Secondary pickets

14.40 A secondary picket is not liable for economic torts, like inducing breach of contract, where he pickets his own place of work and his employer is:

(a) an immediate supplier or customer of the employer in dispute, and the aim is to disrupt services between them; or

(b) an associated employer of the employer in dispute and the aim is to cut off dispute (TULRCA 1992, s 224).

14.41 Even if the picketeer fulfils all the other requirements of secondary action, the picket must be at or near his place of work to attract immunity (see *Mersey Dock and Harbour Co v Verrinder* (1982)). According to the Code of Practice on Picketing, the 'place of work' means 'an entrance to or an exit from the factory, site or office at which the picket works'.

14.42 The immunity has also been narrowly applied by the courts. For example, *Broome v DPP* (1974): 'The section gives no protection in relation to anything the pickets may say or do whilst they are attending if what they say or do is unlawful... The section therefore gives a narrow but nevertheless real immunity to pickets.'

14.43 In contrast, the statute contains no specific restriction on the number of pickets, but clearly large numbers may intimidate more easily than the actions of the few. Lord Reid's opinion has already been reviewed. The Code of Practice describes mass picketing as 'obstruction if not intimidation' and para 31 recommends ensuring that 'in general the number of pickets does not exceed six at any entrance to a workplace: frequently a smaller number will be appropriate'.

Remedies

14.44 Most employers will not seek damages against striking employees. More likely, the employers desire the return of their workforce to full employment capacity. As a result, employers will often seek injunctions to enable this.

Injunctions

14.45 The principles determining whether injunctions are to be granted are found in *Cyanamid Co v Ethicon Ltd* (1975), where the House of Lords postulated that it was only necessary that the plaintiff have an arguable case and that there was a serious issue to be tried. The court should not at this stage express a concluded opinion as to the law unless it is reasonably clear (*Associated British Ports plc v Transport and General Workers Union* (1989)). In *Associated British Ports plc v Transport and General Workers Union* (1989) the Court of Appeal stated that the status quo was to be understood in the sense that work was still proceeding at the time the writ was issued, so that was the status quo position.

14.46 Section 221 TULRCA 1992, provides that if there might be a 'trade dispute' defence to an injunction, the court must not grant without notice relief unless all reasonable steps have been taken: (a) to notify the other side of the application; and (b) to give them an opportunity of putting their case.

14.47 The primary methods of enforcement on the breach of injunctive orders are committal for contempt, up to a maximum of two years. Sequestration is an alternative remedy which is only granted as a last resort to enforce a judgment requiring a person to do an act within a specified time or to abstain from doing a specified act. It operates by sequestrating all the real and personal property of the union or persons subject to the order, and is cumulative to other methods of enforcing an order such as committal.

14.48 For example, in *Anglian Windows Ltd v GMB* (2007), Teare J, found that an application by a company for an interlocutory injunction restraining a trade union from carrying out a strike was refused where it was more likely than not that the union would establish at trial that it had conducted the ballot for the strike in accordance with the Trade Union and Labour Relations (Consolidation) Act 1992, s 226.

Damages

14.49 The amount of damages that can be awarded against a union is limited by s 22 TULRCA 1992. Section 22 grades liability in bands, from a maximum of £10,000 in the case of a union with less than 5,000 members, up to a maximum of £250,000 for a union with 100,000 or more members. Consequently, certain property belonging to trade unions is protected from awards of damages, such as the personal property of the union's trustees, officials, and members and the union's political fund (provided its rules prevent the fund from being used to finance strikes or other industrial action).

FURTHER READING

Bowers, J, Duggan, M, & Reade, D, *The Law on Industrial Action and Trade Union Recognition* (2004) Oxford University Press.

Deakin, S, & Morris, G, *Labour Law* (4th ed, 2005) Hart (chapter 11).

ARTICLES

Simpson, B, (1987) 'The Labour Injunction, Unlawful Means and a Right to Strike', *Modern Law Review*, Vol 50, pp 506–516.

Simpson, B, (2001) 'Code of Practice on Industrial Action Ballots', *Industrial Law Journal*, Vol 30, pp 194–198.

SELF-TEST QUESTIONS

1 'The legal framework governing strike action is so unworkable, as to be irrelevant in the twenty-first century.' Discuss.

2 What must unions do to ensure that any industrial action taken is lawful?

3 Bumpy Cars Ltd is a leading manufacturer of sports cars. Currently it is in dispute with its workforce, whose union, Stand Firm, has held a ballot and is involved in a trade dispute with Bumpy Cars Ltd in relation to overtime pay and working hours. Last week, two-day strike action took place, during which Bumpy Cars Ltd's management found it difficult to enter the premises due to the 11 employees on the picket-line. It also observed four delivery lorries being turned away, hearing one driver being threatened

that 'if he entered, his truck would be overturned'. Finally, it was reported to Bumpy Cars Ltd that some of their regular customers had received letters in the post, advising them not to purchase any of Bumpy Cars Ltd's vehicles in future.

Advise Bumpy Cars Ltd on any available remedies its management has against its employees and Stand Firm, its recognized workforce union.

4 What liabilities do unions and individual union members hold when taking industrial action?

Index